Environmental Law and Compliance Methods

Edward E. Shea

OCEANA PUBLICATIONS, INC.
Dobbs Ferry, New York

Library of Congress Control Number: 2002100630

ISBN 0-379-21426-1

Manufactured in the United States of America on acid-free paper.

THE AUTHOR

Edward E. Shea, the author, is a partner and heads the Environmental Practice Group at Windels Marx Lane & Mittendorf, LLP which has offices in New York City; New Brunswick and Princeton, New Jersey; and Bonita Bay, Florida. Mr. Shea previously was a senior officer, director and general counsel of Reichhold Chemicals, Inc. and then of GAF Corporation, both multinational manufacturers of chemicals and other products with shares traded on The New York Stock Exchange. His responsibilities with those companies included environmental, safety and health programs. Mr. Shea has worked with environmental programs of several industry organizations and presented lectures at their meetings and also at meetings sponsored by the New York State Bar Association, the National Law Journal and Chemical Week. He is the author of The Lead Regulation Handbook, (Government Institutes) and numerous articles for publications such as the National Law Journal, the American Bar Association Journal and the Environmental Management Review. He is also an Adjunct Professor at Pace University's Graduate School of Business and teaches courses at The New York Institute of Finance. Mr. Shea is a graduate of the University of Michigan Law School and served as a Lieutenant in the U.S. Air Force, Strategic Air Command.

SUMMARY TABLE OF CONTENTS

TABLE OF CONTENTS

CHAPTER I
ENVIRONMENTAL LAW AND COMPLIANCE METHODS

I. Introduction

This book is a concise one-volume guide and reference source for use by professionals responsible for daily compliance with the environmental laws of the United States. It should be helpful to company officers and managers who have environmental responsibilities. It should also be helpful to lawyers, engineers, consultants and governmental administrators whose responsibilities include environmental compliance. It can also be helpful to officers and members of environmental organizations interested in compliance activities. However, environmental advocates should be aware that the book does not advocate environmental regulation, but focuses on the practical tasks of achieving compliance including critical discussions of problems in the regulatory programs that make environmental compliance a challenge to accomplish.

The major environmental laws in the United States are federal laws administered primarily by the Environmental Protection Agency (USEPA). However, much of the administration of these laws has been delegated to the states which have adopted and implemented laws at least as strict as the federal laws. When administration is delegated, the USEPA continues to support administration with funding, research, development of standards and methods, and a secondary enforcement role. Local government units (such as regions, counties and cities) also have laws which supplement, but cannot contradict, the federal and state laws. The states and many municipalities also have many environmental laws which are not part of the federal pattern.

The environmental laws are lengthy and detailed. The federal laws alone total thousands of pages. The USEPA's regulations interpreting and implementing the federal laws total many thousands of pages including lists of chemical substances and their characteristics, test methods and equipment, and control methods and equipment.

Each law has its own enforcement provisions and civil and criminal penalties. In general, the laws require record keeping and periodic reporting, provide for inspections, and impose civil and criminal fines and jail terms for violations. They are strictly enforced, primarily by orders for compliance and corrective action. However, civil penalties and fines are frequently imposed. Criminal actions are less common, but relatively frequent. Jail terms are reserved for the most serious cases.

Many environmental laws also allow private citizens and groups to file lawsuits for enforcement and to obtain money damages. Many of these lawsuits are successful. Thus, compliance with government programs is not always the end of environmental responsibilities.

Factors stimulating adoption of environmental laws have included scientific advancements in analytical chemistry, computer and communications technology. Development of analytical equipment such as chromatographs and spectrophotometers made possible the detection of contaminants at parts per trillion and lower. Computer and communications advances made it possible to collect data from widespread sources and rapidly analyze and distribute the results throughout the United States. Using these advances, the field of toxicology (including risk assessment) has grown into a major field. Environmental engineering, geology, industrial hygiene and law have also grown from a few courses into major fields taught at universities and practiced in specialized firms and in departments of government agencies and large companies.

CHAPTER II

RIVERS, HARBORS AND WETLANDS: THE U.S. ARMY CORPS OF ENGINEERS

A. Dredging and Filling Restrictions and Permits

The Rivers and Harbors Appropriation Act of 1899, 33 U.S.C. § 401 *et* seq. restricts excavation, filling and other activities in navigable waters of the United States without the approval of the U.S. Army Corps of Engineers and, in some cases, other governmental authorities such as the U.S. Secretary of Transportation. The Corps of Engineers is also authorized to regulate and issue permits for dredging and filling in navigable waters and adjacent wetlands pursuant to Section 404 of the Clean Water Act. 33 U.S.C. § 1344.The regulations of the Corps of Engineers are at 33 C.F.R. Part 203 *et seq*. Of important environmental interest are the parts on general regulatory policies (Part 320), permits (Parts 321 to 330), and projects involving the discharge of dredged or fill material (Parts 335 and 336).

Many lawsuits have been brought against the Corps of Engineers by environmental groups who believed that some permits were granted without sufficient consideration of environmental effects. See, e.g., *California v. Sierra Club,* 451 U.S. 287, 68 L.Ed. 2d 101 (1981); *Roanoke River Basin Ass'n v. Hudson*, 940 F.2d 58 (4th Cir. 1991); *Van Abbema v. Fornell*, 807 F.2d 633 (7th Cir. 1986). Property owners and developers have also engaged in litigation with the Corps of Engineers, contending that it is too strict in exercising its authority to deny, restrict or enforce permits. See, e.g., *Fox Bay Partners v. U.S. Corps of Engineers*, 831 F. Supp. 605 (N.D. Ill. 1993); *United States v. Members of the Estate of Boothby*, 16 F.3d 19 (1st Cir. 1994).

B. The Refuse Act

Section 13 of the Rivers and Harbors Appropriation Act of 1899, 33 U.S.C. § 407, (sometimes called the Refuse Act) was for decades the only federal environmental law restricting the discharge of pollutants that was not primarily directed to safety. Section 10 of the Act prohibits the discharge or deposit of refuse, other than liquid flows from streets and sewers, into any navigable water (or tributary) of the United States.

Refuse is any substance not naturally occurring in the water. The courts have consistently found that waste from industrial processes, such as taconite tailings, are refuse. *Reserve Mining Co. v. Environmental Protection Agency*, 514 F.2d 492 (8th Cir. 1975). Violations are punishable by fines up to $2,500 and a jail term up to one year.

Most courts have ruled that private individuals do not have rights to sue under the Refuse Act. *National Sea Clammers Ass'n. v. New York*, 616 F.2d 1222 (3d Cir. 1980) and cases cited therein; *Yates v. Island Creek Coal Co.*, 485 F. Supp. 995 (W.D. Va. 1980).

The Refuse Act has been partially preempted or supplemented by later federal environmental laws. *U.S. v. M/V Big Sam*, 681 F.2d 432 (5th Cir. 1982); *U.S. v. Outboard Marine Corp.*, 789 F.2d 497 (7th Cir. 1986).

C. Violation of Permit Restrictions

An owner of residential property on a riverbank obtained a permit from the Corps of Engineers to stabilize the bank of depositing 275 cubic yards of concrete rubble, limestone riprap and topsoil as fill material. However, the owner actually placed 1,225 cubic yards of fill material on the riverbank and also in the river. A federal district court found, among other things, that the deposit violated the Refuse Act and ordered removal of the excess fill. *U.S. v. Lambert*, 915 F. Supp. 797 (S.D.W. Va. 1996).

D. Federal Wetlands Regulation

As stated earlier, the Corps of Engineers is authorized to issue permits for dredging and filling in navigable waters pursuant to Section 404 of the Clean Water Act. The Corps maintains that navigable waters include adjacent wetlands and has been upheld in that interpretation by the U.S. Supreme Court. *United States v. Riverside Bayview Homes, Inc.*, 474 U.S. 121, 88 L.Ed. 2d 419 (1985).

The Corps defines wetlands as ". . . areas that are inundated or saturated by surface or groundwater at the frequency and duration sufficient to support, and that under normal conditions do support, a prevalence of vegetation typically adopted for life in saturated soil conditions." 33 C.F.R. § 328.3(b). The USEPA uses the same definition. Phragmytes are an example of plants that typically grow in wetlands. For further information, see the *Federal Manual for Identifying and Delineating Jurisdictional Wetlands, 1989.*

Section 404 exempts the following activities from the permit requirement:

(A) normal farming, silviculture, and ranching activities such as plowing, seeding, cultivating, minor drainage, harvesting for the production of food, fiber, and forest products, or upland and water conservation practices;

(B) maintenance, including emergency reconstruction of recently damaged parts, of currently serviceable structures such as dikes, dams, levees, groins, riprap, breakwaters, causeways, and bridge abutments or approaches, and transportation structures;

(C) construction or maintenance of farm or stock ponds or irrigation ditches, or the maintenance of drainage ditches;

(D) construction of temporary sedimentation basins on a construction site which does not include placement of fill material into the navigable waters;

(E) construction or maintenance of farm roads or forest roads, or temporary roads for moving mining equipment, where such roads are constructed and maintained, in accordance with best management practices and other requirements are met.

The exemptions have been interpreted narrowly by the courts to allow only the continuance of preexisting activities and not the conversion of wetlands for new farming or other activities. *United States v. Brace*, 41 F.3d 341 (3d Cir. 1994). Concentrated animal feeding operations (CAFOs) were held to be engaged in activities beyond normal farming activities and their discharges are strictly regulated.

However, the U.S. Supreme Court ruled that Corps of Engineers did not have authority to regulate gravel pits where no wetlands existed on grounds that migratory birds used ponds in the pits so they could be called waters of the United States. *Solid Waste Agency of Northern Illinois v. U.S. Army Corps of Engineers*, 531 U.S. 159 (2001).

The Corps has two kinds of permits, general and individual.

General permits (nationwide and regional) are prescribed in the Corps' regulations including the activities authorized and the conditions that apply to their use. An application is not necessary for dredging and filling wetlands authorized by a general permit, although a pre-discharge notice is required in some cases. Examples of activities authorized by a general permit are stabilization of river banks to prevent erosion and maintenance, dredging of existing basins, and cleanup of spills of oil and hazardous substances.

Individual permits require an application on Form ENG 4345 supported by extensive detail. See Pamphlet 1145-2-1. The application must demonstrate that there is no practical alternative. The Corps must make a "public interest" review to determine whether the proposed activities could contribute to significant degradation and whether the applicant will take steps to minimize adverse effects on the wetlands by means such as creation of new wetlands areas equal to or greater than the areas to be dredged or filled. The Corps must also consider whether the permit is a major federal action requiring preparation of an environmental impact statement under the National Environmental Policy Act. The permit is issued on Form ENG 1721 and contains general conditions and special conditions governing the authorized activity.

If a person innocently engages in activities that would be covered by a general permit except for failure to meet one or more conditions, the Corps may suspend enforcement if the person modifies the activities to comply. However, the Corps will not do so if a violation was knowing or intentional.

The Corps must notify the USEPA and state and local agencies before it issues an individual permit and the USEPA may block a permit if it would allow activities harmful to water supplies, shellfish beds, wildlife, or fishing and recreational areas. A state may also block a permit if the activities would not comply with its water quality regulations. As a result, it is difficult to obtain an individual permit. Any applicant should plan for an extensive effort and allow considerable time.

Both the Corps and the USEPA have authority to enforce Section 404 by administrative penalties and proceedings for injunctions and to impose civil and criminal penalties. In addition, citizen suits are authorized. *U.S. Department of Energy v. Ohio*, 503 U.S. 607,118 L. Ed. 2d 255 (1992). However, citizen's suits for wholly past violations are not authorized. *Gwaltney of Smithfield Ltd. v. Chesapeake Bay Foundation, Inc.*, 484 U.S. 49, 98 L. Ed. 2d 306 (1987).

See Chapter V for further information on wetlands permits under the Clean Water Act.

E. State Wetlands Laws

Section 404 expressly authorizes the states to adopt their own regulatory programs to control dredging and filling in navigable waters within their jurisdiction. The states have generally adopted such programs, including programs governing discharges into freshwater wetlands. In addition, the States of Michigan and New Jersey, which have extensive shorelines, have obtained authority to administer the federal wetlands program.

New Jersey has a Wetlands Act that applies to tidal wetlands. N.J.S.A. § 13:9A-1 *et seq*. New Jersey also has a Freshwater Wetlands Protection Act that regulates both wetlands and transition areas near them. N.J.S.A. § 13:9B-1 *et seq*. These laws and related laws allow its Department of Environment Protection to exercise extensive control over real estate development and land use in New Jersey:

Coastal Area Facilities Review Act, N.J.S.A. § 13:19-1 *et seq*.

Soil Erosion and Sediment Control Act, N.J.S.A. § 4:24-39 *et seq*.

Flood Hazard Area Control Act, N.J.S.A., N.J.S.A. § 58:16A-50 *et seq*.

Waterfront and Harbor Facilities Act, N.J.S.A. § 12:5-1 *et seq*.

Construction Permit Act, N.J.S.A. § 13:1D-29 *et seq*.

Pinelands Protection Act, N.J.S.A. § 13:18A-2 *et seq*.

Hackensack Meadowlands Reclamation and Development Act, N.J.S.A. § 13:17-1 *et seq.*

New York has a Tidal Wetlands Act. *Environmental Conservation Law*, § 25-0101 *et seq.* New York also has a Freshwater Wetlands Act. *Environmental Conservation Act*, § 24-0101 *et seq.* In New York, persons seeking to perform dredging or filling activities must often apply both to the Corps and to the New York Department of Environmental Conservation.

CHAPTER III
NATIONAL ENVIRONMENTAL POLICY ACT

A. Introduction

The National Environmental Policy Act (NEPA), 42 U.S.C. § 4321 *et seq.*, was adopted upon its signature by President Richard Nixon effective January 1, 1970. It established a national environmental policy to require federal government agencies to consider the environmental impacts of their major activities. It also established the Council on Environmental Quality (CEQ). President Nixon later gave practical life to NEPA by issuing Executive Order 11514 authorizing the CEQ to issue guidelines to the federal agencies on the preparation of environmental impact statements. The CEQ's regulations are found at 40 C.F.R. Part 1500 *et seq*. Related USEPA regulations are found at 40 C.F.R. Part 6.

B. The CEQ's Procedures for NEPA Compliance

NEPA requires that all federal government agencies prepare an environmental impact statement (EIS) for every proposal of a major federal action significantly affecting the human environment. Where several agencies are involved, a lead agency assumes primary responsibility.

The CEQ's regulations extend the application of NEPA to include state, local and private actions partially subject to federal control and responsibility. For example, if a federal air, water, waste or other permit is required for part of a project, the regulations indicate that NEPA applies. Acceptance of federal grants or other assistance may also subject a project to NEPA. For example, if project sponsors accept federal categorical grants, they must include in their plans the effort, time and cost of NEPA compliance. However, if funds are derived from block grants to the states or revenue sharing, NEPA compliance may not be necessary.

The CEQ's procedures begin with an evaluation of the scope of the proposal because an EIS, if required, must include all connected actions which are closely related. An agency may not split an action into segments in order to avoid treatment as a major action.

The next step is to make determination whether it is necessary to prepare an EIS. Unless the action is known to be one which normally does not require an

EIS or is an action categorically excluded, the agency should prepare an environmental assessment (EA). To do so, the agency obtains information from the applicant, environmental agencies and the public. Applicants customarily submit extensive information that, once verified, can be used in the EA with information from other sources. The EA is used as a screening service to determine whether the proposed action will have a significant impact on the environment.

An EIS need not be prepared if an agency finds based on the EA that a proposed action is not major or has no significant impact on the environment. A finding of no significant impact is commonly called a "FONSI." A FONSI is often an essential condition to the feasibility of a development project because business and financing arrangements cannot be held together during a lengthy EIS proceeding.

If the agency finds, based on the environmental assessment, that the proposed federal action is major and may have a significant impact upon the environment, the next step is the EIS. The preparation of an EIS is a process involving several steps:

1. Identify the lead agency and cooperating agencies
2. Determine the scope of the issues to be included in the EIS
3. Establish a time schedule and time limits
4. Prepare a draft environmental impact statement (DEIS) in accordance with the scope determined.
5. Invite comments by government agencies, the applicant and the public on the DEIS and hold public hearings
6. Explore and evaluate the alternatives, their effects, and the direct and indirect environmental consequences.
7. Prepare the final environmental impact statement (FEIS) including responses to the comments on the DEIS.
8. Make decisions on the proposed federal action based on the FEIS including selection of the appropriate environmental actions.
9. Prepare a record of decision (ROD).
10. Implement the decisions in a manner that monitors compliance with the conditions established by the FEIS.

NEPA requires that an EIS describe for the proposed action (1) the environmental impacts; (2) any environmental impacts that cannot be avoided if the proposal is implemented; (3) the reasonable alternatives to the proposed action; (4) the relationship between local short-term uses of man's environment and the maintenance and improvement of long term productivity; and (5) any irreversible commitments of resources if the proposed action is implemented.

The CEQ's regulations require discussion of direct and indirect impacts and impacts that are alone insignificant, but cumulatively significant. They require discussion of all reasonable alternatives, including the "no action" alternative. They also require discussion of measures that can be taken to mitigate any adverse impacts.

The impacts that must be discussed include difficult and unpredictable subjects such as energy requirements and conservation; natural or depletable resource requirements and conservation; and urban quality, historic and cultural resources. Executive Order 12898 dated February 11, 1994 on "environmental justice" requires discussion of environmental affects and also of health, economic and social impacts on minority and low-income communities.

The CEQ's regulations do not require "worst case" analysis. However, preparers of EAs and EISs must anticipate and be ready to respond to questions and challenges from project opponents who claim that "worst case" impacts will happen.

The CEQ's regulations provide guidance in addition to specific requirements. For example, the regulations state that EISs should be a means to assess the environmental impact of proposed actions rather than to justify decisions already made. Thus, they should be prepared as part of the decision process. An agency should not prematurely take steps or commit resources that will prejudice consideration of reasonable environmental alternatives. A major action should be considered to have a major effect on the environment if it will *or may* have such an effect. EISs should be concise and use plain language and graphics so as to communicate effectively to other agencies involved and the public. The EIS should identify methodologies used and refer by footnotes to scientific and other sources relied upon for conclusions, although discussions of methodology and supporting scientific data may be placed in an appendix. The agency must hold public hearings on the DEIS and include the public comments and the agency's responses to the public comments in the FEIS. The agency should take steps to assure that its decisions based on the FEIS are implemented by such means as conditions in permits and funding arrangements.

When new conditions are discovered after completion of an FEIS that may have a significant impact on the human environment, the agency should prepare a supplemental environmental impact statement (SEIS) for use in identifying and evaluating the environmental alternatives and selecting among them.

Federal agencies are authorized to prepare programmatic environmental impact statements (PEISs) in tiers for actions that will have national, regional and local aspects. Preparers of EISs for particular projects at the local level can incorporate materials by reference to the national and regional PEISs. This tiered method allows EISs for specific projects to focus on project-related issues and persons interested in national or regional aspects can review the PEISs.

The CEQ's regulations prescribe that EISs be brief and readable and focus on important environmental impacts. Nevertheless, EAs and EISs tend to be very lengthy and detailed. The reason is that opponents of federal actions scrutinize them and claim that they are insufficient if any subject is omitted or covered only briefly. Although a court may eventually uphold the federal agency, months and even years of time could be lost. Thus, it is customary to cover a wide range of issues in considerable detail.

The table of contents from an SEIS prepared for the renovation of a large public building in a major city appears at the end of this chapter. Readers will see that the coverage is extensive and detailed.

The U.S. Environmental Protection Agency (EPA) reviews EISs and discusses them with the lead agency. If the lead agency and the EPA do not agree, the EPA may refer the issue to the CEQ for resolution.

C. NEPA in the Courts

1. Applicability of NEPA

NEPA does not apply to actions that do not affect the physical environment, i.e., air, land or water. *Metropolitan Edison v. People Against Nuclear Energy*, 460 *U.S. 766 (1983); Sabine River Auth. V. U.S. Dept of Interior*, 951 F.3d 669 (5th Cir. 1992); *Pacific Legal Foundation v. Andrus*, 657 F.2d 829 (6th Cir. 1981).

The Clean Air Act and the Clean Water Act contain express provisions exempting the EPA from the need to comply with NEPA. NEPA also does not apply to the designation of the critical habitat of an endangered or threatened species under the Endangered Species Act. *Douglas County v. Babbitt*, 48 F.3d 1495 (9th Cir. 1995); *Pacific Legal Foundation v. Andrus*, 657 F.2d 829 (6th Cir. 1981). The courts have also held that it is not necessary to comply with NEPA when equivalent proceedings are conducted under other laws such as the Federal Insecticide, Fungicide and Rodenticide Act, the Resource Conservation and Recovery Act, the Safe Drinking Water Act and the Toxic Substances Control Act.

NEPA does not apply when another federal statute imposes on a federal agency a conflicting duty that is nondiscretionary. *Flint Ridge v. Scenic Rivers*, 426 U.S. 776, 49 L.Ed.2d 205 (1976); *Sierra Club v. Babbitt*, 65 F.3d 1502 (9th Cir. 1995); *Prairie Wood Products v. Glickman*, 971 F. Supp. 457 (D. Ore. 1997). NEPA was also held not to apply to a transfer of title to a mortgagee by the Farmer's Home Administration although the transfer resulted in continued use of wetlands for grazing. *National Wildlife Federation v. Espy, 49 F.3d 1337 (9th Cir. 1995).*

2. Standing to Challenge Agency Compliance with NEPA

Environmentalists have standing to challenge an alleged failure to comply with NEPA if they would be injured by the agency's failure. However, environmentalists having only peripheral interests do not have standing to sue. *Lujan v. Na-*

tional Wildlife, 497 U.S. 871, 111 L. Ed. 2d 695 (1990). The injury must be actual and imminent and not conjectural, hypothetical or the result of actions of a third party. *Lujan v. Defenders of Wildlife*, 504 U.S. 555, 119 L.Ed.2d 351 (1992).

3. Major Federal Action

Mere participation by a federal agency in a state project is not sufficient to be a major federal action. *Almond Hill School v. U.S. Dept. of Agriculture*, 768 F.2d 1030 (9th Cir. 1985); *Ramsey v. Kantor,* 96 F.3d 434 (9th Cir. 1996).

4. Significant Effect on the Human Environment

A federal district court held that a person suing to require preparation of an EIS for a proposed project need not show that a significant effect on the human environment will occur, but only that the project may have a significant effect. *Idaho Sporting Congress v. Thomas*, 137 F.3d 1146 (9th Cir. 1998).

The courts have frequently upheld FONSI's adopted by federal agencies. *Mt. Lookout—Mt. Nebo v. F.E.R.C.*, 143 F.3d 165 (4th Cir. 1998); *Sierra Club v. Babbitt,* 65 F.3d 1502 (9th Cir. 1995); *Kelley v. Sellin,* 42 F.3d 1501 (6th Cir. 1995); cert. den, 515 U.S. 1159 (1995); *D'Agnillo v. U.S. Dept. of Housing and Urban Dev.*, 965 F. Supp. 535 (S.D.N.Y. 1997).

The courts have sometimes held that a FONSI was adopted without a sufficient "hard look" and ordered an agency to conduct further proceedings under NEPA before proceeding with its proposed action. *Swanson v. U.S. Forest Service,* 87 F.3d 339 (9th Cir. 1996); *Prairie Wood v. Glickman,* 971 F. Supp. 457 (D. Ore. 1997); *Virgin Islands Tree Boa v. Witt,* 918 F. Supp. 879 (D.V.I. 1996), *aff'd,* 82 F.3d 408 (3d Cir. 1996).

5. The "Hard Look" Test

The courts have held that a federal agency must (1) accurately identify the relevant environmental concerns (2) take a "hard look" at the problems (3) if it finds no significant environmental impact, prepare a convincing case for its finding, and (4) if it finds an impact of true significance, prepare an EIS unless it finds that changes or safeguards in a project sufficiently reduce the impact to a minimum. *Sierra Club v. U.S. Dept. of Transportation*, 753 F.2d 120 (D.C. Cir. 1985). The agency must consider all reasonable alternatives, including a "no action" alternative. However, it need not use "worst case analysis" or analyze the environmental consequences of alternatives found too remote, speculative, impractical or ineffective. *Marsh v. Oregon Natural Resources Council,* 490 U.S. 360, 104 L.Ed.2d 377 (1989). *All Indian Pueblo Council v. U.S.*, 975 F.2d 1437 (10th Cir. 1992).

6. Scientific Methods and Data

Scientific methods used by a federal agency must be supported by adequate scientific data. If so, the courts will not overturn the agency's decisions because opponents of a project disagree with the scientific conclusions in the FEIS or submit contradictory studies. *Wright v. Inman*, 923 F. Supp. 1295 (D. Nev. 1996); *Price Road Neighborhood Ass'n v. U.S. Dept of Transportation*, 113 F.3d 1505 (9th Cir. 1997).

7. Agency Decisions Based on Final Environmental Impact Statements

The U.S. Supreme Court has ruled that an agency's final decision cannot be overturned if the agency has complied with NEPA procedures and its decision is not arbitrary or capricious. *Marsh v. Oregon Natural Resources Council*, 490 U.S. 360 (1989); *Vermont Yankee Nuclear Corporation*, 435 U.S. 519 (1978) and numerous later decisions. NEPA exists to ensure a process, not a result. *Northwest Environmental Defense Ctr. v. BPA*, 117 F.3d 1520 (9th Cir. 1997); *Sierra Club v. U.S. Forest Service*, 46 F.3d 835 (8th Cir. 1995).

However, when a federal agency failed to consider all reasonable alternatives in an EIS, a court ordered that a permit be granted on the basis of the EIS be vacated. *Simmons v. U.S. Corps of Engineers*, 120 F.3d 664 (7th Cir. 1997).

8. Supplemental Environmental Impact Statements

A federal agency must take a "hard look" at the question whether an SEIS is required when it considers changes of a project previously considered in an FEIS. *Hughes River v. Glickman*, 81 F.3d 437 (4th Cir. 1996). If the changes substantially affect the alternative chosen on the basis of the FEIS, an SEIS must be prepared. *Du Bois v. U.S. Dept of Agriculture*, 102 F.3d 1273 (1st Cir. 1996). If a change is not a significant new circumstance, an SEIS is not required. *Swanson v. U.S. Forest Service*, 87 F.3d 339 (9th Cir. 1996). An agency need not hold public hearings when evaluating whether a partial redesign of a project requires an SEIS. *Price Road Neighborhood Ass'n v. U.S. Dept. of Transportation*, 113 F.3d 1505 (9th Cir. 1997).

D. Some NEPA Anomalies

Both NEPA and the corresponding state laws can be used to seek a commercial objective. For example, existing businesses may seek to prevent or delay a competitive business by claiming that government agencies should not grant permits or take other enabling actions without requiring the competitive business to go through EIS procedures. Individuals and groups in affluent suburban neighborhoods sometimes assert claims under NEPA or similar state laws to require environmental evaluation of the construction of housing, roads, bridges, water and sewer systems and other facilities needed by middle and lower income groups. Political and governmental organizations sometimes use NEPA or state laws to block or delay projects when they cannot muster a vote against them through customary legislative or governmental procedures.

In 1993, for example, opponents of the North American Free Trade Agreement sought unsuccessfully to block that treaty because an EIS had not been prepared.

Public Citizen v. U.S. Trade Representative, 5 F.3d 549 (D.C. Cir. 1993); see also *Public Citizen v. Office of the U.S. Trade Representative*, 970 F.2d 916 (D.C. Cir. 1992). In several cases, the courts have denied standing to competitors or persons asserting economic interests to challenge agency actions alleged to have violated NEPA. For example, see *Western Radio v. Espy*, 79 F.3d 896 (9th Cir. 1996); cert. den. 136 L. Ed. 2d 38 (1996); *City of Los Angeles v. U.S. Dept of Agriculture*, 950 F. Supp. 1005 (C.D. Cal. 1996). For another example, a federal court ordered that federal housing entities attempt to prepare an EIS to consider the cumulative impact on vehicular traffic and the waste disposal system of the construction an additional 4,200 units of low-income housing in the City of Yonkers, New York, but later upheld a FONSI based on an environmental assessment they prepared. *D'Agnillo v. U.S. Dept. of Housing and Urban Development*, 965 F. Supp. 535 (S.D.N.Y. 1997).

Some environmental groups opposed the development of Hudson River Park which is planned to extend for five miles along the west side of Manhattan in New York City. As described in The New York Times, the Park will have a continuous riverfront esplanade with lawns and flowers, bicycle and running trails and playgrounds and will replace 13 huge rotting piers now located in the river. An extensive study of environmental impacts was made under the State Environmental Quality Review Act and significant changes in the initial plans were made to accommodate environmentalists' objections including cancellation of a marina and restrictions on dredging and construction activities. Twenty years ago, environmental groups blocked a larger similar project, called Westway, thus continuing for two decades the decay, unsanitary conditions, and criminal activities in the area. Since the tragedy at the World Trade Center, there has been a new outlook on development in Manhattan that may allow the Park to be built.

E. State Laws Similar to NEPA

NEPA does not apply to state government agencies. However, some states have laws similar to NEPA. Examples are the California Environmental Quality Act, Public Resources Code § 21000 *et seq*.; the Connecticut Environmental Policy Act, G.G.S.A. § 22a-1a *et seq*.; and the New York State Environmental Quality Review Act, New York Envtl. Conserv. Law § 8-0101 *et seq*.

EXHIBITS

1. Final Supplement Environmental Impact Statement

Table of Contents

Redevelopment Final Supplemental EIS

<u>Redevelopment Final Supplemental EIS</u>

CHAPTER IV
THE CLEAN AIR ACT

A. Legislative History

The Clean Air Act (CAA), 42 U.S.C. § 7401 *et seq.*, was adopted in 1963, but its provisions were then quite modest. In 1970, extensive amendments to the CAA were adopted. They provided for air quality control regions (AQCR), primary and secondary national ambient air quality standards (NAAQS), new source performance standards (NSPS), and national emission standards for hazardous air pollutants (NESHAPs).

The 1970 amendments also directed each state to adopt a state implementation plan (SIP) to attain the NAAQS; to regulate construction, modification and operation of specific pollution sources; to enforce emission limitations, and to establish monitoring and other programs. Each SIP, including amendments, must be approved by the USEPA and can be stricter, but not less strict, than the federal law and regulations. The USEPA was authorized to adopt a federal implementation plan (FIP) for any state that did not adopt a SIP. 42 U.S.C. § 7410.

In 1977 and 1982, amendments to the CAA required that the states add stricter requirements to their SIPs for prevention of significant deterioration (PSD) of air quality in areas which meet the NAAQS. 42 U.S.C. §§ 7471-7479. The amendments also established stricter requirements for major new sources of pollution in areas not attaining the NAAQS. 42 U.S.C. §§ 7501-7507.

The Clean Air Act Amendments of 1990 (CAAA of 1990) amended and extensively supplemented the CAA. Among other things, the CAAA of 1990 established stricter ambient air quality standards for nonattainment areas and new NAAQS compliance deadlines; major programs governing vehicles and fuels; an expanded program to establish NESHAPs for at least 189 air toxics; a program to reduce sulfur dioxide emissions by electric utilities perceived to be causing "acid rain"; an expanded permit program which state environmental agencies must adopt in their SIPs; a phaseout of chlorofluorocarbons (CFCs) and certain other products perceived to deplete stratospheric ozone; new enforcement powers for the USEPA; stricter criminal and civil penalties for violation of the CAA; and a variety of programs including assistance to workers terminated or laid off as a consequence of compliance with the CAA.

1. Ambient Air Quality

a. USEPA Administration

The USEPA's Office of Air and Radiation administers the CAA at the federal level.

b. Air Quality Control Regions and Pollutant Standards

The USEPA has adopted 264 AQCRs. 40 C.F.R. Part 81. The USEPA has also adopted national primary and secondary NAAQS for sulfur oxides, particulate matter, carbon monoxide, ozone, nitrogen dioxide, and lead and its compounds. 40 C.F.R. Part 50.

These pollutants were selected by the USEPA based on criteria prescribed in the CAA. The national primary standards for these "criteria" pollutants are based on the USEPA's determinations of their effects on health with an adequate margin of safety. The secondary standards are based on the USEPA's determinations of what is necessary to protect the public welfare from their known or anticipated effects. *Lead Industries Ass'n. v. EPA,* 647 F.2d 1130 (D.C. Cir. 1980).

The standards are as follows:

Sulfur Oxides. The national primary standard for sulfur oxides states that the annual average per calendar year, measured as sulfur dioxide, may not exceed 0.03 parts per million (ppm) and the 24 hour average may not exceed 0.14 ppm more than once per calendar year. The secondary standard states that the 3 hour average may not exceed 0.5 ppm more than once per calendar year.

Particulate Matter. The national annual and primary standards for particulate matter, which are the same, state that the annual arithmetic mean concentration of particles equal to or less than 10 microns in diameter (PM_{10}) shall not exceed 50 micrograms per cubic meter (ug/m^3) and the 24 hour average concentration shall not exceed 150 ug/m^3.

NOTE: See the status described below of a revised standard adopted in 1997 by the USEPA.

Carbon Monoxide. The national primary standard for carbon monoxide states that the 8 hour average concentration shall not exceed 9 ppm and the 1 hour average concentration shall not exceed 35 ppm more than once per calendar year.

Ozone. The national primary and secondary standards for ozone, which are the same, state that the one hour average concentration shall not exceed 0.12 ppm more than once per year.

NOTE: See the status described below of a revised standard adopted in 1997 by the USEPA.

Nitrogen Dioxide. The national primary and secondary standards for nitrogen dioxide, which are the same, state that the annual arithmetic mean concentration for a calendar year may not exceed 0.053 ppm (100 ug/m^3).

Lead and its Compounds. The national primary and secondary standards for lead and its compounds, which are the same and are measured as elemental lead, state that their concentration may not exceed 1.5 ug/m^3 arithmetic mean average over a calendar quarter.

In 1997, the USEPA tightened the particulate matter standards by adopting new primary and secondary standards, which are again the same, stating that the annual arithmetic mean concentration of particles equal to 2.5 microns in diameter ($PM_{2.5}$) shall not exceed 15 ug/m^3 and the 24 hour average concentration shall not exceed 65 ug/m^3. The USEPA also tightened the ozone standards by adopting new primary and secondary standards, which are the same, to state that the eight hour average concentration shall not exceed a daily maximum of 0.08 ppm. In a lawsuit challenging these regulations, the U.S. Circuit Court of Appeals for the District of Columbia reaffirmed that the USEPA is not allowed to consider cost or use cost-benefit analysis in setting ambient air quality standards. However, the Court ordered the USEPA to reconsider the standards on other grounds. *American Trucking Associations, Inc. v. U.S.E.P.A.*, 175 F.3d 1027 (D.C. Cir. 1999). The U.S. Supreme Court reversed the decision of the Circuit Court of Appeals except that it found the USEPA's ozone nonattainment implementation provisions were unlawful. *Whitman v. American Trucking Association*, 531 U.S. 457, 149 L.Ed.2d 1(2001). The Circuit Court of Appeals then upheld the standards except for the further actions required of the USEPA by the Supreme Court. 283 F.3d 355 (D.C. Cir. 2002).

The NAAQS are general air quality standards and do not apply to particular plants or equipment. They are implemented by the SIPs adopted by the states.

The USEPA has adopted ambient air quality surveillance regulations. They provide for national air monitoring stations (NAMS), state and local air monitoring stations (SLAMS), and photochemical assessment monitoring stations (PAMS). 40 C.F.R. Part 58.

c. State Implementation Plans

The states adopted SIPs as required by Section 110 of the CAA, 42 U.S.C. § 7410, and the USEPA's regulations at 40 C.F.R. Part 51. The USEPA has disapproved SIP proposals where it believed the state program was inadequate. Thus, the submission and approval of SIPs has been a long term process.

The CAA requires that each SIP must (A) contain enforceable emission limitations and other control measures; (B) provide for monitoring, compilation and analysis of ambient air quality data; (C) include an enforcement program and regulation of modification and construction of stationary sources including a permit program; (D) contain provisions prohibiting emissions of air pollutants in amounts which interfere with attainment or maintenance of the NAAQS, PSD or visibility requirements of any other state and insuring compliance with certain interstate and international pollution abatement requirements; (E) provide for adequate personnel, funding and authority and state responsibility for ensuring adequate implementation of SIP provisions delegated to local or regional authorities; (F) require monitoring and periodic reporting of emissions data; (G) provide authority comparable to the emergency powers of the USEPA relating to pollutant emissions presenting an imminent and substantial danger to public health or welfare or the environment and related contingency plans; (H) provide for revision of the SIP to take into account NAAQS revisions and other matters; (I) meet requirements applicable to nonattainment areas; (J) meet PSD and visibility requirements; (K) provide for air quality modelling and submission of data to the USEPA; (L) require permit fees payable by the owner or operator of each major stationary source; and (M) provide for consultation and participation by local political subdivisions affected by the SIP. 42 U.S.C. § 7410(a)(2).

The SIPs provide, among other things, for permit programs which limit emissions from specific stationary sources such as facility stacks, vents, pipes, tanks and boilers as well as fugitive emissions from sources such as equipment leaks and loading and unloading activities. The permits typically require monitoring, record keeping and reporting to the state environmental agency and are also enforced by surveillance and inspections. In addition to NAAQS pollutants, SIPs control other pollutants from designated sources such as fluoride emissions from phosphate fertilizer and aluminum plants, sulfur emissions from kraft pulp mills, and sulfuric acid mist from sulfuric acid production plants. 40 C.F.R. Parts 52 and 62.

The USEPA's regulations on preparation, adoption and submittal of SIPs are published in 40 C.F.R. Part 51. They prescribe requirements for control strategies to attain and maintain the national standards; prevention of air pollution emergency episodes; review of new sources; surveillance; enactment of legal authority to carry out the SIP; compliance schedules; protection of visibility; reporting of air quality data and source emissions; and inspection and maintenance programs.

The USEPA's regulations on approval and promulgation of SIPs are published at 40 C.F.R. Part 52. This Part also contains a summary of the SIP for each state, the District of Columbia, Puerto Rico, the Virgin Islands, American Samoa and the Northern Mariana Islands.

The USEPA must allow the states freedom to choose their own methods to meet the SIP requirements to comply with the NAAQS and may not require specific control methods or methods stricter than those required by the CAA. *Commonwealth of Virginia v. EPA*, 108 F.3d 1397 (D.C. Cir. 1997).

The USEPA has adopted regulations prescribing methods that SIPs must require to monitor and measure pollutant emissions for compliance with emission limitations. When proposed, the regulations were called the "credible evidence rule" and were accomplished by amendments throughout 40 C.F.R. Parts 51, 52, 60 and 61. The USEPA has also adopted regulations imposing compliance assurance monitoring (CAM) requirements on owners and operators of major stationary sources, although these regulations are actually part of the Title V permit program described later. 40 C.F.R. Part 64. The CAM rule was upheld in a court challenge, except that the court held that the CAA requires a certification whether compliance is continuous or intermittent. The court reserved for future consideration the issues raised concerning the use of "any credible evidence" to show a violation. *NRDC v. EPA*, 194 F.3d 130 (D.C. Cir. 1999).

The CAA contains provisions penalizing states and commercial and industrial activities for failure to conform to the air quality standards. For example the CAA forbids any federal department to engage in support, financially assist, license or approve any activity that does not conform to a SIP. The USEPA has adopted transportation conformity regulations that can lead to a loss of federal highway funds for failure to conform to a SIP. 40 C.F.R. § 51.390 *et seq*. The EPA has also adopted general conformity regulations requiring federal agencies to take punitive actions for nonconformity. 40 C.F.R. § 51.850 *et seq*.

When the USEPA approves a SIP or an action taken by a state under its SIP, environmental groups may sue to block the approval. *Wall v. EPA*, 265 F.3rd 426 (6th Cir. 2001).

The USEPA has regulations requiring reductions of NO_x emissions in two phases. The regulations are at 40 C.F.R. Part 76. Lists of the coal-fired utility units included in Phase I are contained in Appendix A to Part 76 and the emission limitations are in §§ 76.5 and 76.6. The limitations for coal-fired utility units included in Phase II are in §§ 76.7 and 76.8. Provisions for permit applications and compliance plans are in § 76.9. Alternative emission limitations are in § 76.10.

A recent article presented a thoughtful and detailed analysis of the economics of the electric utility industry and of existing and potential technologies for the control of its NO_x emissions. Among other things, the article describes the success during 1999 of a cap and trade program of the 12 states comprising the Northeast Transport Region in achieving 30% reductions of NO_x emissions through operational charges alone with significant capital additions. The article recommends changes to the existing regulatory standards to recognize and optimize the advantages of modern gas-fired turbine generation. "Grandfathering, New Source Review, and NO_x–Making Sense of a Flawed System," Byron Swift, 31 Environment Reporter 1538 (July 21, 2000). Although the author of this book recommends the article to readers, the author is concerned about the trend to burn valuable natural gas to provide heat and electric power. The world has limited natural gas resources and the author would prefer to see it used for more valuable uses such as raw material for fertilizers and building materials.

In 1998, the USEPA announced a so-called "SIP Call" rule that would require 22 states east of the Mississippi to revise their SIPs to impose stricter controls on NO_x emissions by public utilities. The USEPA also proposed a related program for transferrable NO_x emission allowances that could be used by the states as a means to comply with the SIP Call. 63 Fed. Reg. 57355 (Oct. 27, 1998); 40 C.F.R. Part 96. The SIP Call was supported by the northeastern states who claim that their ozone nonattainment areas are caused by windblown NO_x emissions of midwestern and southern electrical generating plants. These states' urban voters are major supporters of the USEPA. These voters also support the "deregulation" programs that require midwestern and southern electric utilities to "wheel" inexpensive electricity to the eastern cities where environmental requirements have driven up electric power rates.

Faced with growing electricity demands in their own states and demands for cheap electricity from the northeastern states, the midwestern states and utilities challenged the SIP Call. The District of Columbia Circuit Court of Appeals upheld the SIP Call as to 22 states, but vacated the rule as to Georgia, Missouri and Wisconsin because the USEPA did not show that emissions from those states contributed significantly to pollution in other states. *Michigan v. EPA*, 213 F.3d 663 (D.C.Cir. 2000). The Court also ordered the USEPA to reconsider the heat input growth rates used in setting emissions budgets in the SIP Call. Appalachian Power v. U.S.E.P.A., 249 F.3d 1032 and 251 F.3d 1026 (D.C. Cir. 2001). The USEPA reconsidered and decided that the rates were reasonable. 67 Fed. Reg. 21,868 (May 1, 2002).

The USEPA's SIP Call will increase electricity generation costs. However, the USEPA and environmental groups see increased fossil fuel electric power costs as necessary to switch public preference to solar and other power sources and to energy conservation.

d. Nonattainment Areas

Many areas throughout the United States are in compliance with the NAAQS standards. However, many areas are in nonattainment status for one or more of the criteria pollutants and are working under extensions granted by the USEPA. 40 C.F.R. Part 52. The USEPA publishes the nonattainment areas on its Internet website.

The CAA requires that SIPs provide for annual incremental reductions of emissions of nonattainment pollutants and authorizes the EPA to order further reductions to attain compliance by the required dates. To measure progress, SIPs must provide for current inventories of nonattainment pollutants, identify and quantify emissions from new permitted sources, and contain measures that will automatically be implemented if there is a failure to make reasonable progress or to attain compliance by the required date. 42 U.S.C. § 7501 *et seq*. The USEPA has granted extensions of time to the states to meet their SIPs.

In addition to the general steps already described, the CAA imposes specific requirements applicable to existing sources and new or modified sources and to particular pollutants. SIPs must require that all existing major stationary sources in nonattainment areas implement reasonably available control technology (RACT). SIPs must also require that permits be obtained for construction and operation of all new or modified major stationary sources in nonattainment areas and that the grant of such permits be subject to strict nonattainment new source review requirements. These requirements include emission controls that provide the lowest achievable emission rate (LAER) and to arrange or obtain offsetting emission reductions equal to or greater than the emissions created. 42 U.S.C. § 7502 *et seq*. In effect, the CAA requires that the SIPs impose rationing systems on development in nonattainment areas.

For states having areas that have not attained the NAAQS, the SIP must contain additional requirements applicable to nitrogen oxides, volatile organic compounds, carbon monoxide and particulate matter (PM_{10}), sulfur oxides, nitrogen dioxide and lead. 42 U.S.C. §§ 7511 to 7514a. For example, ozone nonattainment areas were divided into five categories: marginal, moderate, serious, severe and extreme with design values and compliance deadlines for each ranging from 3 to 20 years. Depending on the degree of ozone nonattainment, increasingly strict control programs must be imposed on existing and stationary sources of ozone precursors, i.e., volatile organic compounds and nitrogen oxides. See 40 C.F.R. § 52.24 and provisions throughout 40 C.F.R. Part 52. In ozone nonattainment areas, the states must also implement new or stricter programs such as vehicle inspection and maintenance, transportation controls and clean fuels or advanced control technology systems.

In 1997, the EPA created many new nonattainment areas by adopting stricter 8-hour standards to replace its 1-hour standards for ozone and particulate matter. As described earlier, a federal appellate court ordered the USEPA to reconsider the standards. As an interim measure, the USEPA reinstated its 1-hour standards until such time as the 8-hour standards may be held fully enforceable and no longer subject to legal challenge. 65 Fed. Reg. 45182 (July 20, 2000). In 2002, the court upheld the stricter standards, so industrial and commercial activities will be restricted in many areas which had attained compliance with the old standards but do not meet the new standards.

As enacted, the CAAA of 1990 contained a provision requiring that SIPs impose on firms with 100 or more employees in severe nonattainment areas a requirement to reduce work-related use of vehicles by such steps as carpools. Due to widespread opposition, Congress amended the CAA in 1995 to make these provisions optional. 42 U.S.C. § 7511a(d).

e. Attainment Areas; Prevention of Significant Deterioration

For areas in compliance with the NAAQS, the CAA imposes PSD requirements. The CAA divides the areas into three classes. Class I includes parks and wilderness areas where only the smallest increases of air pollution are allowed. Other areas are considered Class II, unless redesignated, and must meet primary and secondary NAAQS and additional limits on increases of particulate matter and sulfur dioxide. The initial increments and ceilings are prescribed in the CAA and the USEPA is required to adopt regulations applying PSD restrictions to additional pollutants. By following specified procedures, states can redesignate areas as Class III which has more lenient limits for pollutant emission increases. However, no "major emitting facility" may be constructed without a permit in any area to which the PSD requirements apply. The permit may be issued only after demonstration that emissions from the facility will meet specified requirements including control of each emitted pollutant by the best available control technology (BACT). 42 U.S.C. § 7470 *et seq*. See also 40 C.F.R. §§ 51.166 and 52.24.

The PSD requirements also include a program to remedy impairment of visibility in Class I federal areas and to prevent future visibility impairment. For example, restrictions were imposed on a Navajo power generating station in Arizona that was linked to haze over the Grand Canyon. Visibility is a factor which must be considered before a construction permit can be issued for a new or modified major stationary source. In addition, certain existing sources can be required to install and operate best available retrofit technology (BART). 42 U.S.C. § 7491 *et seq.*; 40 C.F.R. § 51.300 *et seq.;* 40 C.F.R. §§ 52.26 to 52.29; 66 Fed. Reg. 38,107 (7/20/01). In 2002, the USEPA's "regional haze rule" mandating BART to be invalid because it infringed on state authority to establish programs granted by the CAA. *American Corn Growers v. EPA,* _F.3d_, 2002 WL 1040579 (D.C. Cir. 2002).

f. New Source Review

The USEPA has requirements in its regulations on nonattainment areas and prevention of significant deterioration that persons who propose to construct large new facilities that will be air pollution sources must apply for a construction permit before commencing construction.

Under the nonattainment regulations, a permit application and preconstruction review are required for sources with potential to emit quantities of pollutants ranging from 10 tons to 100 tons per year depending on the pollutant for which the area is in nonattainment and how seriously the area is in nonattainment. New and modified major sources in a nonattainment area must use emission controls that provide the lowest achievable emission rate (LAER). Their owners or operators must also arrange or obtain offsetting emission reductions equal or greater than the emissions created. 40 C.F.R. § 50.165(a)(i).

Under the PSD regulations, the permit and preconstruction review requirements apply to sources with potential to emit 250 tons per year of a regulated pollutant or, if the source is among certain listed industrial categories, 100 tons per year of a regulated pollutant. 40 C.F.R. § 52.21.

The USEPA and state environmental agencies take an expansive view of potential to emit. They assume that a facility will operate at design capacity, but will typically take into account regulatory limits on emissions. When the USEPA adopted a rule that only federally enforceable emission limits would be considered in determining whether a plant site was a "major source", the U.S. District Court for the District of Columbia vacated the rule and said that any effective limit should be considered. *Nat'l Mining Ass'n v. EPA*, 59 F.3d 1351 (D.C. Cir. 1995).

The CAA states that a major modification resulting in a significant emissions increase is subject to new source review. See 40 C.F.R. §§ 51.165 and .166 and *Wisconsin v. Reilly*, 893 F.3d 901 (7th Cir. 1990).

During the Clinton Administration, the USEPA imposed large penalties on electric utilities based on a revised interpretation of the exclusion for routine maintenance, repair and replacement. The USEPA contended that capital expenditures performed infrequently that constitute a replacement or redesign of component with a long useful life are subject to new source compliance if they increase capacity, regain lost capacity, and/or extend the life of major equipment such as coal-fired boiler unit. This interpretation was questioned in a well-written article titled "Reinterpretation of NSR Regulations Could Have Costly Implications for Business," Domike and Zaracoli, 31 Env. Rptr. (BNA) 407 (March 3, 2000). See also *TVA v. EPA.*, 2002 U.S. App. LEXIS 249 (11th Cir. Jan. 8, 2002). In 2002, the USEPA proposed to allow electric utilities to produce more electricity without penalties.

2. New Source Performance Standards

The USEPA has adopted new source performance standards (NSPS) for about 70 categories of industrial plants (such as cement and glass plants) and equipment (such as incinerators and stationary gas turbines). New plants and equipment in these categories must meet technology based standards which require the best system of emission reduction adequately demonstrated (BADT), taking into account cost and other factors. NSPS regulations must be nationally uniform for each industry category and also archievable. *National Lime Ass'n. v. EPA*, 627 F.2d 416 (D.C. Cir. 1980). The NSPS regulations typically apply mass emission limits to quantities of pollutants emitted by a plant or equipment and also apply opacity (visible emission) limits. The regulations also prescribe emission controls and operating standards. If an existing plant or equipment is reconstructed or modified, it is treated as a new source and must comply with NSPS. Compliance with NSPS must be demonstrated by monitoring, reporting and recordkeeping. 42 U.S.C. § 7411; 40 C.F.R. Part 60.

The NSPS regulations apply regardless of whether a plant is in an area subject to nonattainment or PSD requirements. An owner or operator seeking a permit to construct, reconstruct or modify a plant must to comply with the NSPS regulations and may also be subject to a SIP requiring a nonattainment area, new source performance review or a PSD review. If so, the plant may also have to meet RACT, BACT or LAER technology. If the plant will emit hazardous air pollutants, it will also have to meet maximum achievable control technology (MACT). The resulting duplication and cost have resulted in decisions by many manufacturers to build new plants in other nations where environmental requirements, however strict, can be met by a single design that will remain in effect for the life of the permit granted by the government.

In recent years, the USEPA issued standards for new and existing municipal waste combustion units, municipal solid waste landfills, and medical waste incinerators as well as revised SO_2 and NO_x standards for fossil fueled steam boilers. The new standards were sometimes challenged in court. For example, the Sierra Club challenged the MACT floors in the standard for medical waste incinerators and the U.S. Court of Appeals for the District of Columbia remanded it for further explanation by the USEPA. *Sierra Club v. EPA*, 167 F.3d 658 (D.C. 1999). The standard for municipal waste combustion units was vacated by the same Court. *Davis County v. EPA*, 101 F.3d.1395 (D.C.Cir. 1996).

The regulations requiring compliance with the NSPS if a plant or equipment are reconstructed or modified contain an exclusion allowing routine maintenance, repair and replacement. In the author's experience, many companies have been allowed by the USEPA or state air permit authorities to make repairs and replacements that significantly improved the efficiency, quality and even capacity of a plant or equipment if the changes also reduced (or did not increase) emissions of pollutants. However, owners or operators must be careful to limit changes to steps which will not be a reconstruction or modification a state agency or the USEPA may contend that a new permit is required containing NSPS limits. Companies have sometimes successfully challenged a decision by an environmental agency to require an NSPS permit for the installation of replacement facilities or equipment. *Celebrezze v. National Lime*, 68 Ohio 3d 377, 627 N.E. 2d 538 (1994); *Allstead Inc. v. EPA*, No. 94-3179, 1994 U.S. App. LEXIS 12385 (6th Cir., 3/26/94). *U.S. v. AM General*, 34 F.3d 472 (7th Cir. 1994).

3. National Emission Standards for Hazardous Air Pollutants

a. Pre-1990 NESHAPs

Prior to 1990, the USEPA adopted national emission standards for hazardous air pollutants (NESHAPs) for eight pollutants which it found may cause or contribute to air pollution reasonably anticipated to result in mortality or an increase in serious irreversible, or incapacitating reversible, illness. They were beryllium, mercury, vinyl chloride, radionuclides from specified sources, benzene from specified sources, asbestos, inorganic arsenic from specified sources, and Radon-222 from uranium mill tailings. A NESHAP was also adopted to cover equipment leaks (fugitive emissions) of a lengthy list of hazardous air pollutants from manufacturing equipment. When the USEPA found that it was not feasible to adopt a NESHAP prescribing an emission standard, the USEPA adopted a NESHAP prescribing operating standards as it did in the NESHAP for asbestos. Both new and existing sources were required to comply with NESHAPs, although existing sources could seek exemptions and time extensions. 42 U.S.C. § 7412; 40 C.F.R. Part 61.

By 1990, environmentalists were dissatisfied with the relatively small number of standards adopted by the USEPA. Manufacturers were concerned about the authorization given to the EPA to adopt standards based on its extremely cautious assessments of mortality and health risks without regard to the availability of technology to meet them. For example, the USEPA adopted its vinyl chloride monomer (VCM) standard as a technology-forcing standard. Although VCM manufacturers developed technology that enabled them to meet the standard, manufacturers realized that they would not always be able to do so.

b. Post-1990 NESHAPs

The CAAA of 1990 amended the CAA to require the USEPA to adopt standards limiting emissions of hazardous air pollutants from new and existing major sources and also from smaller sources, called "area sources," such as paint shops and dry cleaning stores. The CAA requires that the USEPA adopt standards for control of emissions of a list of 189 hazardous air pollutants (HAPs) using maximum available control technology (MACT). The USEPA may add or delete chemicals from this list and private parties may petition the USEPA to make additions or deletions. 42 U.S.C. § 7412. The USEPA has deleted caprolactam, a chemical used in making nylon, from the list which now has 188 HAPs.

The USEPA was also required to issue a list of major sources and area sources of the listed HAPs. The USEPA published the required list at 57 Fed. Reg. 31,576 (7/16/92). See 40 C.F.R. Part 61.

The CAA also require the USEPA to review and revise the pre-1990 NESHAPs to conform to the new standards.

c. Major Sources

A major source is any source or group of sources in a contiguous area under common control that emits or has potential to emit 10 tons per year of any one of the listed HAPs or 25 tons per year of any combination of them.

The USEPA defines potential to omit as operation of a source at full capacity for the entire year, even though it is shut down for part of the year. However, source operators can commit to maintain emissions below a cap that is enforcable by the USEPA or a state environmental agency. *National Mining Ass'n. v. EPA*, 59 F.3d 1351 (D.C. Cir. 1995).

The USEPA published its final schedule for promulgating NESHAPs for toxic air pollutants based on MACT standards on November 16, 1993. Among the early important actions taken by the USEPA was its issuance of the Hazardous Organic NESHAP, or the HON, requiring the synthetic organic chemical industry and certain other chemical processors operating major sources to apply MACT to reduce emissions (including leaks) of 112 of the HAPs listed in the CAA. 40 C.F.R. Part 63, Subpart F, § 63.100 et seq.

Another early action with widespread effect was the USEPA's issuance of a final NESHAP regulating emissions of several HAPs by halogenated solvent cleaners. 40 C.F.R. Part 63, Subpart T, § 63.460 *et seq.*

The USEPA has also issued a rule providing guidance for state programs regulating HAPs. 40 C.F.R. Part 63, Subpart E, § 63.90.

d. Area Sources

Area sources are any sources of HAPs in the source categories designated by the USEPA other than a major source. They include many small businesses as well as many sources whose emissions are small, although their cumulative effect may be important in some areas. Accordingly, the CAA requires that the USEPA list only those categories or subcategories of area sources that it finds present a threat of adverse effects to human health or the environment, individually or in the aggregate. However, the USEPA was required to list sufficient categories or subcategories of area sources to ensure that area sources representing 90% of the area source emissions of the 30 hazardous air pollutants that present the greatest threat to public health in the largest number of urban areas are subject to regulations. Such regulations may require the use of generally available control technology (GACT) or management practices. 42 U.S.C. § 7412(k). An important action to control area source emissions was taken by the USEPA in its Perchloroethylene Dry Cleaning Facilities NESHAP. 40 C.F.R. Part 63, Subpart M, § 63.320 *et seq.*

e. Technology-Based Standards for NESHAPS

i. MACT Standards

As described earlier, the CAAA of 1999 required that the EPA establish technology-based standards for the list of HAPs that would be not less stringent than the emission control level achieved in practice by the best controlled similar source. 42 U.S.C. § 7412(d)(3). If an existing source is modified, the modified facility must meet the standards for a new source.

The CAA provides that the USEPA use strict criteria in developing MACT standards and even authorizes a prohibition of HAP emissions if achievable. However, the CAA also requires that the USEPA consider cost and other measures including, without limitation, measures that:

(A) Reduce the volume of, or eliminate emissions of, such pollutants through process changes, substitution of materials or other modifications;

(B) enclose systems or processes to eliminate emissions;

(C) collect, capture or treat such pollutants when released from a process, stack, storage or fugitive emissions point;

(D) are design, equipment, work practice, or operational standards (including requirements for operator training or certification);

(E) are a combination of the above.

For existing sources, the MACT standards may be less stringent than standards for new sources in the same category, but must not be less stringent, and may be more stringent, than (A) the average emission limitations achieved by the best 12% of the existing sources *excluding* certain sources that have within specified recent time periods first achieved compliance with the lowest achievable emission rate (LAER), or (B) the average emission limitation achieved by the best performing five sources in any category with fewer than 30 sources. 42 U.S.C. § 7412(d)(3). In its interpretation of the CAAA of 1990, the USEPA chose a strict (or "higher flow") standard for MACT. See 59 Fed. Reg. 29,196 (6/16/94).

Qualifying facilities which achieve a 90% reduction of certain HAPs may be entitled to defer. compliance with the MACT standards for six years under the USEPA's Early Reductions Program. 40 C.F.R. § 63.70 *et seq.*

The CAA requires the USEPA to issue MACT standards according to a schedule to be met within 10 years after enactment, i.e., November 15, 2000. Owners and operators must comply with a new MACT standard within 3 years after its effective date. Extensions for achieving compliance are available to companies making significant improvements which do not fully achieve the MACT standards.

A helpful article titled "Maximum Achievable Control Technology" discussed the USEPA's methods for setting floors (or minimum stringency levels) for NSPS and NESHAP standards and court decisions affecting the methods. "Maximum Achievable Control Technology," Friedland and Doster, 33 *Env. Rep. (BNA)*, April 26, 2002. The article discusses decisions by the U.S. Circuit Court of Appeals for the District of Columbia which sometimes question the USEPA's methods, but generally uphold them anyway. *National Lime Ass'n v. EPA*, 233 F.3d 625 (D.C. Cir. 2001); *Cement Kiln Recycling Ass'n v. EPA*, 255 F.3d 855 (D.C. Cir. 2001); *Sierra Club v. EPA*, 167 F.3d 658 (D.C. Cir. 1996).

ii. GACT Standards

The CAA does not define generally available control technology (GACT) and the USEPA has not adopted a regulatory definition. The USEPA has moved cautiously in regulating area sources, many of which are located in urban areas. Voters in the large cities provide strong support for the USEPA's programs to regulate industry in industrial, rural and undeveloped areas of the nation.

By early 1999, the USEPA had published a few regulations applicable to area sources. The best known were the regulations on dry cleaning facilities and halogenated solvent cleaners. Others applied to medical waste incinerators, municipal waste combustors and chromium electroplating.

In 1999, the USEPA published an Integral Urban Air Toxics Strategy, 64 Fed. Reg. 38705 (July 19, 1999) linking 33 of the 198 HAPs listed in the CAAA of 1990 to urban problems. In the Strategy document, the USEPA said that the CAA allows it flexibility to decide which level of control to apply to a given area source category. The USEPA said that it can adopt rules that set emission levels based on specific controls or management practices or rules that establish permitting or other regulatory processes that result in the identification and application of GACT. The USEPA also reminded readers of the Strategy that it has authority to apply MACT to area sources.

f. Health-Based Standards for NESHAPs

In addition to the MACT standards, the CAA provides that the USEPA must develop health-based standards unless Congress acts to defer or delete that requirement. The health standards applicable to pollutants classified as known, probable or possible human carcinogens will be designed to reduce lifetime excess cancer risk to the individual most exposed to less than one in one million.

The CAAA of 1990 required the USEPA to submit a report to Congress within six years on any risks to public health remaining after compliance with the MACT standards. The USEPA submitted the report in 1999 and informed Congress that it has not completed the required MACT standards for all 188 HAPs. The USEPA also informed Congress that its work to evaluate the risk reduction likely to be achieved by the MACT standards and the risks remaining after compliance is incomplete. The risk assessments used by the USEPA are extremely cautious so it is likely to propose health based standards that would actually reduce risk to less than one in one billion for most HAPs and even lower for some HAPs.

g. Court Review of HAP Listing

The courts may nullify a listing of a substance as a HAP if the USEPA's methods in reaching its decision are found to be arbitrary. For example, its listing of methylene diphenyl diisocyanate (MDI) was nullified in *Chemical Manufacturers Association v. EPA*, 28 F.3d 1259 (D.C. Cir. 1994).

B. Accidental Releases of Chemicals

1. Requirements of the CAAA of 1990

The CAAA of 1990 created a new program intended to prevent or mitigate accidental releases of hazardous chemical substances and any other extremely hazardous substances. A general duty was imposed directly on owners and operators of stationary sources producing, processing, handling or storing such substances to identify hazards which may result from accidental releases, to design and maintain a safe facility so as to prevent such releases, and to minimize the consequences for such releases as do occur. The USEPA was instructed to issue regulations requiring that owners and operators of stationary sources adopt and register with the USEPA a risk management plan (RMP). The USEPA was also required to issue within 24 months an initial list of at least 100 substances which pose the greatest risk of causing death, injury or serious adverse effects to human health or the environment from accidental releases. A Chemical Safety and Hazard Investigation Board was created with broad investigative and other powers relating to accidental releases. 42 U.S.C. § 7412(r).

2. Rulemaking Controversies

The USEPA proposed a rule governing RMPs in 58 Fed. Reg. 54, 190 (10/20/93), but it encountered widespread opposition because it would have required hazard assessments of worst-case scenarios based on very unrealistic assumptions. The USEPA issued the initial list of regulated substances including 77 toxic substances, 63 flammable substances, and substances defined by the U.S. Department of Transportation as those that have an explosion hazard. 40 C.F.R. Part 68.

The CAA contemplated that the USEPA's rules would be coordinated with the chemical process safety management standard of the Occupational Safety and Health Administration (OSHA) described later. 29 C.F.R. § 1910.119. However, the USEPA proposed regulations imposing many additional and different requirements.

Responding to extensive public comments, the USEPA published a supplemental notice of proposed rulemaking. 60 Fed. Reg. 13,526 (3/13/95). The USEPA revised some of its assumptions for worst case scenarios and proposed three tiers for RMPs. A Tier 1 source would prepare a brief RMP demonstrating and certifying that its worst case release would not reach any public or environmental receptors of concern. A Tier 2 source would conduct an offsite consequence analysis, document a 5-year accident history, implement prevention steps, prepare an emergency response plan, and submit an RMP, but need not take steps to comply with the prevention and emergency response programs. A Tier 3 source would be required to develop and implement the full risk management program. After further modifications, the USEPA adopted the final regulations on June 20, 1996 and has amended them several times thereafter. The list now includes 77 toxic and 63 flammable substances.

3. USEPA's Chemical Accident Prevention Regulations

a. Covered Processes

The USEPA's chemical accident prevention (CAP) regulations apply to the owner or operator of any stationary source that has more than a threshold quantity of a regulated substance in a process. 40 C.F.R. § 68.10(a). Any such stationary source is called a covered process.

Ammonia used as an agricultural nutrient, when held by farmers, is exempt. 40 C.F.R. § 68.175. As amended in 1999, the CAA also excludes any flammable substance when used as fuel or held for sale as fuel at a retail facility unless a fire or explosion caused by the substance will result in adverse health effects from human exposure other than those caused by heat or explosion impact. 42 U.S.C. § 7412.

b. Stationary Sources

A stationary source means any buildings, structures, equipments, installations, or substance emitting stationary activities, but does not include transportation or any regulated or extremely hazardous substance or storage incident to transportation. Thus, a stationary source does not include pipeline natural gas and hazardous liquid transportation subject to oversight or regulation by the U.S. Department of Transportation (DOT) under 40 C.F.R. Parts 192, 193 or 195 and any state natural gas or hazardous liquid program certified by the DOT under 49 U.S.C. § 60105. However, transportation containers used for storage that is not incident to transportation or connected to a stationary source for loading or unloading are not excluded. 40 C.F.R. § 68.3.

c. Regulated Substances and Threshold Quantities

Lists of regulated substances and their threshold quantities are provided in 40 C.F.R. § 68.130. The chemicals designated as toxic by the CAA are listed alphabetically in Table 1 and by CAS numbers in Table 2. The chemicals designated as flammable are listed alphabetically in Table 3 and by CAS numbers in Table 4. For example, acrolein is the first regulated substance listed in Table 1 and its threshold is 5,000 pounds.

In its proposed regulations, the USEPA also sought to regulate explosives. However, explosives present serious imminent hazards and the USEPA is not experienced in regulation of such hazards. Thus, the proposal to regulate explosives was dropped and they continue to be regulated by the International Makers of Explosives (IME), DOT, the Department of Energy, and the military departments.

If a new regulated substance is listed, owners and operators have three years to achieve compliance. 40 C.F.R. § 68.10(a)(2).

The regulations on threshold determination allow certain substances to be excluded in determining whether a threshold quantity is present at a stationary source:

1. A mixture containing a concentration below 1% by weight of the regulated substance.

2. A mixture containing a concentration above 1% by weight of a regulated toxic substance if the owner or operator can demonstrate that the partial pressure of the regulated toxic substance in the mixture is less than 10 millimeters of mercury, but this exclusion does not apply to oleum or toluene diisocyanate (TDI).

3. A mixture containing a concentration above 1% by weight of a regulated flammable substance if the owner or operator can demonstrate that the mix-

ture itself does not have a National Fire Protection Association (NFPA) flammability hazard rating of 4.

4. Regulated substances in gasoline when in distribution for use as fuel for internal combustion engines.

5. Regulated substances in naturally occurring hydrocarbon mixtures prior to entry into a natural gas processing plant or petroleum refining process unit.

6. Regulated substances in manufactured articles

7. Regulated substances used as a structural component of a stationary source; for routine janitorial maintenance; or by employees as food, drugs, cosmetics or other personal items.

8. Regulated substances used in process water or non-contact cooling water as drawn from the environment or municipal sources or used as compressed air or combustion air.

9. Regulated substances manufactured, processed, or used in a laboratory under the supervision of a technically qualified person, but this exemption does not apply to specialty chemical production, pilot plant operations, or activities outside a laboratory. 40 C.F.R. § 68.115.

To be eligible for Program 1, a covered process must not have had for five years an accidental release of a regulated substance that led to an offsite death, injury, or response or restoration activity for an exposure of an environmental receptor. Further, the distance to a toxic or flammable endpoint of a worst-case release assessed by the USEPA's methods must be less than the distance to any public receptor. In addition, its emergency response procedures must have been coordinated with local emergency planning and response organizations. 40 C.F.R. § 68.10(b).

A covered process that is not eligible for Program 1 must comply with the Program 2 requirements unless it is in one of the categories subject to Program 3. 40 C.F.R. § 68.10(a).

A covered process that is not eligible for Program 1 must comply with the Program 3 requirements if it is either:

(1) a process in North American Industry Classification Systems (NAICS) code 32211 (pulp mills); 32411 (petroleum refineries); 325181 (alkalies and chlorine); 325188 (all other organic chemical manufacturing); 325192 (other cyclic crude and intermediate manufacturing); 325199 (all other basic organic chemical manufacturing); 325211 (plastics and resins); 325311 (nitrogen fertilizer); or 32532 (pesticides and other agricultural chemicals); or

(2) a process subject to the OSHA Process Safety Management Standard, 29 C.F.R. § 1910.119.

d. Risk Management Programs

An owner or operator of a stationary source subject to the CAP regulations must submit to the USEPA a registration which includes all its covered processes and a Risk Management Plan (RMP). The covered processes are divided into three programs according to the USEPA's perceptions of their hazard levels:

Program 1. An owner or operator eligible for Program 1 must register and submit an RMP and also (1) analyze the worst case scenario for its processes and document that the nearest public receptor is beyond the distance to a toxic or flammable endpoint; (2) complete a 5-year accident history for the process; (3) ensure that response actions have been coordinated with local emergency planning and response agencies; and (4) sign a certification prescribed by the regulations as to its eligibility for Program 1 and as to the accuracy of information in the RMP.

Program 2. An owner or operator subject to Program 2 must register and submit an RMP and also (1) develop and implement a management system; (2) conduct a hazard assessment; (3) implement Program 2 prevention steps; (4) develop and implement an emergency response program and (5) submit as part of its RMP certain prevention program data on its Program 2 processes.

Program 3. An owner or operator subject to Program 3 must register and submit an RMP and also (1) develop and implement a management system; (2) conduct a hazard assessment; (3) implement the Program 3 prevention requirements; (4) develop and implement an emergency response program; and (5) submit as part of its RMP certain prevention program data for its Program 3 processes. 40 C.F.R. § 68.12.

e. Program Documents

The documentation required by the regulations is extensive and detailed. The major items are as follows:

1. *Registration.* The registration form calls for 13 mandatory items and 5 optional items of information. The mandatory items include the latitude and longitude of the stationary source and the Dun and Bradstreet numbers of the source and its parent company. 40 C.F.R. § 68.160.

2. *Risk Management Plan.* The RMP requirements include an executive summary; registration information; offsite consequence analyses including worst case scenario information; five-year accident history; prevention program; emergency response program; and certification. 40 C.F.R. § 68.150 *et seq.*

3. *Hazard Assessment.* The hazard assessment requirements are based on worst case release scenarios using assumptions prescribed by the USEPA regardless of whether they could actually happen. 40 C.F.R.§ 68.20 *et seq.* Alternative release scenario analysis is also required. 40 C.F.R. § 68.28.

4. *Prevention Programs*. The Program 2 prevention program requires the owner or operator to compile and maintain safety information; conduct a hazard review; prepare written operating procedures; provide employee training; prepare and implement equipment maintenance procedures; conduct compliance audits and retain the two most recent reports; investigate each incident which did or could reasonably have resulted in a catastrophic release; and retain investigation summaries for five years.

The Program 3 prevention program requires the owner or operator to compile and document process safety information; perform process hazard analyses using specified methods and update them; develop and implement written operating procedures; perform initial and refresher employee training in process safety and health; establish and implement written procedures to manage process and other changes; perform pre-startup reviews; perform compliance audits and retain the two most recent reports; investigate each incident that did or could reasonably have resulted in a catastrophic release and retain the reports for five years; develop and implement a written employee participation plan; develop and implement hot work permit procedures; and develop and implement safety procedures to outside contractors hired to perform work at a covered process.

The prevention programs parallel OSHA's Process Safety Management Standard described in another chapter of this book.

5. *Emergency Response Programs*. An owner or operator subject to Program 2 or Program 3 must develop and implement an emergency response program if its employees will respond to accidental releases of regulated substances. The program must include a written emergency response plan; procedures on emergency response equipment; employee training; and procedures to review and update the plan. If employees will not respond to accidental releases, an emergency response program is not required if the stationary source is included in the community emergency response plan, response actions relating to regulated flammable substances are coordinated with the local fire department, and appropriate mechanisms are in place to notify emergency responders when needed.

In 2002, the USEPA proposed acute exposure guideline levels (AEGLs) for eight chemicals for use in emergency planning, prevention, or response programs. As proposed, the AEGLs would be set at three levels: AEG-1 (nondisabling), AEGL-2 (disabling), and AEGL-3 (lethal). 67 Fed. Reg. 7167 (Feb. 15, 2002). The USEPA's National Advisory Committee for Acute Exposure Guideline Levels for Hazardous Substances published a second lengthy list of priority chemcials for guideline development at 67 Fed. Reg. 38, 107 (May 31, 2002).

f. Worst Case and Alternative Case Analyses

The USEPA's requirement of worst case release scenario analysis has been the most controversial part of the regulations, especially because of the extremely pessimistic assumptions required.

For example, the owner or operator must assume a release of the greatest amount held in a vessel or pipe. Toxic gases must be assumed to release over 10 minutes. Toxic liquids must be assumed to spill instantaneously to form a liquid pool. The volatilization rate must account for the highest daily maximum temperature in the last three years. Similarly pessimistic assumptions must be used in calculating the distance to the endpoint of a vapor cloud explosion resulting from an accidental release of flammable gases or liquids. 40 C.F.R. § 68.25.

An owner or operator subject to Program 2 or Program 3 must identify and analyze at least one alternative release scenario for each regulated toxic substance and each regulated flammable substance. These analyses need not use assumptions as pessimistic as those used in the worst case analysis. 40 C.F.R. § 68.28.

As of August 5, 1999, Congress adopted the Chemical Safety Information, Site Security and Fuels Regulatory Relief Act making amendments to the accidental release provisions of the CAA. The Act instructs the President to adopt regulations within a year governing the disclosure of offsite consequence analysis information after assessing the increased risk of terrorist and other criminal activity associated with posting of such information on the Internet together with the incentives created by public disclosure for reduction of accidental releases. After the regulations are adopted, the information will no longer be furnished under the Freedom of Information Act. The regulations must allow access for official use by federal, state and local authorities and also public access "as appropriate." The USEPA and the Attorney General must develop and implement a system for providing offsite consequence analysis information to qualified researchers, including researchers from industry and public interest groups, but they must be restricted from making the information available on the Internet. The Act provides criminal penalties for federal, state and local government employees and other persons, including qualified researchers, who violate its provisions.

In view of the several exceptions and the limited ability of government authorities to control information placed on the Internet, the Act does not seem sufficient to prevent the disclosure of offsite consequences analysis information on the Internet or to prevent its delivery to terrorists or other criminals. After the attack on the World Trade Center on September 11, 2001, the USEPA withdrew some information from the Internet for national security purposes.

g. The Chemical Safety and Hazard Investigation Board

The CAA created a Chemical Safety and Hazard Investigation Board (CSB) to investigate any accidental release that results in death, serious injury or substantial property damage and to issue periodic reports recommending measured to reduce accidental releases, corrective actions, and proposed rules and orders for consideration by the USEPA and OSHA. The CSB is also authorized to adopt accident reporting regulations. 42 U.S.C. § 7412(r).

The members of Congress elected during the 1990s were doubtful about the role of the CSB and did not fund its activities until 1997. The CAA instructs the CSB to coordinate its accident investigations with the USEPA, OSHA and the National Transportation Safety Board. Its reports are not to be admitted as evidence in any action or suit for damages arising out of an accident. In 2002, the CSB issued a report stating that the process safety management standards of the USEPA and ASHA for reactive chemicals are insufficient and that information available through professional societies and trade associations is limited, although reactive chemcials were involved in many serious accidents.

C. Motor Vehicles and Clean Fuels

1. Background

There are over 200 million motor vehicles in the United States and they are operated for trillions of miles annually. They emit to the air conventional pollutants such as carbon dioxide (CO_2), carbon monoxide (CO), nitrogen dioxide (NO_2), sulfur dioxide (SO_2) and particulate matter (PM). They emit volatile organic components and nitrogen oxides that are ozone precursors. They also emit relatively small quantities of substances, such as formaldehyde (HCHO), classed as air toxics by the USEPA.

On the other hand, motor vehicles are vital to the national economy and very popular among the general public. Thus, the USEPA regulates by imposing obligations on vehicle manufacturers and fuel producers who bear the burden of persuading the pubic to accept the changes and increased costs.

The USEPA's regulations prescribe limits on "tailpipe" exhaust emissions of pollutants from fuel burned by the internal combustion engines in vehicles. The regulations also limit evaporative emissions while vehicles are in operation, parked and being refueled.

2. Exhaust Emissions and Oxygenated Gasoline

The "tailpipe" exhaust regulations focus primarily on passenger vehicles and light-duty trucks. The regulations are extensive and detailed and apply to imported vehicles and engines as well as those manufactured in the United States. They prescribe standards and test methods for emission control systems, such as catalytic converters and on-board diagnostic systems. They also prescribe standards for performance warranties, labelling, testing, recordkeeping, emission defect reporting and recalls of vehicles and engines. The regulations are intended to reduce "tailpipe" emissions in phases running into the early years of the new century. Many reductions are already scheduled and important further reductions are scheduled, especially for the model year 2003. 40 C.F.R. Parts 85 and 86.

The USEPA issues certificates of conformity to manufacturers for prototype engines based on review of test data submitted by the manufacturers. Motor vehicles using the engines must conform to the emission standards for their useful lives. The USPEA can order a recall if it finds that a substantial number of them fail to meet the standards.

The USEPA has adopted regulations prescribing technology based exhaust emission standards for heavy duty vehicles and engines. They include equipment requirements; test procedures for pollutant emissions; certificates of conformity; maintenance of records; calculation and reporting of test results; suspension and revocation of certificates of conformity; and penalties for nonconformity. 40 C.F.R. Part 86, Subparts D, I, K and L.

The USEPA has also adopted regulations prescribing emission standards for motorcycles. Among other things, the regulations prescribe sampling and analytical methods; certificates of conformity; lubricant specifications; labelling; and a prohibition of defeat devices. 40 C.F.R. Part 86, Subparts E and F.

USEPA's standards require special designs to meet conditions that create emissions beyond those resulting from normal vehicle operation. For example, special standards apply to CO emissions during cold weather (20°F) when thin air would otherwise lead to incomplete fuel combustion. Gasoline sold in CO nonattainment areas during winter months must be oxygenated gasoline. Refiners complied with the requirement to provide oxygenated gasoline by adding 2.7% by weight of methyl tertiary butyl ether (MTBE). Similarly, there are also standards applicable to high altitudes and to starting and restarting engines. 40 C.F.R. Part 86, §§ 86.094-8 and 9.

3. Evaporative Emissions

In addition to exhaust emissions, vehicles emit hydrocarbon vapors by evaporation while parked, while running in operation or idling, and while being refueled. These evaporation losses occur most extensively during summer months. The USEPA's evaporation test procedures are at 40 C.F.R. § 86. 1201-90 *et seq.* They apply to testing of new vehicles, whether fueled by gasoline, natural gas, liquified petroleum gas (LPG) or methanol. The USEPA proposed and then withdrew regulations requiring installation of onboard vapor recovery systems because they were potentially hazardous.

The USEPA's fuel regulations contain requirements designed to reduce evaporative emissions by limiting the volatility of gasoline and controlling the flow rate of gasoline pumped during fueling. They are described under "Fuels and Fuel Additives."

4. Fuels and Fuel Additives

The USEPA has adopted regulations requiring the registration of fuels and fuel additives and also prescribing standards for them. 40 C.F.R. Parts 79 and 80. Fuel manufacturers are prohibited from selling fuels and additives until they have been tested and registered with the USEPA. When a manufacturer wishes to introduce a fuel or fuel additive, it must submit information characterizing both evaporative and combustion emissions, their health and welfare effects, and a toxicological literature survey as Tier 1 information. The manufacturer will also submit the results of biological testing as Tier 2 information and may be required to submit additional test results as Tier 3 information in order to obtain a decision by the USEPA on registration.

The regulations banned the sale of gasoline with lead additives after December 31, 1995. The regulations require that fuel sold as unleaded gasoline meet specifications which prohibit any more than 0.05 gram of lead and 0.005 gram of phosphorous per gallon. Extensive testing requirements have discouraged the substitution of other metallic additives in refinery gasoline. Ethyl Corporation, the former maker of tetraethyl lead, was able to obtain registration of manganese based additive, MMT. *Ethyl Corp. v. Browner*, 67 F.3d 941 (D.C.Cir. 1995). However, although extensive testing indicated it was safe, environmentalists opposed the manganese additive with adverse publicity that has limited its use. In July 2000, the USEPA announced that the Ethyl had agreed to perform further testing of MMT.

The fuel regulations reduce evaporative emissions by restricting the volatility of gasoline by prescribing Reid vapor pressure standards in pounds per square inch (psi) that must be met during the months from May through September with lower psi requirements for the southern states where temperatures are warmer than in other states. 40 C.F.R. § 80.27.

The fuel regulations reduce evaporative emissions during refueling by prescribing specifications for gasoline pump nozzle spouts and limiting nozzle flow rate to 10 gallons per minute except for pumps dedicated exclusively to heavy duty vehicles, boats or airplanes. 40 C.F.R. § 80.22.

The fuel regulations set specifications for diesel fuel quality including a limit on sulfur content to 0.05% by weight. 40 C.F.R. 80.29.

The fuel regulations require labeling of pump stands dispensing oxygenated gasoline to state that the gasoline is oxygenated to reduce carbon monoxide pollution. 40 C.F.R.§ 80.33.

The fuel regulations contain extensive standards and requirements, including certification procedures, for reformulated gasoline and detergent gasoline. 40 C.F.R. § 80.40 *et seq.* They are described in the next paragraphs.

In 2001, the USEPA adopted new regulations for diesel fuel to be effective in 2006 and for diesel engines to be effective between 2007 and 2010. The regulations would drastically reduce the sulfur in diesel fuel from 500 to 15 parts per million. The USEPA said cleaner diesel fuel is essential so that the catalytic converters and soot traps it proposes for diesel trucks will be effective. The USEPA estimated that the regulations would increase diesel fuel cost by three to four cents per gallon and new trucks by $1,000 to $1,600. Engine producers said that they might not be able to develop technology sufficient to achieve compliance and that fuel meeting the standards might not be available by the scheduled compliance dates. Fuel producers estimated the increased cost of diesel fuel at 10 to 20 cents per gallon. The USEPA and environmentalists said the regulations would prevent thousands of deaths and illnesses. A court challenge was rejected. *National Petrochemical & Refineries Assoc. v. Environmental Protection Agency*, 287 F.3d 1130 (D.C. Cir. 2002).

The USEPA has regulations requiring SIPs to include vehicle inspection/maintenance (I/M) program requirements such as on-road testing of vehicles by as remote sensing devices or roadside pull over, tailpipe testing. 40 C.F.R. Part 51, Subpart S, § 51.350 *et seq.* These programs are unpopular with the public. Thus, they are also unpopular with state governments which resist imposing them on the public with the strictness that the USEPA wants. In July 2000, the USEPA published amendments to the I/M program regulations that delay their milestone dates to 2002 and thereafter. 65 Fed. Reg. 45526 (July 24, 2000).

5. Reformulated Gasoline

The reformulated gasoline (RFG) regulations carry out requirements of the CAAA of 1990 to mandate the use of new gasoline formulations in certain nonattainment areas in the United States. The primary objectives are to reduce ozone precursors, especially during summer months, and air toxics. 40 C.F.R. § 80.40 *et seq.*

The CAA requires that RFG have no greater NO_x emissions than nonreformulated gasoline; contain at least 2% oxygen; and contain no more than 1% benzene and no heavy metals. At least 30% of the oxygen content of RFG must come from renewable feedstocks, meaning ethanol for practical purposes.

The CAA also required that the USEPA to determine emissions of VOCs and air toxics by baseline vehicles and baseline fuels early in the 1990s and to require a reduction of 25% of those pollutants by the year 2000 as to further limit the aromatic content of gasoline. RFG was also required to reduce NO_x emissions by 5% to 7% beginning in the year 2000.

The CAA required the sale of RFG in the nine highest ozone nonattaiment areas and other nonattainment areas where a state governor elected to "opt in" to the use of RFG as a way to move toward ozone attainment. Several states, including New York, made "opt-in" elections because it was initially popular to do so. However, when RFG met widespread public dislike, some asked to withdraw, including New York. A U.S. Circuit Court of Appeals held invalid the provisions of the USEPA's regulations allowing areas that are in attainment with the ozone standard to opt into the RFG program. *American Petroleum Institute v. EPA*, 198 F.3d 275 (D.C. Cir. 2000).

During the spring and summer of 2000, sales of RFG combined with price increases for petroleum by the Organization of Petroleum Exporting Countries (OPEC) to cause sharp increases of gasoline prices throughout the nation and especially in the midwestern states. The USEPA announced that it might eliminate its requirement that all gasoline contain at least 1.5 percent oxygen by weight, thus allowing fuel producers flexibility in maintaining a national average of 2.1 percent oxygen by weight.

The USEPA's mandated addition of oxygenating additives led to widespread use of methyl tertiary butyl ether (MTBE) in gasoline. However, the USEPA later decided that MTBE may be a carcinogen and has been seeking a rapid regulatory method to prohibit or phase out its use. In the meantime, MTBE has been detected in leaks from thousands of underground storage tanks. Thus, plaintiff attorneys are pursuing MTBE lawsuits in many areas of the nation. The USEPA announced that it would consider reducing its summer VOC emission standards for RFG mixed with ethanol, thus providing an incentive to use ethanol rather than MTBE in RFG.

In July 2000, the governors of many states proposed amendments to the CAA to eliminate RFG requirements or to allow states to opt out of the program. They expressed concern that an MTBE ban or limit would compel increased use of ethanol as an oxygenate, although supplies of ethanol are not available for that use at reasonable cost throughout the United States. In the meantime, the USEPA and its environmental supporters proposed a limit on benzene concentrations in gasoline based on levels achieved by the use of MTBE, although MTBE may soon be banned or limited. The USEPA also issued a list of 21 other compounds present in gasoline and diesel fuel that it said should be studied because they present cancer and other health hazards in urban areas.

6. "Clean Fuel" Vehicles

The CAAA of 1990 established two programs to promote the development of vehicles that would use alternative fuels perceived by environmentalists as clean. These fuels include alcohols, RFG, diesel, natural gas, liquified petroleum gas, hydrogen and electricity. One program is a pilot program conducted in California and the other is a fleet vehicle program. The USEPA's regulations for clean fuel vehicles are at 40 C.F.R. Part 88.

The USEPA's regulations for the California Pilot Test Program prescribe standards for emissions for nonmethane organic gases, carbon monoxide, nitrogen oxides, formaldehyde and particulate matter. They are applied to transitional low-emission vehicles (TLEVs), low-emission vehicles (LEVs), ultra low-emission vehicles (ULEVs), zero-emission vehicles (ZEVs), and also heavy engines. The regulations established annual sales requirements such as 300,000 clean fuel vehicles for the year 1999. The regulations provide a system of credits applicable to the sales requirements. Other states are authorized to opt into the California Pilot Test Program if they contain all or part of a ozone nonattainment area classified as serious, severe or extreme. However, as discussed later, these states cannot change the program requirements. 40 C.F.R. § 88.201-94 *et seq.*

The mandated sales have not been achieved because the public is not willing to undertake the difficulties and costs presented by experimental vehicles that do not perform as well as traditional vehicles. In 1996, California withdrew its requirement that ZEVs be sold for the model years 1998 to 2002 and entered into memoranda of agreement with vehicle manufacturers to develop ZEV technology and introduce smaller numbers of vehicles than had been required. The CARB continues to maintain its requirement that ZEVs be sold notwithstanding their disadvantages in technology, costs and other factors.

The CAA requires states having an ozone nonattainment area that is serious, severe or extreme or a CO nonattainment area at a 16 ppm level revise their SIPs to include a fleet vehicle program. The programs are designed to require owners and operators of fleets of ten or more vehicles that can be fueled at a central location to buy and use clean fuel vehicles. The regulations apply, for example, to package delivery, taxi and bus fleets. However, exemptions apply to dealer demonstration vehicles, fire trucks and other emergency vehicles, law enforcement vehicles, and vehicles held for lease or rental tot he general public. 40 C.F.R. § 88.301-93 *et seq.*

7. Preemption of State Laws

The CAA preempts the power of the states to regulate new motor vehicle and engine emissions. 42 U.S.C. § 7543. However, the CAA requires the USEPA to grant a waiver of the preemption upon application by the California Air Resources Board (CARB) when it adopts a standard that is at least as strict and is consistent with the USEPA's standards. To grant the waiver, the USEPA must find that California needs the new standard to meet compelling and extraordinary conditions and the standards are not arbitrary or capricious. However, the USEPA is likely to make the required findings whenever requested by the CARB because it shares the CARB's views on strict regulation.

When a waiver is granted, the CARB can enforce its standard as to new vehicles and engines in California. Other states may then, if they wish, adopt the same standard for any new vehicle model year that California set for that model year. However, the CAA provides that other states may not adopt their own standards because vehicle and engine manufacturers might be subjected to the impossible task of producing different models for each of the 50 states.

The practical effect is that CARB creates new vehicle and engine emission standards for much of the nation. When the CARB sets a standard, environmentalists campaign vigorously for it to be adopted in other states. Not wishing to appear less protective of the environment or to be lenient to large manufacturers, state officials are inclined to adopt the standard even though environmental conditions in their states are different from California.

In New York, the Department of Environmental Conservation (DEC) adopted CARB standards requiring sales of LEVs and ZEVs in New York for the model years 1998 to 2002. This requirement was popular because the burdens were imposed on manufacturers located in other states. However, the DEC did not adopt the CARB's clean fuels standards. Automotive manufacturers sued to set aside the DEC's requirements on grounds that the DEC's regulations were not identical to those of the CARB and that they would have to design vehicles specially for New York to achieve LEV and ZEV standards without the benefit of clean fuels. However, the DEC told the court that RFG would soon be required in New York and that it did not require clean fuels because it was not cost effective to do so. The court upheld the DEC's right to impose the LEV and ZEV sales requirements. *Motor Vehicle Manufacturers v. NYS Dept. of Env. Cons.*, 17 F.3d 521 (2d Cir. 1994). Later, the DEC withdrew its requirement that RFG be sold in nonattainment areas outside New York City because the public complained of its poor performance and cost.

The Commonwealth of Virginia chose not to adopt the CARB's requirements for sales of LEVs and ZEVs. The USEPA then issued a "SIP call" declaring that Virginia's SIP was inadequate and must be revised to include the CARB requirements. The Commonwealth and associations representing automobile manufacturers and dealers challenged the USEPA's end run around the CAA's provisions. A U.S. Court of Appeals held that the USEPA did not have authority to issue the SIP call. *Commonwealth of Virginia v. E.P.A.*, 108 F.3d 1397 (D.C.Cir. 1997).

In the meantime, the CARB withdrew its requirement that ZEVs be sold for the model years 1998 to 2002 because it became clear that the public would not buy them due to their inability to perform as well as traditional vehicles. In its place, the CARB entered into memoranda of agreement with vehicle manufacturers under which they undertook to produce improved LEVs. In New York, the automobile manufacturers sued the DEC to cancel its requirement that ZEVs for the model years 1998 to 2002 be sold in New York. The U.S. Court of Appeals agreed that the DEC's requirement was based on a CARB standard that no longer existed, so it was preempted by the CAA. *American Auto Mfrs. Ass'n.*, 152 F.3d 196 (2d Cir. 1998). Subsequently, another U.S. Court of Appeals vacated a requirement by the Massachusetts Department of Environmental Protection that ZEVs for the model years 1998 to 2002 be sold in Massachusetts and held that the requirement could not be based on the memoranda of agreement made by the CARB. *Ass'n of Int'l Auto Manufacturers v. Massachusetts DEP*, 208 F.3d 1 (1st Cir. 2002).

8. Fuel Economy Regulations

Faced with intense competition from foreign imports and investment by foreign competitors in domestic manufacturing operations, motor vehicle manufacturers began years ago to design vehicles that would improve fuel economy, i.e., more miles per gallon of fuel. The USEPA has adopted fuel economy regulations for motor vehicles and retrofit devices. The regulations require, among other things, labels that prominently link the USEPA to the manufacturers' improved mileage per gallon which is popular among the public. 40 C.F.R. Parts 600 and 610.

9. Hand Held Engines

In early 2000, the USEPA adopted a new regulation mandating a 70% cut in emissions from hand held equipment and engines, such as chainsaws and weedcutters, between 2000 and 2007. John Deere and Komatsu Zenoah reportedly supported the new regulations which give a competitive advantage to new products they have developed.

D. Acid Deposition Control (Acid Rain)

The CAAA of 1990 established programs to control and reduce emissions of SO_2 and NO_x from electric utilities that are believed to create "acid rain" damaging forests and lakes. These programs are in addition to the other programs regulating SO_s and NO_x described earlier in this Chapter. The purpose of the programs is to reduce annual emissions from 1980 levels by 10 million tons of SO_2 and by 2 million tons of NO_x in the 48 continental states and the District of Columbia. The "acid rain" programs consist of a complex package of permit requirements and emission allowances that can be used for new or modified sources or can be transferred. 42 U.S.C. § 7651.

The sulfur dioxide limitations were implemented in two phases. The CAA's Phase I required that, after January 1, 1995, 111 electric utility plants located primarily in the Midwestern United States reduce sulfur dioxide emissions to 2.5 pounds per million BTU multiplied by their average 1985-87 fuel consumption. However, a reserve of bonus allowances administered by the USEPA to provide flexibility during this first phase were provided as well as numerous exceptions. Plants that elected to repower their facilities using qualifying clean coal technologies could obtain extended compliance dates and extra allowances for reducing sulfur dioxide emissions below 1.2 pounds per million BTU.

The Phase II provisions required that, after January 1, 2000, all steam-electric utilities must reduce SO_2 emissions below 1.2 pounds per million BTU. Again, a system of allowances and other requirements and exceptions was provided. The CAA authorized matching grants up to $2.5 billion for the development of clean coal technology processes and equipment.

The USEPA adopted an acid rain permits regulation that requires certain public utilities to apply for an acid rain permit limiting SO_2 and NO_x emissions. With exceptions, the regulations apply to fossil fuel fired combustion units that are new or have a nameplate capacity in excess of 25 Mwe per year. There is an exemption for new units which have a nameplate capacity of 25 Mwe or less and which burn low sulfur gaseous fuel. The regulation also requires an annual compliance certification report. 40 C.F.R. Part 72.

The USEPA has a sulfur dioxide allowance system regulation. It provides for the (a) allocation of SO_2 emission allowances among listed public utility combustion units; (b) the tracking, holding in accounts and transfer of the allowances; (c) the deduction of allowances for compliance purposes and to offset excess emissions; (d) the sale of allowances through EPA-sponsored auctions and their direct sale, including an independent power producer's written guarantee programs; (e) the application for, and distribution of, allowances from the Conservation and Renewable Energy Reserve; and (f) the application for, and distribution of, allowances for desulfurizing of fuel by small diesel refineries. 40 C.F.R. Part 73.

The USEPA has held annual auctions of allowances which have often sold for over $100 per allowance. The allowances are traded on the Chicago Board of Trade. The USEPA and some environmentalists consider the allowances program to be a major success because there have been important reductions of SO_2 and NO_x emissions by public utilities. Further, utilities whose compliance efforts result in a lack of need for all their allowances can earn a profit by selling them to utilities that need them for expansion. However, some environmentalists have been lobbying the legislatures in the eastern states to enact laws prohibiting their state utilities from selling their allowances to midwestern utilities.

A recent article described the success achieved by the acid rain program between 1995 and 2000. The article reported that the program set an overall cap of 8.95 million tons, half of historic levels, on industrial SO_2 emissions. The phase 1 program required 263 units to reduce their annual emissions to 5.7 million tons and they actually reduced them to 4.6 million tons. The market price of allowances averaged $150, far below the $250 to $700 range predicted by some analysts at the start of the program. "Allowance Trading and SO_2 Hot Spots–Good News from the Acid Rain Program, "Byron Swift, 31 Environment Reporter 954 (May 12, 2000).

The USEPA also adopted rules under which owners and operators of small utility boilers, industrial boilers and other combustion sources can opt into the compliance program in order to sell and buy allowances. 40 C.F.R. Part 74.

The USEPA has regulations mandating continuous emissions monitoring of SO_2 NO_x and CO_2 emissions as well as volumetric flow and opacity data. The regulations include NO_x and quality control and assurance, recordkeeping and reporting requirements. These regulations also include provisions for utilities subject to NO_x mass emission reduction programs. 40 C.F.R. Part 75.

Compliance by electric utilities with the acid deposition control regulations creates difficult choices whether and how to use high or low sulfur coal, oil or nuclear fuels and whether to incur the cost of capital equipment to control emissions. These choices were made more difficult by government-mandated programs requiring utilities to purchase power from cogeneration plants and to "wheel" power through their lines and facilities for the benefit of customers who wish to purchase power from distant sources. The USEPA opposed the adoption of these so-called "deregulation" programs adopted by Congress and administered by the Federal Energy Regulatory Commission (FERC) and continues to oppose them indirectly.

The USEPA has regulations allowing the deduction of allowances to offset excess emissions. 40 C.F.R. Part 77. The CAA imposed a penalty of $2,000 per ton on emissions by utilities in excess of their SO_2 and NO_x limits and provided for its annual escalation based on the Consumer Price Index. The USEPA calculated the excess emissions penalty for 2000 at $2,623 per ton. 64 Fed. Reg. 52,725 (Sept. 30 1999). The USEPA's appeal procedures are at 40 C.F.R. Part 78.

E. Stratospheric Ozone Provisions

The CAAA of 1990 added provisions to the CAA to restrict chemical substances suspected of depleting stratospheric ozone. The amendments required eventual elimination of these substances in cooperation with the Montreal Protocol. Class I chemicals include chlorofluorocarbons (CFCs), halons, carbon tetrachloride, methyl chloroform and methyl bromide. They were scheduled to be phased out by the year 2000 except for methyl chloroform which was scheduled for 2002. Class II chemicals consist of hydrochlorofluorocarbons (HCFCs). They are to be phased out between 2003 and 2030. Other requirements include monitoring and reporting, recycling and disposal, standards for servicing motor vehicle air conditioners and labelling. The USEPA was directed to adopt regulations governing replacement chemicals and processes and was authorized to recommend research programs to promote their development and sale. The USEPA was authorized to add to the lists of Class I and Class II chemicals. The USEPA was also required to publish a list of substitutes for Class I and II chemicals that it determined to be safe and unsafe and to ban the use of substitutes it determined to be unsafe. 42 U.S.C. § 7671.

The Internal Revenue Code imposes an excise tax on so-called ozone-depleting chemicals. The tax is based on sale or use after 1995. The rate per pound is $5.35 (plus 45¢ for each year after 1995) multiplied by an ozone-depleting factor assigned to each chemical. There is an exception for certain recycling activities and an exemption for metered-dose inhalers. 26 U.S.C. §§ 4681 and 4682.

Many CFCs have very valuable uses in refrigerant, fire retardant and medical dose-metering products. For example, halons are the only chemical compounds capable of effectively extinguishing some fires. Other essential uses are in metered-dose inhalers for asthma and chronic obstructive pulmonary disease and cleaning, bonding and surface active applications for space shuttle rockets and Titan missile rockets. Several exceptions to the phase out programs are provided in 42 U.S.C. § 7671c.

The USEPA's regulations define the regulated chemical compounds as Class I controlled substances and Class II controlled substances. Class I is subdivided into seven groups. Each substance is assigned an ozone depletion percentage (ODP) that the USEPA treats as its potential to harm the stratospheric ozone layer. 40 C.F.R. Part 82.

The USEPA's regulations apportioned baseline production allowances during the phaseout periods among the manufacturers such as Allied Signal, Inc., E.I. du Pont de Nemours & Co., Elf Atochem, N.A., Great Lakes Chemical Corp., Kali Chemie Corporation, and Vulcan Chemicals. The largest allocations were made for refrigerants such as CFC-11 and CFC-12. Significant allocations were also made for Halon 1211 and Halon 1301, methyl chloride, methyl chloroform and methyl bromide. 42 C.F.R. § 82.5 and 82.6.

The USEPA's regulations include production and consumption controls including baseline allowances and allocations; servicing of motor vehicle air conditioners; labelling; and recycling of controlled substances. The USEPA adopted a Significant New Alternatives Policy (SNAP) under which it receives notices from companies which propose to produce subsititutes for Class I and II substances; assesses the risks of the substitutes and either accepts or refuses them; and publishes lists of the accepted substitutes. 59 Fed. Reg. 13044, (March 18, 1994) and periodically thereafter, including additions published in 67 Fed. Reg. 13272 (March 22, 2002). The full list is at http://www.epa.gov/ozone/title6/snap/. See also 40 C.F.R. Part 82.

The USEPA has regulations requiring that service, maintenance, repair and disposal of appliances containing Class I and Class II substances be performed only by certified technicians. 40 C.F.R. §§ 82.150 to .166. The USEPA also has regulations requiring labelling of containers of Class I and II substances. 40 C.F.R. §§ 82.102 to .116.

In general, industry has moved rapidly to comply with the new laws and regulations and to develop substitute products. However, the adequacy of substitute products for all uses has not so far been demonstrated to the public. Thus, the press has reported the existence of "black markets" for CFCs.

In 1998, Congress amended § 7671c to forbid the USEPA to prohibit the production of methyl bromide before January 1, 2005 and to authorize the USEPA to allow production of limited quantities for sanitation and food protection in developing countries that are parties to the Copenhagen Amendments to the Montreal Protocol.

F. Operating Permits

1. The Title V Programs

Before 1990, The CAA created a variety of overlapping and conflicting regulatory programs at the federal level which multiplied when extended to the state level where the basic permitting and enforcement functions are performed. Faced with vague and inconsistent requirements and unwilling to shut down local industry, state environmental agencies developed their own methods that varied from state to state, but worked fairly effectively.

Title V of the Clean Air Act Amendments of 1990 established a new permit program using experience developed in administering the national pollutant discharge elimination system (NPDES) under the Clean Water Act. Title V also extended the USEPA's authority to control and require uniformity among the state programs, 42 U.S.C. § 7661.

Title V states the minimum elements of each state permit program must include: (1) adoption of forms and procedures for applications; (2) establishing procedures and forms for monitoring and reporting; (3) annual or other fees sufficient to cover all reasonable costs required to develop and implement the program; (4) adequate personnel and funding; (5) adequate authority for the permitting agency to issue permits for a fixed term not to exceed five years incorporating emission limits and other requirements, to enforce the permits and to terminate, modify or revoke and reissue them for cause; (6) assurance that no permit will be issued if the USEPA objects in a timely manner; (7) permit processing procedures including public notice opportunity and for public comment and hearings; (8) provisions authorizing judicial review in the event of unreasonable delay; (9) procedures to afford public access to permit files; (10) requirements that major source permits with a term of three or more years be subject to revision to incorporate standards and regulations adopted after their issuance; and (11) provisions allowing changes within a permitted facility without requiring a permit revision if the changes are not modifications and do not exceed the emissions allowed by the permit.

Title V requires that the fees charged to obtain and maintain permits must cover direct and indirect costs for activities such as permit reviews; monitoring; preparing generally applicable regulations; modelling, analysis and demonstrations; preparing inventories; and tracking emissions. Thus, the cost of the programs will be borne by the owners and operators of regulated sources. Failure to pay fees is subject to a 50% penalty plus interest.

Title V requires that permit applications must be submitted with a compliance plan and schedule including progress reports no less often than six months until compliance is achieved. Permitting authorities are required to approve or disapprove a permit application within 18 months. Each permit must contain conditions including enforceable emission limits and standards, a compliance schedule, and periodic submission of any required monitoring reports. Each permit must also contain inspection, entry, monitoring, compliance certification, and reporting requirements. Permit holders must be required to certify compliance no less often than annually and to promptly report any deviations from permit requirements.

Title V requires that permitting authorities must provide to the USEPA a copy of each permit application and compliance plan and each proposed and final permit. If any permit contains provisions not in compliance with the CAA, the USEPA is required to object to its issuance and state its reasons. If the USEPA objects, the permitting authority may not issue the permit unless it is revised to meet the objection.

Title V requires that permitting authorities must notify all states (A) whose air quality may be affected and that are contiguous to the state in which an emission originates, or (B) that are within 50 miles of the source. They must provide an opportunity for these states to submit written recommendations.

2. The USEPA's Permit Regulations

The USEPA's regulations on state operating permit programs are at 40 C.F.R. Part 70. The regulations are intended to achieve permits that assure compliance with all applicable CAA requirements and may be coordinated with permits issued under other laws such as the CWA and RCRA whether issued by the state, the USEPA or the U.S. Army Corps of Engineers. The regulations are not intended to impose substantive requirements, but to require that the states adopt certain procedural requirements and impose fees on air emission sources. The threshold requirement is that the states submit their programs for review and approval by the USEPA. To be approved, they must be as strict as the USEPA's requirements, but may be stricter. The approval status of state and local operating permit programs is listed in 40 C.F.R. Part 70, Appendix A. Many state, district or county air management authorities obtained interim approvals. Some have obtained final approvals.

The USEPA has also adopted federal operating permit regulations that it can apply in any states that do not obtain and maintain approved programs. The requirements are similar to those applicable to state programs. 40 C.F. R. Part 71.

The state program regulations use the term "part 70 source" to refer to any of the sources, including area sources, that are subject to their permitting requirements. They call the permit a "part 70 permit."

An owner or operator of a part 70 source must apply for a part 70 permit within 12 months after the source becomes subject to the part 70 program. An application for renewal must be submitted at least 6 months before the permit expiration date. The application must be on standard forms calling for extensive detail, including a compliance plan, and must be certified to be true, accurate and complete. § 70.5. If a timely and complete application is submitted, a source's failure to have a permit is not a violation. However, if the permitting authority requests additional information needed to process the application and the applicant fails to submit it by a deadline specified in writing, the "application shield" protection ceases to apply. § 70.7(b).

Part 70 sources include (1) any major source of a criteria pollutant; (2) any source subject to preconstruction review under the nonattainment or PSD programs; (3) any stationary source emitting or having potential to emit 10 tons per year of any hazardous air pollutant or 25 tons per year of a combination of hazardous air pollutants; (4) any source, including an area source, subject to the hazardous air pollutant regulations; (5) any source subject to the acid deposition control regulations; and (6) any other source designated by the USEPA's regulations. 40 C.F.R. § 70.3. See also the definitions in § 70.2.

A major source is a source emitting or having potential to emit 100 tons per year of any criteria pollutant so long as it is in an attainment area for the pollutant. In a serious CO nonattainment area, the threshold is 50 tons. In a serious PM_{10} nonattainment are, the threshold is 70 tons. In ozone nonattainment areas, the thresholds for VOCs and NO_x drop to 50 tons per year for an area classed as serious, 25 tons per year for an area classed as severe, and 10 tons per year for an area classed as extreme. 40 C.F.R. § 70.2.

The USEPA defines potential to emit as operation of a source at full capacity for the entire year, even though it may be shut down for maintenance or other reasons for part of the year. However, source operators can agree to maintain emissions below a cap that is enforceable by the USEPA or a state environmental agency. *Clean Air Implementation Project v. EPA,* 1996 WL 393118, 65 USLW 2059 (D.C. Cir. 1996).

A part 70 permit must contain (1) standard requirements including emission limitations and standards; (2) a fixed term not to exceed 5 years except that the term may be 12 years for municipal solid waste incinerators; (3) monitoring and related recordkeeping and reporting requirements; (4) a prohibition against exceeding any allowance the source may hold; (5) a severability clause; (6) several provisions on noncompliance, enforcement, modification, termination, furnishing of information, and related subjects; (7) a provision to ensure that the part 70 source pays appropriate fees; (8) a provision that no permit revision is required for approved economic incentive programs; (9) terms and conditions for various operating scenarios identified by the source in its application; and (10) terms and conditions for the trading of emission increases and decreases in the permitted facility, if the applicant requests them and the applicable requirements allow such trading without case by case approval. § 70.6.

A part 70 permit must also contain provisions with respect to compliance including (1) compliance certification, testing, monitoring, reporting and recordkeeping requirements; (2) inspection and entry requirements; (3) a compliance schedule; and (4) progress reports. A part 70 permit may contain "permit shield" provisions stating that compliance with the permit shall be deemed compliance with any applicable requirements as of the date of permit issuance, but the provisions must be specific and in writing § 70.6.

Among other provisions, the regulations contain detailed requirements on permit issuance, renewal, reopenings and revisions. For example, permitting authorities are required to take final action on each permit application within 18 months, but a permitting authority that wants more time can notify the applicant that the application is incomplete. § 70.7. The regulations also require that permits contain broad reopener provisions, so that owners and operators who receive a five year permit should not assume that the permit will remain unchanged for five years. 40 C.F.R. § 70.7.

The regulations also require that state and local authorities submit a copy of each application, each proposed permit and each final permit to the USEPA. If the USEPA objects to a proposed permit, the permitting authority must revise and submit a proposed permit in response to the objection. If it fails to do so, the USEPA will issue or deny the permit in accordance with its federal program regulations. The USEPA has been using this authority to negate the CAA's grant of permitting authority to state and local agencies and make itself the actual permitting authority. For example, the USEPA has been mandating that permits require continuous monitoring of emissions even when state and local authorities consider strict periodic monitoring to be enough. See "Negotiating Title V Operating Permits: A View from the Provinces," Ternes and Macfarlane; *Natural Resources & Environment, ABA Section on Natural Resources, Energy and Environmental Law*, Fall 1998. See also *Appalachian Power v. EPA*, 2000 U.S. App. LEXIS 6826 (D.C. Cir., April 14, 2000).

G. Lakes, Bays and Coastal Waters

The CAA authorizes the USEPA to consider and establish monitoring networks to measure HAPs affecting the Great Lakes, the Chesapeake Bay, Lake Champlain and coastal waters. The USEPA is required to submit reports to the U.S. Congress every two years beginning in 1993 on the monitoring results and a determination whether the existing regulations are adequate to protect those waterbodies from serious adverse health and environmental effects. 42 U.S.C. § 7412(m)(6).

H. Enforcement

The CAA grants extensive enforcement powers to the USEPA against state and local governments, private industry and individuals.

For example, if the USEPA determines that a person has violated a SIP or a state has failed to enforce its SIP, the USEPA can issue an order prohibiting the violation and imposing administrative penalties. The USEPA may also commence a civil action in court to obtain an order enjoining a violation and imposing civil penalties. The USEPA may also refer charges to the U.S. Department of Justice for criminal prosecution. The USEPA can also directly enforce the SIP. 42 U.S.C. § 7413.

As mentioned earlier, the USEPA can also replace a SIP that it considers inadequate with a FIP. 42 U.S.C. §§ 7410 and 7411. The USEPA is also authorized to prevent states from receiving federal highway construction funds. 42 U.S.C. § 7509(b).

The CAA authorizes administrative and civil penalties up to $27,500 per day plus inflation adjustments for certain violations. 42 U.S.C. 7413(d) and (e). The USEPA can also assess penalties equal to any economic benefits that it finds a violator gained from noncompliance. 42 U.S.C. § 7420. The USEPA can also impose excess emissions penalties of $2,000 per day, plus inflation adjustments, on excess emissions of SO_2 and NO_x 42 U.S.C. § 7651j.

The USEPA has adopted regulations for assessment and collection of noncompliance penalties. 40 C.F.R. Part 66. The USEPA has also adopted regulations for federal approval of state noncompliance penalty programs. 40 C.F.R. Part 67.

The CAA also imposes numerous criminal penalties including imprisonment for terms up to 15 years and penalties up to $1,000,000. They are doubled for repeat offenses. 42 U.S.C. § 7413(c). The CAA authorizes the USEPA to pay bounties to "whistleblowers" who furnish information about violations. 42 U.S.C. § 7413(f). (Retaliation against "whistleblowers" is forbidden.) Persons convicted of criminal violations are disqualified from receiving federal contracts, loans, and grants unless the President grants an exemption. 42 U.S.C. § 7606.

The CAA provides for "citizen suits" which are often brought by environmental organizations. The CAA authorizes the courts to award attorneys fees, costs and expert witness fees. Civil penalties recovered can sometimes be used for projects to enhance public health or the environment. Employers are forbidden to retaliate or discriminate against employees who participate in a "citizen suit." 42 U.S.C. § § 7604 and 7622.

A lawsuit seeking to enjoin issuance of a state air permit for a cement processing plant on "environmental justice" grounds (i.e., racially disparate adverse impact) was denied in *South Camden Citizens v. New Jersey DEP*, 274 F.3rd 771 (3d Cir. 2001).

The CAA grants broad powers to the USEPA to inspect the premises and records of owners and operators of emission sources. 42 U.S.C. § 7414. The USEPA can issue its own administrative inspection warrants and is not limited to records required by the CAA, but may not impose unreasonably burdensome requirements such as records of every type. *Matter of Investigation Pursuant to Clean Air Act*, 728 F. Supp. 626 (D. Idaho 1990); *Public Service Co. of Indiana v. U.S. Environmental Protection Agency*, 509 F. Supp. 720, (D.C. Ind. 1981), *aff'd*, 682 F.2d 626, cert. denied 459 U.S. 1127.

Liability of corporate employees is generally limited to senior management personnel and officers and, except for knowing and willful violations, does not include stationary engineers, technicians and other such employees who are carrying out normal activities and acting under orders from the employer.

The Joint Explanatory Statement of the Senate/House Conference Committee on the CAAA of 1990 contains several interesting statements about the enforcement provisions. First, the criminal sanctions for recordkeeping, filing and other omissions are not intended to penalize inadvertent errors. Second, the criminal penalties are not intended to discourage owners or operators from conducting self-evaluations or self-audits and acting to correct any problems identified. On the contrary, they are to be encouraged. The criminal penalties should not be applied to persons acting in good faith who promptly report the results of an audit and act to correct any deviation. Knowledge gained solely in these activities should not ordinarily form the basis of the intent that results in a finding of criminal activities.

EXHIBITS

EPA **Risk Management Plan Form** **CEPP**
Section 112(r) of the Clean Air Act

Form Approved: 2/22/1999
OMB Control Number: 2050-0144

IMPORTANT: Type or print; read instructions before completing form.

Submission Type:	**Where to Send Completed Forms:**
❑ First-Time RMP Submission ❑ Correction to My Current RMP ❑ Re-Submission (all 9 sections are updated and certified)	RMP Reporting Center P.O. Box 3346 Merrifield, VA 22116-3346 Attention: RMP*Submit

Facility Name: ______________________

_ _ _ _ – _ _ _ _ – _ _ _ _
EPA Facility ID# (leave blank for first submission only)

ES **Executive Summary**

(attach a separate piece of paper if you need additional space)

EPA Form 8700-25 (Date 2/1999)

Page ES–____

Appendix A

EPA **Risk Management Plan**

Facility Name: ______________________

EPA Facility ID# (leave blank for first submission only)

1 Section 1. Registration

1.1 Source Identification

1.1.a. Facility Name (maximum 50 characters)

1.1.b. Parent Company #1 Name (maximum 50 characters)

1.1.c. Parent Company #2 Name (maximum 50 characters)

1.2. EPA Facility Identifier (12 characters)

(leave blank for first submission only)

1.3. Other EPA Systems Facility Identifier (15 characters)

1.4. Dun and Bradstreet Numbers (DUNS) (9 characters)

1.4.a. Facility DUNS	1.4.b. Parent Company #1 DUNS	1.4.c. Parent Company #2 DUNS

1.5 Facility Location

1.5.a. Street - Line 1 (maximum 35 characters)

1.5.b. Street - Line 2 (maximum 35 characters)

1.5.c. City (maximum 19 characters)	1.5.d. State
1.5.e. Zip Code Zip +4 Code	1.5.f. County (maximum 20 characters)
1.5.g. Facility Latitude (report in degrees, minutes, and seconds) +/- D D M M S S . S	1.5.h. Facility Longitude (report in degrees, minutes, and seconds) +/- D D D M M S S . S
1.5.i. Method for determining Lat/Long (see User Manual for codes)	1.5.j. Description of location identified by Lat/Long (see User Manual for codes)

EPA Form 8700-25 (Date 2/1999)

Page 1–1

EPA **Risk Management Plan**

Facility Name: ______________________

EPA Facility ID# (leave blank for first submission only) ____-____-____

1 Section 1. Registration

1.6. Owner or Operator

1.6.a. Name (maximum 35 characters)
1.6.b. Phone (___) ___ - ____

Owner or Operator Mailing Address

1.6.c. Street - Line 1 (maximum 35 characters)	
1.6.d. Street - Line 2 (maximum 35 characters)	
1.6.e. City (maximum 19 characters)	1.6.f. State
1.6.g. Zip Code ______ - Zip +4 Code ____	

1.7. Name and title of person or position responsible for RMP (part 68) implementation

1.7.a. Name of person (maximum 35 characters)	1.7.b. Title of person or position (maximum 35 characters)

1.8. Emergency Contact

1.8.a. Name (maximum 35 characters)	1.8.b. Title of person or position (maximum 35 characters)
1.8.c. Phone (___) ___ - ____	1.8.d. 24-Hour Phone (___) ___ - ____
1.8.e. 24-Hour Phone Extension/PIN # (maximum 35 characters)	

1.9. Other Points of Contact (Optional)

1.9.a. Facility or Parent Company E-mail Address (maximum 100 characters)	1.9.b. Facility Public Contact Phone Number (___) ___ - ____
1.9.c. Facility or Parent Company WWW Homepage Address (maximum 100 characters)	

EPA Form 8700-25 (Date 2/1999)

Page 1–2

EPA **Risk Management Plan**

Facility Name: ______________________

EPA Facility ID# (leave blank for first submission only)

1 Section 1. Registration

1.10. Local Emergency Planning Committee (LEPC) (optional) (maximum 30 characters)

1.11. Number of full-time employees (FTEs) on site

1.12. Covered by (select all that apply)

- ❑ 1.12.a. OSHA PSM
- ❑ 1.12.b. EPCRA section 302
- ❑ 1.12.c. CAA Title V Air Operating Permit Program. If covered, specify permit ID# below.

1.13. OSHA Star or Merit Ranking (optional)

❑ Yes ❑ No

1.14. Last Safety Inspection (by an External Agency) Date

MM DD YYYY

1.15. Last Safety Inspection Performed by an External Agency (select one)

- ❑ 1.15.a. OSHA
- ❑ 1.15.b. State occupational safety agency
- ❑ 1.15.c. EPA
- ❑ 1.15.d. State environmental agency
- ❑ 1.15.e. Fire department
- ❑ 1.15.f. Never had one
- ❑ 1.15.g. Other (specify) (maximum 50 characters)

____

____

1.16. Will this RMP involve Predictive Filing? (optional)

❑ Yes ❑ No

EPA Form 8700-25 (Date 2/1999)

Page 1–3

EPA Risk Management Plan

Facility Name: ______________________

EPA Facility ID# (leave blank for first submission only)

1 Section 1. Registration

1.17. Process Specific Information. For each covered process, fill in this page. If you are reporting more than one process, make a photocopy of this page and report each process on a separate sheet.

Process ID# (optional–for your reference only)

Process Description (optional–for your reference only)

1.17.a. Program Level (select one)

❑ 1 ❑ 2 ❑ 3

1.17.b. NAICS Code(s) (five or six digits)

1.17.c. Chemical(s) (regulated substance(s))

1.17.c.1. Name (maximum 100 characters)	1.17.c.2. CAS Number (10 characters)	1.17.c.3. Quantity (lbs) (max. 12 chars.)

If you need more space to list NAICS codes or chemicals, please make a photocopy of this sheet.

EPA Form 8700-25 (Date 2/1999)

Page 1–4

Are you claiming confidential business information in this section? ❑

EPA **Risk Management Plan**

Facility Name: ______________________________

EPA Facility ID# (leave blank for first submission only)

2 Section 2. Toxics: Worst Case

(If you need to report a worst-case scenario, make a photocopy of pages 2-1 and 2-2 and report each scenario separately)

2.1. Chemical

2.1.a. Name (maximum 100 characters)

2.1.b. Percent weight of chemical (if in a mixture) ___ . ___%

2.2. Physical state (select one)

- ❑ 2.2.a. Gas
- ❑ 2.2.b. Liquid
- ❑ 2.2.c. Gas liquified by pressure
- ❑ 2.2.d. Gas liquified by refrigeration

2.3. Model Used (select one or enter another model name in Other below)

- ❑ 2.3.a. EPA's OCA Guidance Reference Tables or Equations
- ❑ 2.3.b. EPA's RMP Guidance for Ammonia Refrigeration Reference Tables or Equations
- ❑ 2.3.d. EPA's RMP Guidance for Waste Water Treatment Plants Reference Tables or Equations
- ❑ 2.3.e. EPA's RMP Guidance for Warehouses Reference Tables or Equations
- ❑ 2.3.f. EPA's RMP Guidance for Chemical Distributors Reference Tables or Equations
- ❑ 2.3.g. EPA's RMP*Comp™
- ❑ 2.3.h. Areal Locations of Hazardous Atmospheres (ALOHA®)
- ❑ 2.3.z. Other model (specify) (maximum 255 characters)

____

2.4. Scenario (select one)

- ❑ 2.4.a. Gas Release
- ❑ 2.4.b. Liquid Spill and Vaporization

2.5. Quantity released (lbs)

2.6. Release rate (lbs/minute) ___ . ___

2.7. Release duration (minutes) ___ . ___

2.8. Wind speed (meters/second) ___ . ___

2.9. Atmospheric stability class (A-F) ___

2.10. Topography (select one)

- ❑ 2.10.a. Urban
- ❑ 2.10.b. Rural

2.11. Distance to endpoint (miles) ___ . ___

EPA Form 8700-25 (Date 2/1999)

Page 2–1

Are you claiming confidential business information in this section? ❑

EPA **Risk Management Plan**

Facility Name: ____________________

|__|__|__|__|–|__|__|__|__|–|__|__|__|__|
EPA Facility ID# (leave blank for first submission only)

2 Section 2. Toxics: Worst Case

2.12. Estimated residential population within distance to endpoint (numeric)

|__|__|__| , |__|__|__| , |__|__|__|

2.13. Public receptors within distance to endpoint (select all that apply)

- ❑ 2.13.a. Schools
- ❑ 2.13.b. Residences
- ❑ 2.13.c. Hospitals
- ❑ 2.13.d. Prison/Correctional Facilities
- ❑ 2.13.e. Recreation Areas
- ❑ 2.13.f. Major commercial, office, or industrial areas
- ❑ 2.13.g. Other (specify) (maximum 200 characters)

____

____

____

2.14. Environmental receptors within distance to endpoint (select all that apply)

- ❑ 2.14.a. National or State Parks, Forests, or Monuments
- ❑ 2.14.b. Officially Designated Wildlife Sanctuaries, Preserves, or Refuges
- ❑ 2.14.c. Federal Wilderness Area
- ❑ 2.14.d. Other (specify) (maximum 200 characters)

____

____

2.15. Passive mitigation considered (select all that apply)

- ❑ 2.15.a. Dikes
- ❑ 2.15.b. Enclosures
- ❑ 2.15.c. Berms
- ❑ 2.15.d. Drains
- ❑ 2.15.e. Sumps
- ❑ 2.15.f. Other (specify) (maximum 200 characters)

____

____

2.16. Graphics file name (optional) (maximum 12 characters)

EPA Form 8700-25 (Date 2/1999)

Page 2–2

Are you claiming confidential business information in this section? ❑

⊕EPA   Risk Management Plan

Facility Name: _____

EPA Facility ID# ☐☐☐☐-☐☐☐☐-☐☐☐☐ (leave blank for first submission only)

3 Section 3. Toxics: Alternative Releases

(If you need to report more than one alternative release scenario, make a copy of pages 3-1 and 3-2 and report each scenario separately)

3.1. Chemical

3.1.a. Name (maximum 100 characters)

3.1.b. Percent weight of chemical (if in a mixture) ☐☐.☐%

3.2. Physical State (select one)

☐ 3.2.a. Gas
☐ 3.2.b. Liquid
☐ 3.2.c. Gas liquified by pressure
☐ 3.2.c. Gas liquified by refrigeration

3.3. Model Used (select one or enter another model name in Other below)

☐ 3.3.a. EPA's OCA Guidance Reference Tables or Equations
☐ 3.3.b. EPA's RMP Guidance for Ammonia Refrigeration Reference Tables or Equations
☐ 3.3.d. EPA's RMP Guidance for Waste Water Treatment Plants Reference Tables or Equations
☐ 3.3.e. EPA's RMP Guidance for Warehouses Reference Tables or Equations
☐ 3.3.f. EPA's RMP Guidance for Chemical Distributors Reference Tables or Equations
☐ 3.3.g. EPA's RMP*Comp™
☐ 3.3.h. Areal Locations of Hazardous Atmospheres (ALOHA®)
☐ 3.3.z. Other model (specify) (maximum 200 characters)

_____

3.4. Scenario (select one)

☐ 3.4.a. Transfer hose failure
☐ 3.4.b. Pipe leak
☐ 3.4.c. Vessel leak
☐ 3.4.d. Overfilling
☐ 3.4.e. Rupture disk/relief valve failure
☐ 3.4.f. Excess flow device failure
☐ 3.4.g. Other (specify) (maximum 35 characters)

_____

3.5. Quantity released (lbs)	3.6. Release rate (lbs/minute)
☐☐☐☐☐☐☐☐	☐☐☐☐☐☐☐.☐
3.7. Release duration (minutes)	3.8. Wind speed (meters/second)
☐☐☐☐.☐	☐☐☐.☐
3.9. Atmospheric stability class (A-F) ☐	

EPA Form 8700-25 (Date 2/1999)   Page 3-1   Are you claiming confidential business information in this section? ☐

EPA **Risk Management Plan**

Facility Name: ______________________

EPA Facility ID# (leave blank for first submission only)

3 **Section 3. Toxics: Alternative Releases**

3.10. Topography (select one)

- ❑ 3.10.a. Urban
- ❑ 3.10.b. Rural

3.11. Distance to endpoint (miles)

___ . ___

3.12. Estimated residential population within distance to endpoint

___ , ___ , ___

3.13. Public receptors within distance to endpoint (select all that apply)

- ❑ 3.13.a. Schools
- ❑ 3.13.b. Residences
- ❑ 3.13.c. Hospitals
- ❑ 3.13.d. Prisons/Correctional facilities
- ❑ 3.13.e. Recreation areas
- ❑ 3.13.f. Major commercial, office, or industrial areas
- ❑ 3.13.g. Other (specify) (maximum 200 characters)

____

3.14. Environmental receptors within distance to endpoint (select all that apply)

- ❑ 3.14.a. National or State Parks, Forests, or Monuments
- ❑ 3.14.b. Officially Designated Wildlife Sanctuaries, Preserves, or Refuges
- ❑ 3.14.c. Federal Wilderness Area
- ❑ 3.14.d. Other (specify) (maximum 200 characters)

____

____

3.15. Passive mitigation considered (select all that apply)

- ❑ 3.15.a. Dikes
- ❑ 3.15.b. Enclosures
- ❑ 3.15.c. Berms
- ❑ 3.15.d. Drains
- ❑ 3.15.e. Sumps
- ❑ 3.15.f. Other (specify) (maximum 200 characters)

____

3.16. Active mitigation considered (select all that apply)

- ❑ 3.16.a. Sprinkler systems
- ❑ 3.16.b. Deluge systems
- ❑ 3.16.c. Water curtain
- ❑ 3.16.d. Neutralization
- ❑ 3.16.e. Excess flow valve
- ❑ 3.16.f. Flares
- ❑ 3.16.g. Scrubbers
- ❑ 3.16.h. Emergency shutdown systems
- ❑ 3.16.i. Other (specify) (maximum 200 characters)

____

____

3.17 Graphics file name (optional) (maximum 12 characters)

EPA Form 8700-25 (Date 2/1999) Page 3–2

Are you claiming confidential business information in this section? ❑

EPA **Risk Management Plan**

Facility Name: ______________________

EPA Facility ID# (leave blank for first submission only)

4 Section 4. Flammables: Worst Case

(If you need to report more than one worst-case scenario, make a photocopy of pages 4-1 and 4-2 and report each scenario separately)

4.1. Chemical Name (maximum 100 characters)

4.2. Model Used (select one or enter another model name in Other below)

- ❑ 4.2.a. EPA's OCA Guidance Reference Tables or Equations
- ❑ 4.2.c. EPA's RMP Guidance for Propane Storage Facilities Reference Tables or Equations
- ❑ 4.2.d. EPA's RMP Guidance for Waste Water Treatment Plants Reference Tables or Equations
- ❑ 4.2.e. EPA's RMP Guidance for Warehouses Reference Tables or Equations
- ❑ 4.2.f. EPA's RMP Guidance for Chemical Distributors Reference Tables or Equations
- ❑ 4.2.g. EPA's RMP*Comp™
- ❑ 4.2.z. Other model (specify) (maximum 235 characters)

____

4.3. Scenario (only one option)

Vapor Cloud Explosion

4.4. Quantity released (lbs)

4.5. Endpoint Used (only one option)

1 PSI

4.6. Distance to endpoint (miles)

___ . ___

4.7. Estimated residential population within distance to endpoint

___ , ___ , ___

4.8. Public receptors within distance to endpoint (select all that apply)

- ❑ 4.8.a. Schools
- ❑ 4.8.b. Residences
- ❑ 4.8.c. Hospitals
- ❑ 4.8.d. Prisons/Correctional Facilities
- ❑ 4.8.e. Recreation Areas
- ❑ 4.8.f. Major commercial, office, or industrial areas
- ❑ 4.8.g. Other (specify) (maximum 200 characters)

____

4.9. Environmental receptors within distance to endpoint (select all that apply)

- ❑ 4.9.a. National or State Parks, Forests, or Monuments
- ❑ 4.9.b. Officially Designated Wildlife Sanctuaries, Preserves, or Refuges
- ❑ 4.9.c. Federal Wilderness Area
- ❑ 4.9.d. Other (specify) (maximum 200 characters)

____

EPA Form 8700-25 (Date 2/1999)

Page 4–1

Are you claiming confidential business information in this section? ❑

EPA Risk Management Plan

Facility Name: ______________________

|_|_|_|_|-|_|_|_|_|-|_|_|_|_|
EPA Facility ID# (leave blank for first submission only)

4 Section 4. Flammables: Worst Case

4.10. Passive mitigation considered (select all that were considered in defining the release quantity or rate for the worst-case scenario)

❑ 4.10.a. Blast walls

❑ 4.10.b. Other (specify) (maximum 200 characters)

____

____

4.11. Graphics file name (optional) (maximum 12 characters)

EPA Form 8700-25 (Date 2/1999)

Page 4–2

Are you claiming confidential business information in this section? ❑

EPA **Risk Management Plan**

Facility Name: ______________________

EPA Facility ID# (leave blank for first submission only)

5 Section 5. Flammables: Alternative Releases

(If you need to report more than one alternative release scenario, make a copy of pages 5-1 and 5-2 and report each scenario separately)

5.1. Chemical Name (maximum 100 characters)

5.2. Model Used (select one or enter another model name in Other below)

- ❑ 5.2.a. EPA's OCA Guidance Reference Tables or Equations
- ❑ 5.2.c. EPA's RMP Guidance for Propane Storage Facilities Reference Tables or Equations
- ❑ 5.2.d. EPA's RMP Guidance for Waste Water Treatment Plants Reference Tables or Equations
- ❑ 5.2.e. EPA's RMP Guidance for Warehouses Reference Tables or Equations
- ❑ 5.2.f. EPA's RMP Guidance for Chemical Distributors Reference Tables or Equations
- ❑ 5.2.g. EPA's RMP*Comp™
- ❑ 5.2.z. Other model (specify) (maximum 255 characters)

____

5.3. Scenario (select one)

- ❑ 5.3.a. Vapor cloud explosion
- ❑ 5.3.b. Fireball
- ❑ 5.3.c. BLEVE
- ❑ 5.3.d. Pool fire
- ❑ 5.3.e. Jet fire
- ❑ 5.3.f. Vapor cloud fire
- ❑ 5.3.g. Other (specify) (maximum 30 characters)

____

5.4. Quantity released (lbs)

5.5. Endpoint used (select one)

- ❑ 5.5.a. 1 PSI
- ❑ 5.5.b. 5 kw/m² for 40 seconds
- ❑ 5.5.c. Lower flammability limit (specify) __ . __

5.6. Distance to endpoint (miles)

__ . __

5.7. Estimated residential population within distance to endpoint

__ , __ , __

EPA Form 8700-25 (Date 2/1999)

Page 5–1

Are you claiming confidential business information in this section? ❑

EPA **Risk Management Plan**

Facility Name: ______________________

EPA Facility ID# (leave blank for first submission only)

5 Section 5. Flammables: Alternative Releases

5.8. Public receptors within distance to endpoint (select all that apply)

- ❑ 5.8.a. Schools
- ❑ 5.8.b. Residences
- ❑ 5.8.c. Hospitals
- ❑ 5.8.d. Prisons/Correctional facilities
- ❑ 5.8.e. Recreation areas
- ❑ 5.8.f. Major commercial, office, or industrial areas
- ❑ 5.8.g. Other (specify) (maximum 200 characters)

5.9. Environmental receptors within distance to endpoint (select all that apply)

- ❑ 5.9.a. National or State Parks, Forests, or Monuments
- ❑ 5.9.b. Officially Designated Wildlife Sanctuaries, Preserves, or Refuges
- ❑ 5.9.c. Federal Wilderness Area
- ❑ 5.9.d. Other (specify) (maximum 200 characters)

5.10. Passive mitigation considered (select all that apply)

- ❑ 5.10.a. Dikes
- ❑ 5.10.b. Fire walls
- ❑ 5.10.c. Blast walls
- ❑ 5.10.d. Enclosures
- ❑ 5.10.e. Other (specify) (maximum 200 characters)

5.11. Active mitigation considered (select all that apply)

- ❑ 5.11.a. Sprinkler system
- ❑ 5.11.b. Deluge system
- ❑ 5.11.c. Water curtain
- ❑ 5.11.d. Excess flow valve
- ❑ 5.11.e. Other (specify) (maximum 200 characters)

5.12. Graphics file name (optional) (maximum 12 characters)

EPA Form 8700-25 (Date 2/1999)

Page 5–2

Are you claiming confidential business information in this section? ❑

⊕EPA Risk Management Plan

Facility Name: _____

EPA Facility ID# (leave blank for first submission only)

6 Section 6. Five-Year Accident History

(If you need to report more than one accident history, make a photocopy of pages 6-1 through 6-3 and report each accident separately)

Would you like to certify that your facility *did not have* any reportable accidents in the last 5 years?

☐ Yes; leave the rest of this section blank   ☐ No; fill out this section for each accident

---

6.1. Date of accident (day, month, and year)

M M   D D   Y Y Y Y

6.2. Time accident began (hours and minutes)

H H   M M   ☐ a.m. ☐ p.m.

6.3. NAICS code of process involved

6.4. Release duration (hours and minutes)

H H H   M M

6.5. Chemical(s) released (if you need more space to list chemicals, please make a photocopy of this sheet)

6.5.a.i. Chemical name (maximum 100 characters)	6.5.a.ii CAS number	6.5.b. Quantity released (lbs.)	6.5.c. Percent weight of chemical if in a mixture (toxics only)
			___ . _ %
			___ . _ %
			___ . _ %
			___ . _ %

6.6. Release event (select at least one)

☐ a. Gas release
☐ b. Liquid spill/evaporation
☐ c. Fire
☐ d. Explosion

6.7. Release source (select at least one)

☐ a. Storage vessel
☐ b. Piping
☐ c. Process vessel
☐ d. Transfer hose
☐ e. Valve
☐ f. Pump
☐ g. Joint
☐ h. Other (specify) (maximum 200 characters)

_____
_____

EPA Form 8700-25 (Date 2/1999)

Are you claiming confidential business information in this section? ☐

EPA Risk Management Plan

Facility Name: ______________________

EPA Facility ID# (leave blank for first submission only)

6 Section 6. Five-Year Accident History

6.8. Weather conditions at time of event

a.i. Wind speed (numerical)	Wind speed unit ❑ miles/hr. ❑ knots ❑ meters/sec.	a.ii. Wind direction
b. Temperature (°F)	c. Atmospheric stability class (A-F)	❑ d. Precipitation present
❑ e. Unknown weather conditions (check if a-d are all unknown)		

6.9. On-site Impacts

a. Deaths (enter numbers)	b. Injuries (enter numbers)
a.i. Employees or contractors	b.i. Employees or contractors
a.ii. Public responders	b.ii. Public responders
a.iii. Public	b.iii. Public
c. Property damage $ ___,___,___	

6.10. Known off-site impacts (enter numbers)

a. Deaths	d. Evacuated
b. Hospitalizations	e. Sheltered-in-place
c. Other medical treatment	f. Property damage ($):

6.10.g. Environmental damage (select all that apply)

❑ g.1. Fish or animal kills
❑ g.2. Tree, lawn, shrub, or crop damage
❑ g.3. Water contamination
❑ g.4. Soil contamination
❑ g.5. Other (specify) (maximum 200 characters)

____

____

EPA Form 8700-25 (Date 2/1999)

Page 6–2

Are you claiming confidential business information in this section? ❑

EPA **Risk Management Plan**

Facility Name: ______________________

EPA Facility ID# (leave blank for first submission only)

6 Section 6. Five-Year Accident History

6.11. Initiating event (select one)

- ❑ a. Equipment failure
- ❑ b. Human error
- ❑ c. Natural (weather conditions, earthquake)
- ❑ d. Unknown

6.12. Contributing factors (select all that apply)

- ❑ a. Equipment failure
- ❑ b. Human error
- ❑ c. Improper procedure
- ❑ d. Overpressurization
- ❑ e. Upset condition
- ❑ f. By-pass condition
- ❑ g. Maintenance activity/inactivity
- ❑ h. Process design failure
- ❑ i. Unsuitable equipment
- ❑ j. Unusual weather conditions
- ❑ k. Management error
- ❑ l. Other (specify) (maximum 200 characters)

____

____

6.13. Off-site responders notified (select one)

- ❑ a. Notified only
- ❑ b. Notified and responded
- ❑ c. No, not notified
- ❑ d. Unknown

6.14. Changes introduced as a result of the accident (select at least one)

- ❑ a. Improved/upgraded equipment
- ❑ b. Revised maintenance
- ❑ c. Revised training
- ❑ d. Revised operating procedures
- ❑ e. New process controls
- ❑ f. New mitigation systems
- ❑ g. Revised emergency response plan
- ❑ h. Changed process
- ❑ i. Reduced inventory
- ❑ j. None
- ❑ k. Other (specify) (maximum 200 characters)

____

____

____

____

EPA Form 8700-25 (Date 2/1999)

Page 6–3

Are you claiming confidential business information in this section? ❑

EPA Risk Management Plan

Facility Name: ____________________

EPA Facility ID# (leave blank for first submission only)

7 Section 7. Prevention Program: Program 3

(If you need to report more than one prevention program, make a photocopy of pages 7-1 through 7-4 and report each separately)

Prevention program description:

7.1 NAICS code for process

7.2 Chemical name(s) (maximum 100 characters)	

If you need more space to list chemicals, please make a photo copy of this sheet.

7.3. Date on which the safety information was last reviewed or revised

MM DD YYYY

7.4. Process Hazards Analysis (PHA)

7.4.a. Date of last PHA or PHA update

MM DD YYYY

7.4.b. Technique used (select at least one)

- ❑ 7.4.b.1. What If
- ❑ 7.4.b.2. Checklist
- ❑ 7.4.b.3. What If/Checklist (combined)
- ❑ 7.4.b.4. HAZOP
- ❑ 7.4.b.5. Failure Mode & Effects Analysis
- ❑ 7.4.b.6. Fault Tree Analysis
- ❑ 7.4.b.7. Other (Specify) (maximum 200 characters)

EPA Form 8700-25 (Date 2/1999)

Page 7–1

Are you claiming confidential business information in this section? ❑

EPA **Risk Management Plan**

Facility Name: ______________________

|_|_|_|_|-|_|_|_|_|-|_|_|_|_|
EPA Facility ID# (leave blank for first submission only)

7 **Section 7. Prevention Program: Program 3**

7.4.c. Expected or actual date of completion of all changes resulting from last PHA or PHA update

|_|_| |_|_| |_|_|_|_|
M M D D Y Y Y Y

7.4.d. Major hazards identified (select at least one)

- ☐ 7.4.d.1. Toxic release
- ☐ 7.4.d.2. Fire
- ☐ 7.4.d.3. Explosion
- ☐ 7.4.d.4. Runaway reaction
- ☐ 7.4.d.5. Polymerization
- ☐ 7.4.d.6. Overpressurization
- ☐ 7.4.d.7. Corrosion
- ☐ 7.4.d.8. Overfilling
- ☐ 7.4.d.9. Contamination
- ☐ 7.4.d.10. Equipment failure
- ☐ 7.4.d.11. Loss of cooling, heating, electricity, instrument air
- ☐ 7.4.d.12. Earthquake
- ☐ 7.4.d.13. Floods (flood plain)
- ☐ 7.4.d.14. Tornado
- ☐ 7.4.d.15. Hurricanes
- ☐ 7.4.d.16. Other (specify) (maximum 200 characters)

____

7.4.e. Process controls in use (select at least one)

- ☐ 7.4.e.1. Vents
- ☐ 7.4.e.2. Relief valves
- ☐ 7.4.e.3. Check valves
- ☐ 7.4.e.4. Scrubbers
- ☐ 7.4.e.5. Flares
- ☐ 7.4.e.6. Manual shutoffs
- ☐ 7.4.e.7. Automatic shutoffs
- ☐ 7.4.e.8. Interlocks
- ☐ 7.4.e.9. Alarms and procedures
- ☐ 7.4.e.10. Keyed bypass
- ☐ 7.4.e.11. Emergency air supply
- ☐ 7.4.e.12. Emergency power
- ☐ 7.4.e.13. Backup pump
- ☐ 7.4.e.14. Grounding equipment
- ☐ 7.4.e.15. Inhibitor addition
- ☐ 7.4.e.16. Rupture disks
- ☐ 7.4.e.17. Excess flow device
- ☐ 7.4.e.18. Quench system
- ☐ 7.4.e.19. Purge system
- ☐ 7.4.e.20. None
- ☐ 7.4.e.21. Other (specify) (maximum 200 characters)

____

7.4.f. Mitigation systems in use (select at least one)

- ☐ 7.4.f.1. Sprinkler system
- ☐ 7.4.f.2. Dikes
- ☐ 7.4.f.3. Fire walls
- ☐ 7.4.f.4. Blast walls
- ☐ 7.4.f.5. Deluge system
- ☐ 7.4.f.6. Water curtain
- ☐ 7.4.f.7. Enclosure
- ☐ 7.4.f.8. Neutralization
- ☐ 7.4.f.9. None
- ☐ 7.4.f.10. Other (specify) (maximum 200 characters)

____

7.4.g. Monitoring/detection systems in use (select at least one)

- ☐ 7.4.g.1. Process area detectors
- ☐ 7.4.g.2. Perimeter monitors
- ☐ 7.4.g.3. None
- ☐ 7.4.g.4. Other (specify) (maximum 200 characters)

____

EPA Form 8700-25 (Date 2/1999) Page 7–2

Are you claiming confidential business information in this section? ☐

EPA **Risk Management Plan**

Facility Name: ______________________

EPA Facility ID# (leave blank for first submission only) |_|_|_|_|-|_|_|_|_|-|_|_|_|_|

7 Section 7. Prevention Program: Program 3

7.4.h. Changes since last PHA or PHA update (select at least one)

- ❑ 7.4.h.1. Reduction in chemical inventory
- ❑ 7.4.h.2. Increase in chemical inventory
- ❑ 7.4.h.3. Change in process parameters
- ❑ 7.4.h.4. Installation of process controls
- ❑ 7.4.h.5. Installation of process detection systems
- ❑ 7.4.h.6. Installation of perimeter monitoring systems
- ❑ 7.4.h.7. Installation of mitigation systems
- ❑ 7.4.h.8. None recommended
- ❑ 7.4.h.9. None
- ❑ 7.4.h.10. Other (specify) (maximum 200 characters) ______________________

7.5 Date of most recent review or revision of operating procedures |_|_| M M |_|_| D D |_|_|_|_| Y Y Y Y

7.6 Training

7.6.a. Date of most recent review or revision of training programs |_|_| M M |_|_| D D |_|_|_|_| Y Y Y Y

7.6.b. Type of training provided (select at least one)

- ❑ 7.6.b.1. Classroom
- ❑ 7.6.b.2. On the job
- ❑ 7.6.b.3. Other (specify) (maximum 200 characters) ______________________

7.6.c. Type of competency testing used (select at least one)

- ❑ 7.6.c.1. Written test
- ❑ 7.6.c.2. Oral test
- ❑ 7.6.c.3. Demonstration
- ❑ 7.6.c.4. Observation
- ❑ 7.6.c.5. Other (specify) (maximum 200 characters) ______________________

7.7. Maintenance

7.7.a. Date of most recent review or revision of maintenance procedures |_|_| M M |_|_| D D |_|_|_|_| Y Y Y Y

7.7.b. Date of most recent equipment inspection or test |_|_| M M |_|_| D D |_|_|_|_| Y Y Y Y

7.7.c. Equipment most recently inspected or tested (list equipment) (maximum 200 characters)

EPA Form 8700-25 (Date 2/1999) Page 7–3 Are you claiming confidential business information in this section? ❑

EPA Risk Management Plan

Facility Name: ______________________

EPA Facility ID# (leave blank for first submission only)

7 Section 7. Prevention Program: Program 3

7.8. Management of Change

7.8.a. Date of most recent change that triggered management of change procedures

MM DD YYYY

7.8.b. Date of most recent review or revision of management of change procedures

MM DD YYYY

7.9. Date of most recent pre-startup review

MM DD YYYY

7.10. Compliance audits

7.10.a. Date of most recent compliance audit

MM DD YYYY

7.10.b. Expected or actual date of completion of all changes resulting from the compliance audit

MM DD YYYY

7.11. Incident investigation

7.11.a. Date of your most recent incident investigation (if any)

MM DD YYYY

7.11.b. Expected or actual date of completion of all changes resulting from the incident investigation

MM DD YYYY

7.12. Date of most recent review or revision of employee participation plans

MM DD YYYY

7.13. Date of most recent review or revision of hot work permit procedures

MM DD YYYY

7.14. Date of most recent review or revision of contractor safety procedures

MM DD YYYY

7.15. Date of most recent evaluation of contractor safety performance

MM DD YYYY

EPA Form 8700-25 (Date 2/1999)

Page 7–4

Are you claiming confidential business information in this section? ☐

EPA **Risk Management Plan**

Facility Name: ______________________

EPA Facility ID# (leave blank for first submission only) ____-____-____

8 Section 8. Prevention Program: Program 2

(If you need to report more than one prevention program, make a photocopy of pages 8-1 through 8-4 and report each separately)

Prevention program description:

____

8.1. NAICS Code for process: __ __ __ __ __ __

8.2. Chemical name(s): (maximum 100 characters)

8.2. Chemical name(s): (maximum 100 characters)	

If you need more space to list chemicals, please make a photo copy of this sheet.

8.3. Safety information

8.3.a. Date of most recent review or revision of safety information __ __ (M M) __ __ (D D) __ __ __ __ (Y Y Y Y)

8.3.b. Federal/state regulations or industry-specific design codes and standards used to demonstrate compliance with the safety information requirement (select at least one)

- ☐ 8.3.b.1. NFPA 58 (or state law based on NFPA 58)
- ☐ 8.3.b.2. OSHA (29 CFR 1910.111)
- ☐ 8.3.b.3. ASTM Standards
- ☐ 8.3.b.4. ANSI Standards
- ☐ 8.3.b.5. ASME Standards
- ☐ 8.3.b.6. None
- ☐ 8.3.b.7. Other (specify) (maximum 200 characters) ______________________
- ☐ 8.3.b.8. Comments (maximum 100 characters) ______________________

EPA Form 8700-25 (Date 2/1999)

Page 8–1

Are you claiming confidential business information in this section? ☐

EPA Risk Management Plan

Facility Name: ____________________

EPA Facility ID# (leave blank for first submission only)

8 Section 8. Prevention Program: Program 2

8.4. Hazard review

8.4.a. Date of completion of most recent hazard review or update

MM DD YYYY

8.4.b. Expected or actual date of completion of all changes resulting from the hazard review

MM DD YYYY

8.4.c. Major hazards identified (select at least one)

- ❑ 8.4.c.1. Toxic release
- ❑ 8.4.c.2. Fire
- ❑ 8.4.c.3. Explosion
- ❑ 8.4.c.4. Runaway reaction
- ❑ 8.4.c.5. Polymerization
- ❑ 8.4.c.6. Overpressurization
- ❑ 8.4.c.7. Corrosion
- ❑ 8.4.c.8. Overfilling
- ❑ 8.4.c.9. Contamination
- ❑ 8.4.c.10. Equipment failure
- ❑ 8.4.c.11. Loss of cooling, heating, electricity, instrument air
- ❑ 8.4.c.12. Earthquake
- ❑ 8.4.c.13. Floods (flood plain
- ❑ 8.4.c.14. Tornado
- ❑ 8.4.c.15. Hurricanes
- ❑ 8.4.c.16. Other (specify) (maximum 200 characters)

____

8.4.d. Process controls in use (select at least one)

- ❑ 8.4.d.1. Vents
- ❑ 8.4.d.2. Relief valves
- ❑ 8.4.d.3. Check valves
- ❑ 8.4.d.4. Scrubbers
- ❑ 8.4.d.5. Flares
- ❑ 8.4.d.6. Manual shutoffs
- ❑ 8.4.d.7. Automatic shutoffs
- ❑ 8.4.d.8. Interlocks
- ❑ 8.4.d.9. Alarms and procedures
- ❑ 8.4.d.10. Keyed bypass
- ❑ 8.4.d.11. Emergency air supply
- ❑ 8.4.d.12. Emergency power
- ❑ 8.4.d.13. Backup pump
- ❑ 8.4.d.14. Grounding equipment
- ❑ 8.4.d.15. Inhibitor addition
- ❑ 8.4.d.16. Rupture disks
- ❑ 8.4.d.17. Excess flow device
- ❑ 8.4.d.18. Quench system
- ❑ 8.4.d.19. Purge system
- ❑ 8.4.d.20. None
- ❑ 8.4.d.21. Other (specify) (maximum 200 characters)

____

EPA Form 8700-25 (Date 2/1999) Page 8–2 Are you claiming confidential business information in this section? ❑

EPA **Risk Management Plan**

Facility Name: ______________________

EPA Facility ID# (leave blank for first submission only)

8 **Section 8. Prevention Program: Program 2**

8.4.e. Mitigation systems in use (select at least one)

- ❑ 8.4.e.1. Sprinkler system
- ❑ 8.4.e.2. Dikes
- ❑ 8.4.e.3. Fire walls
- ❑ 8.4.e.4. Blast walls
- ❑ 8.4.e.5. Deluge system
- ❑ 8.4.e.6. Water curtain
- ❑ 8.4.e.7. Enclosure
- ❑ 8.4.e.8. Neutralization
- ❑ 8.4.e.9. None
- ❑ 8.4.e.10. Other (specify) (maximum 200 characters)

8.4.f. Monitoring/detection systems in use (select at least one)

- ❑ 8.4.f.1. Process area detectors
- ❑ 8.4.f.2. Perimeter monitors
- ❑ 8.4.f.3. None
- ❑ 8.4.f.4. Other (specify) (maximum 200 characters)

8.4.g. Changes since last hazard review or hazard review update (select at least one)

- ❑ 8.4.g.1. Reduction in chemical inventory
- ❑ 8.4.g.2. Increase in chemical inventory
- ❑ 8.4.g.3. Change in process parameters
- ❑ 8.4.g.4. Installation of process controls
- ❑ 8.4.g.5. Installation of process detection systems
- ❑ 8.4.g.6. Installation of perimeter monitoring systems
- ❑ 8.4.g.7. Installation of mitigation systems
- ❑ 8.4.g.8. None recommended
- ❑ 8.4.g.9. None
- ❑ 8.4.g.10. Other (specify) (maximum 200 characters)

8.5. Date of most recent review or revision of operating procedures

M M / D D / Y Y Y Y

8.6. Training

8.6.a. Date of most recent review or revision of training programs

M M / D D / Y Y Y Y

8.6.b. Type of training provided (select at least one)

- ❑ 8.6.b.1. Classroom
- ❑ 8.6.b.2. On the job
- ❑ 8.6.b.3. Other (specify) (maximum 200 characters)

EPA Form 8700-25 (Date 2/1999) Page 8–3

Are you claiming confidential business information in this section? ❑

EPA **Risk Management Plan**

Facility Name: ____________________

EPA Facility ID# (leave blank for first submission only)

8 Section 8. Prevention Program: Program 2

8.6.c. Type of competency test used (select at least one)

- ❑ 8.6.c.1. Written test
- ❑ 8.6.c.2. Oral test
- ❑ 8.6.c.3. Demonstration
- ❑ 8.6.c.4. Observation
- ❑ 8.6.c.5. Other (specify) (maximum 200 characters)

____

____

8.7. Maintenance

8.7.a. Date of most recent review or revision of maintenance procedures

M M / D D / Y Y Y Y

8.7.b. Date of most recent equipment inspection or test

M M / D D / Y Y Y Y

8.7.c. Equipment most recently inspected or tested (list equipment) (maximum 200 characters)

8.8. Compliance audits

8.8.a. Date of most recent compliance audit

M M / D D / Y Y Y Y

8.8.b. Expected or actual date of completion of all changes resulting from the compliance audit

M M / D D / Y Y Y Y

8.9. Incident investigation

8.9.a. Date of your most recent incident investigation (if any)

M M / D D / Y Y Y Y

8.9.b. Expected or actual date of completion of all changes resulting from the incident investigation

M M / D D / Y Y Y Y

8.10. Date of most recent change that triggered a review or a revision of safety information, the hazard review, operating or maintenance procedures, or training

M M / D D / Y Y Y Y

EPA Form 8700-25 (Date 2/1999)

Page 8–4

Are you claiming confidential business information in this section? ❑

EPA Risk Management Plan

Facility Name: ____________________

EPA Facility ID# (leave blank for first submission only)

9 Section 9. Emergency Response

9.1. Written emergency response (ER) plan

9.1.a. ❑ Is your facility included in the written community emergency response plan?

9.1.b. ❑ Does your facility have its own written emergency response plan?

9.2. ❑ Does your facility's ER plan include specific actions to be taken in response to accidental releases of regulated substance(s)?

9.3. ❑ Does your facility's ER plan include procedures for informing the public and local agencies responding to accidental releases?

9.4. ❑ Does your facility's ER plan include information on emergency health care?

9.5. Date of most recent review or update of your facility's ER plan

MM DD YYYY

9.6. Date of most recent ER training for your facility's employees

MM DD YYYY

9.7. Local agency with which your facility's ER plan or response activities are coordinated

9.7.a. Name of agency (maximum 35 characters)

9.7.b. Phone number ( ) -

9.8. Subject to (select all that apply)

- ❑ 9.8.a. OSHA Regulations at 29 CFR 1910.38
- ❑ 9.8.b. OSHA Regulations at 29 CFR 1910.120
- ❑ 9.8.c. Clean Water Act Regulations at 40 CFR 112
- ❑ 9.8.d. RCRA Regulations at 40 CFR 264, 265, 279.52
- ❑ 9.8.e. OPA-90 Regulations at 40 CFR 112, 33 CFR 154, 49 CFR 194, 30 CFR 254
- ❑ 9.8.f. State EPCRA Rules or Laws
- ❑ 9.8.g. Other (specify) (maximum 200 characters)

EPA Form 8700-25 (Date 2/1999)

Page 9–1

Are you claiming confidential business information in this section? ❑

APPENDIX B

Form Approved: February 22, 1999
OMB Control Number: 2050-0144

ELECTRONIC WAIVER FORM

Facility Name:______________________________

EPA Facility ID#: □□□□ - □□□□ - □□□□
(Leave blank for first submission only)

Risk Management Plan Electronic Waiver Form

Note: check all that apply.

(1) The reason(s) I am not submitting in electronic format is:

- □ I have no computers on site
- □ The software is incompatible (Ex: I only have access to a Macintosh computer)
- □ Other (specify)____

(2) I considered alternative means to file electronically (visiting a local copy store which rents computers, going to my State or local government office to use their computer, etc.), but for the following reason I am not submitting in electronic format:

- □ No commercial or public computer access available within 5 miles
- □ Contractor costs too great
- □ Computer use rental/lease costs too great
- □ No trained personnel
- □ Other (specify)__________________________

____________________________ __________________________
Signature Print Name

____________________________ _____________
Title Date

EPA Form 8700-26 (Date 2/1999)
RMP*Submit User Manual February 1999 Appendix B B-1

APPENDIX C

SAMPLE CERTIFICATION LETTERS

Certification Statement for Program 1 Process(es):

Based on the criteria in 40 CFR 68.10, the distance to the specified endpoint for the worst-case accidental release scenario for the following process(es) is less than the distance to the nearest public receptor:

- [insert description for first program 1 process from executive summary]
- [insert description for second program 1 process from executive summary]]
- etc.

Within the past five years, the process(es) has (have) had no accidental release that caused offsite impacts provided in the risk management program rule (40 CFR 68.10(b)(1)). No additional measures are necessary to prevent offsite impacts from accidental releases. In the event of fire, explosion, or a release of a regulated substance from the process(es), entry within the distance to the specified endpoints may pose a danger to public emergency responders. Therefore, public emergency responders should not enter this area except as arranged with the emergency contact indicated in the RMP. The undersigned certifies that, to the best of my knowledge, information, and belief, formed after reasonable inquiry, the information submitted is true, accurate, and complete.

______________________ ______________________

Signature Print Name

______________________ ____________

Title Date

Certification Statement for Program Level 2 & 3 Processes:

To the best of the undersigned's knowledge, information, and belief formed after reasonable inquiry, the information submitted is true, accurate, and complete.

______________________ ______________________

Signature Print Name

______________________ ____________

Title Date

RMP*Submit User Manual February 1999 Appendix C C-1

Certification Statement for a Correction:

To the best of the undersigned's knowledge, information, and belief formed after reasonable inquiry, these corrections and/or administrative changes are true, accurate, and complete.

____
Signature

____
Print Name

____
Title

____
Date

EPA Facility ID # ☐☐☐☐ - ☐☐☐☐ - ☐☐☐☐

RMP*Submit User Manual February 1999 Appendix C C-2

CHAPTER V
CLEAN WATER ACT

A. General

The Federal Water Pollution Control Act, usually called the Clean Water Act (CWA), 33 U.S.C. § 1251 *et seq.*, was adopted to protect fish, shellfish and wildlife, restore water recreation, and eliminate discharge of pollutants into U.S. waters. The CWA provides several programs such as: (1) technology based national effluent standards by industry; (2) water quality standards; (3) a permit program restricting discharges from point sources known as the national pollutant discharge elimination system (NPDES); (4) programs for the regulation of nonpoint source effluent discharges such as surface water runoff from industrial plant sites; (5) stormwater permit programs; (6) a spill control program; (7) permit programs for dredging and filling in tidal and freshwater wetlands; and (8) construction grants for publicly owned treatment works (POTWs).

B. Industrial and Commercial Effluent Discharges

Owners and operators of many industrial and commercial facilities discharge their process and other effluents directly to a river, stream or other waterbody. The discharge is usually through a pipe or other outfall. Before the CWA, some direct dischargers pretreated their effluent before its discharge to a waterbody, but many did not.

Many other owners and operators of industrial and commercial facilities discharge their effluents to public sewer systems leading to POTWs. Their wastes commingle with the sanitary and other wastes discharged by countless residential and other dischargers. Before the CWA, some industrial dischargers pretreated their process effluents before discharge to a sewer, but most did not.

Before the CWA, POTWs treated the effluents they received from their sewer systems before discharging them to a river, stream or waterbody. However, their treatment facilities were limited. A few POTWs also used other methods such as incineration.

The effluents that industrial and commercial firms and POTWs discharged to waterbodies and sewers contained large quantities of conventional pollutants, such as suspended and dissolved solid materials, oil and grease, and sanitary waste. They also contained hazardous materials (such as acids) and toxic materials (such as arsenic compounds).

Before the CWA, facility owners and operators who pretreated their effluent before direct discharge to a waterbody or a sewer used simple methods. For example, some of them separated solid material by filtering, clarifying or settling the effluent. Some neutralized the effluent by adding an acid or caustic compound. A few also used chemical or biooxidation methods with varying degrees of effectiveness. However, much of the effluent was discharged untreated or partially treated, thus causing a variety of adverse effects on the receiving waters. Some of the effects included loss of fish and other forms of marine life and loss of clean water available for drinking, recreation and other purposes.

Before the CWA, facility owners and operators who pretreated their effluent before discharging it to a sewer also used simple methods. Few went beyond separation of solids and neutralization.

Before the CWA, the POTWs also used simple methods. They received a wide variety of industrial, commercial and residential effluents and treated them by methods such as separation and neutralization. Some POTWs also had the capability to apply chemical and biological treatment or to incinerate effluents. However, much effluent passed through POTWs to public waterbodies with treatment that was able to remove or control only some of its potential adverse effects on the receiving waters.

Readers may wonder why such conditions existed. The answer is that the nation went through the desperate years of the great depression in the 1930s; the patriotic defense production years of the 1940s; and the rapid postwar growth years in which the nation and the world achieved more scientific, economic and social progress in a few decades than had been achieved in centuries of world history. In those years, the public feared tuberculosis, dyphtheria, infantile paralysis, scarlet fever, malaria and other environmentally caused diseases that killed and sickened millions of humans. Proud of developing pharmaceuticals and other chemical products that improved life span and health and living standards, industry focussed on protection against imminent hazards, but had little experience to foresee the long-term side-effects of their products and processes such as discharges of insufficiently treated effluent.

C. Prohibition of Unpermitted Discharges

The CWA prohibits all discharges of pollutants from point sources into navigable waters unless allowed by an NPDES permit. The term "pollutant" includes chemical, biological and other industrial substances as well as sewage, solid waste and dredging spoils. A point source is a means of conveyance such as a pipe, ditch, conduit or vessel, but also may include surface runoff from land.

Navigable waters include coastal waters, lakes, rivers and their tributaries such as non-navigable creeks and streams.

The USEPA's regulations and court decisions have held that some events are not discharges. For example, passive migration through soil and groundwater of contamination released years ago has been held not to be a discharge. *Friends of Santa Fe County v. LAC Minerals*, 892 F.Supp. 1333 (D. N.M. 1995). Dredging and excavation activities that move material from one place to another have also been held not to be a discharge. *National Mining Ass'n v. Army Corps of Engineers*, 145 F.3d 1399 (D.C. Cir. 1998); *U.S. v. Wilson*, 133 F.3d 251 (4th Cir. 1997); but see *Du Bois v. U.S. Dept. of Agriculture*, 102 F.3d 1273 (1st Cir. 1996).

The USEPA's regulations and court decisions have interpreted the terms "pollutant," "point source" and "navigable waters," so broadly that it is difficult to identify matters not within their scope. For example, even harmless materials (such as rock and sand) and nonmaterial physical characteristics (such as heat) are treated as pollutants. 33 U.S.C. § 1362(6) *Driscoll v. Adams*, 181 F.3d 1285 (11th Cir. 1999); *Piney Run v. County Commissioners*, 268 F.3d 255 (4th Cir. 2001). The CWA specifically regulates thermal discharges, primarily by electricity generating utilities, together with their cooling water intake structures because of their effects on fish and other marine life. 33 U.S.C. § 1326.

Ditches and gullies carrying surfacewater runoff from spoil piles and detention ponds created by mining activities have been held to be point sources. *Sierra Club v. Abston Construction*, 620 F.2d 41 (5th Cir. 1980). A pumping station was required to obtain a discharge permit, *Miccosukee Tribe v. South Florida Water Mgt. Dist.*, 2002 U.S. App. LEXIS 1588 (11th Cir. 2002). Even vehicles have been held to be point sources. A U.S. District Court held that a dam was a point source and that a change of oxygen content and other characteristics of water downstream was the addition of pollutants. However, the EPA's interpretation that dams should be treated as nonpoint sources was upheld on appeal. *National Wildlife Federation v. Gorsuch*, 693 F.2d 156 (D.C. Cir. 1982). A human being is not a point source. *U.S. v. Plaza Health*, 3 F.3d 643 (2d Cir. 1993).

Navigable waters have been held to include not only waters that are not navigable by even the smallest watercraft but also dry areas (such as arroyos) in arid regions that might contain water in the event of rain. *Leslie Salt Co. v. U.S.*, 896 F.2d 354 (9th Cir. 1990); *Quivira Mining v. EPA*, 765 F.2d 126 (10th Cir. 1985); *Friends of Santa Fe County v. LAC Minerals*, 892 F. Supp. 1333 (D.N.M. 1995). Navigable waters have also been held to include a discharge to a sewer that discharged to navigable waters. *U.S. v. Edison*, 108 F.3d 1336 (11th Cir. 1997).

A few court decisions, however, have restrained the long arm of the CWA. Isolated wetland areas have sometimes been held not to be waters of the United States. *Solid Waste Agency v. U.S. Army Corps of Engineers*, 531 U.S. 159 (2001); *Hoffman Homes, Inc. v. Environmental Protection Agency*, 999 F.2d 256 (7th Cir. 1993); *U.S. v. Wilson*, 133 F.3d 251 (4th Cir. 1997). See also *Kelley v. U.S.*, 618 F.

Supp. 1103 (W.D. Mich. 1985) and *U.S. v. GAF Corp.*, 389 F. Supp. 1379 (S.D. Tex. 1975).

In determining the amount of pollutants discharged, a discharger may subtract pollutants present in its intake water. 40 C.F.R. § 122.45(h). The regulations limit this credit to technology-based criteria or standards. See *American Iron & Steel Institute v. EPA*, 526 F.2d 1022 (3d Cir. 1975). Such subtraction should be made for all purposes unless the discharger contributed the pollutants to its intake water.

Some courts have also found that groundwater is neither navigable nor waters of the United States, thus leaving groundwater within the regulatory jurisdiction of the state environmental agencies. A few courts, however, have found that even groundwater is subject to the CWA if it can be linked to surfacewater. *Williams Pipe Line Co. v. Bayer Corp.*, 964 F. Supp. 1300 (S.D. Iowa 1997); *Sierra Club v. Colorado Refining*, 838 F. Supp. 1428 (D. Colo. 1993).

In a series of court battles, environmental groups and the USEPA have been successful in expanding the reach of the CWA to include agricultural operations that were formerly regarded as exempt by characterizing them as concentrated animal feeding operations (CAFOs). The courts have found that numerous agricultural operations were point sources (including vehicles and irrigation systems) and that irrigation ditches were navigable waters, i.e., waters of the United States. *Community Ass'n v. Henry Bosna Dairy*, 65 F. Supp. 2d 1129 (E.D. Wash. 1999). See also *Concerned Area Residents v. Southview Farm* 34 F.3d 114 (2d Cir. 1994) and *Carr v. Alta Verde Industries*, 931 F.2d 1055 (5th Cir. 1991). The USEPA's regulations on CAFOs are at 40 C.F.R. §§ 122.23 and 123.25.

In a series of lawsuits, environmental organizations have obtained court orders against organizations engaged in the sport of trap shooting. The courts have supported their arguments that the ranges and the shooting stations are point sources of lead shot that impact navigable waters. Efforts to resist were rejected in *Stone v. Naperville Park District*, 38 F. Supp. 2d 651 (N.D. Ill. 1999) and *Long Island Soundkeeper Fund v. New York Athletic Club*, 42 Env. Rep. Cases (BNA) 1421, 1996 WL 131863 (S.D.N.Y. March 22, 1996).

D. Permits under the NPDES Program

The principal regulatory mechanism established by the CWA is the discharge permit requirement of the NPDES program. 33 U.S.C. § 1342. A discharge from a point source to waters of the United States without an NPDES permit granted by the USEPA, or a permit granted by a state agency that has permitting authority, is prohibited.

The USEPA regulations governing the NPDES permits are at 40 C.F.R. Parts 122-125. A great majority of the states have adopted programs approved by the USEPA so that their state environmental agencies can grant permits and administer the programs. As described later in this Chapter, the permits set limits for conventional pollutants, other pollutants not classed as toxic, toxic pollutants, and pollutants in effluents from particular categories of industrial processes. The limits are derived from health-based standards, technology-based standards, and water quality based standards determined by the USEPA.

The USEPA's regulations for reviewing and approving state permit programs are at 40 C.F.R. Part 123. The USEPA's Regional Offices issue permits in states and other jurisdictions which have not obtained permit authority.

State permit programs are implemented by laws and regulations that must be as strict as the CWA and the USEPA's regulations and may be stricter. 40 C.F.R. § 123.1. Most states follow the USEPA's regulations and the state environmental agencies often incorporate them by reference into its regulations. However, a few state agencies, such as the New Jersey Department of Environmental Protection, adopt stricter standards.

Permit applications must be submitted 180 days before a discharge will commence. Obtaining issuance can be a lengthy and detailed effort, especially for a new source where the application must be accompanied by a new source questionnaire containing detailed manufacturing process data. Several government agencies, private environmental organizations, the media and the public may become involved. Each permit requires periodic or continuous monitoring and testing of effluent discharges, record keeping and reporting including any violations.

Proposed permits to be issued by state environmental agencies must be submitted for review by the USEPA which has 90 days to require changes. The state agencies must make the changes or the USEPA is entitled to issue the permit directly. 33 U.S.C. § 1342(d). 40 C.F.R. § 123.44(a).

Permits are usually issued by the state agencies and the USEPA for five year terms. It is common to issue a draft permit for comments by the applicant and others including the USEPA and the public. If there are errors in the permit, the applicant should object and request that they be corrected or it may waive its right to object. The draft permit is typically published in a local newspaper and a public hearing is scheduled if there is a significant degree of public interest. The permit typically states in detail the narrative and numerical criteria that apply to the effluent and the monitoring, testing and reporting requirements. To assure that testing is done properly, it is common to specify the applicable test methods which are usually methods prescribed by the USEPA. The permit may also require the use of best management practices. If a permit requires that the applicant comply with new or other criteria that it cannot meet, the permit may contain a compliance schedule for steps such as installation of control equipment and will impose penalties for failure to comply in a timely manner. Renewal applications must be submitted at least 180 days before the permit expiration date. The USEPA can require monitoring of an internal waste stream, although it cannot ordinarily require that it meet effluent limits. *American Iron & Steel Institute v. E.P.A.*, 115 F.3d 979 (D.C. Cir. 1997).

Permitholders must recognize that the monitoring, sampling, testing, recordkeeping and reporting obligations in permits are very serious. The state agencies and the USEPA impose significant penalties for simple failures to comply. Tampering, falsification and other knowing failures are subject to criminal penalties that are imposed not only on corporations but also their responsible officers.

An applicant's best opportunity to obtain a permit containing requirements with which it can comply without excessive burdens is to acquaint the agency personnel as early and fully as possible with the nature of its facilities and processes as well as its effluent discharges. This is specially important when they do not fit neatly into regulatory categories or criteria. The author recalls plants that were issued permits mandating control equipment and methods appropriate for petrochemicals, but unworkable for the chemical intermediates that the applicants manufactured. The case manager was in a quandary because the agency's only other related standards were for polymers or compounds which were also inappropriate. Eventually, after reviewing the applicant's technical information and the state of the art, the agency adopted a new subcategory of technology-based standards for the intermediates that achieved results as good as those achieved by the petrochemical standards but required methods that were technically and economically feasible for manufacturers of chemical intermediates.

When negotiating a permit, it is important to obtain a clear provision that "upset" conditions beyond the reasonable control of the permitholder will not be regarded as a violation, provided that it gives timely notice of the upset and meets other requirements. 40 C.F.R. § 122.41(n). It is also important to include a clear provision allowing the permitholder to "bypass" its treatment system under emergency conditions, including prior notice when possible, allowed by the regulations. 40 C.F.R. § 122.41(m).

The USEPA's regulations allow a permit applicant to seek a variance from its effluent limitations because of fundamental factors relating to its facilities, equipment, processes or other conditions that are fundamentally different from the factors considered by the USEPA in setting the limits. 40 C.F.R. § 125.30-32. *E.I. du Pont v. Train*, 40 U.S.112 (1977); *Appalachian Power v. Train*, 545 F.2d 1351 (4th Cir. 1976). Variances are seldom granted.

Both the USEPA and the state agencies provide internal review procedures at which an applicant can challenge permit requirements. 40 C.F.R. Parts 123 and 124. Although not often used, their existence is important because agency personnel are aware that their actions can be reviewed. The state laws and the CWA also authorize appeal to a court after an applicant has exhausted its remedies within an agency and it has taken final action. An applicant which wishes to challenge an NPDES permit issued by final action of the USEPA can appeal to the appropriate U.S. Circuit Court of Appeals. However, the applicant will not prevail by merely showing that an agency was wrong. It must prove that the agency was arbitrary and capricious or that its action was contrary to law. The courts rarely find that the USEPA was arbitrary and capricious.

In addition to applicants, the states must allow citizens to challenge final actions or permits in court. 40 C.F.R. § 123.30.

Once an applicant obtains a permit, it serves as a shield against enforcement actions and citizen suits seeking to prohibit or impose liability for discharges that do not violate the permit. The shield applies not only to discharges within the limits authorized by the permit, but also to discharges of pollutants not limited by the permit. *E.I. du Pont v. Train*, 430 U.S. 112 (1977); *Atlantic States Legal Foundation v. Eastman Kodak,* 12 F.3d 353 (2d Cir. 1994), cert. denied 115 S.Ct. 62 (1994). *Piney Run Pres. Assn. v. Carroll County,* 268 F.3d 255 (4th Cir. 2001).

E. Water Quality and Wastewater Management Programs

In addition to its permit-based programs, the CWA has major programs that impose planning requirements on the states and link compliance to appropriations of federal funds for construction and other purposes.

The CWA requires that the states adopt and implement a continuing water quality planning process. 33 U.S.C. § 1313(e). The USEPA's regulations require that the states adopt water quality management (WQM) plans and prescribe their content and use. 40 C.F.R. Part 130. The states may designate area-wide planning agencies to assume responsibility for water quality management planning. 40 C.F.R. § 130.9.

The CWA requires that a state's continuing planning process include (1) water quality based effluent limitations and compliance schedules; (2) elements for area-wide management plans and basin plans; (3) total maximum daily load (TMDL) requirements for pollutants based on water quality standards; (4) controls over the disposition of residual waste from water treatment processing; and (5) an inventory and ranking in order of priority of needs for construction of waste treatment works to meet the new effluent limitations and standards. 33 U.S.C. § 1313(e).

The USEPA's regulations amplify the CWA by requiring that WQM plans include, among many other things, the following elements:

1. TMDLs.

2. Effluent limitations, including water quality based limitations, and schedules of compliance.

3. Identification of anticipated municipal and industrial waste treatment works including information on sewer overflows, financial arrangements, and construction priorities and schedules.

4. Descriptions of regulatory and nonregulatory programs, activities and best management practices selected to control nonpoint source pollution from

sources such as residual waste, land disposal of pollutants, agricultural and silvicultural activities; mines, construction, saltwater intrusion, and urban stormwater.

5. Identification of the agencies to carry out the plan and their capabilities to carry out their responsibilities.

6. Implementation of measures to carry out the plan including financing, time, and economic, social and environmental impacts.

7. Identification and development of programs to control dredge or fill material.

8. Identification of any relationship to basin plans.

9. Identification and development of programs for control of groundwater pollution.

The CWA also contains programs providing billions of dollars of funds for construction of wastewater treatment facilities. 33 U.S.C. § 1281 *et seq.* These funds are linked to the adoption of a continuing wastewater management planning process including wastewater management plans. 33 U.S.C. § 1288. The CWA provides for grants to the states to carry out water quality management planning, including determination of publicly owned treatment works (FOTWs) that should be constructed with federal assistance. 33 U.S.C. § 1285(j).

F. Technology-Based Effluent Standards

1. Introduction

The CWA requires the states to adopt and implement technology-based effluent standards. 33 U.S.C. §§ 1311, 1314(b) and (c), 1316(b) and (c) and 1317(c). The standards are implemented primarily by the permit requirements described later in this chapter.

The USEPA's regulations distinguish between sources discharging directly into waterbodies and those discharging to POTWs. They also distinguish between existing sources and new sources. An existing source which is substantially modified is treated as a new source.

2. Direct Dischargers

a. Existing Sources

Owners and operators of sources directly discharging to a waterbody are required to treat their effluent before discharge using technology-based standards. The CWA originally required that industrial direct dischargers implement the best practicable technology (BPT) on or before July 1, 1977. The CWA required them to implement the best available technology economically feasible (BAT) by July 1, 1983, but allowed them to use the best conventional technology

(BCT) for conventional pollutants, i.e., biological oxygen demand (BOD), total suspended solids (TSS), pH, fecal coliform, and oil and grease. The BCT exception is important for industrial dischargers because BAT standards do not require cost-benefit justification and must be implemented if they are economically achievable. On the other hand, BCT standards for conventional pollutants must be based on reasonable costs.

The CWA authorizes the USEPA to modify the BAT requirements for dischargers of ammonia, chlorine, color, iron and total phenols, and any other nonconventional pollutant that it lists as a pollutant, but not as a toxic pollutant, and which meets other requirements in 33 U.S.C. § 1311(g).

The USEPA's Effluent Guidelines and Standards for the states are published in 40 C.F.R. Parts 400 to 471. They list the conventional pollutants described in the previous paragraph. 40 C.F.R. § 401.16. They also provide a list of 65 toxic pollutants designated as required by § 307(a)(1) of the CWA. 40 C.F.R. § 401.15. They go on to provide guidelines and standards for over 50 industrial categories. For each industrial category, the regulations prescribe effluent limits based on BAT, BCT and BAT. They also prescribe the limits for new and modified sources described in the next section of this chapter. They also contain the national pretreatment standards for indirect dischargers described later in this chapter. These regulations are commonly called "categorical standards."

In industries for which no categorical standard has been adopted, permits are based on the best professional judgment of the agency issuing the discharge permit. The agency reviewing the permit application assembles and evaluates information on the industry and develops limits corresponding to the applicable technology standard. 40 C.F.R. § 125.3. If the USEPA should thereafter adopt a stricter categorical standard, the discharger must comply with the new standard. If the new standard is more lenient, the discharger is not allowed to use it. *NRDC v. EPA*, 859 F.2d 156 (D.C. Cir. 1988).

b. New and Modified Sources

Owners and operators of new (or modified) direct discharge sources must meet new source performance standards (NSPS) which require use of the best available demonstrated control technology (BADCT). In developing NSPS, the USEPA must consider not only discharge controls but other controls achieved by process and operating methods. NSPS standards based on BADCT may be the same as, or stricter than, BAT and the selection does not require cost-benefit analysis. Thus, when a source must implement BADCT, the state authorities and the USEPA can insist on "state of the art" control processes and equipment if they have been demonstrated and are not in a conceptual or development stage. Issuance of a permit for a major new source may also require an EIS under NEPA. 33 U.S.C. §1316; 40 C.F.R. § 122.29(c).

To provide some relief to owners and operators of sources required to meet NSPS requirements, a source that meets NSPS may not be required to met stricter technology-based standards for 10 years after the completion of construction or the depreciation life prescribed by the Internal Revenue Code, whichever is shorter. However, this relief may be taken away as these sources are subjected to the allocation requirements of the USEPA's TDML regulations described later in this chapter.

c. POTWs

POTWs are direct dischargers and are required to treat their effluent like other direct dischargers. POTWs typically must treat a much larger volume and wider range of pollutants then commercial and industrial dischargers.

3. Indirect Dischargers

The CWA requires that owners and operators of sources discharging to sewers leading to a POTW may not discharge their effluent without pretreatment in compliance with standards adopted by the USEPA. 33 U.S.C. § 1317.

The USEPA's general pretreatment regulations prohibit some discharges entirely. For example, discharge of ignitable, reactive and other pollutants which may create a fire or explosion hazard in a POTW is prohibited, including those with a flashpoint of less than 140° F (60° C) as determined by closed cup testers in accordance with specified ASTM methods. Discharge of pollutants which result in toxic gases, vapors or fumes within a POTW in a quantity that may cause acute worker health and safety problems is prohibited. Discharge of petroleum oil, nonbiodegradable cutting oil, or products of mineral oil origin in amounts that would cause interference or pass through the POTW is prohibited. Discharge of trucked or hauled wastes, except at specific discharge points designated by a POTW, is prohibited. 40 C.F.R. § 403.5.

The USEPA's general pretreatment regulations also provide that POTWs with a design flow of 5,000,000 gallons per day must adopt a pretreatment program by which they require industrial facilities to pretreat their effluents. 40 C.F.R. § 403.8. The POTWs must require indirect dischargers to comply with pretreatment standards for existing sources (PSES) and pretreatment standards for new sources (PSNS). The USEPA's regulations provide national pretreatment standards for existing and new industrial users in specific industrial categories. 40 C.F.R. § 403.6; 40 C.F.R. Parts 405 *et seq.* They are commonly called categorical standards. The POTWs must prescribe pretreatment standards as strict or stricter than those in the USEPA's categorical standards. The POTW programs must be approved by the USEPA.

The regulations prohibit any industrial user from adding process water or otherwise diluting a discharge as a substitute for compliance with a pretreatment standard. 40 C.F.R. § 403.6(d).

If a POTW has an approved pretreatment program, it can charge user fees for its treatment capability and can grant removal credits for its treatment operations to indirect dischargers using its facilities. 40 C.F.R. §§ 403.7 and 1403.11. The removal credits may not include any elements attributable to dilution (or volatilization) as effluent passes through sewer systems and is handled at the POTW. 40 C.F.R. § 403.7(a). However, they may include sludge disposed of at municipal landfills or applied for beneficial uses at land application sites. 40 C.F.R. Part 403 An attempt by large environmental organizations to block the grant of removal credits by POTWs was rejected. *Sierra Club v. EPA*, 992 F.2d 337 (D.C. Cir. 1993).

POTWs with approved pretreatment plans must issue permits or to establish equivalent control mechanisms for each industrial user. POTWs must prohibit discharges of pollutants from passing untreated through their facilities or interfering with their operations, but an upset that is unintentional, temporary and beyond a user's control maybe excused. 40 C.F.R. § 403.16. POTWs must also take enforcement action against any industrial user for any intentional bypass (diversion) of its wastestream from any portion of its treatment facility unless it is unavoidable, there are no feasible alternatives, and the user submits prior notice to the POTW if the user has advance knowledge of the bypass. 40 C.F.R. § 403.17.

The regulations impose reporting requirements on significant industrial users, i.e., those that discharge 25,000 gallons per day of process wastewater to a POTW excluding sanitary, noncontact cooling and boiler blowdown waters. Each industrial user must notify the POTW, the USEPA Regional Waste Management Division Director and state hazardous waste authorities in writing of any discharge to a POTW of a substance considered a hazardous waste under the Resource Conservation and Recovery Act (RCRA). Industrial users are required to file semiannual reports of effluent monitoring data including a description of the concentration and flow of pollutants to the POTW. All industrial users must also notify the POTW in advance of any substantial change in the volume or character of pollutants in their discharge. Sampling and analysis may be performed by the POTW in lieu of the industrial user.

POTWs with approved pretreatment programs are required to conduct at least one inspection and sampling visit annually for each significant industrial user. They must also evaluate whether each significant industrial user needs a plan to control slug discharges, i.e., accidental spills or nonroutine batch discharges. 40 C.F.R. § 403.8.

The regulations impose testing requirements and restrictions on POTWs that compel them to impose strict pretreatment requirements on industrial dischargers. For example, POTWs with a design influent flow equal to or greater than one million gallons per day and any POTW having (or required to have) an approved pretreatment program must submit the results of a whole effluent biological toxicity test to the USEPA as part of its NPDES permit application. The regulations also create specific numeric limits for certain toxic pollutants in sewage sludge, specify acceptable sludge management practices and encourage the development of local limits to keep pollutants out of sludge which interfere with its beneficial use or disposal. 40 C.F.R. Part 403.

G. Toxicity Based Standards

In the early days of regulation of effluent discharges, the states regulated discharges of toxic substances under their own laws and then under the CWA when it was interpreted by court decision to require federal regulation of such discharges. *EDF v. Costle*, 636 F.2d 1229 (D.C. Cir. 1980). The CWA was subsequently amended several times to increase federal regulation of discharges of toxic substances.

State environmental regulators originally wrote narrative standards into permits issued to industrial dischargers. Examples of narrative standards were provided by the court on page 990 of *American Iron & Steel Institute v. E.P.A.*, 115 F.3d 979 (D.C. Cir. 1997). For example, the court quoted a familiar narrative requiring that effluent be free from substances in concentrations or combinations harmful to humans or aquatic life. Industry understood the intent of the narrative standards and adopted controls to achieve compliance by using a variety of traditional toxicity tests. In addition to narrative standards, state environmental agencies sometimes issued permits limiting concentrations of specific toxic pollutants to levels that would not have harmful effects.

Among the early tests for toxicity were acute toxicity tests performed periodically using dilute effluent samples. The tests were typically LC_{50} tests using very sensitive tiny fish (such as fathead minnows), crustaceans (such as mysid shrimp) or invertebrates (such as ceriodophnia water fleas). Subchronic and chronic tests were less common. Some states did not insist that an exceedance of the criteria be treated as a violation, but only as a trigger for toxicity reduction evaluation (TRE) obligations to identify, evaluate and reduce or eliminate the effluent toxicity.

For a while, some states issued narrative standards for toxic pollutants as well as numeric standards. However, the CWA was amended in 1987 to require all states to issue numeric standards. If numerical criteria are not available, the states may adopt criteria based on biological monitoring or assessment methods. 33 U.S.C. § 1313(c)(2)(B). The USEPA issues national standards that apply to states that fail to adopt standards satisfactory to the USEPA.

In recent years, the states and the USEPA have required tests for subchronic and chronic toxicity including carcinogenicity. For example, see 40 C.F.R. Part 132, Appendix A and 40 C.F.R. Part 136. They have also required use of bioaccumulation factors, especially for very stable chemical compounds that resist biodegradation. For example, see 40 C.F.R. Part 132, Appendix B, and the discussion in *American Iron & Steel Institute v. E.P.A.*, 115 F.3d 979 (D.C. Cir. 1997).

State agencies and the USEPA also developed and implemented whole effluent toxicity (WET) methods that reflect the presence of all toxic pollutants in an effluent and their effects on the receiving water and other receptors such as fish, wildlife and plantlife. The USEPA issued regulations on WET requirements as early as 1980 and in 1995 issued tests methods for measuring acute and subchronic toxicity and published corrections in January 1999. 40 C.F.R. § 136.3, Table IA. The USEPA consented to revise the WET test methods in *Edison Electric Institute v. EPA*, D.C. Cir No. 96-1062, July 25, 1998.

The author recommends that interested persons read the article "Whole Effluent Toxicity a Status Report," Koorse, *Natural Resources & Environment (ABA)*, Vol. 14, No.1, Summer, 1999.

Industry organizations have contended that the USEPA's methods for setting WET limits are scientifically indefensible and overly conservative. However, the court upheld the right of the USEPA to use such methods in the *American Iron & Steel Institute* decision. The USEPA refused to approve more scientifically reasonable methods adopted by the environmental agencies of Indiana, Michigan and Ohio. 65 Fed. Reg. 47864 (Aug. 4, 2000).

The USEPA's NPDES criteria and standards provide that permits for dischargers other than POTWs must require that BATEA be implemented for all toxic pollutants referred to in Committee Print No. 95-30, House Committee on Public Works. 40 C.F.R. § 125.3(a)(2)(iii). They are the 65 toxic pollutants that were the subject of the consent decree in *EDF v. Costle*, supra. A discharge must not result in an accumulation of toxic pollutants or pesticides at levels which exert adverse effects on the biota within the zone of initial dilution (ZID). 40 C.F.R. § 125.62. A permit applicant must submit at the time of application a chemical analysis of its current discharge for all toxic pollutants listed in 40 C.F.R. § 401.15 and the pesticides demeton, guthion, malathion, mirex, methoxychlor and parathion, and must also adopt and implement a toxic control program if its effluent contains toxic pollutants or pesticides. 40 C.F.R. § 125.66.

The CWA requires the states to develop and implement a surface water toxics program. 33 U.S.C. § 1314(l). The states were required to submit four lists for approval by the USEPA. Three of the lists are of waters that cannot reasonably be expected to attain or maintain water quality standards for specified seasons. The fourth list is of point sources discharging priority (toxic) pollutants to the waters on the first three lists. The states must require each permitholder, including each POTW, to adopt an individual control strategy (ICS) to reduce discharges of priority pollutants.

H. Water Quality Based Standards

The CWA requires that the states adopt water quality standards for waters within their jurisdiction in accordance with USEPA regulations. 40 C.F.R. Part 131, 33 U.S.C. § 1313.

The USEPA's regulations prescribe requirements for state water quality planning and management. They require the states to adopt water quality standards and to prescribe water quality methods and procedures; continuous planning processes; total maximum daily load (TMDL) and individual water quality based limitations; and water quality reports. 40 C.F.R. Part 130.

The CWA also requires that the states establish use classifications for state water such as drinking water, recreational, fish and wildlife, agricultural and industrial. The states must establish water quality criteria that protect those uses. 33 U.S.C. § 1313(c)(2). The states must include in their standards an antidegradation policy so that waters exceeding the standards are not impaired. 40 C.F.R. Part 131. The CWA and the USEPA have published water quality criteria for numerous pollutants. In theory, the states can adopt their own criteria, but in reality they must adopt the federal criteria or the USEPA will not approve them. The states are free to adopt criteria stricter than the federal criteria. 33 U.S.C. § 1370. Many states are reluctant to impose on their industries criteria that their competitors in other states need not observe. These states simply adopt the USEPA's criteria. However, states such as California and New Jersey tend to adopt criteria that are stricter than the federal criteria.

The USEPA has prescribed methods for the states to use in developing limits for permits issued to industrial dischargers based on water quality standards. They require very conservative assumptions as to the concentrations of pollutants in the receiving waters and as to their acute and chronic health effects. Thus, although the technology-based effluent limits have combined with industrial initiatives to greatly impose water quality, there are numerous waterbodies that at least partially fail to meet the water quality standards as to one or more pollutants. Nonpoint source pollution that is unregulated or only partially regulated contributes significantly to these failures.

The CWA requires the states to identify and list waters within their boundaries where technology-based limits are not stringent enough to implement any water quality standards for toxic pollutants, the specific point sources believed to be preventing or impairing achievement of the standards for each segment of the listed waters; and an individual control strategy for each segment to achieve reductions through the established TMDL restrictions on point and nonpoint sources to achieve the applicable standards. 33 U.S.C. § 1313; 40 C.F.R. § 130.7.

The CWA requires the states to list these water quality limited segments of waterbodies and develop TMDLs for each pollutant causing the segment to fail to meet the applicable standard. 33 U.S.C. § 1313(d). The TMDLs must include a margin of safety for any lack of knowledge about the relation between effluent limits and water quality. The CWA provides that the states use the permit system to allocate the TMDL among all point sources and nonpoint sources of the pollutant, thus creating water quality based effluent limits that are stricter than the technology-based limits. 33 U.S.C. § 1313(d); 40 C.F.R. Part 130.7.

The TMDL requirements were written into the CWA at the urging of environmentalists, including the USEPA, who dislike technology-based standards which industrial dischargers have widely met after overcoming technical and financial hurdles. The TMDL requirements were not discussed in a meaningful way with the state officials required to implement them.

As a result, some states and the District of Columbia were slow in submitting the lists. Other states submitted lists, but the USEPA added to them. For example, without consulting Indiana, the USEPA reportedly added dozens of allegedly impaired waters to the list.

Rather than directly confront the states, the USEPA waited for environmental organizations to file friendly lawsuits to obtain court orders directing the USEPA to require the states establish TMDLs. Several courts rendered decisions or issued orders directing compliance, including consent orders signed by the USEPA. *American Canoe Ass'n v. EPA*, 54 F. Supp. 2d 621 (E.D. Va. 1999); *Kingman Park v. EPA*, 29 Envtl. L. Rep. 10716 (Nov. 1999); *Hayes v. EPA*, 48 Env't Rep. Cases (BNA) 1078 (N.D. Okla. 1998). However, one U.S. Court of Appeals rejected a lawsuit seeking to compel the USEPA to establish TMDLs for California because the State of California had been diligently working on TMDLs, *San Francisco Baykeeper v. EPA*, 54 ERC 1225 (9th Cir. 2002). See also *Hayes v. Whitman*, 204 F.3d 1017 (10th Cir. 2001).

Some of the lawsuits seek to stretch the statutory language to require TMDLs for water segments impacted only by nonpoint source pollution. Other lawsuits seek to require the USEPA to link the TMDL requirements to the Endangered Species Act.

On July 13, 2000, the USEPA published new regulations greatly extending the TMDL program. The regulations were published just before Congressional legislation to block their adoption. However, Congress denied funding to implement the regulations until fiscal year 2002. Reportedly, both Democrats and Republicans criticized the USEPA for including provisions beyond its authority, particularly those relating to nonpoint source pollution.

The new regulations require that the states develop TMDLs for the waterbodies they are required to list as impaired. The methodology is prescribed in detail. The states must include waterbodies impaired by pollution from any source including point sources, nonpoint sources, stormwater sources that are not subject to point source permits, groundwater and atmospheric deposition. 40 C.F.R. § 130.25. The states must develop TMDLs over a period of ten years from July 10, 2000 with priority assigned to drinking water and water where endangered species are present. 40 C.F.R. § 130.28. The states must assign wasteload allocations to point sources and load allocations to nonpoint sources including stormwater, atmospheric, groundwater and background sources. NPDES permits must be reissued or revised to implement the new wasteload allocations. 40 C.F.R. §§130.2 and.32. Thus, allocations for pollution from unregulated sources reduce the allocations available for revised permits of industrial and commercial sources that have already complied with the technology based effluent standards.

The states may base wasteload allocation to regulated point sources on anticipated or expected reductions of pollutants from other sources if the reductions are supported by reasonable assurance they will occur. 40 C.F.R. § 130.2(g). To provide reasonable assurance, the regulations require the development of extensive regulatory or voluntary programs. 40 C.F.R. § 130.2(p). If any state fails to comply with the regulations, the USEPA will implement the TMDL program directly. 40 C.F.R. § 130.35.

Despite the doubt about the USEPA's authority, the new regulations were supported by a resolution adopted on July 19, 2000 by the Association of Metropolitan Sewage Associations (AMSA) which views them as an opportunity to require agricultural, urban stormwater and other nonpoint sources of pollution to share responsibility for water quality. On the other hand, it is far from clear that states (or anyone else) can identify owners and operators of nonpoint sources having the ability and financial capability to make meaningful improvements. For example, older cities with large low-income populations are likely to refuse to pay for major stormwater improvements, just as they have declined to pay for other environmental improvements.

In 2001, the USEPA announced that it planned to revise the TMDL rule and delayed its effective date for 18 months. 66 Fed. Reg. 53,044 (Oct. 18, 2001).

On the other hand, some states are already moving to implement TMDL programs. For example, the New Jersey Department of Environmental Protection has announced broad new watershed regulatory programs that will be based on TMDL and other restrictive criteria. Environmental groups reacted enthusiastically, predicting that the new program will block land development causing "urban sprawl" for years into the future.

I. Nonpointsource Effluent

Much of the pollution discharged to the nation's waters comes from surface runoff and other nonpoint sources. Major nonpoint sources include farms and municipalities which cannot readily be regulated like private industry. The CWA requires the states to provide inventories and reports on compliance with water quality standards showing failure to attain compliance traceable to nonpoint source discharges of toxic pollutants. The CWA also provides funding for state studies of nonpoint source controls.

In its definition of a point source, the CWA excludes agriculturally and silviculturally related nonpoint sources of pollution, including runoff from manure disposal areas and from land used for livestock and crop production. However, it includes a concentrated animal feeding operation. Environmental groups oppose this agricultural exclusion. A federal appellate court held that a large dairy farm should be treated as a concentrated animal feeding operation and that its entire operation was a point source subject to regulation under the CWA. *Concerned Residents v. Southview Farm*, 34 F.3d 114 (2nd Cir. 1994).

A federal appellate court held that the CWA does not authorize the USEPA to regulate nonpoint source efficient. The CWA also does not require the USEPA to overrule state regulations so as to require states to adopt requirements favored by the environmental organizations. *American Wildlands v. EPA,* 260 F.3d 1192 (10th Cir. 2001).

J. Stormwater

The CWA, as amended by the Water Quality Act of 1987, regulates stormwater discharges from industrial activities and larger municipalities, even when they are not point source discharges. Stormwater permit regulations were adopted in 1990 applicable to large and medium-sized cities, some counties and certain industries. The final rule establishing general permit requirements and reporting requirements for stormwater discharges associated with industrial activity was published in April, 1992. 40 C.F.R. § 122.26.

Federal and state regulations allow some discharges to be covered by general or group permits rather than requiring industrial facility permits. Pollution control methods required by stormwater permits include finding and removing illegal sewer connections, halting dumping in sewers and preventing spills. State environmental agencies may impose "best management practices" rather than numerical limits in appropriate situations.

Stormwater regulatory programs were delayed for many years, partially because of a challenge of the USEPA's early regulations in *Natural Resources Defense Council v. EPA*, 966 F.2d 1292 (9th Cir. 1992). The NRDC, a large environmental organization, successfully objected to exemptions in the rules for light industry and small construction sites and to brief delays authorized by the USEPA. The USEPA eventually reinforced its factual support and again exempted the light industries and construction sites smaller than five acres. 40 C.F.R. § 122.26(b)(14).

A U.S. Circuit Court of Appeals declined to hold a real estate developer liable for unpermitted discharges during the long delay where the developer could not obtain a permit because the Georgia Department of Natural Resources was not ready to issue them. *Hughey v. JMS Development*, 78 F.3d 1522 (1st Cir. 1996).

The USEPA subdivided its stormwater sewer system permitting requirements into two phases. Phase I applies to discharges associated with industrial activity including any discharge through large and medium separate storm water to waters of the United States. 40 C.F.R. § 122.26(a)(4). These industrial activities are defined in the regulations to include a wide range of activities are defined in the regulations to include a wide range of activities including many identified by standard industrial code (SIC) numbers. 40 C.F.R. § 122.26(b)(14).

Phase I also applies to municipal separate stormwater systems located in incorporated areas with a population of 250,000 or more (large systems) and a population of 100,000 or more (medium systems). Phase I also applies to discharges for which a permit was issued before February 4, 1987 and any discharge that a state agency or the USEPA determines to contribute to a violation of a water quality standard to be a significant contributor of pollutants to waters of the United States. 40 C.F.R. § 122.26. See 40 C.F.R. § 123.25(a)(9) for permits issued by state agencies.

Phase II applies to stormwater dischargers not covered by Phase I. These dischargers were not required to apply for a permit until August 7, 2001 unless required to apply sooner by a notice from the USEPA or a state agency. 40 C.F.R. § 122.26(g). 64 Fed. Reg. 68722 (Dec. 8, 1999).

The stormwater permit requirements are subject to several exclusions such as discharges to POTWs by certain mining and oil and gas operations, and conveyances or conveyance systems for precipitation runoff that are not contaminated with or that have not come in contact with any onsite overburden, raw material, intermediate products, finished product, byproduct or waste products. 40 C.F.R. §§ 122.3 and 122.26(a)(2).

Important activities not considered to be industrial include wholesale, retail, service and commercial activities. If a facility is industrial, the permit requirement applies to discharges from the plant yards, access roads, dedicated rail lines, shipping and receiving areas drainage ponds, and materials storage areas. However, it does not apply to separate parking lots, administrative building areas and other nonindustrial areas if the stormwater from those areas is not commingled with stormwater from industrial areas. 40 C.F.R. § 122.26(b)(14).

The permit requirements were held applicable to mining properties that had formerly carried on industrial activities, even though the mines were inactive. *American Mining Congress v. EPA*, 965 F.2d 759 (9th Cir. 1992).

To avoid a massive program to issue individual stormwater permits that would close thousands of plants, the USEPA's Regional Offices issued in 1992 a stormwater baseline general permit (not including construction activities) for many areas of the United States, the District of Columbia and the U.S. territories. Thousands of industrial dischargers that met the eligibility requirements were authorized to elect the general permit by filing a notice with the USEPA and thereafter complying with its terms and conditions.

In 1995, the USEPA began to phase out the general permit program and replace it with a multi-sector general permit (MSGP) program applicable to 11,000 industrial dischargers in industrial sectors. The MSGP permit prescribed best management practices (BMP) for these industrial sectors. The MSGP for industrial activities was modified extensively in 1998. 63 Fed. Reg. 52430 (Sept. 30, 1998).

K. Spills and Leaks

1. Notification

The CWA prohibits discharges of oil and hazardous substances into waters of the United States in quantities that may be harmful. 33 U.S.C. § 1321(b)(3). Any person in charge of a facility (or vessel) who fails to notify the National Response Center as soon as he has knowledge of such a discharge may be sentenced to imprisonment for up to five years. 33 U.S.C. § 1321(b)(5); 40 C.F.R. §§ 110.6 (oil) and § 117.21 (hazardous substances). The reporting requirement does not apply to discharges in compliance with an NPDES permit and certain other dischargers. 40 C.F.R. § 117.12.

Many persons assume the notification requirement applies to large spills by companies such as Exxon Corporation. However, it also applies to spills of small quantities. The USEPA has defined a quantity of oil that may be harmful to include any quantity that causes a film, sheen or discoloration of the surface of the water, or a sludge or emulsion below the surface of the water, or upon adjoining shorelines. 40 C.F.R. § 110.32. Fats and vegetable oils are considered to be oil as well as petroleum. 62 Fed. Reg. 54,508 (Oct. 20, 1997).

The USEPA has established a table of reportable quantities of hazardous substances that are subject to the reporting requirements. 40 C.F.R. § 117.3, Table 117.3. It is important to refer to the Table because reportable quantities are difficult to predict. For example, a dangerous substance such as hydrochloric acid has a reportable quantity of 1,000 pounds, but the relatively mild termiticide, chlorpyrifos, has a reportable quantity of one pound.

The CWA's notification requirements are in addition to the notification requirements under other laws such as CERCLA and EPCRA.

2. Spill Control and Countermeasure Plans; Facility Response Plans

Owners and operators of onshore and offshore facilities that have discharged or, due to their location, could reasonably be expected to discharge oil in harmful quantities to navigable waters must prepare and maintain a Spill Control and Countermeasure (SPCC) Plan which must be reviewed and certified by a Professional Engineer. 40 C.F.R. Part 112.

A facility is exempt if it has less than (A) 42,000 gallons of underground buried oil storage capacity *and* (B) 1,320 gallons of unburied oil storage capacity, provided that no container has a capacity in excess of 660 gallons. 40 C.F.R. § 112.1(d)(2).

The SPCC Plan must describe any spills which the facility has experienced. It must also describe actions that the owner or operator has taken and will take to prevent spills and to control and remove any spills that occur. The guidelines for preparation of SPCC Plans require that a facility provide minimal prevention measures such as containment and/or diversionary structures or equipment to prevent discharged oil from reaching a navigable watercourse such as dikes, berms and retention ponds. For example, material and construction of bulk storage tanks must be compatible with the materials stored in them and the pressure, temperature and other conditions of storage. Bulk storage tanks must also have secondary containment that will hold the entire contents of the largest single tank plus sufficient freeboard to allow for rain. The SPCC Plan should also cover facility drainage systems; facility pipeline and other transfer operations; and facility tank truck and tank car loading operations. 40 C.F.R. § 112.7.

The SPCC Plan need not be filed with the USEPA, but must be maintained at the facility and available for onsite review during normal working hours. 40 C.F.R. § 112.3(e).

3. Facility Response Plans

The owner or operator of any nontransportation related onshore facility that, because of its location, could reasonably be expected to cause substantial harm to the environment by discharging oil to navigable waters or adjoining shorelines must prepare and submit a facility response plan (FRP) to the appropriate USEPA Regional Administrator. 33 U.S.C. § 1321(j)(5)(B)(iii). 40 C.F.R. § 112.20 *et seq*.

An onshore facility must submit an FRP if it either (A) transfers oil over water to or from vessels that have a total oil storage capacity greater than or equal to 42,000 gallons or (B) has total oil storage capacity of at least 1,000,000 gallons if any of four conditions are true. The conditions, stated briefly, are lack of adequate secondary containment; location where a discharge could injure fish, wildlife or sensitive environments or shut down operations at a public drinking water intake; or a reportable spill greater than or equal to 10,000 gallons within the past five years. 40 C.F.R. § 112.20(f).

An FRP must determine the worst case discharge of oil and the steps that would be taken to contain and respond to it as well as planning scenarios for lesser discharges. 40 C.F.R. § 112.20(f)(5). The owner or operator must also develop and implement facility response training and drill/exercise programs. 40 C.F.R. § 112.21.

L. Wetlands

The CWA regulates dredging and filling in tidal and fresh water wetlands. Wetlands are areas inundated or saturated by groundwater and normally supporting vegetation typically adapted for life in saturated soil conditions, *i.e.*, swamps, marshes, bogs and the like. Prior to dredging or filling, a permit must be obtained from the U.S. Army Corps of Engineers and any state agency having similar jurisdiction. Normal farming, agriculture and ranching and certain maintenance and construction activities are exempt. 33 U.S.C. § 1344. However, see *Borden Ranch v. U.S. Army Corps*, 261 F.3d 810 (9th Cir. 2001).

A permit application must describe in detail not only the dredging and filling activities, but also related construction projects such as buildings, bridges and docks. The Corps of Engineers must notify other interested government agencies and the public. It must also determine whether an environmental impact statement is required under NEPA. The Corps of Engineers considers the public interest, effects on wetlands and adjacent waters, wildlife resources, water quality and other factors in deciding whether to grant a permit. 33 C.F.R. § 320.4. Permits can be challenged in a U.S. District Court which is limited to determining whether the permit decision was arbitrary and capricious.

See Chapter II for further information on wetlands.

M. Sewage Sludge

The USEPA's regulations governing sewage sludge are contained in 40 C.F.R. Parts 501 *et seq*. Part 501 sets forth the USEPA's procedures for approval of state sludge management programs. Part 503 sets national standards for use and disposal of sewage sludge including standards for certain metals and pathogens in sewage sludge.

The USEPA has considered, but not so far adopted, limits for organic compounds, including polychlorinated biphenyls and chlorodioxins and furans. In early 2000, the USEPA proposed a strict standard of 300 parts per trillion for chlorodioxins and furans measured by a 17 congener toxic equivalency quotient (TEQ). In general, sewage sludge and biosolids products made from sewage sludge can meet this standard. Environmental groups are urging the USEPA to adopt a lower standard.

N. Enforcement

1. Federal and State Jurisdiction

The CWA is enforced by the USEPA. States that have clean water programs approved by the USEPA also enforce the CWA by enforcing their own laws and regulations which often incorporate by reference provisions of the CWA and the USEPA's regulations. The USEPA directly enforces the CWA in states which do not have a clean water program approved by the USEPA.

The USEPA has the right to take enforcement action in states which have an approved program under some circumstances. The USEPA may do so if it notifies the alleged violator and the state of its finding that the person is in violation and allows the state 30 days to commence appropriate enforcement action. 33 U.S.C. § 1319(a)(1). The USEPA may also take enforcement action if it finds widespread violations that appear to result from a failure of a state to enforce permit conditions and limitations and, after notice to the state, finds that the failure has extended 30 days beyond the notice. 33 U.S.C. § 1319(a)(2). *E.P.A. v. Smithfield Food, Inc.*, 191 F.3d 516 (4th Cir. 1999).

The USEPA has been engaging in a controversial practice called "overfiling" by taking enforcement action under the CWA and other laws even when a state with an approved program is also currently taking enforcement action. However, a U.S. Court of Appeals recently held that the USEPA cannot take enforcement action under the Resource Conservation and Recovery Act to impose large penalties for the same violations already resolved without penalties in a state enforcement proceeding. *Harmon Industries v. Browner*, 191 F.3d 894 (8th Cir. 1999). For decisions to the same effect under the CWA, see *U.S. v. ITT Rayonier, Inc.*, 627 F.2d 996 (9th Cir. 1980) and *The Old Timer, Inc. v. Blackhawk-Central City*, 51 F. Supp. 2d 1109 (D. Colo. 1999). However, see also *U.S. v. Town of Lowell*, 637 F. Supp. 254 (N.D. Ind. 1985).

2. Administrative Orders

The most common and effective enforcement action by the USEPA is the issuance of an administrative order directing that a person cease violating the CWA and usually also assessing administrative penalties. When the violation is failure to have a required permit or to comply with a permit, the permit cannot be obtained or compliance achieved without taking steps such as filing a permit application and installing control equipment. Thus, the administrative order will contain a compliance schedule to accomplish the necessary steps with penalties for failure to comply in a proper and timely manner. Administrative orders are not subject to review in court until the USEPA commences enforcement action in the U.S. District Court. 33 U.S.C. § 1319(b). However, when an alleged violator is cooperative, the USEPA is often willing to negotiate a consent order that resolves issues which might be otherwise contested.

The USEPA is authorized to assess class I and class II civil penalties. A class I penalty may not exceed $10,000 per violation and may not exceed a total of $25,000. The alleged violator is entitled to prior written notice and an opportunity to request a hearing which need not follow formal hearing procedures. A class II penalty may not exceed $10,000 per day per violation and may not exceed a total of $125,000. The alleged violator is entitled to prior written notice and a formal hearing including discovery procedures. 33 U.S.C. § 1319(g).

3. Civil Enforcement in a U.S. District Court

The USEPA can also request the U.S. Department of Justice to commence a civil enforcement action on its behalf in a U.S. District Court to obtain an injunction and impose civil penalties for violation of the CWA. 33 U.S.C. § 1319(b) and (d). The USEPA may take such action, for example, if the alleged violator is not willing to cooperate and plans to contest the facts or legal interpretations asserted by the USEPA. The USEPA may also take such action in order to obtain a court order that can be enforced by contempt proceedings and/or to seek penalties larger than administrative penalties.

In addition to issuing an injunction, the U.S. District Court may impose civil penalties up to $25,000 per day per violation. Although the alleged violator is entitled to a jury trial on liability issues, the civil penalties are imposed by the District Judge who may impose very large amounts if violations occurred several times per day over a long period of time. For example, in upholding a civil penalty of $186,070, a U.S. Court of Appeals observed that the District Court could have imposed statutory penalties totalling $20,225,000. *Sierra Club v. Cedar Point Oil*, 73 F.3d 546 (5th Cir. 1996).

The USEPA has published a Clean Water Act Penalty Policy for Civil Settlement Negotiations that lists the criteria it will apply in determining a penalty in settlement of a civil enforcement action. In addition to typical factors considered in settling enforcement actions, such as gravity of the offense and the alleged violator's past record and current cooperation, the USEPA will also consider any economic benefit obtained from the alleged violations.

4. Criminal Enforcement

The USEPA may also request the U.S. Department of Justice to commence criminal action for knowing or negligent violations of the CWA. 33 U.S.C. § 1319(c). Upon conviction of a knowing violation, the violator may be imprisoned for not more than three years and fined from $5,000 to $50,000 per day per violation. A convicted negligent violator may be imprisoned for not more than one year and fined from $2,500 to $25,000 per day per violation. All of the foregoing punishments are increased for persons who are convicted and then commit further violations.

The courts have held that the USEPA can establish a knowing violation by simply showing that alleged violators know of their conduct, but need not prove they know the conduct was unlawful. *U.S. v. Wilson*, 133 F.3d 251 (4th Cir. 1997); *U.S. v. Sinskey*, 119 F.3d 712 (8th Cir. 1997); *U.S. v. Hopkins*, 53 F.3d 533 (2d Cir. 1995); *U.S. v. Weitzenhoff*, 1 F.3d 1523 (9th Cir. 1993).

A responsible corporate officer who can be held criminally liable for violating the CWA includes a president and chief executive officer who had authority to exercise control over corporate activity that caused a discharge without need to prove actual exercise of the control or an express duty to oversee the activity. *U.S. v. Iverson*, 162 F.3d 1015 (9th Cir. 1998). As the facts were described by the Court, however, it appeared that the defendant actively encouraged the violations.

In a recent decision, a U.S. Court of Appeals held that a roadmaster for a railroad company was properly convicted of a criminally negligent violation resulting from actions of a contractor hired by the railroad company. The conviction was upheld even though District Court did not provide an instruction to the jury that it had to find criminal negligence and not just ordinary negligence. *U.S. v. Hanousek*, 176 F.3d 1116 (9th Cir. 1999).

The CWA provides even stricter punishments for any person who commits a knowing violation and who knows at that time that he thereby places another person in imminent danger of death or serious bodily injury. Such a person may be imprisoned for up to 15 years and fined up to $250,000, if an individual, or $1,000,000, if an organization.

Under the Debt Collection Improvement Act of 1996, the USEPA increased the penalties by 10% in 1998 and 13.6% in 2002. Thus, for example, a $25,000 penalty is now $31,500.

5. Citizen's Suits

The CWA authorizes lawsuits by persons adversely affected by a violation or seeking to require the USEPA or a state agency to perform a duty it is failing to perform. 33 U.S.C. § 1319(c)(6). Environmental organizations make use of this authorization to commence lawsuits, called "citizen's suits," because evidence is readily available and attorneys fees are can be recovered. However, any civil penalties awarded must be paid to the U.S. Treasury. *Friends of the Earth v. Archer-Daniels-Midland*, 780 F.Supp. 95 (N.D.N.Y. 1992).

An environmental organization must show that it has standing to maintain a citizen's suit. An environmental organization successfully demonstrated standing in *Piney Run Preservation Ass'n. v. Carroll County,* 268 F.3d 255 (4th Cir. 2001). When an environmental group fails to demonstrate standing the lawsuit will be dismissed. *Public Interest Research Group v. Magnesium Elektron, Inc.*, 123 F.3d 111 (3d Cir. 1997); *Friends of the Earth v. Crown Central Petroleum*, 95 F.3d 358 (5th Cir. 1996).

An environmental organization is not entitled to commence a citizen's suit if the USEPA or a state agency is diligently prosecuting a violation. *Arkansas Wildlife Federation v. ICI Americas, Inc.*, 29 F.3d 376 (1994); cert. denied 513 U.S. 1147 (1994); *Connecticut Coastal Fishermen's Ass'n. v. Remington Arms*, 777 F. Supp. 173 (1991); aff'd in part, reversed in part 989 F.2d 1305 (1st cir. 1991). However, if the USEPA or a state agency settles a violation on terms that can be perceived as lenient, an organization may be allowed to sue. *Friends of the Earth v. Laidlaw Environmental*, 890 F. Supp. 470 (D.S.C., 1995). As to jurisdiction, see *Sierra Club v. Whitman*, 268 F.3d 898 (9th Cir. 2001).

CHAPTER VI
RESOURCE CONSERVATION AND RECOVERY ACT

A. General

The Resource Conservation and Recovery Act (RCRA), 42 U.S.C. § 6901 *et seq.*, governs the generation, transportation, treatment, storage and disposal of solid waste including hazardous waste. Under RCRA, the USEPA has adopted regulations establishing a Hazardous Waste Management System which applies throughout the United States. 40 C.F.R. Part 260 *et seq.* RCRA establishes permit requirements for hazardous waste related activities and the use of a "cradle to the grave" manifest system which accounts for hazardous waste from the generator's facility to final disposal. RCRA also establishes methods for the management and reuse or disposal of hazardous and nonhazardous waste by methods such as recycling, incineration and disposal in modern well-designed and managed landfills.

B. Background

For centuries, humans have generated and discarded waste. Archaeologists are able to study ancient civilizations by excavating discarded remnants that often provide more insight into daily lives than the writings of historians.

For thousands of years, the usual disposal choice was an open dump in an undeveloped area. Although never praised, the open dump had the advantages of ease and low cost. There was little incentive to do better so long as dumps were in remote locations and the materials dumped were relatively small quantities that were biodegradable or harmless.

Other historical choices included minimization, reuse, burning and dumping into water. A tradesman who could use a higher portion of raw materials in making products saved material costs and disposal costs. Anyone who could reuse products saved effort and cost. Burning saved transportation and disposal cost and eliminated hazardous materials that could not safely be stored or sent for disposal. Dumping into water was an inexpensive method to cause waste to be transported and dispersed.

During the last century, populations grew rapidly. Remote locations became scarce and locations that had been remote became populated. Numerous products were designed to have long useful lives by resisting biodegradation. Many of them also had characteristics that were potentially hazardous to human health or the environment when discarded as waste. Manufacturers were generally able to identify and minimize imminent hazards. However, experience gradually showed that some wastes created potential chronic hazards to human health and the environment that did not reveal themselves for many years.

Ironically, the adoption of clean air and clean water laws increased waste disposal volumes and problems. Manufacturers who could no longer allow air emissions and wastewater effluent discharges beyond permit limits began to extract and store wastes and to seek ways to dispose of them. Because they could not stop production without going out of business, they sometimes chose unwise methods of disposal including burial on their own property or pumping into containers which were transported by waste haulers to open dumps.

In those years, many waste haulers and dump operators were small firms eager to earn extra revenues, but lacking skills and resources to handle disposal properly. Large quantities of abandoned chemical containers were found at locations such as Chemical Control Center in New Jersey and the "Valley of the Drums" in Kentucky. Large quantities of chemicals were sent to open dumps such as the Winthrop Landfill in Maine, Picillo's Pig Farm in Rhode Island, and Price's Pit in New Jersey. Well-publicized investigations revealed that some haulers who contracted to transport waste dumped it along highways or in rural locations. Investigations also revealed that some disposal firms who contracted to incinerate waste or to place it in a permitted landfill actually dumped it into municipal sewers or arranged for it to be retransported to open dumps.

Environmental organizations and also industrial organizations called on the federal and state governments to adopt a regulatory program. The result was RCRA and numerous state laws that implemented and supplemented RCRA.

Of necessity, RCRA and the state waste management laws were designed to apply to both large and small industrial and commercial firms throughout the United States. As a result, both Congress and the USEPA and state environmental agencies set requirements that were strict, but more attainable then those set under other environmental laws. In turn, industry, recognizing the need for regulation and, appreciating that compliance was attainable, devoted the effort and resources to cooperate widely with RCRA's Hazardous Waste Management System. Thus, although there have been significant exceptions, the System has been far more successful than other regulatory programs that imposed requirements with less consideration of how they would be achieved.

C. Definition of Solid Waste

For a material to be subject to the waste management requirements of RCRA, it must be "solid waste". Solid waste is broadly defined to include any garbage, refuse, certain sludges and any other discarded material including solid, liquid, semisolid or contained gaseous materials. However, the definition excludes a few wastes such as domestic sewage, effluent discharges allowed by NPDES permits, irrigation return flows, some nuclear materials, some mining residues, some recyclable wastes; wastes still in the manufacturing process; residues in "empty" containers and liners removed from containers; and samples collected for testing. 42 U.S.C. § 6903(27) and 40 C.F.R. §§ 261.2 to 261.7.

The USEPA has defined discarded material as a material which is abandoned, recycled or inherently waste-like. Certain military munitions are also included. A material is abandoned if it is (i) disposed of; (ii)burned or incinerated; or (iii) accumulated, stored, or treated (but not recycled) before or in lieu of being abandoned by being disposed, burned or incinerated. A material is inherently waste-like if it is listed as such by the USEPA. 40 C.F.R. § 261.2(a)(2).

Recycled materials are not solid waste if they are recycled by being used or reused as (i) ingredients in an industrial process to make a product and are not being reclaimed or (ii) effective substitutes for commercial products. They are also not solid waste if returned to the original process as a substitute for feedstock materials without being reclaimed or land disposed. 40 C.F.R.§ 261.2(e). However, a material is recycled solid waste if it is recycled (or accumulated, stored or treated before recycling) and (1) used in a manner constituting disposal by being applied to land or used in products applied to land; (2) burned for energy recovery; (3) reclaimed; or (4) accumulated speculatively.

When material is stored temporarily before recycling, a question arises whether it should be considered discarded and subject to regulation as solid waste. The authority of the USEPA to regulate a slag recycling area in a steel manufacturing plant as a solid waste management unit was upheld where the slag was held several months for curing before being sold to the construction industry for road base material and other commercial purposes. *Owen Electric Steel v. Browner*, 37 F.3d 146 (4th Cir. 1994). However, this decision is questionable in light of a recent decision by the U.S. Circuit Court of Appeals for the District of Columbia discussed later in this chapter. *Association of Battery Recyclers v. EPA*, 208 F.3d 1047 (D.C. Cir. 2000).

Persons who claim that materials are not solid waste or are exempt must be prepared to document their claim. 40 C.F.R. § 261.2(f). See *American Mining Congress v. E.P.A.*, 824 F.2d 1177 (D.C. Cir. 1987).

RCRA assigned the management of nonhazardous solid wastes primarily to the states which are required to ban "open dumping" and adopt solid waste management plans implemented by laws and regulations. RCRA instructed the USEPA to establish minimum criteria and to review and approve state plans, but did not authorize the USEPA any direct enforcement authority. 40 C.F.R. Parts 240 to 258. See *Sierra Club v. USEPA*, 992 F.2d 337 (D.C. Cir. 1993). However, the USEPA adopted regulations in 1998 assuming a much more extensive role, including a claimed right to exercise direct enforcement authority if states do not meet its requirements. In 2000, the USEPA proposed rules that would reinforce its claimed authority. For further information, see "Nonhazardous Solid Waste Regulation" later in this Chapter.

D. Definition of Hazardous Waste

RCRA states that a solid waste is a hazardous waste if, among other things, it poses a substantial potential threat to human health or the environment, even when *improperly* treated, stored, transported, disposed of, or otherwise managed. 42 U.S.C. § 9604(5). This statutory authority granted broad power to the USEPA to define hazardous waste.

Hazardous waste is solid waste which either (1) appears on any of the hazardous waste lists adopted by the USEPA in 40 C.F.R. Part 261 including series designated as F, K, P and U or (2) has specific characteristics of ignitability, corrosivity, reactivity or toxicity measured by a toxicity characteristic leaching procedure (TCLP). However, exceptions for certain solid wastes are provided in 40 C.F.R. § 261.4(b). For example, they include household waste; agricultural crops and animal manures returned to soil as fertilizer; mining overburden returned to the minesite; fly ash and certain other wastes from combustion of coal or other fuels but not from burning hazardous waste; and drilling fluids and other wastes associated with exploration, development or production of crude oil, natural gas or geothermal energy. However, see *City of Chicago v. Environmental Defense Fund*, 511 U.S. 328, 114 S. Ct. 1588, 128 L.Ed.2d 302 (1994).

The so-called "Bevill Amendment" to RCRA statutorily excludes certain wastes generated by the mineral and ore mining industry and the oil and gas industry and also ash and other wastes from combustion of coal and fossil fuels. 42 U.S.C. § 6921(b)(2) and (3) and § 6982(m) and (n).

The listed hazardous wastes are fairly easy to identify and most firms which generate them did so years ago. The "F" series consists of wastes from non-specific sources such as spent solvents. The "K" series consists of wastes from specific sources such as wood preservative bottom sediment sludges that use creosote and/or pentachlorophenol. The "P" series consists of a lengthy list of commercial chemical products and intermediates which are acute hazardous wastes if and when discarded or used in other ways that amount to disposal. The "U" series consists of other toxic chemicals. 40 C.F.R. § 261.31 *et seq.*

"Characteristic" wastes are not easy to identify. The identification depends on the results of tests for the applicable characteristics. For example, wastes containing many common paints, solvents and adhesives may be hazardous because they are ignitable, i.e., flashpoint less than 140° F as measured by the regulatory tests. Waste may be corrosive, i.e., pH less than 2.0 or higher than 12.5. Waste containing peroxide residues may be reactive. Wastes containing soluble heavy metals may be toxic if toxic characteristic leaching procedure (TCLP) tests show they may leach into groundwater.

E. Universal Wastes

The USEPA exempted certain solid wastes, which it called "universal wastes," from the definition of "hazardous waste" and subjected them to special regulatory programs. These wastes are (1) certain batteries other than spent lead-acid batteries; (2) certain stocks of pesticides that have been recalled or are part of a collection program; (3) certain mercury thermostats; and (4) certain lamps that may contain mercury. The regulations recognize that universal wastes are very widely generated in small quantities and are often returned to their manufacturer or another person which manages their recycling or disposal. 40 C.F.R. Part 273.

F. Mixtures; Wastes Derived from Hazardous Waste; Recyclable Wastes

The USEPA adopted a rule in 1980 that a mixture of listed hazardous waste and a nonhazardous solid waste was considered a hazardous waste unless it meets certain exemption requirements. 40 C.F.R. § 261.3(a)(2).

The USEPA also adopted a rule in 1980 that a waste generated from treatment, storage or disposal of hazardous waste was considered a hazardous waste unless it meets exemption requirements. Among other things, the rule included any sludge, spill residue, ash, emission control dust, or leachate, but not precipitation runoff. 40 C.F.R. § 261.3(b)(2).

The two rules were held invalid in *Shell Oil Company v. EPA*, 950 F.2d 741 (D.C. Cir. 1991) on grounds that they had been adopted without sufficient notice and opportunity for comment. In 1992, The USEPA reissued the rules as temporary rules with the approval of the Court. Congress adopted legislation allowing the rules to remain temporarily in effect, but directed the USEPA to reconsider the rules by October 1, 1994. A challenge to the temporary rules was held to be moot in *Mobil Oil Corp. v. EPA*, 35 F.3d 579 (D.C. Cir. 1994). After extensive further proceedings, the USEPA published a revised rule at 66 Fed. Reg. 27,266 (May 16, 2001).

The mixture rule has important practical effects. The listed wastes are deemed hazardous even though the concentrations of hazardous constituents in them may be very small. The mixtures rule makes it clear that mixing a listed hazardous waste with a nonhazardous solid waste will not change its status as hazardous waste. On the contrary, the entire mixture will be deemed hazardous waste unless an exclusion applies.

The rule on wastes derived from hazardous waste has important practical consequences. The rule makes it clear that hazardous waste continues to have that status notwithstanding treatment, storage or disposal activity unless and until steps are taken to meet the requirements of one of the exemptions.

The rules have advantages and disadvantages. The USEPA can use them to regulate hazardous waste that might be mixed or transformed by irresponsible persons. On the other hand, they discourage innovative efforts by responsible persons to improve the quality of hazardous waste.

The mixtures rule contains an exception for certain mixtures containing waste from extraction, benefication and processing of ores and minerals. It also contains an exclusion for a mixture containing a hazardous waste that is listed solely because it exhibits one or more hazardous characteristics if the mixture no longer demonstrates any hazardous characteristic. This exclusion was extended by the amendments adopted in 2001. The rule also contains an exception for certain mixtures consisting of wastewater subject to regulation under CWA §§ 307(b) or 402. Readers should keep in mind that the mixtures rule applies to listed hazardous wastes, not characteristic wastes. Subject to the rule against dilution, the mixture rule does not apply to a mixture of a waste that is hazardous solely because it exhibits one or more hazardous characteristics with a nonhazardous solid waste as a result of normal manufacturing activities.

The rule on solid waste derived from hazardous waste does not apply to materials reclaimed from hazardous waste and used beneficially, unless the reclaimed materials are burned for energy recovery or used in a manner constituting disposal.

The revised rule published in 2001 added a conditional exemption for "mixed waste" containing wastes that are both hazardous and radioactive. The USEPA also adopted new regulations exempting certain low-level mixed waste regulated by the Nuclear Regulatory Commission. 66 Fed. Reg. 27,218 (May 16, 2001).

Certain hazardous wastes that qualify as "recyclable materials" are exempted from part of the hazardous waste management system regulations, but are required to comply with other requirements. They include recyclable materials applied to land; hazardous wastes burned for energy recovery in boilers and industrial furnaces; recyclable materials from which precious metals are reclaimed; and spent lead-acid batteries being reclaimed. 40 C.F.R. § 261.6. The USEPA regulates recycling of hazardous wastes so strictly that only a small minority of hazardous wastes are recycled because persons interested in recycling cannot incur the costs and take the risks of violating the regulations.

G. Generator Responsibilities

1. General Duties

The USEPA's regulations require generators of solid waste to (1) determine whether their solid waste is a listed or characteristic hazardous waste and, if so, (2) notify the USEPA by filing Form 8700-22 and obtain an identification number from the USEPA, (3) obtain, prepare, sign, use and retain the uniform hazardous waste manifests prescribed by the regulations, (4) package, label, mark and placard the hazardous waste as required by regulations of the U.S. Department of Transportation, (5) deliver waste only to transporters having an USEPA identification number for delivery only to permitted disposal facilities, (6) store hazardous waste only for the 90 day or other accumulation times permitted by the regulations and in compliance with dating and labelling requirements, and (7) keep records and submit reports to the USEPA. Generators must also certify that they have a plan to minimize volume and toxicity of the waste generated. These and other rules (including rules applicable to exports and imports) are contained in 40 C.F.R. Part 262.

Generators who store hazardous waste longer than the 90 day (or other) permissible limit must obtain a storage permit under the treatment, storage and disposal facility regulations described later in this Chapter.

If a generator transfers hazardous waste to a transporter and does not receive a copy signed by the disposal facility, the generator must contact the transporter and the disposal facility to inquire about the waste. If the signed manifest copy is not received within 45 days, the generator must file an exception report with the USEPA. 40 C.F.R. Part 262.

The USEPA adopted Form 8700-22 as a uniform form of manifest. States adopted similar forms. In 2001, the USEPA proposed amendments to the uniform manifest system to standardize and provide for electronification of the system. However, the states would not be required to use the proposed electronic manifest. 66 Fed. Reg. 28,240 (May 22, 2001).

2. Small Quantity Generators

Small quantity generators are subject to somewhat more lenient regulations which allow, for example, six months storage without a storage permit. 40 C.F.R. § 261.5 and § 262.34 (d)-(f). A generator may move in and out of the small quantity generator provisions each month as production rates and waste quantities change. A generator should document these changes to avoid potential liability for noncompliance.

The regulations divide small quantity generators into two groups. The first group is conditionally exempt from most of the hazardous waste management regulations. The second group is exempt from only a few regulations. If a generator in either group generates *acute* hazardous waste, stricter provisions apply.

a. Conditionally Exempt Small Quantity Generators

A generator is a conditionally exempt small quantity generator in a calendar month if he generates no more than *100 kilograms* of hazardous waste in that month. 40 C.F.R § 261.5. 100kg (220 lbs.) Is roughly equivalent to half a 55 gallon drum in volume. A conditionally exempt small quantity generator is exempt from most of the regulatory and reporting requirements, but remains subject to (1) requirements applicable to acutely hazardous waste, (2) rules requiring a determination whether waste is as hazardous or acutely hazardous, (3) a limitation on accumulation of hazardous waste on-site to not more than 1,000 kg at anytime, (4) disposal of the hazardous waste in a proper manner such as delivery to a permitted offsite disposal facility, and (5) compliance with regulations applicable to mixtures including wastes are mixed with used oil destined to be burned for energy recovery. 40 C.F.R. § 261.5.

b. Other Small Quantity Generators

Small quantity generators who generate more than 100 kilograms, but less than 1,000 kilograms, of hazardous waste in a calendar month must comply with most of the hazardous waste management regulations. However, they are excused from several requirements:

1. They need not comply with the manifest requirements if their waste is reclaimed under a contractual agreement meeting specific requirements. 40 C.F.R. § 262.20.

2. They may accumulate hazardous waste on site for up to 180 days without a permit, provided that the quantity of waste accumulated onsite never exceeds 6,000 kilograms and they comply with all but one of the interim status regulations pertaining to the onsite storage. If the waste must be transported over 200 miles or more for offsite treatment, they may accumulate onsite for up to 270 days. 40 C.F.R. § 262.34.

3. They need not comply with some of the recordkeeping and reporting requirements. 40 C.F.R. § 262.44.

4. They need not prepare a formal contingency plan and conduct formal personnel training, but must establish the limited emergency procedures outlined in 40 C.F.R. § 262.34(d).

5. They need not maintain a 50-foot buffer zone for container storage of ignitable or reactive wastes. 40 C.F.R. § 262.34(d)(2).

6. They may accumulate up to 55 gallons of nonacutely hazardous waste in a "satellite" area without meeting the storage requirements. Satellite areas are places where wastes are generated in an industrial process and may initially accumulate prior to removal to a central area, provided that the containers are marked to identify clearly their contents as hazardous waste and certain requirements as to the containers are met. 40 C.F.R. § 262.34(c) and § 264.171-173(a).

7. They are subject to several special requirements relating to storage of hazardous waste in storage tanks imposed by 49 C.F.R. § 265.201.

3. Acute Hazardous Waste

If a small quantity generator, even though conditionally exempt, generates in a calendar month more than one *kilogram* (2.2 pounds) of acutely hazardous waste or *100 kilograms* (220 pounds) of any residue or contaminated soil, waste or other debris resulting from the cleanup of a spill of acute hazardous waste, all quantities of the acute hazardous waste are subject to the full regulatory and notification requirements. 40 C.F.R. § 261.5(f).

H. Transporter Responsibilities

Transporters of hazardous waste must obtain an identification number from the USEPA, accept hazardous waste only in conformity with a manifest signed by the generator, complete their part of each manifest and return a signed copy to the generator before leaving its property, make and keep records, file reports, and deliver waste only to facilities having a permit authorizing receipt of the waste. They must ensure that the manifest accompanies the waste throughout its transportation. They can store the waste up to 10 days at a transfer facility without a storage permit. A transporter must obtain a signed copy of the manifest from any other transporter to whom waste is delivered or from the operator of the designated disposal facility. Transporters must report discharges of hazardous waste to the National Response Center and local authorities, take immediate action to protect health and the environment, and clean up the discharges. 40 C.F.R. Part 263. Manifest copies must be retained for three years.

RCRA mandated that the USEPA coordinate with the U.S. Department of Transportation (DOT) and that the USEPA's standards be consistent with the DOT's regulations under the Hazardous Materials Transportation Act (HMTA). 42 U.S.C. § 6923(b). This was an important requirement because the DOT's Research and Special Programs Administration (RSPA) has extensive experience and long established programs for protecting the public against imminent hazards. RSPA's programs are also coordinated with the transportation safety programs of the United Nations.

In the author's experience, transporters do not agree to transport waste until the generator has obtained and furnished the results of physical and chemical analytical tests performed in compliance with the USEPA's regulations and Manual SW-846. They are anticipating the requirements of the TSD facility pursuant to 40 C.F.R. § 264.13.

I. Treatment, Storage and Disposal Facilities

1. TSD Permits

Each owner or operator of a treatment storage disposal (TSD) facility (including those who are also generators or transporters) must obtain a permit for each facility. TSD facilities in operation on November 19, 1980, when the RCRA regulations of USEPA became effective, were automatically granted interim status permits and required to meet interim standards. These facilities were also required to apply for final permits by filing Part A and Part B applications, and can be closed only in compliance with comprehensive closing and post-closing requirements. New TSD facilities must have a final permit before commencing operation. 40 C.F.R. Parts 264-266 and Part 270.

Several kinds of TSD facilities are excluded from the permit requirement such as (1) publicly owned treatment works (POTWs); (2) TSD facilities regulated by a state environment agency administering an approved RCRA program; (3) municipal and industrial nonhazardous solid waste facilities permitted by the state environmental agencies if they accept hazardous waste only from conditionally exempt small quantity generators of less than 100 kilograms; (4) onsite storage facilities used by generators to accumulate for up to 90 days or other periods permitted by 40 C.F.R. § 260.34; (5) facilities of small quantity generators exempt under 40 C.F.R. §§ 261.4 and 5; (6) transfer station facilities where transporters may store up to 10 days; (7) underground injection facilities permitted under the Safe Drinking Water Act; (8) elementary neutralization units; (9) totally enclosed treatment facilities; (10) wastewater treatment facilities permitted under the CWA or a state program; and (11) farms where farmers dispose of waste pesticides from their own use in compliance with 40 C.F.R. § 262.70.

RCRA provides that each TSD facility in existence or under construction in November 19, 1980 must have a permit issued by the USEPA or a state environmental agency authorized to administer the RCRA program. 42 U.S.C. § 6925(a). Historically, many owners and operators closed their TSD facilities before that date because they could not undertake the obligations imposed by RCRA. The USEPA's regulations indicate that it may require corrective action at any facility closed before November 19, 1980 unless the closure was equivalent to its Part 264 closure standards. 40 C.F.R. § 270.1(c)(6).

Owners and operators who continued to operate facilities existing on November 19, 1980 were required to apply for a permit by filing a Part A application with the USEPA. The Part A application required relatively limited information intended to enable the USEPA to identify TSD facilities and regulate them. For several years, many existing facilities were allowed to defer filing Part B applications, which requires far more extensive information, because the USEPA was not ready to review them. Existing facilities which filed Part A were granted an interim status permit that required compliance with the USEPA's interim standards at 40 C.F.R. Part 265. Later, the USEPA adopted schedules requiring submission of Part B information.

Anyone who wishes to propose a new TSD facility is required to submit both Part A and Part B for review by the USEPA and may not commence physical construction until it receives a finally effective RCRA permit. 40 C.F.R. § 270.10(f).

A Part A application must provide such information as the name, address and telephone number of the facility owner and operator; the SIC codes for its products or services; the activities requiring a RCRA permit; an indication whether the facility is new or existing; scale drawings and photographs of existing facilities; a description of the TSD processes and their design capacities; descriptions of the hazardous wastes and debris to be treated, stored or disposed of and their quantities; a list of other environmental permits and permit applications; a topographic map; and a brief description of the applicant's business. 40 C.F.R. § 270.13.

A Part B application requires far more information. The general requirements include (1) a facility description; (2) chemical and physical analyses of hazardous waste and debris handled at the facility; (3) waste analysis plan; (4) security procedures and equipment; (5) general inspection schedule; (6) any request for waivers of preparedness and prevention standards; (7) contingency plan; (8) hazard prevention procedures, structures and equipment; (9) precautions to prevent accidental ignition or reaction of ignitable, reactive or incompatible wastes; (10) traffic data; (11) facility location information including the political jurisdiction, seismic data geological fault data, and flood maps and data; (12) training program descriptions; (13) a closure plan and, if applicable, postclosure plan; (14) documentation that notices of closed hazardous waste disposal units were filed; (15) a recent closure cost estimate and financial assurance documentation; (16) if applicable, a recent postclosure cost estimate and financial assurance documentation; (17) if applicable, insurance policy or other documentation; (18) if applicable, proof of coverage by a state financial mechanism; (19) a topographic map with contours and other data; and (20) other information 40 C.F.R. § 270.14.

In addition, a Part B application must also include specific design and operating information based on the kind of facility, i.e., containers, tank systems, surface impoundments, waste piles, incinerators, land treatment facilities, landfills, boilers and industrial furnaces, miscellaneous units, process vents, equipment subject to air emission leak restrictions, drip pads, air emission controls for certain facilities, and information for postclosure permits. 40 C.F.R. §§ 270.15 to .28.

The USEPA's regulations also provide for several kinds of special permits including emergency permits; hazardous waste incinerator permits; land treatment demonstration permits; interim permits for underground injection wells; research, development and demonstration permits; boiler and industrial furnace permits; and remedial action plans (RAPs) which are given the status of permits. 40 C.F.R. §§ 270.60 to 68.

Compliance with a RCRA permit constitutes compliance with RCRA for enforcement purposes, subject to a few exceptions. 40 C.F.R. § 270.4. This sometimes called the "permit shield' provision and is important to justify the effort and expenses incurred by permitholders to achieve compliance. A challenge to this rule by the Environmental Defense Fund was rejected. *Shell Oil v. EPA*, 950 F.2d 741 (D.C. Cir. 1991).

2. TSD Standards

Both the interim and final standards for TSD facilities are extensive and detailed. They include design specifications for treatment facilities, such as bio-oxidation ponds, and for disposal facilities, such as landfills and incinerators. For example, land disposal facilities must be double-lined and include leachate collection systems and groundwater monitoring systems. Wastes must be analyzed in accordance with specified methods and handled in compliance with the "cradle to the grave" requirements of the Hazardous Waste Management System. The regulations require personnel training, inspections and emergency response procedures, alarms and communication equipment, spill plans, record keeping and reporting, groundwater monitoring, a contingency plan, insurance, cooperation with community officials, closure plans, and post closure plans including monitoring for at least 30 years. The owner or operator of each TSD facility must maintain liability insurance and provide financial assurance for its closure and post-closure obligations by a trust fund, surety bond, letter of credit or other sufficient demonstration that adequate funds will be available. 40 C.F.R. Parts 264-266 and Part 270.

A brief survey of the topics covered by the USEPA's standards for owners and operators of hazardous waste TSD facilities holding final permits under 40 C.F.R. Part 264 illustrates their extensive detail:

1. General applicability provisions

2. General facility standards including waste analysis, security procedures, inspections, location standards, and construction quality assurance requirements.

3. Preparedness and prevention requirements including design and operation, required equipment, testing and maintenance of equipment, access to communications or alarm systems, required aisle space, and arrangements with local authorities.

4. Contingency plan and emergency procedures.

5. Manifest systems, recordkeeping and reporting.

6. Releases including a groundwater protection standard with concentration limits for hazardous constituents and monitoring and corrective action programs.

7. Closure and post closure requirements including plans and certifications; decontamination of equipment, structures and soils; postclosure notices; and postclosure care and use of property.

8. Financial responsibility and liability insurance requirements including cost estimates and financial assurances for closure and post closure care by means such as a trust fund; surety bond; letter of credit; demonstration that the owner passes a financial test; or a corporate guarantee with a demonstration that the guarantor passes a financial test.

9. Use and management of containers including maintenance of their condition; inspections; special requirements for ignitable, reactive and incompatible wastes; closure; and air emission standards.

10. Tank systems including assessment of integrity; design and installation; containment and detection of releases; general operating requirements; response to releases and spills; closure and post-closure care; special requirements for ignitable, reactive and incompatible wastes; and air emission standards.

11. Surface impoundments including design and operating requirements; action leakage rate; response actions; monitoring and inspections; emergency repairs and contingency plans; closure and post-closure care; special requirements for ignitable, reactive, incompatible and certain listed wastes; and air emission standards.

12. Waste piles including design and operating requirements; action leakage rate; response actions; monitoring and inspections; emergency repairs and contingency plans; closure and post-closure care; special requirements for ignitable, reactive, incompatible and certain listed wastes; and air emission standards.

13. Land treatment requirements including treatment programs and demonstrations; design and operating requirements; growth of food chain crops in the treatment area; unsaturated zone monitoring; recordkeeping; closure and post-closure care; and special requirements for ignitable, reactive, incompatible and certain listed wastes.

14. Landfill requirements including design and operating requirements such as impervious liner and leachate collection system specifications; action leakage rate; monitoring and inspection; response actions; surveying and recordkeeping; closure and post-closure care; special requirements for containers and lab packs; special requirements for bulk and containerized liquids; and special requirements for ignitable, reactive, incompatible and certain listed wastes.

15. Incinerator requirements including waste analysis, performance standards, permits, operating requirements, monitoring, inspections and closure.

16. Corrective action requirements including corrective action management units and temporary units.

17. Drip pad requirements including assessment of existing pad integrity; design and installation of new pads; design and operating requirements; inspections; and closure.

18. Miscellaneous unit requirements including environmental performance standards, monitoring, analysis, inspection, response, reporting, corrective action, and post-closure care.

19. Air emission standards for process vents including closed vent systems and control devices; test methods and procedures; and recordkeeping and reporting requirements.

20. Air emission standards for equipment leaks including standards for various kinds of pumps, compressors, valves, pressure relief devices, flanges and other connecting systems as well as test methods and procedures and recordkeeping and reporting requirements.

21. Air emission standards for tanks, surface impoundment and containers.

22. Containment building requirements including design and operating standards and closure and post-closure care.

23. Hazardous waste munitions and explosives requirements including design and operating standards and post-closure care.

The USEPA's standards for TSD facilities holding interim status permits under 40 C.F.R. Part 265 impose requirements similar to those in 40 C.F.R. Part 264.

The USEPA's regulations set specially strict standards for incinerators. For example, an incinerator burning hazardous waste must achieve a destruction and removal efficiency (DRE) of 99.99% for each principal organic hazardous constituent and 99.9999% for chlorodioxins and furans. 40 C.F.R. § 264.340 *et seq.* and § 265.340 *et seq.* Similarly strict standards are imposed on boilers and industrial furnaces that burn hazardous waste. 40 C.F.R. § 266.100 *et seq.* The standards are very difficult to meet consistently. As a result, large volumes of hazardous wastes continue to be sent for disposal to landfills.

The USEPA has regulations that provide standards for management of recyclable and other materials that are used in a manner constituting disposal, used for precious metals recovery, or burned in boilers and industrial furnaces. These regulations are necessary because the USEPA deems recycled products as continuing to be hazardous waste if they are applied to land or burned as fuel. 40 C.F.R. Part 266. These regulations also apply to spent lead-acid batteries being reclaimed. As described in another chapter, recycling and secondary smelting of used lead-acid batteries are important and successful environment-based industries in the United States.

For workers at TSD facilities, important and practical protection is provided by OSHA's Hazardous Waste Operations and Emergency Response Standard (the "HAZWOPER"). 29 C.F.R. § 1910.120(p). Ordered to do so by Congress, the USEPA has accepted the HAZWOPER which is widely implemented by industry organizations and industry

The USEPA's regulations impose special requirements on TSD facilities located in floodplains. They must be designed, constructed, maintained and operated to prevent a release of hazardous wastes that could be caused by the worst flood that could occur in a 100-year period. The regulations contain exceptions for facilities that can demonstrate a capability to remove the wastes to a safe location or that any releases resulting from a flood would not have adverse effects on human health or the environment. 40 C.F.R. § 264.18.

J. Corrective Action

Hazardous waste TSD facilities subject to the RCRA permit requirements must have a corrective action program. 40 C.F.R. § 270.100. Their owners and operators must take corrective actions to protect human health and the environment from all past or present releases of hazardous wastes or constituents. The corrective actions are specified in the facility permit and may include releases that migrated beyond the facility boundary. Assurances of financial responsibility for corrective action must be provided. 40 C.F.R. § 264.101.

Many owners and operators of industrial facilities have carefully avoided commencing any treatment, storage or disposal activities that would require a TSD permit under RCRA. Other owners and operators closed their TSD facilities before November 19, 1980 so they would not be required to comply with the TSD permit requirements. 42 U.S.C. § 6924(u) to (v). However, many owners and operators needed their facilities and became subject to the interim permit regulations in 40 C.F.R. Part 265 and the obligation to apply for a permit requiring compliance with 40 C.F.R. Part 264. These owners became subject to the corrective action requirements.

Owners and operators who attempted to take corrective actions soon found that the USEPA's TSD regulations created serious obstacles. For example, removal or treatment of contaminated soil and groundwater required compliance with design, construction and other minimum technology standards that were impossible or excessively costly for limited and temporary remedial work. Further, the concentration limits for hazardous constituents established by the treatment standards for currently generated wastes were found to be impossible or excessively costly to achieve for hazardous wastes released many years ago. As a result, many industrial facilities became "ghost towns" reduced to limited or nominal operations. Other facilities took corrective actions, but could use only a limited range of remedies such as capping contaminated soil and recording a restrictive deed giving notice of the need for continuing compliance with engineering and institutional controls.

As "rust belt" states sought to rebuild their industrial bases, they urged the USEPA to amend its regulations to allow corrective actions to be accomplished realistically. Faced with strong opposition by environmental groups and its own staff, the USEPA was willing to make only limited amendments. A significant step was the adoption in 1993 of regulations exempting corrective management units (CAMUs) and temporary units (TUs) from the minimum technology regulations for TSD facilities and the treatment standards for hazardous wastes. In lieu of those requirements, the USEPA's Regional Administrators were authorized to set facility standards based on several stated criteria. 40 C.F.R. §§ 264.552 and .553.

The Environmental Defense Fund and other environmentalists challenged the regulations in court and claimed that the exemptions would leave human health and the environment unprotected. In February 2000, the lawsuit was settled and the USEPA agreed to adopt stricter CAMU and TU regulations. The USEPA published the proposed regulations in August 2000. 65 Fed. Reg. 51059 (Aug. 22, 2000). The proposed regulations did not apply to CAMUs already approved or for which substantially complete applications are submitted within 90 days after the publication of the proposed rule. The USEPA said that the proposed regulations would apply to as many as 6,000 facilities.

The proposed regulations would (1) require additional information in applications; (2) clarify the waste eligible for CAMUs to exclude, among other things, currently generated process wastes; (3) prescribe design and operating standards for temporary CAMUs, now called TUs; (4) prescribe design standards for CAMUs used for permanent disposal that would include, for example, a composite liner and leachate collection system meeting specified requirements unless the Regional Administrator approves alternative requirements; (5) prescribe treatment standards for principal hazardous constituents placed in CAMUs for permanent disposal that would apply unless the Regional Administrator authorizes adjustment of the treatment levels or methods. State environmental agencies authorized to regulate CAMUs would continue to do so if their state does not have an audit privilege or immunity law that USEPA claims raises a concern about adequate enforcement.

The Regional Administrators would be authorized to designate the principal hazardous constituents based on prescribed criteria. In general, treatment would have to achieve 90% reduction in concentrations of the designated principal hazardous constituents. When such treatment would result in a concentration less than ten times the universal treatment standard for a constituent, treatment below that level would not be required. However, waste exhibiting a hazardous characteristic of ignitability, corrosivity or reactivity, must be treated to eliminate the characteristic.

The USEPA adopted the proposed CAMU regulations in December, 2001.

Another step taken by the USEPA to expedite remediation of contaminated facilities was the adoption of its regulations authorizing owners and operators of remediation waste treatment sites to apply for a remedial action plan

(RAP) rather than a more extensive RCRA permit. 40 C.F.R. § 270.80 *et seq*. In 2001, the USEPA published a Handbook of Groundwater Protection and Cleanup Policies for RCRA Corrective Action, No. 530-F-01-021. It also issued a fact sheet on treatment methods titled "Treatment Experiences at RCRA Corrective Action Facilities," No. 542-F-00-020.

K. Underground Storage Tanks

1. Background

The useful life of underground storage tanks (USTs) depends on a number of factors such as age, design, material composition, contents, and corrosivity of the surrounding soil. With time, corrosion may affect a tank's walls and cause holes which permit the contents to leak out and contaminate surrounding soil. The contamination may then migrate into groundwater and eventually contaminate nearby properties and also wells, creeks, rivers and lakes which may be drinking water sources.

In 1984, the USEPA persuaded Congress to adopt amendments to RCRA to provide federal regulation of USTs. The USEPA was authorized, among other things, to promulgate regulations on detection and correction of leaks and to set standards for USTs.

2. Tanks Regulated

USTs which contain an accumulation of regulated substances (i.e., hazardous substances or petroleum), the volume of which is 10% or more beneath the surface of the ground, are underground tanks. This means that many tanks which are primarily above ground are USTs. Hazardous substances are those defined as hazardous in 42 U.S.C. § 9601(14) and include a long list of common substances contained in paints, solvents, adhesives, degreasers, inks, pigments and pesticides and other widely used products. Petroleum includes crude oil and derivatives such as gasoline, diesel fuel, aviation fuel, lubricants and solvents. 40 C.F.R.§ 280.12.

Some tanks excluded from the UST definition are (A) farm and residential tanks with capacities of 1,100 gallons or less used to store motor fuel for noncommercial purposes; (B) tanks storing heating oil for consumptive use on the premises (i.e. heating oil tanks); (C) septic tanks; (D) regulated pipeline facilities; (E) surface impoundments, pits, ponds or lagoons; (F) stormwater or wastewater collection systems; (G) flow-through process tanks; (H) liquid traps and gathering lines for oil and gas gathering operations (I) tanks in a subsurface area situated upon or above the surface of the floor; and (J) pipeline connected to the foregoing tanks. 42 U.S.C. § 6991(1); 40 C.F.R. § 280.12.

An "UST system" means an UST, connected underground piping, underground ancillary equipment and any containment system. 40 C.F.R. § 280.12. The

USEPA's regulations exclude (1) any UST system holding hazardous waste listed or identified under RCRA, Subtitle C; (2) any wastewater treatment tank systems regulated under CWA §§ 307(b) or 402; (3) equipment or machinery containing regulated substances for operational purposes such as hydraulic lifts or electrical equipment; (4) any UST system whose capacity is 110 gallons or less or contains a *de minimis* concentration of regulated substances; or (5) any emergency spill or overflow containment system emptied expeditiously after use. 40 C.F.R. § 280.10.

3. Persons Regulated

RCRA places responsibility for an UST system on its owner and operator. An owner is a person who owns an UST system used to store, use or dispense regulated substances on or after November 8, 1984 and any person who owned a UST immediately before its use was discontinued prior to that date. 42 U.S.C. § 6991(3); 40 C.F.R. § 280.12. An operator is any person controlling or responsible for daily operation of an UST system. 42 U.S.C. § 6991(4); 40 C.F.R. § 280.12.

RCRA contains an exclusion from the definition of an "owner" for a secured lender which does not participate in management of a petroleum UST or UST system and is not engaged in petroleum refining, distribution or marketing. 42 U.S.C. § 6991b (h)(9); 40 C.F.R. § 280.220. The USEPA's regulations provide an exclusion from the definition of an "operator" to a secured lender before foreclosure if the lender is not in control of and does not have responsibility for the daily operation of the petroleum UST or UST system. 40 C.F.R. § 280.230. The regulations also exclude a secured lender from the definition of an operator after foreclosure, but only if (1) there is an operator, other than the lender, who is in control or has responsibility for daily operating and can be held responsible for compliance or (2) the lender performs specified requirements with respect to the UST or UST system. 40 C.F.R. § 280.230. The regulations are silent on UST systems containing hazardous substances.

4. New v. Existing USTs

The regulations contain different standards for existing and new UST systems. Existing UST systems are those whose installation was commenced on or before December 22, 1988. 40 C.F.R. § 280.12. All other UST systems are "new."

5. Standards for New USTs

The USEPA performance standards for new UST systems (and piping that routinely contains regulated substances) requires that they be properly designed and constructed and that any portions underground that routinely contain product must be protected from corrosion in accordance with a code of practice developed by a nationally recognized association such as Underwriters Laboratories (UL), the American Society of Testing Materials, Inc. (ASTM), or the National Association of Corrosion Engineers (NACE). The requirements vary with the design and construction materials such as steel or fiberglass reinforced plastic composite. The regulations also prescribe requirements for spill and overfill prevention equipment, installation, and certification of installation to demonstrate compliance to the applicable state or local agency. 40 C.F.R.§ 280.20.

Any owner who brings an UST system into use must within 30 days submit notice of its existence on a prescribed form to the applicable state or local agency. The notice includes a certification of compliance with the key requirements of the regulations. Sellers of tanks to be used as USTs are required to notify purchasers of the notification requirements. 40 C.F.R. § 280.22.

6. Upgrading Existing Tank Systems

Owners and operators of existing UST systems were given three choices: (1) comply with the standards for UST systems; (2) upgrade to standards for existing UST systems; (3) close the existing UST systems and take any necessary corrective actions.40 C.F.R.§ 280.21.

The purpose of upgrading an existing UST or complying with the new tank standards was to ensure adequate protection against corrosion which might result in leaks. Steel tanks could be upgraded three ways: (1) internal lining; (2) cathodic protection; (3) owners and operators performing upgrades; (4) a combination of the above methods. The connective piping was also to be upgraded. In addition, owners and operators performing upgrades were required to comply with the new UST system spill and overfill prevention equipment requirements. 40 C.F.R.§ 280.21.

COMMENT: While working with owners of UST systems throughout the United States since the regulations were adopted, the author has never met or heard of an owner who decided to incur the effort and cost of upgrading an existing UST system. They always decided that the best choice was to close the existing UST system and to replace it with either a new UST system, an aboveground system, or another storage or supply arrangement that eliminated the need for a storage tank system.

The deadline for compliance with the upgrading requirements was December 22, 1998. Non-upgraded systems could be tightness-tested annually until December 22, 1998 and, if not upgraded by that date, they should have been permanently closed by removal or other methods prescribed by the USEPA and state regulatory agencies. Although owners and operators had ten years to do so, many thousands throughout the nation failed to comply and became subject to enforcement action. The USEPA and most state environmental agencies adopted policies allowing leniency for small business owners and operators. However, the New Jersey Department of Environmental Protection imposes substantial fines on those who failed to comply, even when they come forward voluntarily.

7. General Operating Requirements

a. Spill and Overfill Control

Owners and operators must ensure that releases due to spilling or overfilling do not occur. Owners and operators must make certain that the tank volume exceeds the volume of product that will be transferred to it and must constantly monitor the transfer operation. Monitoring can be achieved by electronic or mechanical means or by having an attendant present. The owner and operator must report, investigate and clean up any spills immediately. The regulations require owners and operators to report spills and releases to the USEPA or the applicable state implementing agency. 40 C.F.R. § 280.30.

New and existing USTs must have spill and overfill prevention equipment. 40 C.F.R.§ 280.20(c). Examples are a catch basin to collect product when the transfer hose is detached from the fill pipe, a system to alert an attendant when the tank is 90% full ,and an automatic cut-off before the tank exceeds 95% capacity.

An owner and operator cannot avoid responsibility for damage caused by spills through contract provisions with transport carriers or others. However, an owner and operator can and should require carriers, construction contractors and others to provide contractual indemnities which will reimburse any liability, cost or expense imposed by law for which they are responsible.

b. Operation and Maintenance of Corrosion Protection

Owners and operators of steel UST systems with corrosion protection must continuously operate and maintain the corrosion protection systems and inspect them within six months of installation and at least every three years thereafter in accordance with a code of practice developed by a nationally recognized association such as NACE, 40 C.F.R. § 280.31.

c. Compatibility, Repairs, Reporting and Recordkeeping

Owners and operators must use an UST system made of or lined with materials that are compatible with the materials stored. 40 C.F.R.§ 280.32. They must repair the UST system in accordance with a code of practice developed by a nationally recognized association (such as the National Fire Protection Association or the American Petroleum Institute) to prevent releases due to structural failure or corrosion. 40 C.F.R.§ 280.33. They must also comply with reporting and recordkeeping requirements including reports of releases, suspected releases, spills, overfills and confirmed releases to the implementing agency. 40 C.F.R. § 280.34.

8. Release Detection

New USTs must have release detection equipment upon installation. If an existing UST cannot does not have release detection equipment, it must be added or the UST must be closed.

Compliance requires careful adherence to the performance standards that address inventory control, volume measurements and other requirements. The following examples are acceptable methods for release detection: (1) monthly inventory control; (2) manual tank gauging; (3) automatic tank gauging; (4) tank tightness-testing; (5) vapor monitoring; (6) ground-water monitoring; (7) interstitial monitoring; and (8) any other method approved by the implementing agency. Piping must also be equipped with release detection equipment. Release detection recordkeeping is required. 40 C.F.R. §§ 280.40 to .45.

9. Reporting, Investigation and Confirmation

The USEPA's regulations require reporting to the USEPA or the state implementing agency within 24 hours (or another reasonable time prescribed by a state implementing agency) of the discovery of released regulated substances or, with some exceptions, unusual operating conditions or monitoring results from a release detection method, that indicate that a release may have occurred. 40 C.F.R. § 280.50

The regulations also require investigation and confirmation of all suspected releases requiring reporting including, when required, any offsite impacts. Owners and operators must also contain and immediately clean up any spill or overfill that exceeds specified quantities and report to the implementing agency. 40 C.F.R. § 280.51 to .53.

10. Release Response and Corrective Action

Upon confirmation of a release, an owner or operator must take a series of steps beginning with an initial response consisting of reporting, immediate action to prevent any further release, and identification and mitigation of fire, explosion and vapor hazards. Owners and operators must also remove any free product and investigate for soil and groundwater contamination. Unless otherwise directed by the implementing agency, owners and operators must undertake initial abatement measures and an initial site check and characterization, including submission of the collected information to the implementing agency. They must also investigate the extent and location of soils contaminated by the release and any concentrations of dissolved product contamination in groundwater. The implementing agency may require owners and operators to develop and submit a corrective action plan for responding to contaminated soils and groundwater. If so, the agency must provide notice to members of the public directly affected by the release and may hold a public hearing before approving the plan. 42 C.F.R. § 280.60 to .67.

11. Out-of-Service UST Systems and Closure

When an UST is temporarily closed, the owner or operator must continue operation and maintenance of corrosion protection and also release detection if a release is suspected or confirmed. Release detection is not necessary so long as the UST is empty. If an UST is temporarily closed for 3 months or more, the requirements are to (1) leave vent lines open and functioning and (2) cap and secure all other lines, pumps, manways, and ancillary equipment. When an UST system is temporarily closed for more than 12 months, it must be permanently closed unless it meets either the performance standards for new UST systems or the upgrading requirements for existing UST system. 40 C.F.R. § 280.70

Owners and operators must notify the appropriate federal or state agency of their intent to permanently close a UST or commence a change-in-service. This notification should precede the closure or change-in-service by at least 30 days or within a reasonable time period determined by the appropriate agency. Permanent closure requires removal of all liquids and sludges from the UST which then must either be removed from the ground or filled with an inert solid material. A change-in-service occurs when a UST will store a non-regulated substance. Owners or operators must empty and clean the tank and conduct a site assessment before a change-in-service.

Owners and operators must assess an UST site before a permanent closure or change-in-service for the presence of any release or contamination. If free product or contaminated soil or groundwater is discovered, the owners or operators must commence corrective action such as removal or other remediation of contaminated soil or groundwater. Owners and operators must maintain closure records demonstrating compliance with the closure requirements.

If a UST was closed before December 22, 1988, the appropriate implementing agency may still require compliance with the closure regulations if the agency determines a current or potential contamination threat on the UST site. 40 C.F.R. §§ 280.70 to .74.

12. Financial Responsibility

Owners and operators must demonstrate financial responsibility to maintain a UST system. If the owner and operator are two separate entities, only one need demonstrate financial responsibility. However, both are liable in the event of noncompliance. Financial responsibility includes the necessary financial resources to take corrective action and to compensate third parties for bodily injury and property damage. The regulations prescribe the amounts per occurrence that must be provided. 40 C.F.R. § 280.93.

Financial responsibility may be shown by a guarantee or surety bond, insurance or risk retention group coverage, a letter of credit, a trust fund or a state-required mechanism in states without approved programs, or a combination of the above. An owner or operator which passes financial test requirements may elect to be self-insured.

Current owners/operators are responsible for obtaining financial responsibility even if previous owners or operators are responsible for contamination. In this situation the current owner/operator may pursue appropriate legal remedies against the previous owner/operator. 40 C.F.R. § 280.90 to .116.

13. State Laws

Many states have their own laws regulating USTs. These laws may impose additional requirements on owners and operators of USTs. They cannot contradict or excuse nonperformance with the federal standards.

For example, New York requires all new underground storage facilities to meet the following requirements (1) tanks must be made of fiberglass, reinforced plastic, steel which is cathodically protected, or steel which is clad with fiberglass, (2) a secondary containment system which prevents any materials spilled or leaked from reaching the land or water outside the containment area must be installed, and (3) a leak monitoring system must be installed.

All required equipment must meet the New York Department of Environmental Conservation (DEC) specifications and installation regulations. The DEC also regulates new USTs, labeling, and pressure testing. The DEC also sets specifications for (1) secondary containment, (2) monitoring, (3) reconditioning, and (4) installation methods. The DEC also has regulations and guidance memoranda on the remediation of releases and spills.

K. "Land Ban" Regulations

RCRA prohibits placement on land of bulk or noncontainerized liquid hazardous waste or free liquids contained in hazardous waste including liquids in materials that biodegrade or release liquids when compressed. 42 V.S.C. § 6924(c).

RCRA instructs the USEPA to prohibit land disposal of hazardous wastes by any other methods except those that the USEPA finds are protective of human health and the environment for so long as the waste remain hazardous. 42 U.S.C. § 6924(g)(5). Land disposal includes disposal in a landfill, surface impoundment, injection well, land treatment facility, salt dome or bed formation, or underground mine or cave. 42 U.S.C. § 6924(k).

RCRA requires the USEPA to prescribe treatment methods that will substantially diminish the toxicity of waste or reduce the likelihood of migration of hazardous constituents from waste. Wastes treated as required by the USEPA and their residues are no longer subject to the prohibition against land disposal. 42 U.S.C. § 6924(m).

In general, the USEPA has chosen the set pretreatment standards rather than to prohibit disposal. However, some of its standards have been so strict that they were equivalent to a prohibition for generators who could not meet them and were, therefore, required to discontinue the related business activities.

In 1986, the USEPA banned land disposal without pretreatment of listed wastes containing chlorodioxin and furan constituents (F021 to F023 and F026 to

F028) and spent solvents listed at 40 C.F.R. § 261.31 (F001 to F005). The USEPA prescribed incineration as the pretreatment method for the wastes containing chlorodioxin and furan constituents, but many generators could not use that method because it is very difficult to obtain a permit for a hazardous waste incinerator. 40 C.F.R. § 268.31.

In 1987, the USEPA banned land disposal without pretreatment of a group of wastes called the "California List" because California had previously banned them. They included wastes containing as constituents specified concentrations of free cyanide (100mg/L); partially soluble heavy metals; polychlorinated biphenyls (50 mg/L); and halogenated organic compounds (1,000 mg/L). The list also included acids below 2.0 pH. The ban formerly appeared at 40 C.F.R. § 268.32 which the USEPA removed in 1997 because the listed substances had been included in other treatment standards applicable to their specific constituents or characteristics.

The USEPA then undertook a program to prohibit land disposal and to prescribe pretreatment standards for the rest of the listed and characteristic hazardous wastes based on priority criteria which it developed. The USEPA divided the wastes into a first-third, a second-third and a third-third and adopted the regulations for them by 1990 after some delays and controversy. 42 U.S.C. § 6924(c)(2); 40 C.F.R. Part 268.

In general, the USEPA developed pretreatment standards based on best available demonstrated technology (BADT). Its choice was upheld in *Hazardous Waste Treatment Counsel v. E.P.A.*, 886 F.2d 355 (D.C.Cir. 1989). In practice, the USEPA set maximum concentration limits for hazardous constituents that it determined could be achieved by BADT. The USEPA sometimes required that a specific technology be used, but sometimes allowed use of any method that could achieve the concentration limit.

For ignitable, corrosive, reactive and TCLP characteristic wastes, the USEPA generally required pretreatment before land disposal sufficient to reduce the hazardous constituents below the level set for determination of the characteristic in 40 C.F.R. Part 261. Asserting that the pretreatment standards for characteristic wastes allowed generators to comply by simply diluting their wastes, the Natural Resources Defense Council challenged the standards in the U.S. District Court for the District of Columbia. The Court held that the USEPA must adopt pretreatment standards for characteristic waste waters in surface impoundments that treat hazardous constituents including those which did not cause the wastewaters to be characterized as hazardous. *Chemical Waste Management v. E.P.A.*, 976 F.2d 2 (D.C.Cir. 1992).

The Court's decision applied to wastewaters that were part of treatment systems permitted under the CWA. However, The Land Disposal Program Flexibility Act of 1986 superseded the Court's decision by providing that characteristic wastewaters are eligible for land disposal if managed in a treatment system regulated under the CWA (or an equivalent system) or in a Class I nonhazardous injection well, provided that the wastes are no longer hazardous when applied to land. 42 U.S.C. § 6924(7) and (8). Except for reactive cyanide wastes and certain other wastes, the methods by which the hazardous characteristics are removed are not restricted. It is not necessary to treat constituents that do not cause the waste to be considered hazardous. Unhappy with this law, some environmental groups have been claiming that sewage sludges applied as biosolids to land are threatening public health and the environment. See also the discussion of the sewage sludge regulations (40 C.F.R. Part 503) in the chapter on the Clean Water Act.

The USEPA's regulations assign a specific waste code to each listed and characteristic waste together with treatment standards for wastewater and nonwastewaters that are listed at length in 40 C.F.R. § 268.40. This section includes the standards expressed as concentrations in waste extract, as specified technologies, and as waste concentrations that were formerly contained in 40 C.F.R. §§ 268.41 to .43. Dilution is prohibited as a substitute for treatment. 40 C.F.R. § 268.3.

In general, listed wastes must be treated to meet the requirements for their specific waste codes and need not be treated beyond those requirements. However, if a listed waste displays a hazardous characteristic, the generator must determine the hazardous constituents and also comply with the requirements applicable to the characteristic waste. However, if the treatment standard for a listed waste includes a treatment standard for the constituent that causes the waste to exhibit the characteristic, compliance with that standard is sufficient. 40 C.F.R. § 268.9.

In general, characteristic wastes must be treated for the hazardous constituents that cause the characteristics and also for any underlying hazardous constituents listed in the Universal Treatment Standards (UTS) that can reasonably be expected to be present at the point of generation at a concentration above the constituent specific UTS treatment standards. 40 C.F.R. §§ 268.9, 268.2(i) and 268.48.

In 1994, the USEPA adopted the UTS wastewater and nonwastewater treatment standards to establish compliance standards for hazardous constituents that may not be exceeded in spite of inconsistencies in the standards for listed and characteristic wastes that resulted from their development based on BDAT. The UTS standards are expressed as concentrations for wastewaters and as TCLP concentrations for nonwastewaters. Compliance is measured by analysis of grab samples unless otherwise provided. 40 C.F.R. § 268.48 and Table UTS.

An important addition to the regulations were the treatment standards for hazardous debris using a variety of alternative extraction, destruction and immobilization technologies. For example, extraction technologies include such physical methods as abrasive blasting and high pressure steam and water sprays and chemical methods such as liquid phase and vapor phase solvent extraction. Destruction technologies include biodegradation, chemical or electrolytic reduction, chemical reduction and incineration. Immobilization technologies include macroencapsulation, microencapsulation and sealing. 40 C.F.R. § 268.45.

L. Used Oil

The USEPA has made a commendable effort to be practical about listing used oil as hazardous waste in spite of efforts by environmental groups to compel it to do otherwise. In 1986, the USEPA decided not to list used oil as hazardous waste and stated candidly that it did not want to discourage recycling by stigmatizing used oil as hazardous. The Natural Resources Defense Council challenged the decision in court and won. The U.S. Circuit Court of Appeals for the District of Columbia held that the USEPA had to determine whether used oil is hazardous. *Hazardous Waste Treatment Council v. E.P.A.* 861 F.2d 270 (D.C. Cir. 1988). The decision became a Pyrrhic victory for the NRDC because the USEPA determined that recycled used oil is not usually hazardous. Thus, the USEPA adopted separate regulations governing the management of recycled used oils that do not require management as hazardous waste except when mixed with other hazardous waste that causes the used oil to exceed limits for halogens or to exhibit an ignitability, corrosivity, reactivity or TCLP characteristic. 40 C.F.R. Part 279.

The USEPA's practicality has been rewarded by a nationwide transformation of thousands of gasoline automobile stations and other small shops from sloppy operations into clean orderly workplaces. Serviced by Safety Kleen and other firms, used oil and other wastes are recycled on a basis that achieves benefits for the recycler, the shop owners and operators, employees and customers.

M. Medical Waste

Finally, RCRA sponsored a medical waste tracking program in which the USEPA and several states participated. 42 U.S.C. §§ 6912 and 6992; 40 C.F.R. Part 259.

During and since the program, most states adopted legislation regulating medical waste. Although not uniform, the state laws follow similar patterns. In addition, the U.S. Occupational Safety and Health Administration (OSHA) adopted strict and detailed requirements in its standard Occupational Exposure to Bloodborne Pathogens. 29 C.F.R. § 1910.1030. The Research and Special Programs Administration (RSPA) of the U.S. Department of Transportation also adopted a regulation on packaging of medical waste. C.F.R. § 173.197.

Although medical waste is now extensively regulated, some environmental advocates are disappointed that Congress did not extend the USEPA's authority to regulate medical waste. See "Medical Waste Regulation in the United States," Jensen, *Natural Resources & Environment* (ABA), Vol. 9, No.2, Fall 1994.

N. State Hazardous Waste Regulation

RCRA authorizes the states to adopt laws regulating hazardous waste. If a state program is approved by the USEPA, the state may administer the RCRA hazardous waste program instead of the USEPA. To obtain approval, the state program must be at least as strict as the USEPA's program. 42 U.S.C. §§ 6926(b) and 6929. If the USEPA determines that a state is not properly administering or enforcing its program, the USEPA can withdraw its approval and resume direct administration and enforcement of the RCRA hazardous waste program. 42 U.S.C. § 6926(e).

The USEPA's regulations stating its requirements for authorization of state hazardous waste programs are at 40 C.F.R. Part 271. The regulations prescribe the content of state programs in detail to assure that there cannot be significant differences between state programs and the USEPA's program.

O. State Nonhazardous Solid Waste Regulation

Until October 1998, it was widely believed that RCRA granted primary authority to regulate nonhazardous solid waste to the states. The USEPA's role was perceived as using its extensive resources to provide criteria for use in state programs. Using this authority, many states made extensive and innovative progress.

Under state programs, modern landfills and recycling and reclamation programs were developed in cooperation with industrial owners and operators. Materials such as foundry sand and paper sludge that were once simply discarded were beneficially used as daily cover and capping materials. Methane gas generated by municipal landfills that had been a hazard was recovered for use as an inexpensive substitute for natural gas.

The USEPA adopted regulations on criteria for classification of solid waste disposal facilities. 40 C.F.R. Part 257. The regulations establish criteria relating to floodplains, endangered species; surface water; groundwater; application of waste containing cadmium or PCBs to land used for production of food chain crops; disease vectors; open burning; and certain safety practices. Facilities failing to satisfy the criteria are considered open dumps prohibited by RCRA. 40 C.F.R. § 157.1. The regulations contain separate standards applicable to non-municipal nonhazardous waste units that receive waste from conditionally exempt small quantity generators. 40 C.F.R. §§ 257.5 to 257.29. Among other things, these regulations also prescribe maximum contaminant levels (MCLs) and other criteria for the disposal of sewage sludge when the sewage sludge is not used or disposed of by practices regulated by the Part 503 regulations 40 C.F.R. Part 257, Appendix A. The regulations also describe processes to significantly reduce pathogens in sludge such as aerobic and anaerobic digestion, air drying, composting, line stabilization, irradiation, and pasteurization. 40 C.F.R. Part 257, Appendix B.

The USEPA also adopted regulations prescribing criteria under RCRA for municipal solid waste landfills (MSWLFs) and under the CWA for MSWLFs that are used to dispose of sewage sludge. 40 C.F.R. Part 258. The regulations establish location restrictions; operating criteria; design criteria; groundwater monitoring and corrective action requirements; closure and post-closure area requirements; and financial assurance criteria. MSWLF units failing to satisfy the criteria are considered prohibited open dumps under RCRA. MSWLF units containing sewage sludge and failing to satisfy the criteria violate the CWA. 40 C.F.R. § 258.1(g).

In October 1998, the USEPA adopted regulations requiring that all states submit their solid waste permit programs to the USEPA for a determination of adequacy. 40 C.F. R. Part 239. The regulations require that each state's program adopt and enforce the USEPA's criteria under 40 C.F.R. Parts 257 and 258 and numerous other requirements prescribed by the USEPA. The USEPA declared that, if it determines that a state program is inadequate, the USEPA will have the authority to enforce the solid waste program on facilities under the state's jurisdiction that may receive hazardous waste from households or small quantity generators. 40 C.F.R. § 239.2(a). In effect, the regulations curtail the states' primary authority over many solid waste facilities, leaving the states only the right to add stricter requirements to the USEPA's extensive program. In 2000, the USEPA announced that it will move to strengthen its claim of direct enforcement authority.

Some states, such as New Jersey, adopted elaborate solid waste management laws and regulations designed to allow the state environmental agency to control and manage all aspects of solid waste including generation, collection, transportation, disposal, recycling, reclamation and beneficial reuse. One effect of this intense regulation was to shut down many landfills and other waste disposal facilities and make it almost impossible to open new facilities. Another effect was to increase dramatically the cost of waste disposal. Companies began to ship their waste to other states. To force the companies to pay the costs of the highly regulated facilities. These states created district waste flow laws and rules under which franchise monopolies were granted and prohibitions, restrictions and charges were imposed on the movement into and out of the state or the districts. The restrictive "waste flow" laws of these states were held in violation of the U.S. Constitution because of their discriminatory effect on interstate commerce. *Fort Gratiot Sanitary Landfill, Inc. v. Michigan Department of Natural Resources*, 112 S.Ct. 2019, 34 ERC 1721 (1992); *Chemical Waste Management v. Templet*, 967 F.2d 1058, (5th Cir. 1992), *cert. denied,* 61 USLW 3498 (1993); *Clarkstown v. C&A Carbone, Inc.*, 511 U.S. 383, 128 L. Ed. 2d 399 (1994).

After the decisions by the U.S. Supreme Court, state and local officials adopted revised laws and regulations that enable them to maintain at least partial waste flow monopolies or oligopolies. The courts have so far upheld these laws, although they obtain some of the same results as the laws declared unconstitutional. *United Haulers Association, Inc. v. Oneida-Herkimer Solid Waste Management Authority*, 261 F.3d 245 (2d Cir. 2001) *cert. denied*, 122 S.Ct. 815, 151 L. Ed. 2d 699 (2002); *Mahary, Inc. v. Van Wert Solid Waste*, 249 F.3d 544 (6th Cir. 2001).

The states also were confronted by the political problem that the public creates waste, but believes its disposal should be somewhere far away and "Not in my back yard," commonly called the "NIMBY" factor. This factor is particularly troublesome for disposal of low level radioactive wastes from hospitals. Ironically, people willingly have X-ray pictures taken by doctors and dentists and have radiation treatment in hospitals that involves direct exposure to radiation. However, they protest against safe disposal of low level radioactive wastes from hospitals in sealed specially designed steel containers in concrete encased disposal facilities in their state. Thus hospitals must retain the wastes or ship them to a facility such as the Chem Risk facility at Barnwell, South Carolina at very high cost.

Some states adopted laws prohibiting shipments of hazardous wastes from other states. Other states imposed fees or other charges on disposal of out of state wastes that were dramatically higher than those for disposal of local wastes. For example, Alabama imposed a high fee on hazardous wastes sent from other states for disposal at the Chemical Waste facility at Emelle, Alabama. Such laws have been declared unconstitutional. *City of Philadelphia v. New Jersey*, 119 L. Ed. 2d 121 (1992); *National Solid Waste Management v. Meyer*, 165 F.3d 11151 (7th Cir. 1999).

P. Enforcement

RCRA authorizes the USEPA to issue orders requiring compliance immediately or within a specified time period and also to suspend or revoke a permit and assess a penalty not exceeding $25,000 per day of noncompliance for each violation. 42 U.S.C. § 6928. The USEPA can also seek enforcement by a civil action in the U.S. District Court which can issue orders and impose civil penalties up to $25,000 for each violation. 42 U.S.C. § 6928(g).

> *NOTE*: The $25,000 amount is stated in RCRA. However, the Debt Collection Improvement Act of 1996 requires the USEPA to adjust penalties for inflation at least once every four years. Thus, the USEPA periodically increases the penalty amounts. The increase in 1998 was 10% and in 2002 was 13.6%.

RCRA also imposes criminal penalties for knowing violations up to $50,000 for each day of violation and imprisonment up to two years for some violations and five years for others. 42 U.S.C. § 6928(d). For repeat convictions, the maximum punishment is doubled. For violations by an individual who knows that he or she thereby places another person in imminent danger of death or serious bodily injury, the penalty is up to $250,000 or 15 years imprisonment. For a knowing endangerment violation by an organization, the penalty is up to $1,000,000. 42 U.S.C. § 6928(f). *U.S. v. Elias*, 269 F.3d 1003 (9th Cir. 2001); *U.S. v. Hanson*, 262 F.3d 1217 (11th Cir. 2001); *U.S. v. Hong*, 242 F.3d 528 (4th Cir. 2001). *U.S. v. Wagner*, 29

F.3d 264 (7th Cir. 1994); *U.S. v. Laughlin*, 10 F.3d 961 (2d Cir. 1993); *U.S. v. Heuer*, 3 F.3d 723 (9th Cir. 1993); *U.S. v. Dean*, 969 F.2d 187 (6th Cir. 1992);

Q. Citizen Suits

RCRA authorizes "citizen suits" which are frequently commenced on behalf of environmental organizations. The plaintiffs can recover attorneys fees and costs if they prevail or substantially prevail. 42 U.S.C. § 6972. However, RCRA prohibits citizen suits without prior notice to the USEPA and other specified persons including the alleged violator and under several circumstances where a citizen suit could interfere with actions being taken by the USEPA or a state.

The U.S. Supreme Court held that a citizen suit may not be used as a means to recover costs which have been spent to remediate hazardous wastes which no longer endanger human health or the environment. *Meghrig v. KFC Western*, 516 U.S. 479, 134 L. Ed.2d 121 (1996). The Court pointed to the remedies, including the contribution recovery provisions in CERCLA, for recovery of such costs.

Homeowners had standing to sue the City of Dallas for unlawful dumping at two garbage disposal sites where the dumping had attracted vectors such as rats and snakes and resulted in fires. They also had standing to seek an injunction requiring the Texas National Resource Conservation Commission to classify the sites for listing on the USEPA's Open Dump Inventory. *Cox v. City of Dallas*, 256 F.3d 281 (5th Cir. 2001).

An attempt to sue under RCRA to prevent the City of New York from spraying malathion to control West Nile Virus which had caused the death of several people was rejected in *No Spray Coalition, Inc. v. The City of New York*, 252 F.3d 148 (2d Cir. 2001). The Court held that the sprayed insecticide is not discarded until it achieves its intended purpose.

EXHIBITS

Please print or type with ELITE type (12 characters per inch) in the unshaded areas only

Form Approved, OMB No. 2050-0034 Expires 10/31/02
GSA No. 0248-EPA-OT

For EPA Regional Use Only

Date Received
Month Day Year

✿EPA
United States Environmental Protection Agency
Washington, DC 20460

Hazardous Waste Permit Application Part A
(Read the Instructions before starting)

I. Facility's EPA ID Number *(Mark 'X' in the appropriate box)*

☐ A. First Part A Submission ☐ B. Revised Part A Submission (Amendment # _____)

C. Facility's EPA ID Number

D. Secondary ID Number *(If applicable)*

II. Name of Facility

III. Facility Location *(Physical address not P.O. Box or Route Number)*

A. Street

Street *(Continued)*

City or Town State Zip Code

County Code *(If known)* County Name

B. Land Type *(Enter code)* C. Geographic Location LATITUDE *(Degrees, minutes, & seconds)* LONGITUDE *(Degrees, minutes & seconds)* D. Facility Existence Date Month Day Year

IV. Facility Mailing Address

Street or P.O. Box

City or Town State Zip Code

V. Facility Contact *(Person to be contacted regarding waste activities at facility)*

Name *(Last)* *(First)*

Job Title Phone Number *(Area Code and Number)*

VI. Facility Contact Address *(See instructions)*

A. Contact Address ☐ Location ☐ Mailing ☐ Other   B. Street or P.O. Box

City or Town State Zip Code

EPA Form 8700-23 (Rev. 10/99)

Please print or type with ELITE type (12 characters per inch) in the unshaded areas only

Form Approved, OMB No. 2050-0034 Expires 10/31/02
GSA No. 0248-EPA-OT

EPA ID Number *(Enter from page 1)*

Secondary ID Number *(Enter from page 1)*

VII. Operator Information *(See instructions)*

A. Name of Operator

Street or P.O. Box

City or Town

State

ZIP Code —

Phone Number *(Area Code and Number)* — —

B. Operator Type

C. Change of Operator Indicator: Yes No

Date Changed: Month Day Year

VIII. Facility Owner *(See instructions)*

A. Name of Facility's Legal Owner

Street or P.O. Box

City or Town

State

ZIP Code —

Phone Number *(Area Code and Number)* — —

B. Owner Type

C. Change of Owner Indicator: Yes No

Date Changed: Month Day Year

IX. NAICS Codes *(in order of significance; start in left box)*

First	Third
(Description)	*(Description)*
Second	Fourth
(Description)	*(Description)*

X. Other Environmental Permits *(See instructions)*

A. Permit Type *(Enter code)*	B. Permit Number	C. Description

EPA Form 8700-23 (Rev. 10/99)

- 2 of 7 -

Please print or type with ELITE type (12 characters per inch) in the unshaded areas only

Form Approved, OMB No. 2050-0034 Expires 10/31/02
GSA No. 0248-EPA-OT

EPA ID Number *(Enter from page 1)* | **Secondary ID Number** *(Enter from page 1)*

XI. Nature of Business *(Provide a brief description)*

XII. Process Codes and Design Capacities

A. **PROCESS CODE** - *Enter the code from the list of process codes below that best describes each process to be used at the facility. Thirteen lines are provided for entering codes. If more lines are needed, attach a separate sheet of paper with the additional information. For "other" processes (i.e., D99, S99, T04 and X99), describe the process (including its design capacity) in the space provided in item XIII.*

B. **PROCESS DESIGN CAPACITY** - *For each code entered in column A, enter the capacity of the process.*
1. **AMOUNT** - *Enter the amount. In a case where design capacity is not applicable (such as in a closure/post-closure or enforcement action) enter the total amount of waste for that process.*
2. **UNIT OF MEASURE** - *For each amount entered in column B(1), enter the code from the list of unit measure codes below that describes the unit of measure used. Only the units of measure that are listed below should be used.*

C. **PROCESS TOTAL NUMBER OF UNITS** - *Enter the total number of units used with the corresponding process code.*

PROCESS CODE	PROCESS	APPROPRIATE UNITS OF MEASURE FOR PROCESS DESIGN CAPACITY
	<u>Disposal:</u>	
D79	Underground Injection Well Disposal	Gallons; Liters; Gallons Per Day; or Liters Per Day
D80	Landfill	Acre-feet; Hectare-meter; Acres; Cubic Meters; Hectares; Cubic Yards
D81	Land Treatment	Acres or Hectares
D82	Ocean Disposal	Gallons Per Day or Liters Per Day
D83	Surface Impoundment Disposal	Gallons; Liters; Cubic Meters; or Cubic Yards
D99	Other Disposal	Any Unit of Measure Listed Below
	<u>Storage:</u>	
S01	Container	Gallons; Liters; Cubic Meters; or Cubic Yards
S02	Tank Storage	Gallons; Liters; Cubic Meters; or Cubic Yards
S03	Waste Pile	Cubic Yards or Cubic Meters
S04	Surface Impoundment Storage	Gallons; Liters; Cubic Meters; or Cubic Yards
S05	Drip Pad	Gallons; Liters; Acres; Cubic Meters; Hectares; or Cubic Yards
S06	Containment Building Storage	Cubic Yards or Cubic Meters
S99	Other Storage	Any Unit of Measure Listed Below
	<u>Treatment:</u>	
T01	Tank Treatment	Gallons Per Day; Liters Per Day; Short Tons Per Hour; Gallons Per Hour; Liters Per Hour; Pounds Per Hour; Short Tons Per Day; Kilograms Per Hour; Metric Tons Per Day; or Metric Tons Per Hour
T02	Surface Impoundment Treatment	Gallons Per Day; Liters Per Day; Short Tons Per Hour; Gallons Per Hour; Liters Per Hour; Pounds Per Hour; Short Tons Per Day; Kilograms Per Hour; Metric Tons Per Day; or Metric Tons Per Hour
T03	Incinerator	Short Tons Per Hour; Metric Tons Per Hour; Gallons Per Hour; Liters Per Hour; Btu Per Hour; Pounds Per Hour; Short Tons Per Day; Kilograms Per Hour; Gallons Per Day; Liters Per Day; Metric Tons Per Hour; or Million Btu Per Hour
T04	Other Treatment	Gallons Per Day; Liters Per Day; Pounds Per Hour; Short Tons Per Hour; Kilograms Per Hour; Metric Tons Per Day; Metric Tons Per Hour; Short Tons Per Day; Btu Per Hour; Gallons Per Day; Liters Per Hour; or Million Btu Per Hour
T80	Boiler	Gallons; Liters; Gallons Per Hour; Liters Per Hour; Btu Per Hour; or Million Btu Per Hour

PROCESS CODE	PROCESS	APPROPRIATE UNITS OF MEASURE FOR PROCESS DESIGN CAPACITY
T81	Cement Kiln	Gallons Per Day; Liters Per Day; Pounds Per Hour; Short Tons Per Hour; Kilograms Per Hour; Metric Tons Per Day; Metric Tons Per Hour; Short Tons Per Day; Btu Per Hour; Liters Per Hour; Kilograms Per Hour; or Million Btu Per Hour (T81–T86)
T82	Lime Kiln	
T83	Aggregate Kiln	
T84	Phosphate Kiln	
T85	Coke Oven	
T86	Blast Furnace	
T87	Smelting, Melting, Or Refining Furnace	Gallons Per Day; Liters Per Day; Pounds Per Hour; Short Tons Per Hour; Kilograms Per Hour; Metric Tons Per Day; Metric Tons Per Hour; Short Tons Per Day; Btu Per Hour; Gallons Per Hour; Liters Per Hour; or Miilion Btu Per Hour (T87–T93)
T88	Titanium Dioxide Chloride Oxidation Reactor	
T89	Methane Reforming Furnace	
T90	Pulping Liquor Recovery Furnace	
T91	Combustion Device Used In The Recovery Of Sulfur Values From Spent Sulfuric Acid	
T92	Halogen Acid Furnaces	
T93	Other Industrial Furnaces Listed in 40 CFR §260.10	
T94	Containment Building - Treatment	Cubic Yards; Cubic Meters; Short Tons Per Hour; Gallons Per Hour; Liters Per Hour; Btu Per Hour; Pounds Per Hour; Short Tons Per Day; Kilograms Per Hour; Metric Tons Per Day; Gallons Per Day; Liters Per Day; Metric Tons Per Hour; or Million Btu Per Hour
	<u>Miscellaneous (Subpart X):</u>	
X01	Open Burning/Open Detonation	Any Unit of Measure Listed Below
X02	Mechanical Processing	Short Tons Per Hour; Metric Tons Per Hour; Short Tons Per Day; Metric Tons Per Day; Pounds Per Hour; Kilograms Per Hour; Gallons Per Hour; Liters Per Hour; or Gallons Per Day
X03	Thermal Unit	Gallons Per Day; Liters Per Day; Pounds Per Hour; Short Tons Per Hour; Kilograms Per Hour; Metric Tons Per Day; Metric Tons Per Hour; Short Tons Per Day; Btu Per Hour; or Million Btu Per Hour
X04	Geologic Repository	Cubic Yards; Cubic Meters; Acre-feet; Hectare-meter; Gallons; or Liters
X99	Other Subpart X	Any Unit of Measure Listed Below

UNIT OF MEASURE	UNIT OF MEASURE CODE
Gallons	G
Gallons Per Hour	E
Gallons Per Day	U
Liters	L
Liters Per Hour	H
Liters Per Day	V
Short Tons Per Hour	D
Metric Tons Per Hour	W
Short Tons Per Day	N
Metric Tons Per Day	S
Pounds Per Hour	J
Kilograms Per Hour	R
Million Btu Per Hour	X
Cubic Yards	Y
Cubic Meters	C
Acres	B
Acre-feet	A
Hectares	Q
Hectare-meter	F
Btu Per Hour	I

EPA Form 8700-23 (Rev. 10/99) - 3 of 7 -

Please print or type with ELITE type (12 characters per inch) in the unshaded areas only

Form Approved, OMB No. 2050-0034 Expires 10/31/02
GSA No. 0248-EPA-OT

EPA ID Number *(Enter from page 1)* | **Secondary ID Number** *(Enter from page 1)*

XII. Process Codes and Design Capabilities *(Continued)*

EXAMPLE FOR COMPLETING ITEM XII (shown in line number X-1 below): A facility has a storage tank, which can hold 533.788 gallons.

Line Number		A. Process Code (From list above)			B. PROCESS DESIGN CAPACITY 1. Amount (Specify)	2. Unit Of Measure (Enter code)	C. Process Total Number Of Units	For Official Use Only
X	1	S	0	2	5 3 3 . 7 8 8	G	0 0 1	
	1				.			
	2				.			
	3				.			
	4				.			
	5				.			
	6				.			
	7				.			
	8				.			
	9				.			
1	0				.			
1	1				.			
1	2				.			
1	3				.			

NOTE: If you need to list more than 13 process codes, attach an additional sheet(s) with the information in the same format as above. Number the lines sequentially, taking into account any lines that will be used for "other" processes (i.e., D99, S99, T04 and X99) in item XIII.

XIII. Other Processes *(Follow instructions from item XII for D99, S99, T04 and X99 process codes)*

Line Number (Enter #s in seq w/XII)		A. Process Code (From list above)			B. PROCESS DESIGN CAPACITY 1. Amount (Specify)	2. Unit Of Measure (Enter code)	C. Process Total Number Of Units	D. Description Of Process
X	1	T	0	4	.			In-situ Vitrification
	1				.			
	2				.			
	3				.			
	4				.			

EPA Form 8700-23 (Rev. 10/99) - 4 of 7 -

Please print or type with ELITE type (12 characters per inch) in the unshaded areas only

Form Approved, OMB No. 2050-0034 Expires 10/31/02
GSA No. 0248-EPA-OT

EPA ID Number *(Enter from page 1)* | **Secondary ID Number** *(Enter from page 1)*

XIV. Description of Hazardous Wastes

A. **EPA HAZARDOUS WASTE NUMBER** - *Enter the four-digit number from 40 CFR, Part 261 Subpart D of each listed hazardous waste you will handle. For hazardous wastes which are not listed in 40 CFR, Part 261 Subpart D, enter the four-digit number(s) from 40 CFR, Part 261 Subpart C that describes the characteristics and/or the toxic contaminants of those hazardous wastes.*

B. **ESTIMATED ANNUAL QUANTITY** - *For each listed waste entered in column A estimate the quantity of that waste that will be handled on an annual basis. For each characteristic or toxic contaminant entered in column A estimate the total annual quantity of all the non-listed waste(s) that will be handled which possess that characteristic or contaminant.*

C **UNIT OF MEASURE** - *For each quantity entered in column B enter the unit of measure code. Units of measure which must be used and the appropriate codes are:*

ENGLISH UNIT OF MEASURE	CODE	METRIC UNIT OF MEASURE	CODE
POUNDS	P	KILOGRAMS	K
TONS	T	METRIC TONS	M

If facility records use any other unit of measure for quantity, the units of measure must be converted into one of the required units of measure taking into account the appropriate density or specific gravity of the waste.

D. **PROCESSES**

1. **PROCESS CODES:**

For listed hazardous waste: For each listed hazardous waste entered in column A select the code(s) from the list of process codes contained in item XII A. on page 3 to indicate how the waste will be stored, treated, and/or disposed of at the facility.

For non-listed hazardous waste: For each characteristic or toxic contaminant entered in column A, select the code(s) from the list of process codes contained in item XII A. on page 3 to indicate all the processes that will be used to store, treat, and/ or dispose of all the non-listed hazardous wastes that possess that characteristic or toxic contaminant.

NOTE: THREE SPACES ARE PROVIDED FOR ENTERING PROCESS CODES. IF MORE ARE NEEDED:

1. Enter the first two as described above.
2. Enter "000" in the extreme right box of item XIV-D(1).
3. Use additional sheet, enter line number from previous sheet, and enter additional code(s) in item XIV-E.

2. **PROCESS DESCRIPTION:** *If a code is not listed for a process that will be used, describe the process in the space provided on the form (D.(2)).*

NOTE: HAZARDOUS WASTES DESCRIBED BY MORE THAN ONE EPA HAZARDOUS WASTE NUMBER - Hazardous wastes that can be described by more than one EPA Hazardous Waste Number shall be described on the form as follows:

1. Select one of the EPA Hazardous Waste Numbers and enter it in column A. On the same line complete columns B, C and D by estimating the total annual quantity of the waste and describing all the processes to be used to treat, store, and/or dispose of the waste.

2. In column A of the next line enter the other EPA Hazardous Waste Number that can be used to describe the waste. In column D(2) on that line enter "included with above" and make no other entries on that line.

3. Repeat step 2 for each EPA Hazardous Waste Number that can be used to describe the hazardous waste.

EXAMPLE FOR COMPLETING ITEM XIV (shown in line numbers X-1, X-2, X-3, and X-4 below) - A facility will treat and dispose of an estimated 900 pounds per year of chrome shavings from leather tanning and finishing operation. In addition, the facility will treat and dispose of three non-listed wastes. Two wastes are corrosive only and there will be an estimated 200 pounds per year of each waste. The other waste is corrosive and ignitable and there will be an estimated 100 pounds per year of that waste. Treatment will be in an incinerator and disposal will be in a landfill.

Line Number		A. EPA HAZARD WASTE NO. (Enter code)				B. ESTIMATED ANNUAL QUANTITY OF WASTE	C. UNIT OF MEASURE (Enter code)	D. PROCESS (1) PROCESS CODES (Enter)									D. PROCESS (2) PROCESS DESCRIPTION (If a code is not entered in D(1))
X	1	K	0	5	4	900	p	T	0	3	D	8	0				
X	2	D	0	0	2	400	P	T	0	3	D	8	0				
X	3	D	0	0	1	100	P	T	0	3	D	8	0				
X	4	D	0	0	2												Included With Above

EPA Form 8700-23 (Rev. 10/99) - 5 of 7 -

Form Approved, OMB No. 2050-0034 Expires 10/31/02
GSA No. 0248-EPA-OT

Please print or type with ELITE type (12 characters per inch) in the unshaded areas only

EPA ID Number *(Enter from page 1)*

Secondary ID Number *(Enter from page 1)*

XIV. Description of Hazardous Wastes *(Continued; use additional sheets as necessary)*

Line Number	*A. EPA Hazardous Waste No. (Enter code)*	*B. Estimated Annual Quantity of Waste*	*C. Unit of Measure (Enter code)*	*D. PROCESSES* *(1) PROCESS CODES (Enter code)*	*(2) PROCESS DESCRIPTION (If a code is not entered in D(1))*
1					
2					
3					
4					
5					
6					
7					
8					
9					
1 0					
1 1					
1 2					
1 3					
1 4					
1 5					
1 6					
1 7					
1 8					
1 9					
2 0					
2 1					
2 2					
2 3					
2 4					
2 5					
2 6					
2 7					
2 8					
2 9					
3 0					
3 1					
3 2					
3 3					

EPA Form 8700-23 (Rev. 10/99)

- 6 of 7 -

Please print or type with ELITE type (12 characters per inch) in the unshaded areas only

Form Approved, OMB No. 2050-0034 Expires 10/31/02
GSA No. 0248-EPA-OT

EPA ID Number *(Enter from page 1)*	Secondary ID Number *(Enter from page 1)*

XV. Map

Attach to this application a topographic map, or other equivalent map, of the area extending to at least one mile beyond property boundaries. The map must show the outline of the facility, the location of each of its existing and proposed intake and discharge structures, each of its hazardous waste treatment, storage, or disposal facilities, and each well where it injects fluids underground. Include all springs, rivers and other surface water bodies in this map area. See instructions for precise requirements.

XVI. Facility Drawing

All existing facilities must include a scale drawing of the facility (See instructions for more detail).

XVII. Photographs

All existing facilities must include photographs (aerial or ground-level) that clearly delineate all existing structures; existing storage, treatment and disposal areas; and sites of future storage, treatment or disposal areas (see instructions for more detail).

XVIII. Certification(s)

I certify under penalty of law that this document and all attachments were prepared under my direction or supervision in accordance with a system designed to assure that qualified personnel properly gather and evaluate the information submitted. Based on my inquiry of the person or persons who manage the system, or those persons directly responsible for gathering the information, the information submitted is, to the best of my knowledge and belief, true, accurate, and complete. I am aware that there are significant penalties for submitting false information, including the possibility of fine and imprisonment for knowing violations.

Owner Signature	Date Signed
Name and Official Title (Type or print)	
Owner Signature	Date Signed
Name and Official Title (Type or print)	
Operator Signature	Date Signed
Name and Official Title (Type or print)	
Operator Signature	Date Signed
Name and Official Title (Type or print)	

XIX. Comments

Note: Mail completed form to the appropriate EPA Regional or State Office. (Refer to instructions for more information).

EPA Form 8700-23 (Rev. 10/99) - 7 of 7 -

Form Approved, OMB No. 2050-0034 Expires 10/31/02
GSA No. 0248-EPA-OT

Please print or type with ELITE type (12 characters per inch) in the unshaded areas only

EPA ID Number *(Enter from page 1)* **Secondary ID Number** *(Enter from page 1)*

XIV. Description of Hazardous Wastes *(Continued; Additional Sheet)*

Line Number	*A. EPA Hazardous Waste No. (Enter code)*	*B. Estimated Annual Quantity of Waste*	*C. Unit of Measure (Enter code)*	*E. PROCESSES*	
				(1) PROCESS CODES (Enter code)	*(2) PROCESS DESCRIPTION (If a code is not entered in E(1))*

EPA Form 8700-23 (Rev. 10/99)

NYG 3269727

STATE OF NEW YORK
DEPARTMENT OF ENVIRONMENTAL CONSERVATION
DIVISION OF SOLID & HAZARDOUS MATERIALS

HAZARDOUS WASTE MANIFEST
P.O. Box 12820, Albany, New York 12212

Please type or print. Do not staple

(Hazardous Waste Manifest 1/5/99)

In case of emergency or spill immediately call the National Response Center (800) 424-8802 and the NYS Department of Environmental Conservation (518) 457-7362

UNIFORM HAZARDOUS WASTE MANIFEST

1. Generator's US EPA ID No.
Manifest Doc. No.
2. Page 1 of
Information within heavy bold line is not required by Federal Law.

GENERATOR

3. Generator's Name and Mailing Address

SAMPLE

4. Generator's Telephone Number ( )
5. Transporter 1 (Company Name)
6. US EPA ID Number
7 Transporter 2 (Company Name)
8. US EPA ID Number
9. Designated Facility Name and Site Address
10. US EPA ID Number

A. NYG 3269727
B. Generator's ID
C. State Transporter's ID
D. Transporter's Telephone ( )
E. State Transporter's ID
F. Transporter's Telephone ( )
G. State Facility ID
H. Facility Telephone ( )

11. US DOT Description (Including Proper Shipping Name, Hazard Class and ID Number)	12. Containers Number	Type	13. Total Quantity	14. Unit Wt/Vol	I. Waste No.
a.					EPA STATE
b.					EPA STATE
c					EPA STATE
d.					EPA STATE

J. Additional Descriptions for Materials listed Above
a
b
c
d

K. Handling Codes for Wastes Listed Above
a
b
c
d

15. Special Handling Instructions and Additional Information

16. GENERATOR'S CERTIFICATION: I hereby declare that the contents of this consignment are fully and accurately described above by proper shipping name and are classified, packed, marked and labeled, and are in all respects in proper condition for transport by highway according to applicable international and national government regulations and state laws and regulations.
If I am a large quantity generator, I certify that I have a program in place to reduce the volume and toxicity of waste generated to the degree I have determined to be economically practicable and that I have selected the practicable method of treatment, storage, or disposal currently available to me which minimizes the present and future threat to human health and the environment; OR if I am a small quantity generator, I have made a good faith effort to minimize my waste generation and select the best waste management method that is available to me and that I can afford.

Printed/Typed Name | Signature | Mo. Day Year

TRANSPORTER

17. Transporter 1 Acknowledgement of Receipt of Materials
Printed/Typed Name | Signature | Mo. Day Year

18. Transporter 2 Acknowledgement of Receipt of Materials
Printed/Typed Name | Signature | Mo. Day Year

FACILITY

19. Discrepancy Indication Space

20. Facility Owner or Operator: Certification of receipt of hazardous materials covered by this manifest except as noted in Item 19.
Printed/Typed Name | Signature | Mo. Day Year

COPY 1—Disposer State—Mailed by TSD Facility

EPA

United States
Environmental Protection Agency
Washington, DC 20460

Form Approved.
OMB No.2050-0068

Notification for Underground Storage Tanks

State Agency Name and Address:

STATE USE ONLY
ID NUMBER:
DATE RECEIVED:
DATE ENTERED INTO COMPUTER:
DATA ENTRY CLERK INITIALS:
OWNER WAS CONTACTED TO CLARIFY RESPONSES, COMMENTS:

TYPE OF NOTIFICATION

☐ A. NEW FACILITY	☐ B. AMENDED	☐ C. CLOSURE
____ Number of tanks at facility	____ Number of continuation sheets attached	

INSTRUCTIONS AND GENERAL INFORMATION

Please type or print in ink. Also, be sure you have signatures in ink for sections VIII and XI. Complete a notification form for each location containing underground storage tanks. If more than 5 tanks are owned at this location, you may photocopy pages 3 through 5 and use them for additional tanks.

The primary purpose of this notification program is to locate and evaluate underground storage tank systems (USTs) that store or have stored petroleum or hazardous substances. The information you provide will be based on reasonably available records, or in the absence of such records, your knowledge or recollection.

Federal law requires UST owners to use this notification form for all USTs storing regulated substances that are brought into use after May 8, 1986, or USTs in the ground as of May 8, 1986 that have stored regulated substances at any time since January 1, 1974. The information requested is required by Section 9002 of the Resource Conservation and Recovery Act (RCRA), as amended.

Who Must Notify? Section 9002 of RCRA, as amended, requires owners of USTs that store regulated substances (unless exempted) to notify designated State or local agencies of the existence of their USTs. "Owner" is defined as:

- In the case of an UST in use on November 8, 1984, or brought into use after that date, any person who owns an UST used for storage, use, or dispensing of regulated substances; or
- In the case of an UST in use before November 8, 1984, but no longer in use on that date, any person who owned the UST immediately before its discontinuation.

Also, if the State so requires, any facility that has made any changes to facility information or UST system status, must submit a notification form (only amended information needs to be included).

What USTs Are Included? An UST system is defined as any one or combination of tanks that (1) is used to contain an accumulation of regulated substances, and (2) whose volume (including connected underground piping) is 10% or more beneath the ground. Regulated USTs store petroleum or hazardous substances (see the following "What Substances Are Covered").

What Tanks Are Excluded From Notification?

- Tanks removed from the ground before May 8, 1986;
- Farm or residential tanks of 1,100 gallons or less capacity storing motor fuel for noncommercial purposes;
- Tanks storing heating oil for use on the premises where stored;
- Septic tanks;
- Pipeline facilities (including gathering lines) regulated under the Natural Gas Pipeline Safety Act of 1968, or the Hazardous Liquid Pipeline Safety Act of 1979, or which is an intrastate pipeline facility regulated under State laws;
- Surface impoundments, pits, ponds, or lagoons;
- Storm water or waste water collection systems;
- Flow-through process tanks;
- Liquid traps or associated gathering lines directly related to oil or gas production and gathering operations;
- Tanks on or above the floor of underground areas, such as basements or tunnels;
- Tanks with a capacity of 110 gallons or less.

What Substances Are Covered? The notification requirements apply to USTs containing petroleum or certain hazardous substances. Petroleum includes gasoline, used oil, diesel fuel, crude oil or any fraction thereof which is liquid at standard conditions of temperature and pressure (60 degrees Fahrenheit and 14.7 pounds per square inch absolute). Hazardous substances are those found in Section 101 (14) of the Comprehensive Environmental Response, Compensation and Liability Act of 1980 (CERCLA), with the exception of those substances regulated as hazardous waste under Subtitle C of RCRA.

Where To Notify? Send completed forms to:

When To Notify? 1. Owners of USTs in use or that have been taken out of operation after January 1, 1974, but still in the ground, must notify by May 8, 1986. 2. Owners who bring USTs into use after May 8, 1986, must notify within 30 days of bringing the UST into use. 3. If the State requires notification of any amendments to facility, send information to State agency immediately.

Penalties: Any owner who knowingly fails to notify or submits false information shall be subject to a civil penalty not to exceed $11,000 for each tank for which notification is not given or for which false information is given.

I. OWNERSHIP OF UST(s)

Owner Name (Corporation, Individual, Public Agency, or Other Entity)		
Street Address County		
City	State	Zip Code
Phone Number (Include Area Code)		

II. LOCATION OF UST(s)

If required by State, give the geographic location of USTs by degrees, minutes, and seconds. Example: Latitude 42° 36' 12" N, Longitude 85° 24' 17" W

Latitude ____________ **Longitude** ____________

Facility Name or Company Site Identifier, as applicable		
☐ If address is the same as in Section I, check the box and proceed to section III. If address is different, enter address below. Street Address County		
City	State	Zip Code

EPA Form 7530-1 (Rev. 9-98) Electronic and paper versions acceptable.
Previous editions may be used while supplies last.

Page 1 of 5

EPA

United States
Environmental Protection Agency
Washington, DC 20460

Form Approved.
OMB No.2050-0068

Notification for Underground Storage Tanks

III. TYPE OF OWNER	IV. INDIAN COUNTRY	
☐ Federal Government ☐ State Government ☐ Commercial ☐ Local Government ☐ Private	USTs are located on land within an Indian Reservation or on trust lands outside reservation boundaries. ☐ USTs are owned by a Native American nation or tribe. ☐	Tribe or Nation where USTs are located:

V. TYPE OF FACILITY

☐ Gas Station	☐ Railroad	☐ Trucking/Transport
☐ Petroleum Distributor	☐ Federal - Non-Military	☐ Utilities
☐ Air Taxi (Airline)	☐ Federal - Military	☐ Residential
☐ Aircraft Owner	☐ Industrial	☐ Farm
☐ Auto Dealership	☐ Contractor	☐ Other (Explain) ____________

VI. CONTACT PERSON IN CHARGE OF TANKS

Name:	Job Title:	Address:	Phone Number (Include Area Code):

VII. FINANCIAL RESPONSIBILITY

☐ I have met the financial responsibility requirements (in accordance with 40 CFR Subpart H) by using the following mechanisms:

Check All that Apply

☐ Self Insurance	☐ Guarantee	☐ State Funds
☐ Commercial Insurance	☐ Surety Bond	☐ Trust Fund
☐ Risk Retention Group	☐ Letter of Credit	☐ Other Method (describe here)
☐ Local Government Financial Test	☐ Bond Rating Test	____________

VIII. CERTIFICATION (Read and sign after completing ALL SECTIONS of this notification form)

I certify under penalty of law that I have personally examined and am familiar with the information submitted in Sections I through XI of this notification form and all attached documents, and that based on my inquiry of those individuals immediately responsible for obtaining the information, I believe that the submitted information is true, accurate, and complete.

Name and official title of owner or owner's authorized representative (Print)	Signature	Date Signed

Paperwork Reduction Act Notice

EPA estimates public reporting burden for this form to average 30 minutes per response including time for reviewing instructions, gathering and maintaining the data needed and completing and reviewing the form. Send comments regarding this burden estimate to Director, OP, Regulatory Information Division (2137), U.S. Environmental Protection Agency, 401 M Street Washington D.C. 20460, marked "Attention Desk Officer for EPA." This form amends the previous notification form as printed in 40 CFR Part 280, Appendix I. Previous editions of this notification form may be used while supplies last.

EPA Form 7530-1 (Rev. 9-98) Electronic and paper versions acceptable.
Previous editions may be used while supplies last.

Page 2 of 5

EPA

United States
Environmental Protection Agency
Washington, DC 20460

Form Approved.
OMB No.2050-0068

Notification for Underground Storage Tanks

IX. DESCRIPTION OF UNDERGROUND STORAGE TANKS (Complete for all tanks and piping at this location.)

Tank Identification Number	Tank No. ____	Tank No. ____	Tank No. ____	Tank No. ____	Tank No. ____
1. Status of Tank (check only one) Currently In Use	☐	☐	☐	☐	☐
Temporarily Closed	☐	☐	☐	☐	☐
Permanently Closed	☐	☐	☐	☐	☐
2. Date of Installation (month/year)					
3. Estimated Total Capacity (gallons)					
4. Material of Construction (check all that apply)					
Asphalt Coated or Bare Steel	☐	☐	☐	☐	☐
Cathodically Protected Steel	☐	☐	☐	☐	☐
Coated and Cathodically Protected Steel	☐	☐	☐	☐	☐
Composite (Steel Clad with Fiberglass)	☐	☐	☐	☐	☐
Fiberglass Reinforced Plastic	☐	☐	☐	☐	☐
Lined Interior	☐	☐	☐	☐	☐
Excavation Liner	☐	☐	☐	☐	☐
Double Walled	☐	☐	☐	☐	☐
Polyethylene Tank Jacket	☐	☐	☐	☐	☐
Concrete	☐	☐	☐	☐	☐
Unknown	☐	☐	☐	☐	☐
If Other, please specify here	____	____	____	____	____
Check box if tank has ever been repaired	☐	☐	☐	☐	☐
5. Piping Material (check all that apply) Bare Steel	☐	☐	☐	☐	☐
Galvanized Steel	☐	☐	☐	☐	☐
Fiberglass Reinforced Plastic	☐	☐	☐	☐	☐
Copper	☐	☐	☐	☐	☐
Cathodically Protected	☐	☐	☐	☐	☐
Double Walled	☐	☐	☐	☐	☐
Secondary Containment	☐	☐	☐	☐	☐
Unknown	☐	☐	☐	☐	☐
Other, please specify	____	____	____	____	____
6. Piping Type (Check all that apply) "Safe" Suction (no valve at tank)	☐	☐	☐	☐	☐
"U.S." Suction (valve at tank)	☐	☐	☐	☐	☐
Pressure	☐	☐	☐	☐	☐
Gravity Feed	☐	☐	☐	☐	☐
Check box if piping has ever been repaired	☐	☐	☐	☐	☐

EPA Form 7530-1 (Rev. 9-98) Electronic and paper versions acceptable.
Previous editions may be used while supplies last.

Page 3 of 5

EPA

United States
Environmental Protection Agency
Washington, DC 20460

Form Approved.
OMB No.2050-0068

Notification for Underground Storage Tanks

Tank Identification Number	Tank No. ____	Tank No. ____	Tank No. ____	Tank No. ____	Tank No. ____
7. Substance Currently Stored (or last stored in the case of closed tanks) (Check all that apply) Gasoline	☐	☐	☐	☐	☐
Diesel	☐	☐	☐	☐	☐
Gasohol	☐	☐	☐	☐	☐
Kerosene	☐	☐	☐	☐	☐
Heating Oil	☐	☐	☐	☐	☐
Used Oil	☐	☐	☐	☐	☐
If Other, please specify here	____	____	____	____	____
Hazardous Substance	☐	☐	☐	☐	☐
CERCLA name and/or CAS number	____	____	____	____	____
Mixture of Substances	☐	☐	☐	☐	☐
Please specify here	____	____	____	____	____

8. **Release Detection** (check all that apply)	TANK	PIPE	TANK	PIPE	TANK	PIPE	TANK	PIPE	TANK	PIPE
Manual tank gauging	☐		☐		☐		☐		☐	
Tank tightness testing	☐		☐		☐		☐		☐	
Inventory Control	☐		☐		☐		☐		☐	
Automatic tank gauging	☐	☐	☐	☐	☐	☐	☐	☐	☐	☐
Vapor monitoring	☐	☐	☐	☐	☐	☐	☐	☐	☐	☐
Groundwater monitoring	☐	☐	☐	☐	☐	☐	☐	☐	☐	☐
Interstitial monitoring	☐	☐	☐	☐	☐	☐	☐	☐	☐	☐
Automatic line leak detectors		☐		☐		☐		☐		☐
Line tightness testing		☐		☐		☐		☐		☐
No release detection required (such as some types of suction piping, emergency generator tanks or field constructed tanks)	☐	☐	☐	☐	☐	☐	☐	☐	☐	☐
Other method allowed by implementing agency (such as SIR)	☐		☐		☐		☐		☐	
Please specify other method here	____		____		____		____		____	

9. Spill and Overfill Protection					
Overfill device installed	☐	☐	☐	☐	☐
Spill device installed	☐	☐	☐	☐	☐

EPA Form 7530-1 (Rev. 9-98) Electronic and paper versions acceptable.
Previous editions may be used while supplies last.

Page 4 of 5

EPA

United States
Environmental Protection Agency
Washington, DC 20460

Form Approved.
OMB No.2050-0068

Notification for Underground Storage Tanks

Tank Identification Number	Tank No. ____	Tank No. ____	Tank No. ____	Tank No. ____	Tank No. ____
X. CLOSURE OR CHANGE IN SERVICE					
1. **Closure or Change in Service**					
Estimated date the UST was last used for storing regulated substances (month/day/year)	____	____	____	____	____
Check box if this is a change in service	☐	☐	☐	☐	☐
2. **Tank Closure**					
Estimated date tank closed (month/day/year)	____	____	____	____	____
(check all that apply below)					
Tank was removed from ground	☐	☐	☐	☐	☐
Tank was closed in ground	☐	☐	☐	☐	☐
Tank filled with inert material	☐	☐	☐	☐	☐
Describe the inert fill material here	____	____	____	____	____
3. **Site Assessment**					
Check box if the site assessment was completed	☐	☐	☐	☐	☐
Check box if evidence of a leak was detected	☐	☐	☐	☐	☐
XI. CERTIFICATION OF INSTALLATION (COMPLETE FOR UST SYSTEMS INSTALLED AFTER DECEMBER 22, 1988)					
Installer Of Tank And Piping Must Check All That Apply:					
Installer certified by tank and piping manufacturers	☐	☐	☐	☐	☐
Installer certified or licensed by the implementing agency	☐	☐	☐	☐	☐
Installation inspected by a registered engineer	☐	☐	☐	☐	☐
Installation inspected and approved by implementing agency	☐	☐	☐	☐	☐
Manufacturer's installation checklists have been completed	☐	☐	☐	☐	☐
Another method allowed by State agency If so, please specify here	☐ ____	☐ ____	☐ ____	☐ ____	☐ ____

Signature of UST Installer Certifying Proper Installation of UST System

____________ Name ____________ Signature ____________ Date

____________ Position ____________ Company

EPA Form 7530-1 (Rev. 9-98) Electronic and paper versions acceptable.
Previous editions may be used while supplies last

Page 5 of 5

Please print or type with ELITE type (12 characters per inch) in the unshaded areas only

Form Approved, OMB No. 2050-0028 Expires 12/31/02
GSA No. 0246-EPA-OT

Please refer to Section V. Line-by-Line Instructions for Completing EPA Form 8700-12 before completing this form. The information requested here is required by law (Section 3010 of the *Resource Conservation and Recovery Act*).

Notification of Regulated Waste Activity

EPA United States Environmental Protection Agency

Date Received
(For Official Use Only)

I. Installation's EPA ID Number *(Mark 'X' in the appropriate box)*

☐ A. Initial Notification

☐ B. Subsequent Notification *(Complete item C)*

C. Installation's EPA ID Number

II. Name of Installation *(Include company and specific site name)*

III. Location of Installation *(Physical address not P.O. Box or Route Number)*

Street

Street *(Continued)*

City or Town | State | Zip Code

County Code | County Name

IV. Installation Mailing Address *(See instructions)*

Street or P.O. Box

City or Town | State | Zip Code

V. Installation Contact *(Person to be contacted regarding waste activities at site)*

Name *(Last)* | *(First)*

Job Title | Phone Number *(Area Code and Number)*

VI. Installation Contact Address *(See instructions)*

A. Contact Address: Location ☐ Mailing ☐

B. Street or P.O. Box

City or Town | State | Zip Code

VII. Ownership *(See instructions)*

A. Name of Installation's Legal Owner

Street, P.O. Box, or Route Number

City or Town | State | Zip Code

Phone Number *(Area Code and Number)* | B. Land Type | C. Owner Type | D. Change of Owner Indicator: Yes ☐ No ☐ | Date Changed: Month Day Year

EPA Form 8700-12 (Rev. 12/99)

- 1 of 2 -

Please print or type with ELITE type (12 characters per inch) in the unshaded areas only

Form Approved, OMB No. 2050-0028 Expires 12/31/02
GSA No. 0246-EPA-OT

ID - For Official Use Only

VIII. Type of Regulated Waste Activity *(Mark 'X' in the appropriate boxes. Refer to Instructions)*

A. Hazardous Waste Activities

1. Generator (See Instructions)
   - ☐ a. Greater than 1000kg/mo (2,200 lbs.)
   - ☐ b. 100 to 1000 kg/mo (220-2,200 lbs.)
   - ☐ c. Less than 100 kg/mo (220 lbs)
2. Transporter (Indicate Mode in boxes 1-5 below)
   - ☐ a. For own waste only
   - ☐ b. For commercial purposes

Mode of Transportation
- ☐ 1. Air
- ☐ 2. Rail
- ☐ 3. Highway
- ☐ 4. Water
- ☐ *5. Other - specify* ________

☐ 3. Treater, Storer, Disposer (at installation) Note: A permit is required for this activity, see instructions.

4. Exempt Boiler and/or Industrial Furnace
   - ☐ a. Smelting, Melting, and Refining Furnace Exemption
   - ☐ b. Small Quantity On-Site Burner Exemption

☐ 5. Underground Injection Control

B. Universal Waste Activity

☐ Large Quantity Handler of Universal Waste

C. Used Oil Management Activities

1. Used Oil Transporter/Transfer Facility - Indicate Type(s) of Activity(ies)
   - ☐ a. Transporter
   - ☐ b. Transfer Facility
2. Used Oil Processor/Re-refiner - Indicate Type(s) of Activity(ies)
   - ☐ a. Processor
   - ☐ b. Re-refiner

☐ 3. Off-Specification Used Oil Burner

4. Used Oil Fuel Marketer
   - ☐ a. Marketer Who Directs Shipment of Off-Specification Used Oil to Used Oil Burner
   - ☐ b. Marketer Who First Claims the Used Oil Meets the Specifications

IX. Description of Hazardous Wastes *(Use additional sheets if necessary)*

A. Listed Hazardous Wastes. *(See 40 CFR 261.31 - 33; See instructions if you need to list more than 12 waste codes.)*

1	2	3	4	5	6
7	8	9	10	11	12

B. Characteristics of Nonlisted Hazardous Wastes. *(Mark 'X' in the boxes corresponding to the characteristics of nonlisted hazardous wastes your installation handles; See 40 CFR Parts 261.20 - 261.24; See instructions if you need to list more than 4 toxicity characteristic waste codes.)*

1. Ignitable *(D001)*	2. Corrosive *(D002)*	3. Reactive *(D003)*	4. Toxicity Characteristic	(List specific EPA hazardous waste number(s) for the Toxicity Characteristic contaminant(s)) 1	2	3	4
☐	☐	☐	☐				

C. Other Wastes. *(State-regulated or other wastes requiring a handler to have an I.D. number; See instructions.)*

1	2	3	4	5	6

X. Certification

I certify under penalty of law that this document and all attachments were prepared under my direction or supervision in accordance with a system designed to assure that qualified personnel properly gather and evaluate the information submitted. Based on my inquiry of the person or persons who manage the system, or those persons directly responsible for gathering the information, the information submitted is, to the best of my knowledge and belief, true, accurate, and complete. I am aware that there are significant penalties for submitting false information, including the possibility of fine and imprisonment for knowing violations.

Signature	Name and Official Title *(Type or print)*	Date Signed

XI. Comments

Note: Mail completed form to the appropriate EPA Regional or State Office. *(See Section IV of the booklet for addresses.)*

EPA Form 8700-12 (Rev. 12/99) - 2 of 2 -

Please print or type with ELITE type (12 characters per inch) in the unshaded areas only

Form Approved, OMB No. 2050-0028 Expires 12/31/02
GSA No. 0246-EPA-OT

ID - For Official Use Only

IX. Description of Hazardous Wastes *(Continued; Additional Sheet)*

A. Listed Hazardous Wastes. ***(See 40 CFR 261.31 - 33; Use this page only if you need to list more than 12 waste codes.)***

13	14	15	16	17	18
19	20	21	22	23	24
25	26	27	28	29	30
31	32	33	34	35	36
37	38	39	40	41	42
43	44	45	46	47	48
49	50	51	52	53	54
55	56	57	58	59	60
61	62	63	64	65	66
67	68	69	70	71	72
73	74	75	76	77	78
79	80	81	82	83	84
85	86	87	88	89	90
91	92	93	94	95	96

B. Toxicity Characteristic Hazardous Wastes. ***(See 40 CFR 261.24; Use this page only if you need to list more than 4 waste codes.)***

5	6	7	8	9	10
11	12	13	14	15	16
17	18	19	20	21	22

EPA Form 8700-12 (Rev. 12/99)

CHAPTER VII

THE COMPREHENSIVE ENVIRONMENTAL RESPONSE, COMPENSATION AND LIABILITY ACT

A. Background

In the early 1970s, state and federal clean air laws and water laws were adopted without recognition of the major redesign and reconstruction of industrial and municipal facilities that they would require throughout the nation. Faced with the need to make rapid reductions of contaminants in air emissions and water effluent discharges, many companies extracted them from their process streams and stored them in pits, ponds, tanks and drums. The companies then sought methods to dispose of the growing volume of waste.

Some companies increased the volume of wastes sent to municipal landfills. The waste haulers and landfills operators were happy to receive increased transportation and tipping fees, but found themselves handling wastes at volume levels and with characteristics they could not manage. Some municipal landfill operators stored wastes in unlined or poorly lined pits. Some stored drums and other containers until they rusted and leaked. Some poured wastes onto landfill surfaces and burnt them, except for the content that migrated into soil and groundwater. When RCRA was adopted, these landfills were prohibited as open dumps and many were abandoned.

Other companies sent wastes to private contractors which began to offer incineration and other disposal services. However, as state and federal regulation grew, many of these companies found they did not have facilities, technical knowledge or financial resources to meet increasingly strict requirements. Environmental government agencies issued fines and penalties and ordered them to make major improvements of their facilities and operating methods. Criminal actions were taken against some waste transportation and disposal operators. Many went out of business and abandoned their facilities, leaving large accumulations of waste.

Many chemical manufacturers and other large industrial companies decided that most responsible choice was to design, construct and operate storage, treatment and disposal facilities on their own properties. The author participated in projects throughout the 1970s to install storage areas with secondary containment and ponds in which wastes could be neutralized, clarified and oxidized by the organisms in activated sludge. Although well-intentioned, some of these new facilities were only partially successful. Some spills overflowed the secondary containment. Some early pond liners cracked and leaked. The organisms in sludge sometimes died or were ineffective and left wastes partially untreated.

Specially unfortunate events occurred at Niagara Falls. Between 1947 and 1953, Hooker Chemical built a relatively modern capped landfill for its chemical wastes at Love Canal. The result was an attractive property which municipal officials asked Hooker Chemical to donate to the city school board which would otherwise acquire the property by eminent domain. Hooker placed a warning in the deed. However, despite the warning, Niagara Falls and the State of New York performed construction that disturbed the landfill and some of the chemicals leaked out of the landfill into the canal. Residents were relocated as claims and fear of illness spread and years of litigation followed. The U.S. District court eventually held both Occidental Chemical (which had acquired Hooker Chemical) and the City of Niagara Falls responsible for the releases of chemicals. *U.S. v. Occidental Chemical*, 965 F. Supp. 408 (W.D.N.Y. 1997).

In addition, urban areas, especially in northeastern states, had thousands of old manufacturing plants operating with facilities and equipment that had become wholly or partially obsolete. These plants were able to operate with modest profits or at breakeven because their fully depreciated facilities and equipment created no depreciation charges against income. The environmental laws required major capital and operating expenses that resulted in large losses. Further, each time compliance was achieved, the laws and regulations were tightened again. Eventually, many owners closed their plants, wholly or partially, or sold them to buyers who later closed them. These closings left industrial "ghost towns" in many urban areas where old plants sat idle with many still containing storage tanks and containers with waste residues and contaminated soil and groundwater.

In 1980, Congress recognized that there were throughout the nation a growing number of abandoned municipal and private waste disposal facilities and former manufacturing plants that were an existing or potential threat to human health and the environment. Congress enacted a law, popularly called the "Superfund Law, to authorize and require the USEPA to clean up these sites or order their owners, operators and others named as responsible parties to do so.

B. "The Superfund" Law

The Comprehensive Environmental Response, Compensation and Liability Act (CERCLA), 42 U.S.C. § 9601 *et seq*. authorizes and requires the USEPA to clean up contaminated facilities where there is a release or threatened release of hazardous substances, pollutants or contaminants at levels high enough to place them on the National Priority List (NPL). CERCLA also created a multi-billion dollar trust fund (the "Superfund") derived from excise taxes on oil and chemical feedstocks and other sources for the use of the USEPA in removal and other response actions. The excise taxes expired in 1995 and were not extended because the President made it clear that he would veto CERCLA reform legislation being considered by Congress. The reform legislation is discussed later in this chapter.

CERCLA also requires any person in charge of a vessel or facility to report any release of a reportable quantity of a hazardous substance from the vessel or facility to the National Response Center. 42 U.S.C. §§ 9602 and 9603. The USEPA has issued an extensive list of hazardous substances and reportable quantities at 40 C.F.R. § 302.

C. Some Key Definitions

1. Hazardous Substance

The USEPA's authority to take response actions and to list facilities on the NPL depends importantly on the question whether a release or threatened release of a "hazardous substance" has occurred. The meaning of the term "hazardous substance" is important. Although CERCLA authorizes the USEPA to clean up pollutants and contaminants which present an imminent and substantive danger to public health or welfare as well as hazardous substances, it only authorizes the USEPA to recover response costs for cleanup of hazardous substances.

As interpreted by the USEPA and the courts, the term "hazardous substance" is very broadly defined in CERCLA and includes substances designated as hazardous by the USEPA under the Clean Air Act, Clean Water Act, Resource Conservation Recovery Act (RCRA) and the Toxic Substances Control Act (TSCA) including any waste designated as hazardous waste under RCRA. Petroleum and natural gas are excluded. 42 U.S.C. § 9601(14); 40 C.F.R. Part 302.

The courts have held that materials containing low levels of hazardous substances are subject to CERCLA even though they are below the reportable quantities established under CERCLA and the strict criteria for hazardous waste under RCRA. *U.S. v. Alcan Aluminum Corp.*, 990 F.2d 711 (2d Cir. 1993); *U.S. v. Alcan Aluminum Corp.*, 964 F.2d 252 (3d Cir. 1992). Only a few courts have found any substance to be nonhazardous. The U.S. Circuit Court of Appeals for the Ninth Circuit described the situation as follows:

> "CERCLA seems to give the agency carte blanche to hold liable anybody who disposes of about anything. Drop an old nickel that actually contains nickel? A CERCLA violation. Throw out an old lemon? It's full of citric acid, another hazardous substance?"

A&W Smelter v. Clinton, 146 F.3d 1107 (9th Cir. 1998).

The practical effect of these court decisions is that many persons who sent ordinary nonhazardous solid waste to municipal and other landfills were forced to pay legal fees and liability settlements. The courts granted relief to some defendants such as very small businesses. However, even household waste was not excluded as it was under RCRA. *B.F. Goodrich v. Murtha*, 815 F. Supp. 539 (D.C. Conn. 1993); later proceedings in the same case 840 F. Supp. 180 (D.C. Conn. 1994); *Transportation Leasing v. California*, 32 Env. Rep. (C.D. Cal. 1990). See the discussions of *de minimis* and municipal solid waste exemptions and settlements later this chapter under "Settlements with the USEPA" and "Brownfields Programs."

CERCLA's definition of a hazardous substance excludes petroleum. The courts have disagreed in interpreting the petroleum exclusion. For example, one court interpreted it broadly to cover gasoline. *Wilshire Westwood Associates v. Atlantic Richfield Co.*, 881 F.2d 801 (9th Cir. 1989). Another court held that the exclusion applies to both used and unused petroleum products. *Organic Chemical Site PRP Group v. Total Petroleum, Inc.*, 58 F. Supp. 2d 755 (W.D. Mich. 1999). Other courts interpreted it narrowly and found distilled petroleum products and oil wastes to be hazardous substances. *U.S. v. Western Processing Co.*, 761 F. Supp. 713 (W.D. Wash. 1991); *City of New York v. Exxon Corp.*, 744 F. Supp. 474 (S.D.N.Y. 1990).

CERCLA does not authorize response actions for removal or remediation of useful products. *Freeman v. Glaxo Wellcome, Inc.*, 189 F.3d 160 (2d Cir. 1999); *Pneumo Abex Corp. v. High Point, Thomasville & Denton PR Co.*, 142 F.3d (4th Cir. 1998); *A&W Smelter v. Clinton*, 146 F.3d 1107 (9th Cir. 1998); *RSR Corp. v. Avanti Development, Inc.*, 69 F. Supp. 2d 1119 (S.D. Ind. 1999). Useful products include those which are part of the structure of residential buildings or business or community structures. Accordingly, CERCLA does not authorize recovery of costs for removal of asbestos-containing materials from buildings and structures. *First United Methodist Church v. U.S. Gypsum*, 882 F.2d 862 (4th Cir. 1989) and cases cited therein. The courts may reach the same result in lead-based paint cases. On the other hand, used PCB containing transformers purchased for a nominal price and stored and handled using questionable practices were not found to be useful products. *Carter-Jones Lumber v. Dixie Distributing*, 166 F.3d 840 (6th Cir. 1999).

In 1999, an exemption from liability under CERCLA was adopted for persons who arrange for recycling or transportation of recyclable materials such as scrap paper, plastic, glass, textiles, rubber (other than whole tires), metals or batteries. 42 U.S.C. § 9627.

2. Release

The USEPA's authority to incur response costs is triggered by a release or a substantial threat of a release of a hazardous substance. A "release" means any spilling, leaking, pumping, pouring, emitting, emptying, discharging, injecting, escaping, leaching, dumping or disposing into the environment including abandonment of barrels, containers and other receptacles. Releases do not include releases solely within a workplace, vehicle engine exhausts, certain radioactive materials, normal fertilizer applications and federally permitted releases.

3. Facility

A release or threatened release that triggers CERCLA must be from a facility which is broadly defined to include not only buildings, fixtures, structures and equipment but also any site or area where a hazardous substance has come to be located. 42 U.S.C. § 9607(j). Thus, almost anything can be considered a facility. For example, abandoned drums were found to be facilities. *U.S. v. R.W. Meyer, Inc.*, 889 F.2d 1497 (6th Cir. 1989). Contiguous parcels have been held to be a single facility. *U.S. v. 150 Acres of Land*, 204 F.3d 698 (6th Cir. 2000), but see the later discussion under "Brownfields Programs."

However, the definition specifically excludes consumer products in consumer use. This exclusion allows the public to continue to use valuable old products such as nonfriable asbestos-containing materials, properly maintained lead-based paint, fully enclosed PCB dielectric fluids, and fully enclosed chlorofluorocarbon refrigerants.

The definition also excludes a vessel, meaning any craft used as a means of water transportation. 42 U.S.C. § 9601. Although CERCLA applies to vessels, the author has not discussed vessels in this chapter because the subject is too specialized.

4. The Environment

A release or threatened release that triggers CERCLA must be into the environment. CERCLA defines the environment to include surface and groundwater and ambient air.

D. Removal Actions

The USEPA can take immediate removal actions at any site where they are needed to prevent or mitigate imminent and substantial danger to the public health or welfare or the environment. The USEPA can also take planned removal actions limited in cost and time. 42 U.S.C. §§ 9601(23) and 9604(a). However, remedial actions of a long term nature may be taken and funded from the Superfund only at sites listed on the National Priority List.

E. Investigations and Administrative Cleanup Orders

1. Investigations and § 104(e) Letters

The USEPA has extensive authority to investigate facilities where releases of hazardous substances, pollutants or contaminants have or may have occurred. One of the most common methods is to send letters pursuant to § 104(e) of CERCLA requiring that persons furnish information and documents relating to the facility. A § 104(e) letter is not an accusation or a claim, but it often requires that the recipient to undertake an extensive review of old documents and the recollections of older employees in order to answer the detailed questions.

Corporations preparing answers to § 104(e) letters must be aware that they are not protected by the right to refuse to furnish self-incriminating information afforded to individuals by the Fifth Amendment to the U.S. Constitution. They must provide information in their possession or control regardless of the consequences. On the other hand, their employees have rights under the Fifth Amendment and those rights must be respected.

Persons answering § 104(e) letters should do so carefully and responsively. Failures to answer and nonresponsive answers may provoke further investigation by the USEPA. When the § 104(e) letter asks about events that occurred years ago or facilities no longer owned or operated, a call to the USEPA to ask about the circumstances that led to the letter can save a lot of time and effort. It is generally appropriate to provide brief factual answers to the questions asked. However, the response should procide sufficient information and explanations to protect against possible misunderstandings.

§ 104 also grants extensive investigation powers to the USEPA. The USEPA can enter and examine facilities and documents and can even take and test samples. Major penalties may be imposed for noncompliance.

2. § 106 Unilateral Administrative Orders

§ 106(a) of CERCLA authorizes the USEPA to issue unilateral administrative orders to PRPs to take or finance response actions at an NPL site if it finds there is an imminent and substantial endangerment to the public health or welfare or the environment. A PRP may not refuse to comply with such an order on grounds that another PRP previously entered into a consent decree with USEPA by which it agreed to perform the remedial work. *U.S. v. Occidental Chemical Corp.*, 200 F.3d 143 (3d Cir. 1999).

F. The National Contingency Plan

The National Oil and Hazardous Substance Pollution Contingency Plan, commonly called the National Contingency Plan (NCP), is an extensive set of regulations covering over 270 pages. 40 C.F.R. Part 301. Although generally used for smaller situations, the NCP is written to respond to major oil spills and other disasters.

The NCP begins with delegation of responsibilities of the President to the USEPA and coordination with the Federal Emergency Management Agency (FEMA) and the Nuclear Regulatory Commission (NRC). 40 C.F.R. §§ 300.2 and 300.100.

The NCP establishes a National Response Team (NRT) headed by the USEPA. Since the USEPA has limited experience with major emergencies, the NRT members include federal government agencies which have major emergency experience such as the Department of Defense, the Department of Transportation, the Department of Energy, the Department of Labor, FEMA and the NRC. 40 C.F.R.

§ 110. The regulations also provide for state and local participation and even encourage commitments of resources from industry groups, academic organizations and others 40 C.F.R. §§ 300.180 and 300.181. The regulations provide for selection of a lead agency to coordinate response actions at particular sites.

The regulations provide for response to oil discharges in four phases. They are (1) discovery and notification; (2) preliminary assessment and initiation of action; (3) containment, countermeasures, cleanup and disposal; and (4) documentation and cost recovery. 40 C.F.R. § 300 *et seq.* The USEPA also regulates the dispersants and other chemicals used to control and mitigate oil spills and maintains a schedule of products authorized for such use. 40 C.F.R. § 300.900 *et seq.*

The most frequently used parts of the NCP are those providing for hazardous substance response because they govern the identification and evaluation of facilities for listing on the National Priority List (NPL) and for their investigation and remediation and recovery of the related costs. 40 C.F.R. § 300,400 *et seq.*, § 300.700 *et seq.* and § 300.800 *et seq.* The requirements for state involvement in hazardous substance response are provided at 40 C.F.R. § 300.500 *et seq.*

The Appendices to the regulations are of special importance. For example, the extensive methods that the USEPA uses in its hazard ranking system (HRS) are prescribed in Appendix A. The NPL sites are listed in Appendix B. Lists of appropriate actions and methods of remedying releases are provided in Appendix D. The HRS and NPL are described later in this chapter.

G. The Hazardous Substance Response Regulations

1. A Very Structured System

The USEPA's hazardous substance response regulations provide very structured methods and criteria for the identification, evaluation and remediation of facilities where releases of hazardous substances have occurred. 40 C.F.R. § 300.400 *et seq.*

2. Natural and Other Releases Not Subject to Response Actions

The regulations provide that action will not usually be taken in response to a release of a naturally occurring substance through naturally occurring processes or phenomena from a location where it is naturally found, i.e., a release of lava or dust from a volcano. Action will also not usually be taken in response to a release from products that are part of, and result in exposure within, residential buildings or business or community structures, i.e., asbestos-containing insulation or lead-based paint. (Programs for remediation of these materials have been developed under the Toxic Substances Control Act). Action will also not usually be taken in response to a release into public or private drinking water supplies due to deterioration of the system through ordinary use. (Programs to protect drinking water are provided by the Safe Drinking Water Act). 40 C.F.R. § 300.400(b).

3. Response Actions Financed by the Superfund

The regulations provide criteria for determining when the USEPA should undertake response actions financed from the Superfund. Among the criteria is conservation of the Superfund monies by encouraging private party response. 40 C.F.R. § 300.400(c).

4. Entry and Access to the Facility

The regulations provide procedures to gain entry and access to a facility to investigate whether a release has occurred and, if so, to take response action. If the owner or operator of a facility does not consent to access, the USEPA is authorized to issue an administrative order directing compliance with its request for access. The USEPA may not use force to compel compliance with its administrative order. However, it may ask the Attorney General to commence a civil action to compel compliance and impose civil penalties. 40 C.F.R. § 300.400(d).

5. Exemption from Permit Requirements

No federal, state or local permits are required for onsite response actions conducted pursuant to CERCLA. This avoids the lengthy delays that would be involved in applying for and obtaining permits. 40 C.F.R. § 300.400(e), Of course, USEPA managers supervising response actions can be expected to impose requirements similar to those that would be imposed by the permit authorities to the extent necessary to protect human health and the environment.

6. Health Assessments

The regulations provide for health assessments by the Agency for Toxic Substance and Disease Registry (ATSDR) and for identification of applicable or relevant and appropriate requirements. 40 C.F.R. §§ 300.400(f) and (g).

7. Oversight for PRP Response Actions

The regulations authorize the lead agency to provide oversight for response actions taken by potentially responsible parties (PRPs) rather than government agencies. 40 C.F.R. § 300.400(h). These regulations will be further discussed later in this chapter.

8. Discovery and Reporting of Releases

Releases may be discovered by a variety of methods including the reports of releases of reportable quantities (RQs) required by 40 C.F.R. Part 302 and even random or incidental observations reported by government agencies or the public. 40 C.F.R. § 300.405. Notification is made or routed to the National Response

Center (NRC) and the on-scene coordinator (OSC) and, as appropriate, to other agencies such as the U.S. Coast Guard (USCG) and the NRC. 40 C.F.R. § 300.405.

9. Planned Removal Actions

The response action at a facility begins with a removal site evaluation including a removal preliminary assessment and, if warranted, a removal inspection. The evaluation must be documented. 40 C.F.R. § 300.410.

If indicated by the evaluation, a planned removal action may be undertaken. (This is not the same as the emergency removal action authorized by 42 U.S.C. § 9604(a)). The lead agency must consider several factors in determining the appropriateness of a removal action including actual or potential exposure to nearby human population, animals or the food chain and contamination of drinking water supplies or sensitive ecosystems. If a planning period of a least six months exists, the lead agency is required to conduct an engineering evaluation/cost analysis (EE/CA). Removal actions may include the following: (1) fences, warning signs or other security or site control precautions; (2) drainage controls; (3) stabilization of berms, dikes or impoundments or drainage or closing of lagoons; (4) capping of contaminated soils or sludges; (5) use of chemicals to retard the spread of releases or mitigate their effects; (6) excavation, consolidation or removal of highly contaminated soils; (7) removal of containers of hazardous substances, contaminants or pollutants; (8) containment, treatment, disposal or incineration of hazardous materials; and (9) provision of an alternate water supply. These removal actions, if financed by the Superfund, must be limited to $2,000,000 or 12 months unless the lead agency makes determinations supporting necessity for continuation. 40 C.F.R. § 300.415.

10. Preliminary Site Evaluation

Beyond removal actions, the regulations prescribe methods, procedures and criteria for remedial site evaluation which consist of a remedial preliminary assessment (PA) and a remedial site inspection (SI).

The lead agency must perform a PA for all sites listed in the CERCLIS database to (1) eliminate sites that pose no threat to public health or the environment; (2) determine any potential need for removal action; (3) set priorities for site inspections; and (4) gather data for later evaluation pursuant to the HRS.

An SI may include field sampling and analysis of soil and groundwater that should be performed after development of a sampling and analysis plan and a quality assurance project plan. Upon completion of a remedial SI, the lead agency must prepare a report that includes the following: (1) a description of the history and nature of waste handling at the site; (2) a description of known contaminants; (3) a description of pathways of migration of contaminants; (4) an identification and description of human and environmental targets; and (5) a recommendation whether further action is warranted. 40 C.F.R. § 300.420.

11. Priorities for Remedial Actions; The Hazard Ranking System

The regulations establish criteria, methods and procedures that the USEPA uses to establish priorities for remedial actions. The National Priority List (NPL) is the list of sites having priority for long term remedial evaluation and response. Only sites on the NPL are eligible for remedial action financed from the Superfund. Removal and other actions pursuant to 42 U.S.C. § 9604(b) are not limited to NPL sites. A site may be included on the NPL if the release meets one of three criteria (1) the release scores sufficiently high on the HRS; (2) a state designates a release as its single highest priority; or (3) the release is the subject of an ASTDR health advisory recommending dissociation of individuals from the release and the USEPA determines that the release poses a significant threat to public health and anticipates that it will be more cost effective to use its remedial authority than its removal authority. The regulations also contain procedures for placing sites on the NPL and removing them from the NPL, including publication for public comment in the Federal Register. 40 C.F.R. § 300.425.

The HRS is a very detailed risk assessment device to evaluate the potential for releases of uncontrolled hazardous substances to cause human health or environmental damage. It measures relative rather than absolute risk. The HRS score is the result of evaluation of four pathways: groundwater migration, surface water migration, soil exposure and air migration.

The HRS evaluates the four pathways by four primary factors. *First*, the sources are characterized by identifying the hazardous substances associated with each source and identifying those available to each pathway. *Second*, a score is calculated for any observed release or exposure or potential for release or exposure if there is no release or exposure. *Third*, a score is calculated for the waste characteristics including toxicity, mobility, persistence, bioaccumulation potential and quantity. *Fourth*, a score is calculated for targets including individuals, human population, resources and sensitive environments. The HRS prescribes higher scores for actual releases and exposures than those for potential releases and exposures. However, the HRS considers potential effects on such targets as drinking water wells near an NPL site, the human food chain and sensitive ecological receptors.

12. The National Priority List

The NPL includes over 1,200 sites, including some sites in every state and many facilities owned or operated by the federal government. Many new sites are proposed each year. A cutoff score of 28.5 is used by the USEPA as a numerical criteria in deciding whether to list sites on the NPL. 40 C.F.R. Part 300, Appendices A and B. When sites are remediated, they are removed from the NPL after publication in the Federal Register and review of public comments. The USEPA may also allow partial site deletions. 60 Fed. Reg. 55466, Nov. 1, 1995.

It is possible to challenge a decision by the USEPA to list a site on the NPL by appealing to the U.S. Circuit Court of Appeals for the District of Columbia. For the first decade of CERCLA, no successful court challenges of NPL listings were made. However, several challenges were upheld during the 1990s. *Tex Tin Corp. v. USEPA*, 935 F.2d 1321 (1991) and 992 F.2d 353 (1993); *Kent County v. USEPA*, 963 F.2d 391 (1992); *Anne Arundel County v. USEPA*, 963 F.2d 412 (1992); *National Gypsum Co. v. USEPA*, 968 F.2d 40 (1992); *Mead Corp. v. Browner*, 100 F.3d 152 (D.C. Cir. 1996); *Harbour Gateway v. USEPA*, 167 F.3d 602 (D.C. Cir. 1999).

The USEPA agreed to delist a hardwood sawmill site at Plymouth, North Carolina in order to settle an appeal by Georgia-Pacific Corporation to the U.S. Circuit Court of Appeals for the District of Columbia. 65 Fed. Reg. 58,225 (Sept. 28, 2000)

13. Remedy Selection and Remedial Methods

The regulations prescribe a remedy selection process consisting of several steps. The goal is to select remedies protective of human health and the environment that maintain protection over time and minimize untreated waste. Sites may be divided into operable units if they are large or complex or if it would expedite completion of the total site cleanup. In developing remedial alternatives, the USEPA expects to use treatment to address the principal threats posed by a site, wherever practicable. However, the USEPA also expects to use engineering controls (such as containment) and institutional controls (such as water use restrictions and deed notice restrictions) where hazardous substances, pollutants or contaminants pose a relatively low long term threat or treatment is impracticable. In order to assess site conditions and evaluate alternative, the regulations require preparation of a remedial investigation/feasibility study (RI/FS).

14. Remedial Investigations

Preparation to conduct a remedial investigation (RI) begins with a scoping phase including collection and evaluation of existing data; identification of data to be collected; preparation of site-specific health and safety plans; notification of federal and state trustees of natural resources that may be affected; development of sampling and analysis plans and quality assurance plans; and identification of applicable or relevant and appropriate requirements (ARARs) and other criteria. 40 C.F.R. § 300.430(b).

The lead agency must also carry out extensive community relations requirements including (1) interviews with local officials, community residents, "public interest" groups, and others; (2) preparation of a formal community relations plan; (3) establishing at least one local information repository; and (4) informing the community of the availability of technical assistance grants. When PRPs are taking response actions, a lead agency which conducts technical discussions with PRPs must also conduct technical discussions concurrently with the public. The lead agency must also provide advance notice and opportunity for the public to comment on proposed settlement agreements and consent decrees. 40 C.F.R. §300.430(c).

The RI is then conducted to characterize the site to develop and evaluate remedial alternatives. The methods include field investigations, treatability studies and a baseline risk assessment. Bench and pilot scale studies may also be conducted to support engineering design remedial alternatives. The RI should assess (1) the physical characteristics of the site including surface features, soils, geology, hydrogeology, meteorology and ecology; (2) characteristics or classifications of air, surface water and groundwater; (3) general characteristics of waste including quantities, state, concentration, toxicity, propensity to bioaccumulate, persistence and mobility; (4) the extent to which the source can be identified and characterized; (5) actual and potential exposure pathways through environmental media; (6) actual and potential exposure routes such as inhalation and ingestion; and (7) other factors, such as sensitive populations. ARARs and other advisories, criteria and guidance must be identified and a site-specific baseline risk assessment performed. 40 C.F.R. § 300.430(d).

15. Feasibility Studies

The next step is a feasibility study (FS). The objective is to develop and evaluate remedial alternatives by considering a multitude of factors including ARARs, MCLs, MCLGs and EPA-determined acceptable exposure levels. The acceptable levels range from one in 10,000 to one in 1,000,000 excess lifetime risk of cancer or other adverse health effects. (Note: Due to the repetitive conservative assumptions mandated by the USEPA for risk assessment, the actual risks are far more remote then indicated by calculations using the USEPA's methods). The FS must consider the habitats of species protected by the Endangered Species Act. The FS must also develop and consider innovative treatment technologies if they offer comparable or superior performance or implementability.

16. Remedy Selection Methods and Criteria

The lead agency must develop a range of alternative remedial actions, including a no further action alternative, and evaluate them using three groups of criteria: (1) effectiveness, (2) implementability, and (3) cost.

The alternatives identified by the FS are evaluated for selection using nine criteria:

(A) Overall protection of human health and the environment;

(B) Compliance with ARARs;

(C) Long-term effectiveness and permanence;

(D) Reduction of toxicity, mobility or volume;

(E) Short-term effectiveness;

(F) Implementability;

(G) Cost, including direct and indirect capital costs; and annual operation and maintenance costs;

(H) State acceptance; and

(I) Community acceptance.

Criteria (A) and (B) are threshold criteria and each remedial alternative must meet them to be eligible for selection. Criteria (C) through (G) are balancing criteria. Criteria (H) and (I) are modifying criteria. The lead agency and the support agency use them to select a preferred alternative and present it to the public in a proposed plan for review and comment. The lead agency then reviews the public comments and consults with the state (or the support agency) to determine whether the preferred alternative remains the most appropriate remedial action. The lead agency then makes the final remedy selection decision which it must document in a record of decision (ROD).

The FS regulations contain provisions reinforcing the requirement that the remedy selected must comply with ARARs, but allow some exceptions. For example, compliance with an ARAR is not required if technically impracticable from an engineering perspective. The FS regulations prescribe how cost is to be used with the other balancing criteria. The FS regulations require use of permanent solutions and treatment or resource recovery technologies to the maximum extent practicable and discourage offsite land disposal of untreated waste.

17. Public Relations

The regulations require repeated attention to public relations. Among other things, the lead agency must communicate with the public throughout the remedial process, even on technical matters. The lead agency must publish its preferred remedial alternative for public comment and furnish access to the RI/FS. The lead agency must provide an opportunity for a public meeting on remedy selection and a transcript of the meeting must be kept. The lead agency must provide opportunities for public review and comments on any changes in the plan.

18. The Record of Decision

The lead agency must support the selection of a remedial action by preparing a formal record of decision (ROD) containing all facts, analyses of facts, and site-specific policy decisions. The ROD must explain how the remedy selection criteria were used to select the remedy and how it will protect human health and the environment by eliminating, reducing or controlling exposures to human and environmental receptors. The ROD must explain the remediation goals and how performance will be measured at appropriate locations in the ground water, surface water, soils, air and other affected environmental media. It must describe significant changes in response to public comments.

The ROD must also describe hazardous substances, pollutants or contaminants that will remain at the site such that five year reviews will be required. The ROD may also describe any commitment for further analysis and selection of long term response measures.

After the ROD is signed, the lead agency must publish a notice of its availability in a major local newspaper of general circulation and make it available for inspection and copying at or near the facility before commencement of any remedial action.

19. Remedial Design and Remedial Action

The remedial design and remedial action (RD/RA) stage includes the development of the actual design of the selected remedy and implementation of the remedy through construction. A period of operation and maintenance may follow these activities.

RD/RA activities must conform to the remedy selected in the ROD and to QA/QC requirements. They must also conform to ARARs and other USEPA requirements. Before initiation of an RD, the lead agency must determine whether the community relations plan should be revised to describe further public involvement activities. Any changes from the ROD require detailed and formal procedures including public notice and opportunities for public comment and a public meeting. Arrangements must be made for the state where the site is located to assume responsibility for operations and maintenance (O&M) after the remedy is determined to be operational and functional. For example, a state must assure that it will assume responsibility for maintaining institutional controls after the remedy is complete. The regulations limit to ten years the period during which Superfund-financed remedial actions to remediate groundwater or surfacewater quality may continue and the states must assume responsibility thereafter. 40 C.F.R. § 300.435.

20. Transfers to Offsite Locations

Any transfer of a hazardous substance, pollutant or contaminant from a CERCLA facility to an offsite location must meet acceptability requirements, except for emergencies determined by the On-Scene Coordinator and except for samples sent to laboratories for testing and hazardous wastes sent for treatability studies. 40 C.F.R. § 300.440.

Waste may be transferred from a CERCLA facility for the following purposes: (1) treatment to meet the universal waste standards in 40 C.F.R. Part 268, Subpart D; (2) treatment to substantially reduce its mobility, toxicity or persistence in the absence of a defined treatment standard; or (3) storage or ultimate disposal of waste not treated to the previous criteria at the same CERCLA facility. With a few exceptions, transfers must be made to receiving units at facilities holding permits under RCRA that do not have significant violations or uncontrolled releases. 40 C.F.R. § 300.440.

21. Review of Remedy Effectiveness

CERCLA provides that the USEPA must review every five years the adequacy of any remedy that leaves hazardous substances at an NPL site. If the USEPA finds the remedy to be inadequate, it must select another remedy. 42 U.S.C. § 9621(c).

H. Remediation by Potentially Responsible Parties

After initial investigation at NPL facilities, the USEPA sends notices to potentially responsible parties (PRPs). It also informs them of the kinds and volumes of wastes found at the site and the identity of the PRPs ranked by volume of waste. *See* Interim Settlement Policy, 50 Fed. Reg. 5,034 (2/5/85). *See also* OSWER Directive No. 7834.10, 53 Fed. Reg. 5,298 (2/23/88) on notice letters, negotiations and information exchange.

In the early years after CERCLA was adopted, the USEPA learned that many companies, government agencies and other persons that caused the primary contamination at NPL sites had closed or sold their operations long ago. Some could not be found and some had no records or recoverable financial assets. Thus, the USEPA focussed its enforcement program on claims against current site owners and operators because they were clearly liable without fault under CERCLA regardless of whether they caused or contributed to the contamination. The USEPA also focussed on claims against other currently active businesses that could be linked to the site. USEPA investigators sometimes identified businesses that had arranged for disposal of significant quantities of hazardous wastes at NPL sites. However, the USEPA also named companies as PRPs on fragmentary evidence that was no more than finding their labels on containers at a site or a mention of their names in the site records. PRPs erroneously named tried to persuade the USEPA to withdraw the designation, but it seldom did so. The courts also refused relief that would allow erroneously-named PRPs to free themselves of potential liability.[1]

The courts also ruled that liability to reimburse the USEPA for response costs is usually joint and several and could be imposed on PRPs for nonhazardous wastes that contained diminimous amounts of hazardous substances. This meant that companies named as PRPs were potentially liable without fault for millions of dollars of liabilities of other PRPs who could not pay. Companies also found that PRP status, even when unjustified, meant difficulty raising financing from lenders and other investors.

---

1 In recent years, the courts have been more inclined to require meaningful evidence that a person was responsible for the presence of hazardous substances at a site before imposing liability. *New Jersey Turnpike Authority v. PPG Industries*, 1999 U.S. App. LEXIS 30389 (3d Cir. 1999); *Freeport-McMoran v. B-B Paint Corp.*, 56 F. Supp. 2d 823 (E.D. Mich. 2000).

Companies named as PRPs also saw that USEPA personnel were inexperienced in handling hazardous substances. They become concerned that USEPA personnel might cause bodily injury and property damage to themselves and others while handling hazardous materials with characteristics they did not know. They were also concerned that the USEPA personnel would incur needlessly high response costs due to lack of experience.

For these reasons, companies named as PRPs generally stepped forward and agreed to provide the skills and money to remediate the NPL sites. The USEPA personnel were willing to have the PRPs do the work, provided that the PRPs agreed to procedures that allowed the USEPA to review in advance and approve all aspects of the work.

The PRPs usually organized a committee to represent them in performing the response actions. As a first step, the PRP committee negotiated an agreement with the USEPA for some or all the PRPs to perform and pay for remediation of the site. The agreement sometimes also required the PRPs to perform or reimburse the cost of a removal action already performed by a contractor hired by the USEPA. The USEPA published a model consent decree at 56 Fed. Reg. 30,996 (7/8/91) and said it would seldom negotiate changes.

The PRP committee then hired an experienced environmental engineering firm to perform the RI/FS. The PRPs hoped to propose remedial alternatives in the RI/FS that would enable them to perform the remedial work rapidly and economically. Among the remedial alternatives commonly proposed were soil removal; soil caps; slurry walls; soil treatment by such methods as reduction of the valence of metals and biooxidation of organics; and groundwater remediation by air stripping or carbon adsorption. However, remedial alternatives proposed by PRPs were widely opposed by environmental groups and seldom approved by the USEPA until extensively modified. The USEPA often found that an RI/FS was insufficient and directed the PRPs to perform further investigation and to develop more extensive and costly remedial alternatives. The alternatives at many NPL sites were studied in extensive detail over many years.

I. Remedy Selection Criteria ("How Clean is Clean")

CERCLA § 121 provides that, if any hazardous substance, pollutant or contaminant will remain onsite, the remedial action selected must provide a level or standard of control which at least attains compliance with each applicable or relevant and appropriate federal or state standard, requirement, criteria or limitation, whichever is more stringent. Among other things, the remedy must provide a level or standard of control which at least attains the maximum contaminant level goals (MCLGs) under the Safe Drinking Water Act (SDWA) and the water quality criteria under the Clean Water Act (CWA) where such goals or criteria are relevant and appropriate under the circumstances. However, alternate concentration limits for hazardous constituents in groundwater may be established after careful study of hydrologic, geologic and other factors bearing on human exposure. 42 U.S.C. §9621(d).

As described earlier, the USEPA included in the NCP a list of factors to be used in determining the applicable or relevant and appropriate requirement (ARAR) standards to be used at an NPL site. 40 C.F.R. § 300.400(q). The USEPA has also included threshold criteria, primary balancing criteria and modifying criteria to be used in remedy selection. 40 C.F.R. § 300.400(f). The threshold criteria are protection of human health and the environment and compliance with ARAR standards. A remedy must meet the threshold ARAR criteria to be seriously considered for selection. Among the alternative remedies that meet the threshold criteria, selection is then based on the primary balancing criteria, including cost, and the modifying criteria.

The requirement that remedies comply with the strictest federal or state ARAR standards made the cleanup of NPL sites extremely complex and costly. For years, the USEPA and environmental groups resisted any relaxation of criteria or selection of remedies for industrial and commercial sites. The primary activity at many NPL sites became lengthy efforts by PRPs to support their proposed remedies and similarly lengthy efforts by the USEPA and environmental groups to oppose them. Environmental groups could obtain grants from the USEPA enabling them to oppose the PRPs and contributions from private donors to fight both the PRPs and the USEPA. The PRPs hired environmental consulting firms to perform investigations and develop remedial proposals and the USEPA and environmental groups hired consultants to contend that the proposals were inadequate. As the years passed, some observers concluded that the primary function of CERCLA was to provide employment for consultants.

PRPs who disagree with the USEPA's selection of a remedy can not seek court review of the selection until the USEPA sues to recover its costs. 42 U.S.C. § 9613(h).

J. Reforms Adopted During the 1990s

1. Directions and Guidance Documents

During the economic recession in the early 1990s, the Superfund program was criticized not only by industry but also by state and local governments and the public. The criticism focussed on the long delays and high costs and also on the unrealistic remedial criteria and methods required by the USEPA. Several states adopted their own remediation programs and demonstrated that contaminated sites could be restored to productive use. These states proudly publicized their "brownfields" programs that reopened industrial sites to provide jobs and pay taxes. Legislation was proposed to the U.S. Congress to make fundamental amendments to CERCLA. While opposing the amendments, the USEPA adopted a series of directives and guidance documents intended to make investigation and remediation of NPL sites more realistic:

- Role of Baseline Risk Assessment in Superfund Remedy Selection, OSWER Directive 9355.0-30, April 22, 1991.
- Guide to Principal Threat and Low Level Threat Wastes, OSWER Directive 9380.3-06 FS, Nov. 1992.
- Guidance on Implementation of the Superfund Accelerated Cleanup Model (SACM) under CERCLA and the NCP. OSWER Directive 9203.1-03, July 7, 1992.
- Presumptive Remedies: Policy and Procedures, OSWER Directive 9355.0-47 FS, Sept. 1993.
- Presumptive Remedies: Site Characterization and Technology Selection for CERCLA Sites With Volatile Organic Compounds in Soils, OSWER Directive 9355.0-48 FS, Sept. 1993.
- Presumptive Remedy for CERCLA Municipal Landfill Sites, OSWER Directive 9355.0-49 FS. Sept. 1993.
- Guidance for Evaluating the Technical Impracticability of Ground-Water Restoration, EPA No. 540-R-93-080, Sept. 1993.
- Land Use in the CERCLA Remedy Selection Process, OSWER Directive 9355.7-04, May 25, 1995.
- Directive allowing PRPs to perform the risk assessment part of an RI/FS. OSWER Directive 9340.1-02 (Jan. 26, 1996).
- Guidance on consistency in remedy selection, EPA Guidance 9200.0-21 (Sept. 25, 1996).
- Superfund Reforms: Updating Remedy Decisions, OSWER Directive 9200.0-22 (Sept. 27, 1996).
- Directive limiting the extent of oversight by the USEPA at NPL sites being remediated by cooperative and capable PRPs. OSWER Directive 9200.4-15 (July 31, 1996).
- The Role of Cost in the Superfund Remedy Selection Process, EPA Guidance 540-F-96-018, Sept. 1996.
- Presumptive Response Strategy and Ex-Situ Treatment Technologies for Contaminated Groundwater at CERCLA Sites, OSWER Directive 9283.1-12, Oct. 1996.
- The Role of CSGWPPs in EPA Remediation Programs, OSWER Directive 9283.1-09, August 4, 1997.
- Presumptive Remedy: Supplemental Bulletin Multi-Phase Extraction (MPE) Technology for VOCs in Soil and Groundwater, OSWER Directive 93550.0-485, April 1997.

- Rules of Thumb for Superfund Remedy Selection, OSWER Directive 9355.0-69, Aug. 1997.
- Interim Soil Lead Guidance for CERCLA Sites and RCRA Corrective Facilities, OSWER Directive 9200.4-27P and Revised Directive 9200.4-29, 1998.
- Use of Monitored Natural Attenuation at Superfund, RCRA Corrective Action, And Underground Storage Tank Sites, OSWER Directive, April 1999.
- Treatment Technologies for Site Cleanup: Annual Status Report, Ninth Ed., OSWER June 1999.
- Improving Site Assessment: Combined PA/SI Assessments, EPA Guidance 540-F-98-038, Oct. 1999.
- Improving Site Assessment: Pre-CERCLIS Screening Assessments, EPA Guidance 540-F-98-039, Oct. 1999.
- Use of Monitored Natural Attenuation at Superfund, RCRA Corrective Action and Underground Storage Tank Sites, OSWER Directive 9200.4-17P, April 1, 1999.
- Reuse Assessments: A Tool to Implement the Superfund Land Use Directive, OSWER 9355.7-06P (June 4, 2001).

2. Risk Assessment Policies

As shown by its directives and guidance documents, the USEPA recognized that ideal of restoring NPL sites to their natural pre-industrial condition is seldom technically feasible or cost-effective. Thus, the USEPA developed risk assessment methods to set criteria and select methods that were achievable but also protective of human health and the environment.

The USEPA's risk assessment methods for NPL sites continue to be very conservative. Preliminary remediation goals (PRGs) are based on ARARs. In the absence of applicable ARARs, PRGs are set for chemicals that pose carcinogenic risks at concentrations that achieve 10^{-6} excess cancer risk and for chemicals that pose noncarcinogenic risks at concentrations that achieve a hazard quotient of one. On a site-specific basis, the USEPA may approve remedies that are somewhat less protective in the range between 10^{-4} and 10^{-6} excess cancer risk. The USEPA may also authorize an ARAR waiver or an alternate concentration limit (ACL) after careful review.

The development of presumptive remedies has helped to standardize and simplify the remedy selection process. In developing the presumptive remedies, the USEPA recognized that some remedies had proven to be failures, such as efforts to pump and treat groundwater containing perchloroethylene or other dense nonaqueous phase liquids (DNAPLs). Examples of presumptive remedies are as follows:

Municipal Landfills. The presumptive remedy is containment using a landfill cap; groundwater control; leachate collection and treatment; gas collection and/or treatment; and institutional controls to assure the cap is preserved.

Volatile Organic Compounds (VOCs) in Soils. The preferred presumptive remedy is soil vapor extraction. The other choices are thermal desorption and incineration.

Wood Treater Sites. The presumptive remedies for wood treater sites are immobilization of metals and other inorganics and bioremediation, thermal desorption or incineration of inorganics.

Contaminated Groundwater. The presumptive remedy is a strategy to develop and evaluate information (including site characterization and evaluation of hydrogeological and other factors favoring or limiting full restoration) to design a treatment train for phased use of one or more presumptive treatment technologies. The presumptive technologies are air stripping, granular activated carbon, chemical/UV oxidation, aerobic biological reactors, chemical precipitation, ion exchange/adsorption, electrochemical methods, and aeration of background metals. These technologies may be followed by monitored natural attenuation.

3. Land Use

The Directive on land use confirms that the USEPA considers current and reasonably anticipated future land use when assessing risk and selecting remedies at NPL sites. The Directive applies to soil remediation, not groundwater remediation which is governed by other directives.

To enable site managers to evaluate reasonably anticipated future land use, the Directive says that extensive independent research should not be necessary. The Directive recommends use of existing information available from local planning authorities. Among the numerous items which should be considered are current land use; zoning laws and maps; comprehensive community master plans; population growth patterns and projections; accessibility of the site to existing infrastructure such as municipal drinking water; engineering and institutional controls currently in place; uses of nearby land areas; any applicable government land use designations such as parklands or military reservations; historical or recent development patterns; cultural factors; natural resources; vulnerability of groundwater to migration of soil contaminants; effects on certain minority populations; location of onsite or nearby wetlands; location in or near a floodplain; location of onsite or nearby wetlands; location in or near a floodplain; location near critical habitats of endangered or threatened species; geographic or geological information; and location of wellhead protection and recharge areas and other areas identified in the state's groundwater protection plan.

The Directive applies primarily to industrial sites located in urban areas that have been industrial for years and will continue to be industrial for the foreseeable future. PRPs and state and municipal authorities had repeatedly complained that it was unrealistic to require remediation of industrial facilities by methods necessary to meet criteria for residential use. When active measures are not practicable, the USEPA now allows remediation of industrial properties to meet somewhat more lenient criteria, provided that appropriate engineering and institutional controls are installed and deed restrictions are recorded to require their long term maintenance.

4. Groundwater Criteria

The guidance on evaluating the technical impracticality of groundwater restoration was a milestone. During the 1980s and early 1990s, PRPs at NPL sites and other persons devoted years and large amounts of effort and cost to pumping and treating chlorinated solvents and other DNAPLs, but were seldom able to achieve the USEPA's extremely strict criteria due to the tendency of DNAPLs to sink through groundwater and form pools on an impermeable surface such as bedrock. The allowance of an alternative remedy of containment, if treatment is not feasible or reaches a "plateau," was an important step forward.

The USEPA's directive that comprehensive state groundwater protection programs (GSGWPPs) be used at NPL sites might improve the state programs. Most states adopted groundwater quality and cleanup standards based on the drinking water maximum contaminant limits (MCLs) issued by the USEPA under the Safe Drinking Water Act. Some states, such as Connecticut, classified groundwater into areas based on use for residential or industrial purposes and the availability of municipal drinking water. Other states, such as New York, included all groundwater in a single class required to meet the drinking water MCLs. However, experience showed that remediation of groundwater at NPL sites to meet ARARs based on drinking water MCLs was often technically impossible or costly far beyond any real benefit.

The USEPA's directive told the states that their CSGWPPs generally cannot be used to set site-specific groundwater remediation criteria. The USEPA recommended that the states add to their CSGWPPs a method for establishing priorities among groundwater resources based on groundwater characteristics or other factors such as current and expected future uses. As an alternative, CSGWPPs may define the relative value, priority or vulnerability of groundwater resources in a manner that enables the USEPA to set site-specific remediation criteria.

5. Natural Attenuation

Natural attenuation of groundwater by biodegradation, dispersion, dilution or adsorption was opposed for years by environmentalists as a "do nothing" alternative. In recent years, however, the USEPA and its Science Advisory Board

(SAB) have developed cautious policies that allow natural attenuation as a remedy if it will effectively reduce contaminants in groundwater to concentrations protective of human health and the environment within a reasonable timeframe.

Reevaluation of natural attenuation resulted from experience at NPL sites. It was usually feasible, although costly, to remove free product liquids and to reduce high concentrations of contaminants by treatment to relatively low levels. However, as efforts were made to reduce concentrations of contaminants to the extremely low criteria set by the USEPA, treatment often reached a "plateau" or point of diminishing returns where little or no progress was being made but significant work and cost was continuing. Under these circumstances, the PRPs often requested that the USEPA allow the remaining concentrations to be reduced to meet applicable criteria by natural attenuation over time at far less cost.

Before allowing natural attenuation, the USEPA requires that PRPs use removal and treatment remedies to the extent feasible and effective. The USEPA requires site characterization to show that natural attenuation will be effective and periodic monitoring to verify the effectiveness. Sources of the contamination must be removed or controlled. The contamination must not biodegrade into harmful compounds and must be subjected to engineering and institutional controls to prevent dispersal from having harmful effects on human health or the environment.

6. Alternate Concentration Limits (ACLs)

At many NPL sites, contamination accumulated during decades of industrial use made remediation to meet ARARs based on drinking water MCLs an impossible task. Where the groundwater was not used for drinking water, the PRPs sought approval from the USEPA to remediate to meet alternate concentration limits (ACLs). The requirements to remediate to ACLs are as follows:

- The contaminated groundwater must have "known or protected" points of entry to a surface water body.
- There must be no "statistically significant increases" of contaminant concentrations in the surface water body at those points of entry, or at points downstream.
- It must be possible to reliably prevent human exposure to the contaminated groundwater through the use of institutional controls.

All three requirements must be met and be supported by site-specific information which must be incorporated into the RI/FS and ROD.

7. Engineering and Institutional Controls

Engineering controls are used at NPL sites when it is not feasible to remove or treat soil contamination to levels that meet applicable criteria. When a decision is made to manage in place the remaining contamination (e.g., partially soluble heavy metals), the USEPA will require installation and long term maintenance of engineering controls to contain and immobilize the contamination. The most common engineering control is an impermeable "cap" over the contaminated soil consisting of clay and/or a paving material such as concrete or asphalt. A slurry wall is another example.

Institutional controls include a variety of measures such as bans on use of water for drinking, fishing or drilling wells. They also include zoning, building permit and deed restrictions. Institutional controls are commonly used with engineering controls. For example, if the USEPA allows metal contamination to remain in soil at concentrations exceeding applicable criteria and requires that a "cap" be installed over the soil, it will also require the landowner to record a deed giving notice of contamination and restricting the current and future owners and operators from actions that may disturb the "cap" without prior notice to and approval by the USEPA. The deed must identify the contamination and its locations and describe the restrictions in detail.

Recognition by the USEPA and state environmental agencies that engineering and institutional controls can be effective remedies has restored to productive use some NPL sites and other sites throughout the United States.

8. Progress Reported by the General Accounting Office

On September 9, 1999, the General Accounting Office (GAO) reported that all remedies were in place or no further action was needed at 595 of the 1,204 NPL sites. At least one remedy was being implemented or had been completed at 424 of the other 609 sites. This report showed the progress that the reforms during the 1990s had achieved. However, a GAO report dated June 10, 1999 said that less than half the annual expenses of the Superfund continued to be for remediation of sites.

K. Recovery of Response Costs

1. Persons Entitled to Recover Response Costs

CERCLA authorizes the USEPA to recover its response costs for removal actions at facilities contaminated with hazardous substances and for remediation of NPL sites from owners, operators, certain arrangers for disposal, and certain transporters. 42 U.S.C. § 9607(a). *U.S. v. Monsanto Company*, 858 F.2d 160 (4th Cir. 1988); *New York v. Shore Realty*, 759 F.2d 1032 (2d cir. 1985).

CERCLA also authorizes innocent landowners and other persons who are not responsible parties to recover their response costs under 42 U.S.C. § 9607(a). A responsible party may not sue to recover response costs under 42 U.S.C. § 9607(a), which imposes joint and several liability, but may sue for contributions under 42 U.S.C. § 9613, which imposes only several liability. *Axel Johnson Inc. v. Carroll Carolina Oil Co.*, 191 F.3d 409 (4th Cir. 1999); *Centerior Serv. Co. v.*

Acme Scrap Iron, 153 F. 3d 344 (6th Cir. 1998) and cases cited on page 349 therein, including *United Technologies v. Browning-Ferris Industries*, 33 F.3d 96 (1st Cir. 1994), cert den. 513 U.S. 1183 (1995).

A landowner who is a responsible party because of its status as an owner, but who alleged it did not contaminate the site, was allowed to sue for response costs by the Seventh Circuit in *Rumpke of Indiana v. Cummins Engine*, 107 F.3d 1235 (7th Cir. 1997). However, the Second Circuit reached the opposite conclusion in *Bedford Affiliates v. Sills*, 156 F.3d 416 (2d Cir. 1999); *Minyard Enterprises v. Southeastern Chemical*, 184 F.3d 373 (4th Cir. 1999).

2. Retroactive Joint and Several Liability; Causation

Several courts have held that the retroactive imposition of liability under CERCLA is not prohibited by the U.S. Constitution. For example, see *U.S. Gurley*, 43 F.3d 1188 (8th Cir. 1994).

Although CERCLA does not expressly so provide, the courts have held that the liability is also joint and several unless a responsible party can prove that its liability is divisible from that of the other parties. The joint liability makes any responsible party fully liable for the entire cleanup cost and related liability, even someone whose role was minor such as a person who sent a few small shipments of waste containing hazardous substances to an NPL site where millions of pounds of hazardous substances are located. *Acushnet Co. v. Mohasco Corp.*, 191 F. 3d 69 (1st Cir. 1999); *Bedford Affiliates v. Sills*, 156 F.3d 416 (2d Cir. 1998); *U.S. v. Alcan Aluminum Corp.*, 990 F. 2d 711 (2d Cir. 1993); *O'Neil v. Picillo*, 883 F.2d 176 (1st Cir. 1989); *U.S. v. Monsanto Company, supra*.

A claimant seeking to recover response costs need not prove causation. The claimant must only show that contaminants in the custody of a PRP could have been deposited at the site and that similar contaminants found at the site caused the claimant to incur response costs. The PRP then has the burden to disprove causation. *Westfarm Associates v. Washington Suburban*, 66 F.3d 669 (4th Cir. 1995). See also *Kalamazoo River Study Group v. Menasha Corp.*, 228 F.3d 648 (6th Cir. 2000) involving claims for contributions.

3. Costs Recoverable

To be recoverable, response costs must be necessary. At many sites, the cleanup consists of clearly necessary steps such as investigation and removal of contamination sources including leaking drums, transformers and storage tanks and excavation of contaminated soil and their disposal in compliance with federal and state waste management regulations. However, the decision process can become very complicated, especially when a site has extensive soil and groundwater contamination that requires characterization and onsite treatment. In general, private parties who perform cleanups seek to limit both the actions taken and their costs and often attempt to persuade personnel at the USEPA or state environmental agencies to withdraw or modify demands for excessive work.

The courts have often used consistency with the NCP as a test to determine whether response costs were necessary and, therefore, recoverable under CERCLA. For example, one court denied recovery of response costs where the claimant, the Washington Department of Transportation, made serious errors during the cleanup including incorrect tests that erroneously showed that a tar-like material was hazardous and had to be sent for disposal to a fully secure landfill at Arlington, Oregon. *Washington State Dept. of Transportation v. Washington Natural Gas Co.*, 59 F.3d 793 (9th Cir. 1995). The court found the claimant's conduct was arbitrary and capricious, particularly when it discovered that it had underestimated the amount of the tar-like material but continued to rely on the erroneous tests and failed to consider available alternatives.

For another example, a court denied a large portion of the response costs incurred by the Minnesota Pollution Control Authority (MPCA) to remediate lead-contaminated soil at a property because the MPCA selected an unsuccessful "soil washing" technology as the remedial method although warned by a USEPA contractor that the method might not be effective and involved relatively high costs. Ultimately, the soil was removed by customary methods. *State of Minnesota v. Kalman W. Abrams Metals, Inc.*, 155 F.3d 1019 (8th Cir. 1998).

Oversight costs of the USEPA and other environmental regulatory agencies are recoverable response costs. *U.S. v. Lowe*, 118 F.3d 399 (5th Cir. 1997).

Attorneys fees for services such as litigation or negotiating a consent decree are not usually recoverable as response costs. *PMC, Inc. v. Sherwin-Williams Co.*, 151 F.3d 610 (7th Cir. 1998); *AM International, Inc. v. Datacard Corp.*, 106 F. 3d 1342 (7th Cir. 1997); *Atlantic Richfield Co. v. American Airlines, Inc.*, 98 F.3d 564 (10th Cir. 1996); *Key Tronic Corp. v. U.S.*, 511 U.S. 809 (1994). However, attorneys fees closely related to the actual cleanup may constitute a necessary response cost. *Pneumo Abex Corp. v. Bessemer & Lake Erie RR Co.*, 936 F. Supp. 1250 (E.D. Va. 1996). For example, many environmental attorneys use their experience to guide clients through environmental cleanups, especially when the attorneys also have scientific or engineering experience in the methods used. *Key Tronic Corp. v. U.S.*, 511 U.S. 809, 128 L. Ed. 2d 797(1994). *Franklin County v. American Premier Underwriters*, 240 F.3d 574 (6th Cir. 2001).

Prejudgment interest should be awarded in both response costs recovery actions and contribution actions. *Bancamerica Commercial Corp. v. Mosher Steel, Inc.*, supra.

At some NPL sites, plaintiff attorneys have sought to include costs of medical monitoring to determine whether releases might cause future human health problems. The courts have held that response costs do not include medical monitoring; *Durfey v. E.I. du Pont*, 59 F.3d 121 (9th Cir. 1995); *Daigle v. Shell Oil*, 972 F.2d 1527 (10th Cir. 1992); *Price v. Navy Department*, 39 F.3d 1101 (9th Cir. 1994).

4. Consistency with the NCP

The USEPA and state environmental agencies are entitled to recover response costs if they are *not inconsistent* with the NCP. Private claimants are entitled to recover response costs or contributions to response costs if they are *consistent* with the NCP. 42 U.S.C. §§ 9607(a)(4).

If the USEPA or a state agency establishes a *prima facie* case to recover response costs, the burden shifts to the defendant to prove the response action was inconsistent with the NCP. *U.S. v. Chapman*, 146 F.3d 1166 (9th Cir. 1998). A private party has the burden of proving consistency with the NCP as an element of its *prima facie* case. *Public Service Co. v. Gates Rubber Co.*, 175 F.3d 1177 (10th Cir. 1999).

Although it is very lengthy, the NCP is nevertheless a general guide that allows room for many choices. Consistency with the NCP can be difficult to prove, even when a cleanup was supervised by the USEPA. Further, the NCP has been amended a number of times. *Louisiana-Pacific Corp. v. Asarco, Inc.*, 204 F.3d 1565 (9th Cir. 1994).

Whether the USEPA or a state environmental agency has performed a cleanup in a manner consistent with the NCP is determined by an arbitrary and capricious standard. In other words, the USEPA or a state agency are entitled to recover response costs unless they were incurred in an arbitrary and capricious manner. *State of Minnesota v. Kalman W. Abrams Metals, Inc.*, 155 F.3d 1024 (8th Cir. 1998) and cases cited therein.

On the other hand, some courts require private parties to prove strict compliance with the NCP, at least with versions of the NCP before it was amended to provide for substantial compliance. *County Line Investment Co. v. Wagco Land*, 933 F.2d 1508 (10th Cir. 1991); *Artesian Water Co. v. New Castle County*, 659 F. Supp. 1269 (D. Del. 1987). Other courts hold that proof of substantial compliance is sufficient. *Louisiana-Pacific Corp. v. Asarco, Inc.*, supra.

When PRPs are sued for response costs or contributions to response costs, they can contest the methods and costs as inconsistent with the NCP and have the advantage of hindsight when doing so. In recent years, several courts have denied recovery of response costs, wholly or partially, because of inconsistency with the NCP. *State of Minnesota v. Kalman W. Abrams Metals, Inc.*, supra; *Washington State Dept. of Transportation v. Washington Natural Gas. Co.*, 59 F.2d 793 (9th Cir. 1995); *County Line Investment Co. v. Wayco Land Development, Inc.*, supra; *Pierson Sand v. Pierson Township*, 43 Env. Rep. Cases (BNA) 1559 (6th Cir. 1996).

Among the most common claims of inconsistency with the NCP is failure to provide for public notice and an opportunity for appropriate public comment as provided in 40 C.F.R. § 300.71. When small and medium-sized cleanups are performed under state programs, cleanup work is typically reviewed by a case manager for the state environmental agency with little or no public participation or solicitation of public comments. The reason is that there are thousands of relatively routine cleanups in progress at any given time. Most involve routine tasks such as removal of containers and underground storage tanks, sampling and testing of contaminated soil and groundwater, and removal of modest amounts of contaminated soil. There is no imminent threat to public health and there are no issues likely to interest the public.

That is specially true when the case manager applies strict standards, as is customary. Nevertheless, one court deprived claimants of their contribution rights, even though two public meetings were held, because the meetings did not involve the citizens in the decision-making process concerning the selection of the cleanup plan. *Pierson Sand v. Pierson Township*, supra.

Another court held that comprehensive oversight of a cleanup by a state environmental agency could be treated as public participation. *Bedford Associates v. Sills*, 156 F.3d 416 (2d Cir. 1998). However, if the state agency's involvement is limited, it will not fulfill the public participation requirement. *Public Service Co. v. Gates Rubber Co.*, 175 F.3d 1177 (10th Cir. 1999).

The courts have so far consistently held that response costs for compliance with a Section 106 administrative cleanup order issued by the USEPA are recoverable even though public comments were not obtained pursuant to the NCP. *Bancamerica Commercial Corp. v. Mosher Steel, Inc.*, 100 F.3d 792 (10th Cir. 1996).

Some courts have held that preliminary investigation, monitoring and evaluation costs may be recovered without proof of consistency with the NCP because there are no guidelines in the NCP for performing those tasks. *Pierson Sand v. Pierson Township*, supra; *Donahey v. Bogel*, 987 F.2d 1250 (6th Cir. 1993), vacated 114 S. Ct. 2688 (1994); *Carlyle Piermont Corp. v. Federal Paper Board*, 742 F. Supp. 814 (S.D.N.Y. 1990).

5. Owner Liability

The current owners of a facility where hazardous substances have been or are being released is strictly and retroactively liable under CERCLA for response costs and certain other damages and costs regardless of whether it caused or contributed to the releases. 42 U.S. C. § 9607(a)(1). The courts have interpreted the term "owner" broadly to include:

- A co-owner of less than 10% of a contaminated area. *U.S. v. Rohm and Haas*, 2 F.3d 1265 (3d Cir. 1993).
- An "alter ego" shell corporation *Atlantic Richfield v. Blorenski*, 847 F. Supp. 1261 (E.D. Pa. 1994).
- A tenant that asserted control over use of the property. *Burlington Northern RR Co. v. Woods Industries* 815 F. Supp. 1384 (E.D. Wash. 1993); *U.S. v. A&N Cleaners*, 788 F. Supp. 1317 (S.D.N.Y. 1992). However, a tenant is not usually subject to liability as an owner unless it has sufficient attributes of ownership

such as may exist after a sale-and-leaseback transaction. *Commander Oil v. Barlo Equipment*, 215 F.3d 321 (2d Cir. 2000).

- A titleholder, but not a land trustee under Illinois law where the beneficiary has full management and control. *U.S. v. Peterson Sand*, 806 F. Supp. 1346 (N.D. Ill. 1992).
- An absentee owner. *U.S. v. R.W. Meyer, Inc.*, 889 F.2d 149 (6th Cir. 1989); *U.S. v. Monsanto Co.*, 858 F.2d 160 (4th Cir. 1988).
- A right of way owner. *City of Toledo v. Beazer Materials*, 923 F. Supp. 1013 (N.D. Ohio 1996). However, a long term easement was held not to be ownership in *Acme Printing Ink Co. v. Menard, Inc.*, 870 F. Supp. 1465 (E.D. Wis. 1994). See also *Long Beach v. Dorothy B. Godwin California Living Trust*, 32 F.3d 1364 (9th Cir. 1994).
- An owner of a storage tank. *Darbouze v. Chevron*, 1998 Westlaw 512941 (E.D. Pa. Aug. 19, 1998). *Minyard Enterprises v. Southeastern Chemical*, 194 F.3d 373 (5th Cir. 1999).
- A developer alleged to be an equitable owner. *Con-Tech Sales v. Cockerham*, 715 F. Supp. 701 (E.D. Pa. 1989). However, a real estate broker and its agent were held not to be equitable owners in *Lentz v. Mason*, 961 F. Supp. 709 (D.N.J. 1997).

A former owner is liable if it owned a facility when the disposal of hazardous substances occurred. 42 U.S.C. § 9607(a)(2). *Axel Johnson, Inc. v. Carroll Carolina Oil Co.*, 191 F.3d 409 (4th Cir. 1999). When the USEPA and others have made claims against former owners, it has sometimes been difficult to determine whether disposal occurred during their periods of ownership or some previous time. The task is specially difficult when a succession of owners have operated the same or similar businesses at a facility over many decades because the intermediate owners argue that their handling of hazardous substances was much better than previous owners.

The USEPA and other claimants have argued that intermediate owners should be held responsible for disposal if they allowed contamination released by prior owners or operators to continue to migrate through soil and groundwater during their periods of ownership. In other words, they argued that the intermediate owners should be liable for allowing passive migration, even though they did nothing to contribute to, or exacerbate, the migration. One U.S. Circuit Court of Appeal has accepted this argument. *Nurad Inc. v. William E. Hooper & Sons Co.*, 906 F.2d 837 (4th Cir. 1992); Five U.S. Circuit Courts of Appeal have rejected the argument. *U.S. v. 150 Acres of Land*, 204 F.3d 698, 2000 U.S. App. LEXIS (6th Cir. 2000). *ABB Industrial v. Prime Technology*, 120 F.3d 351 (2d Cir. 1997); *U.S. v. CMDG Realty Co.*, 96 F.3d 706 (3d Cir. 1996); *Joslyn Mfg. Co. v. Koppers Co.*, 40 F.3d 750 (5th Cir. 1994). *Carson Harbor Village, Ltd. v. Unocal Corp.*, 270 F.3d 863 (9th Cir. 2001).

A downgradient landowner is not liable for hazardous substances that migrated through the subsurface from an adjoining property. *Dent v. Beazer Materials*, 156 F.3d 523 (4th Cir. 1998).

6. Operator Liability

The current operator of a facility where hazardous substances have been or are being released is strictly and retroactively liable under CERCLA for response costs and certain other damages and costs regardless of whether it caused or contributed to the releases. 42 U.S.C. § 9607(a)(2). The courts have interpreted the term "operator" broadly to include any person who had responsibility for, participated in, or had control over the disposal of hazardous substances at a facility. In general, the courts require proof that a person had "actual" control and participation as a basis for operator liability. *U.S. v. Gurley*, 43 F.3d 1188 (8th Cir. 1994); *cert. denied*, 516 U.S. 817 (1995). However, some courts may impose liability on persons who had authority to control, even though unexercised. *U.S. v. Carolina Transformer*, 978 F.2d 832 (4th Cir. 1992).

Tenants are the most common example of persons subject to operator liability. Tenants have been held liable as an operator where they exercised actual control over facilities. *U.S. v. Mexico Feed*, 980 F.2d 478 (8th Cir. 1992). A Circuit Court of Appeals said that tenant liability can be imposed on the basis of authority to control, even if the authority is not exercised, but then found that the tenant defendants in the case did not have authority to control. *Nurad, Inc. v. William E. Hooper & Sons. Co*, 966 F.2d 837 (4th Cir. 1992). "Authority to control" has also been used in other cases. *Pierson Sand v. Pierson Township*, 851 F. Supp. 850 (W.D. Mich. 1994); *Northwestern Mutual v. Atlantic Research*, 847 F. Supp. 389 (E.D. Va., 1994); *U.S. v. TIC Investment Corp.*, 866 F. Supp. 1173 (N.D. Iowa 1994). Whether leases or other transactions are involved, however, some courts require actual control. *Landsford-Coaledale Joint Water Authority v. Tonolli Corp.*, 4 F.3d 1209 (3rd Cir. 1993).

A property management company that is actively involved in the operational activities at a site may be liable as an operator. *Redwing Carriers v. Saraland Apartments*, 94 F.3d 1489 (11th Cir. 1996).

A contractor which excavated contaminated soil and spread it on other areas of a property may be an operator. *Kaiser Aluminum v. Catellus Development*, 976 F.2d 1338 (9th Cir. 1992).

State or local government entities are excluded from the definitions of the terms "owner" and "operator" if they acquire ownership or control of a facility in their function as sovereign involuntarily because of bankruptcy, tax delinquency, abandonment or other involuntary circumstances. 42 U.S.C. § 9601(20)(D). Further, acquisition of a facility by escheat, involuntary transfer or acquisition or eminent domain is a defense against liability. 42 U.S.C. § 9601(35).

State or local governments are not liable for actions taken in response to an emergency created by the release or threatened release of a hazardous substance generated by or from a facility owned by another person except for gross negligence or willful misconduct. 42 U.S.C. 9607 (d)(2).

Any person who renders care, assistance or advice in accordance with the NCP at the direction of an onsite coordination for an NPL site is protected from liability except for gross negligence or willful misconduct. 42 U.S.C. § 9607(d)(1).

7. Third Party Acts or Omissions; Innocent Landowners and Operators

CERCLA excuses acts of God, acts of war, and acts or omissions by a third party if the person seeking excuse proves exercise of all due care and proves that it could not have foreseen the conduct of the third party. This defense includes what is sometimes called the "innocent landowner" or "innocent purchaser"defense. The landowner owner must show that prior to purchase it made a diligent investigation of a kind likely to reveal any contamination. 42 U.S.C. § 9607(b) and 9601(35). *Westfarm Associates v. Washington Suburban Sanitary Com'n*, 66 F.3d 669 (4th Cir. 1995), *cert. denied,* 517 U.S. 1103 (1995); *U.S. v. CDMG Realty*, 96 F.3d 706 (3d Cir. 1996); *Kerr-McGee Chemical v. Lefton Iron*, 14 F.3d 321 (7th Cir. 1994).

The third party defense is also available to an innocent operator.

An owner who fails to exercise due care after discovery of hazardous substances loses the third party defense. *Idylwoods Associates v. Mader Capital*, 915 F. Supp. 1290, reconsidered in part 956 F. Supp. 410 (W.D.N.Y. 1996). An owner who leased property to a business that necessarily used hazardous substances and failed to exercise due care to prevent the tenant from contaminating the property is not eligible for the third party defense. *Briggs & Stratton Corp. v. Concrete Sales*, 20 F. Supp. 2d 1356 (M.D. Ga. 1998); aff'd sub.non. *Concrete Sales v. Blue Bird Body Co.*, 211 F.3d 1333 (11th Cir. 2000).

The courts have been strict in their interpretation of the due care requirement. However, there are a few court decisions in which a federal court found that a landowner exercised due care and was entitled to the third party defense. *Norfolk Southern v. Shulimson Brothers Co.*, 1 F. Supp. 2d 553 (W.D.N.C. 1998). *New York v. Lashins Arcade*, 91 F.3d 353 (2d Cir. 1996); *Redwing Carriers v. Saraland Apartments*, 94 F.3d 1489 (11th Cir. 1996); *Town of New Windsor v. Tesa Tuck, Inc.*, 935 F. Supp. 310 (S.D.N.Y.1996). See also *U.S. v. 150 Acres of Land*, 204 F.3d 698 (6th Cir. 2000).

The innocent landowner defense is available to a former landowner. *ABB Industrial v. Prime Technology*, 120 F.3d 351 (2d Cir. 1997). However, a former landowner who knew that its tenant disposed of waste on the property during the term of a lease was not an innocent landowner. *U.S. v. Broderick Investment*, 862 F. Supp. 272 (D. Colo. 1994).

The third party defense is not available to anyone who fails to notify the National Response Center of a release. 42 U.S.C. § 960 3(c).

As a general policy, the USEPA does not take enforcement action against innocent downgradient landowners (or operators) whose property is contaminated by hazardous substances which migrated from nearby properties. For example, the USEPA issued on May 24, 1995 a "Final Policy Toward Owners of Property Containing Contaminated Aquifers," published at 60 Fed. Reg. 34.790, July 3, 1995. In the Final Policy, the USEPA confirmed that it will not take enforcement actions under CERCLA against owners of property containing aquifers contaminated as a result of migration from outside the property. The USEPA warned that the policy does not apply if the owner caused or contributed to the contamination, made the contamination worse, or was in some other way responsible for the contamination.

See the discussion later in this chapter of additional requirements imposed on persons seeking to claim the innocent purchaser defense by the Small Business Liability Relief and Brownfields Revitalization Act of 2000.

8. Arranger Liability

Any person who arranges for disposal or treatment of hazardous substances which it owns or possess by another party or entity at a facility, incineration vessel or site owned or operated by such party or entity is subject to liability for response costs and other costs and damages under CERCLA. 42 U.S.C. § 9607(a)(3). This includes any person who arranged with a transporter for transport to a disposal or treatment facility. This subsection has been widely used to impose strict liability without fault on waste generators who thought they had made lawful arrangements with licensed transporters, but discovered later that the transporter or the disposal site mishandled the waste. Unforseen and even criminal conduct by the transporter or disposal facility may not excuse the liability.

A company that entered into a toll conversion agreement under which it furnished new materials to another company for production of chemical products was held liable as an arranger for disposal. *U.S. v. Aceto Agricultural*, 699 F. Supp. 1384 (S.D. Iowa); aff'd in part 872 F.2d 1373 (8th Cir. 1988).

A seller of used equipment was held liable as an arranger for disposal where the evidence showed that the buyer had no real use for the equipment. *Carter-Jones Lumber v. Dixie Distributing*, 166 F.3d 840 (6th Cir. 1999); *Catellus Development v. U.S.*, 34 F.3d 748 (9th Cir. 1994).

Although the statutory language imposes liability on a person who arranges for disposal of hazardous substances owned or possessed by such person, a waste broker was found to be in constructive possession and, therefore, liable as an arranger for disposal. *U.S. v. Bliss*, 667 F. Supp. 1298 (E.D. Mo. 1987) *contra, U.S. v. Mottolo*, 695 F. Supp. 615 (D.N.H. 1988). Defendants who returned drums to a supplier and received return of their deposit were not entitled to a summary judgment on grounds that they had no intent to arrange for disposal of the residues in the drums because their intent was an issue of fact. *U.S. v. Cello-Foil Products*, 100 F.3d 1227 (6th Cir. 1996).

Cropgrower customers of two aerial pesticide spraying service companies were held not to be arrangers for disposal of pesticides spilled and drained by the spraying service companies into their airstrip property, even though the customers contracted for the spraying services and owned the pesticides. *South Florida Water Mgmt Dist. v. Montalvo*, 84 F.3d 402 (11th Cir. 1996).

An electroplating company that outsourced production to another electroplater was held not liable as an arranger for disposal even though it loaned money to the other company and knew it would generate hazardous waste. The court found there was, nevertheless, no evidence that the outsourcing company itself took any action to dispose of wastes. *Concrete Sales v. Blue Bird Body Co.*, 211 F.3d 1333 (11th Cir. 2000).

The Superfund Recycling Equity Act provides an exemption from arranger liability for persons who arrange for recycling of items constituting "recyclable material", subject to several conditions. 42 U.S.C. § 9627.

9. Transporter Liability

Any person who accepts or accepted any hazardous substance for transport to disposal or treatment facilities, incineration vessels or sites selected by such person from which there is a release is subject to liability for response costs and other costs and damages. 42 U.S.C. § 9607(a)(4). For example, a transporter who substantially participates in selection of the disposal site by actions such as furnishing a list of sites can be held liable for response costs. 42 U.S.C. § 9607. *Tippins v. USX Corp.* No. 93-3609, 1994 U.S. App. LEXIS 24550 (3d Cir., Sept. 12, 1994). A transporter who took waste to the only available state-licensed disposal facility was held liable in *U.S. v. Hardage*, 750 F. Supp. 1444 (W.D. Okla. 1990); affirmed in part and reversed in part on other issues, 982 F.2d 1436 (10th Cir. 1992).

A landfill owner was unsuccessful in recovering response costs or contributions from three transporters of construction or demolition materials because it failed to prove that they transported hazardous substances to the landfill. *Prisco v. A&D Carting*, 168 F.3d 593 (2d Cir. 1999). See also *B.F. Goodrich v. Betkoski*, 99 F.3d 88 (2nd Cir. 1996); *cert. denied,* 118 S. Ct. 2318, 141 L. Ed. 2d 694.

10. Allocation of Liability

Allocation of liability among responsible parties is often made on a volumetric basis. *Boeing Co. v. Cascade Corp.*, 207 F.3d 1177 (9th Cir. 2000); *Akzo Nobel v. Aigner Corp.*, 197 F.3d 302 (7th Cir. 1999). However, the courts also consider and weigh equitable factors. Among others, the courts often consider factors mentioned in a House of Representatives report on the Superfund Amendments Act of 1986:

1. The amount of hazardous substances involved;

2. The degree of toxicity or hazard of the materials involved;

3. The degree of involvement of the parties in the generation, transportation, treatment, storage or disposal of the substances;

4. The degree of care exercised by the parties with respect to the substances; and

5. The degree of cooperation of the parties with government officials to prevent any harm to public health or the environment.

The courts also consider other factors such as the relative financial resources of the parties and benefits that any of them may receive from the cleanup of the site.

The courts have wide discretion in applying equitable factors. For example, only toxicity and volume were considered in *Bancamerica v. Mosher Steel, Inc.*, 99 F.3d 505 (2d Cir. 1996). A PRP's argument for a reduced allocation based on a claim that a PRP's solvent was less toxic than other wastes at the site was rejected in *Akzo Nobel v. Aigner Corp., supra*. because the lower toxicity did not result in any difference or cost saving in the remedy.

On the other hand, a court allocated a higher percentage of liability to a dry cleaning supply company because of the toxicity of its perchloroethylene solvent waste which was also more difficult to remediate than the other waste at the site and influenced the design and construction of the remediation system because it had to be reduced to a lower concentration than other waste. *Bedford Affiliates v. Sills*, 156 F.3d 416 (2nd Cir. 1998).

In recent years, some of the U.S. Circuit Courts of Appeals have found that a zero allocation of liability to a responsible party may be justified if the waste material containing hazardous substances for which it is responsible is insignificant compared to those of other responsible parties. *Kalamazoo River Study Group v. Rockwell International*, 274 F. 3d 1043 (6th Cir. 2001); *Akzo Nobel Coatings, Inc. v. Aigner Corp.*, 197 F. 3d 302 (7th Cir. 1999); *Acushnet Co. v. Mohasco Corp.*, 191 F. 3d 69 (1st Cir. 1999); *Dent v. Beazer Materials*, 156 F. 3d 523 (4th Cir. 1998); *PMC, Inc. v. Sherwin-Williams Co.*, 151 F. 3d 610 (7th Cir. 1998); *Gopher Oil Co. v. Union Oil Co.*, 955 F. 3d 519 (8th Cir. 1992). *U.S. v. Alcan Aluminum*, 990 F.2d 711 (2d Cir. 1993). *Matter of Bell Petroleum*, 3 F.3d 889 (5th Cir. 1993), later proceedings 64 F.3d 202 (5th Cir. 1995).

11. "Orphan Shares"

The imposition of joint and several liability by the courts made it extremely risky for PRPs to defend mistaken or unjust claims for response costs. The reason is that many NPL sites have large volumes of hazardous waste whose source cannot be identified by any means. This creates a so-called "orphan share" of liability to be absorbed by the other responsible parties. The "orphan share" is increased by the shares of PRPs who cannot pay. The "orphan share" is further increased whenever the USEPA settles with PRPs for less than their fair share of the response costs at a site.

In the early years, some major PRPs sought to move quickly to settlement before the USEPA fully investigated a site. These PRPs hoped to settle before the full extent of their liability was revealed. If they succeeded, the "orphan share" was increased. Some PRPs also sought to dominate a PRP committee and to direct the RI/FS and remedial actions in ways which minimized their liability and increased the "orphan share" to be borne by other PRPs.

At many sites, the PRP committees negotiate a voluntary settlement to share costs among the PRPs. The usual allocation method is volumetric. *De minimis* and other small PRPs who do not undertake the burden of sponsoring the cleanup often pay a premium over their volumetric share. PRPs responsible for wastes (such as PCBs) requiring special cleanup costs pay them separately. Such voluntary settlements can save considerable time and cost, but are difficult to negotiate when the "orphan share" is large. PRPs faced with an "orphan share" liability which seems very unfair or beyond their means may decide to take the risk of litigation.

As a partial answer to the "orphan share" problem the USEPA is authorized to make "mixed funding" settlements in which PRPs agree to fund a substantial portion of the response costs and the USEPA funds the rest from the Superfund. The larger the portion offered by the settling PRPs and the stronger the case the USEPA believes it has against nonsettling PRPs, the more likely it is that a "mixed funding" settlement can be achieved. 53 Fed. Reg. 8,279 (3/14/88).

12. Phase I and II Assessments

It has become customary for prospective purchasers and mortgage lenders to arrange for a so-called phase 1 assessment of the environmental condition of a property prior to a purchase or loan and perhaps also a phase II assessment. In addition to the brief discussion here, see Chapter XXI for information about these assessments.

The American Society for Testing Materials, Inc. (ASTM) issued Standard Practice E1527-00 to define good commercial and customary practice for conducting a phase I environmental site assessment of commercial property. If a phase 1 assessment reveals possible contamination or violations, it may be followed by a phase II assessment in which soil, groundwater and other sampling and testing is performed to verify and quantify the conditions found in the phase I assessment.

The scope of a phase I assessment is limited to conditions affecting commercial properties and its cost is about $2,500. Its scope does not include asbestos-containing materials, lead-based paint, radon, wetlands, lead in drinking water supplied in buildings, regulatory compliance, endangered species, ecological or historical resources, industrial hygiene, indoor air quality, health and safety, or electromagnetic fields from power lines, but it is common to add some of these items. Unless supplemented extensively, the scope is not sufficient to evaluate environmental compliance by an operating industrial business. Further, many environmental consulting firms do not have personnel experienced in reviewing overall environmental compliance by an industrial business.

ASTM issued Standard Guide E 1903-97 to provide a framework for employing good commercial and industrial practices in conducting a phase II environmental site assessment. The Guide describes, among other things quality assurance and quality control procedures; field screening and analytical techniques; environmental media sampling; sample handling methods including the chain of custody record; evaluation of data after verification of assumptions and the data; interpretation of results; preparation of a written report. The Guide refers to ASTM's D5730 Guide to Site Characteristics; D653 Terminology Relating to Soil, Rock and Contained Fluids; and D4750 Test Method for Determining Subsurface Liquid Levels in a Borehole or Monitoring Well.

ASTM also published a transaction screen procedure as ASTM E 1528-96. Without any criticism of the good intentions of ASTM in adopting this transaction screen, the author recommends against using it. In lawsuits, plaintiff attorneys frequently use hindsight to portray standards, however strict, as inadequate. They will surely claim that anyone who uses only a transaction screen failed to exercise due care because the customary phase I environmental site assessment can easily be obtained for modest cost.

L. Contribution Rights

CERCLA does not allow responsible parties to recover response costs from other responsible parties under 42 U.S.C. § 9607. However, Section 113 of CERCLA authorizes responsible parties who incur response costs to recover contributions from other responsible parties. 42 U.S.C. § 9613(f). Liability is retroactive, but several and not joint. *Minyard Enterprises v. Southeastern Chemical*, 184 F.3d 373 (4th Cir. 1999); *Centerior Serv. Co. v. Acme Scrap Iron*, 153 F.3d 344 (6th Cir. 1998). Section 113 does not create a cause of action, but is a mechanism for apportioning costs recoverable under Section 107. *Sun Co. v. Browning-Ferris Industries*, 124 F.3d 1187 (10th Cir. 1997).

Contribution claims may not be made against a party who has resolved its liability to the United States by a settlement with the USEPA pursuant to 42 U.S.C. § 9622(h). 42 U.S.C. § 9613(f)(2).

For information about the statutes of limitations applicable to contribution claims, see *United Technologies Corporation et al. v. Browning-Ferris Industries, Inc. et al.*, 33 F.3d 96 (1st Cir. 1994); *cert. denied*, No. 94-1079, Feb. 17, 1995, in which the author served as counsel for one of the successful defendants. In a questionable decision, the Fifth Circuit reclassified typical remedial work as a removal action in order to allow a lawsuit commenced a decade after the events involved in the lawsuit. *Geraghty & Miller v. Conoco, Inc.*, 234 F.3d 917, (5th Cir. 2000).

Some courts have held that the contribution provisions of CERCLA are an exclusive remedy and parties who have failed to comply with the NCP, as required by CERCLA, may not circumvent that requirement by suing under a state contribution law. *PMC, Inc. v. Sherwin-Williams Co.*, 151 F.3d 610 (7th Cir. 1998); *Matter of Reading Company*, 115 F.3d 1111 (3d Cir. 1997).

To help PRPs to resolve cost sharing problems, CERCLA authorizes the USEPA to prepare a nonbinding allocation of responsibility (NBAR), but it has been reluctant to do so. 42 U.S.C. § 9622(e)(3)(A).

An upgradient responsible party was not excused from contribution liability by an argument that the downgradient owner would have had the same cleanup costs in any event. *Boeing Co. v. Cascade Corp.*, 207 F.3d 1177 (9th Cir. 2000).

M. The CERCLA Lien

CERCLA provides that the costs and damages for which a person is liable under § 107(a) to the U.S. shall constitute a lien in favor of the U.S. upon all real property which belongs to such person and is subject to or affected by a removal or remedial action. The lien arises at the later of (1) the time when the costs are first incurred by the United States or (2) the time when the person is provided written notice by certified or registered mail. As to third parties, the lien is subject to rights perfected before notice of the lien is filed in the appropriate office, as designated by state law, where the property subject to the lien is located. 42 U.S.C. § 9607(1).

A federal court of appeals held that the procedures for imposition of the lien violate constitutional due process requirements by failing to provide notice and a predeprivation hearing to a property owner. *Reardon v. U.S.*, 947 F.2d 1509 (1st Cir. 1991). However, the lien was held valid in a later enforcement proceeding where the USEPA provided a notice of intent and an informal hearing before a "neutral" USEPA hearing officer. *U.S. v. 150 Acres of Land*, 204 F.3d 698 (6th Cir. 2000); *U.S. v. Glidden Co.*, 3 F. Supp.2d 823 (N.D. Ohio 1997).

N. Liability of Lenders and Fiduciaries

1. Lender Liability

During the 1980s, the courts ruled that banks and other lenders may be held liable as an owner or operator if they foreclose a mortgage or exercise powers contained in a loan agreement in a manner which involves them in ownership or operation of a facility. Leading court decisions on these subjects were *U.S. v. Mi-*

rabile, 15 E.L.R. 20,992 (E.D. Pa. 1985); *U.S. v. Maryland Bank & Trust Co.*, 632 F. Supp. 573 (D. Md. 1986); *U.S. v. Fleet Factors*, 901 F.2d 1550 (11th Cir. 1990); and *Giudice v. BFG Electroplating*, 732 F. Supp. 556 (W.D. Pa. 1989). However, a court refused to impose liability on a municipal port authority which served as issuer of industrial revenue bonds with only nominal responsibilities. *In re Bergsoe Metal Corp.*, 910 F.2d 668 (9th Cir. 1990).

In 1993, the USEPA adopted a rule interpreting the security interest exemption afforded to lenders by Section 101(20) of CERCLA. The rule clarified the exemption and also allowed lenders greater latitude to protect a security interest including freedom to engage in workout activities, provided that the borrower continued to be the ultimate decision maker for the facility. The rule clarified that the security interest exemption did not require a lender to meet the requirements of the "innocent landowner" defense by steps such as performing an environmental inspection or audit of the collateral when the loan is made. If foreclosure became necessary, the rule relieved a lender from liability if it did not participate in management prior to foreclosure and if it foreclosed and sold or otherwise divested the property within 12 months. If the property was not divested within 12 months, the lender would not become liable, but should be prepared to demonstrate that it did not participate in management prior to foreclosure and was using reasonable efforts to divest and was not holding the property for investment. In divesting collateral, the rule indicated that a lender must not outbid, reject or fail to act within 90 days of receipt upon a written bona fide offer of fair consideration. 40 C.F.R. §§ 330.1100 and 330.1105.

The USEPA's lender liability rule was held invalid by the U.S. Court of Appeals for the District of Columbia in a lawsuit by the Michigan Attorney General and the Chemical Manufacturers Association. The essential flaw in the rule was that it not only bound the USEPA in its enforcement activities, but also purported to prevent other parties from recovering response costs and contributions to response costs. *Kelley v. E.P.A.*, 15 F.3d 1100 (D.C. Cir. 1994); rehearing denied, 25 F.3d 1088 (D.C. Cir. 1994); *cert. denied,* (No. 94-752, January 17, 1995). However, the Court said that the USEPA was free to use the principles of the rule in its own enforcement policy. In 1995, the USEPA and Department of Justice issued a policy memorandum providing guidance on the exercise of its enforcement discretion and containing principles consistent with the rule. 60 Fed. Reg. 63517, Dec. 11, 1995.

In 1995, Congress adopted the Clinger-Cohen Asset Conservation Act which reinstated the USEPA's lender liability rule retroactive to its original date. Congress also amended Section 9601(20) of CERCLA to correspond to the original lender liability rule. As amended, the exemption protects secured creditors from the USEPA and also other parties seeking to recover response costs and contributions to response costs. Since then, lender liability has subsided as a problem because most lenders have established procedures consistent with the new exemption and the rule. Lenders continue to obtain Phase I and Phase II environmental site assessment reports, but primarily to verify the value of their collateral.

In 1997, the USEPA and the Department of Justice published a clarification that withdrew the 1995 enforcement policy and said that the lender liability rule would be used as a guidance in interpreting the amended secured creditor exemption. 62 Fed. Reg. 36424, July 7, 1997.

The Asset Conservation Act also amended RCRA to protect secured lenders as owners and operators of underground storage tanks.

An example of a state law adopting the same principles as the CERCLA lender liability rule is 13 NJSA § 58: 10-23g-4, enacted in New Jersey in May 1993.

2. Fiduciary Liability

The Clinger-Cohen Asset Conservation Act limited the liability of fiduciaries to the assets held in fiduciary capacity including trustee, executors, administrator, custodian, guardian, receiver, conservators, committee of estate of incapacitated persons, or other capacity deemed similar by the USEPA. However, a fiduciary may be liable (1) for negligent conduct that contributes to a release or threat of a release; (2) for conduct or ownership other than in fiduciary capacity; (2) for any fiduciary relationship or transaction structured to evade liability for a release or threatened release; or (4) if the fiduciary's compensation exceeds customary or reasonable compensation. 42 U.S.C. § 9607 (n).

O. Parent Corporation Liability

Parent corporations are not ordinarily responsible under CERCLA for environmental liabilities of their subsidiaries. However, liability can be imposed on a parent corporation by piercing the corporate veil between the parent and its subsidiary. *Joslyn Manufacturing Corp. v. T.L. James & Co.*, 893 F.2d 80 (5th Cir. 1990). In addition, some courts held that liability could be imposed on a parent without piercing the corporate veil if the parent was found to be an "operator" of the subsidiary's facilities. *U.S. v. Kayser-Roth Corp.*, 724 F. Supp. 15 (D. R.I. 1989), aff'd 910 F.2d 24 (1st Cir. 1990), *cert. denied,* 498 U.S. 1084.

The U.S. Supreme Court held that liability can be imposed under both the "veil piercing" and "operator" concepts. If a claimant seeks to impose derivative liability on a parent corporation under the *respondeat superior* theory, the claimant must prove the elements required to pierce the corporate veil between the parent and its subsidiary. If a claimant seeks to impose liability on a parent because of its own direct conduct as an operator of a subsidiary's facility, the claimant need not pierce the corporate veil but must prove that the parent operated the subsidiary's facility. *U.S. v. Bestfoods Inc.*, 524 U.S. 51, 118 S. Ct.1876 (1998). Two passages from the majority opinion of Justice David Souter are significant:

> "An operator is simply someone who directs the workings of, manages, or conducts the affairs of a facility. To sharpen the definition for purposes of CERCLA's concern

with environmental contamination, an operator must manage, direct, or conduct operations specifically related to pollution, that is, operations having to do with the leakage or disposal of hazardous waste, or decisions about compliance with environmental regulations."

"Activities that involve the facility but which were consistent with the parent's investor status, such as monitoring of the subsidiary's performance, supervision of the subsidiary's finance and capital budget decisions, and articulation of general policies and procedures, should not give rise to direct liability. [citation omitted]. The critical question is whether, in degree and detail, actions directed to the facility by an agent of the parent alone are eccentric under accepted norms of parental oversight of a subsidiary's facility."

Applying *Bestfoods* analysis, a federal appeals court imposed "veil piercing" liability on a parent corporation in *Carter-Jones Lumber v. LTV Steel Co.,* 237 F.3d 745 (6th Cir. 2001).

P. Officer, Director and Individual Shareholder Liability

Officers and directors of a corporation are not ordinarily subject to CERCLA liabilities of a corporation. However, they can become liable by engaging in the activities of an operator or an arranger for disposal.

In early decisions, the courts imposed liability on individuals who were a CEO, director and the sole or a majority shareholder of a corporation by using "operator" analysis. The facts showed that they were personally involved in corporate activities including day to day decisions involving environmental matters. *New York v. Shore Realty,* 759 F.2d 1032 (2nd Cir. 1985); *FMC Corp. v. Aero Industries, Inc.* 998 F.2d 842 (10th Cir. 1993).

Some courts also imposed liability on individuals who were a CEO and major shareholder and supervised overall operations. The courts would not allow such an individual to escape liability because the actual tasks were delegated to junior managers or employees. *Control Data Corp. v. S.C.S.C. Corp,*, 53 F.3d 930 (8th Cir. 1995); *Marriott Corp. v. Simkins Industries, Inc.*, 929 F. Supp. 396 (S.D. Fla. 1996); *Nutra Sweet Co. v. X-L Engineering Corp.*, 933 F. Supp. 1409 (N.D. Ill. 1996). See also *U.S. v. Carolina Transformer Co.*, 978 F.2d 832 (4th Cir. 1992).

On the other hand, the Seventh Circuit held that the president and majority shareholder and a vice president would not be liable unless the plaintiff could prove they were personally involved in a PCB spill rather than on a basis of *respondeat superior. Sidney S. Arst v. Pipefitters Welfare Educ. Fund,* 25 F. 3d 417 (7th Cir. 1994).

The Third Circuit held that individuals who were the sole officers, directors and shareholders would not be liable merely because they supervised and participated in the day to day corporate activities. However, they would be liable if they were aware of and controlled environmental decisions, even though they did not personally participate in a specific decision that resulted in liability. *U.S. v. USX Corp.*, 68 F. 3d 811 (3d Cir. 1995).

The Eighth Circuit imposed operator liability on an individual who was not an officer, director or shareholder because he served as a director of operations and was personally involved in environmental activities including waste disposal that resulted in the liability. *U.S. v. Gurley*, 43 F.3d 1188 (8th Cir. 1994). The individual was unsuccessful in an argument that he acted at the direction of his father who was the president and principal shareholder.

Although the issue involved liability of a parent corporation rather than an individual, the analysis of operator liability by the U.S. Supreme Court in its *Bestfoods* decision has been influential in subsequent cases involving operator liability of officers, directors and individual shareholders. *U.S. v. Bestfoods, Inc.*, 524 U.S. 51, 118 S.Ct. 1876 (1998).

Since the *Bestfoods* decision, two Circuit Courts of Appeal have applied its analysis to the liability of an individual officer, director and shareholder. The Sixth Circuit imposed arranger liability on a president and sole shareholder who personally participated in sales of PCB-contaminated transformers in transactions found to be disposal arrangements. *Carter-Jones Lumber v. Dixie Distributing*, 166 F.3d 840 (6th Cir. 1999). The Seventh Circuit held that a president and principal shareholder was not subject to operator liability based on direction of general operations, but could be liable if he supervised day to day environmental operations such as negotiating waste contracts or directing where wastes were to be dumped. *Browning-Ferris Industries v. Ter Maat*, 195 F.3d 953 (7th Cir. 1999).

On remand, the U.S. District Court imposed joint operator liability of $40 million on Richard Ter Maat based on findings that he exerted control over the day-to-day operations over the corporate landfill; abandoned the landfill site without closure; and intentionally diverted funds from and bankrupted the corporation which operated the landfill.

To be free of liability, directors and shareholders should limit their activities to those appropriate for directors and shareholders. They should not supervise or participate in day to day environmental operations. They should also refrain from any action that diverts funds from environmental compliance or prevents environmental compliance.

Q. Successor Liability

If a corporation acquires another corporation by merging the acquired corporation into itself, the acquiring and surviving corporation succeeds by operation of law to all liabilities of the merged corporation including CERCLA liabilities. *NJDEP v. Ventron Corp.*, 94 N.J. 473, 468 A.2d 150 (1983); *Smith Land and Improvement Corporation v. Celotex Corporation*, 851 F.2d 86 (3d Cir. 1988); *U.S. v. Crown Roll Leaf Inc.*, 29 ERC 2018 (D. N.J. 1987); *Anspec Co. v. Johnson Controls, Inc.*, 922 F.2d 1240 (6th Cir. 1991).

If a corporation acquires a business from another corporation and assumes all its liabilities, the acquirer may be responsible for environmental liabilities of the acquired business even as to a plant sold some years previously. *Philadelphia Electric Co. v. Hercules*, 762 F.2d 303 (3d Cir. 1985), cert den. 474 U.S. 980 (1985).

If a corporation acquires assets of a business and declines to assume liabilities in a good faith arm's length transaction, it should not be responsible for the seller's CERCLA liabilities. *North Shore Gas Co. v. Salomon Inc.*, 152 F.3d 642 (7th Cir. 1998); *U.S. v. Mexico Feed & Grains*, 980 F.2d 478 (8th Cir. 1992). However, some courts have imposed successor liability under CERCLA using an expanded de facto merger doctrine. *In re Acushnet River and New Bedford Harbor Proceedings*, 712 F. Supp. 1010 (D. Mass. 1989); *Philadelphia Electric Co.*, supra; *Louisiana-Pacific Corp. v. Asarco, Inc.*, 909 F.2d 1260 (9th Cir. 1990).

A substantial continuity test has also been used to impose successor liability. *B.F. Goodrich v. Betkoski*, 99 F.3d 505 (2d Cir. 1996); *U.S. v. Carolina Transformer Co.*, 978 F.2d 832 (4th Cir. 1992); *New York v. Westwood Squibb*, 62 F. Supp. 2d 1035 (W.D.N.Y. 1999); aff'd 964 F.2d 85 (2d Cir. 1992).

The federal courts are divided as to whether successor liability should be determined by the customary application of state law or by a so-called "federal common law" that some courts used to impose liability when state law may not have done so. *North Shore Gas Co. v. Salomon Inc.*, 152 F. 3d 642 (7th Cir. 1998) and cases cited therein.

R. Indemnification

Liability for response costs under CERCLA cannot be assigned or otherwise transferred. 42 U.S. § 9607(e). However, the courts have held that indemnification agreements against liability are not contrary to this restriction and may be valid and enforceable if they meet appropriate requirements for such agreements. See, e.g., *Harley-Davidson, Inc. v. Minstar, Inc.*, 41 F.3d 341 (7th Cir. 1994) and cases cited therein.

There are numerous court decisions on contractual indemnification provisions. In several cases, the agreement was made before the enactment of CERCLA and a key issue was whether the parties could have intended that CERCLA liability be covered by the indemnification provisions. The courts also considered other issues such as choice of the applicable state law; the duration and scope of the indemnification provisions; and limitations on the enforceability of indemnification provisions.

For example, the Third Circuit declined to enforce a pre-CERCLA indemnification provision because it could find no clear and unmistakeable intent to indemnify against CERCLA response costs which were unknown when the contract was signed. *Beazer East, Inc. v. Mead Corp.*, 34 F.3d 206 (3d Cir. 1994). However, the Seventh Circuit and Fifth Circuit found pre-CERCLA indemnification provisions to be sufficiently clear to be enforceable. *Kerr-McGee Chemical v. Lefton Iron*, 14 F.3d 321 (7th Cir. 1994); *Joslyn Mfg. Co. v. Koppers Co., Inc.*, 40 F.3d 750 (5th

Cir. 1994). See also *Smith Kline Beecham Corp. v. Rohm & Haas Co.*, 89 F.3d 154 (3d Cir. 1996).

The Seventh Circuit held that the expiration of a seller's two year indemnification provision against breaches of warranties regarding environmental liabilities did not transfer seller's pre-sale environmental liabilities to the buyer and did not prevent the buyer from seeking contributions to response costs under CERCLA. *PMC, Inc. v. Sherwin-Williams*, 151 F.3d 610 (7th Cir. 1998). The Second Circuit reached a contrary conclusion, although it found that only the liabilities expressly mentioned in the indemnification provision were transferred upon its expiration. *Schiavone v. Pearce*, 79 F.3d 248 (2nd Cir. 1996).

Provisions in a Bill of Sale and Assignment and a Restated Assumption Agreement were effective to transfer all CERCLA obligations related to the business and operations of a battery division sold to a buyer including seller's liabilities for facilities of the battery division previously sold to other buyers and seller's liabilities for wastes at dump sites where both seller and buyer previously sent wastes for disposal. *GNB Battery v. Gould, Inc.*, 65 F.3d 617 (7th Cir. 1995).

A seller's indemnity of a buyer for all obligations, responsibilities and liabilities, costs and expenses related to environmental hazards associated with the sale of a lead smelting facility was held to include liability as an arranger for disposal of hazardous substances at an offsite location where a supplier to the smelting facility had performed battery breaking activities. *Taracorp, Inc. v. NL Industries, Inc.*, 73 F.3d 738 (7th Cir. 1996). In reaching its decision, the Seventh Circuit contrasted the indemnity language with narrower language used by the same seller and buyer in a contemporaneous sale of another lead smelting facility for which the language covered only environmental hazards or contamination located at, on, or near the facility.

In a decision based on Delaware law, the Fifth Circuit allowed a buyer to assert contribution claims under CERCLA and held that contractual indemnity provisions given by the buyer to the seller were unenforceable because they failed to state expressly that the indemnity included the consequences of the seller's own negligence. *Fina, Inc., v. ARCO*, 200 F.3d 266 (5th Cir. 2000). In another decision in the same case based on Texas law, the court held that an indemnity provision did not extend to strict liability claims because they were not expressly mentioned. *Fina, Inc. v. ARCO*, supra.

S. Settlements with the USEPA

Faced with strict retroactive joint and several liability for very large amounts and no effective rights to obtain early review of the USEPA's actions, PRPs have almost always been forced to "settle" with the USEPA. In general, a settlement with the USEPA has meant signing a standard agreement prepared by the USEPA containing extensive obligations and few rights for the PRP. In 1986, Congress amended CERCLA to add provisions relating to settlement with the USEPA. 42 U.S.C. § 9622.

The amended provisions encourage the USEPA to enter into settlement agreements with PRPs, but leave the decision to its discretion. As a small element of pressure to settle, the USEPA must give written notice to the PRPs of a decision not to use settlement procedures. However, the decision is not subject to judicial review. 42 U.S.C. § 9622.

The USEPA is authorized to make "mixed funding" settlement agreements in which PRPs agree to remediate an NPL site and the USEPA agrees to finance and reimburse some of the costs attributable to nonsettling PRPs and to "orphan shares." 42 U.S.C. § 9622(b). The USEPA makes "mixed funding" agreements, although sparingly. A factor which the USEPA considers before making a "mixed funding" agreement is whether it has a good chance to recover its reimbursement payments from nonsettling PRPs.

The USEPA is authorized to provide a covenant not to sue to a PRP which is a party to an agreement settling liability under CERCLA, including future liability. The covenant not to sue may limit the PRP's future liability to the same proportion as that established in the original settlement agreement. 42 U.S.C. § 9622(c)(1).

Settlement agreements between the USEPA and a PRP may be entered as a consent decree with the appropriate federal district court. Consistent with the compromise nature of a settlement, the USEPA need not make any finding regarding an imminent or substantial endangerment to the public health or environment because a PRP otherwise willing to settle would often be compelled to contest such a finding. The consent decree is also not to be construed to be an acknowledgment by the PRPs that the release or threatened release constitutes an imminent and substantial endangerment to the public health or welfare or the environment. The USEPA may also fashion a consent decree so that it will not be considered an admission of liability for any purpose. 42 U.S.C. § 9622(d).

Notice to the public and an opportunity for public comments is required before a final judgment is entered. The Department of Justice representing the USEPA must file with the court any written comments, views or allegations relating to the proposed judgment. The Department of Justice may withdraw or withhold its consent to the proposed judgment if the comments, views, and allegations disclose facts or considerations which indicate the proposed judgment is inappropriate, improper, or inadequate. 42 U.S.C. § 9622(d)(2).

The USEPA also has discretionary authority to prove a covenant not to sue to any person concerning liability under CERCLA, including future liability, resulting from a release or threatened release of a hazardous substance addressed by a response action, whether the action is offsite or onsite, if each of several conditions are met. The covenant not to sue must be in the public interest (based on several factors) and expedite response action consistent with the NCP. The covenant not to sue may be granted only to a person in full compliance with a consent decree for a response action approved by the USEPA. It may not take effect concerning future liability until the USEPA certifies that the remedial action has been completed in accordance with the requirements of CERCLA. 42 U.S.C. § 9622(f).

The USEPA has traditionally required "reopener" provisions in covenants not to sue. The USEPA is entitled to reopen if new information reveals a release or threatened release arising out of conditions not previously known. 42 U.S.C. § 9622(f)(6)(A). The USEPA has authority to omit this reopener provision in extraordinary circumstances. The USEPA may also negotiate for a right to reopen if new information reveals that the remedy selected for an NPL site is proving to be ineffective.

Some authors have correctly said that the reopener provisions mean that any settlement with the USEPA is illusory. However, the USEPA requires so much investigation and remediation at NPL sites over such lengthy time periods that exercise of reopener rights is rare. However, the author recommends that PRPs establish programs to monitor long term future use of a remediated facility. Based on the lesson of Love Canal, if the USEPA or other government officials decide to authorize use of the site for purposes that may create hazards, the PRPs should act decisively to prevent such use.

The USEPA is authorized to make expedited *de minimis* settlements with final and unconditional covenants not to sue. These settlements may be made with (1) PRPs responsible for hazardous substances at a facility that are minimal both in amount and hazardous effects in comparison to other hazardous substances at the facility and (2) PRPs responsible as owner of real property in which a facility is located but which did not conduct or permit the generation, transportation, storage, treatment or disposal of any hazardous substance at the facility or contribute to the release or threat of release of any hazardous substance at the facility through any action or omission. However, a real property owner is not entitled to a *de minimis* settlement if it purchased the real property with actual or constructive knowledge that it was used for the generation, transportation, storage, treatment, or disposal of any hazardous substances. 42 U.S.C. § 9622(g).

The USEPA also makes expedited settlements with *de micromis* parties who contributed even less hazardous substances to a site than *de minimis* parties. These contributors of miniscule amounts pay modest cash settlements in return for an immediately effective covenant not to sue with only limited reservations of rights and reopener rights. The settlement provides contribution protection under 42 U.S.C. §§ 9613(b) and 9622(g)(5).

Settlements by the USEPA relating to any facility where the total response costs exceed $500,000 (excluding interest) must have the prior written approval of the U.S. Department of Justice. Any person who resolves its liability to the United States by such a settlement is not liable for contribution claims regarding matters addressed in the settlement. 42 U.S.C. § 9622(h). This "sweeping power" to grant protection from contribution claims is an important incentive to settle with the USEPA. *Akzo Coatings Inc. v. Aigner Corp.*, 30 F.3d 761 (7th Cir. 1994). However, the scope of contribution protection is subject to review and can be set aside if excessive. *Kelley v. Wagner*, 930 F. Supp. 293 (E.D. Mich. 1996); *Waste Management v. City of York*, 910 F. Supp. 1035 (M.D., Pa. 1995).

At least 30 days before a settlement may become final, notice of the proposed settlement must be published in the Federal Register for public comments. The settlement may be withdrawn if the comments disclose facts or considerations indicating that it is inappropriate, improper or inadequate. 42 U.S.C. § 9622(i).

A PRP which is a party to an administrative order or consent decree and which fails or refuses to comply is subject to civil penalties. 42 U.S. § 9622(l). The USEPA customarily recites the civil penalties in the order or decree and related them to the commitments to perform response actions, including time schedules.

The USEPA has published several directives, guidance documents and forms on its settlement policies. Among the relatively recent publications are the following:

Model Administrative Order on Consent for CERCLA Remedial Investigation/Feasibility Study, OSWER Directive 9835.3-1A, Jan. 30, 1990

Model CERCLA RD/RA Consent Decree, 56 Fed. Reg. 30996, July 8, 1991

Streamlined Approaches for Settlement with De Minimis Waste Contributors, OSWER Directive 9834.7-1D, July 30, 1993

Guidance on CERCLA Settlements with De Minimis Waste Contributors, July 30, 1993

Guidance on CERCLA Settlements with De Micromis Waste Contributors, July 30, 1993

Guidance on Agreements with Prospective Purchasers of Contaminated Property, EPA, OSWER, May 24, 1995.

Model CERCLA Section 107 Consent Decree for Recovery of Past Response Costs, 60 Fed. Reg. 62446, Dec. 6, 1995

Model CERCLA Section 122(h)(1) Agreement for Recovery of Past Response Costs, 60 Fed. Reg. 62452, Dec. 6, 1995

Revised Model CERCLA Section 122(g)(4) De Minimis Contributor Consent Decree and Administrative Order on Consent, 60 Fed. Reg. 62849, Dec. 7, 1995

Expediting Requests for the Prospective Purchaser Agreements, EPA, Office of Site Remediation Enforcement (OSRE) (Oct. 1, 1999).

Support of Regional Efforts to Negotiate Prospective Purchaser Agreements at Superfund Sites and Clarification of PPA Guidance, OSRE (Jan. 10, 2001).

T. Brownfields Programs

Responding to widely praised state initiatives to remediate and restore contaminated properties to productive use, the USEPA took several steps during the 1990s under its Superfund Administrative Reform and Brownfields Initiative Programs. The USEPA describes brownfields as abandoned, idled or underused industrial and commercial properties where real or perceived contamination complicates expansion or redevelopment.

The USEPA published a Guidance on Agreements with Prospective Purchasers of Contaminated Property, 60 Fed. Reg. 34792, July 3, 1995. The Guidance restated the USEPA's policy to consider agreements that provide covenants not to sue prospective purchasers of contaminated property, thus encouraging its redevelopment or reuse. The Guidance said that the USEPA will consider such an agreement if it results in either (1) a substantial direct benefit to the USEPA in terms of cleanup actions or funds for cleanup actions or (2) a lesser direct benefit to the USEPA coupled with a substantial indirect benefit to the community in terms of cleanup, creation of jobs, development of property, and the like. The USEPA also published a Model Prospective Purchase Agreement. The Guidance also applies to prospective tenants and others who wish to operate contaminated property.

An early example of a prospective purchaser agreement enabled Boliden to purchase sulfuric acid and other chemical plants at Copperhill, Tennessee without risk of responsibility for major copper mining operations that were historically conducted on a large property which included the chemical plants. Boliden made costly commitments to provide benefits to the USEPA.

A current example is a proposed prospective purchaser agreement enabling The Nature Conservancy to acquire the Palmyra Atoll, a group of coral islets 680 acres in extent located in the Pacific Ocean, to preserve it as a wildlife refuge. The purchaser, a major environmental organization, will pay $10,000 to the USEPA and commit to manage the atoll to protect its conservation values in cooperation with the U.S. Fish and Wildlife Service.

The USEPA has also provided comfort letters to prospective purchasers about properties such as those listed in the CERCLIS database if it was unlikely that any response actions would be taken.

The USEPA issued an OSWER Memorandum dated November 14, 1996 on Interim Approaches for Regional Relations with State Voluntary Cleanup Programs. The Memorandum seeks to coopt the state programs by proposing that the states enter into a Memorandum of Agreement (MOA) in which the states would agree to include a number of procedural and enforcement requirements in their voluntary programs in return for an assurance that the USEPA would not take enforcement action under CERCLA against persons responsible for sites remediated under the programs. The states have been reluctant to sign an MOA because the procedures outlined in the Memorandum are burdensome. Of the states that have signed MOAs, some negotiated changes of the terms proposed by the USEPA to reduce their harmful effects.

During the 1990s, the USEPA established a well-publicized program called its Brownfields Economic Redevelopment Initiative followed by a Brownfields Action Agenda. A major part of this Agenda was the awarding of Brownfields Assessment Demonstration Projects. Centerpieces of the Brownfields Initiative are Brownfields Showcase Communities. The USEPA invited statements of interest to become model brownfields communities. 62 Fed. Reg. 44274, Aug. 20 1997.

In 1997, Congress amended the Internal Revenue Code to allow environmental cleanup costs incurred before December 31, 2001 to be deducted as business expenses in the year incurred rather than capitalized. However, this treatment was limited to pilot areas, high poverty rate areas, empowerment zones and enterprise communities. Thus, the favorable tax treatment in Code Section 198 had limited effectiveness. In December 2000, Congress extended the deadline to January 1, 2004 and amended Section 198 of the Internal Revenue Code to expand the definition of eligible sites to include sites throughout the nation.

Congress adopted the Small Business Liability Relief and Brownfields Revitalization Act of 2001 which provides extensive funding for environmental activities related to "brownfields" sites. Some of the funds will pay for states to expand their lists of contaminated sites and to adopt systems by which environmental groups can require assessments of properties to determine whether they should be listed as brownfields. Other funds are available if a state will enter into an agreement with the USEPA to add further cleanup planning and review procedures including further provisions for notice and opportunities for environmental groups and others to object to cleanup plans. Public Law No. 107-118, 115 Stat. 2356.

The Brownfields Act added a new *de minimis* exemption from arranger or transporter liability for response costs under CERCLA for a person who can demonstrate that the total amount of material containing hazardous substances at a facility for which he, she or it is responsible is less than 110 gallons of liquid materials or 200 pounds of solid materials and all or part of the disposal, treatment or transport occurred before April 1, 2001. A nongovernmental party bringing a contribution action has the burden of proof that the 110 gallon or 200 pound quantities were exceeded or that disposal, treatment of transport occurred on or after April 1, 2001. 42 U.S.C. § 9607(a)(o).

The Brownfields Act added a new municipal solid waste exemption from arranger liability for response costs under CERCLA for a person who can demonstrate that he, she or it is (1) owner, operator or lessee of residential property; (2) is a business entity that employed an average of less than 100 full-time individuals for the past 3 years and is a small business concern as defined in the Small Business Act (15 U.S.C. § 631 *et seq.*); or (3) is an Internal Revenue Code § 501(c)(3) organization that employed not more than 100 persons during the past year. A person claiming the exemption must also show that the exemption applies to all its municipal solid waste at the facility. A nongovernmental party may not bring a contribution action against an owner, operator or lessee of residential property with respect to municipal solid waste at a facility and has the burden of proof in a contribution action to prove that small business or § 501(c)(3) organization exemptions are not met. 42 U.S.C. § 9607(a)(p).

The Brownfields Act amended the definition of an innocent landowner to add to the conditions required to assert the innocent landowner defense. 42 U.S.C. § 9607(35). The Brownfields Act also added a new provision stating that an owner of contiguous property will not be considered to be an owner or operator of a facility if it complies with several conditions. 42 U.S.C. § 9607(g).

The Brownfields Act provides a list of due diligence and cooperation requirements to qualify as a bona fide prospective purchaser of brownfields property. 42 U.S.C. § 9607(40). It also grants to the USEPA a "windfall lien" against a facility for which it has unrecovered response costs in amount equal to the increased fair market value of the property attributable to the response action at the time of sale over its fair market value before the response action was initiated. 42 U.S.C. § 9607(r).

Several recent articles have indicated disappointment with the Brownfields Act. The Act is likely to make brownfields properties more difficult to sell to purchasers seeking to remediate and restore them to productive use.

U. Release Notification Requirements and Reportable Quantities

As stated earlier, any person in charge of a vessel or facility is required by CERCLA to report to the National Response Center any release of a reportable quantity (RQ) of a hazardous substance. The Center's telephone numbers are 1-800-424-8802 and 1-202-426-2675. The RQ for any hazardous substance is one pound unless the USEPA sets a different RQ in its regulations under CERCLA or there is a different RQ under the CWA. 42 U.S.C. § 9602 to 9604.

The USEPA has adopted regulations designating lists of hazardous elements, compounds and wastes as hazardous substances subject to the notification requirements. 40 C.F.R. § 302.4 and Table 302.4. A RCRA solid waste, which is not excluded as a hazardous waste under 40 C.F.R. § 261.4(b), is subject to the notification requirements if it exhibits any of the characteristics (ignitability, corrosivity, reactivity or leaching procedure toxicity) identified in 40 C.F.R. § 261.20 to.24.

The RQs listed in Part 302.4 range from 1 to 5,000 pounds, except those set for radionuclides which range from 0.001 to 1,000 Curies. The RQs for non-listed hazardous substances are set at (1) 100 pounds for hazardous substances other than radionuclides, (2) 1 Curie for radionuclides, and (3) the RQ of the hazardous substance in a solid waste that causes it to be a characteristic hazardous waste.

The regulations exempt from the notification requirements certain naturally occurring releases and permitted releases. Limited reporting obligations apply to certain continuous and stable releases. 40 C.F.R. § 302.8.

The USEPA enforces the notification requirements strictly. For example, in October 2000, it imposed penalties of $37,830 on Apache Nitrogen Products, Inc. of Benson, Arizona for an accidental release of 100 pounds of nitrogen dioxide that it failed to report promptly and also required Apache to contribute $98,000 to fund a supplemental environmental improvement project.

V. Bankruptcy Enforcement

Enforcement of CERCLA against the estate in bankruptcy of a PRP is subject to limitations imposed by the Bankruptcy Code. 11 U.S.C. § 101 *et* seq.

When a petition in bankruptcy is filed, an automatic stay applies to lawsuits and other actions to enforce debts and to create, perfect or enforce liens against the bankrupt debtor. If the USEPA, a state agency or a private claimant has an unsecured pre-petition claim to recover response costs or contributions to response costs, it must file the claim and accept such pro rata payment, if any, as may be distributed to unsecured creditors. These debt claims are allowed by Section 7 of the Bankruptcy Code or by order of the Bankruptcy Court if the debtor is reorganized pursuant to Chapter 11. *Matter of Reading Co.*, 115 F.3d 1111 (3d Cir. 1997).

If the USEPA perfected a lien under CERCLA before the petition was filed, the USEPA will have a secured claim against the property against which the lien was recorded and can recover response costs to the extent the property has realizable value after satisfying the amounts owed to any previously perfected liens or security interests. If the USEPA, obtained a judgment lien before the petition was filed, it would also have a secured claim.

On the other hand, the overall obligation to comply with the environmental laws is not excused by the Bankruptcy Code. For example, a debtor in possession, receiver or trustee in bankruptcy must comply with a cleanup decree or other order issued under CERCLA and the order is not discharged by the Bankruptcy Code. *Ohio v. Kovacs*, 469 U.S. 274, 85 L.Ed 2d 649 (1985); *In re Chateaugay*, 944 F2d 997 (2d Cir. 1991); *In re CMC Heartland Partners*, 966 F.2d 1143 (7th Cir. 1992); *In re Towrico Electronics Inc.*, 8 F.3d 146 (3d Cir. 1993). However, lack of money may make it difficult or impossible for representatives of a bankrupt estate to comply with an order.

If the USEPA, a state agency or private party incurs response costs to remediate property owned or operated by a bankrupt estate during the administration, it can seek administrative priority for the claim as actual, necessary costs and expenses of preserving the estate. The claimant must show that the response costs were necessary to preserve the estate. If successful, the claim will be paid with other administrative expenses before distributions are made to general creditors. Administrative priority has been granted to post-petition cleanup costs in several cases. *In re Smith Douglass Inc.*, 856 F.2d 12 (4th Cit. 1988); *In re Chateaugay*, supra; *In re Hemingway Transport Inc.*, 993 F.2d 915 (1st Cir. 1993); *Pennsylvania v. Conroy*, 24 F.3d 568 (3d Cir. 1994).

A trustee in possession of real property that is burdensome or of inconsequential value and benefit to the estate is entitled to abandon the property unless the USEPA or a state environmental agency can show that the abandonment would aggravate risk of imminent and indentifiable harm. If the property than reverts to the debtor and the mortgagee does not elect to foreclose, remedy any environmental contamination and sell the property, then possession remains in the debtor subject to any obligations imposed by federal and state environmental laws. *In re Lawrence Corp.*, 239 B.R. 720 (Bkrtcy. D.N.J. 1999); *Midlantic National Bank v. NJDEP*, 474 U.S. 494, 88 L.Ed. 2d 859 (1984); *In re Smith-Douglass Inc.*, supra; *In re Wall Tube*, F.2d 118 (6th Cir. 1987).

W. Citizen Suits

CERCLA authorizes any person to commence a civil action against (a) any other person (including the USEPA and other federal government agencies) for violation of any standard, regulation, requirement, condition or order effective under CERCLA and (2) any officer of the United States (including the USEPA) for failure to perform a nondiscretionary act under CERCLA. The person commencing such a "citizen suit" must give 60 days' prior written notice to the USEPA. 42 U.S.C.§ 9659. *Friends of the Earth v. Laidlaw Environmental*, 528 U.S. 167, 145 L. Ed. 2d 610 (2000).

A person must have standing to commence a citizens suit or it will be dismissed. *Steel Co. v. Citizens for a Better Environment*, 523 U.S. 83, 118 S. Ct. 1003 140 L. Ed. 2d 210 (1998). Affidavits or testimony in support of standing that contain only general covenants, conclusive allegations or speculation are insufficient to show the necessary injury in fact. *Lujan v. National Wildlife Federation*, 497 U.S. 871, 111 L. Ed. 2d 695 (1990); *Lujan v. Defenders of Wildlife*, 504 U.S. 555, 119 L. Ed. 2d 351 (1992). However, relatively general affidavits have been held to be sufficient. *Friends of the Earth v. Laidlaw Environmental*, supra.

Environmental groups and PRPs have commenced civil actions seeking to challenge the USEPA's methods and decisions on remediation of NPL sites. The courts have rejected these actions because they would infringe on the freedom from judicial review granted to the USEPA by 42 U.S.C. § 9613(h). *Schalk v. Reilly*, 900 F.2d 1091 (7th Cir. 1990); cert. den. 498 U.S. 987 (1990).

The citizen suit provisions in CERCLA do not abrogate state sovereign immunity under the Eleventh Amendment to the U.S. Constitution. Thus, a citizen suit against government officials of the State of Connecticut alleging that hazardous substances leaked into their water wells from a state prison was dismissed. *Burnette v. Carothers*, 192 F.3d 52 (2d Cir. 1999).

X. Civil Administrative Penalties

CERCLA provides civil administrative penalties for (1) a violation of the requirement to notify the National Response Center of a release; (2) destruction of records required USEPA regulations; (3) a violation of the financial responsibility regulations; (4) a violation of an order issued pursuant to a settlement agreement providing for response actions and costs; and (5) a failure or refusal to comply with a consent order or settlement agreement relating to a federal facility. 42 U.S.C. § 9609.

The penalties are divided into two classes which appear to overlap because each applies to the same five violations. The Class I civil administrative penalty is not more than $25,000 per violation. The Class II civil administrative is not more than $25,000 per day during which a violation continues. The Class II civil administrative penalty for a second or subsequent violation is not more than $75,000 for each day during which a violation continues. In effect, the penalties mean that any small or medium-sized company that seeks to challenge the USEPA can do so only by assuming serious financial risk that it cannot easily afford to undertake.

Under the Debt Collection Improvement Act of 1996, the USEPA increased the penalties for inflation by 10% in 1998 and 13.6% in 2002. Thus, for example, a penalty of $25,000 is now $31,500.

Y. Claims Against the U.S. Government

A number of lawsuits have been commenced against the U.S. Government because of activities that contaminated property or remedial activities that deprived owners of use of their property. The lawsuits have been commenced in the federal district courts under the Federal Tort Claims Act (FTCA), 28 U.S.C. § 2671 *et seq.* and in the Court of Federal Claims under the Tucker Act 28 U.S.C. § 1346 and other sections, and the Fifth Amendment to the U.S. Constitution. The claimants have found little success in these lawsuits.

To sustain a claim under the FTCA, a claimant must prove that government representatives broke the rules. It is not enough to show that they were wrong,, foolish, high-handed or negligent in the exercise of a discretionary function. *Berkovitz v. U.S.*, 486 U.S. 531 (1988); *U.S. v. Gaubert*, 499 U.S. 135 (1991). Environmental cases illustrate the extent to which the federal courts will reach to protect the federal government. Negligent disposal of trichloroethylene at Walker and Reese Air Force Bases was held within the exception for discretionary actions in *Aragon v. U.S.*, 146 F.3d 819 (10th Cir. 1998); and *Western Greenhouses v. U.S.*, 878 Supp. 917 (N.D. Tex. 1995). In *Aragon*, the court even excused failures to follow environmental practices prescribed in Air Force manuals. The courts often impose punitive damages on private industry for conduct less culpable.

To sustain a claim under the Tucker Act, a claimant must prove that an inverse condemnation (or "taking") occurred and that it is permanent and effectively destroys or impairs the owners' right to use its property. *Loretto v. Teleprompter Manhattan*, 458 U.S. 419 (1982). The courts have said that permanent does not mean forever and that migration of contamination can amount to a "taking" if it amounts to permanent destruction or deprivation of the right to use. The installation of monitoring wells can be a taking. *Hendler v. U.S.*, 951 F.2d 1364 (Fed. Cir. 1991); *Juliano v. Montgomery-Otsego-Scholarie*, 983 F. Supp. 319 (N.D.N.Y. 1997); *McKay v. U.S.*, 199 F.3d 1376 (Fed. Cir. 1999).

Nevertheless, the burden of proving a "taking" case under the Tucker Act is formidable. After years of litigation, including successful appeals to the Federal Circuit, landowners lost their case against the U.S. Government based on the USEPA's installation of 20 monitoring wells and activities on their property to monitor groundwater contamination from a nearby NPL site. *Hendler v. U.S.*, 175 F.3d 1374 (Fed. Cir. 1999). The Federal Circuit upheld the finding by the Court of Federal Claims that no "taking" occurred and also upheld its finding that compensation for a taking, if any, was offset by the benefit to the landowners of the investigation conducted by the USEPA.

Z. Possible Reimposition of the Superfund Tax

The Superfund was well over $3 billion dollars when the excise tax providing its funds expired in 1995. By 2001, it was below $1 billion dollars. Environmentalists are campaigning to reinstate the tax, but have been unwilling to agree to reform CERCLA.

Environmentalists claim that CERCLA uses a "polluter pays" principle. As the reader has seen, CERCLA does not impose liability on polluters as such. Rather, CERCLA imposes retroactive strict liability on owners and operators of property without regard to whether they are or were polluters. Long-time owners and operators may be the polluters, but recent owners or operators are often not the polluters. Prospective purchasers are also not the polluters, but are allowed only a narrow defense to strict liability. CERCLA also imposes liability on arrangers and transporters who may well have been polluters, but many of them have been out of business for years and their liability adds to the "orphan shares" paid by others without regard to fault. Further, the Superfund tax is imposed on producers and users of petroleum, chemical and other products regardless of whether they caused pollution or paid directly to remediate pollution they caused.

CERCLA also encourages lengthy and costly cleanups. Over 1,200 sites were still listed on the NPL in early 2002, many for well over a decade.

Industry groups oppose reimposition of the tax and point out that companies named as potentially responsible parties have been directly paying most of the cost to clean up the NPL sites. They also urge amendments to CERCLA that will enable cleanups to be performed more effectively.

CHAPTER VIII

EMERGENCY PLANNING AND COMMUNITY RIGHT-TO-KNOW ACT

A. Overview

The Emergency Planning and Community Right-to-Know Act (EPCRA), was adopted in 1986 as an amendment creating Title III of CERCLA. Impetus for enactment was provided by two major accidents in foreign countries, i.e., the methyl isocyanate leak at Bhopal, India and the nuclear reactor fire at Chernobyl, Russia. 42 U.S.C. § 11001 *et seq.*

EPCRA required that states establish state emergency response commissions (SERCs), planning districts and local emergency planning committees (LEPCs). EPCRA required that these organizations develop comprehensive emergency response plans including identification of facilities having extremely hazardous substances. 42 U.S.C. §§ 11001-11003. The plans were required to establish methods and procedures to be followed by facility owners and operators and local emergency and medical personnel in responding to releases of extremely hazardous substances. The plans were also required to include procedures for notifying safety officials and the public of releases and personnel training programs and evacuation plans. 42 U.S.C. § 11004-11005.

The states established the SERCs and planning districts. Some states established many LEPCs and other states established as few as one.

EPCRA required the USEPA to publish a list of extremely hazardous substances. The list appears (alphabetically and by CAS numbers) as Appendix A to 40 C.F.R. Part 355. It contains several hundred substances which the USEPA has designated as extremely hazardous with a reportable quantity and threshold planning quantity for each of them. A facility having any of these substances in excess of the specified threshold levels must notify the SERC and LEPC of any release of the substance beyond the boundaries of the facility. The notice requirement, however, does not apply to releases within the limits of federal air and water permits and certain other continuous releases. The notice must include extensive information about the release, anticipated health risks, medical advice and precautions to be taken including evacuation. See 42 U.S.C. § 11004-11005 and 40 C.F.R. Part 355.

Facilities having hazardous chemicals in excess of stated thresholds must provide to the SERC, LEPC and local fire departments a list of such chemicals or copies of the material safety data sheets (MSDS) required by the Occupational Safety and Health Act (the "OSH Act"). These hazardous chemicals are more numerous than those on the list of extremely hazardous chemicals. They include any chemical which presents a physical hazard or health hazard subject to the MSDS disclosure requirements of the OSH Act. Chemicals which are physical hazards include flammables, combustibles, explosives, compressed gases, oxidizers, pyrophors and unstable or water reactive substances. Chemicals which are health hazards include those with acute effects (such as ammonia or chlorine) and also those with chronic effects including carcinogens, teratogens, mutagens, toxins and agents affecting blood, lungs and other organs. There are exemptions, however, for consumer products, foods, drugs, cosmetics, household items, substances used in medical and research facilities and other substances including tobacco products. 42 U.S.C. § 11021.

Facility owners or operators must also annually prepare and submit to the SERC, LEPC, and fire department an inventory of hazardous chemicals, including quantity and location data, and other information. 42 U.S.C. § 11022. In addition, facilities must report annually to the USEPA and state environmental agencies on releases of toxic chemicals that can reasonably be expected to cause adverse human health effects or significant adverse effects on the environment. Subject to quantity exemptions which decline each year, these reports must include permitted emissions of toxic chemicals because the reports will be used by the USEPA to maintain a national toxic chemical inventory and related database available to the public. 42 U.S.C. § 11023.

EPCRA contains general provisions providing rights to withhold trade secret information; requiring provision of information to doctors, nurses and other health professionals; imposing civil and criminal penalties; and providing rights to citizens and state and local government agencies to sue for enforcement and damages.

B. The USEPA's Regulations

1. Extremely Hazardous Substances

a. Emergency Planning

EPCRA requires each LEPC to prepare and review at least annually an emergency response plan including the following:

1. Identification of facilities in the district that are subject to the planning requirements, the routes likely to be used for transportation of listed extremely hazardous substances (EHSs), and other facilities contributing or subjected to additional risk (such as hospitals or natural gas facilities) because of their proximity to the facilities subject to the planning requirements.

2. Methods and procedures to be followed by facility owners and operators and local and emergency personnel to respond to any EHS release.

3. Designation of a community emergency coordinator and facility emergency coordinators.

4. Procedures for providing reliable, effective and timely notification to persons specified in the plan and to the general public that a release has occurred.

5. Methods for determining the occurrence of a release and the area or population likely to be affected.

6. A description of emergency equipment and facilities in the community and at each facility and the persons responsible for them.

7. Evacuation plans including alternative traffic routes.

8. Training programs, including schedules for local emergency response and medical personnel.

9. Methods and schedules for exercising the emergency plan.

The owner or operator of any facility where there is present an amount of an extremely hazardous substance (EHS) equal to or exceeding its threshold planning quantity (TPQ) must notify the SERC that it is subject to the emergency planning requirements. The amount present includes amounts present in mixtures at concentrations greater than 1% by weight. The notification must be provided within 60 days after the facility first becomes subject to the requirements.

NOTE: Most facilities furnished the notice on or before May 17, 1987 which was the initial filing deadline for facilities then subject to the requirements. 40 C.F.R. § 355.30(a) and (b).

The USEPA has provided a list of the substances that it considers to be extremely hazardous in Appendices A and B to 40 C.F.R. Part 355. Appendix A lists the chemicals alphabetically and Appendix B lists them by Chemical Abstract Service numbers. The lists set a reportable quantity and a threshold planning quantity for each substance. The lists include such substances as ammonia, chlorine, hydrogen fluoride and methyl isocyanate that have been involved in serious industrial accidents.

The regulations require the owner to designate a facility representative to participate in the local emergency planning process as a facility emergency response coordinator. The owner or operator must also inform the LEPC of information necessary to develop or implement a local emergency plan and of any relevant changes. The regulations prescribe methods for calculation of TPQs for solids and mixtures.

NOTE: Many manufacturers had programs to provide information and exchange resources with local officials for years before the USEPA's regulations were adopted. For example, some chemical manufacturers had mutual fire fighting arrangements with local fire departments under which the chemical facilities also agreed to help fight local fires, if needed. 40 C.F.R. § 355.40(a), (d) and (e).

b. Release Notification

The owner or operator of any facility at which a hazardous chemical is produced, used or stored must immediately notify the SERC and also the LEPC for any area likely to be affected of any release of (1) a reportable quantity of an EHS listed in 40 C.F.R. Part 355 or a reportable quantity of a hazardous substance listed in 40 C.F.R. § 302, Table 302.4 under CERCLA. The notice must include the following information to the extent known and so long as no delay of emergency response results:

1. Chemical name and identity of the substance
2. Whether the substance is an EHS
3. Estimated quantity released
4. Time and duration of the release
5. Media into which the release occurred
6. Known or anticipated acute or chronic health risks and, where appropriate, advice on medical attention necessary for exposed individuals.
7. Precautions, including evacuation, unless that information is readily available to the community emergency coordinator pursuant to the emergency response plan.
8. Names and telephone numbers of information contact persons.

As soon as practicable, the owner or operator must provide written followup notices as information becomes available about (1) response and containment actions, (2) known or anticipated acute or chronic health risks, and (3) advice regarding medical attention necessary for exposed individuals, where appropriate. 40 C.F.R. § 355.40.

As stated above, the obligation to provide notification of emergency releases applies to any facility which produces, uses or stores a hazardous chemical. For this purpose, a hazardous chemical does not include (1) any food, food additive, color additive, drug or cosmetic regulated by the FDA; (2) any substance present as a solid in a manufactured item to the extent exposure to the substance does not occur under normal use conditions; (3) any substance to the extent used for personal, family or household purposes or is present in the same form and concentration as a product packaged for distribution and use by the general public; (4) any substance to the extent used in a research laboratory, hospital or other medical facility under direct supervision of a technically qualified individual; or (5) any substance to the extent it is used in routine agricultural operations or is a fertilizer held for sale by a retailer to the ultimate customer. 40 C.F.R. § 355.20 (Definition of "hazardous chemical").

A release means any spilling, leaking, pumping, pouring, emitting, emptying, discharging, injecting, escaping, leaching, dumping, or disposing into the environment including the abandonment or discarding of barrels, containers and other closed receptacles. 40 C.F.R. § 355.20.

The emergency release notification requirement does not apply to any release which (i) results in exposure to persons solely within the facility boundaries, (2) is a federally permitted release as defined in CERCLA; (3) is continuous and stable in quantity and rate and meets certain other requirements; (4) is a release of a pesticide product exempt from reporting under CERCLA; (5) is a release not defined as a release in CERCLA; or (6) is a release of certain naturally occurring radionuclides and other radionuclides. 40 C.F.R. § 355.40(a).

c. Civil Penalties

Any person who fails to comply with the emergency release notification requirements is subject to civil penalties up to $31,500 for each violation. For continuing violations, civil penalties up to $31,500 per day may be imposed and, in the case of repeat violations, up to $93,000 per day.

Any person who knowingly and willingly fails to provide the required notification may also be imprisoned for up to two years and fined up to $31,500. For repeat violations, the prison sentence may be up to five years and the fine up to $62,000.

2. Hazardous Chemical Inventories; Community Right-to-Know

a. Material Safety Data Sheet Reporting

The owner or operator of any facility required by the OSH Act to prepare or have available a material safety data sheet (MSDS) for a hazardous chemical which is present at the facility in a quantity at or above the applicable threshold must submit to the SERC, LEPC and fire department either the MSDS for each hazardous chemical or a list of hazardous chemicals for which MSDS are required. The submission must be made within three months after the facility first becomes subject to the requirement. The minimum threshold levels for reporting are (1) the lesser of 500 pounds or the TPQ for the EHS; (2) 75,000 gallons for gasoline in compliant underground storage tanks at a retail gas station; (3) 100,000 gallons for diesel fuel in compliant underground storage tanks at a retail gas station; and (4) 10,000 pounds for other hazardous chemicals.

If the owner or operator furnishes a list, it must thereafter submit the MSDS within 30 days after receiving a request from the LEPC, even if the quantity present at the facility is below the threshold level. 40 C.F.R. § 370.21.

NOTE: Most facilities submitted MSDS or a list on or before October 17, 1990, the initial deadline for facilities then subject to the reporting requirements.

The owner or operator of a facility that has submitted an MSDS must provide revised MSDS to the SERC, LEPC and fire department within three months after discovering significant new information about the chemical. 40 C.F.R. § 370.21(c).

OSHA's requirements for preparing and maintaining MSDS as part of its hazard communication requirements are described in Chapter XV of this book. OSHA's hazard communication regulation is found at 29 C.F.R. § 1910.1200.

The obligation to provide MSDS or a list of hazardous chemicals does not apply to substances excluded from the definition of a hazardous chemical: (1) any food, food additive, color additive, drug or cosmetic regulated by the FDA; (2) any substance present as a solid in a manufactured item to the extent exposure to the substance does not occur under normal use conditions; (3) any substance to the extent used for personal, family or household purposes or is present in the same form and concentration as a product packaged for distribution and use by the general public; (4) any substance to the extent used in a research laboratory, hospital or other medical facility under direct supervision of a technically qualified individuals; or (5) any substance to the extent it is used in routine agricultural operation or is a fertilizer held for sale by a retailer to the ultimate customer. 40 C.F.R. § 370.2.

b. Annual Inventory Reporting

The owner or operator of a facility subject to the reporting requirements must also submit an inventory form annually before March 31 to the SERC, LEPC and fire department. The inventory form must contain Tier I information on hazardous chemicals present at the facility during the previous calendar year in quantities above the threshold levels described earlier. 40 C.F.R. § 370.24(a).

An owner or operator may voluntarily submit Tier II information in lieu of Tier I information. An owner must submit Tier II information within 30 days if requested by the SERC, LEPC or fire department. The owner or operator must also allow on-site inspection by the fire department and inform the fire department of the specific locations of hazardous chemicals at the facility. 40 C.F.R. § 370.25(b), (c) and (d).

For hazardous chemicals that are mixtures of hazardous chemicals, an owner or operator may provide the required information on each component which is a hazardous chemical or on the mixture itself. If reporting is by component, each component present at greater than 1% (or 0.1% if carcinogenic) must be reported. If reporting is of the mixture, the total quantity must be reported. To determine whether the threshold for an EHS has been equalled or exceeded, the owner or operator must aggregate all quantities present at the facility, including those present in mixtures. 40 C.F.R. § 370.28.

c. Public Requests for Information

Any person may obtain an MSDS for a specific facility by written request to the LEPC. If the LEPC does not have the MSDS, it must request the MSDS from the owner or operator of the facility. 40 C.F.R. § 370.30(a). In the author's experience, a requester can save time by requesting the MSDS directly from the facility.

Any person may request Tier II information for a specific facility by written request to the SERC or LEPC. If the SERC or LEPC does not have the information, it must request the owner or operator to submit a Tier II form. If a person wants Tier II information for hazardous chemicals stored at the facility in amounts equal to or less than 10,000 pounds, the request must include a general statement of need. 40 C.F.R. § 370.30(b).

The SERC or LEPC must make available to the requesting person the MSDS or Tier II information in its possession or obtained from the owner or operator, but shall withhold the location of any specific chemical identified in the Tier II Form. 40 C.F.R. § 370.31. Withholding the location is a step intended to deter terrorists and thieves who might otherwise take advantage of the information.

d. The Tier One Inventory Form

The USEPA's regulations provide a Tier One Emergency and Hazardous Substance Inventory Form for submission of Tier I information. An owner or operator may submit a state or local form that contains identical information. 40 C.F.R. § 370.40.

The Tier One Form requires, among other things, that maximum amounts of chemicals be provided, even though the instructions concede that the amount will seem artificially high. Chemicals which present more than one hazard must be reported for each hazard. The Form also requires average daily amounts, the greatest number of days on site, and the general location where each hazard may be found.

The Tier One Form groups hazards into three physical hazard categories and two health hazard categories. The categories are a consolidation of the 23 hazard categories in OSHA's Hazard Communication Standard, 29 C.F.R. § 1910.1200.

Chemicals presenting fire hazards include flammable, combustible liquid, pyrophoric and oxidizer chemicals. Chemicals presenting release of pressure hazards include explosives and compressed gases. Chemicals presenting reactive hazards include unstable reactive, organic peroxide and water reactive chemicals. Chemicals presenting acute health hazards include highly toxic, toxic, irritant, sensitizer and corrosive chemicals. Chemicals presenting chronic health hazards include carcinogens and other chemicals "with an adverse effect with long term exposure."

e. The Tier Two Form

The USEPA's regulations provide a Tier Two Emergency and Hazardous Substance Inventory Form for submission of Tier II information. The Tier Two Form requires the information described earlier as required by the Tier One Form and additional and more specific information describing the chemicals and their storage types, conditions and locations at the facility. Confidentiality may be claimed for the storage locations. 40 C.F.R. § 370.41. A copy of the Tier Two Form appears at the end of this Chapter.

3. Toxic Chemical Release Reporting: Community Right-to-Know

a. Introduction

The USEPA's regulations require annual reporting of releases of toxic chemicals using Form R, or an alternate Form A. The regulations also require suppliers to notify persons to whom they distribute mixtures or trade name products containing toxic chemicals that they contain such chemicals. 40 C.F.R. Part 372. The USEPA has listed the chemicals to which it applies the toxic chemical release reporting requirements in 40 C.F.R. § 372.65.

The USEPA uses the reports to prepare its toxic release inventory (TRI). The TRI is published widely as part of the Toxic Release Inventory System (TRIS) and through publicity releases by the USEPA and campaigns by environmental advocacy organizations.

b. Toxicity Criteria

EPCRA provides toxicity criteria to the USEPA for use in evaluating chemicals for addition to the list of toxic chemicals:

> (A) The chemical is known to cause or can reasonably be anticipated to cause significant adverse acute human health effects at concentration levels that tare reasonably likely to exist beyond facility site boundaries as a result of continuous, or frequently recurring, releases.
>
> (B) The chemical is known to cause or can reasonably be anticipated to cause in human–
>
> (i) cancer or teratogenic effects or
>
> (ii) serious or irreversible–
>
> (I) reproductive dysfunctions,
>
> (II) neurological disorders,
>
> (III) heritable genetic mutations, or
>
> (IV) other chronic health effects,
>
> (C) The chemical is know to cause or can reasonable be anticipated to cause, because of
>
> (i) its toxicity,
>
> (ii) its toxicity and persistence in the environment, or
>
> (iii) its toxicity and tendency to bioaccumulate in the environment, a significant adverse effect on the environment of sufficient seriousness, in the

judgment of the Administrator, to warrant reporting under this section. (42 U.S.C. § 11023(d).

c. Covered Facilities

A facility that meets *all three* of the following criteria for a calendar year is a covered facility for which a report must be filed for that calendar year:

(a) The facility had 10 or more full-time employees

(b) The facility was in one or more of the standard industrial classification (SIC) numbers described below.

(c) The facility manufactured (including imported), processed, or otherwise used any toxic chemical in excess of an applicable threshold quantity described below.

Although SIC codes have been replaced by North American Industry Classification System (NAICS) codes, the USEPA's regulation continues to use the SIC codes published by the U.S. Department of Commerce, Bureau of Census, in effect on January 1, 1987. Any facility in SIC codes 20-39 is a covered facility if (1) it is an establishment with a primary SIC major group or industry codes which are in codes 20-39, or (2) it is a multi-establishment complex where all the establishments have primary SIC major group or industry codes which are in codes 20-39. Facilities in a few other SIC codes are also covered. 40 C.F.R. § 372.22.

d. Reporting Thresholds and Threshold Exemptions

The basic reporting thresholds for toxic chemicals are as follows:

(a) 25,000 pounds of the chemical manufactured (including imported) or processed for the calendar year at the facility.

(b) 10,000 pounds of the chemical otherwise used for the calendar year at the facility.

If more than one threshold applies, an owner or operator must report a toxic chemical if it exceeds any applicable threshold. An owner or operator must add all members of any chemical category listed for reporting and report if the total exceeds the threshold. Chemicals recycled or reused must also be included.

COMMENT: The USEPA's requirement that chemicals recycled or reused be reported is confusing to the public because these chemicals are not released to the environment. 40 C.F.R. § 372.25.

The owner or operator of a facility may apply an alternate threshold of 1,000,000 pounds per year to a chemical if the facility would have an annual reportable amount not exceeding 500 pounds for the combined total quantities (1) released at the facility; (2) disposed within the facility; (3) treated by destruction or conversion at the facility; (4) recovered by recycling at the facility; (5) combusted for energy at the facility; and (6) transferred from the facility to offsite locations for recycle, energy recovery, treatment and/or disposal. An owner or operator who applies the alternate threshold need not report for the chemical, but must submit a certification that the chemical did not exceed the alternate threshold. The owner or operator must also keep records including a copy of the certification and supporting materials, documentation and data. 40 C.F.R. §§ 372.27, 372.95 and 372.10(d).

In late 1999, the USEPA established lower thresholds for chemicals which it said were of special concern because they do not readily biodegrade. Thus, they persist in the environment longer than other chemicals and may bioaccumulate under some circumstances. 40 C.F.R. § 372.28; 64 Fed. Reg. 58,665 (Oct. 29, 1999). These chemicals include mercury and its compounds (10 lbs.); several pesticide precursors (10 or 100 lbs.); PCBs (10 lbs.); several polycyclic aromatic compounds (100 lbs.); and several chlorodioxin and furan congeners (0.1 grams). In 2001, the USEPA added lead and lead compounds (other than stainless steel, brass and bronze alloys) to the list of persistent, bioaccumulative or toxic chemicals with a reporting threshold of 100 pounds.

> *NOTE:* The USEPA reported that data for the year 2000 showed that releases continue to decline. Onsite releases by the mining industry are about half of the total.

The regulations exempt *de minimis* concentrations of toxic chemicals in mixtures from inclusion in calculations of thresholds. With some exceptions, a concentration of a toxic chemical below 1% of a mixture need not be considered. A concentration of carcinogen below 0.1% of a mixture need not be considered. However, these exemptions do not apply to the "special concern" chemicals designated by the USEPA. 40 C.F.R. § 372.38(a).

The regulations exempt toxic chemicals contained in articles when determining an applicable threshold 40 C.F.R. § 372.38(b). The regulations also exempt from threshold calculations chemicals used at a covered facility for the following purposes:

1. Structural components of the facility
2. Routine janitorial or facility grounds maintenance
3. Foods, drugs, cosmetics or other personal items for personal use by employees or other persons at a facility such as those used in a cafeteria, store or infirmary
4. Motor vehicle maintenance
5. Process and noncontact cooling water and compressed and combustion air. 40 C.F.R. § 372.38(c).

The regulations also contain exemptions from the threshold calculations for certain laboratory activities, owners of leased properties, coal extraction facilities, and metal mining overburden. 40 C.F.R. § 372.38.

e. Supplier Notification to Customers

The USEPA's regulations require suppliers of toxic chemicals to notify their customers that the chemicals are subject to the reporting requirements.

The notification requirements apply to any person who owns or operates a facility or establishment that (1) is in SIC codes 20 through 39, (2) manufactures, imports or processes a toxic chemical, and (3) sells or distributes a mixture or trade name product containing the toxic chemical to a covered facility or to a person who may sell or distribute the mixture or trade name product to a covered facility. 40 C.F.R. § 372.45(a).

The notification must be in writing and include:

(1) A statement that the mixture or trade name product contains a toxic chemical or chemicals subject to the reporting requirements of section 313 of Title III of the Superfund Amendments and Reauthorization Act of 1986 and 40 C.F.R. Part 372.

(2) The name of each toxic chemical, and the associated Chemical Abstracts Service registry number of each chemical if applicable, as set forth in § 372.65.

(3) The percent by weight of each toxic chemical in the mixture or trade name product.

The notification must be provided with at least the first shipment to each recipient in each calendar year. A revised notification must be provided with at least the first shipment of any product that is changed to add, remove or change the weight percent of any toxic chemical for which notification was previously provided. If a notifier discovers that a product previously sold or distributed during the calendar year contains a toxic chemical and that the previous notice did not properly identify the toxic chemical or the weight percent in the product, the notifier must furnish a new corrected notification within 30 days of the discovery and identify the prior shipments to which the new notification applies. 40 C.F.R. § 372.45(c).

If a person is required to prepare a material safety data sheet (MSDS) for a product in accordance with the hazard communication regulations of OSHA at 29 C.F.R. § 1910.1200, the notification must be attached to or incorporated in the MSDS. If attached, the notice must contain clear instructions that it must not be detached and that any copying and redistribution of the MSDS must include the notice. 40 C.F.R. § 372.45(c)(5).

COMMENT: Customary practice is to include the notification in the MSDS.

The notification requirements do not apply if a product contains no toxic chemical in excess of the applicable *de minimis* concentration threshold. Notification is also not required if a product is (1) an article as defined in § 372.3, (2) a food, drug, cosmetic, alcoholic beverage, tobacco or tobacco product packaged for distribution to the general public, or (3) a consumer product as defined in the

Consumer Product Safety Act, 15 U.S.C. § 1251 *et seq.* packaged for distribution to the general public. 40 C.F.R. § 372.45(d).

If the specific identity of a toxic chemical in a product is a trade secret, the notice may contain a generic name that is descriptive of the toxic chemical. If the percent by weight composition of the toxic chemical is a trade secret, the notice may state that the chemical is present at a concentration value. The value must be no larger than necessary to protect the trade secret. The regulation gives an example of a toxic chemical present in a product at a concentration of 12% which is reported as being present in a concentration up to 15%. 40 C.F.R. § 372.45(f).

f. Form R

The release reports are filed on Form R (EPA Form 9350-1). Form R can be obtained from the EPA's Document Distribution Center, P.O. Box 12505, Cincinnati, Ohio 45212 and is filed with the EPCRA Reporting Center, P.O. Box 3348, Merrifield, Virginia 22116-3348, Attention: Toxic Chemical Release Inventory. A senior management official must sign the certification that it is true and complete and that amounts and values are based upon reasonable estimates using data available to the preparer. 40 C.F.R. § 372.85(a). A copy of Form R appears at the end of this chapter.

Submitters can use the USEPA's automated TRI reporting software. See http://www.epa.gov/tri/report.htm.

Form R requires extensive information. The substantive information includes the activities and uses of the chemical and the maximum amount on site at any time during the reporting year. The information on releases includes an estimate of total releases in pounds except for dioxin and dioxin-like compounds which must be reported in grams. The basis of the estimate must be indicated for (1) fugitive or nonpoint air emissions, (2) stock or point air emissions, (3) discharges to receiving streams or water bodies including the percent of releases due to stormwater, (4) underground injection on site, and (5) releases to land on site. (The names of receiving streams or water bodies must be provided.) The information must also include the distribution of the chemicals included in the dioxin and dioxin-like compounds category. 40 C.F.R. § 372.85(b)(13), (14) and (15).

Form R requires information on of the toxic chemicals in wastes transferred to offsite locations, including publicly owned treatment works (POTWs). Form R also requires information relating to waste treatment and pollution prevention data. 40 C.F.R. § 372.85(b)(16), (17) and (18).

g. Form A

A Form R need not be filed for any toxic chemical if the annual reportable amount of releases for the reporting year did not exceed 500 pounds and the amount manufactured, processed or otherwise used did not exceed 1.0 million pounds for the reporting year. A certification statement as to those facts on a form which the USEPA calls Form A must be signed by a senior management official and filed with the USEPA. 40 C.F.R. § 372.27 and 372.95. A copy of Form A appears at the end of this chapter.

Form A may not be used for any of the chemicals of special concern designated as such because of their persistence and tendency to bioaccumulate. 40 C.F.R. § 372.27(e).

h. Recordkeeping

Each person subject to the reporting requirements must retain for three years from the date of a submission a copy of each report and all supporting material and documentation. 40 C.F.R. § 372.10.

C. Citizen Suits

EPCRA authorizes so-called citizen suits against owners and operators of facilities for failure to comply with the emergency notification and reporting obligations. Before commencing suit, the plaintiff must give 60 days written notice to the USEPA, the state and the facility owner or operator. The suit may not be commenced if the USEPA has commenced and is diligently pursuing either administrative or court proceedings to enforce compliance or impose a penalty. The plaintiff attorney's fees and costs can be recovered as part of a judgment.

EPCRA also authorizes suits against the USEPA, a state governor or a SERC for failure to implement its provisions including failure to provide access to information or respond to requests for information.

Environmental groups sponsoring citizen suits must show they have standing and that there is a case or controversy to be heard. In 1995, an environmental organization sued Chicago Steel and Pickling Company for failure to file hazardous chemical inventory and toxic chemical release reports and sought to impose fines, recover attorneys fees, and obtain future access to the company's reports and facilities. However, the company submitted the reports during the 60 day notice period. The U.S. Supreme Court held that the organization lacked standing and there was no case or controversy because there was no existing violation and no threat of a future violation. *Steel Co. v. Citizens for a Better Environment*, 573 U.S. 83, 118 S. Ct. 1003 (1998). In a later proceeding, a request by the steel company to recover its attorneys fees was denied.

D. Challenges to Listings in the Toxic Release Inventory

Industry organizations and their members have made several efforts to challenge questionable scientific decisions by the USEPA to list chemical substances in the Toxic Release Inventory. They have had only limited success. The courts defer to the USEPA and decline to review the scientific soundness of its decisions. They have vacated the USEPA's decisions only when it made a mistake of law or acted arbitrarily and capriciously by failing to follow its own methods and procedures. The courts have not been willing to review, much less overrule, decisions that were scientifically arbitrary and capricious.

The USEPA's decisions to list six diisocyanates; polychlorinated alkanes; 3-iodo-2-propynyl butyl carbonate (IPBC) and n-methyl-2-pyrrolidone (NMP) were upheld in spite of efforts to challenge the scientific basis for doing so. However, the court set aside the listing of Bronopol because the USSEPA failed to consider exposure and the listing of 2,6-dimethylphenol (DMP) because the USEPA acted on the basis of undocumented testing that did not satisfy its own guidelines. *Troy Corp. v. Browner*, 120 F.3d 277 (D.C. Cir. 1997); petition for rehearing on IPBC denied 129 F. 3d 1290 (D.C. Cir. 1997).

The USEPA's decision to list nitrate compounds under chronic health effects without considering long term exposure based on their production of health effects that persist past the period of exposure was upheld. In reaching its conclusion, the court declined to consider claims that the USEPA's listing of the nitrate compounds was inconsistent with its listing of certain silanes, brucine and phosphine for their acute effects. *Fertilizer Institute v. Browner*, 163 F.3d 774 (3d Cir. 1998).

In 1998, the Fertilizer Institute challenged the listing of phosphoric acid in 40 C.F.R. § 372.65 on grounds that it did not meet the requirements for listing, including toxicity. The District Court for the District of Columbia held that the USEPA had incorrectly listed phosphoric acid because the USEPA had done so on the basis of environmental effects and not because of toxicity as required by EPCRA. *Fertilizer Institute v. Browner*, No. 98-1067 1999 U.S. Dist. LEXIS 9298 (D.D.C. April 15, 1999). Subsequently, the USEPA delisted phosphoric acid. 65 Fed. Reg. 395552, June 27, 2000.

EXHIBITS

1. Form R - Toxic Chemical Release Inventory Reporting Form

Form Approved OMB Number: 2070-0093

(IMPORTANT: Type or print; read instructions before completing form) Approval Expires: 01/31/2003 **Page 1 of 5**

EPA
United States Environmental Protection Agency

FORM R

TOXIC CHEMICAL RELEASE INVENTORY REPORTING FORM

Section 313 of the Emergency Planning and Community Right-to-Know Act of 1986, also known as Title III of the Superfund Amendments and Reauthorization Act

WHERE TO SEND COMPLETED FORMS: 1. EPCRA Reporting Center, P.O Box 3348, Merrifield, VA 22116-3348, ATTN: TOXIC CHEMICAL RELEASE INVENTORY
2. APPROPRIATE STATE OFFICE (See instructions in Appendix F)

Enter "X" here if this is a revision ☐

For EPA use only

Important: See instructions to determine when "Not Applicable (NA)" boxes should be checked.

PART I. FACILITY IDENTIFICATION INFORMATION

SECTION 1. REPORTING YEAR ________

SECTION 2. TRADE SECRET INFORMATION

2.1 Are you claiming the toxic chemical identified on page 2 trade secret?
☐ Yes (Answer question 2.2; Attach substantiation forms) ☐ No (Do not answer 2.2; Go to Section 3)

2.2 Is this copy ☐ Sanitized ☐ Unsanitized
(Answer only if "YES" in 2.1)

SECTION 3. CERTIFICATION (Important: Read and sign after completing all form sections.)

I hereby certify that I have reviewed the attached documents and that, to the best of my knowledge and belief, the submitted information is true and complete and that the amounts and values in this report are accurate based on reasonable estimates using data available to the preparers of this report.

Name and official title of owner/operator or senior management official:	Signature:	Date Signed:

SECTION 4. FACILITY IDENTIFICATION

4.1 TRI Facility ID Number

Facility or Establishment Name	Facility or Establishment Name or Mailing Address(if different from street address)
Street	Mailing Address
City/County/State/Zip Code	City/State/Zip Code; Country (Non-US)

4.2 This report contains information for: (Important : check a or b; check c or d if applicable)
a. ☐ An entire facility b. ☐ Part of a facility c. ☐ A Federal facility d. ☐ GOCO

4.3 Technical Contact Name — Telephone Number (include area code)

4.4 Public Contact Name — Telephone Number (include area code)

4.5 SIC Code (s) (4 digits) — Primary a. — b. — c. — d. — e. — f.

4.6	Latitude			Longitude		
	Degrees	Minutes	Seconds	Degrees	Minutes	Seconds

4.7 Dun & Bradstreet Number(s) (9 digits)	**4.8** EPA Identification Number (RCRA I.D. No.) (12 characters)	**4.9** Facility NPDES Permit Number(s) (9 characters)	**4.10** Underground Injection Well Code (UIC) I.D. Number(s) (12 digits)
a.	a.	a.	a.
b.	b.	b.	b.

SECTION 5. PARENT COMPANY INFORMATION

5.1 Name of Parent Company NA ☐

5.2 Parent Company's Dun & Bradstreet Number NA ☐

EPA Form 9350-1 (Rev. 01/2001) - Previous editions are obsolete.

Page 2 of 5

EPA FORM R PART II. CHEMICAL-SPECIFIC INFORMATION	TRI Facility ID Number
	Toxic Chemical, Category or Generic Name

SECTION 1. TOXIC CHEMICAL IDENTITY (Important: DO NOT complete this section if you completed Section 2 below.)

1.1	CAS Number (Important: Enter only one number exactly as it appears on the Section 313 list. Enter category code if reporting a chemical category.)
1.2	Toxic Chemical or Chemical Category Name (Important: Enter only one name exactly as it appears on the Section 313 list.)
1.3	Generic Chemical Name (Important: Complete only if Part 1, Section 2.1 is checked "yes". Generic Name must be structurally descriptive.)

1.4 Distribution of Each Member of the Dioxin and Dioxin-like Compounds Category.
(If there are any numbers in boxes 1-17, then every field must be filled in with either 0 or some number between 0.01 and 100. Distribution should be reported in percentages and the total should equal 100%. If you do not have speciation data available, indicate NA.)

	1	2	3	4	5	6	7	8	9	10	11	12	13	14	15	16	17
NA ☐																	

SECTION 2. MIXTURE COMPONENT IDENTITY (Important: DO NOT complete this section if you completed Section 1 above.)

2.1	Generic Chemical Name Provided by Supplier (Important: Maximum of 70 characters, including numbers, letters, spaces, and punctuation.)

SECTION 3. ACTIVITIES AND USES OF THE TOXIC CHEMICAL AT THE FACILITY
(Important: Check all that apply.)

3.1 Manufacture the toxic chemical:	3.2 Process the toxic chemical:	3.3 Otherwise use the toxic chemical:
a. ☐ Produce b. ☐ Import		
If produce or import:	a. ☐ As a reactant	a. ☐ As a chemical processing aid
c. ☐ For on-site use/processing	b. ☐ As a formulation component	b. ☐ As a manufacturing aid
d. ☐ For sale/distribution	c. ☐ As an article component	c. ☐ Ancillary or other use
e. ☐ As a byproduct	d. ☐ Repackaging	
f. ☐ As an impurity	e. ☐ As an impurity	

SECTION 4. MAXIMUM AMOUNT OF THE TOXIC CHEMICAL ONSITE AT ANY TIME DURING THE CALENDAR YEAR

4.1	☐ (Enter two-digit code from instruction package.)	

SECTION 5. QUANTITY OF THE TOXIC CHEMICAL ENTERING EACH ENVIRONMENTAL MEDIUM ONSITE

			A. Total Release (pounds/year*) (Enter range code or estimate**)	B. Basis of Estimate (enter code)	C. % From Stormwater
5.1	Fugitive or non-point air emissions	NA ☐			
5.2	Stack or point air emissions	NA ☐			
5.3	Discharges to receiving streams or water bodies (enter one name per box)				
	Stream or Water Body Name				
5.3.1					
5.3.2					
5.3.3					

If additional pages of Part II, Section 5.3 are attached, indicate the total number of pages in this box ☐
and indicate the Part II, Section 5.3 page number in this box. ☐ **(example: 1,2,3, etc.)**

* For Dioxin or Dioxin-like compounds, report in grams/year

EPA Form 9350-1 (Rev. 01/2001) - Previous editions are obsolete.

** Range Codes: A= 1 - 10 pounds; B= 11- 499 pounds; C= 500 - 999 pounds.

EPA FORM R PART II. CHEMICAL - SPECIFIC INFORMATION (CONTINUED)	TRI Facility ID Number
	Toxic Chemical, Category or Generic Name

SECTION 5. QUANTITY OF THE TOXIC CHEMICAL ENTERING EACH ENVIRONMENTAL MEDIUM ONSITE (Continued)

		NA	A. Total Release (pounds/year*) (enter range code** or estimate)	B. Basis of Estimate (enter code)
5.4.1	Underground Injection onsite to Class I Wells	☐		
5.4.2	Underground Injection onsite to Class II-V Wells	☐		
5.5	Disposal to land onsite			
5.5.1A	RCRA Subtitle C landfills	☐		
5.5.1B	Other landfills	☐		
5.5.2	Land treatment/application farming	☐		
5.5.3	Surface Impoundment	☐		
5.5.4	Other disposal	☐		

SECTION 6. TRANSFERS OF THE TOXIC CHEMICAL IN WASTES TO OFF-SITE LOCATIONS

6.1 DISCHARGES TO PUBLICLY OWNED TREATMENT WORKS (POTWs)

6.1.A Total Quantity Transferred to POTWs and Basis of Estimate

6.1.A.1. Total Transfers (pounds/year*) (enter range code** or estimate)	**6.1.A.2 Basis of Estimate** (enter code)

6.1.B.__ POTW Name

POTW Address

City		State		County		Zip	

6.1.B.__ POTW Name

POTW Address

City		State		County		Zip	

If additional pages of Part II, Section 6.1 are attached, indicate the total number of pages in this box ☐ and indicate the Part II, Section 6.1 page number in this box ☐ (example: 1,2,3, etc.)

SECTION 6.2 TRANSFERS TO OTHER OFF-SITE LOCATIONS

6.2. ___ Off-Site EPA Identification Number (RCRA ID No.)

Off-Site Location Name

Off-Site Address

City		State		County		Zip		Country (Non-US)	

Is location under control of reporting facility or parent company? ☐ Yes ☐ No

* For Dioxin or Dioxin-like compounds, report in grams/year

EPA Form 9350-1 (Rev. 01/2001) - Previous editions are obsolete.

** Range Codes: A = 1 - 10 pounds; B = 11 - 499 pounds; C = 500 - 999 pounds.

EPA FORM R PART II. CHEMICAL-SPECIFIC INFORMATION (CONTINUED)	TRI Facility ID Number
	Toxic Chemical, Category or Generic Name

SECTION 6.2 TRANSFERS TO OTHER OFF-SITE LOCATIONS (Continued)

A. Total Transfers (pounds/year*) (enter range code** or estimate)	B. Basis of Estimate (enter code)	C. Type of Waste Treatment/Disposal/ Recycling/Energy Recovery (enter code)
1.	1.	1. M
2.	2.	2. M
3.	3.	3. M
4.	4.	4. M

6.2.___ Off-Site EPA Identification Number (RCRA ID No.)							
Off-Site location Name							
Off-Site Address							
City		State		County		Zip	Country (Non-US)

Is location under control of reporting facility or parent company? ☐ Yes ☐ No

A. Total Transfers (pounds/year*) (enter range code** or estimate)	B. Basis of Estimate (enter code)	C. Type of Waste Treatment/Disposal/ Recycling/Energy Recovery (enter code)
1.	1.	1. M
2.	2.	2. M
3.	3.	3. M
4.	4.	4. M

SECTION 7A. ON-SITE WASTE TREATMENT METHODS AND EFFICIENCY

☐ Not Applicable (NA) - Check here if no on-site waste treatment is applied to any waste stream containing the toxic chemical or chemical category.

a. General Waste Stream (enter code)	b. Waste Treatment Method(s) Sequence [enter 3-character code(s)]	c. Range of Influent Concentration	d. Waste Treatment Efficiency Estimate	e. Based on Operating Data ?
7A.1a	7A. 1b 1 2 3 4 5 6 7 8	7A. 1c	7A. 1d %	7A. 1e Yes ☐ No ☐
7A.2a	7A. 2b 1 2 3 4 5 6 7 8	7A. 2c	7A. 2d %	7A. 2e Yes ☐ No ☐
7A.3a	7A. 3b 1 2 3 4 5 6 7 8	7A. 3c	7A. 3d %	7A. 3e Yes ☐ No ☐
7A.4a	7A. 4b 1 2 3 4 5 6 7 8	7A. 4c	7A. 4d %	7A. 4e Yes ☐ No ☐
7A.5a	7A. 5b 1 2 3 4 5 6 7 8	7A. 5c	7A. 5d %	7A. 5e Yes ☐ No ☐

If additional pages of Part II, Section 6.2/7A are attached, indicate the total number of pages in this box ☐ **and indicate the Part II, Section 6.2/7A page number in this box :** ☐ **(example: 1,2,3, etc)**

EPA Form 9350-1 (Rev. 01/2001) - Previous editions are obsolete.

* For Dioxin or Dioxin-like compounds, report in grams/year

** Range Codes: A = 1 - 10 pounds; B = 11 - 499 pounds; C = 500 - 999 pounds.

Page 5 of 5

EPA FORM R PART II. CHEMICAL-SPECIFIC INFORMATION (CONTINUED)	TRI Facility ID Number
	Toxic Chemical, Category or Generic Name

SECTION 7B. ON-SITE ENERGY RECOVERY PROCESSES

☐ Not Applicable (NA) - Check here if no on-site energy recovery is applied to any waste stream containing the toxic chemical or chemical category.

Energy Recovery Methods [enter 3-character code(s)]

1 ☐ 2 ☐ 3 ☐ 4 ☐

SECTION 7C. ON-SITE RECYCLING PROCESSES

☐ Not Applicable (NA) - Check here if no on-site recycling is applied to any waste stream containing the toxic chemical or chemical category.

Recycling Methods [enter 3-character code(s)]

1. ☐ 2. ☐ 3. ☐ 4. ☐ 5. ☐

6. ☐ 7. ☐ 8. ☐ 9. ☐ 10. ☐

SECTION 8. SOURCE REDUCTION AND RECYCLING ACTIVITIES

		Column A Prior Year (pounds/year*)	Column B Current Reporting Year (pounds/year*)	Column C Following Year (pounds/year*)	Column D Second Following Year (pounds/year*)
8.1	Quantity released ***				
8.2	Quantity used for energy recovery onsite				
8.3	Quantity used for energy recovery offsite				
8.4	Quantity recycled onsite				
8.5	Quantity recycled offsite				
8.6	Quantity treated onsite				
8.7	Quantity treated offsite				
8.8	Quantity released to the environment as a result of remedial actions, catastrophic events, or one-time events not associated with production processes (pounds/year)				
8.9	Production ratio or activity index				

8.10	Did your facility engage in any source reduction activities for this chemical during the reporting year? If not, enter "NA" in Section 8.10.1 and answer Section 8.11.			
	Source Reduction Activities [enter code(s)]	Methods to Identify Activity (enter codes)		
8.10.1		a.	b.	c.
8.10.2		a.	b.	c.
8.10.3		a.	b.	c.
8.10.4		a.	b.	c.
8.11	Is additional information on source reduction, recycling, or pollution control activities included with this report ? (Check one box)			YES ☐ NO ☐

EPA Form 9350-1 (Rev. 01/2001) - Previous editions are obsolete.

* For Dioxin or Dioxin-like compounds, report in grams/year

*** Report releases pursuant to EPCRA Section 329(8) including "any spilling, leaking, pumping, pouring, emitting, emptying, discharging, injecting, escaping, leaching, dumping, or disposing into the environment." Do not include any quantity treated onsite.

2. Form A - Toxic Chemical Release Inventory

(IMPORTANT: Type or print; read instructions before completing form)

Form Approved OMB Number: 2070-0143
Approval Expires: 01/31/2003

Page 1 of __

United States Environmental Protection Agency

TOXIC CHEMICAL RELEASE INVENTORY
FORM A

WHERE TO SEND COMPLETED FORMS: 1. EPCRA Reporting Center, P.O Box 3348, Merrifield, VA 22116-3348, ATTN: TOXIC CHEMICAL RELEASE INVENTORY
2. APPROPRIATE STATE OFFICE (See instructions in Appendix F)

Enter "X" here if this is a revision

For EPA use only

Important: See instructions to determine when "Not Applicable (NA)" boxes should be checked.

PART I. FACILITY IDENTIFICATION INFORMATION

SECTION 1. REPORTING YEAR ________

SECTION 2. TRADE SECRET INFORMATION

2.1	Are you claiming the toxic chemical identified on page 2 trade secret? ☐ Yes (Answer question 2.2; Attach substantiation forms) ☐ No (Do not answer 2.2; Go to Section 3)	2.2	Is this copy ☐ Sanitized ☐ Unsanitized (Answer only if "YES" in 2.1)

SECTION 3. CERTIFICATION (Important: Read and sign after completing all form sections.)

I hereby certify that to the best of my knowledge and belief, for each toxic chemical listed in the statement, the annual reportable amount as defined in 40 CFR 372.27 (a), did not exceed 500 pounds for this reporting year and that the chemical was manufactured, processed, or otherwise used in an amount not exceeding 1 million pounds during this reporting year.

Name and official title of owner/operator or senior management official:	Signature:	Date Signed:

SECTION 4. FACILITY IDENTIFICATION

4.1	TRI Facility ID Number
Facility or Establishment Name	Facility or Establishment Name or Mailing Address(if different from street address)
Street	Mailing Address
City/County/State/Zip Code	City/State/Zip Code; Country (Non-US)

4.2	This report contains information for: (Important: check c or d if applicable)	c. ☐ A Federal facility	d. ☐ GOCO
4.3	Technical Contact Name		Telephone Number (include area code)
4.4	Intentionally left blank		

4.5	SIC Code (s) (4 digits)	Primary a.	b.	c.	d.	e.	f.

4.6	Latitude	Degrees	Minutes	Seconds	Longitude	Degrees	Minutes	Seconds

4.7	Dun & Bradstreet Number(s) (9 digits)	4.8	EPA Identification Number (RCRA I.D. No.) (12 characters)	4.9	Facility NPDES Permit Number(s) (9 characters)	4.10	Underground Injection Well Code (UIC) I.D. Number(s) (12 digits)
a.		a.		a.		a.	
b.		b.		b.		b.	

SECTION 5. PARENT COMPANY INFORMATION

5.1	Name of Parent Company	NA ☐
5.2	Parent Company's Dun & Bradstreet Number	NA ☐

EPA Form 9350-2 (Rev. 01/2001) - Previous editions are obsolete.

IMPORTANT: Type or print; read instructions before completing form — Page ___ of ___

EPA FORM A

PART II. CHEMICAL IDENTIFICATION — **TRIFID:**

Do not use this form for reporting PBT chemicals including Dioxin and Dioxin-like Compounds*

SECTION 1. TOXIC CHEMICAL IDENTITY	Report ___ of ___
1.1	CAS Number (Important: Enter only one number exactly as it appears on the Section 313 list. Enter category code if reporting a chemical category.)
1.2	Toxic Chemical or Chemical Category Name (Important: Enter only one name exactly as it appears on the Section 313 list.)
1.3	Generic Chemical Name (Important: Complete only if Part 1, Section 2.1 is checked "yes". Generic Name must be structurally descriptive.)
SECTION 2. MIXTURE COMPONENT IDENTITY (Important: DO NOT complete this section if you completed Section 1 above.)	
2.1	Generic Chemical Name Provided by Supplier (Important: Maximum of 70 characters, including numbers, letters, spaces, and punctuation.)

SECTION 1. TOXIC CHEMICAL IDENTITY	Report ___ of ___
1.1	CAS Number (Important: Enter only one number exactly as it appears on the Section 313 list. Enter category code if reporting a chemical category.)
1.2	Toxic Chemical or Chemical Category Name (Important: Enter only one name exactly as it appears on the Section 313 list.)
1.3	Generic Chemical Name (Important: Complete only if Part 1, Section 2.1 is checked "yes". Generic Name must be structurally descriptive.)
SECTION 2. MIXTURE COMPONENT IDENTITY (Important: DO NOT complete this section if you completed Section 1 above.)	
2.1	Generic Chemical Name Provided by Supplier (Important: Maximum of 70 characters, including numbers, letters, spaces, and punctuation.)

SECTION 1. TOXIC CHEMICAL IDENTITY	Report ___ of ___
1.1	CAS Number (Important: Enter only one number exactly as it appears on the Section 313 list. Enter category code if reporting a chemical category.)
1.2	Toxic Chemical or Chemical Category Name (Important: Enter only one name exactly as it appears on the Section 313 list.)
1.3	Generic Chemical Name (Important: Complete only if Part 1, Section 2.1 is checked "yes". Generic Name must be structurally descriptive.)
SECTION 2. MIXTURE COMPONENT IDENTITY (Important: DO NOT complete this section if you completed Section 1 above.)	
2.1	Generic Chemical Name Provided by Supplier (Important: Maximum of 70 characters, including numbers, letters, spaces, and punctuation.)

SECTION 1. TOXIC CHEMICAL IDENTITY	Report ___ of ___
1.1	CAS Number (Important: Enter only one number exactly as it appears on the Section 313 list. Enter category code if reporting a chemical category.)
1.2	Toxic Chemical or Chemical Category Name (Important: Enter only one name exactly as it appears on the Section 313 list.)
1.3	Generic Chemical Name (Important: Complete only if Part 1, Section 2.1 is checked "yes". Generic Name must be structurally descriptive.)
SECTION 2. MIXTURE COMPONENT IDENTITY (Important: DO NOT complete this section if you completed Section 1 above.)	
2.1	Generic Chemical Name Provided by Supplier (Important: Maximum of 70 characters, including numbers, letters, spaces, and punctuation.)

* See the TRI Reporting Forms and Instructions Manual for the list of PBT Chemicals (including Dioxin and Dioxin-like Compounds)

EPA Form 9350-2 (Rev. 01/2001) - Previous editions are obsolete.

(Make additional copies of this page, if needed)

IMPORTANT: Type or print; read instructions before completing form

Page ___ of ___

EPA FORM A

PART II. CHEMICAL IDENTIFICATION **TRIFID:**

SECTION 1. TOXIC CHEMICAL IDENTITY **Report ___ of ___**

1.1	CAS Number (Important: Enter only one number exactly as it appears on the Section 313 list. Enter category code if reporting a chemical category.)
1.2	Toxic Chemical or Chemical Category Name (Important: Enter only one name exactly as it appears on the Section 313 list.)
1.3	Generic Chemical Name (Important: Complete only if Part I, Section 2.1 is checked "yes". Generic Name must be structurally descriptive.)

SECTION 2. MIXTURE COMPONENT IDENTITY (Important: DO NOT complete this section if you completed Section 1 above.)

2.1	Generic Chemical Name Provided by Supplier (Important: Maximum of 70 characters, including numbers, letters, spaces and punctuation.)

SECTION 1. TOXIC CHEMICAL IDENTITY **Report ___ of ___**

1.1	CAS Number (Important: Enter only one number exactly as it appears on the Section 313 list. Enter category code if reporting a chemical category.)
1.2	Toxic Chemical or Chemical Category Name (Important: Enter only one name exactly as it appears on the Section 313 list.)
1.3	Generic Chemical Name (Important: Complete only if Part I, Section 2.1 is checked "yes". Generic Name must be structurally descriptive.)

SECTION 2. MIXTURE COMPONENT IDENTITY (Important: DO NOT complete this section if you completed Section 1 above.)

2.1	Generic Chemical Name Provided by Supplier (Important: Maximum of 70 characters, including numbers, letters, spaces and punctuation.)

SECTION 1. TOXIC CHEMICAL IDENTITY **Report ___ of ___**

1.1	CAS Number (Important: Enter only one number exactly as it appears on the Section 313 list. Enter category code if reporting a chemical category.)
1.2	Toxic Chemical or Chemical Category Name (Important: Enter only one name exactly as it appears on the Section 313 list.)
1.3	Generic Chemical Name (Important: Complete only if Part I, Section 2.1 is checked "yes". Generic Name must be structurally descriptive.)

SECTION 2. MIXTURE COMPONENT IDENTITY (Important: DO NOT complete this section if you completed Section 1 above.)

2.1	Generic Chemical Name Provided by Supplier (Important: Maximum of 70 characters, including numbers, letters, spaces and punctuation.)

SECTION 1. TOXIC CHEMICAL IDENTITY **Report ___ of ___**

1.1	CAS Number (Important: Enter only one number exactly as it appears on the Section 313 list. Enter category code if reporting a chemical category.)
1.2	Toxic Chemical or Chemical Category Name (Important: Enter only one name exactly as it appears on the Section 313 list.)
1.3	Generic Chemical Name (Important: Complete only if Part I, Section 2.1 is checked "yes". Generic Name must be structurally descriptive.)

SECTION 2. MIXTURE COMPONENT IDENTITY (Important: DO NOT complete this section if you completed Section 1 above.)

2.1	Generic Chemical Name Provided by Supplier (Important: Maximum of 70 characters, including numbers, letters, spaces and punctuation.)

EPA Form 9350-2

(Make additional copies of this page, if needed)

3. Tier One - Emergency and Hazardous Chemical Inventory

Page ____ of ____ pages
Form Approved OMB No. 2050–0072

Revised June 1990

Tier One — EMERGENCY AND HAZARDOUS CHEMICAL INVENTORY
Aggregate Information by Hazard Type

FOR OFFICIAL USE ONLY — ID # ____ Date Received ____

Important: Read instructions before completing form

Reporting Period From January 1 to December 31, 19____

Facility Identification

Name ____
Street ____
City ____ County ____ State ____ Zip ____
SIC Code ☐☐☐☐ Dun & Brad Number ☐☐-☐☐☐-☐☐☐☐

Owner/Operator

Name ____
Mail Address ____
Phone ( )

Emergency Contacts

Name ____
Title ____
Phone ( )
24 Hour Phone ( )

Name ____
Title ____
Phone ( )
24 Hour Phone ( )

☐ Check if information below is identical to the information submitted last year.

☐ Check if site plan is attached

	Hazard Type	*Max Amount**	*Average Daily Amount**	*Number of Days On-Site*	*General Location*
Physical Hazards	Fire	☐☐	☐☐	☐☐☐	
	Sudden Release of Pressure	☐☐	☐☐	☐☐☐	
	Reactivity	☐☐	☐☐	☐☐☐	
Health Hazards	Immediate (acute)	☐☐	☐☐	☐☐☐	
	Delayed (Chronic)	☐☐	☐☐	☐☐☐	

Certification *(Read and sign after completing all sections)*

I certify under penalty of law that I have personally examined and am familiar with the information submitted in pages one through ________, and that based on my inquiry of those individuals responsible for obtaining the information, I believe that the submitted information is true, accurate and complete.

____
Name and official title of owner/operator OR owner/operator's authorized representative

____
Signature

____
Date signed

*** Reporting Ranges**

Range Code	Weight Range in Pounds From...	To...
01	0	99
02	100	999
03	1000	9,999
04	10,000	99,999
05	100,000	999,999
06	1,000,000	9,999,999
07	10,000,000	49,999,999
08	50,000,000	99,999,999
09	100,000,000	499,999,999
10	500,000,000	999,999,999
11	1 billion	higher than 1 billion

4. Tier Two - Emergency and Hazardous Chemical Inventory

Page ____ of ____ pages
Form Approved OMB No. 2050-0072

Tier Two
EMERGENCY AND HAZARDOUS CHEMICAL INVENTORY

Specific Information by Chemical

Facility Identification
Name ________
Street ________
City ________ County ________ State ________ Zip ________
SIC Code ________ Dun & Brad Number ________

FOR OFFICIAL USE ONLY — ID # ________ Date Received ________

Owner/Operator Name
Name ________ Phone ( ) ________
Mail Address ________

Emergency Contact
Name ________ Title ________
Phone ( ) ________ 24 Hr. Phone ( ) ________
Name ________ Title ________
Phone ( ) ________ 24 Hr. Phone ( ) ________

Important: Read all instructions before completing form

Reporting Period From January 1 to December 31, 19 ____

[ ] Check if information below is identical to the information submitted last year.

Chemical Description	Physical and Health Hazards (*check all that apply*)	Inventory	Container Type	Pressure	Temperature	Storage Codes and Locations (Non-Confidential) *Storage Locations*	Optional
CAS ____ Trade Secret ____ Chem. Name ____ *Check all that apply* [ ] Pure [ ] Mix [ ] Solid [ ] Liquid [ ] Gas [ ] EHS EHS Name ____	[ ] Fire [ ] Sudden Release of Pressure [ ] Reactivity [ ] Immediate (acute) [ ] Delayed (chronic)	Max. Daily Amount (code) Avg. Daily Amount (code) No. of Days On-site (days)					[ ]
CAS ____ Trade Secret ____ Chem. Name ____ *Check all that apply* [ ] Pure [ ] Mix [ ] Solid [ ] Liquid [ ] Gas [ ] EHS EHS Name ____	[ ] Fire [ ] Sudden Release of Pressure [ ] Reactivity [ ] Immediate (acute) [ ] Delayed (chronic)	Max. Daily Amount (code) Avg. Daily Amount (code) No. of Days On-site (days)					[ ]
CAS ____ Trade Secret ____ Chem. Name ____ *Check all that apply* [ ] Pure [ ] Mix [ ] Solid [ ] Liquid [ ] Gas [ ] EHS EHS Name ____	[ ] Fire [ ] Sudden Release of Pressure [ ] Reactivity [ ] Immediate (acute) [ ] Delayed (chronic)	Max. Daily Amount (code) Avg. Daily Amount (code) No. of Days On-site (days)					[ ]

Certification ***(Read and sign after completing all sections)***
I certify under penalty of law that I have personally examined and am familiar with the information submitted in pages one through ____, and that based on my inquiry of those individuals responsible for obtaining the information, I believe that the submitted information is true, accurate, and complete.

Name and official title of owner/operator OR owner/operator's authorized representative ________ Signature ________ Date signed ________

Optional Attachments
[ ] I have attached a site plan
[ ] I have attached a list of site coordinate abbreviations
[ ] I have attached a description of dikes and other safeguards measures

4a. Tier Two - Instructions

EPA TIER TWO INSTRUCTIONS

GENERAL INFORMATION

Submission of this Tier Two form (when requested) is required by Title III of the Superfund Amendments and Reauthorization Act of 1986, Section 312, Public Law 99-499, codified at 42 U.S.C. Section 11022. The purpose of this Tier Two form is to provide State and local officials and the public with specific information on hazardous chemicals present at your facility during the past year.

CERTIFICATION

The owner or operator or the officially designated representative of the owner or operator must certify that all information included in the Tier Two submission is true, accurate, and complete. On the first page of the Tier Two report, enter your full name and official title. Sign your name and enter the current date. Also, enter the total number of pages included in the Confidential and Non-Confidential Information Sheets as well as all attachments. An original signature is required on at least the first page of the submission. Submissions to the SERC, LEPC, and fire department must each contain an original signature on at least the first page. Subsequent pages must contain either an original signature, a photocopy of the original signature, or a signature stamp. Each page must contain the date on which the original signature was affixed to the first page of the submission and the total number of pages in the submission.

YOU MUST PROVIDE ALL INFORMATION REQUESTED ON THIS FORM TO FULFILL TIER TWO REPORTING REQUIREMENTS.

This form may also be used as a worksheet for completing the Tier One form or may be submitted in place of the Tier One form.

WHO MUST SUBMIT THIS FORM

Section 312 of Title III requires that the owner or operator of a facility submit their Tier Two form if so requested by a State emergency response commission, a local emergency planning committee, or a fire department with jurisdiction over the facility.

This request may apply to the owner or operator of any facility that is required, under regulations implementing the Occupational Safety and Health Act of 1970, to prepare or have available a Material Safety Data Sheet (MSDS) for a hazardous chemical present at the facility. MSDS requirements are specified in the Occupational Safety and Health Administration (OSHA) Hazard Communication Standard, found in Title 29 of the Code of Federal Regulations at ξ1910.1200.

This form does not have to be submitted if all of the chemicals located at your facility are excluded under Section 311(e) of Title III.

WHAT CHEMICALS ARE INCLUDED

If you are submitting Tier Two forms in lieu of Tier One, you must report the required information on this Tier Two form for each hazardous chemical present at your facility in quantities equal to or greater than established threshold amounts (discussed below), unless the chemicals are excluded under Section 311(e) of Title III. Hazardous chemicals are any substance for which your facility must maintain an MSDS under OSHA's Hazard Communication Standard.

If you elect to submit Tier One rather than Tier Two, you may still be required to submit Tier Two information upon request.

WHAT CHEMICALS ARE EXCLUDED

Section 311(e) of Title III excludes the following substances:

Any food, food additive, color additive, drug, or cosmetic regulated by the Food and Drug Administration:
- Any substance present as a solid in any manu-factured item to the extent exposure to the sub-stance does not occur under normal conditions of use;
- Any substance to the extent it is used for personal, family, or household purposes, or is present in the same form and concentration as a product packaged for distribution and use by the general public;
- Any substance to the extent it is used in a research laboratory or a hospital or other medical facility under the direct supervision of a technically qualified individual;
- Any substance to the extent it is used in routine agricultural operations or is a fertilizer held for sale by a retailer to the ultimate customer.

OSHA regulations, Section 1910.1200(b), stipulate exemptions from the requirement to prepare to have available an MSDS.

REPORTING THRESHOLDS

Minimum thresholds have been established for Tier One/ Tier Two reporting under Title III, Section 312. These thresholds are as follows:

For Extremely Hazardous Substances (EHSs) designated under Section 302 of Title III, the reporting threshold is 500 pounds (or 227 kg.) or the threshold planning quantity (TPQ), whichever is lower.

For all other hazardous chemicals for which facilities are required to have or prepare an MSDS, the minimum reporting threshold is 10,000 pounds (or 4.540 kg.).

You need to report hazardous chemicals that were present at your facility at any time during the previous calendar year at levels that equal or exceed these thresholds. For instructions on threshold determinations for components of mixtures, see "What About Mixtures?" on page 2 of these instructions.

A requesting official may limit the responses required under Tier Two by specifying particular chemicals or groups of chemicals. Such requests apply to hazardous chemicals regardless of established thresholds.

INSTRUCTIONS

Please read these instructions carefully. Print or type all responses.

WHEN TO SUBMIT THIS FORM

Owners or operators of facilities that have hazardous chemicals on hand in quantities equal to or greater than set threshold levels must submit either Tier One or Tier Two forms by March 1.

If you choose to submit Tier One, rather than Tier Two, be aware that you may have to submit Tier Two Information later, upon request of any authorized official. You must submit the Tier Two form within 30 days of receipt of a written request.

WHERE TO SUBMIT THIS FORM

Send either a completed Tier One form or Tier Two form(s) to each of the following organizations:
Your State Emergency Response Commission.
Your Local Emergency Planning Committee.
The fire department with jurisdiction over your facility.
If a Tier Two form is submitted in response to a request, send the completed form to the requesting agency.

PENALTIES

Any owner or operator who violates any Tier Two reporting requirements shall be liable to the United States for a civil penalty of up to $25,000 for each such violation. Each day a violation continues shall constitute a separate violation.

If your Tier Two responses require more than one page, use additional forms and fill in the page number at the top of the form.

REPORTING PERIOD

Enter the appropriate calendar year, beginning January 1 and ending December 31.

FACILITY IDENTIFICATION

Enter the full name of your facility (and company identifier where appropriate).

Enter the full street address or state road. If a street address is not available, enter other appropriate identifiers that describe the physical location of your facility (e.g., longitude and latitude). Include city, county, state and zip code.

Enter the primary Standard Industrial Classification (SIC) code and the Dun & Bradstreet number for your facility. The financial officer of your facility should be able to provide the Dun & Bradstreet number. If your firm does not have this information, contact the State or regional office of Dun & Bradstreet to obtain your facility number or have one assigned.

OWNER/OPERATOR

Enter the owner's or operator's full name, mailing address, and phone number.

EMERGENCY CONTACT

Enter the name, title, and work phone number of at least one local person or office who can act as a referral if emergency responders need assistance in responding to a chemical accident at the facility.

Provide an emergency phone number where such emer-gency information will be available 24 hours a day, everyday. The requirement is mandatory. The facility must make some arrangement to ensure that a 24 hour contact is available.

IDENTICAL INFORMATION

Check the box indicating identical information, located below the emergency contacts on the Tier Two form, if the current chemical information being reported is identical to that submitted last year. Chemical descriptions, hazards, amounts, and locations must be provided in this year's form, even if the information is identical to that submitted last year.

CHEMICAL INFORMATION: Description, Hazards, Amounts, and Locations

The main section of the Tier Two form requires specific information on amounts and locations of hazardous chemicals, as defined in the OSHA Hazard Communication Standard.

If you choose to indicate that all of the information on a specific hazardous chemical is identical to that submitted last year, check the appropriate optional box provided at the right side of the storage codes and locations on the Tier Two form. Chemical descriptions, hazards, amounts, and locations must be provided even if the information is identical to that submitted last year.

What units should I use?

Calculate all amounts as *weight in pounds*. To convert gas or liquid volume to weight in pounds, multiply by an appropriate density factor.

What about mixtures?

If a chemical is part of a mixture, *you have the option* of reporting either the weight of the entire mixture or only the portion of the mixture that is a particular hazardous chemical (e.g., if a hazardous solution weighs 100 lbs. but is composed of only 5% of a particular hazardous chemical, you can indicate either 100 lbs. of the mixture *or* 5 lbs. of the chemical).

The option used for each mixture must be consistent with the option used in your Section 311 reporting.

Because EHSs are important to Section 303 planning, EHSs have lower thresholds. The amount of an EHS at a facility (both pure EHS substances and EHSs in mixtures) must be aggregated for purposes of threshold determination. It is suggested that the aggregation calculation be done as a first step in making the threshold determination. Once you determine whether a threshold for an EHS has been reached, you should report either the total weight of the EHS at your facility, or the weight of each mixture containing the EHS.

CHEMICAL DESCRIPTION

Enter the Chemical Abstract Service registry number (CAS). For mixtures, enter the CAS number of the mixture as a whole if it has been assigned a number distinct from its constituents. For a mixture that has no CAS number, leave this item blank or report the CAS numbers of as many constituent chemicals as possible.

If you are withholding the name of a chemical in accordance with criteria specified in Title III, Section 322, enter the generic class or category that is structurally descriptive of the chemical (e.g., list toulene diisocyanate as organic isocyanate) and check the box marked Trade Secret. Trade secret information should be submitted to EPA and must include a substantiation. Please refer to EPA's final regulation on trade secrecy (53 FR 28772, July 29, 1988) for detailed information on how to submit trade secrecy claims.

Enter the chemical name or common name of each hazardous chemical.

Check box for *ALL* applicable descriptors: pure or mixture; *and* solid, liquid, or gas; and whether the chemical is or contains an EHS.

If the chemical is a mixture containing an EHS, enter the chemical name of each EHS in the mixture.

EXAMPLE:

You have pure chlorine gas on hand, as well as two mixtures that contain liquid chlorine. You write "chlorine" and enter the CAS number. Then you check "pure" *and* "mix" -- as well as "liquid" *and* "gas".

PHYSICAL AND HEALTH HAZARDS

For each chemical you have listed, check all the physical and health hazard boxes that apply. These hazard categories are defined in 40 CFR 370.2. The two health hazard categories and three physical hazard categories are a consolidation of the 23 hazard categories defined in the OSHA Hazard Communication Standard, 29 CFR 1910.1200.

Hazard Category Comparison
For Reporting Under Sections 311 and 312

EPA's Hazard Categories	OSHA's Hazard Categories
Fire Hazard	Flammable Combustion Liquid Pyrophoric Oxidizer
Sudden Release of Pressure	Explosive Compressed Gas
Reactive	Unstable Reactive Organic Peroxide Water Reactive
Immediate (Acute) Health Hazards	Highly Toxic Toxic Irritant Sensitizer Corrosive
	Other hazardous chemicals with an adverse effect with short term exposure
Delayed (Chronic) Health Hazard	Carcinogens
	Other hazardous chemicals with an adverse effect with long term exposure

MAXIMUM AMOUNT

For each hazardous chemical, estimate the greatest amount present at your facility on any single day during the reporting period.

Find the appropriate range value code in Table I.

Enter this range value as the Maximum Amount.

Table I REPORTING RANGES

Range Value	Weight Range in Pounds From...	To...
01	0	99
02	100	999
03	1,000	9,999
04	10,000	99,999
05	100,000	999,999
06	1,000,000	9,999,999
07	10,000,000	49,999,999
08	50,000,000	99,999,999
09	100,000,000	499,999,999
10	500,000,000	999,999,999
11	1 billion	higher than 1 billion

If you are using this form as a worksheet for completing Tier One, enter the actual weight in pounds in the shaded space below the response blocks. Do this for both Maximum Amount and Average Daily Amount.

EXAMPLE:

You received one large shipment of a solvent mixture last year. The shipment filled five 5,000-gallon storage tanks. You know that the solvent contains 10% benzene, which is a hazardous chemical.

You figure that 10% of 25,000 gallons is 2,500 gallons. You also know that the density of benzene is 7.29 pounds per gallon, so you multiply 2,500 gallons by 7.29 pounds per gallon to get a weight of 18.225 pounds.

Then you look at Table I and find that the range value 04 corresponds to 18.225. You enter 04 as the Maximum Amount.

(If you are using the form as a worksheet for completing a Tier One form, you should write 18.255 in the shaded area.)

AVERAGE DAILY AMOUNT

For each hazardous chemical, estimate the average weight in pounds that was present at your facility during the year. To do this, total all daily weights and divide by the number of days the chemical was present on the site.

Find the appropriate range value in Table I.

Enter this range value as the Average Daily Amount.

EXAMPLE:

The 25,000-gallon shipment of solvent you received last year was gradually used up and completely gone in 315 days. The sum of the daily volume levels in the tank is 4,536,000 gallons. By dividing 4,536,000 gallons by 315 days on-site, you calculate an average daily amount of 14,400 gallons.

You already know that the solvent contains 10% benzene, which is a hazardous chemical. Since 10% of 14,400 is 1,440, you figure that you had an average of 1,440 gallons of benzene. You also know that the density of benzene is 7.29 pounds per gallon, so you multiply 1,440 by 7.29 to get a weight of 10,500 pounds.

Then you look at Table I and find that the range value 04 corresponds to 10,500. You enter 04 as the Average Daily Amount.

(If you are using the form as a worksheet for completing Tier One form, you should write 10,500 in the shaded area.)

NUMBER OF DAYS ON-SITE

Enter the number of days that the hazardous chemical was found on-site.

EXAMPLE:

The solvent composed of 10% benzene was present for 315 days at your facility. Enter 315 in the space provided.

STORAGE CODES AND STORAGE LOCATIONS

List all non-confidential chemical locations in the column, along with storage types/conditions associated with each location. Please note that a particular chemical may be located in several places around the facility. Each row of boxes followed by a line represents a unique location for the same chemical.

Storage Codes: Indicate the types and conditions of storage present:

Look at Table II. For each location, find the appropriate storage type and enter the corresponding code in the first box.
Look at Table III. For each location, find the appropriate storage types for pressure and temperature conditions. Enter the applicable pressure code in the second box. Enter the applicable temperature code in the third box.

Table II - STORAGE TYPES

CODES	Types of Storage
A	Above ground tank
B	Below ground tank
C	Tank inside building
D	Steel drum
E	Plastic or non-metallic drum
F	Can
G	Carboy
H	Silo
I	Fiber drum
J	Bag
K	Box
L	Cylinder
M	Glass bottles or jugs
N	Plastic bottles or jugs
O	Tote bin
P	Tank wagon
Q	Rail car
R	Other

Table III - PRESSURE AND TEMPERATURE CONDITIONS

CODES	Storage Conditions
	(PRESSURE)
1	Ambient pressure
2	Greater than ambient pressure
3	Less than ambient pressure
	(TEMPERATURE)
4	Ambient temperature
5	Greater than ambient temperature
6	Less than ambient temperature but not cryogenic
7	Cryogenic conditions

EXAMPLE:

The benzene in the main building is kept in a tank inside the building, at ambient pressure and less than ambient temperature.

Table II shows you that the code for a tank inside a building is C. Table III shows you that the code for ambient pressure is 1, and the code for less than ambient temperature is 6.

You enter: | C | 1 | 6 |

STORAGE LOCATIONS:

Provide a brief description of the precise location of the chemical, so that emergency responders can locate the area easily. You may find it advantageous to provide the optional site plan or site coordinates as explained below.

For each chemical, indicate at a minimum the building or lot. Additionally, where practical, the room or area may be indicated. You may respond in narrative form with appropriate site coordinates or abbreviations.

If the chemical is present in more than one building, lot, or area location, continue your responses down the page as needed. If the chemical exists everywhere at the plant site simultaneously, you may report that the chemical is ubiquitous at the site.

Optional attachments: If you choose to attach one of the following, check the appropriate Attachments box at the bottom of the Tier Two form.

A site plan with site coordinates indicated for buildings, lots, areas, etc. throughout your facility.

A list of site coordinate abbreviations that correspond to buildings, lots, areas, etc. throughout your facility.
A description of dikes and other safeguard measures for storage locations throughout your facility.

EXAMPLE:

You may have benzene in the main room of the main building, and in tank 2 in tank field 10. You attach a site plan with coordinates as follows: main building = G-2, tank field 10 = B-6. Fill in the Storage Location as follows:

B-6 [Tank 2] G-2 [Main Room]

CONFIDENTIAL INFORMATION

Under Title III, Section 324, you may elect to withhold location information on a specific chemical from disclosure to the public. If you choose to do so:

Enter the word "confidential" in the Non-Confidential Location section of the Tier Two form on the first line of the storage locations.

On a separate Tier Two Confidential Location Information Sheet, enter the name and CAS number of each chemical for which you are keeping the location confidential.

Enter the appropriate location and storage information, as described above for non-confidential locations.

Attach the Tier Two Confidential Location Information Sheet to the Tier Two form. This separates confidential locations from other information that will be disclosed to the public.

CERTIFICATION

Instructions for this section are included on page one of these instructions.

CHAPTER IX
THE TOXIC SUBSTANCES CONTROL ACT

A. Overview

The Toxic Substances Control Act (TSCA) was adopted in 1976 and regulates the manufacture, processing, distribution, use and disposal of chemical substances and mixtures. 15 U.S.C. § 2601 *et seq.* TSCA is administered by the USEPA. TSCA applies to chemical substances and mixtures manufactured in the United States or imported into the United States. Except for export notification requirements, TSCA does not apply to substances, mixtures and articles manufactured or processed solely for export and not for use in the United States.

B. Definitions; Applicability of TSCA

A chemical substance is any organic or inorganic substance of a particular molecular structure including (i) any combination of such substances occurring in whole or in part as a result of a chemical reaction or occurring in nature and (ii) any element or uncombined radical. In general, a mixture is any combination of two or more substances if the combination does not occur in nature and is not, in whole or part, the result of a chemical reaction. 15 U.S.C. § 2602. Microorganisms and their DNA molecules are considered to be "chemical substances" by the USEPA. 62 Fed. Reg. 17909 (1997); 59 Fed. Reg. 45526 (1994); 51 Fed. Reg. 23302 (June 26, 1986), 49 Fed. Reg. 50886 (December 31, 1984).

TSCA does not apply to (1) pesticides, as defined in the Federal Insecticide Fungicide and Rodenticide Act; (2) tobacco and tobacco products; (3) nuclear materials regulated by the Atomic Energy Act; (4) firearms and ammunition subject to the excise tax provisions of the Internal Revenue Code; or (5) foods, food additives, drugs, cosmetics and devices subject to regulation by the Federal Food, Drug, and Cosmetic Act. All of these substances (except tobacco products) are subject to other regulatory laws. The tobacco industry is a major industry in the southeastern United States which has considerable freedom from environmental and product liability laws applied to other industries.

TSCA defines the term "manufacture" to include importing into the customs territory of the United states. 42 U.S.C. § 2602(7). Thus, importers are generally subject to the same requirements as manufacturers and may not import chemicals or mixtures unless they can persuade foreign manufacturers to provide information and take other steps that enable the importers to comply with TSCA. The USEPA's regulations state that "manufacture" means manufacture for commercial purposes which includes test marketing; internal use for research and development or as an intermediate; and coincidentally produced substances such as by products and impurities. 40 C.F.R. §§ 707.3, 712.3(h), 716.3, 717.3(e) and 720.3(r).

TSCA defines the term "process" to mean preparation of a chemical substance or mixture, *after its manufacture*, for distribution in commerce in the same or a different form or physical state from that in which it was received or as part of an article containing the chemical substance or mixture. 15 U.S.C. § 2602(10). The USEPA has adopted regulations imposing some, but not all, of its test rule, reporting and other requirements on processors.

TSCA defines the terms "distribute in commerce" and "distribution in commerce" as meaning to sell, introduce or deliver a chemical substance or to hold a mixture or article after its introduction into commerce. 15 U.S.C. § 2602(4). The definition is broad and could be interpreted to include activities of an agent or user. In general, however, the USEPA applies the definition in a conventional manner. TSCA does not define the terms "use" or "disposal."

Distributors, users and disposers have only a few obligations which include compliance with rules regulating hazardous chemicals and mixtures, including polychlorinated biphenyls (PCBs), and with any inspection and subpoena requirements. 15 U.S.C.§ 2610. A distributor must also report "substantial risks" as required by Section 8(e). 15 U.S.C. § 2607(e). A user must not use any chemical substance or mixture which it has reason to know was manufactured, processed or distributed in violation of TSCA. 15 U.S.C. § 2614.

C. The TSCA Chemical Substances Inventory

Before considering the substantive provisions of TSCA, it is important to understand the history and functions of the TSCA Chemical Substances Inventory.

When adopted, TSCA required the USEPA to compile, keep current, and publish a list of each chemical substance manufactured or processed in the United States. The list was not to include any chemical substance not manufactured or processed in the United States within three years before the effective date of the USEPA's reporting regulations. 15 U.S.C. § 2607(b). 40 C.F.R. Parts 710 and 720.

Compilation of the list was an enormous task for both the USEPA and industry. Chemical manufacturers and processors gave the work high priority because chemical substances listed in the TSCA Inventory could continue to be manufactured, imported, processed, distributed and used without compliance with the premanufacturing notice requirements of TSCA only if they were listed in the TSCA Inventory.

The author was then a senior officer of a large multinational chemical manufacturer and participated in the work to identify which of its thousands of products should be listed. The answers were far from obvious for a manufacturer which made tens of thousands of synthetic resins and compounds which were essentially intermediates, polymers and mixtures made from chemical substances.

The initial list included over 58,000 chemical substances. The list has subsequently grown to over 75,000 chemical substances. The TSCA Inventory does not include any mixture. The TSCA Inventory also does not include formulated pesticides; tobacco or tobacco products; certain radioactive materials; certain firearms and ammunition; and foods, food additives, drugs, cosmetics and devices because TSCA does not apply to them.

The USEPA allows corrections to the TSCA Inventory if an applicant can comply with detailed and cautious requirements.

The USEPA updates the TSCA Inventory by adding new chemicals that clear its premanufacturing notice requirements and delisting chemicals not currently being manufactured or imported for use in the Unites States.

The USEPA no longer publishes the TSCA Inventory in paper form, although reprints of the 1985 publication and 1990 amendments can be obtained from the National Technical Information Service (NTIS) plus diskettes updating the information to the present date.

D. Testing of Chemicals Listed in the TSCA Inventory

1. Findings Required to Order Testing

Section 4 of TSCA authorizes the USEPA, by rule, to require testing of chemical substances or mixtures of chemical substances listed in the TSCA Inventory if they may present any unreasonable risk of injury or substantial with potential for substantial environmental or human exposure. 15 U.S. C. § 2603. In the case of mixtures, testing is required only if the USEPA finds the effects may not reasonably and more efficiently be determined by testing the chemical substances which comprise the mixture. To adopt a test rule, the USEPA must make a finding based either on *risk* or *exposure*. 15 U.S.C. § 2603(a)(1)(A) and (B). The USEPA must find either that:

> A chemical substance or mixture (1) may present an unreasonable risk of injury to human health or the environment; (2) existing data and experience are insufficient to reasonably determine its effects; and (3) testing is necessary to develop such data, or
>
> A chemical substance or mixture (1) will be produced in substantial quantities and may reasonably be anticipated to enter the environment in substantial quantities or result in significant or substantial human exposure; (2) existing

data and experience are insufficient to determine its effects; and (3) testing is necessary to develop such data.

The federal courts have upheld test rules adopted by the USEPA. *Chemical Manufacturers Ass'n v. EPA*, 859 F.2d 977 (D.C. Cir. 1988). However, the Fifth Circuit remanded the test requirement rule for cumene because the USEPA had not adopted substantiality standards relating to its release into the environment or human exposure. *Chemical Manufacturers Ass'n v. EPA*, 899 F.2d 1344 (5th Cir. 1990).

In 1993, the USEPA adopted substantiality standards for exposure-based test rules which are as follows: (1) production (1,000,000 pounds per year); (2) release to the environment (1,000,000 pounds per year); and (3) human exposure (1,000 workers, 10,000 consumers or 100,000 people in the general population). 58 Fed. Reg. 28735 (May 14, 1993).

2. The Interagency Testing Committee

TSCA established an Interagency Testing Committee (ITC) which makes recommendations to the USEPA on chemical substances and mixtures that should have priority consideration for a test rule. The eight ITC members are appointed by the USEPA, Department of Labor, Council on Environmental Quality, National Institute for Occupational Safety and Health. National Institute for Environmental Health Sciences, National Science Foundation and Department of Commerce. Priority lists of chemical substances appear at 40 C.F.R. §§ 712.30 and 72.120 together with related reporting requirements which will be discussed later in this chapter. Specific chemical test rules are listed in 40 C.F.R. Part 799.

3. Test Guidelines

TSCA provides that test rules contain standards requiring development of test data for environmental and health effects including carcinogenesis, mutagenesis, teratogenesis, behavioral disorders, cumulative or synergistic effects, and other effects which may present an unreasonable risk of injury to human health or the environment. The standards may require measurement of characteristics such as persistence and acute, subchronic and chronic toxicity. The methods may include epidemiological studies, serial or hierarchical tests, in vitro tests, and whole animal tests. 15 U.S.C. § 2603(b)(2)(A).

The tests required by the USEPA's testing guidelines go far beyond those mentioned in the statutory language and are based on its perception of the hazard presented by the chemical substance and the test data needed to supplement existing data. The USEPA's test guidelines are found at 40 C.F.R. Parts 795 to 799 and generally apply to chemical fate, environmental effects and health effects.

The chemical fate testing guidelines prescribe tests to determine physical and chemical properties by absorption and vapor tests; transport processes by sediment and soil absorption isotherms; and transformation processes by tests of aerobic aquatic biodegradation and hydrolysis as a function of pH at 25 degrees C. 40 C.F.R. Part 796.

The environmental effects testing guidelines focus on aquatic toxicity and prescribe methods for testing algae, daphnids, fish and crustaceans. The tests are designed to measure acute and chronic toxicity by subjecting sensitive subjects (such as daphnids, fathead minnows and mysid shrimp) to high concentrations of the chemical substance being tested. 40 C.F.R. Part 797.

The health effects testing guidelines focus on subchronic and chronic toxicity; specific organ and tissue toxicity; genetic toxicity; and neurotoxicity. The subchronic tests use small laboratory animals (primarily rodents) to test for dermal, inhalation and oral toxicity. The chronic tests are for chronic toxicity, oncogenicity and combined chronic toxicity and oncogenicity. The genetic tests are quite numerous and include two important mutagenicity studies, rodent dominant lethal assays and rodent heritable translocation assays, and long-term cancer bioassays. The neurotoxicity tests begin with a functional observational battery and go on to include motor activity; neuropathology and schedule-controlled operant behavior. 40 C.F.R. Part 798. See also Part 799.

Specific chemical test rules are prescribed in 40 C.F.R. Part 799 together with lists of testing consent orders, multichemical test rules and additional health effects test guidelines.

4. Development of Test Rules; Consent Agreements

The USEPA has adopted regulations for developing test rules and consent agreements with manufacturers and processors to sponsor the tests. 40 C.F.R. Part 790.

The regulations begin with procedures for response by the USEPA to ITC recommendations that a chemical substance or mixture warrants testing consideration. If the ITC designates a chemical substance or mixture for testing within 12 months, the USEPA must act within 12 months either to initiate rulemaking proceedings or to publish in the Federal Register its reasons not doing so. 40 C.F.R.§ 790.20 *et seq.*

The regulations continue with procedures for the promulgation of test rules for a chemical substance or mixture. Each test rule is promulgated in Part 799 and identifies the chemical; the health or environmental effects or other characteristics for which testing is required; the substance to be tested; standards for development of test data; the applicable good laboratory practice requirements; who must submit either letters of intent to conduct testing or exemption applications; and equivalence data if more than one substance is to be tested. The USEPA may use a single-phase or a two-phase procedure, both procedures providing for public notice and opportunity to comment. In the two-phase procedure, test standards and schedules are deferred to the second phase because time may be needed to develop special test methods. 40 C.F.R. § 790.40.

Manufacturers and/or processors may submit a letter of intent to conduct testing. Persons who submit a letter of intent must also submit their proposed study plans which must meet detailed requirements for content. 40 C.F.R. § 790.50. If no manufacturer or processor submits a letter of intent, after notice from the USEPA and an opportunity to take corrective action, all manufacturers and processors will be in violation of the test rule. 42 C.F.R. § 790.48. Persons who notify the USEPA of their intent to conduct a test required by a test rule and fail to do so in accordance with the standards and schedules in the test rule will also be in violation of the rule. 42 C.F.R. § 790.59.

The regulations provide for the implementation, enforcement and modification of consent agreements including content, submission of study plans, conduct of testing, penalties for failure to comply, and procedures to seek and approve changes. 40 C.F.R. § 790.60 to .68.

Any manufacturer or processor subject to a test rule in Part 799 may submit an application to the USEPA for an exemption from performing any or all of the tests required by the test rule. However, processors are not required to conduct testing or apply for an exemption unless the USEPA so specifies in a test rule or in a special notice published in the Federal Register. The USEPA will conditionally approve an exemption application if it has received a letter of intent from another person willing to conduct the testing and if the chemical substance or mixture for which the exemption is requested are equivalent to the chemical substance or mixture to be tested. An exemption may be terminated for any of several reasons, most importantly if the person who undertook to perform the testing fails to do so in a timely and proper manner. Each applicant for an exemption must include a sworn statement acknowledging that, if the application is granted, it must pay fair and equitable reimbursement to the person or persons who incurred or shared in the costs of complying with the test rule and upon whose data the exemption was based. 40 C.F.R. § 790.80 to .99.

5. Reimbursement of Testing Costs

The USEPA has adopted a rule establishing procedures to be used in determining fair and equitable reimbursement for testing costs incurred in response to a test rule. The rule takes effect only when private efforts to resolve a dispute have failed and a manufacturer or processor requests the USEPA's assistance.

If persons exempted from the test rules do not reach a voluntary agreement, the USEPA will order them to pay fair and equitable compensation. To resolve disputes, any party can request resolution by the American Arbitration Association (AAA). The USEPA will then base its order on the AAA's decision. A volumetric allocation of the test costs is presumed to be fair and equitable, but other factors may be taken into account. Processors may be excluded from the obligation to reimburse because they will usually absorb the cost as manufacturers increase prices to reflect the test costs. 40 C.F.R. Part 791.

6. Voluntary Testing of High Production Volume Chemicals

In recent years, the USEPA has been negotiating with the chemical industry to develop a program to test about 2,800 high production volume (HPV) chemicals for basic effects on health and the environment. HPV chemicals are considered to be those manufactured or imported at a level of 1,000,000 pounds or more per year. Over 400 companies have agreed to participate in the HPV Voluntary Challenge Program and have reportedly agreed to test 2,100 of the chemicals by 2004. The Program has been complicated by opposition from animal rights activists because much of the testing would be performed using rats, mice and other laboratory animals. For example, the activists strongly criticized Vice President Albert Gore, who advocated the HPV program, and threatened opposition to his presidential campaign which narrowly lost to George W. Bush.

The Alliance for Chemical Awareness (ACA) has agreed to provide exposure data for use in connection with the HPV Voluntary Challenge Program. The ACA is led by the American Chemistry Council, the American Crop Protection Association, the Chemical Specialties Manufacturers Association, the National Association of Chemical Distributors, the Soap and Detergent Association and several of their large company members. In January 2001, the ACA announced that it will be advised in its work by a panel of representatives from the USEPA, the Consumer Product Safety Commission, the National Institute of Environmental Health Sciences, the International Chemical Workers Union Council, the Virginia Department of Environmental Quality, and some universities and environmental advocacy organizations.

In December, 2000, the USEPA announced that it would adopt a test rule or rules under which it would mandate testing of any chemical substances for which a test sponsor (or sponsors) was not identified under the voluntary program. Among the avalanche of new regulations issued by the USEPA during the last months of the Clinton Administration, the USEPA published a proposed rule to require testing of 37 chemicals which it identified as HPV chemicals. 5 Fed. Reg. 81657 (Dec. 26, 2000). However, the USEPA said that it hoped that companies agree to test the 37 chemicals under the voluntary program and it would not be necessary to adopt a final test rule for the 37 chemicals.

E. Premanufacturing Notices (PMNs)—TSCA Section 5

1. PMN Requirements

TSCA requires any person intending to manufacture, process or import a new chemical substance to file a premanufacturing notice (PMN) with the USEPA at least 90 days before doing so. The PMN must be accompanied by test data required by the USEPA. 15 U.S.C. § 2604(a) and (b).

A new chemical substance is a chemical substance not listed in the TSCA Inventory. 40 C.F.R. § 720.3(v) and § 720.25(a). If listed, the person can proceed to manufacture, process or import. If not listed, the person must either prepare and file a PMN on EPA Form 7710-25 with the EPA or find an exclusion or exemption in TSCA or the USEPA's regulations. 40 C.F.R. Part 720.

2. Exclusions and Exemptions

The preparation and clearance of a PMN is costly and may be lengthy. Thus, the first step is to review the exclusions and exemptions. For example, the PMN requirements exclude pesticides as defined in the Federal Insecticide, Fungicide and Rodenticide Act, but they apply to chemical precursors used in making pesticides. They also exclude any food, food additive, drug, cosmetic or device regulated by the Food and Drug Administration (FDA) under the Federal Food, Drug and Cosmetic Act.

There are several exemptions from the PMN requirement. Some exemptions are self-operating and others require prior clearance by the EPA.

The self-operating exemptions include (1) any mixture as defined in 40 C.F.R. § 720.3(u); (2) any new chemical substance that will be manufactured or imported in small quantities solely for research and development under 40 C.F.R. § 720.36; (3) any new chemical substance manufactured solely for export if labeled according to TSCA § 12(a)(1)(B) and the manufacturer knows that the distributor intends to export it or process it solely for export; (4) certain impurities, by-products, reaction products and nonisolated intermediates; and (5) any chemical substance manufactured solely for noncommercial research and development purposes. 40 C.F.R.§§ 720.30 and 720.36.

The polymer exemption is also a self-operating exemption. However, manufacturers and importers of polymers must prepare and maintain records demonstrating that each polymer meets the technical requirements for the exemption. They must also file a report with the EPA of each new polymer manufactured or imported during any year by January 31 of the next year. 40 C.F.R. § 723.250. The polymer exemption is discussed again later.

The test-marketing exemption requires an application to, and approval by, the EPA. 40 C.F.R. § 720.38.

The regulations contain exemptions for chemical substances manufactured in quantities of 10,000 kilograms or less per year and chemical substances with low-environmental releases and human exposures. To obtain these exemptions, a manufacturer or importer must file with the EPA a notice of intent to manufacture at least 30 days before manufacture begins. The notice must be accompanied by supporting information with is subject to review by the EPA. The EPA can extend the 30 day period if it needs more time for the review. The EPA can also deny the exemption. 40 C.F.R. § 723.50.

The regulations also contain an exemption for chemical substances used to manufacture or process instant photographic and peel-apart film articles. This exemption also requires the manufacturer, processor or importer to file with the

EPA a notice and supporting data and prescribes conditions of manufacture or processing in a special production area. The manufacturer, processor or importer is free to commence manufacture or import upon filing the notice and supporting data. However, the EPA can prohibit use of the exemption if it finds that the new chemical substance may present an unreasonable risk of injury to health or the environment 40 C.F.R. § 723.175.

The PMN regulations contain detailed requirements for the preparation and maintenance of records including documents supporting exemptions. 40 C.F.R. § 720.78.

3. The Polymer Exemption

The polymer exemption is one of the most important and practical exemptions adopted by the USEPA. Organic chemists know that it is possible to make many different polymers from the same monomers or oligomers. Although it is true that each polymer is a new chemical substance and will have some different characteristics, the characteristics affecting human health and the environment do not generally differ to significant extent. Thus, the polymer exemption spares manufacturers, importers, processors and the USEPA from the need to submit and review numerous PMNs with results that were predictable before they were filed. 40 C.F.R. § 723.250.

The polymer exemption is a self-executing exemption that can be claimed by manufacturers and importers by compliance with its requirements. No application or notice to the USEPA is required except the brief report described later in this section. However, manufacturers and importers should not assume that every polymer meets the polymer exemption. They must apply five steps to determine whether the exemption is available.

The first step is to assure that the polymer meets the definition of a polymer in § 723.250(b). The definition is as follows:

> Polymer means a chemical substance consisting of molecules characterized by the sequence of one or more types of monomer units and comprising a simple weight majority of molecules containing at least 3 monomer units which are covalently bound to at least one other monomer unit or other reactant and which consists of less than a simple weight majority of molecules of the same molecular weight. Such molecules must be distributed over a range of molecular weights wherein differences in the molecular weight are differences in the molecular weight are primarily attributable to differences in the number of monomer units. In the context of this definition, sequence means that the monomer units under consideration are covalently bound to one another and form a continuous string within the molecule, uninterrupted by units other than monomer units.

The second step is to determine that the polymer is not excluded by Subsection (d) of § 723.250:

1. Subsection (d) excludes cationic polymers and any polymer reasonably anticipated to become a cationic polymer in a natural aquatic environment such

as a river or lake unless (i) the polymer is a solid material that is not soluble or dispersable in water and will be used only in the solid phase, or (ii) the combined (total) functional group equivalent weight of cationic groups in the polymer is equal to or greater than 5,000.

2. Subsection (d) excludes a polymer unless it contains at least two of the elements carbon, hydrogen, nitrogen, oxygen, silicon and sulfur. In addition, Subsequent (d) excludes the polymer if it contains as an integral part of its composition, except as impurities, any elements other than those listed in Subsection(d) (2) (ii) (A) through (D) of § 723.250.

3. Subsection (d) excludes polymers which are designed or reasonably anticipated to degrade, decompose or depolymerize.

4. Subsection (d) excludes polymers manufactured or imported from monomers and reactants not on the TSCA inventory.

5. Subsection (d) excludes water-absorbing polymers with number average molecular weights of 10,000 daltons and greater.

The third step is to determine that the polymer meets one of the three exemption criteria of Subsection(e) of § 723.250:

1. The first exemption criteria is based on molecular weight $\geq$1,000 and $\leq$10,000 daltons; limits the percentages of oligomeric materials of certain molecular weights in the polymer; and excludes reactive functional groups unless the reactive groups and the polymer meet specified criteria.

2. The second exemption criteria is based on molecular weight $\geq$10,000 daltons and limits the percentages of oligomeric materials of certain molecular weights in the polymer.

3. The third exemption criteria applies to polyester polymers made solely from reactants listed in Table 1.

The fourth step is to prepare and submit the report required by § 723.250(f) to the EPA postmarked by January 31 of the year subsequent to initial manufacture or import. The report must include:

1. The manufacturer's name and address and the name and address of a technical contact.

2. The number of polymers manufactured under the exemption for the first time in the year before the notice.

The fifth step is to prepare and maintain for 5 years the records required by § 723.250(j). Stated briefly, the records must show the chemical identity and CAS number of each reactant; records of production volumes; analytical and other data to show that the polymer is eligible for the exemption; and the certification required by subsection (h).

4. Preparation and Submission of a PMN

The USEPA has adopted regulations establishing the procedures for submitting and reviewing PMNs. 40 C.F.R. Part 720. It is best to submit a PMN as far as possible in advance of planned manufacture or import because the USEPA's review may extend well beyond the initial 90 day permit mentioned in TSCA.

The PMN regulations identify the persons who must file a PMN including manufacturers in the United States and importers. 40 C.F.R. § 720.22. They also provide guidance on determining whether chemical substance is on the TSCA Inventory including procedures to request the USEPA to determine whether a substance is listed in the confidential portion of the TSCA Inventory. 40 C.F.R.§ 720.25.

The USEPA no longer publishes the TSCA Inventory in paper form, although reprints of the 1985 publication and 1990 amendments can be obtained from the National Technical Information Service (NTIS) plus diskettes updating the information to the present date. Information on the TSCA Inventory can also be obtained from Cornell University and other sources.

A PMN may be filed on paper using Form No. 7710-25. The original and two complete copies, including all tests data and any other information must be filed with the USEPA, 401 M Street, SW, Washington DC 20460. If the PMN contains information claimed as confidential, a sanitized copy must also be filed that can be placed in the public record. A PMN may also be filed electronically. A PMN may be filed by a designated agent and may also be filed jointly. If a submitter obtains new information during the PMN review period, it must submit the information within ten days, but no later than five days before the end of the review period. 40 C.F.R.§ 720.40.

The regulations require that detailed information be included in and with a PMN. The author cautions readers preparing a PMN that the USEPA is quite serious in insisting that the information be submitted as required and be accurate and complete. It must include information known to, and reasonably ascertainable by, the submitter. However, it need not include information relating solely to exposure of human or ecological populations outside the United States.

In summary, the following information is required in the Form 7710-25:

1. The specific chemical identify of the substance including the name and registry number based on the Chemical Abstracts Service system; the molecular formula; and chemical structure diagram. For a polymer, additional information must be provided including the monomers and reactants.

2. Impurities by name, CAS registry number, and weight percent of the total substance.

3. Known synonyms or trade names of the substance.

4. By-products from the manufacture, processing, use and disposal of the substance.

5. Estimated maximum amount to be manufactured or imported during the first year of production and during any 12 month period during the first three years of production.

NOTE: This information is used by the USEPA to estimate factors such as worker or population exposure and does not restrict sales if a product is more successful than anticipated.

6. Intended use categories by function and application, the estimated percent of production volume devoted to each use category, and the percent of the substance in the formulation for each commercial or consumer use.

7. For sites controlled by the submitter, the (a) identity of the sites where the substance will be manufactured, processed or used; (b) a process description and detailed process flow diagram; (c) worker exposure information; and (d) information on releases to the environment including the quantity and media and the control technology used.

8. For sites not controlled by the submitter, a description of processing and use information including an estimate of the number of sites and information about worker exposure and environmental releases and controls which limit them.

The PMN regulations do not prescribe specific studies or tests which must be performed and submitted because they vary widely from substance to substance. A submitter must, of course, submit sufficient information to enable the USEPA to determine that the substance does not present an unreasonable risk of injury to health or the environment because the USEPA will prohibit or restrict the chemical substance if it has insufficient information.

Manufacturers and importers will usually submit with a PMN at least an acute oral toxicity study, an acute dermal toxicity study and an acute dermal toxicity study. See 40 C.F.R. Subpart C for methods used to perform these tests. If the chemical substance will be discharged as water effluent, they will submit one or more of the aquatic toxicity tests such as an algal acute toxicity test, a daphnid acute or chronic toxicity test, a fish acute toxicity test, and/or a mysid shrimp acute toxicity test. See 40 C.F.R. Part 797 for methods used to perform these tests. They may also submit a mutagenicity test such as the in vitro cytogenics test for detection of chromosomal aberrations in cultured mammalian cells attributed to Dr. Bruce Ames. See 40 C.F.R. § 798.5375. They must submit other tests if they foresee that the USEPA's New Chemical Branch will need them for its risk assessment. However, they may decide to defer expensive long term carcinogenicity or neurotoxicity studies until the USEPA completes its initial risk assessment and decides whether such studies are necessary and would be useful if performed.

The submitter should also provide, of course, the label and material safety data sheet (MSDS) that it proposes to use for distribution of the chemical substance and any mixtures or articles containing the chemical substance.

The submitter must provide with the PMN all test data in its possession or control relating to the effects on health or the environment of any manufacture, processing, distribution, use, or disposal of the new chemical substance or any mixture or article containing it. This includes test data concerning the substance in pure, technical grade, or formulated form. The submitter must also provide all other data in its possession or control or which it knows or could reasonably ascertain. If the data appear in the open scientific literature, the submitter should provide a standard literature citation including the author, title, periodical name, date of publication, volume and pages. If the data do not appear in the open scientific literature, the submitter must provide a full report for (i) health effects data, (ii) ecological effects data, (iii) physical and chemical properties data, (iv) environmental fate characteristics, and (v) monitoring or other test data relating to human exposure to or environmental release of the chemical substance. If a study, report or test is in progress and not complete, the submitter must describe the study in detail including significant preliminary results and anticipated completion date. Upon completion, the submitter must provide the study within ten days, but no later than five days before the end of the review period. 40 C.F.R. § 720.50.

The submitter need not provide information previously submitted to the USEPA if it provides the office or person to whom the data were submitted and the date. The submitter also need not submit efficacy data or data relating only to exposure of humans or the environment outside the United States. However, the submitter must provide nonexposure data from outside the United States such as epidemiological studies. 40 C.F.R. § 50(d).

The importer of a new chemical substance is responsible for submission of a PMN for the substance and for the completeness and truthfulness of all the information it submits. 40 C.F.R. § 720.57.

5. PMN Review Procedures

The USEPA initially reviews a PMN to determine whether the chemical substance is subject to the PMN requirement. The USEPA will notify the submitter if it is not. 40 C.F.R. § 720.62.

If the PMN requirement applies, the USEPA sends a letter to the submitter acknowledging receipt of the PMN and providing the number assigned to the case. Within 30 days, the USEPA may request that the submitter correct errors in the PMN or notify that it is incomplete. If incomplete, the 90 day review period does not begin until the PMN is complete. If the USEPA finds any materially false or misleading statements in the PMN, the USEPA may find the PMN is incomplete and take other appropriate action. 40 C.F.R. § 720.65.

The USEPA publishes notice of the PMN in the Federal Register including the identity of the submitter, the chemical substance and its uses, and summaries of the test data submitted. However, these disclosures are subject to the right of the submitter to claim confidentiality for all or part of the information. 40 C.F.R. § 720.70.

The USEPA may extend the 90 review period by determining there is good cause to do so. The submitter may voluntarily suspend the review period for a specified time period. The USEPA notifies the submitter that the review period has expired or that it has completed the review. This does not constitute an approval or mean that the USEPA may not take future action against the substance. However, if the review period expires, the submitter may manufacture or import the chemical substance even if the submitter has not received notice of expiration. A submitter may withdraw a PMN by notice to the USEPA. 40 C.F.R. § 720.75.

The PMN regulations contain extensive and detailed provisions governing claims that information submitted is confidential business information, commonly called "CBI," and limiting public access to CBI. Recognizing that CBI is important to submitters, the USEPA makes extensive efforts to protect CBI if the claim is valid. 40 C.F.R. §§ 720.80 to 720.95.

Any person who submitted a PMN and thereafter commences to manufacture or import the chemical substance must submit a notice to the USEPA on Form 7710-56 no later than 30 days after the first day of such manufacture or import. This notice is important and not a mere formality. Among other things, it triggers listing of the chemical substance on the TSCA Inventory. 40 C.F.R. § 720.102.

6. PMN Substantive Review; Unilateral and Consent Orders

PMNs are reviewed by the New Chemicals Branch of the USEPA. The Branch consists of several internal staff organizations whose names and functions have been reorganized over the years. The submitter works primarily with a program manager who coordinates the communications between the submitter and the staff review team. The program manager may arrange direct communications or meetings from time to time, especially when complex or new scientific issues arise that can usefully be discussed between specialists for the submitter and specialists for the USEPA.

An early and important question may be the choice of a structural analogue for the new chemical substance. Of course, the new chemical substance will not be identical to any existing substance on the TSCA Inventory. However, it will usually have some resemblance to one or more existing substances in composition and structure. To be conservative, the staff may propose the most hazardous substance as the structural analogue. If the submitter disagrees, it should present facts to overcome the choice. Indeed, the submitter may sometimes be able to show that it formulated the new chemical substance to meet a need in the marketplace for a substitute product having different characteristics from products made from the substance proposed as the structural analogue. Whether the USEPA changes the structural analogue or not, a sound presentation by the submitter at this point can be effective in helping the staff to understand the new chemical substance and its use.

For some PMNs, the review team may decide there is adequate available information which makes it clear there is no unreasonable risk to human health or the environment. This might happen at the first meeting of the review team or at a later meeting after some of the staff have obtained further information from the submitter or through their own efforts. If so, the program manager will notify the submitter.

If the review team decides that there is insufficient information to assess the risk and either (i) the new chemical substance may present an unreasonable risk to human health or the environment or (2) the new chemical substance will be produced in substantial quantities or result in significant or substantial human exposure, the USEPA has authority to issue a unilateral order under Section 5(e) prohibiting or restricting manufacture, distribution, use or disposal until sufficient data becomes available. To issue an unilateral order, the USEPA must notify in writing each manufacturer, importer or processor of its determination that underlies the order at least 45 days before expiration of the 90 day review period. Any such manufacturer, importer or processor then have an opportunity to file objections that stay the order pending consideration by the USEPA. If the USEPA determines that the order should be issued notwithstanding the objections, it can apply for an injunction to the U.S. District Court. 15 U.S.C. § 2604(e).

The USEPA could also issue a rule or order pursuant to Section 5(f) or Section 6 or TSCA. 15 U.S.C. §§ 2604(f) and 2605. A rule issued pursuant to Section 5(f)(2) and Section 6(a) could be immediately effective.

More often, when the USEPA has reason to believe that the submitter will cooperate capably and in good faith, the USEPA will propose a Section 5(e) consent order. The USEPA will also ask whether the submitter wishes to negotiate all terms of the order or use a "fast track" program under which most terms will follow its standard form of consent order. The USEPA furnishes the standard form so that the submitter can read it before making a decision. The USEPA will also outline the restrictions that it plans to include in the consent order. Based on experience, the "fast track" choice tends to work well, although it moves more slowly than the words "fast track" would seem to imply. Even if full negotiation is chosen, the USEPA tends to rely on standard provisions and to depart from them only after cautious review. Further, the standard form has been developed over years and already contains some provisions designed to make compliance practicable. In addition, even under the "fast track" program, the submitter can request and the USEPA will make some changes from the standard form for sound substantive reasons.

The USEPA will not propose a consent order unless and until it has sufficient information to assess the imminent hazards of a new chemical substance with and without engineering and institutional controls. Thus, the USEPA is willing to allow manufacture, processing, distribution, use and/or disposal subject to restrictions so that the submitter can use a part of its revenues to pay for studies of the chronic or long term effects on human health and the environment. If the submitter fails to submit the studies or the studies show an unreasonable chronic risk of injury to human health or the environment, the submitter will either drop the chemical substance or the USEPA can act to prohibit or further restrict it before the chemical substance has been used long enough for the risk to become a reality.

The consent order will recite the history of the PMN including the information submitted and the USEPA's determinations. The consent order will allow manufacture or import and usually also processing, distribution and disposal of the new chemical substance subject to a number of restrictions. For example, the consent order may require workers engaged in manufacturing or processing the substance to wear personal protective equipment such as eye protectors, respirators and impermeable uniforms and gloves. The consent order may limit manufacture or processing to fully enclosed equipment or may limit disposal to a method such as incineration. The restrictions must remain in effect until the submitter performs and submits prescribed additional test studies that are expected to provide sufficient information to enable the USEPA to assess the risks of the new chemical substance. The time schedule for submission of the additional studies is usually linked to the sale of maximum volumes of the chemical substance that may not be exceeded before the studies are submitted.

In the consent order, the USEPA may limit distribution of the chemical substance until such time as it has adopted an expedited significant new use regulation (SNUR) for the substance and the time for legal challenges to the SNUR has expired. The limitations in the consent order will then expire. The reason is that the USEPA does not want the substance to be distributed to persons who are not yet legally bound to obligations corresponding to those in the consent order. Of course, the submitter benefits from the expedited SNUR because potential competitors will be subjected to the same restrictions it has undertaken.

After the consent order is signed, the submitter must furnish notice to the USEPA within 30 days after first commencement of manufacture or import, as described earlier, so that the new chemical substance will be added to the TSCA Inventory. In the meantime, the USEPA will proceed with steps to adopt the expedited SNUR. The USEPA customarily processes and publishes SNURs in groups, so submitters should try to complete a consent order in time to join a group of SNURs that will soon be issued.

F. Regulation of Microorganisms

1. Background

The USEPA has contended since 1984 that the definition of a "chemical substance" in TSCA is broad enough to include the genetically engineered microorganisms developed through biology. Using traditional statutory analysis, the USEPA's interpretation is questionable. However, industry is aware that the courts usually interpret the law to support the USEPA. Further, review and regulation of biotech products by the USEPA may help to rebut publicity seekers who attempt to frighten the public about biotechnology products although they have no sound scientific basis for doing so.

2. Reporting Requirements and Review Processes

Effective June 10, 1997, the USEPA adopted regulations establishing reporting requirements and review processes for microorganisms. 40 C.F.R. Part 725, 62 Fed. Reg. 17909 (1997). The regulations establish a reporting and review program quite similar to the PMN and SNUR programs described elsewhere in this chapter.

A microorganism means an organism classified, using the 5-Kingdom classification system of Whittacker, in the Kingdoms Monera (or Procaryotae), Protista, Fungi and the Chlorophyta and the Rhodophyta of the Plantae, and a virus or virus-like article. A new microorganism means a microorganism not included in the TSCA Inventory. 40 C.F.R. § 725.3.

The regulations require submission of a microbial commercial activity notice (MCAN) at least 90 days before manufacture or import of a new genetically engineered microorganism. Like the PMN regulations, the submitter must include detailed information in the MCAN and also submit health and environmental effects data. The USEPA reviews the MCAN by methods generally similar to its review of a PMN and uses, among other sources, information available from its Biotechnology Science Advisory Committee. When the 90 day review period expires or the submitter becomes entitled to manufacture or import the new microorganism under a consent order, the submitter must file a notice of commencement (NOC) within 30 days. Upon receipt of the NOC, the USEPA adds the new genetically engineered microorganism to the TSCA Inventory. 40 C.F.R. Part 725, §§ 725.100 to 190.

The regulations provide a Tier I exemption under which genetic material meeting prescribed criteria can be introduced into a list of ten recipient microorganisms without submitting an MCAN or other review if the manufacturer meets physical control and containment requirements for any facility in which the new microorganisms will be used under the exemption. The manufacturer must submit a compliance certification to the USEPA at least ten days before commencing initial manufacturer or importer of a new microorganism derived from a listed recipient microorganism. The manufacturer must also maintain records for the initial and subsequent uses of the new microorganism that verify compliance. 40 C.F.R. § 725.424.

A manufacturer which can meet the requirements for a Tier I exemption except the physical control and containment requirements may submit a Tier II exemption request to the USEPA. The review period for the request is 45 days. The request must demonstrate that the physical control and containment requirements will be at least adequate. The Tier II exemption also contains certification and recordkeeping requirements. 40 C.F.R. § 725.428 to .470.

Any manufacturer, importer and processor of a microorganism for any significant new use designated by the USEPA in 42 C.F.R. Subpart M must submit an MCAN to the USEPA unless excluded or exempted. 40 C.F.R. § 725.105(c) 40 C.F.R. Part 725, Subpart L. The exclusions are in § 725.910 and the exemptions are in § 725.912. Expedited procedures may be used to issue significant new use rules (SNURs) for microorganisms subject to Section 5(e) orders. The USEPA has not yet published any SNURs for microorganisms in the Code of Federal Regulations.

The USEPA regulates research and development of microorganisms more strictly than its regulation of research and development of new chemical substances. 40 C.F.R. §§ 725.200 *et seq.* To be excused from submitting an MCAN, a person engaged in commercial research and development (R&D) activities must meet one of several requirements:

> *First*, an MCAN need not be submitted if (1) a microorganism is manufactured, imported or processed solely for R&D activities; (2) use is by or under supervision of a technically qualified individual; (3) there is no intentional testing of the microorganism outside of a structure which effectively surrounds and encloses the microorganism and restricts it from leaving; and (4) containment and/or inactivation controls are implemented under supervision of the technically qualified individual. The manufacturer must also meet employee notification and recordkeeping requirements. 40 C.F.R. § 725.234
>
> *Second*, an MCAN need not be submitted for R&D activities in a structure which are performed under federal agency programs which condition funding on, or legally require, that the research be conducted in accordance with the National Institute of Health guidelines for Research Involving Recombinant DNA Molecules (July 5, 1994). 40 C.F.R. § 725.235.
>
> *Third*, an MCAN need not be submitted for R&D activities outside a structure using Bradyrhizobium Japonicum or Rhizobium meliloti microorganisms if several requirements are met including a limitation of the test site area to ten territorial acres. 40 C.F.R. § 725.238.
>
> *Fourth*, rather than an MCAN, a manufacturer, importer or processor may submit a TSCA experimental release application (TERA) with supporting information at least 60 calendar days before initiating a proposed R&D activity. The advantage of a TERA is that the required information is not so extensive as that required for an MCAN and the review period is 60 days rather than 90. In addition, if the USEPA approves a TERA, the submitter can commence the R&D activity without waiting for the end of the review period as is required when an MCAN is submitted. 40 C.F.R. §§ 725.250 to .288.

In January 2001, the USEPA issued new regulations on plant-incorporated protectants (PIPs) which opponents prefer to call pesticides. The USEPA said it found little or no risk to human health or the environment from the PIPs. This followed a report by the National Academy of Sciences reporting that it found no evidence that foods produced by biotechnical engineering are unsafe. The regulations were issued under the Federal Insecticide, Fungicide, and Rodenticide Act and the Federal Food, Drug and Cosmetic Act, but the science may be useful to testing projects under TSCA.

G. Good Laboratory Practice Standards

1. Background

Among the most important steps taken by the USEPA has been the development and enforcement of good laboratory practice standards, 40 C.F.R. Part 792.

The world owes a great debt to imaginative and courageous scientists who performed experiments for centuries using the methods and equipment available to them. Doctors administered new drugs to themselves rather than risk harm to their patients. Chemists and engineers worked alone with new formulations and processes rather than risk fellow workers. To mention just one well known example, Marie Sklodowska Curie died from prolonged exposures to radiation.

However, only outstanding effort can obtain good scientific results from informal methods and limited equipment. The more likely results are inability to perform projects and limited reliability of the projects performed.

Of course, the USEPA did not invent good laboratory practice standards. Laboratories at leading companies, universities, hospitals and other research and testing institutions developed high standards over the years and shared them to some extent through formal and informal associations. The USEPA made use of many of these standards in developing its regulatory programs. The USEPA was able to use regulatory authority to obtain, further develop and publish good laboratory practices for use throughout the nation and to require their consistent use by all regulated laboratories.

2. Terminology

The GLP regulations provide some definitions that are essential to understanding their meaning. Stated briefly, a "test system" means an animal, plant, microorganism, chemical or physical matrix (such as soil or water) to which a test, control or reference substance is administered or added for study. A "test substance" is a substance or mixture administered to a test system to develop data. A "control substance" is a chemical substance or mixture, or any material other than the test substance, feed or water, that is administered to the test system in the course of a study to establish a basis for comparison with the test substance for chemical or biological measurements. A "reference substance" has the same definition as a "control substance," but also includes an analytical standard used in analyzing a test substance for known chemical or biological measurements. A "specimen" is any material derived from a test system for examination or analysis. 40 C.F.R. § 792.3.

3. Statements of Compliance; Conduct of Tests

Any person who submits a test to the USEPA must include a true and correct statement signed by the sponsor and study director either that the study was conducted in accordance with the GLP regulations or describing in detail all differences between the practices used in the study and those required by the GLP regulations. If a person is required to submit a study that it did not conduct, the person may include a statement that it did not conduct the study and does not know whether the study was conducted in accordance with the GLP regulations. 40 C.F.R. § 792.12.

A sponsor or other person conducting a test violates TSCA if (1) the test is not conducted in accordance with any of the GLP regulations; (2) data or information submitted to the USEPA are false, misleading, contain significant omissions, or otherwise do not fulfill the requirements of the GLP regulations; or (3) it denies entry to audit test data or inspect test facilities. Violations are subject to civil or criminal penalties and other remedies. 40 C.F.R. § 792.17.

4. Organization and Personnel

The GLP regulations prescribe qualifications and responsibilities for testing facility management and personnel including a requirement that each testing facility must have a quality assurance unit. The regulations require that a scientist or person of appropriate education, training and/or experience be identified as the study director and prescribe the study director's responsibilities. Testing facility management must promptly replace a study director if it becomes necessary to do so during the conduct of a study. 40 C.F.R. §§ 792.29 to .35.

5. Facilities

The GLP regulations contain detailed requirements for test system care and supply facilities. The regulations focus on sanitation and separation in order to avoid cross-contamination and mixups and also require control of control of conditions such as temperature and humidity. The regulations require separate areas for handling test, control and reference substances and for laboratory operation areas. The regulations also require limited access space for archives for the storage and retrieval of all raw data and specimens from completed studies. 40 C.F.R. §§ 792.41 to .51.

6. Equipment

The GLP regulations require that equipment be of appropriate design and adequate capacity and be suitably located for operation, inspection, cleaning and maintenance. 40 C.F.R.§ 792.61. The regulations also require that equipment be adequately inspected, cleaned and maintained. Equipment used for generation, measurement or assessment of data must be adequately tested, calibrated and/or standardized. Written standard operating procedures and written records are required including records of nonroutine repairs. 40 C.F.R. §§ 792.61 and .63.

7. Testing Facilities Operation

Testing facilities must establish and maintain standard operating procedures for each of the numerous steps in their operations and they must be immediately available for the laboratory or field procedures being performed. Significant changes must be authorized in writing by management. 40 C.F.R. § 792.81.

Reagents and solutions in laboratory areas must be labeled to indicate identity, titer or concentration, storage requirements and expiration dates. Deteriorated or outdated reagents and solutions must not be used. 40 C.F.R. § 792.83.

Standard operating procedures must be adopted for the housing, feeding, handling and care of animals and other test systems. Among other things, all newly received test systems must be isolated and their health status or appropriateness for study must be evaluated. They must be free of any disease that might interfere with the study. If they will be removed from and returned to their housing units, they must be identified by means such as a tattoo, color code, tag or ear punch. Test systems must be housed separately when necessary and the housing and accessory equipment must be cleaned and sanitized at appropriate intervals. Controls and documentation must also be established for food, soil, water, bedding and pest control materials used for the animals or other test control systems. All plant and animal test systems must be acclimatized to the environmental conditions of a test prior to use in a study. 40 C.F.R. § 792.90.

8. Test, Control and Reference Substance Characterization

For each batch of a test, control or reference substance to be used in a study, the identify, strength, purity, composition or other relevant characteristics must be determined and documented before use in the study. When relevant, solubility must be determined. Stability must also be determined. Storage containers must be labeled and batch samples retained. Procedures must be established to assure proper storage, distribution, identification and documentation. Mixtures of substances with carriers and vehicles must be analyzed as appropriate to assure that solubility, stability or other problems do not interfere with the integrity of a test. 40 C.F.R. §§ 792.105 to .113.

9. Protocols and Conduct of Studies

Each study must have an approved written protocol that clearly indicates the objectives and all methods for the conduct of the study. The protocol must provide step-by-step procedures including such matters as justification for selection of the test system and the number, body weight, sex, source of supply, species, strain, substrain and age of the test system. The protocol must describe the experimental design, including methods for control of bias. The protocol must also include other items such as the route, method and frequency of administration of the test, control and reference substances, expressed in milligrams per kilogram of body or test system, weight or other appropriate units. Protocol changes and the reasons must be documented, signed by the study director, dated, and maintained with the protocol. 40 C.F.R. § 792.120.

The study must be conducted in accordance with the protocol. Specimens must be identified in a manner that precludes error. In animal studies where histopathology is required, records of gross findings for a specimen from post mortem observations must be available to the pathologist when examining the specimen histopathologically. Data must be recorded by detailed procedures. 40 C.F.R. § 792.130.

When studies are limited to determining physical and chemical characteristics of a test, control or reference substance, it is not necessary to comply with several of the GLP standards. 40 C.F.R. § 792.135.

In the author's experience, the USEPA's technical staff prefers to review the protocol for a study before it is performed. Sponsors benefit from the review because it is an opportunity to discuss technical questions and possibly to improve and expedite the study.

10. Records and Reports

The GLP regulations contain detailed requirements for reporting of study results, storage and retrieval of records and data, and retention of records. 40 C.F.R. §§ 792.185 to .195.

H. Significant New Use Notices

TSCA requires any person intending to manufacture, process or import any chemical substance for a use which the USEPA has determined by rule to be a significant new use to submit a significant new use notice to the USEPA at least 90 days before doing so. The USEPA may adopt a significant new use rule (SNUR) for any chemical substance regulated by TSCA including those listed in the TSCA Inventory. If the USEPA adopts and publishes a SNUR, any person planning to manufacture, process or import the chemical substance for the use identified in the SNUR must submit a significant new use notice (SNUN) to the USEPA together with test data required by the USEPA. 15 U.S.C. § 2604(a) and (b).

The USEPA adopts significant new use rules (SNURs) for specific chemical substances that are initially published in the Federal Register and then in 40 C.F.R., Part 721, Subpart E. These chemical substances are subject to restrictions stated for each of them in Subpart E which may include some or all of five standard restrictions contained in Subpart B. They are also subject to 5 year recordkeeping requirements in § 721.40

It is important to understand that SNURs are adopted by the USEPA by rulemaking procedures which require publication of each proposed SNUR for public comment before adoption. The significant new uses become those described in the SNUR as finally adopted and published the Federal Register and 40 C.F.R. Part 721, Subpart E. Thus, manufacturers, processors and importers do not have to guess about new uses that the USEPA considers to be significant. Each SNUR refers by cross reference to the uses considered to be new uses and to related notification and recordkeeping requirements.

SNURs can be difficult to read when a manufacturer, processor or importer is not accustomed to the techniques which the USEPA uses. For example, a SNUR may state that a significant new use is any use of a substance without establishing a worker protection and hazard communication program as described in 40 C.F.R. § 721.63 and 64. The reader will recognize the programs as corresponding to those of the U.S. Occupational Health and Safety Administration (OSHA). Thus, the USEPA used its SNUR authority to extend its jurisdiction to worker protection programs usually regulated by OSHA.

The USEPA also adopts and publishes a SNUR for chemical substances which it authorizes to be manufactured or imported under Section 5(e) consent order. The purpose is to require other persons in the industry to comply with requirements corresponding to those imposed on the person who signed the consent order. 40 C.F.R. § 721.160 *et seq*.

If the USEPA has issued a SNUR, any person who intends to manufacture, import or process for commercial purposes a chemical substance listed in Subpart E and either (1) intends to engage in a significant new use of the substance or (2) intends to distribute the substance must submit a significant new use notice (SNUN) to the USEPA. However, a person who intends to distribute the substance is not required to submit a SNUN if it can document any of the following steps:

(1) The person notified the recipient in writing of the specific section in Subpart E which identifies the substance and its designated significant new uses, or

(2) the recipient knows of the specific subsection in Subpart E which identifies the substance and its designated significant new uses, or

(3) the recipient cannot undertake any significant new use described in the specific section of Subpart E.

The USEPA further requires a person who obtains knowledge, after commencing distribution, that a recipient of the substance is engaging in a significant new use without submitting a SNUN to cease supplying the substance to that recipient and to submit a SNUN, unless the person takes certain steps that excuse the obligation. 40 C.F.R. §721.5.

A SNUN must be submitted on EPA Form 7710-25 which is the same form used for a PMN. The SNUN must be submitted at least ninety (90) calendar days before commencing manufacture, import or processing of the chemical substance identified in Subpart E for a significant new use. The supporting information and the provisions for review by the EPA are similar to those provided for PMNs. However, if the USEPA has previously reviewed the chemical substance as part of a PMN proceeding, it may be able to focus its review of the substance primarily on the significant new use.

The regulations also contain procedures by which the USEPA may approve alternative measures to control worker exposure or environmental releases that USEPA determines provide substantially the same degree of protection as those specified in the SNUR regulations.

The USEPA's regulations also contain several exemptions from the SNUN requirements, including an exemption for significant new use in small quantities solely for research and development.

I. Hazardous Chemical Substances and Mixtures

1. Authority to Impose Restrictions including Prohibitions

Section 6 of TSCA authorizes the USEPA to impose restrictions if it finds there is reasonable basis to conclude that the manufacture, processing, distribution, use or disposal of a chemical substance will result in an unreasonable risk of injury to health or the environment. The possible restrictions include prohibition of the substance or mixture, limitation on concentrations in manufacture or use, warning labels and instructions, record keeping, limitations on use, prohibition or regulation of disposal, and notice and recall or repurchase. The Act requires the USEPA to apply the *least* burdensome requirements to the extent necessary to protect adequately against the risk. If the risk is being caused inadvertently, the USEPA may review the quality control procedures of a manufacturer or processor. 15 U.S.C. § 2605.

The USEPA's rulemaking procedures under Section 6 are at 40 C.F.R. Part 750.

Section 6 grants less power to the USEPA than other laws it administers. The USEPA is accustomed to administering laws that allow it to take actions without regard to their economic consequences or burdensome effects. For example, as described in an earlier chapter, the Clean Air Act has been interpreted to prohibit the USEPA from considering cost when it adopts air quality standard. Thus, the USEPA has made relatively little use of Section 6.

2. Chlorofluorocarbons

Soon after TSCA was enacted, the USEPA used Section 6 to prohibit the manufacture, processing and distribution of aerosol propellants containing chlorofluorocarbons. However, the regulations were withdrawn in 1995 because the USEPA had adopted much broader regulations applicable to chlorofluorocarbons under the Clean Air Act.

3. Halogenated Dibenzodioxins and Dibenzofurans

The USEPA used Section 6 to adopt regulations governing the treatment and disposal of wastes containing tetrachlorodibenzo-para-dioxins, but withdrew the regulations when it issued the "land ban" (i.e., treatment before disposal) regulations under the Resource Conservation and Recovery Act. However, the USEPA continues to maintain regulations adopted under Sections 4 and 6 requiring that manufacturers and processors of certain chemicals test them by prescribed methods for the presence of extremely low levels of halogenated dibenzodioxins (HDDs) and halogenated dibenzofurans (HDFs) and report the results to the USEPA. 40 C.F.R. Part 766.

4. Polychlorinated Biphenyls

Effective July 2, 1979, the USEPA used its Section 6 authority to prohibit the manufacture of polychlorinated biphenyls (PCBs) for use within, or export from, the United States. PCB mixtures had been widely used as dielectric fluids and heat transfer fluids because of their excellent stability and fire resistance and their relatively low toxicity compared to many other chemicals. The Monsanto Company, the only U.S. manufacturer, had previously decided to terminate to manufacture PCB products. The USEPA also prohibited processing and distribution of PCBs and PCB items for use within, or export from, the United States. The USEPA also prohibited use of PCB and PCB Items in any manner other than a totally enclosed manner in the United States. PCB Items include articles, article container, PCB containers, PCB equipment or anything that deliberately or unintentionally contains or has as a part of its any PCB or PCBs. A totally enclosed manner means any manner that ensures no exposure of human beings or the environment to any concentration of PCBs. The regulations contain several exclusions and exemptions, including exclusions for PCB materials with concentrations of PCBs equal to or less than 50 parts per million.

The practical effect of the PCB regulations was to prevent further processing and distribution of PCBs and PCB Items, but to allow continued use as dielectric fluid in existing transformers, capacitors and other fully enclosed electrical equipment subject to marking (labelling); storage; disposal by incineration; decontamination; spill cleanup; testing; recordkeeping and reporting requirements. The regulations preempt the provisions of RCRA, the Hazardous Materials Transportation Act and state and local laws to the extent they are inconsistent, but the USEPA has coordinated the regulations with other regulatory programs by such methods as prescribing use of the RCRA Uniform Hazardous Waste Manifest for shipments of PCB and PCB Item wastes.

On June 29, 1998, the USEPA published amendments to the PCB regulations, called the "Mega Rule," intended to make the rules for storage, use and disposal of PCB-containing electrical equipment somewhat more practical. The Sierra Club sued to challenge some of the amendments as insufficiently strict. Some electric utilities and General Electric Company sued on grounds that the USEPA had not provided substantial evidence to support the amendments, including its refusal to grant a blanket exemption to the electrical industry allowing storage for reuse of articles containing PCBs. General Electric alleged that the USEPA used scientifically erroneous methods to assess the risk of PCBs, resulting in an overestimate of their risks. The U.S. Circuit Court of Appeals for the Fifth Circuit held that the Sierra Club did not have standing and dismissed its petition. The Court also dismissed most of the complaints of the electrical utilities and General Electric on grounds that the USEPA need not have substantial evidence to support its TSCA rules which must be upheld unless they are arbitrary and capricious. However, the Court held that the USEPA was required to provide a reasoned explanation for its refusal to adopt the storage and reuse exemption for the electric utility industry. *Central and Southwest Services v. U.S.E.P.A.*, 220 F.3d 683 (5th Cir. 2000); rehearing denied 237 F.3d 633 (5th Cir. 2000); *cert. denied,* 532 U.S. 1065, 150 L.Ed.2d 209 (2001).

In January 2001, the USEPA adopted two additional PCB rules under TSCA. One rule authorizes the return of PCBs for territories and possessions of the United States to the customs territory of the United States for disposal in compliance with the PCB regulations. The purpose is to allow the return of PCBs from islands which have no proper storage or disposal facilities. The other rule simplified the procedures for converting electrical equipment to a less strictly regulated classification by retrofilling the equipment to reduce concentrations of PCBs in the dielectric fluid. The USEPA's cleanup guidance was held invalid in *General Electric v. EPA,* 290 F.3d 377 (D.C. Cir. 2002).

5. Hexavalent Chromium

Effective February 20, 1990, the USEPA used Section 6 authority to prohibit the distribution and commercial use of hexavalent chromium-based water treatment chemicals in comfort cooling towers. The prohibition does not apply to their use in industrial cooling towers and closed cooling water systems, subject to compliance with labelling, reporting and recordkeeping requirements. 40 U.S.C. § 749.68.

6. Nitrosating Additives for Certain Metalworking Fluids

In 1984, the USEPA used Section 6 authority to prohibit any person from adding nitrosating agents to mixed mono and diamides of an organic acid contained in metal working fluids because of their potential to form nitrosamines which the

USEPA determined had potential to cause cancer to laboratory animals. The prohibition also included adding any nitrosating agent to a triethanolamine salt of a substituted organic acid or tricarboxylic acid. Among other requirements, distributors of metalworking fluids containing organic acids and salts subject to the regulation must label them to warn against the addition of nitrites and other nitrosating agents. 40 C.F.R. Part 747.

7. Asbestos-Containing Products

In 1989, the USEPA used Section 6 authority to adopt regulations prohibiting in phases over several years the manufacture, import, processing and distribution for use in the United States or for export of certain asbestos-containing products. The regulations defined an asbestos-containing material as any product to which asbestos is deliberately added in any concentration or which contains more than 1% asbestos by weight or area. The regulations were vacated by court decision in *Corrosion Proof Fittings v. EPA.*, 947 F.2d 1201 (5th Cir. 1991). The court was specially critical of the USEPA's failure to give full consideration to the limited risks, benefits and alternatives for brake linings and other friction products, asbestos cement pipe products, and roofing shingles and materials. The USEPA modified the regulations and the prohibitions now apply to flooring felt, commercial paper, corrugated paper, rollboard, specialty paper, and new uses of asbestos. Commercial paper includes general insulation or muffler paper. Corrugated paper includes pipe coverings and other thermal system insulation. Specialty paper includes filtration, cooling tower and refrigeration systems. The regulations do not prohibit purchases or acquisitions of small quantities of products made outside the customs territory of the United States for personal use in the United States. 40 C.F.R. §§ 763.160 *et seq.*

J. Imminently Hazardous Chemical Substances and Mixtures

Section 7 of TSCA authorizes the USEPA to commence action in a U.S. District Court for seizure of any imminently hazardous chemical substance or mixture and to seek relief against any person who manufactures, processes, distributes, uses or disposes of any such substance or mixture or article containing the same. 15 U.S.C. § 2606.

K. Lead-Based Paint

The USEPA has adopted extensive regulations under TSCA relating to lead-based paint. These regulations are found at 40 C.F.R. Part 745 and are discussed further in Chapter XVI on Laws Relating to Lead.

L. Reporting Obligations under Section 8

Section 8 of TSCA requires manufacturers and importers to file several reports with the USEPA. 15 U.S.C. § 2607.

1. § 8(a)—Preliminary Assessment Information Reports

Manufacturers and importers must submit for each fiscal year a form 7710-35, Manufacturers Report—Preliminary Assessment Information for the chemical substances listed in 40 C.F.R. § 712.30. See 40 C.F.R., Part 712.

A copy of Form 7710-35, the PAIR Report Form appears at the end of this Chapter. Part 712 does not contain recordkeeping requirements, but EPA inspectors may request copies of the reports and supporting data.

Exempt manufacturers and importers include:

(1) Persons who manufactured or imported during the reporting period solely for scientific experimentation, analysis or research;

(2) persons who manufactured or reported during the reporting period fewer than 500 kg (1100 pounds) of the chemical sub stance at a single plant site;

(3) certain persons who qualify as small manufacturers or importers; and

(4) persons who manufactured or imported the chemical substance during the reporting period only as a byproduct not used or sold that was formed as described in 40 C.F.R. 710.4(d)(3) through (7), as a non-isolated intermediate, or as an impurity. See 40 C.F.R. § 712.25.

2. § 8(a)—Inventory Update Reports

Section 8(a) requires inventory update reports (UIRs) at four year intervals by any person who manufactured (or imported) for commercial purposes 10,000 pounds (4,540 kg) or more of a chemical substance listed in the TSCA Inventory (Master Inventory File) during its latest fiscal year before the report. See 40 C.F.R. Part 710.

Several kinds of chemical substances are excluded from the reporting requirement: (1) inorganic chemical substances; (2) polymers; (3) microorganisms; and (4) naturally occurring substances. Further, a manufacturer or importer is not required to report small quantities solely for research and development, a chemical substance imported as part of an article; certain by-products described in 40 C.F.R. § 720.30(g); and certain impurities, by-products, reaction products, nonisolated intermediates and chemical substances used solely for noncommercial research and development purposes described in 40 C.F.R. § 720.30(h).

A copy of the last Form U appears at the end of this Chapter. The USEPA will issue a new Form U in 2002.

The regulations require keeping of records documenting the information reported to the EPA for four years. For substances less than 10,000 pounds, records must support the decision not to report. 40 C.F.R. § 710.32.

3. § 8(c)—Significant Adverse Reaction Reports

Section 8(c) requires that manufacturers (including importers) and processors and distributors of chemical substances and mixtures keep records of allegations of significant adverse reactions to health or the environment alleged to have been caused by the substance or mixture. The records must contain specific information and be retained for 30 years. 40 C.F.R., Part 717. The records must be made available for inspection by EPA representatives. They need not be submitted to the EPA unless the EPA furnishes a notice requiring them to be submitted.

The regulations exclude some manufacturers, sole distributors, and retailers that are not also the manufacturer or processor. The regulations also exclude certain chemical substances.

A "significant adverse reaction" means a reaction that may indicate a substantial impairment of normal activities or long-lasting or irreversible damage to health or the environment. The regulations describe the kinds of allegations, including verbal allegations, and significant adverse reactions that must be recorded. For example, it is not necessary to record commonly recognized human health effects of a substance or mixture described in scientific articles, publications abstracted in standard reference sources, or in the firm's product labeling or MSDS. However, an effect in these categories must be recorded if (1) it is a significantly more severe toxic effect than previously described; (2) it is a manifestation of a toxic effect after a significantly shorter exposure period or lower exposure level than described; or (3) it is a manifestation of a toxic effect by an exposure route different from that described.

4. § 8(d)—Health and Safety Data Reports

Section 8(d) requires manufacturers and importers to report health and safety studies and underlying data and to submit copies to the EPA under certain circumstances. The obligation includes a responsibility to search records to determine whether a manufacturer or importer has any such studies or data. 40 C.F.R., Part 716.

The regulations exclude certain manufacturers and importers and also certain health studies including studies which have been published in the scientific literature and studies previously submitted to the EPA's Office of Pollution Prevention Toxics. Part 716 does not contain specific recordkeeping requirements, but EPA inspectors may request records sufficient to demonstrate compliance with the reporting requirements.

5. § 8(e)—Substantial Risk Reports

Section 8(e) requires that the manufacturer, processor or distributor of a chemical substance must immediately report to the EPA any information concerning the substance that reasonably supports the conclusion that the chemical substance or mixture presents a substantial risk of injury to health or the environment unless such person has actual knowledge that the EPA has been adequately informed of such information. In TSCA, the term "manufacturer" includes importation, so importers must also report substantial risk information.

A company is considered to have received information when received by an officer or employee capable of appreciating its significance. The information must be reported within 15 days. Most companies have established internal reporting systems headed by committees to screen information and determine whether it is reportable. Such a system relieves officers and employees of the obligation to report directly to the USEPA.

It is difficult to interpret Section 8(e) because the EPA was not required to adopt any regulations to implement the reporting requirement and has chosen not to adopt any regulations voluntarily. Thus, the only guidance is provided by the EPA's Statement of Interpretation and Enforcement Policy, 43 Fed. Reg. 11110 (1978) ("1978 Policy Statement"). The EPA also proposed modifications to the 1978 Policy Statement in 58 Fed. Reg. 37735 (1993) and 60 Fed. Reg. 14756 (1995).

According to the USEPA's guidance, it is not necessary to report information (1) already published by the EPA in its reports; (2) previously submitted to the EPA pursuant to the major environmental laws; (3) published in the scientific literature and referenced in certain abstract services; (4) corroborative of well-established adverse effects already documented and referenced in certain chemical abstract services; or (5) contained in notification of spills under Section 311(b)(5) of the Federal Water Pollution Act. The abstract services are Agricola, Biological Abstracts, Chemical Abstracts, Dissertation Abstracts, Index Medicus, and the National Technology Information Service.

M. Export Notification and Import Certification

1. § 12(b)—Export Notification

An export notice must be filed with the EPA when any person exports, or intends to export, a chemical substance or mixture if (1) data has been required by the EPA under §§ 4 or (5(b) of TSCA; (2) the EPA has issued an order under § 5 of TSCA; (3) the EPA has proposed or issued a rule under §§ 5 or 6 of TSCA; or (4) an action is pending or relief has been granted under §§ 5 or 7 of TSCA. No notice is required for exports of articles, except PCB articles. See 40 C.F.R. §§ 707.60 to 707.75.

The exporter, for this purpose, is the person who, as the principal party in interest in the export transaction, has the power and responsibility for determining and controlling the sending of the chemical substance or mixture to a destination out of the customs territory of the United States.

To determine whether a chemical substance or mixture is subject to export notification, the first step is to check the CORR List which shows "12b" if an export notice is required. However, the CORR List is sometimes out of date and omits some chemical substances or mixtures that have become subject to § 12(b) notification and continues to list others after the notice requirement has terminated. Thus, it is necessary to check the Federal Register, a daily publication of the Superintendent of Documents, to verify the CORR List information.

An export notification is given by a letter because the EPA has not published a form. The letter must include the name of the chemical substance as shown in the regulatory action, i.e., the TSCA Chemical Substance Inventory. The notice must also include the name and address of the exporter; the country(ies) of export; the date(s) of export or intended export; and the Section (4, 5, 6 or 7) of TSCA under which the EPA has taken action.

> *NOTE:* The CORR List shows the section of the EPA's action.

The letter must be marked "Section 12(b) Notice: and be sent to the Document Control (7407), Office of Pollution Prevention and Toxics, U.S. Environmental Protection Agency, Room G-099, 401 M Street S.W., Washington, DC 20460. It is *not* necessary to give the name or address of the customer.

The export notification regulations do not contain specific recordkeeping requirements. However, EPA inspectors verify compliance by requesting to review the notification procedures and copies of notices sent to the EPA. 40 C.F.R. Part 707.

2. Import Certification

The U.S. Customs Service requires importers to sign the following statement for each import of chemical substances for each import of chemical substances subject to TSCA:

> "I certify that all chemical substances in this shipment comply with all applicable rules or orders under TSCA and that I am not offering a chemical substance for entry in violation of TSCA or any applicable rule or order under TSCA."

The U.S. Customs Service requires importers of chemicals not subject to TSCA (e.g., pesticides) to certify that compliance with TSCA is not required. Importers must certify this by signing the statement:

> "I certify that all chemicals in this shipment are not subject to TSCA."

The EPA expects that certification will be based upon actual knowledge of the importer in most cases. However, EPA realizes that sometimes importers may not have actual knowledge of the chemical composition of imported mixtures. The importer should attempt to discover the chemical constituents by contacting another party to the transaction (e.g., the foreign manufacturer). The greater the effort an importer makes, the smaller the chance of committing a violation. If a shipment is ultimately determined to have violated TSCA, good faith efforts of the importer, as evidenced by documents in its files, may obviate or mitigate a civil penalty. See C.LF.R. See 40 C.F.R.§ 707.20.

The export certification regulations do not contain specific recordkeeping requirements. However, EPA inspectors verify compliance with the certification requirements by examining shipping documents to see whether the certifications are present and by comparing the certifications to the TSCA Inventory, the CORR List and other data to see whether they are accurate. 40 C.F.R., Part 707

N. Enforcement Provisions

TSCA provides that the USEPA may assess civil penalties up to $31,500 per violation per day. In addition, any knowing or willful violator is subject, upon conviction, to a fine up to $31,500 per day of violation or imprisonment up to one year or both. 15 U.S.C. § 2615. TSCA also provides for seizure of any chemical substance, mixture or product manufactured, processed or distributed in violation of its requirements. 15 U.S.C.§ 2616.

Citizens' civil actions to restrain violations and to compel the USEPA to perform any nondiscretionary act or duty are expressly authorized by TSCA. However, the right is limited by provisions requiring 60 day notice to the USEPA and is also limited if the USEPA or the Department of Justice has commenced and is diligently prosecuting an order or civil action. 15 U.S.C. § 2619. Citizens' petitions to the USEPA to initiate proceedings for the issuance, amendment, or repeal of a rule are also authorized. 15 U.S.C.§ 2620.

TSCA contains express provisions protecting employees who are "whistleblowers" from discharge or discrimination as to compensation, terms, conditions or privileges of employment. 15 U.S.C. § 2622.

A Statement of Interpretation and Enforcement Policy was issued in 1978 by USEPA providing guidelines on Section 8(e). 43 Fed. Reg. 11,110 (1978). During 1990 and 1991, the USEPA initiated strict enforcement steps against several manufacturers based on interpretations that industry claims are new and the USEPA claims are consistent with its 1978 Policy.

The USEPA issued an enforcement response policies for reporting and recordkeeping rules and requirements for TSCA Sections 5, 8, 12 and 13. They are important documents because the majority of violations of TSCA are recordkeeping and reporting violations and the penalties are in large amounts, but can be reduced in some circumstances. The USEPA has also issued an enforcement policy for violations of TSCA Section 5.

O. Asbestos Abatement in Public Elementary and Secondary Schools

In 1986, Congress adopted the so-called Asbestos Hazard Emergency Response Act (AHERA) which is actually Title II of TSCA, 15 U.S.C. § 2641 to 2655. AHERA mandates and regulates inspections for and abatement of asbestos-containing materials in public elementary and secondary schools. AHERA is discussed in Chapter X of this book

P. Radon Abatement in School and Federal Buildings

Radon is a naturally occurring radioactive gas found in the soil in many areas of the United States. Radon sometimes migrates from the soil into basements and other areas of buildings including schools and homes.

In 1988, Congress adopted Title III of TSCA establishing several programs to study and abate radon in elementary and secondary school buildings and buildings owned by the federal government, 15 U.S.C. § 2661 to 2671. The stated goal is to reduce radon in buildings to the same level as in ambient air outside buildings.

Title III directs the USEPA to publish guides to radon. The USEPA has published several guides which present information about radon. Although disclosing that some scientists dispute the number of deaths, the USEPA states that major health organizations agree with estimates that radon causes thousands of preventable lung cancer deaths per year, especially among smokers. (This statement may be helpful to the tobacco industry in its defense of lawsuits). The home buyer's and seller's guide recommends testing the air in homes and fixing them if the average test level is 4 pico Curies per liter (4 pCi/L) or more. The guide advises that homes can be fixed relatively easily and inexpensively by contractors meeting its proficiency requirements or certified under a state program. The USEPA's regulations prescribing the fees for applicants and participants in its national radon measurement proficiency program and its national radon contractor proficiency program are found at 40 C.F.R. Part 195.

Title III also requires the USEPA to develop model construction standards and techniques for controlling radon levels in new buildings and to conduct studies on the extent of radon in schools and federal buildings and to provide grants for training programs and seminars and to assist the states to develop and implement programs for the assessment and mitigation of radon. See also the Radon Gas and Indoor Air Quality Research Act of 1986 (42 U.S.C. § 7401, footnote) and the national emission standard for radon emissions from facilities of the U.S. Department of Energy (40 C.F.R. Part 61, Subpart Q).

For an example of an extensive state radon program, see the radon provisions in the New Jersey State Uniform Construction Code. N.J.A.C. § 5:23-10.1 *et seq.*

Q. Lead-Based Paint Abatement in Pre-1978 Housing

In 1992, Congress adopted Title IV of TSCA as part of the Residential Lead-Based Paint Hazard Reduction Act of 1992 (RLBPHRA). Title IV of TSCA is found at 15 U.S.C. § 2681 to 2692.

Title IV assigned to the USEPA several tasks to implement the RLBPHRA in cooperation with other federal, state and local government agencies including accreditation of training programs for persons engaged in lead-based paint activities; adoption of guidelines for persons engaged in renovation and remodeling of pre-1978 housing; adoption of regulations identifying lead-based paint hazards and dangerous levels of lead in dust and soil; adoption of standards for laboratories testing lead in paint films, soil and dust; establishing a National Clearinghouse on Childhood Lead Poisoning; establishing by rule appropriate criteria, testing protocols and performance characteristics for products used in lead-based paint activities; publishing a lead hazard information pamphlet; and establishing regulations requiring renovation contractors to provide the pamphlet to the owners and occupants of pre-1978 housing before commencing renovation work.

Title IV is discussed in Chapter XVI of this book.

EXHIBITS

1. 40 C.F.R. PART 798–HEALTH EFFECTS TESTING GUIDELINES

Subpart C-Subchronic Exposure

798.2250 Dermal toxicity

798.2450 Inhalation toxicity

798.2650 Oral toxicity

Subpart D-Chronic Exposure

798.3260 Chronic toxicity

798.3300 Oncogenicity

798.3320 Combined chronic toxicity oncogenicity

Subpart E-Specific Organ/Tissue Toxicity

798.4100 Dermal sensitization

798.4350 Inhalation development toxicity study

798.4700 Reproductive and fertility effects

798.4900 Developmental toxicity study

Subpart F-Genetic Toxicity

798.5195 Mouse biochemical specific locus test

798.5200 Mouse visible specific locus test

798.5265 The salmonella typhimurium reverse mutation assay

798.5275 Sex-linked recessive lethal test in drosophila melanogaster

798.5300 Detection of gene mutations in somatic cells in culture

798.5375 In vitro mammalian cytogenetics.

798.5385 In vivo mammalian bone marrow cytogenetics test: Chromosomal analysis

798.5395 In vivo mammalian bone marrow cytogenetics tests: Micronucleus assay

798.5450 Rodent dominant lethal assay

798.5460 Rodent heritable translocation assays

798.5500 Differential growth inhibition of repair proficients and repair deficient bacteria: Bacterial DNA damage or repair tests

798.5955 Heritable translocation test in drosophila melanogaster

Subpart G-Neurotoxicity

798.6050 Functional observational battery

798.6200 Motor activity

798.6400 Neuropathology

798.6500 Schedule-controlled operant behavior

798.6560 Subchronic delayed neurotoxicity of organophosphorus substances

2. Form U - Inventory Update Report (IUR), 1998

EPA

FORM U

United States
Environmental Protection Agency
Washington, DC 20460
Partial Updating of TSCA Inventory Data Base
Production and Site Report
(Section 8(a) Toxic Substances Control Act 15 USC 2607)

1998

Form Approved OMB 2070-0070

REPORT NUMBER

Certification Statement: I hereby certify to the best of my knowledge and belief that (1) all information entered on this form is complete and accurate, and (2) the confidentiality statements on the back of this form are true and correct as to that information for which I have asserted a confidentiality claim

SIGNATURE	DATE	NAME/TITLE (Type or Print)

TECHNICAL CONTACT NAME	PLANT SITE NAME
COMPANY NAME — CBI	DUN & BRADSTREET NUMBER — FACILITY ID NUMBER (FOR AGENCY USE ONLY)
COMPANY ADDRESS LINE 1	PLANT SITE STREET ADDRESS LINE 1
COMPANY ADDRESS LINE 2	PLANT SITE STREET ADDRESS LINE 2
CITY — STATE	CITY — STATE
ZIP CODE — TELEPHONE (w/Area Code)	ZIP CODE

CHEMICAL SUBSTANCE IDENTITY/ACTIVITY/CONFIDENTIALITY

A.	B. Identifying Number / H. Specific Chemical Name	C. ID Code (See back of form)	D. Activity M or I	CBI	E. Site Limited	CBI	F. Production Volume in Pounds	CBI	G. Plant CBI	Chemical CBI
1										
2										
3										
4										
5										
6										
7										
8										
9										
10										

EPA Form 7740-8 (9-97) IMPORTANT: Before completing this form, carefully ready the accompanying instructions. TYPE or PRINT

EPA

FORM U

United States Environmental Protection Agency

Partial Updating of TSCA Inventory Data Base Production and Site Report

(Section 8(a) Toxic Substances Control Act 15 USC 2607)

1998

Form Approved OMB 2070-0070

REPORT NUMBER

Continuation/Correction Form

Certification Statement: I hereby certify to the best of my knowledge and belief that (1) all information entered on this form is complete and accurate, and (2) the confidentiality statements on the back of this form are true and correct as to that information for which I have asserted a confidentiality claim.

SIGNATURE	DATE	NAME/TITLE (Type or Print)

TECHNICAL CONTACT NAME	PLANT SITE NAME
COMPANY NAME — CBI	DUN & BRADSTREET NUMBER — FACILITY ID NUMBER (FOR AGENCY USE ONLY)
COMPANY ADDRESS LINE 1	PLANT SITE STREET ADDRESS LINE 1
COMPANY ADDRESS LINE 2	PLANT SITE STREET ADDRESS LINE 2
CITY — STATE	CITY — STATE
ZIP CODE — TELEPHONE (w/Area Code)	ZIP CODE

CHEMICAL SUBSTANCE IDENTITY/ACTIVITY/CONFIDENTIALITY

A.	B. Identifying Number	C. ID Code (See back of form)	D. Activity M or I	CBI	E. Site Limited	CBI	F. Production Volume in Pounds	CBI	G. Plant CBI	Chemical CBI
	H. Specific Chemical Name									
A.	B. Identifying Number	C. ID Code (See back of form)	D. Activity M or I	CBI	E. Site Limited	CBI	F. Production Volume in Pounds	CBI	G. Plant CBI	Chemical CBI
	H. Specific Chemical Name									
A.	B. Identifying Number	C. ID Code (See back of form)	D. Activity M or I	CBI	E. Site Limited	CBI	F. Production Volume in Pounds	CBI	G. Plant CBI	Chemical CBI
	H. Specific Chemical Name									
A.	B. Identifying Number	C. ID Code (See back of form)	D. Activity M or I	CBI	E. Site Limited	CBI	F. Production Volume in Pounds	CBI	G. Plant CBI	Chemical CBI
	H. Specific Chemical Name									
A.	B. Identifying Number	C. ID Code (See back of form)	D. Activity M or I	CBI	E. Site Limited	CBI	F. Production Volume in Pounds	CBI	G. Plant CBI	Chemical CBI
	H. Specific Chemical Name									
A.	B. Identifying Number	C. ID Code (See back of form)	D. Activity M or I	CBI	E. Site Limited	CBI	F. Production Volume in Pounds	CBI	G. Plant CBI	Chemical CBI
	H. Specific Chemical Name									
A.	B. Identifying Number	C. ID Code (See back of form)	D. Activity M or I	CBI	E. Site Limited	CBI	F. Production Volume in Pounds	CBI	G. Plant CBI	Chemical CBI
	H. Specific Chemical Name									
A.	B. Identifying Number	C. ID Code (See back of form)	D. Activity M or I	CBI	E. Site Limited	CBI	F. Production Volume in Pounds	CBI	G. Plant CBI	Chemical CBI
	H. Specific Chemical Name									
A.	B. Identifying Number	C. ID Code (See back of form)	D. Activity M or I	CBI	E. Site Limited	CBI	F. Production Volume in Pounds	CBI	G. Plant CBI	Chemical CBI
	H. Specific Chemical Name									
A.	B. Identifying Number	C. ID Code (See back of form)	D. Activity M or I	CBI	E. Site Limited	CBI	F. Production Volume in Pounds	CBI	G. Plant CBI	Chemical CBI
	H. Specific Chemical Name									

EPA Form 7740-8 (9-97) IMPORTANT: Before completing this form, carefully ready the accompanying instructions. TYPE or PRINT

YOU MUST PRINT THIS PAGE AND SUBMIT WITH YOUR FORM U

WHERE TO GET SUPPLIES AND SEND COMPLETED FORMS

TSCA Inventory Update Form U and a copy of the instruction booklet may be obtained from:

TSCA Hotline (7408)
U.S. Environmental Protection Agency
Office of Pollution Prevention & Toxics
401 M Street, SW
Washington, DC 20460
Attn: Inventory Update Rule
Telephone: (202) 554-1404

Completed forms should be sent to:

OPPT Document Control Officer (7407)
U.S. Environmental Protection Agency
Office of Pollution Prevention & Toxics
401 M Street, SW
Washington, Dc 20460
Attn: Inventory Update Rule

Concerning EPA Disclosure Information

If you submit information to EPA and claim any of it as confidential, EPA will publically disclose that information only as allowed by the procedures set forth in 40 CFR Part 2. If no such claim accompanies the information when it is received, EPA may make that information public without further notice to you.

Confidentiality Statements

Chemical substance identity and other information reported to EPA on the above form may be claimed as confidential by checking the appropriate CBI boxes. The person signing the certification statement attests to the truth of the following four statements concerning all information claimed as confidential:

1. My company has taken measures to protect the confidentiality of the information, and intends to continue to take such measures.
2. The information is not, and has not been reasonably obtainable without our consent by other persons (other than discovery based on a showing of special need in a judicial or quasi-judicial proceeding).
3. The information is not publically available elsewhere.
4. Disclosure of the information would cause substantial harm to our competitive position.

The person signing also attests to the truth of the appropriate statement(s) below concerning the information specifically claimed as confidential for the [particular chemical substance. By checking the CBI box under:

Company Name: I assert that the linkage between my company identity (including the names of any persons appearing on the form and the information submitted on the form is confidential.

Chemical Identity: I assert that the identities if the chemica substances so claimed are confidential.

Activity: I assert that the nature if my activity (manufacture vs import) is confidential.

Site Limited: I assert that whether or not the chemical substance i distributed for a commercial purpose outside of the plant sit identified on this form is confidential.

Plant Site: I assert that the link of the chemical substance to th plant site identified on this corn is confidential.

Production Volume: I assert that the production volume of th chemical substance at the plant site identified on the form i confidential.

When claiming the identify of a chemical substance as confidentia you must provide written substantiation for such claims (se reporting instructions). Failure to do so may EPA making th information public without further notice to you.

Codes for Block C

A = Accession Number

B = Bona Fide Number

C = CAS Registry Number

F = Original Inventory Form Number

P = PMN Number

T = TMEA Number

Paperwork Reduction Act Notice

The annual public burden for this collection of information estimated to average 11.5 hours per response. Burden means th total time, effort, or financial resources expended by persons t generate, maintain, retain, or disclose information to or for a Feder agency. For this collection it includes the time needed to revie instructions, search existing data sources, gather and maintain th data needed and completing and reviewing the collection information. An agency may not conduct or sponsor, and a pers is not required to respond to, a collection of information unless displays a current valid OMB number. The OMB control number this collection is OMB No. 2070.

Comments on this collection of information may be provided to t Director, OPPE Regulatory Information Division, U.S. Environment Protection Agency (Mail Code 2137), 401 M Street, SV Washington, DC 20460. Include the OMB control number in a correspondence, but do not submit the form or report to th address. The actual information or form should be submitted accordance with the instructions accompanying the form.

Instructions for Completing 1998 Electronic Form U

1. Fill out information on the screen using the fielded boxes. Enter information only when available or required.

2. Use the "tab" button or mouse to enter the cursor in each field. Type the information in as required. Drop down boxes are used for the entries for State and for the Block C and Block D Codes. The values are as follows:

Block C ID Codes

Code	Definition
A	Accession Number
B	Bona Fide Number
C	CAS Registry Number
F	Original Inventory Form Number
P	PMN Number
T	TMEA Number

Block D Activity Codes

M	Manufacture
I	Import

3. When completed, use the button to export the form data to a local file on a diskette. Print a copy of the form for your records. Mail the diskette...

4. Confidentiality Statements

3. Preliminary Assessment Information Report (PAIR)

IMPORTANT: Before completing this form, please read the accompanying instructions carefully *Form Approved OMB No 2070-0054*

EPA U.S. ENVIRONMENTAL PROTECTION AGENCY
401 M Street, S.W.
Washington, D.C. 20460

MANUFACTURER'S REPORT
PRELIMINARY ASSESSMENT INFORMATION

This information is required under the authority of Section 8(a), Toxic Substances Control Act, 15 U.S.C. 2607.

Send completed form to:
Document Control Office (7407)
Office of Pollution Prevention and Toxics
U.S. EPA
Room G-099
401 M Street, S.W.
Washington, DC 20460
Attn: 8(a) PAIR Reporting

CONTROL NUMBER

PERIOD COVERED
FROM: Mo Yr TO Mo Yr

Section I – CERTIFICATION

TECHNICAL CERTIFICATION STATEMENT

I hereby certify that, to the best of my knowledge and belief, all information entered on this form is complete and accurate. I agree to permit access to, and the copying of records by, a duly authorized representative of the EPA Administrator, in accordance with the Toxic Substances Control Act, to document any information reported here.

Signature | Date

Name and title *Please print or type*

CONCERNING EPA DISCLOSURE OF INFORMATION

Any person who submits information to EPA under the Preliminary Assessment Information Rule (40 CFR 712) should be aware of EPA regulations (40 CFR Part 2) which govern disclosure of such information. Those regulations provide that such person may, if he or she desires, assert a confidentiality claim covering part or all of the information submitted. Information covered by such a claim will be publicly disclosed by EPA only to the extent, and by means of the procedures, set forth in 40 CFR Part 2. However, if no such claim accompanies the information when it is received, EPA may make that information public without notifying the submitter.

CONFIDENTIALITY STATEMENTS

Information disclosed to EPA on this form may be claimed confidential by marking the appropriate boxes below. The person signing the Confidentiality Certification Statement attests to the truth of the following four statements concerning all information that is claimed confidential. Note that chemical substance identity may not be claimed confidential for this rule.

1. My company has taken measures to protect the confidentiality of the information, and it intends to continue to take such measures.
2. The information is not, and has not been, reasonably obtainable without our consent by other persons (other than governmental bodies) by use of legitimate means (other than discovery based on a showing of special need in a judicial or quasi-judicial proceeding).
3. The information is not publicly available elsewhere.
4. Disclosure of the information would cause substantial harm to our competitive position.

CONFIDENTIALITY CERTIFICATION STATEMENT

I hereby certify that the Confidentiality Statements on this form are true as to that information below for which I have asserted a confidentiality claim.

Signature | Date

Name and title – *Please print or type*

Section II – CHEMICAL IDENTIFICATION

Part A

CAS No.

Chemical name (first 15 characters)

Part B

Category name (first 15 characters)

Inventory Form C number

Section III – RESPONDENT IDENTIFICATION

☐ *MARK THIS BOX TO CLAIM THIS SECTION CONFIDENTIAL*

Part A – Plant Site – Physical location

Name

Number and street

City

County

State | ZIP code

Dun and Bradstreet number

Part B – Mailing Address of:

☐ Corporate Headquarters ☐ Plant Site

Name

Number and street

City

State | ZIP code

Dun and Bradstreet number (for corporate headquarters only)

Part C – Technical Contact

Name and title

Telephone *(Area code/number)*

☐ At headquarters

☐ At plant site

Part D – Acknowledgement

EPA will send acknowledgement to – *Name and title*

EPA Form 7710-35 (5-82)

*GPO: 1985-484-526

Section IV — PRELIMINARY ASSESSMENT INFORMATION

NOTE Mark the box to the left of any item below to claim the answer to the item as confidential. Report all quantities in kilograms (1 kilogram = 2.2 pounds). Enter N.A. for any item that does not apply to you; do not leave any blanks.

Part A — Plant Site Activities — *Information in part A must be your best estimate from readily obtainable data. For items 3b, 3c, and 3d, specify the accuracy of your answers.*

☐ 1. Total quantity imported	kg	☐ 2. Quantity manufactured for sale or use	kg
☐ 3 a. Quantity lost during manufacture *(3b + 3c + 3d must equal 3a)*	kg	3 c. Quantity in wastes treated to destroy the chemical	kg ± %
3 b. Quantity lost to the environment	kg ± %	3 d. Quantity in wastes not treated to destroy the chemical	kg ± %

Activity (1)	Process category (2)	Quantity (kilograms) (3)	Total worker-hours (4)	Total workers (5)
☐ 4. Manufacture of the chemical	a. Enclosed			
	b. Controlled release			
	c. Open			
☐ 5. On-site use as reactant	a. Enclosed			
	b. Controlled release			
Total Quantity ________ kg	c. Open			
☐ 6. On-site nonreactant use of the chemical substance	a. Enclosed			
	b. Controlled release			
Total Quantity ________ kg	c. Open			
☐ 7. On-site preparation of products	a. Enclosed			
	b. Controlled release			
Total Quantity ________ kg	c. Open			

☐ 8. MANUFACTURER'S PRODUCTS — Report the quantity of the chemical substance that you prepare for each of the following.

INDUSTRIAL PRODUCTS (domestic)	a. Chemical or mixture	kg	**CONSUMER PRODUCTS (domestic)**	d. Chemical or mixture	kg
	b. Article with some release	kg		e. Article with some release	kg
	c. Article with no release	kg		f. Article with no release	kg
g. Products for export →					kg

Part B — Chemical Substance Processing by Customers — *Information in part B must be accurate to within ± 50%.*

☐ 9. CUSTOMERS' USES AND PRODUCTS — Estimate the quantity of the chemical substance that your customers use or prepare for each of the following.

INDUSTRIAL PRODUCTS (domestic)	a. Chemical or mixture	kg	**CONSUMER PRODUCTS (domestic)**	d. Chemical or mixture	kg
	b. Article with some release	kg		e. Article with some release	kg
	c. Article with no release	kg		f. Article with no release	kg
g. Products for export →					kg
h. Quantity of chemical consumed as reactant →					kg
i. Unknown customer uses →					kg

☐ 10. MARKET NAMES — If you report your customers' uses as unknown (9i above) for more than 20% of the total quantity of chemical substance that you manufacture and import (20% of items 1 and 2 above), list the market names under which you distribute the chemical. (If you need more space, attach an additional sheet.)

a.	c.
b.	d.

☐ 11. CUSTOMERS' PROCESS CATEGORIES — Based on your knowledge of general industry practices, estimate the quantity of chemical substance that you sell to customers as the chemical and that your customers further process in each of the following categories.

a. Enclosed processes	kg	c. Open processes	kg
b. Controlled release processes	kg	d. Unknown	kg

EPA Form 7710-35 (5-82) Reverse

OMB Control No. 2070-0054

NOTICE TO SUBMITTERS

This notice is provided to submitters of EPA Form 7710-35, "Manufacturer's Report -- Preliminary Assessment Information," in accordance with the Paperwork Reduction Act (E.O. 2291), to disclose public reporting burden information. In additional, EPA wishes to inform submitters that the reporting requirements on EPA Form 7710-35 have not changed with this notice. For further information on Preliminary Assessment Information reporting, refer to the Code of Federal Regulations - Title 40 - Part 712.

The public reporting and record keeping burden for this collection is estimated to average 29.57 hours per response, including the time for reviewing instructions, searching existing data sources, gathering and maintaining the data needed, and completing and reviewing the collection of information.

Send comments regarding this burden estimate or any other aspect of this collection of information, including suggestions for reducing the burden, to Director, OPPE Regulatory Information Division, U.S. Environmental Protection Agency (Mail Code 2137), 401 M Street S.W., Washington, D.C. 20460. Include the OMB control number in any correspondence, but do not submit the form or report to this address. The actual information or form should be submitted in accordance with the instructions accompanying the information or form, specified in the corresponding regulation.

SUPPLEMENTAL INSTRUCTIONS

What chemicals to report Do not report on listed chemical substances if these are manufactured or imported incidentally as a byproduct, non-isolated intermediate, or impurity.

A byproduct or co-product must be reported if it's marketed or used as a subject (listed) chemical.

Do not report a listed chemical substance if it is a component of a mixture (imported or manufactured). Note, though, that the mixture itself may be listed as a reportable substance. Reporting is required, however, if the chemical is manufactured separately by a given company, and then blended into a mixture. In such a case, the blending step(s) would be reported as processing activities. Reporting is also required if the manufactured or imported chemical is (1) in aqueous solution; (2) in a solution containing an additive (such as a stabilizer or other chemical) to maintain the integrity or physical form of the substance; or (3) present in any grade or purity.

Reporting --Enter the month and year beginning and ending the 12month period for which you report, for example, July 81 -June 82. This reporting period is listed with the chemical substance in 40 CFR 712.50.

Who must report -In addition to the actual synthesis of a compound, all refining, extracting, and purifying activities of a listed chemical substance are considered manufacturing activities under Section 3(7) of TSCA. Reporting is required for all companies involved in any of these activities.

Repackaging is considered a processing activity and should not be reported as manufacture. A company that only repackages a listed chemical substance is considered only a processor. Note, however, that if the company imports the chemical prior to repackaging it is considered a manufacturer and must report.

1. CERTIFICATION

Confidentiality certification -- You may claim information confidential by marking appropriate boxes in sections III and IV. If you claim any information confidential, you must certify that the Confidentiality Statements are true for all information claimed confidential on the form. Do this by signing and dating the Confidentiality Certification Statement. Remember: To claim confidentiality, both the appropriate box must be marked and the confidentiality certification must be signed by personnel with designated authority (e.g., general counsel or corporate office in charge).

IV. PRELIMINARY ASSESSMENT INFORMATION

TSCA Regulable Quantities -- Eliminate second sentence of second paragraph and replace with following:

If a chemical from a given manufacturing stream is solely for a non-TSCA use, no reporting is required. However, if a company produces a chemical from the same stream that will be used for both TSCA and non-TSC,A purposes, the total quantity must be reported under items 4 and 5. Note that the quantity produced for TSCA purposes only is entered under item 2.

PART A: PLANT SITE ACTIVITIES

Item 1 -- **Change second sentence.**

For a given compound, if a company is not involved in any manufacturing activity, and imports a chemical at one site and processes it at another facility, answers need to be provided only for item 1 and items 9 through 11 (Part B). Note that the transfer of chemical to another site of the same company for processing is treated as if it were a customer use.

Item 2 -- Change to:

Enter the total quantity of chemical domestically manufactured for TSCA use during the reporting period, not counting the losses reported in item 3.

PROCESS CATEGORIES

Open Process -- Change the second sentence.

Routine direct contact would be associated, for example, with reaction vessels that are open vats, the transport or storage of the chemical in open containers (even in an otherwise enclosed process), and the venting of a chemical freely into the workplace atmosphere.

WORKERS

Change the first paragraph to the following:

Report the total number of workers for each process category. Workers are counted in a process category if (1) they are directly involved in manufacturing, processing, and handling the chemical during the reporting period or (2) they are regularly assigned maintenance or inspection personnel who work with the process from a remote control room, and who do not regularly come in contact with the actual chemical stream, are not to be counted unless their exposure to the chemical stream is greater than or equal to that of regularly assigned inspection and maintenance workers. If only control room workers are associated with a process, and their exposure to the chemical stream is less than that of regularly assigned inspection and maintenance workers, the company must nevertheless report the process categories associated with the manufacture and on-site use of the chemical (column 3 in items 4 through 7). The number of workers and total worker-hours however may be listed as zero.

QUESTIONS AND ANSWERS ABOUT REPORTING UNDER TSCA SECTION 8(a) PRELIMINARY ASSESSMENT

INFORMATION RULE 47 FR 2699

1. I manufacture a chemical at one company plant site and then ship it to another plant site (within the same company) where it is processed into another product. Do I separately report the activities of both plant sites?

Answer

No Report on only one form for the plant site where manufacturing actually occurs, and treat the second plant site's activities as customer activities on that form.

2. 1 buy a subject chemical in an impure form and purify it, package it and then sell it as a subject chemical. Should I report this activity?

Answer

Yes. Any company which extracts, refines, separates or purifies a listed chemical substance is considered to be a manufacturer for the purposes of this rule. Thus in the above example, both the company that manufactured and sold the impure subject chemical and the company that further refined it are to report as manufacturers.

3. In the process of producing a non-listed chemical substance, I produce a listed chemical substance as a "byproduct." This waste is shipped to another company plant site where the subject chemical is separated out and sold. Do I report on the byproduct?

Answer

If a company produces a chemical with commercial intent (i.e., the company does not merely intend to dispose of the chemical as waste), then that chemical is a product for purposes of the reporting rule regardless of whether that chemical was a primary or secondary product of the production stream In the above example, the "byproduct" subject chemical is shipped to another site where it is purified and ultimately distributed commercially. This subject chemical is in fact a product, because it is ultimately put to use. The first plant site should therefore report on its production of this subject chemical, since the company considers it to.-be a listed chemical.

(Note: If a company produces a mixture of a subject chemical plus other substances (e.g. , water) as a "byproduct" with commercial intent, and the company refers to that "byproduct" as a subject chemical during commercial sales or intra-company transfers (for commercial use), then the manufacturer should report only on the quantity of the listed chemical in the total "byproduct." In addition, reporting is not necessary if the quantity of the listed chemical is less than 500 kg.

QUESTIONS AND ANSWERS ABOUT REPORTING UNDER TSCA 8(A) PRELIMINARY ASSESSMENT INFORMATION RULE

REPORTING YEAR

1. I produce an 8(a) chemical each year from March to July. Our corporate year is from June 1 to

May 31; on which quantities should I report?

Answer

Information should be reported on tho latest complete corporate fiscal year. Therefore, in the above example the company should report on the quantity or the chemical produced during the previous June 1 through July 31 period, and that quantity produced from March 1 through May 31 of this year.

2. 1 imported an 8(a) chemical during the 1981 fiscal year. Sometime during either that year or the next, I stopped importing the chemical. Will that make any difference in how I fill out the reporting form?

Answer

A company is to report how much of the chemical they manufactured or imported during their latest complete corporate fiscal year from the effective date of the rule. Once this period is determined, a company must report only on how much of the chemical was imported at that time. If during this period the company did not import the chemical, they are not subject to this rule.

PRODUCT IDENTIFICATION

3. Should we use the list of chemicals we reported for the TSCA Inventory to determine our reporting obligations under the section 8(a) rule?

Answer

No. All chemicals which are listed in the section 8(a) Preliminary Assessment Information Rule also appeared on the TSCA Inventory. However, the chemicals that any individual company reported for the Inventory may not dictate that company's reporting obligations under the section 8(a) reporting rule.

The Inventory contains data reported by manufacturers prior to 1977.. The section 8(a) reporting rule requires reporting on chemicals produced during a company's latest complete fiscal year (which would be later than 1980). Some companies may no longer produce chemicals that they reported for the Inventory, and thus should not report on those chemicals for the section 8(a) rule. Alternatively, some companies may now produce chemicals listed in the section 8(a) reporting rule that they did not manufacture prior to the Inventor. In this second example, the company would not have reported for the Inventory, yet would be required to report on these chemicals under the section 8(a) rule. In either case, a manufacturer's reporting obligations under the section 8(a) rule would be different from what they were at the time of the Inventory.

4. We manufacture four different products in"coke batteries." At the time of reporting for the initial TSCA inventory, EPA allowed us to use generic terms for our products instead of figuring out exactly what chemicals were in our product. We believe that in our production we produce 50 or more 8(a) chemicals as byproducts, but we are not sure. What should we do for 8(a) reporting?

Answer

Unless a chemical produced by a company is marketed as an 8(a) subject chemical, it is not reportable. The above example represents merely a product stream which contains one or more of the subject chemicals but is not marketed or used in practice as solely a subject chemical. No reports are required.

5. 1 buy a subject chemical in an impure form and purify it, package it and then sell it as a subject chemical. Should I report this activity?

Answer

Yes. Any company which extracts, refines, separates or purifies a listed chemical substance is considered to be a manufacturer for the purposes of this rule. Thus in the above example, both the company that manufactured and sold the impure subject chemical and the company that further refined it are to report as manufacturers.

IMPORTATION

6. If a chemical is on the TSCA section 8(a) Preliminary Assessment Information Rule, must a company report if: (i) they import it as part of an article? (ii) they import it as part of a mixture?

Answer

(i) Importers of articles are exempt from reporting.

(ii) Importers should report chemical substances imported in bulk in any grade of purity, in aqueous solution, or containing additives (such as stabilizers other chemicals) to maintain the integrity or physical form of the substance. this does not-include formulated mixtures of other kinds.

7. It a company imports a chemical in bulk and then further processes it, must they report?

Answer

Yes. The company must report both on the actual importation activity and how they further process the chemical.

8. If a company imports a chemical in a container and merely repackages the chemical and sells it to someone else, is the chemical reportable?

Answer

Yes. Companies that import a chemical are considered manufacturers. Even companies which only import a chemical in bulk form for commercial purposes and do not further process it are required to report for this rule. Note that repackaging is considered a processing activity and should be reported in the appropriate part of the form.

9. We manufacture a chemical that is not on the TSCA section 8(a) list. We also produce an 8(a) chemical as a byproduct which we incinerate. Are we exempt from reporting under section 712.25(d)(1)?

Answer

Yes. If a company produces a chemical without a separate commercial intent during the manufacture of another chemical, it is producing a byproduct (see definition in section 712.3(a)). Companies which produce subject chemicals solely as unmarketed byproducts are exempt from reporting.

PROCESSING

10. If our company manufacturer an 8(a) chemical and then packages the product in a drum for sale to our customers, how do we report the packaging step?

Answer

If the chemical substance in the drum will be further processed by the customers, the packaging step is considered part of the manufacturing of the chemical and should be reported as such in Section IV, Part A, question 4. However, if the manufactured substance is not to be further processed by customers then packaging of the chemical is considered preparation of a final product for customers and should be reported in question 7.

11. Our company uses an 8(a) chemical as a reactant to make a dyestuff: After the reaction, the chemical no longer exists. For item 8 on the reporting form, does EPA want the amount of (a) the chemical before the reaction, (b) the finished product after the reaction. or (c) the 8(a) chemical after the reaction? (in this case there is no chemical remaining after the reaction.)

Answer

First, the company must also manufacture the chemical if they are to report at all. If they do manufacture a subject chemical and react it to form a new product, this reaction step should be reported in question 5. The resultant product (dyestuff) does not have to be reported. Question 8 refers to products which contain the chemical substance (and will not be further processed by customers).

REPORTING QUANTITIES

12. During the reporting period I produced 500,000 pounds of an 8(a) chemical. During that same period I processed all of the 500,000 pounds plus 200,000 pounds that was in storage from the previous year. Do I report on the additional 200,000 pounds?

Answer

Yes. In the above example, the quantity processed is 700,000 pounds.

13. It is stated in section 712.5 of the rule ("Method of identification of substances for reporting purposes") that substances that are marketed or used in aqueous solution, in the presence of an additive, or in various grades of purity are to be reported as substances, not as mixtures. Does this mean that if we produce 200,000 pounds of a subject chemical and add 1 00,000 pounds of water to it to make a solution for our customers, we should include the 1 00,000 pounds of water as a reportable quantity.

Answer

No. Only report the 200,000 pounds of the substance made and prepared. The statement in section 712.5 simply means that, in reporting, a substance conveyed in the presence of additives, or impurities, or in water is still to be classified as a substance just as it is in commercial practice.

14. My company has three plant sites which all produce the same chemical. I would like to report the quantity processed by customers (section IV, Part B) as one total on a corporate basis. Can I do this?

Answer

A company may report section IV Part B on a corporate total basis if the information is kept only on a corporate basis. IF the individual plant sites have the information, they should report it individually.

To report section IV Part B totals for all plant sites, a company must report the total figures on one form; all other plant site forms must have this section blank with the exception of question 1Oa. Use the space under 1Oa to cross reference the form containing the totals. For example, if plant site A's form (control number 808300001) is to contain all customer information for plant sites A, B, and C, then question 1Oa (Market Names) on the plant site form for B and C should contain the following notation:

See control number 808300001

15. If we import a subject chemical, turn it into an alloy and then form it into an electrical wire which we sell to our customers, do we report the sire or the alloy as a final product?

<u>Answer</u>

If a product to be sold to customers is intended to contain the subject chemical (i.e., the chemical was not previously reacted with other substances) then all steps leading to the product formulation are to be reported. Thus, in the above example, processing of the alloy is considered part of the preparation of product step (question 7), with the electrical wire representing the final product (question 8).

16. We import a subject chemical into the U.S. and then sell the chemical to various customers. We have very little information about chemical production or use. How can we report this information?

<u>Answer</u>

A company which imports a chemical but does not further process it should report the total quantity imported in Part A, question 1 and whatever information they can provide in Part B. If customer uses are not known to within +/-50%, report unknown in Part B.

17. 1 manufacture a chemical at one company plant site and then ship it to another plant site (within the same company) where it is processed into another product. Do I separately report the activities of both plant sites?

<u>Answer</u>

No. Report on only one form for the plant site where manufacturing actually occurs, and treat the second plant site's activities as customer activities on that form.

18. In the process of producing a non-listed chemical substance, I produce a listed chemical substance as a "byproduct." This waste is shipped to another company plant site where the subject chemical is separated out and sold. Do I report on the byproducts?

<u>Answer</u>

If a company produces a chemical with commercial intent (i.e., the company does not merely intend to dispose of the chemical as waste), then that chemical is a product for purposes of the reporting rule regardless of whether that chemical was a primary or secondary product of the production stream. In the above example, the "byproduct" subject chemical is shipped to another site where it is purified and ultimately distributed commercially. This subject chemical is in fact a product, because it is ultimately put to use. The first plant site should therefore report on its production of this subject chemical, since the company considers it to be a listed chemical.

(Note: If a company produces a mixture of a subject chemical plus other substances (e.g., water) as a "byproduct" with commercial intent, ant the company refers to that "byproduct" as a subject chemical during commercial sales or intra-company transfers (for commercial use), then the manufacturer should report only in the quantity of the listed chemical in the total "byproduct." In addition, reporting is not necessary if the quantity of the listed chemical is less than 500 kg.)

19. Should we use the list of chemicals we reported for the TSCA Inventory to determine our reporting obligations under the section 8(a) rule?

<u>Answer</u>

No. All chemicals which are listed in the section 8(a) Preliminary Assessment Information Rule also appeared on the TSCA Inventory. However, the chemicals that any individual company reported for the Inventory may not dictate that company's reporting obligations under the section 8(a) rule.

The Inventory contains data reported by manufacturers prior to 1977. The section 8(a) reporting rule requires reporting on chemicals produced during a company's latest complete fiscal year (which would be later than 1980). Some companies may no longer produce chemicals that they reported for the Inventory, and thus should not report on those chemicals for the section 8(a) rule. Alternatively, some companies may now produce chemicals listed in the section 8(a) reporting rule that they did not manufacture prior to the Inventory. In this second example, the company would not have reported for the Inventory, yet would be required to report on these chemicals under the section 8(a) rule. In either case, a manufacturer's reporting obligations under the section8(a) rule would be different from what they were at the time of the Inventory.

4. Premanufacture Notice (PMN) Form 7710-25

Form Approved. O.M.B. No. 2070-0012. Approval Expires 10-31-96.

U. S. ENVIRONMENTAL PROTECTION AGENCY

EPA

PREMANUFACTURE NOTICE

FOR NEW CHEMICAL SUBSTANCES

AGENCY USE ONLY	
Date of receipt	
Document control number	EPA case number

When completed send this form to

DOCUMENT CONTROL OFFICER
OFFICE OF POLLUTION PREVENTION
AND TOXIC SUBSTANCES, 7407
U.S. E.P.A. 401 M STREET, SW
WASHINGTON, D.C. 20460

Enter the total number of pages in the Premanufacture Notice ▶

GENERAL INSTRUCTIONS

TS- ☐☐☐☐☐☐

- You must provide all information requested in this form to the extent that it is known to or reasonably ascertainable by you. Make reasonable estimates if you do not have actual data.
- Before you complete this form, you should read the "Instructions Manual for Premanufacture Notification" (the Instructions Manual is available from the Toxic Substances Control Act (TSCA) Information Service by calling 202-554-1404, or faxing 202-554-5603).
- If a user fee has been remitted for this notice (40 CFR 700.45), indicate in the boxes above the TS-user fee identification number you have generated. Remember, your user fee ID number must also appear on your corresponding fee remittance, which is sent to: EPA, HQ Accounting Operations Branch (PM-266), P.O. 360399M, Pittsburgh, PA 15251-6399, Attn. TSCA User Fee.

Part I – GENERAL INFORMATION

You must provide the currently correct Chemical Abstracts (CA) Name of the new chemical substance, even if you claim the identity as confidential. You may authorize another person to submit chemical identity information for you, but your submission will not be complete and the review will not begin until EPA receives this information. A letter in support of your submission should reference your TS user fee identification number. You must submit an original and two copies of this notice including all test data. If you claimed any information as confidential, a single sanitized copy must also be submitted.

Part II – HUMAN EXPOSURE AND ENVIRONMENTAL RELEASE

If there are several manufacture, processing, or use operations to be described in Part II, sections A and B of this notice, reproduce the sections as needed.

Part III – LIST OF ATTACHMENTS

Attach additional sheets if there is not enough space to answer a question fully. Label each continuation sheet with the corresponding section heading. In Part III, list these attachments, any test data or other data and any optional information included in the notice.

OPTIONAL INFORMATION

You may include any information that you want EPA to consider in evaluating the new substance. On page 11 of this form, space has been provided for you to describe pollution prevention and recycling information you may have regarding the new substance.

So-called "binding" boxes are included throughout this form for you to indicate your willingness to be bound to certain statements you make in this notice, such as use, production volume, protective equipment . . . This option is intended to reduce delays that routinely accompany the development of consent orders or Significant New Use Rules. Except in the case of exemption applications (such as TMEA, LVE, LOREX) where certain information provided in such notification is binding on the submitter when the Agency approves the exemption application, checking a binding box in this notice does not by itself prohibit the submitter from later deviating from the information (except chemical identity) reported in the form.

CONFIDENTIALITY CLAIMS

You may claim any information in this notice as confidential. To assert a claim on the form, mark (X) the confidential box next to the information that you claim as confidential. To assert a claim in an attachment, circle or bracket the information you claim as confidential. If you claim information in the notice as confidential, you must also provide a sanitized version of the notice, (including attachments). For additional instructions on claiming information as confidential, read the Instructions Manual.

☐ Mark (X) if any information in this notice is claimed as confidential.

TEST DATA AND OTHER DATA

You are required to submit all test data in your possession or control and to provide a description of all other data known to or reasonably ascertainable by you, if these data are related to the health and environmental effects of the manufacture, processing, distribution in commerce, use, or disposal of the new chemical substance. Standard literature citations may be submitted for data in the open scientific literature. Complete test data (written in English), not summaries of data, must be submitted if they do not appear in the open literature. You should clearly identify whether test data is on the substance or on an analog. Also, the chemical composition of the tested material should be characterized. Following are examples of test data and other data. Data should be submitted according to the requirements of §720.50 of the Premanufacture Notification Rule (40 CFR Part 720).

Test Data (Check Below any included in this notice)

- Environmental fate data ☐ Yes
- Health effects data ☐ Yes
- Environmental effects data ☐ Yes
- Physical/Chemical Properties* ☐ Yes

- Other data ☐ Yes
  - Risk assessments
  - Structure/activity relationships
  - Test data not in the possession or control of the submitter

*A physical and chemical properties worksheet is located on the last page of this form.

TYPE OF NOTICE (Check Only One)

- ☐ PMN (Premanufacture Notice)
- ☐ INTERMEDIATE PMN (submitted in sequence with final product PMN)
- ☐ SNUN (Significant New Use Notice)
- ☐ TMEA (Test Marketing Exemption Application)
- ☐ LVE (Low Volume Exemption) @ 40 CFR 723.50 (c)(1)
- ☐ LOREX (Low Release/Low Exposure Exemption) @ 723.50(c)(2)
- ☐ LVE Modification ☐ LOREX Modification

IS THIS A CONSOLIDATED PMN? ☐ Yes

# of chemicals ________
(Prenotice Communication # required, enter # on page 3)

EPA FORM 7710-25 (Rev. 5-95) Replaces previous editions of EPA Form 7710-25

Public reporting burden for this collection of information is estimated to average 110 hours per response, including time for reviewing instructions, searching existing data sources, gathering and maintaining the data needed, and completing and reviewing the collection of information. Send comments regarding the burden estimate or any other aspect of this collection of information, including suggestions for reducing this burden, to Chief, Information Policy Branch, PM-223, U.S. Environmental Protection Agency, 401 M. St., S.W., Washington, D.C. 20460; and to the Office of Management and Budget, Paperwork Reduction Act (2070-0012), Washington, D.C. 20503.

CERTIFICATION

I certify that to the best of my knowledge and belief:

1. The company named in Part I, section A, subsection 1a of this notice form intends to manufacture or import for a commercial purpose, other than in small quantities solely for research and development, the substance identified in Part I, Section B.
2. All information provided in this notice is complete and truthful as of the date of submission.
3. I am submitting with this notice all test data in my possession or control and a description of all other data known to or reasonably ascertainable by me as required by §720.50 of the Premanufacture Notification Rule.

Additional Certification Statements:

If you are submitting a PMN, Intermediate PMN, Consolidated PMN, or SNUN, check the following **user fee** certification statement that applies:

☐ The Company named in Part I, Section A has remitted the fee of $2500 specified in 40 CFR 700.45 (b), or

☐ The Company named in Part I, Section A has remitted the fee of $1000 for an Intermediate PMN (defined @ 40 CFR 700.43) in accordance with 40 CFR 700.45(b), or

☐ The Company named in Part I, Section A is a small business concern under 40 CFR 700.43 and has remitted a fee of $100 in accordance with 40 CFR 700.45 (b).

If you are submitting a **low volume exemption (LVE)** application in accordance with 40 CFR 723.50 (c) (1) or a **Low release and low exposure exemption (LoREX)** application in accordance with 40 CFR 723.50 (c) (2), check the following certification statements:

☐ The manufacturer submitting this notice intends to manufacture or import the new chemical substance for commercial purposes, other than in small quantities solely for research and development, under the terms of 40 CFR 723.50.

☐ The manufacturer is familiar with the terms of this section and will comply with those terms; and

☐ The new chemical substance for which the notice is submitted meets all applicable exemption conditions.

☐ If this application is for an LVE in accordance with 40 CFR 723.50 (c)(1), the manufacturer intends to commence manufacture of the exempted substance for commercial purposes within 1 year of the date of the expiration of the 30 day review period.

The accuracy of the statements you make in this notice should reflect your best prediction of the anticipated facts regarding the chemical substance described herein. Any knowing and willful misinterpretation is subject to criminal penalty pursuant to 18 USC 1001.

		Confidential
Signature and title of Authorized Official (Original Signature Required)	**Date**	
Signature of agent - (if applicable)	**Date**	

FORM EPA 7710-25 (Rev. 5-95) Page 2

Part I -- GENERAL INFORMATION

Section A -- SUBMITTER IDENTIFICATION

Confidential

Mark (X) the "Confidential" box next to any subsection you claim as confidential.

1a. Person Submitting Notice (in U.S.)

- Name of authorized official
- Position
- Company
- Mailing address (number and street)
- City, State, ZIP Code

b. Agent (if applicable)

- Name of authorized official
- Position
- Company
- Mailing address (number and street)
- City, State, ZIP Code
- Telephone: Area Code | Number

c. If you are submitting this notice as part of a joint submission, mark (X) this box. → ☐

Joint Submitter (if applicable)

- Name of authorized official
- Position
- Company
- Mailing address (number and street)
- City, State, ZIP Code
- Telephone: Area Code | Number

2. Technical Contact (in U.S.)

- Name
- Position
- Company
- Mailing address (number and street)
- City, State, ZIP Code
- Telephone: Area Code | Number

3. If you have had a prenotice communication (PC) concerning this notice and EPA assigned a PC Number to the notice, enter the number. → Mark (X) if none → ☐

4. If you previously submitted an exemption application for the chemical substance covered by this notice, enter the exemption number assigned by EPA. If you previously submitted a PMN for this substance enter the PMN number assigned by EPA (i.e. withdrawn or incomplete). → Mark (X) if none → ☐

5. If you have submitted a notice of Bona fide intent to manufacture or import for the chemical substance covered by this notice, enter the notice number assigned by EPA. → Mark (X) if none → ☐

6. Type of Notice -- Mark (X)

1. ☐ Manufacture Only; ☐ Binding Option Mark (x)
2. ☐ Import Only; ☐ BindingOption Mark (x)
3. ☐ Both

FORM EPA 7710-25 (Rev. 5-95) Page 3

Part I – GENERAL INFORMATION – Continued

Section B – CHEMICAL IDENTITY INFORMATION: You **must** provide a currently correct Chemical Abstracts (CA) name of the substance based on the ninth Collective Index (9CI) of CA nomenclature rules and conventions.

Mark (X) the "Confidential" box next to any item you claim as confidential.

Complete either item 1 (Class 1 or 2 substances) or 2 (Polymers) as appropriate. Complete all other items.

If another person will submit chemical identity information for you (for either item 1 or 2), mark (X) the box at the right. Identify the name, company, and address of that person in a continuation sheet. → ☐ | Confidential

1. **Class 1 or 2 chemical substances** (for definitions of class 1 and class 2 substances, see the **Instructions Manual**)

   a. Class of substance – Mark (X) 1 ☐ Class 1 or 2 ☐ Class 2

   b. Chemical name (Currently correct Chemical Abstracts (CA) Name that is consistent with TSCA Inventory listings for similar substances. For Class 1 substances a CA Index Name must be provided. For Class 2 substances either a CA Index Name or CA Preferred Name must be provided, whichever is appropriate based on CA 9CI nomenclature rules and conventions.).

   c. Please identify which method you used to develop or obtain the specified chemical indentity information reported in this notice: (check one).

   ☐ Method 1 (CAS Inventory Expert Service - a copy of the Identification report obtained from the CAS Inventory Expert Service must be submitted as an attachment to this notice) ☐ Method 2 (Other Source)

   d. Molecular formula and CAS Registry Number (if a number already exists for the substance)

   CAS #

   e. For a **class 1** substance, provide a complete and correct chemical structure diagram. For a **class 2** substance – (1) List the immediate precursor substances with their respective CAS Registry Numbers. (2) Describe the nature of the reaction or process. (3) Indicate the range of composition and the typical composition (where appropriate). (4) Provide a correct representative or partial chemical structure diagram, as complete as can be known, if one can be reasonably ascertained.

☐ Mark (X) this box if you attach a continuation sheet.

FORM EPA 7710-25 (Rev. 5-95) Page 4

Part I -- GENERAL INFORMATION -- Continued

Section B -- CHEMICAL IDENTITY INFORMATION -- Continued

2. **Polymers** (For a definition of polymer, see the **Instructions Manual.**) — Confi-dential

a. Indicate the number-average weight of the lowest molecular weight composition of the polymer you intend to manufacture. Indicate **maximum** weight percent of low molecular weight species (not including residual monomers, reactants, or solvents) below 500 and below 1,000 absolute molecular weight of that composition.

Describe the methods of measurement or the basis for your estimates: GPC ☐ Other ☐ : (Specify) ________

i) **lowest** number average molecular weight: ________

ii) maximum weight % below 500 molecular weight: ________

iii) maximum weight % below 1000 molecular weight: ________

☐ Mark (X) this box if you attach a continuation sheet.

b. You must make separate confidentiality claims for monomer or other reactant identity, composition information, and residual information. Mark (X) the "Confidential" box next to any item you claim as confidential.
- (1) – Provide the specific chemical name and CAS Registry Number (if a number exists) of each monomer or other reactant used in the manufacture of the polymer.
- (2) – Mark (X) this column if entry in column (1) is confidential.
- (3) – Indicate the typical weight percent of each monomer or other reactant in the polymer.
- (4) – **Mark (X) the identity column if you want a monomer or other reactant used at two weight percent or less to be listed as part of the polymer description on the TSCA Chemical Substance Inventory.**
- (5) – Mark (X) this column if entries in columns (3) and (4) are confidential.
- (6) – **Indicate** the **maximum** weight percent of each monomer or other reactant that may be present as a residual in the polymer as manufactured for commercial purposes.
- (7) – Mark (X) this column if entry in column (6) is confidential.

Monomer or other reactant and CAS Registry Number (1)	Confi-dential (2)	Typical composition (3)	Identity Mark (X) (4)	Confi-dential (5)	Maximum residual (6)	Confi-dential (7)
		%			%	
		%			%	
		%			%	
		%			%	
		%			%	
		%			%	
		%			%	

☐ Mark (X) this box if you attach a continuation sheet.

c. Please identify which method you used to develop or obtain the specified chemical identity information reported in this notice. (check one).

☐ Method 1 (CAS Inventory Expert Service - a copy of the identification report obtained from CAS Inventory Expert Service must be submitted as an attachment to this notice) ☐ Method 2 (other source)

d. The currently correct Chemical Abstracts (CA) name for the polymer that is consistent with TSCA Inventory listings for similar polymers.

e. Provide a correct representative or partial chemical structure diagram, as complete as can be known, if one can be reasonably ascertained.

☐ Mark (X) this box if you attach a continuation sheet.

FORM EPA 7710-25 (Rev. 5-95) Page 5

Part I – GENERAL INFORMATION – Continued

Section B – CHEMICAL IDENTITY INFORMATION – Continued

3. **Impurities**
(a) – Identify each impurity that may be reasonably anticipated to be present in the chemical substance as manufactured for commercial purposes. Provide the CAS Registry Number if available. If there are unidentified impurities, enter "unidentified."
(b) – Estimate the maximum weight % of each impurity. If there are unidentified impurities, estimate their total weight %.

Impurity and CAS Registry Number (a)	Maximum percent (b)	Confidential
	%	
	%	
	%	
	%	
	%	
	%	
	%	

☐ Mark (X) this box if you attach a continuation sheet.

4. **Synonyms** – Enter any chemical synonyms for the new chemical substance identified in subsection 1 or 2. Confidential

☐ Mark (X) this box if you attach a continuation sheet.

5. **Trade identification** – List trade names for the new chemical substance identified in subsection 1 or 2.

☐ Mark (X) this box if you attach a continuation sheet.

6. **Generic chemical name** – If you claim chemical identity as confidential, you must provide a generic chemical name for your substance that reveals the specific chemical identity of the new chemical substance to the maximum extent possible. Refer to the TSCA Chemical Substance Inventory, 1985 Edition, Appendix B for guidance on developing generic names.

☐ Mark (X) this box if you attach a continuation sheet.

7. **Byproducts** – Describe any byproducts resulting from the manufacture, processing, use, or disposal of the new chemical substance. Provide the CAS Registry Number if available.

Byproduct (1)	CAS Registry Number (2)	Confidential

☐ Mark (X) this box if you attach a continuation sheet.

FORM EPA 7710-25 (Rev. 5-95) Page 6

Part I – GENERAL INFORMATION – Continued

Section C – PRODUCTION, IMPORT, AND USE INFORMATION:

Mark (X) the "Confidential" box next to any item you claim as confidential.

1. **Production volume** – Estimate the **maximum** production volume during the first 12 months of production. Also estimate the maximum production volume for any consecutive 12-month period during the first three years of production. Estimates should be on 100% new chemical substance basis. *For a Low Volume Exemption application, if you choose to have your notice reviewed at a lower production volume than 10,000 kg/yr, specify the volume and mark (x) in the binding box. If granted, you are bound to this volume..*

Maximum first 12-month production (kg/yr) (100% new chemical substance basis)	Maximum 12-month production (kg/yr) (100% new chemical substance basis)	Confi-dential	Binding Option Mark (x)

2. **Use Information** – You must make separate confidentiality claims for the description of the category of use, the percent of production volume devoted to each category, the formulation of the new substance, and other use information. Mark (X) the "Confidential" Box next to any item you claim as confidential.

a. (1) – Describe each intended category of use of the new chemical substance by function and application.
(2) – Mark (X) this column if entry in column (1) is confidential business information (CBI).
(3) – Indicate your willingness to have the information provided in column (1) binding.
(4) – Estimate the percent of total production for the first three years devoted to each category of use.
(5) – Mark (X) this column if entry in column (4) is confidential business information (CBI).
(6) – Estimate the percent of the new substance as formulated in mixtures, suspensions, emulsions, solutions, or gels as manufactured for commercial purposes at sites under your control associated with each category of use.
(7) – Mark (X) this column if entry in column (6) is confidential business information (CBI).
(8) – Indicate % of product volume expected for the listed "use" sectors. Mark more than one box if appropriate. Mark (X) to indicate your willingness to have the use type provided in (8) binding.
(9) – Mark (X) this column if entry(ies) in column (8) is (are) confidential business information (CBI).

Category of use (1) (by function and application i.e. a dispersive dye for finishing polyester fibers)	CBI (2)	Binding Option Mark (x) (3)	Produc-tion % (4)	CBI (5)	% in Form-ulation (6)	CBI (7)	% of substance expected per use (8)					CBI (9)
							Site-limited	Con-* sumer	Indus-trial	Com-mercial	Binding Option	
			%		%							
			%		%							
			%		%							
			%		%							
			%		%							
			%		%							
			%		%							

*If you have identified a "consumer" use, please provide on a continuation sheet a detailed description of the use(s) of this chemical substance in consumer products. In addition include estimates of the concentration of the new chemical substance as expected in consumer products and describe the chemical reactions by which this substance loses its identity in the consumer product.

☐ Mark (X) this box if you attach a continuation sheet.

b. Generic use description — If you claim any category of use description in subsection 2a as confidential, enter a generic description of that category. Read the **Instructions** Manual for examples of generic use descriptions.

☐ Mark (X) this box if you attach a continuation sheet.

3. **Hazard Information** – Include in the notice a copy of reasonable facsimile of any hazard warning statement, label, material safety data sheet, or other information which will be provided to any person who is reasonably likely to be exposed to this substance regarding protective equipment or practices for the safe handling, transport, use, or disposal of the new substance. List in part III hazard information you include. — Binding Option Mark (x)

☐ Mark (X) this box if you attach hazard information.

FORM EPA 7710-25 (Rev. 5-95) Page 7

Part II -- HUMAN EXPOSURE AND ENVIRONMENTAL RELEASE

Section A -- INDUSTRIAL SITES CONTROLLED BY THE SUBMITTER

Mark (X) the "Confidential" box next to any item you claim as confidential.

Complete section A for each type of manufacture, processing, or use operation involving the new chemical substance at industrial sites you control. Importers do not have to complete this section for operations outside the U.S. ; however, you may still have reporting requirements if there are further industrial processing or use operations after import. You must describe these operations. See instructions manual.

1. Operation description

a. Identity -- Enter the identity of the site at which the operation will occur. (Confidential ☐)

Name

Site address (number and street)

City, County, State, ZIP Code

If the same operation will occur at more than one site, enter the number of sites. Identify the additional sites on a continuation sheet, and if any of the sites have significantly different production rates or operations, include all the information requested in this section for those sites as attachments. → # of sites

☐ Mark (X) this box if you attach a continuation sheet.

b. Type -- Mark (X) ☐ Manufacturing ☐ Processing ☐ Use

c. Amount and Duration -- Complete 1 or 2 as appropriate

1. Batch	Maximum kg/batch (100 % new chemical substance)	Hours/batch	Batches/year
2. Continuous	Maximum kg/day (100 % new chemical substance)	Hours/day	Days/year

d. Process description ☐ **Mark (X) to indicate your willingness to have your process description binding.**

(1) Diagram the major unit operation steps and chemical conversions. Include interim storage and transport containers (specify-e.g. 5 gallon pails, 55 gallon drum, rail car, tank truck, etc.).
(2) Provide the identity, the approximate weight (by kg/day or kg/batch on an 100% new chemical substance basis), and entry point of all starting materials and feedstocks (including reactants, solvents, and catalysts, etc.), and of all products, recycle streams, and wastes. Include cleaning chemicals (note frequency if not used daily or per batch.).
(3) Identify by number the points of release, including small or intermittant releases, to the environment of the new chemical substance.

☐ Mark (X) this box if you attach a continuation sheet.

FORM EPA 7710-25 (Rev. 5-95) Page 8

Part II -- HUMAN EXPOSURE AND ENVIRONMENTAL RELEASE -- Continued

Section A -- INDUSTRIAL SITES CONTROLLED BY THE SUBMITTER -- Continued

2. **Occupational Exposure** -- You must make separate confidentiality claims for the description of worker activity, physical form of the new chemical substance, number of workers exposed, and duration of activity. Mark (X) the "Confidential" box next to any item you claim as confidential.
   (1) -- Describe the activities (e.g. bag dumping, tote filling, unloading drums, sampling, cleaning, etc.) in which workers may be exposed to the substance.
   (2) -- Mark (X) this column if entry in column (1) is confidential business information (CBI).
   (3) -- Describe any protective equipment and engineering controls used to protect workers.
   (4) and (6) -- Indicate you willingness to have the information provided in column (3) or (5) binding.
   (5) -- Indicate the physical form(s) of the new chemical substance (e.g. solid: crystal, granule, powder, or dust) and % new chemical substance (if part of a mixture) at the time of exposure.
   (7) -- Mark (X) this column if entry in column (5) is confidential business information (CBI).
   (8) -- Estimate the maximum number of workers involved in each activity for all sites combined.
   (9) -- Mark (X) this column if entry in column (8) is confidential business information (CBI).
   (10) and (11) -- Estimate the maximum duration of the activity for any worker in hours per day and days per year.
   (12) -- Mark (X) this column if entries in columns (10) and (11) are confidential business information (CBI).

Worker activity (e.g. bag dumping, filling drums) (1)	CBI (2)	Protective Equipment/ Engineering Controls (3)	Binding Option Mark (x) (4)	Physical form(s) (e.g. solid:powder) and % new substance (5)	Binding Option Mark (x) (6)	CBI (7)	# of Workers Exposed (8)	CBI (9)	Maximum duration Hrs/day (10)	Days/yr (11)	CBI (12)

☐ Mark (X) this box if you attach a continuation sheet.

3. **Environmental Release and Disposal** -- You must make separate confidentiality claims for the release number and the amount of the new chemical substance released and other release and disposal information. Mark (X) the "Confidential" box next to each item you claim as confidential.
   (1) -- Enter the number of each release point identified in the process description, part II, section A, subsection 1d(3).
   (2) -- Estimate the amount of the new substance released (a) directly to the environment or (b) into control technology (in kg/day or kg/batch).
   (3) -- Mark (X) this column if entries in columns (1) and (2) are confidential business information (CBI).
   (4) -- Identify the media of release i.e. stack air, fugitive air (optional-see Instruction Manual), surface water, on-site or off-site land or incineration, POTW, or other (please specify) to which the new substance will be released from that release point.
   (5) -- a. Describe control technology, if any, ,and control efficiency that will be used to limit the release of the new substance to the environment. For releases disposed of on land, characterize the disposal method and state whether it is approved for disposal of RCRA hazardous waste. On a continuation sheet, for each site describe any additional disposal methods that will be used and whether the waste is subject to secondary or tertiary on-site treatment. b. Estimate the amount released to the environment after control technology (in kg/day).
   (6) -- Mark (X) this column if entries in columns (4) and (5) are confidential business information (CBI).
   (7) -- Identify the destination(s) of releases to water. Please supply NPDES (National Pollutant Discharge Elimination System) numbers for direct dischargers or NPDES numbers of the POTW (Publicly Owned Treatment Works). Mark (X) if the POTW name or NPDES # is confidential business information (CBI).

Release Number (1)	Amount of new substance released (2a)	(2b)	CBI (3)	Media of release e.g. stack air (4)	Control technology and efficiency (you may wish to optionally attach efficiency data) (5a)	Binding Mark (x)	(5b)	CBI (6)

(7) Mark (X) the destination(s) of releases to water.	☐ POTW provide name(s) below:	CBI	☐ Navigable waterway	☐ Other - Specify	provide **NPDES #**	CBI

☐ Mark (X) this box if you attach a continuation sheet.

FORM EPA 7710-25 (Rev. 5-95) Page 9

Part II – HUMAN EXPOSURE AND ENVIRONMENTAL RELEASE – Continued

Section B – INDUSTRIAL SITES CONTROLLED BY OTHERS

Complete section B for typical processing or use operations involving the new chemical substance at sites you do not control. Importers do not have to complete this section for operations outside the U.S.; however, you must report any processing or use activities after import. See the Instructions Manual. *Complete a separate section B for each type of processing, or use operation involving the new chemical substance.* If the same operation is performed at more than one site describe the typical operation common to these sites. Identify additional sites on a continuation sheet.

1. **Operation Description** - To claim information in this section as confidential, circle or bracket the specific information that you claim as confidential.
   (1) – Diagram the major unit operation steps and chemical conversions, including interim storage and transport containers (specify- e.g. 5 gallon pails, 55gallon drums, rail cars, tank trucks, etc). On the diagram, identify by letter and briefly describe each worker activity. **(2)** – Provide the identity, the approximate weight (by kg/day or kg/batch, on an 100% new chemical substance basis), and entry point of all feedstocks (including reactants, solvents and catalysts, etc) and of all products, recycle streams, and wastes. Include cleaning chemicals (note frequency if not used daily or per batch). **(3)** – Identify by number the points of release, including small or intermittent releases, to the environment of the new chemical substance.
   (4) Please enter the # of sites (remember to identify the locations of these sites on a continuation sheet) :

   ______ # of sites

☐ Mark (X) this box if you attach a continuation sheet.

2. **Worker Exposure/Environmental Release**
   (1) – From the diagram above, provide the letter for each worker activity. Complete 2-8 for each worker activity described.
   (2) – Estimate the number of workers exposed for all sites combined.
   (4) – Estimate the typical duration of exposure per worker in (a) hours per day and (b) days per year.
   (6) – Describe physical form of exposure and % new chemical substance (if in mixture), and any protective equipment and engineering controls used to protect workers.
   (7) – Estimate the percent of the new substance as formulated when packaged or used as a final product.
   (9) – From the process diagram above, enter the number of each release point. Complete 9-13 for each release point identified.
   (10) – Estimate the amount of the new substance released (a) directly to the environment or (b) into control technology to the environment (in kg/day or kg/batch).
   (12) – Describe media of release i.e. stack air, fugitive air (optional-see Instructions Manual), surface water, on-site or off-site land or incineration, POTW, or other (specify) and control technology, if any, that will be used to limit the release of the new substance to the environment.
   (14) – Identify byproducts which may result from the operation.
   (3), (5), (8), (11), (13) and (15) - Mark (X) this column if any of the proceeding entries are confidential business information (CBI).

Letter of Activity	# of Workers Exposed	CBI	Duration of Exposure		CBI	Protective Equip. / Engineering Controls/ Physical Form and % new substance	% in Formulation	CBI	Release Number	Amount of New Substance Released		CBI	Media of Release & Control Technology	CBI
(1)	(2)	(3)	(4a)	(4b)	(5)	(6)	(7)	(8)	(9)	(10a)	(10b)	(11)	(12)	(13)

(14) – Byproducts: (15)

☐ Mark (X) this box if you attach a continuation sheet.

FORM EPA 7710-25 (Rev. 5-95) Page 10

OPTIONAL POLLUTION PREVENTION INFORMATION

To claim information in this section as confidential circle or bracket the specific information that you claim as confidential.

In this section you may provide information not reported elsewhere in this form regarding your efforts to reduce or minimize potential risks associated with activities surrounding manufacturing, processing, use and disposal of the PMN substance. Please include new information pertinent to pollution prevention, including source reduction, recycling activities and safer processes or products available due to the new chemical substance. Source reduction includes the reduction in the amount or toxicity of chemical wastes by technological modification, process and procedure modification, product reformulation, raw materials substitution, and/or inventory control. Recycling refers to the reclamation of useful chemical components from wastes that would otherwise be treated or released as air emissions or water discharges, or land disposal. Descriptions of pollution prevention, source reduction and recycling should emphasize potential risk reduction subsequent to compliance with existing regulatory requirements and can be either quantitative or qualitative. The EPA is interested in this information to assess overall net reductions in toxicity or environmental releases and exposures, not the shifting of risks to other environmental media or non-environmental areas (e.g., occupational or consumer exposure). In addition, information on the relative cost or performance characteristics of the PMN substance to potential alternatives may be provided. **All information provided in this section will be taken into consideration during the review of this substance. See the revised Instructions Manual that includes a Pollution Prevention manual for guidance and examples.**

Describe the expected net benefits, such as (1) an overall reduction in risk to human health or the environment; (2) a reduction in the volume manufactured; (3) a reduction in the generation of waste materials through recycling, source reduction or other means; (4) a reduction in potential toxicity or human exposure and/or environmental release; (5) an increase in product performance, a decrease in the cost of production and/or improved operation efficiency of the new chemical substance in comparison to existing chemical substances used in similar applications; or (6) the extent to which the new chemical substance may be a substitute for an existing substance that poses a greater overall risk to human health or the environment.

☐ Mark (X) this box if you attach a continuation sheet.

FORM EPA 7710-25 (Rev. 5-95)

Page 11

Part III -- LIST OF ATTACHMENTS

Attach continuation sheets for sections of the form and test data and other data (including physical/chemical properties and structure/activity information), and optional information after this page. Clearly identify the attachment and the section of the form to which it relates, if appropriate. Number consecutively the pages of the attachments. In the column below, enter the inclusive page numbers of each attachment.

Mark (X) the "Confidential" box next to any attachment name you claim as confidential. Read the **Instructions Manual** for guidance on how to claim any information in an attachment as confidential. You must include with the sanitized copy of the notice form a sanitized version of any attachment in which you claim information as confidential.

Attachment name	Attachment page number(s)	Confi-dential
Material Safety Data Sheet (MSDS)		

☐ Mark (X) this box if you attach a continuation sheet. Enter the attachment name and number.

FORM EPA 7710-25 (Rev. 5-95) Page 12

PHYSICAL AND CHEMICAL PROPERTIES WORKSHEET

To assist EPA's review of physical and chemical properties data, please complete the following worksheet for data you provide and include it in the notice. Identify the property measured, the page of the notice on which the property appears, the value of the property, the units in which the property is measured (as necessary), and whether or not the property is claimed as confidential. The physical state of the neat substance should be provided. These measured properties should be for the neat (100% pure) chemical substance. Properties that are measured for mixtures or formulations should be so noted (% PMN substance in _).You are not required to submit this worksheet; however, EPA strongly recommends that you do so, as it will simplify review and ensure that confidential information is properly protected. You should submit this worksheet as a supplement to your submission of test data. This worksheet is not a substitute for submission of test data.

Property (a)	Mark (X) if provided	Page number (b)	Value (c)	Measured or Estimate (M or E)	Confidential Mark (X) (d)
Physical state of neat substance			____ (s) ____ (l) ____ (g)		
Vapor pressure @ Temperature ____ °C			Torr		
Density/relative density			g/cm3		
Solubility @ Temperature ____ °C Solvent ____			g/L		
Solubility in water @ Temperature ____ °C			°C		
Melting temperature			°C		
Boiling/sublimation temperature @ ____ torr pressure					
Spectra					
Dissociation constant					
Particle size distribution					
Octanol/water partition coefficient					
Henry's Law constant					
Volitalization from water					
Volitalization from soil					
pH @ concentration ____					
Flammability					
Explodability					
Adsorption/coefficient					
Other - Specify					

5. Notice of Commencement of Manufacture or Import

O.M.B. No. 2070-0012 Approval Expires 10/31/96

EPA U.S. Environmental Protection Agency
NOTICE OF COMMENCEMENT OF MANUFACTURE OR IMPORT (40 CFR§720.102)

Agency Use Only | Date of Receipt

Part I - SUBMITTER IDENTIFICATION | Document Control #:

Manu-facturer/ Importer (in U.S.)	Name of Authorized Official	Mailing Address (number and street)	
	Company Name	City, State, ZIP code	CBI*
Technical Contact (in U.S.)	Name	Telephone Number	CBI*

Part II - Premanufacture Notice (PMN) "P" Case Number:

Part III - Check the appropriate box and provide the exact date of manufacture or importation:

☐ First Commercial Manufacture** date: ____________ ☐ First Commercial Importation*** date: ____________

** Date of commencement is the date of completion of non-exempt manufacture of the first amount (batch, drum, etc.)
***For importers, the date of commencement is the date that the new chemical substance clears U.S. customs.

Part IV - Manufacturing Plant Site(s) or Importing Site(s): (Importers, provide street address of destination)

CBI*

Part V - Specific Chemical Identity: (For Consolidated submissions, each substance must have a separate NOC form with the specific identity of each chemical substance.)

CBI*

Part VI - Generic Chemical Name (if chemical identity is claimed CBI*):

Part VII - Substance Identity Confidentiality Status:

☐ I wish to continue to claim the substance identity confidential and the substantiation to support this claim is attached. Failure to submit the required substantiation in accordance with 40 CFR 720.85(b) will result in a waiver of your claim.

☐ I previously claimed the substance identity as confidential and hereby relinquish that claim.

☐ I did not claim the substance identity as confidential in my original PMN submission.

You must submit your completed notice no later than 30 calendar days after the first date of commercial manufacture/importation to the address shown below:

U.S. Environmental Protection Agency
OPPT Document Control Office (7407M)
1200 Pennsylvania Ave., NW
Washington, D.C. 20460
ATTN: Notice of Commencement

Signature of authorized official | Date

Note: CBI* - refers to the term "Confidential Business Information". Mark (X) in the box if the information is to be held Confidential.

EPA Form 7710-56 (8-95)

CHAPTER X
LAWS RELATING TO ASBESTOS CONTAINING MATERIALS

A. History

Asbestos is a natural fibrous mineral mined in Canada, South Africa, Russia and a few other nations and formerly mined in the United States. It is an excellent fire retardant and heat resistant material used historically in a wide range of applications including insulation of boilers and pipes, steel construction materials, ceiling and floor tiles, roofing materials, and brake linings. Asbestos was used to protect warships of the U.S. Navy from fires caused by shelling during World War II and the Navy required manufacturers to mine and produce it for that purpose.

Asbestos is hazardous when it is "friable", thus creating a risk that fibers will become airborne and will be inhaled in excessive quantities. Fully encapsulated asbestos is not hazardous so long as it remains nonfriable.

There are several forms of asbestos. Among them are chrysotile (white), crocidolite (blue), amosite (brown), anthophyllite and tremolite. Each has different characteristics and the hazard levels differ for each. However, there has been no recognition of the hazard differences under the asbestos laws and regulations.

Asbestos was widely misused in shipyards operated by and for the U.S. Government during World War II and the Korean War. The misuse caused asbestosis among many workers. The misuse also caused mesothelioma, a rare disease, and was reported in studies by researchers at Mt. Sinai Medical Center to contribute synergistically to lung cancers among workers who were tobacco smokers. The U.S. Government declined to accept responsibility and was eventually allowed to do so by the federal courts which dismissed lawsuits based on sovereign immunity and other technical grounds.

Personal injury and property damage lawsuits against asbestos product manufacturers and users are described later in this chapter.

B. The Clean Air Act

Asbestos-related activities are regulated by the USEPA under the Clean Air Act (CAA) in a national emission standard for hazardous air pollutants (NESHAP) found at 40 C.F.R. § 61.140 *et seq*. The USEPA enforces the NESHAP strictly, most often against contractors who fail to comply with its requirements during demolition and renovation operations that disturb asbestos-containing material (ACM) so that asbestos becomes airborne and a potential respiratory hazard. A real estate developer was also convicted in *U.S. v. Weintraub*, 273 F.3d 139 (2d Cir. 2001).

The NESHAP for asbestos divides ACM into friable ACM and nonfriable ACM. It defines friable ACM as any material containing more than 1% asbestos by area as determined using polarized light microscopy and that, when dry, can be crumbled, pulverized, or reduced to powder by hand pressure. 40 C.F.R. § 61.141. Examples of friable ACM are sprayon insulation and old, deteriorated pipe and boiler insulation. Examples of nonfriable ACM are vinyl floor tiles and asphalt roofing in which the asbestos is encapsulated in plastic or asphalt material.

The NESHAP includes several standards. The standards for manufacturing, spraying, fabricating and installation of ACM and waste disposal by asbestos mills have limited application today. At present, the most significant standards are those for demolition and renovation (§ 61.145) and for waste disposal (§ 61.150 and .154).

The demolition and renovation standard combines friable and nonfriable ACMs and calls them regulated asbestos-containing material (RACM). It then subdivides them into friable ACM and several categories of nonfriable ACM based on whether they are likely to be handled during renovation or demolition in a manner that will cause them to become friable.

The demolition and renovation standard requires an inspection for ACM prior to renovation or demolition and, if detected, a notice to the USEPA at least 10 working days before the work commences. The standard prescribes detailed procedures for the performance of the work including adequate wetting of all RACM during cutting, disjoining, stripping and other operations. However, the USEPA may approve a request not to comply with the wetting requirement if the wetting would unavoidably damage equipment or present an electrical or other safety hazard and the owner or operator substitutes the use of an adequate local exhaust ventilation and collection system, a glove bag system, and leak tight wrapping. In addition to these and other work practices, the standard prescribes recordkeeping and worker supervision and training requirements. The standard contains exemptions from some of the work practice requirements if the combined amount of RACM is below specified quantities.

The waste disposal standard prescribes methods for transportation to, disposal of, ACMs at active solid waste landfills that are similar to the standards prescribed for the disposal of hazardous waste at landfills by the USEPA's regulations under RCRA. 40 C.F.R. §61.150 and .154.

In 1990, the USEPA published a useful book called "Managing Asbestos in Place—A Building Owner's Guide to operations and Maintenance Programs for Asbestos Containing Materials." The book, called the "Green Book," acknowledges that the average airborne asbestos levels in buildings and, accordingly, the health risk to building occupants seems to be very low. Thus, it recommends management in place under an operations and maintenance (O&M) plan rather than removal, except during building demolition, renovation or other activities which would cause asbestos to become airborne and create health risk.

C. The Occupational Safety and Health Act

Employers must protect employees from exposure to asbestos in the workplace by complying with comprehensive regulations of the Occupational Safety and Health Administration (OSHA). See the OSHA General Industry Standard at 29 C.F.R. § 1910.1001, the Construction Standard at 29 C.F.R. § 1926.58 and the Shipyard Employment Standard at 40 C.F.R. § 1950.1001.

The General Industry Standard requires an employer to ensure that no employee is exposed to an airborne concentration of asbestos in excess of 0.1 fiber per cubic centimeter (0.1 f/cc) of air as an eight hour time-weighted average (TWA), called the permissible exposure limit (PEL). The Standard also prescribes an airborne concentration limit of 1.0 f/cc averaged over a sampling period of 30 minutes, called the excursion limit.

The General Industry Standard also requires exposure monitoring; establishment of regulated areas wherever airborne concentrations of asbestos exceed the PEL and/or excursion limit; compliance methods such as engineering controls and work practices; respiratory protection; protective work clothing and equipment; communication of hazards to employees; housekeeping; medical surveillance; and worker rights to observe monitoring. The Standard also imposes responsibilities on building owners and operators to maintain records of ACM and presumed ACM (called "PACM") and to provide information to tenants and buyers of the buildings. 29 C.F.R. § 1910.1001(j)(1) and (2).

D. The Asbestos Hazard Emergency Response Act

The Asbestos Hazard Emergency Response Act (AHERA), 15 U.S.C. § 2641-2656, is an amendment to TSCA. It requires the USEPA to adopt regulations requiring the inspection of primary and secondary schools for asbestos containing materials and appropriate remedial action; accreditation of asbestos abatement contractors; periodic reinspection after abatement actions; and a study of the alleged danger to human health posed by asbestos in public and commercial buildings. The USEPA's asbestos regulations under TSCA are at 40 C.F.R. § 763.80 *et seq.*

Recognizing that unsupervised removal of asbestos could create hazards for workers and building occupants, AHERA requires accreditation programs for contractors and laboratories that include air testing by polarized light microscope or thermal electron microscope, surveillance, reinspections, warning labels, education, use of respirators and other personal protective equipment and proper disposal of asbestos containing waste.

AHERA allows encapsulation and other preventive measures designed to eliminate damage, deterioration or delamination but the cost of continued monitoring, reinspection and other steps usually lead to a decision to abate by removal.

AHERA does not require remediation of colleges or universities, public buildings, privately owned buildings or homes. However, environmentalists, plaintiff attorneys, labor unions and asbestos removal contractors have urged extension of AHERA to include all public buildings. Thus far, Congress has declined to do so, because costs may well exceed benefits and because many buildings are being remediated voluntarily or as required by state law or the NESHAP when renovation or demolition work is done.

E. Other Federal Environmental Laws

Asbestos is also regulated by the CWA and the USEPA has adopted regulations under the CWA limiting effluent emissions of asbestos by asbestos product manufacturers. (40 C.F.R. Part 427). Asbestos is listed as a hazardous substance under CERCLA (40 C.F.R. § 302.4). Transportation of asbestos is regulated by the Hazardous Materials Transportation Act. 49 U.S.C. § 5101 *et seq*,.; 49 C.F.R. Parts 171 *et seq*. See the listing of asbestos in the Hazardous Materials Table at 49 C.F.R. § 172.101.

F. Discontinuance of the Use of Asbestos as Fire Retardant Insulation

In 1989, the USEPA announced a rule prohibiting the manufacture, importation, processing and distribution of most asbestos-containing products to take effect in three stages over a period of years including roofing, flooring and brake-lining materials in which asbestos is fully encapsulated. 40 C.F.R. § 763.160 *et seq*. However, most of the rule was vacated as unsupported by substantial evidence in *Corrosion Proof Fittings v. E.P.A.*, 947 F.2d 1201 (5th Cir. 1991). In 1993, the USEPA published its determinations of the parts of the rule remaining in effect. Even when adopted, the rule was of limited importance because manufacture of asbestos-containing products in the United States had already been almost entirely discontinued except for a few products in which the asbestos was fully encapsulated.

Some years ago, the Detroit News reported that the O-ring used for the Apollo Space Craft was changed from asbestos to a substitute material that failed to protect the astronauts from the fire which killed them. The New York Times recently reported that steel structure of the World Trade Center which failed due to the heat generated by aviation gasoline fires on September 11, 2001 after crashes caused by terrorist hijackers was originally to have been insulated with asbestos. However, the decision was changed during construction.

G. State and Local Laws

Many states and municipalities have laws or ordinances regulating ACMs and licensing and regulating asbestos abatement contractors and their work methods. One example is Local Law No. 76 of the City of New York. In many cities, building owners and/or asbestos abatement contractors must give notice to the USEPA, OSHA, and a state or local agency before commencing renovation, demolition or abatement work and must comply with all of their rules. As a result, the time and cost of removal or abatement of ACMs is an important factor in any decision to upgrade old urban buildings and tends to favor new construction.

State and local laws licensing and regulating asbestos abatement contractors are today the most important asbestos laws. As the years have passed since asbestos products were widely manufactured and used in the United States, exposure of workers in general industry and of the general public has declined. Thus, the population group with the greatest potential exposure to friable ACM consists of the workers employed by asbestos abatement contractors. Many contractors hire semi-skilled and unskilled workers who could without protection be exposed to airborne asbestos at levels comparable to the former workers in the naval shipyards. The state and local laws protect these workers.

H. Recovery of ACM Abatement Costs

Some courts have held that building owners are entitled to recover removal and other abatement costs from the former asbestos product manufacturers and other persons such as architects and construction contractors. See, for example, *City of New York v. Keene Corporation*, 32 Misc. 2d 745, 505 N.Y.S. Supp. 2d 782; aff'd 513 N.Y.S. 2d 1004 (1st Dept. 1987). One court affirmed a tort law recovery, including operations and maintenance costs pending removal from a city hall, even though acknowledging that the damages claimed were economic in nature. The court also upheld an award of $2,000,000 of punitive damages. *City of Greenville v. W.R. Grace & Co.*, 827 F.2d 975 (4th Cir. 1987).

However, the courts have not been unanimously favorable to property owners seeking to recover ACM removal costs. One reason is that many owners purchased asbestos insulation under warranties for periods such as 10 or 15 years, but actually benefitted from its use for 30 or 40 years. Thus, where no personal injuries are involved, the need to replace old insulation is arguably a normal business expense. Another reason is that it has become fairly well known that most ACMs can safely be managed in place.

The courts have not generally been willing to dismiss a case simply because ACM has been installed for a number of years. However, some courts have upheld jury verdicts for defendant manufacturers where property owners claimed the cost of removal of small amounts of ACM or nonfriable ACM that could be managed in place. *Board of Trustees v. National Gypsum*, 733 F. Supp. 1413 (D. Kans. 1990).

The courts have upheld statute of limitations defenses in some cases. *Wichita v. U.S. Gypsum*, 72 F.3d 1491 (10th Cir. 1996); *Corporation of Mercer University v. National Gypsum*, 877 F.2d 35 (11th Cir. 1989); *St. Joseph Hosp. v. Celotex Corp.* 874 F.2d 764 (11th Cir. 1989).

Some courts have also upheld statute of repose defenses. *Trust Co. Bank v. U.S. Gypsum Co.*, 950 F.2d 1144 (5th Cir. 1992); *First United Methodist Church Board v. U.S. Gypsum*, 360 S.E. 2d 325 (1987); contra, *Uricam Corp. v. W.R. Grace & Co.*, 739 F. Supp. 1493 (W.D. Okla. 1990).

Finally, owners of buildings where ACM was installed many years ago may have difficulty identifying the manufacturers and/or distributors whose ACM products were installed in their buildings. If the ACM cannot be traced or is traced to a bankrupt manufacturer, the building owner may be left with no claim or a claim that is uncollectible. *Reorganized Church v. U.S. Gypsum*, 882 F.2d 335 (8th Cir. 1989).

I. Personal Injury Lawsuits

Hundreds of thousands of lawsuits have been (and continue to be) filed against manufacturers and users of ACMs on behalf of workers and other persons. The lawsuits are based on strict liability including failure to warn of asbestos hazards. In the early years, the lawsuits were filed on behalf of many workers (especially shipyard workers) suffering from asbestosis and lesser numbers of workers suffering from mesothelioma and bronchogenic carcinoma. In the last two decades, thousands of lawsuits have been filed on behalf of persons who suffered illnesses caused by tobacco smoking rather than asbestos. (The claimants sued asbestos manufacturers because they have no effective remedy against tobacco product manufacturers.) The plaintiff attorneys use the Mount Sinai studies to argue that even minor asbestos exposure is responsible for illness because of the reported synergistic effect with tobacco smoke. Juries tend to agree because they cannot require the absent tobacco product manufacturers to pay. Many other lawsuits are filed on behalf of persons who are not ill, but claim they were exposed to asbestos and fear they will suffer illness in the future.

The law applicable to asbestos claims differs from state to state on subjects such as the period of limitations for filing a lawsuit; the admissible evidence including identification of asbestos manufacturers; the extent of liability including liability for fear of future illness; the inability to place responsibility upon tobacco product manufacturers; and liability for large repeated awards of punitive damages. However, plaintiff attorneys file the lawsuits in states where the courts interpret the law favorably to them. For example, many lawsuits are filed in Mississippi and Texas where the courts are among those allowing recovery by claimants for alleged mental anguish from fear of future illness. *Jackson v. Johns-Manville*, 781 F.2d 394 (5th Cir. 1986); *Gideon v. Johns-Manville*, 761 F.2d 1129 (5th Cir. 1985).

Billions of dollars have been paid for judgments and settlements of the personal injury lawsuits. A major factor has been court decisions allowing repeated awards of punitive damages against companies that long ago ceased to manufacture asbestos products and allowing unusually dramatic arguments by plaintiff attorneys to persuade juries to award large amounts of consequential damages. *Dunn v. Hovic*, 1 F.3d 1371 (3d Cir. 1993); *Racich v. Celotex Corp.*, 887 F.2d 393 (2d Cir. 1989).

Bankruptcies of many companies which formerly manufactured or used ACMs have resulted as well as insolvencies and reorganizations of their insurers. For example, asbestos liabilities overwhelmed some underwriting syndicates at Lloyds in the City of London and led to a reorganization after many of the members, called "names," sustained severe losses.

Although decades have passed since asbestos was a major commercial product, asbestos lawsuits continue to be filed in increasing numbers, reportedly over 90,000 in 2001. The lawsuits are filed against numerous defendants including companies which made or used asbestos products, if at all, only briefly or in small quantities. Many companies have agreed to make settlement payments because the cost of investigation and defense is prohibitive.

CHAPTER XI
THE SAFE DRINKING WATER ACT

A. The Act and its Administration

The Safe Drinking Water Act (SDWA), 42 U.S.C. § 300f *et seq.*, requires the USEPA to issue drinking water regulations setting standards for contaminants in drinking water and to establish and administer several other programs. The drinking water regulations apply to public water systems which provide water for human consumption through pipes or other constructed conveyances and which have at least 15 service connections or regularly serve at least 25 individuals. Public water systems include collection, treatment, storage and treatment facilities. 42 U.S.C. § 300f.

The drinking water regulations do not apply to public water systems (such as hotels and office buildings) which consist only of distribution and storage facilities and do not have any collection or treatment facilities if they obtain all their water from a regulated public water system and do not sell water to any person. 42 U.S.C. § 300g.

The states may request that the USEPA authorize them to enforce the SDWA, provided that they adopt regulations as strict as those of the USEPA and meet other requirements set by the USEPA. State administration is discussed later in this chapter.

B. Public Water Systems

In its regulations, the USEPA has adopted a broad definition of a public water system. The definition includes any community water system which has at least 15 service connections used by year round residents or regularly serves at least 25 year round residents. The definition also includes any public water system that is a noncommunity water system, whether transient or nontransient. However, special irrigation districts and water delivered in bottles or packages or by trucks are excluded. 40 C.F.R. § 141.2; 63 Fed. Reg. 41, 940 (Aug. 5, 1998).

The USEPA's regulations authorize it to regulate many persons who do not recognize that they may be a community water system. For example, the USEPA's regulations are broad enough to regulate some owners of buildings and trailer parks supplying municipal drinking water to tenants if they furnish monthly water bills to the tenants. The USEPA takes the position that persons who supply water for purposes other than human consumption are subject to its regulations if they know or should know that it is being used for human consumption. 63 Fed. Reg. 91, 940 (Aug. 5, 1998).

C. Drinking Water Regulations

The USEPA has adopted national primary and secondary drinking water regulations. The primary drinking water regulations impose standards which apply to contaminants found in drinking water that may have an adverse effect on human health. The primary drinking water regulations are enforceable against public water systems. 40 C.F.R. Parts 141 and 142.

The secondary drinking water regulations are not health-based and are issued as guidelines to state agencies in relation to substances which may adversely affect the odor or appearance of water or may cause a substantial number of persons to discontinue use. The USEPA has adopted 15 secondary maximum contaminant levels for contaminants such as foaming agents, odor and total dissolved solids. The secondary limits are guidelines and are not enforceable by the USEPA against public water systems, but are enforced by state agencies which adopt them. 40 C.F.R. Part 143.

In adopting primary drinking water regulations, the SDWA requires the USEPA to prescribe for each contaminant that may have an adverse effect on the health of persons either–

1. A maximum contaminant limit (MCL) that is as protective of health as is technologically feasible and cost justified, or

2. Treatment techniques to reduce the contaminant as required by 42 U.S.C. § 300g-1

The SDWA also requires the USEPA to adopt maximum contaminant level goals (MCLGs). They are set at the level where no known or anticipated adverse effects on the health of persons occur and which allows an adequate safety margin. 42 U.S.C. § 300g-1(b)(4)(A). The MCLGs are not enforceable. The USEPA usually sets them at zero. They should be issued at the same time as the MCL for the contaminant.

In selecting contaminants for the adoption of MCLs and MCLGs, the USEPA is required to make three determinations. First, the contaminant may have an adverse effect on the health of persons. Second, the contaminant is known or likely to occur in public water systems with a frequency and at levels of public health concern. Third, regulation of the contaminant is a meaningful opportunity to reduce health risk for persons served by public water systems. 42 U.S.C. § 300g-1(b)(1)(A).

The SDWA requires the USEPA to adopt an MCL for each contaminant that is as close as feasible to its MCLG. "Feasible" includes use of the best technology, treatment techniques, and other available means, taking cost into consideration. 42 U.S.C. § 300g-1(b)(4)(D). However, the USEPA is not required to set an MCL at a level found to be feasible if (1) the MCL would result in an increase of health risk by increasing the concentration of other contaminants in drinking water or (2) the MCL would interfere with the efficiency of drinking water techniques or processes used to comply with the primary drinking water regulations. 42 U.S.C. § 300g-1(b)(5)

For example, the USEPA determined in 1991 that it was not feasible to establish a single national standard for lead in drinking water and required public water systems to design and implement corrosion control plans for lead. 56 Fed. Reg. 26, 460 (1991). Environmentalists sued the USEPA seeking a court order to require the USEPA to adopt an MCL for lead. However, the court deferred to the USEPA's interpretation of feasibility and upheld the regulation, subject to minor corrective actions. *American Water Works Ass'n v. EPA*, 40 F.3d 1266 (D.C. Cir. 1994).

D. A Decade of Unfunded Mandates and Eventual Relief from Them

Through 1986, the USEPA set primary standards containing MCLs for several partially soluble heavy metals, trihalomethanes, coliform bacteria, turbidity and radionuclides. It also set secondary standards for some additional contaminants and established sampling and analytical methods. The USEPA also published recommended maximum contaminant limits (RCMLs) for a number of contaminants.

In 1986, Congress adopted amendments to the SDWA requiring the USEPA to accelerate adoption of primary drinking water regulations and to establish standards for the filtration and disinfection of drinking water drawn by public water systems. The 1986 amendments mandated that the USEPA adopt 83 additional MCLs within three years. The USEPA published the required regulations at 40 C.F.R. Part 141. The implementation cost was estimated at $3 billion. The amendments also mandated that the USEPA adopt 25 MCLs every three years after 1986. The USEPA accelerated its adoption of regulations, although it did not meet the requirement to adopt 25 MCLs every three years.

The USEPA's drinking water regulations included extensive and detailed monitoring and analytical requirements for regulated contaminants as well as recordkeeping, public notification and reporting requirements. 40 C.F.R. Part 141. In addition to the extensive requirements to monitor for regulated contaminants, the regulations also required public water systems to monitor unregulated contaminants on the Unregulated Contaminant Monitoring Regulation List and to report the results. 40 C.F.R. § 141.35 and .40. Many small and medium-sized systems did not have the expensive analytical test equipment and control equipment or the trained personnel to achieve compliance. The multibillion dollar burdens of these requirements on public water systems were among the reasons why state and local governments complained about "unfunded mandates," especially during the recession of the early 1990s.

Environmentalists responded to the complaint about "unfunded mandates" by recommending that small and medium sized public water systems sell themselves to or merge with larger systems in order to gain access greater resources to comply with the regulations. Some consolidation of the industry did take place. For example, a large multinational water company called Suez Lyonnaise des Eaux made some acquisitions in the United States.

In 1994, the "unfunded mandates" issue was a key issue in an election that swept from office many members of the Congress that passed the 1986 amendments. The new Congress passed the Safe Drinking Water Act Amendments Act of 1996 repealing the requirement to adopt 25 MCLs every three years. The 1996 amendments required that the USEPA review at least five contaminants each five years and authorized the USEPA to determine whether or not it should regulate the contaminants based on the reviews. The 1996 amendments also provided relief for small public water systems and created a Drinking Water Site Revolving Fund to provide financial assistance. 42 U.S.C. § 300j-12. The USEPA's Guidelines for the Revolving Fund were published at 63 Fed. Reg. 59, 844 (Nov. 5, 1998).

E. Selection of Contaminants under the 1996 Amendments

The 1996 amendments to the SDWA required the USEPA to publish a Drinking Water Contaminant Candidate List by February 6, 1998 and every five years thereafter. After consultation with its Science Advisory Board, the USEPA published the List at 63 Fed. Reg. 10,274 (March 2, 1998). Recognizing that environmental advocacy groups would sue to challenge the contaminants the USEPA included in the List, Congress provided that the USEPA's listing decisions are not subject to judicial review. 42 U.S.C. § 300g-1(b)(1)(B)(i)(III).

The USEPA was required to determine by August 6, 2001 and each five years thereafter the contaminants on the List that it selects for regulation. The USEPA must select at least five contaminants using the criteria described earlier. The USEPA can also select contaminants that do not appear on the List. 42 U.S.C. § 300g-1(b)(1)(B)(ii)(I)-(III).

Environmental groups persuaded the Congress and the USEPA to allocate priority to regulation of arsenic, sulfate and radon. In January 2001, the USEPA adopted a new MCL of .01 mg/L for arsenic. The 1996 amendments to the SDWA directed the USEPA and the Centers for Disease Control and Prevention (CDC) to study the health effects of sulfate and its possible association with diarrhea in children. They submitted a report on sulfate in drinking water in January 1997.

The National Academy of Sciences published a risk assessment and cost analysis of radon in drinking water in September 1998 indicating that the risk was small.

The USEPA published a health risk reduction and cost analysis for regulation of radon at 64 Fed. Reg. 9,573 (Feb. 26, 1999) in which it used highly conservative methods to estimate annual fatalities at 160, primarily from inhalation of radon gas released from drinking water during household use. Estimated costs for various levels of treatment ranged from $24 million to $795 million per year and from $6.9 million to $11.3 million per assumed death avoided.

In 2002, the USEPA requested public comments on its review of the existing national primary drinking water regulations. The review concluded that 68 chemical regulations continue to be appropriate, but the total coliform rule should be revised. 67 Fed. Reg. 19030 (April 17, 2002).

F. Court Review of MCLs and MCLGs

The SDWA allows persons who wish to challenge an MCL or MCLG to file a petition for review with the U.S. Circuit Court of Appeals for the District of Columbia within 45 days after the regulation is promulgated. A person who fails to seek review may not challenge the regulation in an enforcement proceeding. 42 U.S.C. § 300j-7(a). However, if the USEPA later changes the regulation, judicial review may be allowed. *Ciba-Geigy Corp. v. USEPA*, 46 F.2d 1209 (D.C. Cir. 1995).

Judicial review is, however, very limited. The Court will set aside an USEPA decision only if it finds a mistake of law or that the USEPA acted in an arbitrary and capricious manner. The Court defers to a presumed expertise of the USEPA in scientific matters and declines to consider whether its scientific decisions are arbitrary and capricious. Thus, the Court will find that the USEPA has been arbitrary and capricious only when it refuses or fails to follow its own rules or to respond to specific challenges that are central to its decision. *International Fabricare Institute v. USEPA*, 972 F.2d 384 (D.C. Cir. 1992).

G. Operator Certification, Treatment Techniques and Monitoring

1. Operator Certification

The 1996 amendments of the SDWA made a major addition to the authority of the USEPA by requiring it to promulgate national standards for certification of operators of public water systems. Each state agency must conform its certification requirements to the USEPA's standards or it will lose 20% of its grants from the Revolving Loan Fund. 42 U.S.C. § 300g-8(a). Through its authority to prescribe certification standards, the USEPA can begin to make rules governing in the operation of public water systems and their facilities.

2. Treatment Techniques

The MCLs and MCLGs in the drinking water regulations are health-based standards rather than technology-based standards such as those widely adopted under the Clean Air Act and the Clean Water Act. Public water systems are required to maintain concentrations of contaminants in drinking water below limits usually expressed as milligrams, micrograms, picograms or nanograms per liter. In general, they are free to choose the methods to achieve the results including selection of treatment techniques and equipment.

As described earlier, if the USEPA determines that an MCL is not feasible, it may prescribe treatment techniques. The USEPA has seldom found it necessary to forego an MCL and substitute treatment techniques.

The SDWA itself prescribes one important treatment technique. Treatment of synthetic organic chemicals must be at least as effective as that achievable by granular activated carbon adsorption technology.

The USEPA's regulations prescribe treatment techniques for acrylamide and epichlorohydrin when used in drinking water systems. 40 C.F.R. § 141.111. However, they are expressed as dose and monomer concentration limits. The combination (or product) level may not exceed the following limits:

Acrylamide = 0.05% dosed at 1ppm (or equivalent)

Epichlorohydrin = 0.01% dosed at 20 ppm (or equivalent)

The USEPA elected to prescribe treatment techniques for lead and copper in drinking water rather than MCLs. 40 C.F.R. § 141.80 *et seq.* They are described later in this chapter. See also the later discussion of disinfection treatment of surfacewater and groundwater influenced by surfacewater if used as sources of drinking water

The author believes that the USEPA will eventually use its authority to prescribe operator certification standards to prescribe treatment techniques in addition to MCLs. As an alternative, the USEPA may request Congress to amend the SDWA to authorize it to set both drinking water quality standards and treatment techniques.

3. Monitoring Requirements

The USEPA's regulations prescribe detailed monitoring requirements including sampling and analytical methods and standards for certified testing laboratories. The general requirements are at 40 C.F.R. § 141.21 *et seq.* However, specific sampling and analytical methods are also found elsewhere in the regulations.

H. Self-Reporting of Violations

Despite the broad powers granted by the SDWA, the USEPA has faced some deterrents to building its regulatory programs. The public is generally satisfied with the public water systems and the quality of the water they supply. It is politically unacceptable for the USEPA to use civil and criminal proceedings and adverse publicity against public water systems to the extent it does against private industry.

It is also politically unacceptable for the USEPA to describe the risks of drinking water contaminants in the dramatic terms that it uses for industrial products. When the USEPA overstates the risk of an industrial product, the manufacturers may stop making the product, but usually also develop a substitute product. However, the USEPA would risk a public panic if it overdramatized contaminant risks in drinking water which has no substitute.

Accordingly, the SDWA prescribes notification and reporting programs which place an obligation on public water systems to furnish adverse information about their own activities to the public and the USEPA:

> *Public Notification*. Public water systems are required to notify everyone they serve of any failure to comply with an MCL, treatment technique, testing procedure, monitoring requirement, or other requirement of the USEPA's regulations. These notifications are designed to link public confidence in their local public water systems to compliance with USEPA rules. 40 C.F.R. § 141.35.
>
> *Consumer Confidence Reports*. Public water systems must mail annually to customers a Consumer Confidence Report describing contaminants in their drinking water. These reports are also designed to link public confidence in their local community water systems to conformity to USEPA rules. 40 C.F.R. § 141.151.63 Fed. Reg. 44, 511 (Aug. 19, 1998).
>
> *Noncompliance and Capacity Development Reports*. The 1996 amendments required state environmental agencies to report to the USEPA a list of public water systems that have a significant history of noncompliance. Each state must develop a capacity development strategy (CDS) to assure that all new community water systems and new nontransient noncommunity water system beginning operation after October 1, 1999 demonstrate technical, managerial and financial capacity to meet the USEPA's drinking water regulations. A state which refuses to comply will lose 20% of its grants from the Revolving Loan Fund. The state environmental agency must provide periodic reports to the USEPA on implementation of the CDS. 42 U.S.C. § 300g-9. The USEPA has published a Guidance on Implementing the Capacity Development Provisions. These reports will be useful to the USEPA and environmental groups in persuading the public to measure the reputation of their public water systems by their extent of compliance with USEPA policies. They can also be used to persuade Congress to extend the authority of the USEPA to regulate the operations of public water systems.

I. Variances, Exemptions and Monitoring Relief

The SDWA authorizes variances for up to five years from compliance with the primary drinking water regulations, provided that no unreasonable risk to health will result. The variances are not easily obtained because, among other things, each application must include a schedule to attain compliance with best available technology. Notice and opportunity for a public hearing is required. 40 C.F.R.§§ 142.20 and 142.40 *et seq.* Special procedures apply to variances for small systems serving up to 3,300 persons or, if approved by the USEPA, up to 10,000 persons. However, even small systems will not be granted a variance from a drinking water regulation issued before January 1, 1986 or with respect to microbial contaminants. 40 C.F.R. § 142.301 *et seq.*

The SDWA authorizes the USEPA to grant exemptions from compliance for a period up to three years if a system can show compelling reasons for noncompliance and the exemption will cause no unreasonable health risk. Among other things, the system must demonstrate that it cannot meet the standard without capital improvements that cannot be completed by the compliance date. The system must also show that it has an agreement for any necessary financial assistance, or that financial assistance is likely to become available during the exemption period, or that it has an agreement to become part of a regional system. Notice and opportunity for a public hearing is required. 40 C.F.R. § 142.50 *et seq.*

The 1996 amendments to the SDWA provided that states authorized to enforce the SDWA may grant interim and permanent relief from the monitoring requirements imposed by the USEPA. The states may also substitute alternative monitoring requirements if a system shows that a contaminant is not present in its water supply or is reliably and consistently below the MCL. The monitoring relief is subject to several conditions and restrictions, but it can save the costly burden of sampling and testing repeatedly for long lists of contaminants that a system does not have or has only at levels consistently below the MCLs.

J. Source Water Assessment and Protection Programs

States having authority to enforce the SDWA must develop source water assessment programs to (1) delineate the boundaries of the areas from which they receive drinking water supplies using all reasonably available hydrogeologic information including water flow, recharge, discharge and other information and (2) identify the origins of regulated contaminants within such areas. Public water systems may not seek monitoring relief until they have submitted these assessments. 42 U.S.C. § 300j-13.

The USEPA may make grants to support state source water quality partnership petition programs to reduce contaminants and otherwise protect source water of community water systems. 42 U.S.C. § 300j.-14.

K. Disinfection, Filtration and Disinfection Byproduct Rules

The USEPA has adopted regulations requiring public water systems supplied by a surface water source or a groundwater source directly influenced by surfacewater to install and properly operate treatment processes to protect against giardia lamblia, viruses, heterotrophic plate count bacteria, legionella and turbidity. If a system does not meet the treatment criteria, it must filter its water as required by the regulations. 40 C.F.R. §§ 141.70-75.

The regulations also prescribe general, analytical, monitoring, compliance, recordkeeping, reporting and treatment requirements for disinfectant residuals, byproducts and precursors. 40 C.F.R. §§ 141.130-.144.

These regulations have received special emphasis since the deaths in Milwaukee from the pathogen, cryptosporidium.

L. Subsurface Water Protection

The SDWA establishes underground injection control (UIC) programs, including permit requirements, to protect drinking water from contamination by disposal of hazardous waste into underground deep well disposal facilities. 40 C.F.R. Parts 144 to 147. The SDWA also provides wellhead protection programs. 49 C.F.R. Part 148. The SDWA also provides sole source aquifer protection programs. 40 C.F.R. Part 149.

M. Bottled Water

The U.S. Food and Drug Administration (FDA) is required to conform its standards for bottled water to each primary drinking water regulation within 180 days after its promulgation or publish in the Federal Register its reasons for not doing so. 21 U.S.C. § 349.

N. Lead and Copper

1. Direct Requirements and Prohibitions Relating to Lead

The SDWA requires that pipe, plumbing fixtures, solder or flux used after June 19, 1986 in construction or repair of any public water system or in plumbing providing water for human consumption be lead free. Public water systems must notify any person who may be affected by lead contamination of their drinking water resulting from lead content in the construction materials of its distribution system or corrosivity of its water sufficient to cause leaching of lead. No person may sell or otherwise introduce into commerce after August 6, 1996 any pipe, plumbing fitting or fixture that is not lead free except for a pipe used in manufacturing or industrial processing. Further, no person engaged in the business of selling plumbing supplies, except manufacturers, may sell solder or flux that is not lead free. Any manufacturer or person (other than a plumbing supplier) who sells solder or flux that is not lead free must affix a prominent label stating that it is illegal to use the solder or flux in the installation of any plumbing providing water for human consumption. The term "lead free" means (1) not more than 0.2% lead in solders and flux; (2) 8.0% lead in pipes and pipe fittings; and (3) and not more than the level allowed in fittings and fixtures by Standard 61, Section 9 of the National Sanitation Foundation. 42 U.S.C. § 300g-6

2. The Lead and Copper Rule

Having determined that national MCLs and MCLGs for lead and copper were not feasible, the USEPA issued in 1991 a national drinking water regulation for those contaminants based on monitoring; system corrosion control treatment techniques; and, if necessary, source water treatment and lead service line replacement. 40 C.F.R. § 141.80 *et seq.*

In considering the regulation, the USEPA recognized that the trace amounts of lead and copper in drinking water consumed in homes throughout the United States resulted in large part from lead and copper in the water piping and solder in the homes. Public water systems could not have complied with an MCL by taking steps within their own control and it was politically unacceptable to require homeowners to undertake the effort and cost of removing water piping from their homes.

The regulation established detailed procedures to shift the direct burden and cost of reducing lead and copper in drinking water from the public to their water systems. The regulation also established "educational" programs so that the public would not object to gradually increasing charges for water by their water systems.

The regulation applies to community water systems and to non-transient, non-community water systems. These water systems are required to monitor and analyze tap water in single family homes and other buildings by tiers and using specified test methods. The regulation sets an "action level" for lead of 0.015 mg/L and an "action level" for copper of 1.3 mg/L.

The regulation divides water systems into three groups: large (serving over 50,000 persons), medium-size (serving over 3,300 persons up to 50,000 persons), and small (serving up to 3,000 persons). All large systems, and those medium-sized and small systems with test results over an action level, must test their water factors indicating corrosivity, i.e., pH, alkalinity, orthophosphate or silica, calcium, conductivity and temperature. All large systems, and those medium-sized and small systems whose water is corrosive, must install and operate optimal corrosion control treatment as specified by the regulations.

If sampling and testing after implementation of corrosion control shows that an "action level" is still exceeded, the water system must undertake a program to sample, test and treat its source water to control lead and/or copper. If both corrosion control and source water treatment fails to reduce copper or lead to the action level, the water system must begin a program to replace at least 7% of its lead service lines per year, although it need not replace lines which it can demonstrate contribute less than 0.015 mg/L to drinking water at the tap. The water system must continue replacing the lines until it meets the action levels and must, if necessary, replace all the lines within 15 years.

In the meantime, water systems that exceed the lead action level must send printed materials to customers with their water bills. The materials must inform the customers that some homes in the community have lead above the action level and that the system is required to have a program to reduce lead in their drinking water that will be completed by a specified date. The materials must also warn the customers about the health effects of lead in drinking water and tell them about steps they can take in the home to reduce their exposure, such as letting tap water run for about 15 to 30 seconds before using it for drinking or cooking. The water systems must also send the materials to major newspapers, and radio and televisions stations serving the community and to facilities and organizations likely to be visited regularly by pregnant women and children.

The regulation prescribes the text to be recited in the materials, so that public water systems are not free to present different viewpoints. The materials must be sent each 12 months until lead is reduced to the action level.

O. State Administration

The states may apply to the USEPA for authorization to administer and enforce the SDWA. The authorization is sometimes called "primacy," but that term is a misnomer because a state can obtain the authorization only by demonstrating that it has adopted laws and regulations that are the same as (or stricter than) those of the USEPA. The state must retain records and submit reports required by the USEPA. The USEPA is authorized to withdraw the authorization if it is not satisfied with state enforcement. 40 U.S.C. § 300g-2(a)(1)-(6).

The USEPA has adopted regulations on primary enforcement responsibility. 40 C.F.R. § 142.10 *et seq.* The regulations contain the requirements for a state to obtain a determination of primary enforcement responsibility. They also provide for recordkeeping and reporting obligations and reviews by the USEPA. They also provide for direct enforcement by the USEPA and for withdrawal of the "primacy" authorization if it is not satisfied with state enforcement.

The National Wildlife Federation filed two lawsuits challenging provisions in the USEPA's regulations allowing delays to the states. The court upheld a provision allowing a temporary stay of the process of withdrawal when a state fails to meet a deadline for conforming to new or revised standards for reasons beyond its control. However, the court declared a provision to be invalid that allowed the USEPA discretion to defer withdrawal proceedings after it determines that a state is no longer in compliance with the SDWA. *National Wildlife Fed. v. USEPA*, 925 F.2d 470 (D.C. Cir. 1991); *National Wildlife Fed. v. USEPA*, 980 F.2d 765 (D.C. Cir. 1992).

Another environmental advocacy foundation obtained a court order directing the USEPA to initiate proceedings to withdraw authorization for the State of Alabama's underground injection program because it did not restrict hydraulic fracturing to recover methane gas, a secondary recovery method used in the oil and gas industry. *LEAF v. EPA*, 118 F.3d 1467 (11th Cir. 1997).

P. Application to Federal Government Departments and Agencies

The 1996 amendments to the SDWA require that federal government departments and agencies must comply with the SDWA to the extent that they (1) own or operate a public water system or any facility in a wellhead protection area or (2) engage in any activity that results or may result in contamination of water supplies in a wellhead protection area or underground injection which endangers drinking water. 42 U.S.C. § 300 j-6. The President may grant exemptions, and renewals of exemptions, for periods up to one year if he determines it to be in the paramount interest of the United States to do so.

Q. Enforcement and Penalties

The SDWA authorizes the USEPA to take direct action to enforce the drinking water regulations against a public water system if a state holding enforcement authority fails to do so within 30 days after notice of a violation from the USEPA. 42 U.S.C. § 300g-3(a)(1). The USEPA must also provide the state an opportunity to confer with the USEPA. *U.S. v. Wright*, 988 F.3d 1036 (10th Cir. 1993). However, if a state has not been authorized to enforce the SDWA, the USEPA may issue an administrative order or commence a civil action after notifying the appropriate local elected official having jurisdiction over the public water system. 42 U.S.C. § 300g-3(b).

The USEPA may bring a civil action in an appropriate U.S. District Court to enforce orders and other requirements of the drinking water regulations. If the court finds a violation, it may impose a civil penalty up to $25,000 for each day in which the violation occurs. 42 U.S.C. § 300g-3(a).

Anyone who fails to comply with the monitoring, recordkeeping and inspection requirements is subject to a civil penalty up to $25,000. U.S.C. § 300j-4(c).

The USEPA may issue an order requiring compliance in any case in which it is authorized to bring a civil action. Any person who violates, fails or refuses to comply with the order is liable for a civil penalty up to $25,000 per day of violation. If the proposed penalty exceeds $5,000, but is less than $25,000, the USEPA may assess the penalty only after notice and an opportunity for a hearing. If the proposed penalty exceeds $25,000, the USEPA must bring an action in the appropriate U.S. District Court to assess the penalty. 42 U.S.C. § 300g-3(g).

Any person who tampers with a public water system by introducing a contaminant into, or otherwise interfering with the operation of, the system with the intention of harming persons is subject to a civil penalty up to $50,000. Attempts or threats of such actions are subject to a civil penalty up to $20,000. These actions are also subject to a criminal penalty including a fine and imprisonment up to five years for tampering and up to three years for attempts or threats. 42 U.S.C. § 300i-1.

The SDWA authorizes the USEPA to exercise emergency powers if a contaminant in, or likely to enter, a public water system or underground water source may present an imminent and substantial endangerment to public health and state and local authorities have not acted. The USEPA may issue orders to protect health, including provision of alternate water supplies, and may commence a civil action seeking court orders. Anyone who violates or fails to comply with any such order is subject to a civil penalty up to $15,000 per day in which the violation occurs or fails to comply continues. One court has held that the USEPA can exercise the emergency powers in a case where state and local authorities acted, but the USEPA was not satisfied with the adequacy of their actions. The court also held the USEPA need not show actual imminent and substantial endangerment, but only risk of harm. *Trinity American Corp. v. USEPA*, 150 F.3d 389 (4th Cir. 1998).

The SDWA also contains other provisions for civil and criminal penalties such as a specific civil penalty up to $5,000 for manufacturing or selling a drinking water cooler that is not lead free. The penalty for repeated violations is up to $50,000. A criminal fine and imprisonment up to five years may be imposed for a knowing violation. 42 U.S.C. § 300j-23.

The foregoing penalty amounts are to be adjusted every four years to reflect inflation as provided in the Debt Collection Improvements Act of 1996. Thus, each amount was increased by 10% in 1998 and 13.6% in 2002.

R. Citizen's Civil Actions

The SDWA authorizes any person to commence a civil action on his own behalf in a U.S. District Court against (1) any person alleged to be in violation of the SDWA, (2) the USEPA for an alleged failure to perform any act or duty under the SDWA, or (3) any federal agency that fails to pay a penalty assessed by the USEPA. The right to commence such an action is subject to a requirement to give 60 days notice to the USEPA and any alleged violator in order to provide an opportunity for voluntary correction of the alleged violation. 42 U.S.C. § 300g-8.

A person who commences a civil action must also show that it has standing. For example, an organization with members who owned a well near to coal beds where hydraulic fracturing activities were conducted to recover natural gas was found to have standing for a lawsuit to compel the USEPA to withdraw authorization of Alabama's underground injection program. *LEAF v. USEPA*, 118 F.3d 1467 (11th Cir. 1997).

Environmental groups and their attorneys often commence civil actions under the SDWA which allows them to recover costs, attorneys fees and expert witness fees in addition to other remedies. 42 U.S.C. § 300g-8(d). *Colorado Environmental Coalition v. Romer*, 796 F. Supp. 457 (D. Colo. 1992). However, environmental groups cannot always be sure of success. For example, if there is no ongoing violation, the court will dismiss the lawsuit for lack of jurisdiction. *Mattoon v. City of Pittsfield*, 980 F.2d 1 (1st Cir. 1992). An environmental group which sued the State of Louisiana despite its extensive steps to comply with the SDWA was denied attorneys fees and the denial was upheld through appellate review. *ACORN v. Edwards*, 81 F.3d 1387 (5th Cir. 1996), cert. den. 521 U.S. 1129, 138 L. Ed. 2d 1031 (1987).

CHAPTER XII
FEDERAL INSECTICIDE, FUNGICIDE AND RODENTICIDE ACT

A. Overview and History

1. Introduction

The Federal Insecticide, Fungicide and Rodenticide Act (FIFRA), 7 U.S.C. § 136 *et seq.*, was originally enacted in 1947 and was for many years administered by the U.S. Department of Agriculture (USDA). The administration of FIFRA was transferred to the USEPA in 1970 by President Richard Nixon.

Stringent requirements were added to FIFRA by amendments contained in the Federal Environmental Pesticide Control Act of 1972. Political impetus came from lawsuits that plaintiff attorneys were pursuing on behalf of veterans alleged to be suffering illnesses resulting from use of a mixture of the herbicides, 2, 4, 5-T and 2, 4-D, as a defoliant called "Agent Orange" to detect deployment of enemy tanks and other weapons under jungle foliage in Viet Nam. Political impetus also came from a popular book called *Silent Spring* written by Rachel Carson.

As amended in 1972 and thereafter, FIFRA requires the registration of pesticides with the USEPA and prohibits sale, receipt and other transfers of unregistered pesticides. FIFRA also regulates traps and other devices (except firearms) used for pest, animal and plant control. USEPA regulations are at 40 C.F.R. Parts 152 *et seq*. Establishments producing pesticides and their ingredients must be registered with the USEPA and are subject to inspection, recordkeeping and reporting requirements.

FIFRA also authorizes the USEPA to review and approve state programs for the certification of applicators of restricted use pesticides and to conduct certification programs for applicators in states not having an approved plan. Restricted use pesticides may be applied only by persons who are certified commercial applicators on property other than their own property.

A pesticide is any substance or mixture intended for preventing, destroying, repelling or mitigating any pest or as a plant regulator, defoliant or desiccant. The definition includes insecticides, herbicides, rodenticides and other economic poisons. Certain substances are excluded such as substances regulated by the Food and Drug Administration. Pesticides contribute importantly to the protection of public health from diseases carried by insects, germs, rodents and other pests and to the abundance of food that has made famines a rarity in a world which once feared starvation resulting from population growth, as predicted by Thomas Malthus.

Registration of a pesticide requires the applicant to file (1) the complete formula, (2) the label including a statement of all claims made for the pesticide and directions for its use, (3) a description of studies and other data on which claims for the pesticide are based, and (4) a request for classification for general or restricted use, or both. Limited trade secret protection is available.

The USEPA must approve an application for registration of a pesticide if (1) its composition warrants the proposed claims, (2) its labelling and other submitted materials comply with FIFRA, (3) it will perform its intended function without unreasonable adverse effects on the environment, and (4) it will not generally cause unreasonable adverse effects when used in accordance with widespread and generally recognized practice. Each registration is for specific uses and is for a period of 15 years, subject to rereview by the USEPA.

FIFRA imposes detailed labelling requirements (including the familiar "skull and crossbones" and "poison" warnings) and a statement of practical treatment (first aid or otherwise) in case of poisoning. FIFRA prohibits claims and compositions which differ from the registration. FIFRA also prohibits a variety of other practices including miscoloring, misbranding, adulteration and misbranding; use of a pesticide in a manner inconsistent with its labeling; and use of a pesticide classified for restricted use for other purposes.

FIFRA applies to imports and also contains limited provisions applicable to exports. Unregistered pesticides can be exported subject to several conditions including notice to the applicable foreign government and appropriate international agencies.

A major FIFRA program has been the reregistration of many pesticides registered when standards were more lenient. Many traditional pesticides have been discontinued by their manufacturers or denied registration as a result of inability to bear the complexity and cost of reregistration.

The USEPA is authorized to commence proceedings to cancel a registration if it believes that a pesticide presents a substantial question of safety to man or the environment. The USEPA can also suspend (i.e., impose an immediate prohibition on production and distribution) a pesticide if it finds it is an "imminent hazard." In customary usage, an "imminent" hazard refers to an acute hazard associated with a significant exposure risk. However, the U.S. Circuit Court of Appeals for the District of Columbia required only a finding by the USEPA of any serious threat to public health, whether acute or chronic, including a threat to animals and fish, to support a suspension of a pesticide registration by the USEPA. FIFRA formerly provided indemnity payments to end users, dealers and distributors of a suspended pesticide under some circumstances, but the indemnity payments were later repealed.

The USEPA may order manufacturers to recall a pesticide when its registration is cancelled or suspended, but may allow existing inventories to be used for some period of time.

2. Accelerated Reregistration and Deregistration (1988)

In 1988, amendments to FIFRA were adopted to make its provisions stricter, although less strict than environmental advocates urged. The reregistration process for all pesticides registered before November 1, 1984 was accelerated. During 1989, the USEPA published lists of active ingredients according to priorities based on the possibility that the pesticides would contaminate food or animal feed or leach into groundwater. Companies wishing to maintain registration were required to provide extensive data within a year including tests, studies and any adverse information about the active ingredient. In October 1990, the USEPA published a list of some 1,100 pesticide registration requests for cancellation and many more cancellations have followed in subsequent years. Many cancellations were of older products no longer used or unable to compete with newer products. However, the extraordinary registration fees and the burden of the registration requirements upon small businesses contributed to these cancellations. Fees were increased to between $50,000 and $100,000 for a new registration and $75,000 and $150,000 for a reregistration. Annual maintenance fees are $650 for the first product, subject to limits for companies having multiple registrations.

The 1988 amendments rescinded indemnity payments to manufacturers and limited payments to dealers and distributors. They also authorized the USEPA to adopt storage, transport and packaging regulations including design, use, reuse and disposal of containers. They also eliminated any responsibility of the USEPA to share costs of recall and disposal of suspended and cancelled pesticides. Criminal penalties for violations were increased.

The USEPA has adopted extensive regulations implementing FIFRA. They include labelling and packaging standards, laboratory practice standards, certification of usefulness, disposal and storage, worker protection, and tolerances (maximum residue limits) for pesticides used in or on raw agricultural commodities and in or on processed food and animal feeds. 40 C.F.R. Parts 152 to 186. FIFRA requires the packaging standards set by the USEPA be consistent with those established under the Poison Prevention Packaging Act which protects children from poisoning by inadequately packaged drugs or other toxic products used in households. 15 U.S.C. § 1471 *et seq.*

3. The Food Quality Protection Act (1996)

In 1996, Congress adopted important and fundamental amendments to FIFRA and also to the Federal Food Drug and Cosmetic Act. (FFDCA).

The FQPA greatly added to the powers of the USEPA by amendments to the FFDCA. Most important, the FQPA eliminated the former risk-benefit standard for establishing tolerances for many pesticide residues used in or on raw agricultural commodities or processed food. The FQPA states that the USEPA may establish or leave in effect a tolerance for a pesticide chemical residue in or on a food only if it determines that the tolerance is "safe," meaning that there is a reasonable certainty that no harm will result from aggregate exposure to the pesticide chemical residue, including all anticipated dietary exposures and all other exposures or which there is reliable information. 21 U.S.C. § 346a.

For residues containing chemical substances for which the USEPA recognizes a "threshold," a "safe" level is determined by applying extremely conservative risk assessment methods to calculate a no observed adverse effect level (NOAEL) and multiplying by 100 as an additional conservative safety actor. The result, as stated by the USEPA, is usually a considerable overestimate of the likely actual risk.

In determining tolerances and exemptions from tolerances, the USEPA must also assess the risk of a pesticide chemical residue based on available information about any disproportionately high consumption patterns; any special susceptibilities of infants and children including neurological differences from adults and effects of *in utero* exposure; and cumulative effects of the residues and other substances with a common mechanism of toxicity. The threshold thus determined (including the 100 multiple) is again multiplied by 10 for risks to infants and children.

The USEPA is authorized to determine tolerances for so-called "eligible pesticide chemicals residues" using risk-benefit criteria. Eligible pesticide chemical residues are those for which the USEPA does not recognize a threshold effect because they contain chemical substances which the USEPA treats as carcinogens. The USEPA may determine a tolerance for an eligible pesticide chemical residue if use of the pesticide chemical that produces the residue either (1) protects consumers from adverse affects on health that pose a greater risk than the dietary risk from the residue or (2) is necessary to avoid a significant disruption in domestic production of an adequate, wholesome and economical food supply. However, the USEPA may establish the tolerance only if both of the following conditions are met: (1) the yearly risk of the nonthreshold effect from aggregate exposure to the residue does not exceed 10 times the yearly risk allowed by the general safety standard *and* (2) the tolerance is limited so as to ensure that the risk over a lifetime associated with the nonthreshold effect from aggregate exposure to the residue is not greater than twice the lifetime risk allowed by the general standard. Any such determination must meet the requirements for protection of infants and children and be reviewed again five years after it is established.

The extremely conservative standards in the FQPA were negotiated by the USEPA and environmental organizations in exchange for repeal of the "Delaney Clause" which formerly prohibited use in food of any substance that induces cancer in man or animal. The "Delaney Clause" was adopted before advances in analytical equipment made it possible to detect infinitesimal traces of potentially carcinogenic substances in residues. The U.S. Circuit Court of Appeals for the Ninth Circuit held that the Delaney Clause should be interpreted and enforced literally. *LES v. Reilly*, 968 F.2d 985 (9th Cir. 1992); cert. den. 507 U.S. 950 (1993). Thus, until its repeal by the FQPA, the Delaney Clause prohibited a tolerance for any pesticide residue that, when fed continuously in very high dosages to laboratory rats or mice, induced any cancerous lesions, even though an assessment by the extremely conservative methods used by the USEPA showed that the risk was negligible.

The FQPA amendments to the FFDCA directed that USEPA review all tolerances and exemptions in effect on the day before its enactment on a schedule to be completed within 10 years. The FQPA required the USEPA to consider a list of nine factors among the relevant factors in determining tolerances as well as data regarding anticipated and actual residue levels in or on food. A helpful provision stated that a tolerance shall not be established or modified to a level lower than the method detection limit for the residue. Thus, nondetections should not be assigned values. Another helpful provision required that the USEPA publish for public comment any proposal to adopt a tolerance different from any maximum level established by the Codex Alimentarius Commission established in 1962 by food and health organizations of the United Nations.

The USEPA published for public comment a notice of nine scientific policies proposed for use in its tolerance reassessment work under the FQPA. The nine policies were (1) how to apply the 10-fold factor when assessing dietary risk; (2) whether and how to use probablistic "Monte Carlo" analysis in assessing dietary exposure; (3) interpreting "non detects" in test results and their use in risk assessments; (4) determining whether and how to make dietary (food) exposure assessments taking into account that tolerances already assume "worst case" residue levels; (5) determining whether and how to make dietary (drinking water) exposure assessments taking into account that tolerances already overestimate the concentration of pesticides in most drinking water sources; (6) assessing residential exposure; (7) aggregating exposures from organophosphate insecticides or other pesticides with a common mechanism of toxicity; and (9) selection of appropriate toxicity endpoints for risk assessments of organophosphates. 63 Fed. Reg. 58,038 (Oct. 29, 1998).

The FQPA also made several amendments to FIFRA including the following:

1. The USEPA was authorized to issue an emergency order suspending a pesticide before issuing a notice of intention to cancel.

2. A new Science Review Board was established consisting of 60 scientists to assist in reviews conducted by the Scientific Advisory Panel.

3. Nitrogen stabilizers were included in the definition of a pesticide, but subject to some exceptions.

4. The USEPA was instructed to rereview pesticide registrations periodically with a goal to rereview each registration every 15 years. However, no registration is to be cancelled due to a failure to rereview it.

5. The USEPA was authorized to set minimum requirements for training of maintenance applicators and service technicians for use by state regulators.

6. The USEPA was instructed to develop programs for minor use pesticides that would take into account their benefits in managing pests and the fact that their use may not provide sufficient economic incentive to support initial registration or continuing registration. The FQPA instructs the USEPA to expedite minor use registrations, but not to use the instruction to deny registration without allowing adequate time for submission of data.

7. The USEPA was instructed to reform its programs for registration of antimicrobial pesticides, meaning pesticides intended to (i) disinfect, sanitize, reduce, or mitigate growth or development of microbial organisms, or (ii) protect inanimate objects, industrial processes or systems, surfaces, water or other chemical substances from contamination, fouling or deterioration caused by bacteria, viruses, fungi, protozoa, algae or slime. Among the reforms, the USEPA was instructed to reduce time schedules for reviews of antimicrobial pesticides by giving them higher priority; to conform its reviews to the actual risks, benefits and uses; and to allow antimicrobial pesticides to maintain their efficacy and meet product performance standards and effectiveness levels.

8. The USEPA was instructed to consider the risks and benefits of public health pesticides separate from those of other pesticides and to include the health risks of the diseases transmitted by the vector controlled by the pesticide. Thus, the USEPA is required to consider the diseases, discomforts or injuries caused by mosquitoes, flies. fleas, cockroaches, other insects and ticks, mites and rats.

9. The USEPA was instructed to develop procedures to provide expedited reviews of pesticides formulated to reduce risks to human health or nontarget organisms; reduce potential for contamination of groundwater, surfacewater or other valued environmental resources; or improve integrated pest management strategies.

4. Pesticides as Protectors of Health and the Environment

Pesticides are among the most important protectors of health and the environment developed in world history. They have saved millions of people from death and illness from diseases such as malaria carried by pests. They have also contributed to the a abundance of wholesome food available in most areas of the world.

The author remembers shopping in grocery stores in the 1930s and 1940s when it was necessary to examine each fruit and vegetable for worms, bugs and "spoil spots." In those relatively recent days, adults and especially children suffered annually from contagious diseases carried by rodents, germs and insects. We are now troubled that such conditions continue to exist in underdeveloped nations and in some lower income areas in the United States. However, not long ago, they affected everyone. To young readers who never experienced serious plagues of rodents and insects, the author recommends reading "The Glittering Cloud," a chapter in "On the Banks of Plum Creek," one of the famous "Little House" books by Laura Ingalls Wilder. Young readers can also read how the Marines and Seabees rejoiced when DDT became available to fight mosquitoes and malaria in the South Pacific during World War II.

Early pesticides were formulated to be relatively strong in order to assure effectiveness as economic poisons. Resistance to biodegradation was perceived as a favorable characteristic because a pesticide could be applied to kill migrating swarms of insects and it would also kill their later born larvae or other offspring.

Considering their rapid growth and widespread use, the early pesticides were used quite safely. Manufacturers and distributors provided instructions for use and warnings. However, as time passed, some users applied pesticides in excessive quantities or by improper methods. Although such misapplications were uncommon, they were widely publicized and manufacturers were blamed rather than the users. As a result, many of the early pesticides have been banned or withdrawn from registration and sale in the United States. Examples are DDT, 2,4,5-T and Lindane.

Pesticides are being reformulated to become less effective as the USEPA uses default assumptions and multipliers to evaluate risk. By overestimating chronic pesticide risks, the USEPA and environmental advocates expose the public to real and serious acute risks of death and illness from disease carrying mosquitos and other pests.

Regulation has also led to industry concentration. Regulatory complexity and costs have eliminated many of the pesticides that were once in the market and driven small competitors out of the business. Pesticides are increasingly manufactured by a few large companies which can afford regulatory compliance. As described in a recent article in The New York Times, the predominant manufacturers of pesticides are giants such as Monsanto, Bayer and Syngenta. Monsanto's glyphosate herbicide product, sold under the trademark Roundup®, has a very large market share, so much so that another giant, E.I. du Pont, has reportedly filed antitrust lawsuits against Monsanto. Another large manufacturer is Dow Agro Sciences. These companies, necessarily pass on their regulatory compliance costs to the public by increasing prices which are then added to the cost of food.

B. The USEPA's Regulations

1. Pesticide Definition and Exclusions

A pesticide is any substance or mixture intended for preventing, destroying, repelling, or mitigating any pest or intended for use as a plant regulator, defoliant or dessicant other than certain animal drugs and animal feeds identified by reference to the Federal Food, Drug and Cosmetic Act (FFDCA). 40 C.F.R. § 152.3(s).

An organism is a pest under circumstances that make it deleterious to man or the environment, if it is:

(a) Any vertebrate animal other than man

(b) Any invertebrate animal including any insect, other arthropod, nematode, or mollusk such as slug or snail, but excluding any internal parasite of living man or other living animals;

(c) Any plant growing where not wanted including any moss, alga, liverwort, or other plant of any higher order and any plant part such as a root; or

(d) Any fungus, bacterium, virus or other microorganisms except those on or in living man or other living animals and those on or in processed food or processed animal feed, beverages, drugs and cosmetics as defined in the FFDCA. (40 C.F.R. § 152.5)

Deer are an example of an animal which is well-liked and often protected, but which sometimes become so numerous that they become pests. Water lilies have been the subject of great impressionist paintings, but can grow so widely that they choke waterways and destroy other aquatic life.

A product is not a pesticide if it is not intended for use against pests. For example, a product is not a pesticide if it is intended for use only for the control of fungi, bacteria, viruses, or other microorganisms in or on living man or animals and is labeled accordingly. (This exclusion protects the right to make and sell athlete's foot and similar products). A product is also not a pesticide if intended for use only for control of internal invertebrate parasites or nematodes in living man or animals and is labeled accordingly. 40 C.F.R. § 152.8(a) and (b).

The following product types are not pesticides if intended only to aid the growth of desirable plants:

1. A fertilizer product not containing a pesticide.

2. A plant nutrient product consisting of one or more macronutrients or micronutrent trace elements necessary to normal growth of plants and in a form readily usable by plants.

3. A plant innoculant product consisting of microorganisms applied to the plant or soil to enhance availability or uptake of plant nutrients through the root system.

4. A soil amendment product containing a substance or substances added to the soil to improve soil characteristics favorable for plant growth. (40 C.F.R. § 152.8(c)).

A product is not a pesticide if intended to force bees from hives for the collection of honey crops. 40 C.F.R. § 152.8(d).

The following products or articles are not considered to be pesticides because they are not used for a pesticidal effect, unless a pesticide claim is made on their labelling or in connection with their sale and distribution:

1. Deodorizers, bleaches and cleaning agents;

2. Products not containing toxicants intended only to attract pests for survey or detection and labelled accordingly; and

3. Products intended to exclude pests only by providing a physical barrier against pest access and containing no toxicants. (40 C.F.R.§ 152.10)

The USEPA considers a substance or mixture to be a pesticide if the distributor or seller claims, states or implies, by labeling or otherwise, that (1) the substance (either by itself or with any other substance) can or should be used as a pesticide, or (2) the substance is or contains an active ingredient and can be used to manufacture a pesticide. The USEPA takes the same position if a substance contains one or more active ingredients and has no other significant commercially valuable use. In a questionable interpretation, the USEPA also contends that a substance is a pesticide if the person who distributes or sells it has actual or constructive knowledge that it will be used, or is intended to be used, for a pesticidal purpose. 40 C.F.R. § 152.15.

2. Active and Inert Ingredients; Biological Control Agents

An active ingredient is any substance that will prevent, destroy, repel or mitigate any pest or that functions as a plant regulator, desiccant or defoliant. 40 C.F.R. § 152.3(b).

An inert ingredient is a substance, other than the active ingredient, which is intentionally included in a pesticide product. 40 C.F.R. § 152.3(m).

A biological control agent is a living organism applied to or introduced into the environment that is intended to function as a pesticide against another organism declared to be pest by the USEPA. 40 C.F.R. § 150.3(i).

3. Exemptions

With some exceptions, the USEPA's regulations exempt biological control agents; human drugs regulated by the FFDCA; articles or substances treated with a pesticide for their own protection; pheromones and pheromone traps; preservatives for biological specimens including embalming fluids; vitamin hormone products; foods; natural cedar; and a list of minimum risk pesticides. 40 C.F.R. § 152.25. The list of minimum risk pesticides consists of common food additives.

The foregoing exemptions are subject to conditions. For example, the listed minimum risk pesticides may contain only inert ingredients listed in the most current List 4A published by the USEPA. The list may be obtained from the Registration Support Branch (4A Inserts List), Registration Division (7505C), Office of Pesticide Programs, USEPA, 401 M Street, S.W., Washington, D.C. 20460. Labeling and claim restrictions also apply.

The regulations also provide exemptions for transportation of pesticides between registered establishments; distribution and sale under an experimental use permit; transfers solely for export; transfers solely for disposal; and distribution and sale of existing stocks of a formerly registered product to the extent and in the manner specified in an order by the USEPA. 40 C.F.R. § 152.30.

4. Applications for New Registrations and Amendments

The regulations provide procedures to apply for new registration of a pesticide product and for amendment on existing registration. An application for new registration must be approved by the USEPA before the product may be distributed or sold. 40 C.F.R. § 152.40 and .42. Applications and correspondence should be mailed to the Registration Division (TS-767C), USEPA, Washington, DC 20460. § 152.45.

The application must contain extensive information including:

1. The applicant's identity, address and company number, if one has been assigned.

2. An application summary.

3. The product name; trade names, if different; and registration number, if currently registered.

4. Five copies of the draft labeling.

5. Materials demonstrating compliance with the regulations protecting data submitters' rights.

6. Studies and other data required by 40 C.F.R. Part 158 with a statement whether the studies were conducted in accordance with good laboratory practices required by 40 C.F.R. Part 160 and any factual information of which the applicant is aware regarding unreasonable adverse effects of the pesticide on man or the environment.

7. A certification that the product will be distributed or sold only in child-resistant packaging if required by 40 C.F.R. Part 157.

8. A request for classification, if the applicant wishes a classification different from that established by the USEPA.

9. A statement concerning tolerances if the proposed labeling bears instructions for use on food or feed crops or if the intended use results, or may be expected to result, directly or indirectly, in use in or on food or feed. 40 C.F.R. § 152.50.

An application for amended registration must be submitted for any modification in the composition, labeling or packaging of a registered product, including the information required by § 152.50, as applicable to the change requested. 40 C.F.R. § 152.44.

5. Protection of Submitters' Rights

The regulations contain procedures to protect the rights granted by FIFRA to exclusive use of, or compensation for, valid original studies submitted in support of an application for registration, amended registration, reregistration or experimental use permit, or to maintain an existing registration in effect. 40 C.F.R. §§ 152.80 to .99.

The submitters' rights are important to companies which sponsor a study or studies because some studies take years to perform and cost millions of dollars. Companies which seek to register "me too" pesticide products with the USEPA must contribute to the cost of studies used in their evaluation by the USEPA and do not get a free ride on studies previously submitted.

An applicant must submit information sufficient to comply with the submitters' rights procedures and to enable the USEPA to determine compliance. Failure to comply may result in denial of an application or cancellation of a registration. 40 C.F.R. § 152.80. Submission should be made with the application. Later submission is allowed, but must be made prior to the USEPA's approval of the application. 40 C.F.R. § 152.84.

Formulators who distribute or sell products containing ingredients (or mixtures) derived solely from one or more USEPA-registered products which they purchase from another producer are exempt from the submitters' rights procedures if they submit an appropriate certification to the USEPA. 40 C.F.R. § 152.85.

The USEPA maintains a Data Submitters List. Each original data submitter has a right to be included on the List. 40 C.F.R. § 152.97.

Applicants may use either a cite-all method or a selective method. If the applicant cites data in the USEPA's files from a person or persons on the Data Submitters List, the applicant must certify to the USEPA either that (1) he has obtained written authorization from each person listed as exclusive use data submitter for the chemical or (2) he has furnished a notification to that person including an offer to pay compensation and to commence negotiations to determine the amount and terms of the compensation. 40 C.F.R. §152.86 and .90.

When using the selective method, an applicant may demonstrate compliance by any of several alternative means. For example, an applicant may submit for the data requirement a new valid study. 40 C.F.R.§ 152.92. An applicant may also cite for the data requirement a valid study from the public literature or generated by any federal, state or local government agency. 40 C.F.R. § 152.94. An applicant may also request a waiver of the data requirement if there are grounds for such a waiver. 40 C.F.R. § 152.91. Thus, an applicant is not compelled to rely on a study or studies previously submitted by other persons claiming exclusive use or compensation rights if the data requirement can be fulfilled by other means.

An original data submitter may petition the USEPA to deny or cancel a product registration if he submitted to the USEPA a valid study which, he claims, satisfies a data requirement that an applicant purportedly failed to satisfy. If an applicant has offered to pay compensation, the original data submitter must show that the applicant failed to cooperate with the procedures, including arbitration, to determine the compensation or to comply with an agreement or arbitration decision relating to the compensation. 40 C.F.R. § 152.99.

6. Review of Applications (Unconditional and Conditional Regulation)

a. Applications

The USEPA publishes notice in the Federal Register of each application for registration of a product that contains a new active ingredient or that proposes a new use. 40 C.F.R. § 152.102. The USEPA will not review an incomplete application. The USEPA notifies the applicant and allows 75 days for additions and corrections to complete the application. 40 C.F.R. § 152.105.

The USEPA has discretion to review applications using unconditional registration criteria or conditional registration criteria provided in FIFRA. Except for applications for review of a new active ingredient or in special cases, the USEPA reviews the application using the criteria for conditional registration. 40 C.F.R. § 152.111. This policy has enabled the USEPA to accomplish part of its registration obligations under FIFRA.

b. Unconditional Registration

The criteria for unconditional registration require the USEPA to review all relevant data in its possession and to determine that no additional data are necessary to make determinations of no unreasonable adverse effects as required by § 3(e)(5) of FIFRA. The USEPA must also determine that the product (1) warrants the efficacy claims made for it; (2) will perform its intended function without unreasonable adverse effects on the environment; (3) will not, when used in accordance with widespread and commonly recognized practices, generally cause unreasonable adverse effects on the environment; (4) is not misbranded; and (5) is labeled and packaged in compliance with FIFRA. The USEPA must also verify that any necessary tolerances, tolerance exemptions and food additive regulations have been issued under the FFDCA. If the product is also a drug, the USEPA will require a notice from the FDA as to compliance with its drug requirements. 40 C.F.R. § 152.112.

c. Conditional Registration

Before the USEPA will approve a conditional registration, the applicant must agree to submit or cite all data required for unconditional registration no later than the time such data are required for similar pesticide products already registered or upon notice from the USEPA. If a conditionally approved product contains new active ingredients, the applicant must agree that (1) it will submit the remaining required data in accordance with a schedule approved by the USEPA; (2) the registration will expire upon a date established by the USEPA if it fails to submit data as required by the USEPA; and (3) it will submit an annual report of production of the product. The USEPA may also establish other conditions on a case by case basis. A conditional registration may be cancelled if any condition is not satisfied or the USEPA determines that the registrant has failed to initiate or pursue appropriate action towards fulfillment of any condition. 40 C.F.R. § 152.115.

The USEPA may deny an application if it determines that the pesticide product does not meet the registration criteria. The USEPA must notify the applicant by a certified letter stating the reasons and factual basis for the determinations and the conditions, if any, which must be fulfilled for the registration to be approved. The applicant has 30 days from receipt of the letter to take the specified corrective action. If the applicant does not do so, the USEPA may issue a denial notice which is published in the Federal Register with the reasons and factual basis for the denial. A hearing to review the denial may be requested within 30 days after publication of the notice. 40 C.F.R. § 152.118.

The criteria for conditional registration of a product having only active ingredients contained in one or more other registered pesticide products are similar to the criteria for unconditional registration. However, the USEPA need not undertake the extensive and time-consuming task of reviewing all relevant date in its possession and need not determine that no additional data are necessary to make "no unreasonable risk" determinations. USEPA must only determine that it possesses, at a minimum, data needed to characterize any incremental risk that would result from approval of the application and that such approval would not significantly increase the risk of any unreasonable effect on the environment. 40 C.F.R. § 152.113.

An application for conditional registration of a pesticide containing an active ingredient not in any currently registered product may also be approved. The conditional approval is limited to a time period sufficient to generate and submit some of the data necessary for the findings required for unconditional registrability. To support such a temporary conditional approval, the USEPA must determine that insufficient time has elapsed for the data to have been developed. The USEPA must also determine that all other required test data and materials have been submitted and criteria met. Further, the USEPA must determine that use of the pesticide product will not cause during the conditional registration period any unreasonable adverse effect on the environment and that such registration and use are in the public interest. 40 C.F.R. § 152.114.

7. Sale and Distribution of Registered Products

A registrant may sell or distribute a registered product only with the composition, packaging and labelling currently approved by the USEPA. Any subset of the approved directions for use may be used, provided that in limiting the uses listed on the label no changes would be necessary in precautionary statements, use classifications, or packaging. 40 C.F.R. § 152.130.

A registrant may sell its registered product to a distributor or distributors, but only upon compliance with several conditions. The regulations do not recognize the independent status of a distributor. They treat a distributor as an agent of the registrant and declare that both may be held liable for violations. Thus, the regulations provide that so-called "supplemental distribution" by a distributor is permitted only upon notice to the USEPA and provided that the following conditions are met:

(a) The registrant submits to the USEPA a statement signed by both the registrant and the distributor listing their names and addresses, the distributor's company number, any additional brand names to be used, and the registration number of the registered product.

(b) The distributor product is produced, packaged and labelled in a registered establishment operated by the same producer, or the same contact producer, packager and labeller.

(c) The distributor product is not repackaged.

(d) The label of the distributor product is the same as that of the registered producer with minor exceptions. 40 C.F.R. § 152.132.

A registrant must keep the USEPA informed of its current name and address. 40 C.F.R. § 152.122. If the registrant receives or becomes aware of any factual information regarding unreasonable adverse effects of the pesticide or the environment that has not previously been submitted to the USEPA, the registrant must provide such information to the USEPA in accordance with § 6(a)(2) of FIFRA. The information must be clearly identified as FIFRA § 6(a)(2) data. 40 C.F.R. § 152.125.

A registration may be transferred to another person if detailed requirements are met. 40 C.F.R. § 152.135.

8. Classification of Pesticides (Use Restrictions)

A pesticide product may be unclassified. To the extent that products have not been restricted, they remain unclassified. However, the USEPA does not normally classify products for general use, so most are classified for restricted use. 40 C.F.R. § 152.160.

The USEPA may restrict a pesticide product or its uses to use by, or under direct supervision of, a certified applicator. The USEPA may also, by regulation, prescribe restrictions relating to the product's composition, labeling; packaging, uses, or distribution and sale, or to the status or qualifications of the user. 40 C.F.R. § 152.160.

In its classification procedures, the USEPA may identify a group of products having common characteristics or uses and may classify for restricted use some or all of the products or uses included in that group. For example, a group may be comprised of products that (1) contain the same active ingredients; (2) contain the same active ingredients in a particular concentration range, formulation type or combination thereof; (3) have common uses; or (4) have other common characteristics such as toxicity, flammability or other physical properties. 40 C.F.R. § 152.164.

If a product label bears instructions for end use and the product has been classified for restricted use, it must be labelled in accordance with the labelling requirements described later in this chapter. If a product label does not bear instructions for end use, but is intended and labelled solely for further formulation into other pesticide products, the product is not subject to the labelling requirements. 40 C.F.R. § 152.166.

If the USEPA classifies a product for restricted use, the product may not be distributed or sold after the 120th day after the effective date of the classification unless the product either (1) bears an amended label containing the restricted use terms; (2) bears a sticker containing the product name, EPA registration number and the restricted use terms; or (3) is accompanied by supplemental labelling bearing the information described in clause (2). If a registrant chooses to delete the restricted uses from its product label, the product may not be distributed or sold after the 180th day after the effective date unless the product bears amended labelling with the restricted uses deleted. After the 270th day after the effective date of a classification, the product may not be distributed or sold by a registrant or producer unless it bears the approved amended label. However, a retailer or other person (who is not a registrant or producer) may continue to distribute or sell using stickers or supplemental labelling. 40 C.F.R. § 152.167.

COMMENT: Under normal conditions, retailers sell their product inventories soon after the 270th day and receive new supplies of products bearing the amended label.

A product classified for restricted use must not be advertised unless the advertisement contains a statement of its restricted use classification. The statement must include the term "Restricted Use Pesticide" or describe the restriction terms prominently in the advertisement. 40 C.F.R. § 152.168.

The USEPA uses several criteria when determining whether to restrict a pesticide product to use by certified applicators or persons under their direct supervision. The general criteria for an end-use pesticide product are as follows:

1. Its toxicity exceeds one or more specific hazard criteria or evidence substantiates that the product or use poses a serious hazard that may be mitigated by restricting its use;
2. Its labelling is not adequate to mitigate the hazards;
3. Restriction of the product would decrease the risk of adverse effects; and
4. The decrease in risks of the pesticide as a result of the restriction would exceed the decrease in benefits.

The classification regulations establish criteria for human hazards of pesticide products intended for residential or institutional use and separate human hazard criteria for pesticide products intended for other uses. The regulations also establish criteria for hazards to mammalian wildlife, birds and other species from pesticide products intended for outdoor use. In addition to these criteria, the USEPA may consider evidence such as filed studies, use history, accident data, monitoring data, or other pertinent evidence. 40 C.F.R. § 152.170.

The criteria for acute hazards, which present the most serious real risks, are specific. For example, the first three human hazard criteria for residential or institutional use are (1) an acute oral LD_{50} of 1.5 g/kg or less for the pesticide as diluted for use; (2) an acute dermal LD_{50} of 2,000 mg/kg or less for the pesticide as formulated; and (3) an acute inhalation LC_{50} of 0.5 mg/liter or less for the pesticide as formulated. The criteria for corrosion or irritation to eyes and skin are less specific, but are familiar toxicological approaches. Unfortunately, the criteria for subchronic, chronic or delayed toxic effects are vague. They require only that the USEPA determine that the pesticide *may* cause significant subchronic, chronic or delayed toxic effects as a result of single or multiple exposures to the product ingredients or residues. 40 C.F.R § 152.170. Thus, when it applies repetitive default assumptions, upper bound estimates and other "worse case" risk assessment methods, the USEPA greatly overstates subchronic, chronic or delayed toxic effects and readily finds effects that may be "significant."

The USEPA may also impose restrictions other than those relating to use by certified applicators. 40 C.F.R. § 152.171.

The regulations contain a list of pesticides classified for restricted use only by or under the direct supervision of a certified applicator. The list actually uses chemical names of active ingredients rather than the tradenames of formulated pesticides. Thus, the list provides for each active ingredient the formulation, use patterns, classification and criteria influencing the restrictions. The active ingredients listed are acrolein, aldicarb, aluminum phosphide, azinphos methyl, carbofuran, chloropicrin, clonitralid, dicrotophos, disulfoton, ethoprop, ethyl parathion, fenamiphos, fonofos, methamidophos, methidathion, methomyl, methyl bromide, methyl parathion, nicotine (alkoloid), paraquat (dichloride), paraquat bis (methyl sulfate), phorate, phosphamidon, picloram, sodium cyanide, sodium fluoroacetate, strychnine, sulfotepp and zinc phosphide.

9. Registration Fees

The registration fees provided in the regulations are based on the type of review: new chemical ($184,500); new biochemical or microbial ($64,000); new use pattern ($33,800); experimental use permit ($4,500); old chemical ($4,000); and amendment ($700). 40 C.F.R. § 152.404. The fees are subject to annual adjustment based on the Federal General Schedule (GS) pay scale and are published in the Federal Register. 40 C.F.R. § 152.412

10. Devices

A device is any instrument or contrivance (other than a firearm) intended for trapping, destroying, repelling, or mitigating any pest or other form of plant or animal life other than man and other than a bacterium, virus or other microorganism in or on living man or living animals. However, it does not include equipment used for the application of pesticides (such as tamper-resistant bait boxes for rodenticides) when sold separately. 40 C.F.R. § 152.500(a).

A device is not required to be registered. However, it is subject to compliance with several other sections of FIFRA, i.e., labelling; establishment registration and reporting; books and records; inspection of establishments; violations, enforcement and penalties; import and export; child-resistant packaging; and the USEPA's authority to declare devices subject to certain provisions of FIFRA. 40 C.F.R. § 152.500(b)

11. Labels and Labelling; Worker Protection Statement

FIFRA defines a "label" as the written, printed, or graphic matter on, or attached to, a pesticide or device or any of its containers or wrappers. 7 U.S.C. § 136(p)(1). FIFRA defines "labelling" more broadly as all labels and all other written, printed, or graphic matter accompanying a pesticide or device at any time or to which reference is made on the label or in accompanying literature except for certain references to current official publications of government agencies and agricultural colleges. 7 U.S.C. § 136(p)(2).

Every pesticide product must bear a label showing clearly and prominently (1) its name, brand or trademark; (2) the name and address of the producer, registrant or person for whom produced; (3) the net contents; (4) the product registration number; (5) the producing establishment number; (6) an ingredient statement; (7) warning or precautionary statements; (8) directions for use; and (9) the use classification or classifications. 40 C.F.R. § 156.10.

The regulations contain detailed requirements for labels including prominence, legibility and placement. All required text must be in English, but additional text in other languages may be required or permitted to protect the public. False and misleading statements are prohibited including nonnumerical or other claims as to safety. 40 C.F.R. § 156.10.

The requirements for warnings and precautionary statements illustrate the detailed requirements prescribed in the regulations. For example, all pesticide products in Toxic Category I must bear on the front label panel the signal word "Danger" and, if assigned to that category on the basis of oral, inhalation or dermal toxicity, the word "Poison" must appear in red with a skull and crossbones. A statement of practical treatment (first aid and other) must also appear on the front panel, although the USEPA may allow it to appear on the back panel if a reference to it is provided on the front panel. The child hazard warning "Keep out of the reach of children" must also appear on the front panel. 40 C.F.R. § 156.10.

For other toxicity categories, the signal words are less urgent. Toxicity Category II requires the word "Warning." Toxicity Categories III and IV require the word "Caution," Additional warnings and precautionary statements about environmental and physical or chemical hazards are required. For example, if applicable, the label may be required to warn of toxicity to wildlife or fish or of flammability or explosivity. Restricted use classification statements must appear on the front panel. 40 C.F.R. § 156.10.

A pesticide label must also include references to the USEPA's Worker Protection Standard. 40 C.F.R. § 156.200 *et seq.* Each product must bear prescribed general statements including the following:

> "Do not apply this product in a way that contact workers or other persons, either directly or through drift. Only protected handlers may be in the area during application."

> "Use this product only in accordance with its labelling and with the worker protection standard. 40 C.F.R. Part 170."

If a product is classified in toxicity categories I or II, the signal word must appear both in English and also in Spanish, i.e., "PELIGRO" and "AVISO." A statement must also be added for workers who cannot read the label, telling them to find someone to explain it to them in detail:

> "Si usted no intiende la etiqueta, busque a alguien para que se la explique a Usted en detalle."

When applicable, each product must also bear a restricted entry statement, a notification to workers statement, and personal protective equipment statements. Examples of these statements are as follows:

> "Do not enter or allow worker entry into treated areas during the restricted-entry interval."
>
> "Notify workers of the application by warning them orally and by posting warning signs at entrances to treated areas."
>
> "Applicators and other handlers must wear chemical-resistant gloves meeting the following specifications: ____________________."

12. Packaging

a. Child Resistant Packaging

Unless exempted, a pesticide product which meets certain toxicity criteria must be distributed and sold in child resistant packaging meeting effectiveness, compatibility and durability standards. 40 C.F.R. § 157.22. Child resistant packaging means packaging designed and constructed to be significantly difficult for children under 5 years of age to open or obtain a toxic or harmful amount of the substance contained therein within a reasonable time and that is not difficult for normal adults to use properly. 40 C.F.R. § 157.21(b).

The regulations provide general exemptions for products classified for restricted use and products packaged in specified large sizes. Upon request, the USEPA may also grant exemptions for lack of toxicity or technical factors. 40 C.F.R. § 157.24.

b. Proposed Container Regulations

FIFRA instructs the USEPA to adopt regulations for the design of pesticide containers and procedures and standards for the removal of pesticides from containers before disposal. 7 U.S.C. § 136(p)(2). In 1994, the USEPA published a notice of proposed rulemaking to impose container design and pesticide removal and disposal standards. However, the USEPA has not adopted the proposed regulations. It will be in the public interest if the delay becomes permanent because the subjects are already regulated effectively by several programs including the regulations of the Research and Special Programs Administration (RSPA) of the U.S. Department of Transportation, the Occupational Safety and Health Administration (OSHA) of the U.S. Department of Labor, and the USEPA under the Resource Conservation and Recovery Act (RCRA).

13. Data Requirements for Pesticide Registration

The USEPA has centralized its requirements for data and information that an applicant must submit in support of an application for registration, amended registration or reregistration in 40 C.F.R. Part 158. Part 158 also specifies the types and minimum amounts of data and information that the USEPA requires in order to make judgments about risks and benefits of pesticide products and to decide whether to approve experimental use permits under FIFRA. 40 C.F.R. § 158.20(b).

The data requirements pertain to product chemistry, residue chemistry, environmental fate, toxicology, reentry protection, aerial drift evaluation, wildlife and aquatic organisms, plant protection, nontarget insects, product performance, and biochemical and microbial pesticides. 40 C.F.R. § 158.20(a).

The data requirements do not include the standards for conducting acceptable tests, guidance on evaluation and reporting of data, further guidance on when data are required, definitions of most terms, and examples of most protocols. This information is available in advisory documents called the Pesticide Assessment Guidelines from the National Technical Information Service (NTIS), 5285 Part Royal Road, Springfield, VA 22161 (Tel. 703-487-4650).

> *COMMENT*: The author recommends that applicants obtain these documents, review them and discuss any questions with the technical staff of the USEPA before devoting significant amounts of time and money on studies or other data. Otherwise, the technical staff may reject the data.

For a currently registered pesticide product, the registrant is not required to submit any data until it receives a notice from the USEPA that additional data are required to support continued registration. However, if the registrant applies for an amendment or the product becomes subject to reregistration, the data requirements will apply. 40 C.F.R. § 158.30(a).

The amount of data required to evaluate an application depends on whether the product is being evaluated for unconditional registration under § 3(c)(5) or conditional registration under § 3(c)(7) of FIFRA:

1. For applications for *unconditional registration*, all data required by Part 158 that have not been waived must be available for the USEPA to review.

2. For an application for *conditional registration* of a pesticide containing an active ingredient not in any currently registered product, all data required by Part 158 must be available for the USEPA to review except data for which the requirement has not had sufficient time to produce the data.

3. For an application for *conditional registration* of a pesticide product which is identical or substantially similar to a currently registered pesticide, the product chemistry data required by Subpart C of Part 158 must be available for the USEPA to review.

4. For an application for *conditional registration* of a new use of a currently registered pesticide, product chemistry and product performance data and any other data pertaining solely to the new use must be available for the USEPA to review 40 C.F.R. § 158.30.

Applicants should be aware that even the requirements for data submission are quite formal and detailed. For example, the transmittal letter must contain specified information. The format and number of copies of studies is prescribed including such details as title page contents, statement of confidentiality claims, and certification of good laboratory practice standards. 40 C.F.R. § 158.32.

A formal requirement which is also important and substantive is to flag studies which show potential adverse effects. Anyone who submits a study must submit with it a statement certifying that the study does or does not meet or exceed specified criteria for the following kinds of toxicity studies: (1) oncogenicity or combined oncogenicity chronic feeding study or subchronic feeding study; (2) teratogenicity; (3) neurotoxicity; (4) chronic feeding study or combined chronic feeding/oncogenicity study; (5) reproduction study; or (6) subchronic feeding study. For example, if an oncogenicity study shows an increase of neoplasms in male or female animals which increases with dose, the reporting code for that criteria must be included in the statement. Similarly, if treated animals show a response indicative of acute delayed neurotoxicity, the reporting code for that criteria must be included in the statement. 40 C.F.R. § 158.34.

Although the data requirements are very detailed and strict, the regulations allow some flexibility. The USEPA encourages each applicant to consult with its Product Manager for the product to resolve questions relating to protocols or data requirements before undertaking extensive testing. The Product Managers may also arrange conferences on issues such as an unique or unanticipated aspect of a product's use pattern or composition. 40 C.F.R. § 158.40.

The regulations contain a formulator's exemption. An applicant for registration of an end-use pesticide product need not submit or cite any data that pertain to the safety of another registered pesticide which is purchased by the applicant and used in the manufacture or formulation of the product for which registration is sought. 40 C.F.R. § 158.50.

14. Minor Uses

A minor use of a pesticide is a use on a minor crop (i.e., a crop planted on a small total amount of acreage) or a use which is otherwise limited so that potential market volume for the use is inherently small. The USEPA's policy is to adjust the data requirements for a minor use appropriately. For example, the USEPA will accept extrapolations and regional data to support establishment of individual minor use tolerances. Group tolerances will be established pursuant to 40 C.F.R. § 180.34. Applicants can contact the Minor Use Office for advice. 40 C.F.R. § 158.60.

The USEPA published a policy statement on minor uses of pesticides in 1986. 51 Fed. Reg. 11341, April 2, 1986. In its statement, the USEPA said it recognized that the continued availability of pesticides registered for minor uses is essential in the production of a diverse food supply. The USEPA also recognized that market incentives were inadequate to justify development of the data needed to obtain or maintain registration for many minor uses. The need to develop extensive and costly data to establish a tolerance or tolerance exemption was especially a problem. Accordingly, the USEPA published a list of crops with low dietary intakes for which it would consider for approval tolerances based on residue data from limited geographical areas where the pesticides are used. The USEPA also expanded its programs for fee waivers and refunds applicable to minor use.

15. Biochemical and Microbial Pesticides

The USEPA's regulations say that biochemical and microbial pesticides are generally distinguished from conventional chemical pesticides by their unique modes of action, low use volume, target species specificity or natural occurrence. These pesticides are subject to different sets of data requirements, as specified for biochemical pesticides in 40 C.F.R. § 158.690 and for microbial pesticides in 40 C.F.R. § 158.740.

Biochemical pesticides include some chemicals (such as insect pheromones); hormones (such as insect juvenile growth hormones); natural plant and insect regulators; and enzymes. 40 C.F.R. § 158.65(b).

Microbial pesticides include entities such as bacteria, fungi, viruses and protozoans that are naturally occurring or genetically modified. Each new variety, subspecies or strain of an already registered microbial pest control agent must be evaluated and may be subject to additional requirements. 40 C.F.R. § 158.65(c).

Novel microbial pesticides (such as genetically modified or non-indigenous microbial pesticides) are subject to additional data requirements on a case-by-case basis depending on the particular microorganism, its parent microorganism, the proposed pesticide use pattern, and the manner and extent to which the organism has been genetically modified. The additional requirements may include information on the genetic engineering techniques used; the identity of the inserted or deleted gene segment as shown by base sequence data or an enzyme restriction map of the gene; information on the control region of the gene; a description of the new traits or characteristics; tests to evaluate genetic stability and exchange; and/or selected Tier II environmental expression and toxicology tests. 40 C.F.R. § 158.65(b)(2).

Pest control organisms (such as insect predators, nematodes, and macroscopic parasites) are exempt from the requirements of FIFRA. 40 C.F.R. § 158.65(b)(3).

16. Test Protocols

Before performing studies or extensive tests, applicants should assure that the test protocols are acceptable to the technical staff of the USEPA. Otherwise, costly and well-performed work may be found to be insufficient.

The regulations state that any appropriate protocol may be used provided that it meets the purpose of the test standards specified in the guidelines and provides data of suitable quality and completeness as typified by the protocols cited in the guidelines. For example, tests using protocols of the Organization for Economic Cooperation and Development (OECD) in Europe can be used. However, the USEPA cautions that some OECD standards, such as test duration and selection of test species, are less restrictive than those recommended by the USEPA. Thus, care should be taken to assure that data generated by studies using OECD protocols will meet the requirements of Part 158. 40 C.F.R. § 158.70.

The author has had mixed results with studies using OECD protocols. For example, a 28-day study using an OECD protocol might be accepted in place of a 90-day study if the USEPA staff agrees that extension to 90 days would obviously reach the same result. However, if the staff does not agree, the test will have to be redone. The staff may also use a default assumption rather than the results of the OECD study in its risk assessment.

Questions about protocols should be directed, preferrably in writing, to the Product Manager in the Registration Division of the Office of Pesticide Programs. 40 C.F.R. § 158.70(c). The Manager coordinates the review and response to questions with members of the technical staff. At times, it can be helpful to ask the Manager to arrange direct discussion with the technical staff, especially when the tests are advanced in nature.

17. Data

The USEPA expects that the data requirements prescribed in Part 158 will be adequate in most cases for an assessment of the properties of a pesticide, but may impose additional requirements. The USEPA determines whether data submitted are acceptable based on the design and conduct of the experiment and whether the data fulfill the purposes of the data requirements. Among other things, the USEPA will consider whether generally accepted methods were used; sufficient numbers of measurements were made to achieve statistical reliability; sufficient controls were built into all phases of the experiment; the study was conducted in accordance with its design; good laboratory practices were observed; and the results were reproducible. Data requirements are revised from time to time to keep up with policy changes and technology. 40 C.F.R. §§ 158.75, 158.80 and 158.85.

18. Product Chemistry Data Requirements

An applicant must submit data fulfilling the product chemistry data requirements with each application for registration, amended registration or reregistration if the data has not been submitted previously or if the previously submitted information is not complete and accurate. 40 C.F.R. § 158.150.

The required data include (1) product composition (both active and inactive ingredients); (2) certified upper and lower limits for the active and inactive ingredients and also for impurities if the product is a technical grade; (3) nominal concentrations of active ingredients most likely to be present in the product when produced; and (4) physical and chemical characteristics. 40 C.F.R. §§ 158.150 and 158.155.

Other required information includes raw materials; process description (whether batch or continuous) including flow chart and description of equipment and operating conditions; description of formulation process; discussion of the formation of impurities; a preliminary analysis of each technical grade of active ingredient to identify impurities; a certification statement as to the accuracy of the certified limits; an analytical method for each ingredient to be used for enforcement purposes; and the physical and chemical characteristics. 40 C.F.R. § 158.60 to .90.

The physical and chemical characteristics for which data are required are listed in a table as follows: color; physical state; odor; melting point; boiling point; density, bulk density or specific gravity; solubility; vapor pressure; dissociation constant; octanol/water partition coefficient; pH; stability; oxidizing or reducing action; flammability; explodability; storage stability; viscosity; miscibility; corrosion characteristics; dielectric breakdown constant; and other requirements based on samples submitted. 40 C.F.R. § 158.190.

The regulations include elaborate data requirement tables and instructions for their use. 40 C.F.R. § 158.100 to 108 and § 158.202 to .740. They include data requirements for residue chemistry; environmental fate; toxicology; reentry protection; spray drift; wildlife and aquatic organisms; plant protection; nontarget insects; and product performance. Separate data requirements are provided for biochemical and microbial pesticides. A Use Pattern Index is attached to Part 158 as Appendix A.

19. Reporting Adverse Effects

The USEPA has regulations implementing the requirement of Section 65(a)(2) of FIFRA to report to the USEPA factual information regarding unreasonable adverse effects of a pesticide on the environment. 40 C.F.R. Part 159.

If a registrant possesses or receives information relevant to the assessment of the risks or benefits of a pesticide registration which it presently holds or formerly held, the registrant must submit the information to the USEPA. The reportable information includes the following:

1. Toxicological and ecological studies—§ 159.165
2. Discontinued studies—§ 159.167
3. Human epidemiological and exposure studies—§ 159.170
4. Excess levels of pesticides in food, feed or water—§ 159.178
5. Metabolites, degradates, contaminants and impurities—§ 159.179
6. Toxic or adverse affect incidents—§ 159.184
7. Failure of pesticide performance—§ 159.188
8. Other information—§ 159.195

Most information must be reported so as to be received by the USEPA not later than the 30th day after the registrant first possesses or knows the information. However, some information must be reported within different time periods specified for particular categories of information. 49 C.F.R. § 159.155. For example, a human fatality incident must be reported within 15 days.

The most complex of the reporting requirements is the obligation to report toxic or adverse effect incidents. The effects are those which apply to humans and to all other organisms that are not the proper target of the pesticide such as domestic animals, fish or wildlife, plants, beneficial insects, water contamination, and property damage. Information must be submitted if three conditions are met:

1. The registrant is aware, or has been informed, that a person or nontarget organism may have been exposed to a pesticide.

2. The registrant is aware, or has been informed, that the person or nontarget organism suffered a toxic or adverse effect or may suffer a delayed or chronic adverse effect in the future.

3. The registrant has or could obtain information concerning where the incident occurred, the pesticide or product involved, and the name of the person or contact regarding the incident.

Several exceptions are allowed for minor incidents and incidents where the facts clearly establish that the reported toxic effect or reported exposure did not or will not occur. 40 C.F.R. § 159.184.

The requirements for submission of information are quite detailed to assure that it is identified as FIFRA § 6(a)(2) information and can easily be processed and reviewed by the USEPA. The information may be mailed by certified or registered mail to the Document Processing Desk—6(a)(2), Office of Pesticide Programs—7504C, U.S. Environmental Protection Agency, 401 M Street, SW, Washington, DC 20460. Information may also be delivered in person or by courier service or other means allowed by the USEPA to Document Processing Desk—6(a)(2), Office of Pesticide Programs, Room 266A, Crystal Mall #2, 1921 Jefferson Davis Highway, Arlington, VA 22202.

The information relevant to the assessment of risks or benefits also includes conclusions or opinions rendered by any of the following persons:

1. A person who was employed or retained (directly or indirectly) by the registrant and was likely to receive the information

2. A person from whom the registrant requested an opinion or conclusion

3. A person who is a qualified expert as described in § 159.153(b).

The foregoing requirements can be helpful to plaintiff attorneys because they require reporting of information that may not be subject to discovery in product liability lawsuits. They may require submission of information otherwise protected by attorney-client privilege and the attorney work product doctrine. 62 Fed. Reg. 49377 (Sept. 19, 1997).

Information need not be submitted if it is demonstrated to be clearly erroneous before the submission date by detailed written procedures. Information need not be submitted if it was previously submitted to the USEPA in a proper manner or was published in scientific articles or publications such as Medline, ENBASE, Toxline or Index Medicus or in certain government reports and publications. 40 C.F.R. § 159.158.

20. Good Laboratory Practice Standards

The USEPA has adopted regulations prescribing good laboratory practice (GLP) standards for conducting studies to support applications for research or marketing permits for pesticide products regulated by the USEPA. 40 C.F.R. Part 160.

An applicant who submits a study must include a statement signed by the applicant, the sponsor and the study director of one of the following types:

(a) The study was conducted in accordance with the GLP standards;

(b) A description in detail of all differences between the practices used in the study and the GLP standards; or

(c) The person was not a sponsor of the study, did not conduct the study, and does not know whether the study was conducted in accordance with the GLP standards. 40 C.F.R. § 160.12.

The USEPA may refuse to consider reliable any data from a study which was not conducted in accordance with the GLP standards. 40 C.F.R. § 160.17. The USEPA will not consider reliable any data developed by a testing facility or sponsor that refuses to permit inspection. A testing facility must permit an authorized employee or representative of the USEPA or FDA at reasonable times and in a reasonable manner to inspect the facility and to inspect and copy all records and specimens required to be maintained regarding studies subject to the GLP standards. 40 C.F.R. § 160.15.

The GLP standards prescribe numerous requirements. Organization and personnel requirements include personnel qualifications and training; management of testing facilities; a qualified study director for each study; and a quality assurance unit to monitor each study. Facility requirements include suitable size and construction; facilities for care of animals and other test systems; facilities for handling test, control and reference substances; separate laboratory operation areas; and specimen and data storage areas. Equipment requirements include design, maintenance and calibration. Testing facility operating requirements include establishment and documentation of standard operating procedures; labelling and proper use of reagents and solutions; and animal and other test system care. Test, control and reference substance requirements include proper characterization and handling procedures that apply also to mixtures of substances with carriers. Protocol and study conduct requirements include a requirement that each study have an approved written protocol that clearly indicates the objectives and all methods for conduct of the study and that the study be conducted in accordance with the protocol. The GLP standards also include recordkeeping and reporting requirements. 40 C.F.R. Part 160.

21. Certificates of Usefulness

The first step toward an application for the tolerance or tolerance exemption that is required to obtain registration of a pesticide is to request that the USEPA issue a certificate of usefulness as an economic poison. The request must be accompanied by a copy of the petition for registration. 40 C.F.R. Part 163.

A request for a certificate of usefulness must be supported by (1) a complete report of the results of any experimental work by the petitioner on the effectiveness of the pesticide chemical for the purposes intended; (2) data relating to the usefulness of the pesticide chemical obtained by other qualified investigators; and (3) any other material which the petitioner believes will justify a finding of usefulness. If the material is fully shown in the petition for registration, it need not be set forth separately in the request for certification. 40 C.F.R. § 163.6.

In determining usefulness, the USEPA considers factors such as percentage reduction or control of pests or, when appropriate, increase in yield or quality of crop following application of the pesticide under the conditions prescribed as compared with the results from adequate controls. The USEPA may also consider economy or ease of production, harvest or storage of crop; flexibility as to the time of planting or harvest; and general benefit to livestock, plants or human welfare. 40 C.F.R. § 163.8.

22. Exemption of Federal and State Agencies for Emergency Uses

The regulations contain procedures by which federal and state agencies may apply for exemptions allowing use of pesticides under emergency conditions. 40 C.F.R. Part 166.

Four types of emergency exemptions may be authorized. They are specific, quarantine, public health and crisis exemptions. A *specific exemption* may be authorized in an emergency condition to avert a significant economic loss or a significant risk to endangered or threatened species, beneficial organisms or the environment. A *quarantine exemption* may be authorized in an emergency condition to control the introduction or spread of any pest new to or not previously known to be widely prevalent or distributed within and throughout the United States and its territories. A *public health exemption* may be authorized in an emergency condition to control a pest that will cause a significant risk to human health. A *crisis exemption* may be used in an emergency condition when the time from discovery of the emergency to the time when the pesticide use is needed is insufficient to allow authorization of a specific, quarantine or public health exemption. 40 C.F.R. § 166.2.

An application for a specific, quarantine or public health exemption must be submitted in writing by the head of the federal or state agency, the Governor of the State involved, or their official designee. Written evidence of delegated authority must accompany the application or be on file with the USEPA. The application must contain extensive and detailed information including a detailed explanation why alternative methods of control would be ineffective. The USEPA may publish a notice of the application in the Federal Register and request public comment. 40 C.F.R. § 166.24.

The head of a federal or state agency, the Governor of a State, or their official designee may issue a crisis exemption, but may not do so if the USEPA informs them not to issue the exemption. They also may not do so if the USEPA has suspended or cancelled the registration of the pesticide to be used, the pesticide contains a new chemical, or the application proposes the first food use of a pesticide. 40 C.F.R. § 166.41. The USEPA may review and revoke a crisis exemption. 40 C.F.R. § 166.53.

23. Registration of Pesticidal Product Establishments

Any establishment where a pesticide product is produced must be registered with the USEPA. A pesticidal product means a pesticide, active ingredient or device. The registration requirement does not apply to certain custom blenders who operate within specified limits. 40 C.F.R. § 167.20.

The registration requirements apply to an establishment where a substance is produced if the producer intends the substance to be used as an active ingredient of a pesticide or has actual or constructive knowledge that the substance will be used by any person as an active ingredient of a pesticide. 40 C.F.R. § 167.20.

The registration requirements also apply to any domestic establishment producing a pesticidal product for export or producing any unregistered pesticide. They also apply to any foreign establishment producing a pesticidal product for import into the United States. 40 C.F.R. § 167.20.

An applicant for establishment registration must submit (1) the name and address of the company; (2) the type of ownership (such as individual, partnership or corporation); and (3) the name and address of each producing establishment for which registration is sought. If the application is complete and accurate, the USEPA will assign a registration number to the establishment. Registration remains effective indefinitely so long as pesticide reports for the establishment are submitted annually to the USEPA. Any changes in the registration information must be reported to the USEPA within 30 days after the change occurs. 40 C.F.R. § 167.20.

Each producer operating an establishment must submit an initial report within 30 days after the first registration of the establishment and thereafter an annual report on or before March 1 of each year. The report must include (1) the name and address of the establishment; (2) the amount of each pesticidal product produced during the past year; (3) the amount of each pesticidal product sold or distributed during the past year; and (4) the amount of each pesticidal product estimated to be produced during the current year. The reports must be submitted to the applicable USEPA Regional Office. Foreign exporters to the United States must submit reports to the U.S. Environmental Protection Agency, Office of Enforcement and Compliance, Agriculture and Ecosystems Division (2225A), Ariel Rios Building, 1200 Pennsylvania Avenue, NW, Washington, DC 20460, Attn: FIFRA Foreign Establishment Registration Contact. 42 C.F.R. § 167.85.

24. Advertising Policy; Export Requirements

FIFRA makes it unlawful for any person to offer for sale any pesticide if it is unregistered or if claims made as part of its distribution or sale differ substantially from any claims made as part of the statement required for its registration. The USEPA interprets these provisions as extending to advertising. Accordingly, the USEPA has adopted several restrictions on pesticide advertising. 40 C.F.R. § 168.22.

Some other nations disagree with the decisions made by the USEPA in its regulation of pesticides. For example, some nations continue to regard DDT as a useful and valuable product. Thus, pesticides no longer registered in the United States continue to be used in those nations. FIFRA does not authorize the USEPA to prohibit exports of unregistered pesticides manufactured in the United States to nations where their use is lawful.

The USEPA has adopted regulations requiring that the labels and labelling of exported pesticides, devices and active ingredients provide specific information including warnings and cautionary statements. If an exported pesticide, device or active ingredient is not registered with the USEPA, the label must prominently state: "Not Registered for Use in the United States of America." 40 C.F.R. § 168.65. The exporter must also obtain prior to the export an acknowledgment statement from the foreign purchaser that the purchaser understands that the pesticide is not registered for use in the United States and cannot be sold in the United States. A copy of the statement must be transmitted to an appropriate official of the importing country. 40 C.F.R. § 168.75.

25. Books and Records of Pesticide Production and Distribution

All producers of pesticides, devices, or active ingredients used in producing pesticides subject to FIFRA are required to keep books and records and to submit to inspections. These producers include those producing under an experimental use permit and those producing for export. 40 C.F.R. Part 169.

26. Worker Protection Standard

In 1992, the USEPA adopted worker protection standards to protect agricultural workers and other persons who handle pesticides from occupational exposures to pesticides used in the production of agricultural plants on farms or in nurseries, greenhouses and forests. 40 C.F.R. Part 170.

The agricultural worker standard applies when any pesticide product is used on an agricultural establishment in the production of agricultural plants, but is subject to numerous exceptions. The exceptions include application for mosquito abatement; on livestock or other animals; on plants grown for other than commercial or research purposes such as home fruit and vegetable gardens; on plants in ornamental gardens, parks or private lawns and gardens; by injection directly into agricultural plants with some exceptions; in a manner not directly related to the production of agricultural plants; for control of vertebrate pests; as attractants or repellants in traps; on the harvested portions of agricultural plants or harvested timberland; or for research uses of unregistered pesticides. 40 C.F.R. § 170.3.

Owners of agricultural establishments performing tasks related to production of agricultural plants on their own establishments and certified crop advisors are exempt from some of the requirements of the worker standard. 40 C.F.R. § 104.

The standard for agricultural workers imposes restrictions on entry by persons other than appropriately trained and equipped handlers into areas where pesticides are being or have been applied for specified time periods which are called the restricted entry interval (REI). The restricted areas and REIs differ for farm and forest areas, nurseries and greenhouses. Exceptions are allowed for some short-term activities and for emergencies if specified requirements are met, including provision and proper use of personal protective equipment. 40 C.F.R. § 170.110 and 112.

An agricultural employer must notify workers of any pesticide applications in greenhouses, on farms, in nurseries, or in forests by specific methods including posted warning signs including key words "DANGER" and "PELIGRO," "PESTICIDES," and "KEEP OUT" and "NO ENTRE." 40 C.F.R. § 170.120. The employer must also post the following information before the application and maintain it until 30 days after the application or REI:

1. Location and description of the treated area.

2. Product name, USEPA registration number, and the pesticide's active ingredients.

3. Time and date the pesticide will be applied.

4. The restricted entry interval.

An agricultural employer must also notify handler employers of proposed pesticide applications; provide pesticide safety training for workers; post pesticide safety information; provide water, soap and single-use towels to workers as decontamination supplies; and make available emergency assistance to anyone who is or has been employed on an agricultural establishment if there is reason to believe the person has been poisoned or injured by exposure to pesticides used on the agricultural establishment. 40 C.F.R. § 170.124 to .160.

The standard for pesticide handlers contains generally similar requirements and exceptions insofar as applicable. In addition, before applying pesticide, a handler employer must notify any agricultural employer and provide information about the application. 40 C.F.R. § 170.224. Handler employers are required to have knowledge of pesticide labelling and site-specific information about the agricultural establishment where their pesticide handling tasks will be performed. 40 C.F.R. § 170.232.

27. Certification of Pesticide Applicators

The USEPA's regulations on certification of applicators of restricted use pesticides are designed to require state environmental agencies to regulate pesticide applicators at least as strictly as the USEPA. If any state agency fails to adopt regulations as strict as the USEPA's regulations or fails to enforce its regulations, the USEPA has authority to implement its own regulatory program in the state. 40 C.F.R. Part 171.

The regulations divide applicators into two major categories, private and commercial. A private applicator is a certified applicator who uses or supervises the use of any restricted use pesticide for producing any agricultural commodity on (1) property owned by him or his employer or (2) property of another person if applied without compensation other than trading of personal services between the agricultural commodity producers. A commercial applicator is any certified applicator who uses or supervises the use of a restricted use pesticide and does not meet the definition of a private applicator 40 C.F.R. § 171.2.

Commercial applicators are further divided into categories based on the type of use: plant; animal; forest pest control; ornamental and turf pest control; seed treatment; aquatic pest control; right-of way pest control; industrial, institutional, structural and health related pest control; public health pest control; regulatory pest control; and demonstration and research pest control. 40 C.F.R. § 171.3.

The regulations prescribe standards for certification of commercial applicators. Their competence must be determined on the basis of written examinations and, as appropriate, performance testing. All commercial applicators must demonstrate practical knowledge of the general principles and practices of pest control and safe use of pesticides including (1) label and labelling comprehension; (2) safety factors including pesticide toxicity, common types and causes of pesticide accidents, precautions to guard against injury, protective clothing and equipment, and first aid and other accident procedures; (3) environmental consequences of use and misuse; (4) equipment; (5) pesticide characteristics;

(6) equipment; (7) application techniques; and (8) applicable state and federal laws and regulations. Each commercial applicator must also demonstrate competency in the types of activities carried out by applicators in its category or categories. For example, agricultural applicators must have practical knowledge of drift problems that do not affect seed treatment applicators. However, seed treatment applicators should know the hazards of misuse of treated seed and the necessary precautionary techniques. 40 C.F.R. §171.4.

The regulations also prescribe standards for certification of private applicators and standards for supervision of noncertified applicators by certified private and commercial applicators. The standards prescribe steps required for proper supervision, but do not require a supervisor to be physically present in all situations. 40 C.F.R. § 171.5 and 6.

State plans to certify commercial and private applicators of restricted use pesticides must be submitted to the USEPA for review and approval. Once approved, the state must maintain its certification program in accordance with the plan. 40 C.F.R. §§ 171.7 and 8.

28. Experimental Use Permits

An experimental use permit (EUP) is generally required for testing of any unregistered pesticide or any registered pesticide being tested for an unregistered use. 40 C.F.R. § 172.3(a).

Some tests do not require an EUP:

1. Laboratory or greenhouse tests, limited field trials, and other tests only to assess a pesticide's potential efficacy, toxicity or other properties.

2. Other tests only to assess a pesticide's potential efficacy, toxicity or other properties within the limitations prescribed in § 172.3(c).

An application for an EUP (or an amendment) must be submitted to the Registration Division, USEPA, Washington, DC 20460. The application must be supported by extensive information including a detailed description of the purpose, objectives and parameters of the testing program. If a residue can be expected to result in or on food or feed, the applicant must (1) submit evidence that a tolerance or tolerance exemption has been established for residues of the pesticide, or (2) submit a petition to establish of a tolerance or tolerance exemption; or (3) certify that the food or feed from the experimental program will be fed to experimental animals or otherwise disposed of in a manner which will not endanger man or the environment. The disposal method must be described in the application. The USEPA has authority to issue a temporary tolerance for use of a pesticide under an EUP. 40 C.F.R. § 172.4.

The USEPA publishes notice of receipt of an application for an EUP in the Federal Register with information about the proposed test program and a request for comments from interested persons. An EUP is issued when the USEPA determines that the applicable requirements have been met. The EUP must be for a specified time period, normally one year, that may be renewed if circumstances warrant. The USEPA may include conditions and limitations in the EUP including a limit on the quantity of pesticide to be used. The USEPA may require that additional studies be conducted during the time period to support the establishment of tolerances and/or registration. All producers of pesticides pursuant to an EUP must maintain records pursuant to Part 169. 40 C.F.R. § 172.5.

The EUP regulations contain provisions governing state issuance of EUPs and authorization by the USEPA of state EUP programs. 40 C.F.R. §§ 172.20 to 24.

As an alternative to an EUP application, a person who plans to conduct small scale testing of certain microbial pesticides may submit a notification to the USEPA and obtain approval of the tests. The pesticides subject to the notification and approval requirement are the following:

1. Microbial pesticides whose pesticidal properties have been imparted or enhanced by the introduction of genetic material that has been deliberately modified.

2. Nonindigenous microbial pesticides that have not been acted upon by the U.S. Department of Agriculture.

The notification and approval requirement applies to small scale tests that involve intentional introduction of the microbial pesticide or are performed in a facility without adequate containment and inactivation controls. 40 C.F.R. § 172.45.

The notification and approval requirement does not apply to microbial pesticides resulting from deletions or rearrangements within a single genome that are brought about by the introduction of deliberately modified genetic material. It also does not apply to testing conducted in a facility with adequate containment and inactivation controls. 40 C.F.R. § 172.45.

An exemption petition may be submitted under 40 C.F.R. § 172.52. Any person using a microbial pesticide in small scale testing (including exempt testing) who obtains information regarding potential unreasonable adverse effects on health or the environment must within 30 days submit the information to the USEPA. 40 C.F.R. § 172.57.

29. Plant—Incorporated Protectants

On July 19, 2001, the USEPA published a final rule adopting regulations for some plant-incorporated protectants. The rule did so by adding definitions to 40 C.F.R. § 152.3 and adding a new 40 C.F.R. Part 174.66. Fed. Reg. 37,772 (July 19, 2001).

Part 174 exempts a plant-incorporated protectant from the requirements of FIFRA, other than submission of information regarding adverse effects, if it meets the following criteria:

1. The genetic material that encodes or leads to the production of the pesticidal substance is from a plant that is sexually compatible with the recipient plant and has never been derived from any other source.

2. When intended to be produced and used in a crop used as food, the residues are either exempted from a tolerance or no tolerance would otherwise be required; and

3. Any inert ingredient that is part of the plant-incorporated protectant is on a list of approved inert ingredients in 40 C.F.R. §§ 174.480 to .485.

In § 174.485, the USEPA listed as approved inert ingredients only those which meet the same conditions as the exempt genetic material. In addition, the residues must not be present in food from the plant at levels injurious or deleterious to human health. 40 C.F.R. § 174.485.

On July 19, 2001, the USEPA adopted a rule granting an exemption from the requirement of a tolerance for residues of nucleic acids that are part of plant-incorporated protectant. 40 C.F.R. § 174.475.

On July 17, 2001, the USEPA published a notice that it is engaged in a comprehensive reassessment of all time-limited registrations for all existing bacillus thuringiensis plant-incorporated protectants to assure that decisions on renewal and/or extensions of these registrations are based on the most current scientific data including recommendations of the Scientific Advisory Panel and public comments. The notice invited the public to submit comments. 66 Fed. Reg. 37,228 (July 17, 2001).

On July 19, 2001, the USEPA published a supplemental proposal soliciting additional comments on the exemptions it proposed in 1994 for plant-incorporated protectants derived from sexually compatible plants. In doing so, the USEPA made available for public review and comment a report issued by the National Academy of Sciences (NAS) titled "Genetically Modified Plants: Science and Regulation." The USEPA requested comments on alternative regulatory methods. The first alternative is an exemption of all plant-incorporated protectants derived from plants sexually compatible with the recipient plant, such as the USEPA issued concurrently with the proposal. The second alternative would is case-by-case reviews for exemption through a notification process. On risk issues, the USEPA specifically requested comments on (1) levels of naturally occurring or other toxicants; (2) potential for production of a novel toxicant; (3) consequences of transfer of ability to produce higher levels of a plant-incorporated protectant to wild or weedy relatives; (4) the comparative risks of plant-incorporated protectants derived through genetic engineering with those derived through conventional breeding and the use of antibiotic or herbicide resistance or other selectable markers; and (5) inclusion of protoplast fusion in the definition of wide crosses. 66 Fed Reg. 37,855 (July 19, 2001).

Biotechnology products used as plant-incorporated protectants are discussed later in this Chapter.

30. Food Additive Regulations

The USEPA has authority under Section 409 of the Federal Food, Drug and Cosmetic Act (FFDCA) to adopt food additive regulations for food additives that may result from pesticide residues in or on processed food or which may otherwise affect the characteristics of such food. 21 U.S.C. § 348.

The USEPA has established procedures for the establishment, modification or revocation of food additive regulations including authorization for any person to file a petition with the USEPA for adaption of a food additive regulation and the data and information required to support the petition. 40 U.S.C. Part 177.

A food additive is any substance the intended use of which results or may reasonably be expected to result, directly or indirectly, in its becoming a component or otherwise affecting the characteristics of any food. However, it does not include (1) a pesticide chemical in or on any raw agricultural commodity; (2) a pesticide chemical intended for use or used in production, storage or transportation of any raw agricultural commodity; (3) a color additive; (4) any substance used in accordance with a sanction or approval granted before September 8, 1958 pursuant to the FFDCA, the Poultry Products Inspection Act, or the Federal Meat Inspection Act; (5) a new animal drug; or (6) a substance generally recognized, among experts qualified by scientific training and experience to evaluate its safety, as having been shown to be safe for its intended use through scientific procedures or, in the case of a substance used in food before January 1, 1958, through either scientific procedures or experience based on common use in food. 40 C.F.R. § 177.3.

31. Tolerances and Tolerance Exemptions for Pesticide Residue in or on Raw Agricultural Commodities and Processed Food

The USEPA has authority to set limits (called "tolerances") for the amounts of pesticide residues in or on raw agricultural commodities and processed food. The authority rests on Section 408 of the Federal Food, Drug and Cosmetic Act (FFDCA), as amended by the Food Quality Protection Act of 1996 (FQPA). Pesticide residues for which there is no tolerance or which exceed a tolerance are treated as unsafe and the raw agricultural commodity or processed food are treated as adulterated. The USEPA has established several thousand tolerances which appear in 40 C.F.R. Part 180. Enforcement of the tolerances is performed by the Food and Drug Administration (FDA).

In general, the establishment of a tolerance or tolerance exemption is essential for registration of a pesticide. As described earlier, the first steps toward obtaining a tolerance or tolerance exemption is to request a certificate of usefulness from the USEPA.

For many years, the FDA has maintained a lengthy list of food additives which are generally recognized as safe. The list is called the "GRAS" list. The USEPA's list of pesticide chemicals that are generally recognized as safe is short. The chemicals are benzaldehyde when used as a bee repellant in honey harvesting; ferrous sulfate; lime; lime-sulfur; potassium sorbate; sodium carbonate; sodium hypochlorite; sulfur; sodium metasilicate when used as a plant desiccant at not more than 4% by weight in aqueous solution and when used as a postharvest fungicide; citric acid; fumaric acid; oil of lemon; and oil of orange. 40 C.F.R. § 180.2.

The USEPA's regulations provide that the raw agricultural commodity to be examined for pesticide residues shall generally consist of the whole commodity. However, some "common sense" exceptions are allowed such as exclusion of the crown and stalk when examining bananas and removing the shells before examining nuts. 40 C.F.R. § 180.1.

Processed foods are not considered unsafe if the raw agricultural commodities used in them have a tolerance exemption or are within a tolerance *and if*:

1. Poisonous or deleterious pesticide residues have been removed to the extent possible in good manufacturing practice; and

2. The concentration of the pesticide in the preserved or processed food when ready to eat is not greater than the tolerance permitted on the raw agricultural commodity. 40 C.F.R. § 180.1.

Pesticide chemicals that cause related pharmacological effects are regarded by the USEPA as having additive deleterious action in the absence of evidence to the contrary. Tolerances for related pesticide chemicals may limit the amount of a common component, a biological activity, or the total amount of related pesticide chemicals. When two or more pesticide chemicals are used in a formulation, the tolerance is often set at the highest of the separate applicable tolerances. 40 C.F.R. § 180.3.

The USEPA may set a zero tolerance for a pesticide chemical. This means that no amount of the pesticide chemical may remain on the raw agricultural commodity when offered for shipment. The USEPA may establish a zero tolerance if (1) a safe level in the diet of two different species of warm-blooded animals has not been reliably determined or (2) the chemical is carcinogenic or has other alarming physiological effects on one or more species of test animals when fed in the diet of such animals. 40 C.F.R. § 180.5 (a) and (b).

The USEPA may set a zero tolerance if a pesticide chemical is toxic, but is normally used at times when, or in such manner that, raw agricultural commodities will not bear or contain it. 40 C.F.R. § 180.5(c) The USEPA may also set a zero tolerance for a pesticide chemical if it is normally removed through good agricultural practice such as washing or brushing or through other changes in the pesticide chemical before introduction of the raw agricultural commodity into interstate commerce. 40 C.F.R. §180.5(d).

When establishing tolerances for pesticide residues in or on raw agricultural commodities, the USEPA considers whether the residues may enter human diet through ingestion of milk, eggs, meat and/or poultry produced by animals fed agricultural products bearing such pesticide residues. The USEPA will establish a tolerance for the commodity if there is no reason to expect finite residues in these foods. However, if there is reason to expect that finite residues in the foods will actually be incurred, the USEPA will establish a tolerance for the commodity only if tolerances can be established at the same time for the foods. The analytical methods used for such purpose are set forth in the Pesticide Analytical Manual. 40 C.F.R. § 180.6. See the previous discussion of the USEPA's procedures to adopt food additive regulations for pesticide residues under 40 C.F.R. Part 177.

The regulations prescribe procedures for the establishment of temporary tolerances and tolerance exemptions. Temporary tolerances are commonly established in connection with the issuance of an EUP. A temporary tolerance is customarily issued subject to conditions including: (1) a limit on the amount of the chemical to be used; (2) a limit to use on designated crops by qualified persons; (3) a requirement to immediately inform the USEPA of any reports or findings from the experimental use that have a bearing on safety; and (4) a requirement to keep records for two years and make them available, upon request, to the USEPA. 40 C.F.R. § 180.31.

If there is reason to believe that a pesticide chemical may interact with other pesticide chemicals to be more toxic than their individual toxicities, the USEPA may require special experimental data on potentiation capacities to evaluate a proposed tolerance. 40 C.F.R. § 180.35.

The regulations contain crop group tables and lengthy lists of specific tolerances for pesticide chemicals. The tolerances apply to residues resulting from their application prior to harvest or slaughter, unless otherwise stated. 40 C.F.R. § 180.101.

C. Reregistration

FIFRA granted authority to the USEPA to require that pesticides first registered before November 1, 1984 be reregistered. 7 U.S.C. § 136a-1. The reregistration process has resulted in loss of reregistration for thousands of products because their producers could not afford the lengthy and costly process of reregistration.

In 1989, the USEPA published lists of active ingredients subject to reregistration, known as Lists A, B, C and D. Registrants were required to notify the USEPA by 1990 if they wished to reregister. If so, they were required to identify and commit to furnish studies to fill "data gaps," i.e., data required by current regulations that was not required when their products were registered. Thereafter, the registrants were required to sponsor studies and submit the data required by the USEPA. For much of the past decade, the USEPA has been reviewing the data and issuing reregistration eligibility decisions (REDs). The REDs are accompanied by a data call-in (DCI) requiring the pesticide producer, or registrant, to submit further product specific data and revised labelling. After further review, the USEPA may reregister the pesticide product. However, if the product contains multiple active ingredients, reregistration will not take place until the last active ingredient is eligible for reregistration.

In its year 2000 report on pesticide reregistration performance measures and goals, the USEPA said that, in order to be eligible for registration:

> ". . . an older pesticide must have a substantially complete data base, and must be found not to cause unreasonable risks to human health or the environment when used in accordance with Agency approved label directions and precautions. In addition, all pesticides with food uses must meet the safety standard of the FQPA of 1996. Under FQPA, EPA must make a determination that the pesticide residues remaining in or on food are"safe;" that is, "that there is reasonable certainty that no harm will result from aggregate exposure to the pesticide chemical residue" from dietary and other sources. In determining allowable levels of pesticide residues in food, EPA must perform a more comprehensive assessment of each pesticide's risks, considering:
>
> - Aggregate exposure (from food, drinking water, and residential uses);
> - Cumulative effects from all pesticides sharing a common mechanism of toxicity;
> - Possible increased susceptibility of infants and children; and
> - Possible endocrine or estrogenic effects."

Thus, reregistration is linked to the USEPA's program to reassess within 10 years all tolerances and tolerance exemptions that were in existence on August 3, 1996, the date set by the FQPA.

The USEPA's year 2000 report showed progress in the reregistration program. However, much of the progress consisted of cancellations resulting from decisions by producers or registrants to accept "voluntary" cancellation rather than fulfill the USEPA's extensive and costly data requirements, only to face opposition to reregistration after submission of the data. The year 2000 report contains the following statistics on product reregistration as of September 30, 1999:

Products reregistered	1,281
Products amended	185
Products cancelled	2,671
Products sent for suspension	144
Total products completed	4,281
Products with actions pending	2,764
Total products in reregistration	7,045

The year 2000 report also described progress toward a major goal of the USEPA to cancel and/or restrict uses of organophosphate pesticides by reassessing their previous tolerances and tolerance exemptions. 65 Fed. Reg. 37375, June 14, 2000.

> *COMMENT*: These pesticides include chlorpyrifos, diazinon and malathion which are very widely used to protect food and other crops from pests. In addition to its major use to protect corn crops, chlorpyrifos has also been used to protect commercial buildings and homes from termites, although it is not very strong and repeated applications may be necessary to kill termites. In addition to its major use to protect cotton crops, malathion is being used to combat mosquitos carrying West Nile Virus, but it also requires repeated applications to affect the mosquitoes which have caused a number of deaths.

Subsequent publications indicate that the USEPA and its supporters have been successful in causing the producers of chlorpyrifos and diazinon to drop their efforts to challenge its risk assessment methods and agree to phase out many of their uses. Farm organizations informed the USEPA of their need to continue use of these pesticides for some crops, so the two pesticides remain registered for limited uses.

D. Special Reviews

The USEPA has adopted regulations for conducting special reviews to help determine whether to initiate proceedings to cancel, deny or reclassify the registration of a pesticide product. 40 C.F.R. Part 154.

A special review is a formal proceeding. A docket is established containing a written record of notices, documents, comments, transcripts of public meetings, memoranda describing meetings between USEPA personnel and other parties or persons, and other materials. The regulations provide for public comment and hearings; participation in some matters by the Secretary of Agriculture and the USEPA's Scientific Advisory Panel; and publication of decisions in the Federal Registers.

FIFRA provides that the USEPA may not initiate a special review unless it bases the decision on a validated test or other significant evidence raising prudent concerns of unreasonable adverse risk to man or the environment. 7 U.S.C. § 136a(c)(8). The USEPA expanded those criteria at 40 C.F.R. § 154.7. As described in the next sections of this chapter, the USEPA can commence cancellation and suspension proceedings without undertaking a special review. Further, the USEPA can usually persuade a registrant to "voluntarily" cancel or restrict the use of a pesticide by other means such as adverse publicity and lengthy and costly testing requirements.

E. Cancellation

The USEPA may issue a notice of intent to cancel or modify a registration if it appears that a pesticide or its labelling, when used in accordance with widespread and commonly recognized practice, generally causes unreasonable effects on the environment. 7 U.S.C. § 136d(b). Before issuing the notice, the USEPA must furnish the proposed notice to the Secretary of Agriculture and the USEPA's Scientific Advisory Panel and must publish their comments, evaluations and recommendations in the final notice of intent to cancel. 40 C.F.R. Part 164.

To support its decision to issue a notice of intent to cancel, the USEPA must determine that use of the pesticide creates unreasonable risks, though not necessarily actual adverse consequences, with considerable frequency. *Ciba-Geigy Corp. v. EPA*, 874 F.2d 277 (5th Cir. 1989). A violation of the Endangered Species Act may support such a determination. *Defenders of Wildlife v. EPA*, 882 F.2d 1294 (8th Cir. 1989).

When considering a notice of intent to cancel, the USEPA is required to consider the effects on production and prices of agricultural commodities, retail food prices, and the agricultural economy and to publish its analysis of the effects with the notice.

A notice of cancellation becomes final 30 days after publication in the Federal Register unless the registrant requests a hearing. The USEPA issues an order that states, among other things, the time period allowed for sale or distribution of existing inventories.

A registrant has a right to request a hearing before an USEPA Administrative Law Judge. However, the chance that an Administrative Law Judge will decide in favor of registrant and be upheld by the USEPA's Environmental Appeals Board is not good. As explained elsewhere, the courts do not review the validity of the USEPA's scientific decisions and review other issues only for a mistake of law or an arbitrary and capricious decision. Thus, when facing cancellation, many registrants accept "voluntary" cancellation. Users who need a pesticide can participate in a hearing, but cannot insist that a registrant defend its pesticide product at a hearing or prevent a settlement between the registrant and the USEPA. *McGill v. EPA*, 593 F.2d 631 (5th Cir. 1979).

F. Suspension

When it wishes to cancel or modify a registration, the USEPA can issue a suspension order banning sale and distribution of the pesticide without waiting for the results of a pending cancellation proceeding. 7 U.S.C. § 136d(c)(1). A suspension order, of course, severely damages the reputation of the pesticide product in the perception of the general public.

FIFRA originally required that the USEPA determine that a suspension is necessary to prevent an "imminent hazard." However, the U.S. Circuit Court of Appeals for the District of Columbia essentially nullified the requirement by holding that the USEPA need only make a determination that there is substantial likelihood of serious harm from a chronic hazard during the period projected for cancellation proceedings. *Environmental Defense Fund v. EPA*, 548 F.2d 998 (D.C. Cir. 1976).

A registrant has a right to request a hearing if it does so within 5 days. Users and other adversely may intervene and file proposed findings, conclusions and briefs. 40 C.F.R. § 164.121. Nonregistrant users are also entitled to seek an order of a U.S. District Court to stay the suspension. *Love v. Thomas*, 858 F.2d 1347 (9th Cir. 1988).

G. Inert Ingredients

For many decades, the ingredients in formulated pesticide products (other than the economic poisons which are their active ingredients) have been called "inert" ingredients because no claims were made that they had any effect on pests.

Registrants have for years informed the USEPA of the inert ingredients in pesticide products as part of their applications for registration and reregistration. The USEPA also has authority to require data about new inert ingredients. However, FIFRA and the USEPA's regulations do not require that labels and labelling identify inert ingredients unless the USEPA determines that they are a hazard to human health or the environment. 40 C.F.R. § 156.10(g)(7). The USEPA has required that a few inert ingredients be identified in pesticide labelling after finding they were of toxicological concern.

Pesticide producers also provide information about inert ingredients to the extent their quantities and characteristics require warning labels or other communications under the product liability, worker safety and health and hazardous materials transportation laws.

Nevertheless, environmental groups and lawyers have filed administrative proceedings and lawsuits demanding that the USEPA require disclosure of all inert ingredients in labelling. Although its authority under FIFRA to impose such a requirement is questionable, the USEPA may do so.

H. Antimicrobial Products

An antimicrobial pesticide is a pesticide which is intended:

> (1) either to disinfect, sanitize, reduce, or mitigate growth or development of microbiological organisms or to protect inanimate objects, industrial processes or systems, surfaces, water, or other chemical substances from contaminations, fouling or deterioration caused by bacteria, viruses, fungi, protozoa, algae, or slime; and
>
> (2) in the intended use, is exempt from, or otherwise not subject to USEPA tolerance requirements or FDA food additive regulations. 7 U.S.C. § 136(mm)(1).

Examples of antimicrobial pesticides are chemical sterilants, disinfectants, industrial microbiocides and other preservatives. However, some chemical sterilants are excluded because they are not pesticides. Further, some preservatives which are pesticides are excluded from the definition of an antimicrobial pesticide.

The following pesticides are expressly excluded from the definition of an antimicrobial pesticide; (1) agricultural fungicides, (2) aquatic herbicides, and (3) wood preservatives or antifouling paints if a claim is made for them of pesticidal activity other than or in addition to claims applicable to antimicrobial pesticides. 7 U.S.C. § 136(mm)(2).

Before the FQPA was adopted in 1996, the USEPA regulated those antimicrobial pesticides that were applied to raw agricultural commodities including their registration, labelling, tolerances and tolerance exemptions. The FDA regulated other antimicrobial products to the extent they became direct or indirect food additives. The FDA did so by determining whether or not their residues in food or in food contact coatings, adhesives and paper or paperboard used in food packaging were generally recognized as safe or could meet the requirements for a tolerance or tolerance exemption.

In the FQPA, Congress gave the USEPA the authority to regulate all antimicrobial pesticides. However, Congress directed the USEPA to set prompt time schedules to review antimicrobial pesticides and to consider their benefits as well as their risks. Congress also required the USEPA to consider cost-effective certification processes as part of its regulatory program.

These statutory restrictions meant that the USEPA could not readily ban or compel manufacturers, distributors and users to "voluntarily" discontinue antimicrobial pesticides. In addition, the USEPA recognized that many simple germicides, fungicides and other antimicrobial pesticides have been well known by the public for decades. Thus, a regulatory program could encounter public resistance.

In 1998, the EPA and FDA published a notice of policy interpretation describing how they would share regulation of antimicrobial substances. 63 Fed. Reg. 54,532, Oct. 9, 1998. In the notice, the USEPA returned full or partial jurisdiction to regulate some antimicrobial substances to the FDA. Later in 1998, Congress amended the FFDCA to clarify that the FDA (rather than the USEPA) will determine whether antimicrobial substances used making paper and paperboard for food contact packaging should be generally recognized as safe or should be reviewed for a tolerance or tolerance exemption.

The Antimicrobials Division of the USEPA's Office of Pesticide Programs is developing requirements to describe possible hazards specifically in labelling. The Division will also review labelling claims of public health benefits and disallow those which it determines to be insufficiently supported or excessive.

In an important recent development, the USEPA recently authorized the U.S. Department of Agriculture to make emergency use of mild disinfectants if needed to respond to hoof and mouth disease which has devastated European farms raising cattle for milk and meat production.

I. Biotechnology Products Used as Plant-Incorporated Protectants

Because of the intense regulation of pesticide products, industry used biotechnological research to develop substitute products which cause plants to resist pests. The USEPA regulates these products as microbial pesticides under FIFRA. In 2001, the USEPA renamed them as "plant-incorporated protectants."

An example of the USEPA's extensive review of the new plant-incorporated protectants is its final rule granting a tolerance exemption for the bacillus thuringiensis Cry 3Bb1 protein and the genetic material necessary for its production in corn on field corn, sweet corn and popcorn and the bacillus thuringiensis Cry 2Ab2 protein and the genetic material necessary for its production in corn on field corn, sweet corn, popcorn or in cotton on cotton seed, cotton oil, cotton meal, cotton hay, cotton hulls, cotton forage and cotton by products. The tolerance exemptions were granted in response to a petition submitted by Monsanto Company. 66 Fed. Reg. 24,061, May 11, 2001.

Another example of the USEPA's extensive review is its final rule granting a tolerance exemption for the bacillus thuringiensis Cry 1 F protein and the genetic material necessary for its production in corn on field corn, sweet corn and popcorn. The tolerance exemption was granted in response to a petition submitted by Mycogen Seeds c/o Dow Agro Sciences LLC.

For all three proteins, the genetic materials necessary for their production are the nucleic acids, DNA and RNA, which encode the proteins and their regulatory regions. As the USEPA said, these nucleic acids are common to all forms of plant and animal life and it knows of no instance where they have been associated with toxic effects related to their consumption as a component of food.

The USEPA described its reviews of the three proteins for acute oral toxicity; amino acid sequence comparisons; allergenic sensitivity comparisons including evidence that the proteins are completely degraded by gastric fluid within minutes or seconds; consideration of possible toxicity to the immune system; aggregate exposure; cumulative effects; effects on infants and children; and effects on the endocrine system. All materials for extraction and analysis were validated and found acceptable.

Some environmentalists have for years opposed the use of biotechnology to enable plants to resist pests. Some environmentalists have conducted widespread publicity campaigns against the protein-enhanced crops, calling them names such as "Frankenfood."

Some environmentalists have focused special attention on the StarLink product of Aventis CropScience that produces Cry 9 C protein in corn. The USEPA authorized use of the Cry 9 C protein in corn crops used for animal feed, but not for human food until further tests are performed. Environmental groups then claimed that Star Link corn had become mixed with human food and caused allergenic reactions in a number of individuals.

In June 2001, after environmental publicity forced widespread food recalls, the Centers for Disease Control and Prevention reported that its investigation had found no evidence that the StarLink corn caused the claimed allergenic reactions. The USEPA and its Scientific Advisory Panel were to review the report in connection with Aventis CropScience's application for a tolerance exemption for the Cry 9 C protein. However, the USEPA announced in July 2001 that it did not have enough information to clear the StarLink corn.

J. Inspections

FIFRA authorizes the USEPA to enter at reasonable times (A) any establishment or other place where pesticides are being held for distribution or sale, for the purpose of inspecting and obtaining samples or (B) any place where any suspended or cancelled pesticide is held, for the purpose of determining compliance. 7 U.S.C. § 136g (a) (1).

Before an inspection, the USEPA representative must present to the owner, operator or agent in charge appropriate credentials and a written statement of the reason for the inspection, including whether a violation is suspected. If no violation is suspected, a written alternate and sufficient reason must be given. Before leaving, the USEPA representative must give a receipt for any samples obtained and, if requested, an equal portion of the samples. If the samples are analyzed, the results must be furnished promptly to the owner, operator or agent in charge. 7 U.S.C. § 136g (a) (2).

The USEPA is also authorized to obtain and execute warrants authorizing entry, inspection and copying of records and to seize any pesticide or device which is in violation of FIFRA. 7 U.S.C. § 136g (b). If it appears from examination of a pesticide or device that it fails to comply with FIFRA, the USEPA must give notice to the person against whom criminal or civil proceedings are contemplated and an opportunity to present the person's views, whether orally or in writing. If it appears that the person violated FIFRA, the USEPA then certifies the facts to the Department of Justice with a copy of the results of the analysis or examination for the institution of a criminal or civil proceeding. However, the USEPA is not required to prosecute minor violations and may instead serve a suitable written warning notice. 7. U.S.C. § 136g(c).

K. Violations and Enforcement

Violations of FIFRA, stated briefly, include distribution or sale of (1) an unregistered, cancelled or suspended pesticide except as authorized the USEPA; (2) a registered pesticide using claims different from the statement made with its registration; (3) a registered pesticide with a composition different from the statement made with its registration; (4) a pesticide that has not been colored or discolored if required by USEPA regulations; (5) a pesticide which is adulterated or misbranded; or (6) any misbranded device. 7 U.S.C. § 136j(a)(1).

The penalties for the foregoing violations do not apply to (1) persons who obtain certain written compliance guarantees from suppliers; (2) carriers who cooperate with requests by the USEPA to copy their records; (3) public officials engaged in performance of their official duties; (4) persons using or possessing a pesticide as provided in an experimental use permit; and (5) persons who ship solely for testing purposes.

It is also unlawful for any person (1) to detach, alter, deface or destroy any required labelling; (2) to refuse to prepare, maintain or submit required records or reports or allow entry, inspection, copying of records or sampling authorized by FIFRA; (3) to give a false guaranty or undertaking as to a pesticide; (4) to reveal confidential information except as authorized by law; (5) who is a registrant, wholesaler, dealer, retailer or distributor to advertise a product registered for restricted use without giving its assigned classification; (6) to distribute, sell, make available or use a classified restricted use pesticide for other purposes; (7) to use a registered pesticide in a manner inconsistent with its labelling; (8) to use any pesticide under an experimental use permit contrary to the permit provisions; (9) to violate any stop sale, use, removal or seizure order; (10) to violate any suspension order; (11) to violate any cancellation order or fail to submit a related notice; (12) who is a producer to violate any requirements relating to registration of establishments; (13) to knowingly falsify an application or other records or information filed, required or submitted pursuant to FIFRA; (14) who is a registrant, wholesaler, dealer, retailer or other distributor to fail to file required reports; (15) to add any substance to, or take any substance from, any pesticide in a manner that may defeat the purpose of FIFRA; (16) to use any pesticide in tests on human beings unless they are fully informed and freely volunteer to participate; (17) to falsify test information; (18) to submit to the USEPA information known to be false in support of a registration; or (19) to violate a regulation issued by the USEPA under FIFRA. 7 U.S.C. § 136j(a)(2).

An applicator which allowed a pesticide to contaminate exposed surfaces of a room and did not apply it directly into cracks and crevices as required by the label was found to have used the pesticide in a manner inconsistent with its labelling. *George's Pest Control Service v. USEPA*, 572 F.2d 204 (9th Cir. 1977). Defendants who used a pesticide containing carbofuran and labelled as insecticide nematacide to kill blackbirds and white egrets were found to have used the pesticide in a manner inconsistent with its labelling. *U.S. v. Saul*, 955 F. Supp. 1076 (E.D. Ark., 1996).

L. Adulteration and Misbranding

FIFRA forbids any person to sell or distribute any unregistered pesticide and also any registered pesticide (1) with claims substantially different than those in its registration statement submitted to the USEPA; (2) with a composition different from the composition in its registration statement submitted to the USEPA; (3) without coloring or discoloring, if coloration is required by the USEPA; or (4) that is adulterated or misbranded. 7 U.S.C. §136j(a)(1).

A pesticide is adulterated if (1) its strength or purity falls below the quality standard expressed on its labeling; (2) any substance has been substituted wholly or in part for the pesticide; or (3) any valuable constituent of the pesticide has been wholly or in part abstracted. 7 U.S.C. § 136(c).

A pesticide is misbranded if, among other things, its labelling bears any false or misleading statement, design or graphic representation or its labelling omits any required information such as the establishment, registration number, classification number, or directions for use with warnings adequate to protect health and the environment. A pesticide is also misbranded if it is not packaged in compliance with USEPA regulations. 7 U.S.C. § 136(g)(1) and (2).

FIFRA also prohibits detaching, altering, defacing or destroying pesticide labelling. 7 U.S.C. § 136j(a)(2).

M. Stop Sale, Use, or Removal Orders

The USEPA has authority to issue a "stop sale, use, or removal order" if there is reason to believe on the basis of inspection or tests that a pesticide or device is in violation of FIFRA or has been or is intended to be distributed or sold in violation of FIFRA or when a pesticide's registration has been cancelled by a final order or has been suspended. 7 U.S.C. § 136k(a).

The USEPA is also authorized to commence an *in rem* condemnation proceeding against a pesticide or device in any district court in the district where it is found and seized for confiscation if—

1. The pesticide is adulterated, misbranded or not registered; its labelling fails to bear acquired information; it is not colored or discolored if required; or any claims made for it or directions for its use differ in substance with the representations made in connection with its registration;

2. The device is misbranded; or

3. The pesticide or device, even though used properly, causes unreasonable adverse effects on the environment. 7 U.S.C. § 136k(b)

When a plant regulator, defoliant or desiccant is used according to the label claims and recommendations, the intended physical or physiological effects on plants are not deemed to be injury. 7 U.S.C. § 136k(b).

If a pesticide or device is condemned, it is disposed of by destruction or sale as the court may direct, but not in a manner contrary to FIFRA. 7 U.S.C. § 136 k(c).

N. Penalties

Any registrant, commercial applicator, wholesale, dealer, retailer or other distributor who violates FIFRA may be assessed a civil penalty by the USEPA up to $5,000 per offense. Private applicators are subject to more lenient penalties 7 U.S.C. § 136 l(a).

Any registrant, applicant for registration, or producer who knowingly violates FIFRA can be fined up to $50,000 or imprisoned for up to one year, or both. Any commercial applicator of a restricted use pesticide, or any other person except those already described who distribute or sells pesticides or devices, who knowingly violates FIFRA can be fined up to $25,000 or imprisoned for up to one year, or both. 7 U.S.C. § 136 l(b)(1).

A defendant can be convicted of a knowing violation by proof that its actions were taken intentionally. It is not necessary to prove that the defendant intended to violate FIFRA. *U.S. v. Corbin Farm Service*, 444 F. Supp. 510 (E.D. Cal. 1978).

Any private applicator or other person not described in the previous paragraph who knowingly violates FIFRA is guilty of a misdemeanor and shall, on conviction, be fined up to $1,000 or imprisoned up to 30 days, or both. 7 U.S.C. § 136 l(b)(2).

Any person who, with intent to defraud, uses or reveals information relative to product formulas acquired by the USEPA under the registration requirements of FIFRA shall be fined up to $10,000 or imprisoned up to three years, or both. 7 U.S.C. § 136 l(b)(3).

Under the Debt Collection and Improvement Act of 1996, the USEPA increases the foregoing penalties for inflation every four years. The increase for 1998 was 10% and for 2002 was 13.6%. Thus, for example, a $25,000 penalty is now $31,500.

The USEPA issued an enforcement response policy document on July 2, 1990 providing guidance as to the appropriate level of action to be taken in response to violations and the methods to be used in assessing penalties. The policy includes a civil penalty matrix that, among other things, adjusts penalties for factors such as the size of the business, gravity of the violation, and voluntary disclosure. 3 *Chemical Reg. Rep. (CCH)* 71:1441

O. Partial Preemption of State Regulation

FIFRA does not preempt state and local laws regulating pesticides except for those which require labelling or packaging in addition to or different from those required by FIFRA. *Wisconsin Public Intervenor v. Mortier*, 501 U.S. 597, 111

S.Ct. 2476 (1991); *Papas v. Zoecon Corporation*, 926 F.2d 1019 (11th Cir. 1991); vacated and remanded 505 U.S. 1215, 112 S.Ct. 3020, 120 L.Ed.2d 892 (1992). Thus, a number of states and municipalities have adopted their own laws and regulatory programs which supplement FIFRA and the federal courts have upheld them.

P. Partial Preemption of Lawsuits

The federal courts have found that tort law claims based on alleged inadequacy of the warning labels prescribed by FIFRA were preempted. *Hawkins v. Leslie's Pool Mart, Inc.*, 184 F.3d 244 (3rd Cir. 1999); *Lowe v. Sporicidin International*, 47 F.3d 124 (4th Cir. 1995); *King v. E.I. Du Pont*, 996 F.2d 1346 (1st Cir. 1993); *Worm v. American Cyanamid*, 5 F.3d 744 (4th Cir. 1993); *McDonald v. Monsanto Co.*, 27 F.3d 1021 (5th Cir. 1994); *Shaw v. Dow Brands, Inc.*, 994 F.2d 364 (7th Cir. 1993); *Arkansas Platte & Gulf v. Van Waters & Rogers*, 981 F.2d 1177 (10th Cir. 1993); and *Papas v. Upjohn Co.*, 985 F.2d 516 (11th Cir. 1993). Some federal courts have held that FIFRA does not preempt strict liability claims alleging misdesign or mismanufacture of a pesticide product. *Johnson v. Monsanto Chemical*, 129 F. Supp. 2d 189 (N.D.N.Y 2001); *Lewis v. American Cyanamid Co.*, 715 A.2d 967 (N.J. 1998). However, an allegation of a design or manufacturing defect that was effectively no more than an attack on failure to warn against residential use was preempted. *Grenier v. Vermont Log Buildings, Inc.*, 96 F.3d 559 (1st Cir. 1996). A federal appellate court held that claims of defective packaging of swimming pool disinfectant chemicals were not preempted because the USEPA has adopted regulations only for child-resistant packaging. *Hawkins v. Leslie's Pool Mart, Inc., supra*.

EXHIBITS

1. Application for Pesticide Registration - Section 1

Please read instructions on reverse before completing form. Form Approved. OMB No. 2070-0060

EPA United States Environmental Protection Agency Washington, DC 20460

☐ Registration
☐ Amendment
☐ Other

OPP Identifier Number 285452

Application for Pesticide - Section I

1. Company/Product Number	2. EPA Product Manager	3. Proposed Classification
4. Company/Product (Name)	PM#	☐ None ☐ Restricted

5. Name and Address of Applicant *(Include ZIP Code)*

☐ *Check if this is a new address*

6. **Expedited Review.** In accordance with FIFRA Section 3(c)(3)(b)(i), my product is similar or identical in composition and labeling to:

EPA Reg. No. ____________________

Product Name ____________________

Section - II

☐ Amendment - Explain below.
☐ Resubmission in response to Agency letter dated ____________
☐ Notification - Explain below.
☐ Final printed labels in response to Agency letter dated ____________
☐ "Me Too" Application.
☐ Other - Explain below.

Explanation: Use additional page(s) if necessary. (For section I and Section II.)

Section - III

1. Material This Product Will Be Packaged In:

Child-Resistant Packaging	Unit Packaging		Water Soluble Packaging		2. Type of Container
☐ Yes* ☐ No	☐ Yes ☐ No		☐ Yes ☐ No		☐ Metal ☐ Plastic ☐ Glass ☐ Paper ☐ Other (Specify) ________
** Certification must be submitted*	If "Yes" Unit Packaging wgt.	No. per container	If "Yes" Package wgt	No. per container	

3. Location of Net Contents Information	4. Size(s) Retail Container	5. Location of Label Directions
☐ Label ☐ Container		☐ On Label ☐ On Labeling accompanying product

6. Manner in Which Label is Affixed to Product: ☐ Lithograph ☐ Paper glued ☐ Stenciled ☐ Other ____________

Section - IV

1. Contact Point *(Complete items directly below for identification of individual to be contacted, if necessary, to process this application.)*

Name	Title	Telephone No. (Include Area Code)

Certification

I certify that the statements I have made on this form and all attachments thereto are true, accurate and complete. I acknowledge that any knowingly false or misleading statement may be punishable by fine or imprisonment or both under applicable law.

6. Date Application Received (Stamped)

2. Signature	3. Title
4. Typed Name	5. Date

EPA Form 8570-1 (Rev. 8-94) Previous editions are obsolete. White - EPA File Copy (original) Yellow - Applicant Copy

PAPERWORK REDUCTION ACT NOTICE and INSTRUCTIONS

PAPERWORK REDUCTION ACT NOTICE: Public reporting burden for this collection of information is estimated to average 0.85 hour per response, including time for reviewing instructions, searching existing data sources, gathering and maintaining the data needed, and completing and reviewing the collection of information. Send comments regarding the burden estimate or any other aspect of this collection of information, including suggestions for reducing this burden, to Chief, Information Policy Branch, (2136), U.S. Environmental Protection Agency, 401 M Street, SW, Washington, DC 20460.

INSTRUCTIONS: This form is to be used for all applications for new registration, end use reregistration, amendment, resubmission, to applications for notifications, final printed labeling, reregistration, etc. In order to process an application for a new registration submitted on this form, the following material must accompany the application:

1. Certification with Respect to Citation of Data (EPA Form 8570-29). [If not exempted by 40 CFR 152.81 (b) (4)];
2. Confidential Statement of Formula (EPA Form 8570-4);
3. Formulator's Exemption Statement (EPA Form 8570-27);
4. Five copies of draft labeling;
5. Three copies of any data submitted;
6. Authorization letter where applicable;
7. Matrices where applicable.

Submission of Labeling - Labeling should first be submitted in the form of draft labels with all applications for new registration. Such draft labels may be in the form of typed label text on 8.5 x 11 inch paper for submission or a mockup of the proposed label. If prepared for mockup, it should be constructed in a way as to facilitate storage in an 8.5 x 11 inch file. Mockup labels significantly smaller than 8.5 x 11 inches should be mounted on 8.5 x 11 inch paper for submission.

Submission of Data - Data submitted in support of this application must be submitted in accordance with PR Notice 86-5.

SPECIFIC INSTRUCTIONS: Please read the instructions listed below before completing this application. First determine the type of registration action, listed in Block A, for which you are submitting this application. For applications submitted in connection with New Registration actions, Sections I, III, and IV must be completed by the applicant. For applications submitted in connection with amended reregistration actions, resubmissions, notifications, reregistrations, etc., Sections I, II, and IV must be completed by the applicant.

Block A - Check the appropriate action for which you are submitting this form.

SECTION I - This section must be completed, as applicable, for all registration actions.

1. **Company/Product Number** - Insert your Company Number, if one has been assigned by EPA. This number may have been assigned to you as a basic registrant, a distributor, or as an establishment. If your product is registered, insert the Product Number.
2. **EPA Product Manager** - If known, fill in the name and PM number of the EPA Product Manager.
3. **Proposed Classification** - Specify the proposed classification of this product.
4. **Product Name** - Enter the complete product name of this pesticide as it will appear on the label. The name must be specific to this product only. Duplication of names is not permitted among products of the same company. Do not include any brand name or company line designations.
5. **Name and Address of Applicant** - The name of the firm or person and address shown in your application is the person or firm to whom the registration will be issued. If you are acting in behalf of another party, you must submit authorization from that party to act for them in registration matters. An applicant not residing in the United States must have an authorized agent residing in the United States to act for them in all registration matters. The name and complete mailing address of such an agent must accompany this application.
6. **Expedited Review** - FIFRA section 3 (c) 3 (B) provides for expedited review of applications for registration, or amendments to existing registrations, that are similar or identical to other pesticide products that are currently registered with the EPA. In order for your application to be eligible for expedited review, you must provide us with the EPA Registration Number and product name of the product you believe is similar to or identical to your product. The product must be similar or identical in both formulation and labeled uses.

SECTION II - This section must be completed for all applications submitted to amend the registration only of a currently registered product (Amendment), for a resubmission in response to an Agency letter, for notifications to the Agency, for the submission of final printed labeling, for reregistration and for any other action that pertains to a specific EPA-registered product. This section is not to be used for a new application for registration.

1. **Subject of submission** - Check the applicable block and provide the Agency letter date if appropriate. Provide a brief explanation of the purpose(s) for the submission, such as "the addition of a site, pest or crop (specify)"; "amend the Confidential Statement of Formula by..."; "reregistration submission"; "general label revision of use directions." Attach a separate page if additional space is needed.

SECTION III (Packaging and Container Information) - This Section must be completed for all applications submitted in connection with new registration or applicable amendments.

1. **Type of Packaging** - Check the appropriate block if your product will be packaged in the indicated packaging types. Indicate the size of the individual packets and number per retail container.
2. **Type of Retail Container** - Indicate type of container in which product will be marketed.
3. **Location of Net Contents** - Indicate the location of the net contents information for your product.
4. **Size(s) of Retail Container** - Specify the net contents of all retail containers for your product.
5. **Location of Use Directions** - Indicate the location of the use directions for your product.
6. **Manner in which label is affixed to product** - Indicated the method product label is attached to retail container.

SECTION IV (Contact Point) - This Section must be completed for all applications for Registration actions, i.e., new products registration, resubmission, "me-too," reregistration, etc.

1-5. Self-explanatory.
6. EPA Use Only.

2. Office of Pesticide Programs (7505C) - Confidential Statement of Formula

Confidential Business Information: Does Not Contain National Security Information (E.O. 12065)

Form Approved. OMB No. 2070-0060 Approval expires 5-31-98

EPA United States Environmental Protection Agency
Washington, DC 20460

A. ☐ Basic Formulation ☐ Alternative Formulation

B. Page ☐ of ☐

See Instructions on Back

Office of Pesticide Programs (7505C) - Confidential Statement of Formula

1. Name and Address of Applicant/Registrant *(Include ZIP Code)*

2. Name and Address of Producer *(Include ZIP Code)*

3. Product Name

4. Registration No./File Symbol

5. EPA Product Mgr/Team No.

6. Country Where Formulated

7. Pounds/Gal or Bulk Density

8. pH

9. Flash Point/Flame Extension

EPA USE ONLY	10. Components in Formulation *(List as actually introduced into the formulation. Give commonly accepted chemical name, trade name, and CAS number.)*	11. Supplier Name & Address	12. EPA Reg. No.	13. Each Component in Formulation: a. Amount	13. b. % by Weight	14. Certified Limits % by Weight: a. Upper Limit	14. b. Lower Limit	15. Purpose in Formulation

16. Typed Name of Approving Official

17. Total Weight 100%

18. Signature of Approving Official

19. Title

20. Phone No. (Include Area Code)

21. Date

EPA Form 8570-4 (Rev. 8-94)

White - EPA File Copy (original) Pink - Applicant

Instructions and Paperwork Reduction Act Notice
Please Read Carefully Before Completing This Form

Paperwork Reduction Act Notice

The public reporting burden for this collection of information is estimated to average 1.0 hour per response, including familiarization with the form, organizing the necessary information, and completing the form. Send any comments regarding the burden estimate or any other aspect of this collection of information, including suggestions for reducing this burden to: Chief, Information Policy Branch, 2136, U.S. Environmental Protection Agency, 401 M Street, S.W., Washington, DC 20460.

Instructions

The complete chemical composition of each pesticide must be known so it can be evaluated for registration under the Federal Insecticide, Fungicide, and Rodenticide Act, as amended.

This form is designed for reporting the ingredients used in the formulation of a pesticide product. It must be completed and submitted with each application for new registration of a pesticide and application for amended registration if the revision involves a formula change.

Block A: Check the appropriate action for which you are submitting the form.

Block B: Number all pages consecutively. Enter on each page the total number of pages submitted. If more than one page is required, number them "1of 2", "2 of 3", "3 of 3", etc.

1. Name and Address of Applicant/Registrant: Enter the name and address of your firm or authorized agent.

2. Name and Address of Producer: Specify the name of the producer and the address of the site where this product will be produced.

3. Product Name: Specify the complete name of this pesticide product as it will appear on the label. This name must be the same as that which appears on the application form.

4. Registration Number/File Symbol: Enter the EPA registration number or file symbol, if known, for this product.

5. EPA Product Manager/Team Number: Enter the name and team number of the EPA Product Manager assigned to this product, if known.

6. Country Where Formulated: Specify the country where this product is formulated.

7. Weight per Gallon/Bulk Density: For a liquid product specify pounds per gallon of formulated product. For a powder or granular product, enter the bulk density of formulated product (as used). Enter weight per unit if the product is produced as a tablet, briquette, or other uniformly shaped product.

8. pH: Enter the pH of aqueous formulations and products which are either dispersible or soluble in water. If not applicable enter "N/A."

9. Flash Point/Flame Extension: Specify the flash point as determined by the regulations for pressurized products and/or products known or suspected to burn. State the results of the flame extension test for pressurized products including positive flashbacks.

10. Components in Formulation: List as actually introduced into the formulation. For each component in your formulation, provide the product name, commonly accepted chemical, the trade name, and the Chemical Abstract (CAS) number for each identifiable ingredient present in that product. CAS numbers may be obtained from the Chemical Abstract Service of the American Chemical Society, Columbus, OH. For each original and alternate source of each active ingredient in the product, indicate the percent purity of the manufacturing use product, technical product, or other source of active ingredient. If one or more components will be obtained from more than one source, enter all alternate sources and all alternate EPA Reg Nos. in blocks 10, 11, and 12 or on a separate attachment.

Attention: *(Special Instructions for Columns 10, 13, and 14)* Any impurities greater than or equal to 0.1% (or less than 0.1% if the impurity is toxicologically significant) which are associated with the active ingredient(s) of a technical grade (manufacturing or reformulating use) product or an end use product produced by an integrated formulations system should also be listed in column 10, and the corresponding amount, percent by weight, and upper certified limits in columns 13 and 14.

11. Supplier Name and Address: Provide the name and address of the supplier of each component in the formulation. If one or more components will be obtained from more than one source, specify the names and addresses of the alternate sources also.

12. EPA Reg. No.: Specify the EPA registration number, if any, for each active ingredient in the formulation. If an unregistered active ingredient is used, have the suppliers submit the chemical specifications, as well as any data required under 40 CFR Part 158.

13. Each Component in Formulation

a. Amount: Specify the quantity of each component as actually introduced into the formulation. Units (e.g., pounds, grams, gallons, liters) should be expressed as used in the formulation. If the quantity is a liquid measure, enter the volume and the specific gravity or the pounds per gallon of the component.

b. Percent by Weight: Specify the weight percentage of each component in your formulation. Check Your Calculations. Note that the weight percentage in many cases will not agree with that shown on the label ingredient statement where the weight percentage of the pure active ingredient(s) must be declared.

Attention: Producers of Microbial Products: (Special Instructions for Column 13b.) Please state the percent of active ingredient in British International Units (BIUs), International Toxic Units (ITUs), Polyhedral Inclusion Bodies (PIBs) (viruses), or Colony Forming Units (CFUs) (Fungi), as appropriate, and include an equivalent statement of active ingredient per milligram, ounce, pound, etc., of product (e.g., a 50% active Bacillus thuringiensis product may have an equivalency value of 1.59 million Aedis aegypti ITU per pound of product.

14. Certified Limits: These limits are to be set based on representative sampling and chemical analysis (i.e., quality control) of the product.

a. Upper Limit: Specify the maximum percentage of each active ingredient, intentionally added inert ingredient, and any impurities greater than 0.1%, to be permitted in the product.

b. Lower Limit: Specify the minimum percentage of each active ingredient and intentionally added inert ingredient to be permitted in the product.

15. Purpose in Formulation: Specify the purpose of each ingredient both active and inert. (For example, disinfectant, herbicide, synergist, surfactant, defoamer, sequestrant, etc.) If space is insufficient, abbreviate.

16. Typed Name of Approving Official: Complete this item for identification of individual to be contacted if necessary.

17. Total Weight: Specify the total weight of the batch (column 13a.)

18-21.: Complete these items for identification of individual to be contacted if necessary.

EPA Form 8570-4 (Rev. 8-94) Reverse

*U.S. GPO: 2000-519-239/94558

3. Pesticide Report for Pesticide-Producing and Device-Producing Establishments

EPA

United Sates
Environmental Protection Agency
Washington, DC 20460

FORM APPROVED
OMB NO. 2070-0078

Pesticide Report for Pesticide-Producing and Device-Producing Establishments

Section 7, Federal Insecticide, Fungicide, and Rodenticide Act, (7 U.S.C. 136e)

Note: Read all instructions before completing. Production and distribution/sales volumes information reported on this form is treated as business confidential.

1. **Mailing Address**		8. EPA Est. No.
		9. Establishment Name
2. City		10. Site Address
3. State or Country	4. Zip Code	
5. Name of Establishment Officer		11. City
6. Title	7. Date *(Mo., Day, Year)*	12. State or Country / 13. Zip Code
14. Telephone Number		16.
15. Signature of Establishment Officer		

PESTICIDE PRODUCTION INFORMATION

17. Product Code (If "4" and chemical, attatch formulation per instructions. If "4" and Device, go to Item 19) ☐	18. EPA Product Registration Number		
19. Product Name		20. Product Classification ☐ ☐	
21. Product Type ☐	22. Market Sold To ☐	23. Use Classification ☐	24. Unit of measure: P=Pound G=Gallons K= Kilograms L=Liters T=Tons U=Units ☐
25. Amount Produced, Repackaged or Relabeled Last Year	[2001]		
26. Amount Sold or Distributed Last Year - US	[2001]		
27. Amount Sold or Distributed Last Year - Foreign	[2001]		
28. Amount To Be Produced, Repackaged, Relabeled This Year	[2002]		

17. Product Code (If "4" and chemical, attatch formulation per instructions. If "4" and Device, go to Item 19) ☐	18. EPA Product Registration Number		
19. Product Name		20. Product Classification ☐ ☐	
21. Product Type ☐	22. Market Sold To ☐	23. Use Classification ☐	24. Unit of measure: P=Pound G=Gallons K= Kilograms L=Liters T=Tons U=Units ☐
25. Amount Produced, Repackaged or Relabeled Last Year	[2001]		
26. Amount Sold or Distributed Last Year - US	[2001]		
27. Amount Sold or Distributed Last Year - Foreign	[2001]		
28. Amount To Be Produced, Repackaged, Relabeled This Year	[2002]		

17. Product Code (If "4" and chemical, attatch formulation per instructions. If "4" and Device, go to Item 19) ☐	18. EPA Product Registration Number		
19. Product Name		20. Product Classification ☐ ☐	
21. Product Type ☐	22. Market Sold To ☐	23. Use Classification ☐	24. Unit of measure: P=Pound G=Gallons K= Kilograms L=Liters T=Tons U=Units ☐
25. Amount Produced, Repackaged, or Relabeled Last Year	[2001]		
26. Amount Sold or Distributed Last Year - US	[2001]		
27. Amount Sold or Distributed Last Year - Foreign	[2001]		
28. Amount To Be Produced, Repackaged, Relabeled This Year	[2002]		

CONTINUED ON ATTACHED SHEET (   )   THIS IS PAGE ___ OF ___

EPA Reviewer	EPA Office	Postmark Date or Report Received Date	Date Reviewed	29. Reporting Year **2001**

EPA Form 3540-16 (Rev. 08-01) Previous editions are obsolete.

4. Certification with Respect to Citation of Data

Form Approved OMB No. 2070-0060

UNITED STATES ENVIRONMENTAL PROTECTION AGENCY
401 M Street, S.W.
WASHINGTON, D.C. 20460

Paperwork Reduction Act Notice: The public reporting burden for this collection of information is estimated to average 1.25 hours per response for registration and 0.25 hours per response for reregistration and special review activities, including time for reading the instructions and completing the necessary forms. Send comments regarding burden estimate or any other aspect of this collection of information, including suggestions for reducing the burden to: Director, OPPE Information Management Division (2137), U.S. Environmental Protection Agency, 401 M Street, S.W., Washington, DC 20460.
Do not send the completed form to this address.

Certification with Respect to Citation of Data

Applicant's/Registrant's Name, Address, and Telephone Number	EPA Registration Number/File Symbol
Active Ingredient(s) and/or representative test compound(s)	Date
General Use Pattern(s) (list all those claimed for this product using 40 CFR Part 158)	Product Name

NOTE: If your product is a 100% repackaging of another purchased EPA-registered product labeled for all the same uses on your label, you do not need to submit this form. You must submit the Formulator's Exemption Statement (EPA Form 8570-27).

☐ I am responding to a Data-Call-In Notice, and have included with this form a list of companies sent offers of compensation (the Data Matrix form should be used for this purpose).

SECTION I: METHOD OF DATA SUPPORT (Check one method only)

☐ I am using the cite-all method of support, and have included with this form a list of companies sent offers of compensation (the Data Matrix form should be used for this purpose).

☐ I am using the selective method of support (or cite-all option under the selective method), and have included with this form a completed list of data requirements (the Data Matrix form must be used).

SECTION II: GENERAL OFFER TO PAY

[Required if using the cite-all method or when using the cite-all option under the selective method to satisfy one or more data requirements]

☐ I hereby offer and agree to pay compensation, to other persons, with regard to the approval of this application, to the extent required by FIFRA.

SECTION III: CERTIFICATION

I certify that this application for registration, this form for reregistration, or this Data-Call-In response is supported by all data submitted or cited in the application for registration, the form for reregistration, or the Data-Call-In response. In addition, if the cite-all option or cite-all option under the selective method is indicated in Section I, this application is supported by all data in the Agency's files that (1) concern the properties or effects of this product or an identical or substantially similar product, or one or more of the ingredients in this product; and (2) is a type of data that would be required to be submitted under the data requirements in effect on the date of approval of this application if the application sought the initial registration of a product of identical or similar composition and uses.

I certify that for each exclusive use study cited in support of this registration or reregistration, that I am the original data submitter or that I have obtained the written permission of the original data submitter to cite that study.

I certify that for each study cited in support of this registration or reregistration that is not an exclusive use study, either: (a) I am the original data submitter; (b) I have obtained the permission of the original data submitter to use the study in support of this application; (c) all periods of eligibility for compensation have expired for the study; (d) the study is in the public literature; or (e) I have notified in writing the company that submitted the study and have offered (I) to pay compensation to the extent required by sections 3(c)(1)(F) and/or 3(c)(2)(B) of FIFRA; and (ii) to commence negotiations to determine the amount and terms of compensation, if any, to be paid for the use of the study.

I certify that in all instances where an offer of compensation is required, copies of all offers to pay compensation and evidence of their delivery in accordance with sections 3(c)(1)(F) and/or 3(c)(2)(B) of FIFRA are available and will be submitted to the Agency upon request. Should I fail to produce such evidence to the Agency upon request, I understand that the Agency may initiate action to deny, cancel or suspend the registration of my product in conformity with FIFRA.

I certify that the statements I have made on this form and all attachments to it are true, accurate, and complete. I acknowledge that any knowingly false or misleading statement may be punishable by fine or imprisonment or both under applicable law.

Signature	Date	Typed or Printed Name and Title

EPA Form 8570-34 (9-97) Electronic and Paper versions available. Submit only Paper version.

5. Registration Kit Containing Information to Register a Pesticide Product

UNITED STATES ENVIRONMENTAL PROTECTION AGENCY
WASHINGTON, D.C. 20460

OFFICE OF
PREVENTION, PESTICIDES AND
TOXIC SUBSTANCES

May 2000

Dear Prospective Registrant:

For your convenience, we have assembled a registration kit which contains the following pertinent forms and information needed to register a pesticide product with the U.S. Environmental Protection Agency's Office of Pesticide Programs (OPP):

1. The Federal Insecticide, Fungicide, and Rodenticide Act (FIFRA) and the Federal Food, Drug and Cosmetic Act (FFDCA) as Amended by the Food Quality Protection Act (FQPA) of August 3, 1996

2. Pesticide Registration (PR) Notices:

   A. 83-3: LIP - Storage and Disposal Statements
   B. 84-1: Clarification of Label Improvement Program
   C. 86-5: Standard Format for Data Submitted under FIFRA
   D. 87-1: Label Improvement Program for Pesticides Applied through Irrigation Systems (Chemigation)
   E. 87-6: Inert Ingredients in Pesticide Products Policy Statement
   F. 90-1: Inert Ingredients in Pesticide Products, Revised Policy Statement
   G. 98-1: Self Certification of Product Chemistry Data with Attachments
   H. 98-10: Notifications, Non-notifications, and Minor Formulation Amendments
   I. 2000-5: Guidance for Mandatory and Advisory Labeling Statements

   Other PR Notices can be found at http://www.epa.gov/opppmsd1/PR_Notices.

3. Pesticide Product Registration Application Forms

   A. EPA Form No. 8570-1: Application for Pesticide Registration/Amendment
   B. EPA Form No. 8570-4: Confidential Statement of Formula
   C. EPA Form No. 8570-27: Formulator's Exemption Statement
   D. EPA Form No. 8570-34: Certification with Respect to Citation of Data
   E. EPA Form No. 8570-35: Data Matrix

Recycled/Recyclable • Printed with Vegetable Oil Based Inks on 100% Recycled Paper (40% Postconsumer)

4. Pesticide General Information

   A. Registration Division Personnel Contact List
      Biopesticides and Pollution Prevention Division Personnel Contact List
      Antimicrobial Division Organizational Structure/Contact List
   B. 53 FR 15952: Pesticide Registration Procedures: Pesticide Data Requirements
   C. 40 CFR Labeling Requirements for Pesticides and Devices
   D. 40 CFR Part 158: Data Requirements for Registration
   E. 50 FR 48833: Disclosure of Reviews of Pesticide Data (November 27, 1985)

Before submitting your application for registration, you may wish to consult some additional sources of information. These include:

1. The Office of Pesticide Programs' Web Site at http://www.epa.gov/pesticides
2. The booklet "*General Information on Applying for Registration of Pesticide in the United States*," PB92-221811, available through the National Technical Information Services (NTIS) at the following address: 5285 Port Royal Road, Springfield, VA, 22161. The telephone number for NTIS is 1-800-553-6847. Please note that EPA is currently in the process of updating this booklet to reflect the changes in the registration program resulting from the passage of the FQPA and the reorganization of the Office of Pesticide Programs. We anticipate that this publication will become available soon.
3. The National Pesticide Information Retrieval System (NPIRS) of Purdue University's Center for Environmental and Regulatory Information Systems. This service does charge a fee for subscriptions and custom searches. You can contact NPIRS by telephone at (765) 494-6614 or through their Web Site at http://ceris.purdue.edu/npirs
4. The National Pesticide Telecommunication Network (NPTN) can provide information on active ingredients, uses, toxicology, and chemistry of pesticides. You can contact NPTN by telephone at 1-800-858-7378 or through their Web Site at http://ace.orst/edu/info/nptn/

The Agency will return a notice of receipt of an application for registration or amended registration, experimental use permit, or amendment to a petition if the applicant or petitioner encloses with his submission a stamped, self-addressed postcard. The postcard must contain the following entries to be completed by OPP: Date of receipt, EPA identifying number, and the Product Manager assignment.

Other identifying information may be included by the applicant to link the acknowledgment of receipt to the specific application submitted. EPA will stamp the date of receipt and provide the identifying File Symbol or petition number for the new submission. The identifying number should be used whenever you contact the Agency concerning an application for registration, experimental use permit, or tolerance petition.

To assist us in ensuring that all data you have submitted for the chemical are properly coded and assigned to your company, please include a list of all synonyms, common and trade names, company experimental codes, and other names which identify the chemical (including "blind" codes used when a sample was submitted for testing by commercial or academic facilities). Please provide a CAS number if one has been assigned.

All questions regarding specific registration actions should be directed to the appropriate regulatory contact person in charge of the applicable chemical (see the enclosed personnel contact sheets). The regulatory contact is responsible for managing the regulatory review during the registration process to ensure compliance with FIFRA and the FFDCA. Therefore, the regulatory contact is the only person to contact for information on your submission. If you have general questions on pesticide registration procedures, please contact one of the following individuals:

Antimicrobial products:	Yvette Hopkins	(703) 308-6214
Biological and biochemical products:	Robert Torla	(703) 308-8098
Conventional pesticide products:	Linda Arrington	(703) 305-5446

In order to promote efficient use of time and resources, those wishing to meet with OPP staff must schedule meetings in advance. The subject of the meeting must be identified, and the contact person may reject a request for a meeting of the agenda does not warrant discussion, the purpose of the meeting is vague, or there hasn't been adequate advance notice of the meeting. If applicants/registrants wish to meet with Agency scientists, such meetings must also be coordinated through the regulatory contact.

Additional copies of the materials in this kit may be obtained by calling (703) 305-6549 or by contacting the Registration Support Branch, Registration Division (7505C), Office of Pesticide Programs, Washington, DC 20460.

CHAPTER XIII
HAZARDOUS MATERIALS TRANSPORTATION ACT

A. Introduction

The Hazardous Materials Transportation Act (HMTA), 49 U.S.C. § 5101 *et seq.* was enacted in 1975, but its origins can be traced to the Explosives and Combustibles Act of 1908, then administered by the Interstate Commerce Commission. The HMTA regulates shippers, transporters and persons who manufacture, sell or perform services related to packages or containers of hazardous, radioactive or explosive materials and is administered by the U.S. Department of Transportation (DOT). Although little known to the general public, the programs and experience of the DOT and its Research and Special Programs Administration (RSPA) have long provided expert protection of public safety. RSPA's programs focus on imminent hazards (such as fires or acid spills) that can and will cause death, injury or illness within seconds, but also provide protection against chronic hazards. Thus, RSPA's programs provide a foundation for the other environmental programs.

Hazardous materials are defined by the HMTA as substances and materials in quantities or forms that pose an unreasonable risk to health and safety or property when transported in commerce. They include explosives, radioactive materials, etiological agents, flammable liquids and solids, poisons, oxidizing and corrosive materials, and compressed gases.

Hazardous materials also include hazardous waste. 49 C.F.R. §§ 171.3 and 171.8. The definition of hazardous waste is any waste subject to the manifest requirements of RCRA specified in 40 C.F.R. Part 262.

Under the HMTA and earlier laws, the DOT has adopted regulations creating a comprehensive system for the safe transportation of hazardous materials by rail, aircraft, vessel and public highway. 49 C.F.R. Parts 171 *et seq.* The DOT regulations prescribe methods for identification and classification of hazardous materials such as "flash point" tests to determine flammability. They require marking and warning labels on containers and packages and warning placards on vehicles. For example, the familiar red diamond-shaped placards on trucks and red labels on 55-gallon steel drums indicating flammability are required by RSPA's regulations. The regulations prescribe the use and content of shipping papers. They prescribe specifications for containers and packages and safe loading and unloading procedures. They require training of transport personnel and that emergency response information be available at shipper's locations and be with shipments throughout their transportation. They require accident reports and remedial action as well as more routine record keeping and reporting. They provide for inspections to monitor compliance. RSPA regulations also cover pipeline gas. 49 C.F.R. Part 190 *et seq.*

RSPA's regulations are enforced by other DOT administrations for shipments by the rail, air, water and motor vehicle carriers which they regulate, i.e., the Federal Railway Administration (FRA), the Federal Aviation Administration (FAA), the U.S. Coast Guard (USCG), and the Federal Motor Carrier Safety Administration (FMCSA). Each of these administrations has adopted implementing regulations. RSPA itself enforces regulations as to intermodal shipments.

The HMTA applies not only to shippers and carriers, but also to those who manufacture or provide services for packages or containers for transporting hazardous matèrial. They include any person who fabricates, makes, maintains, reconditions, repairs or tests a package or container that is represented, marked, certified or sold by that person as qualified for use in transportation hazardous material. 49 U.S.C. § 5103(b)(1).

In 1990, the DOT adopted a comprehensive new rule, known as HM-181, restructuring its regulations for packaging and transporting hazardous materials. The rules were intended to align U.S. rules with those of other United Nations member countries and thus avoid dual markings for domestic and international packaging.

HM-181 made fundamental changes in testing, classification, packaging, labelling and shipping document requirements. For example, the 22 classes of materials formerly used by DOT became 9 classes based on chemical reactions. Many packaging standards became performance-based rather than specification-based. Warning labels and placards were revised to correspond to those prescribed in the United Nations Convention on the Transport of Dangerous Goods. The revised rules required extensive training and retraining of employees. The term "HM-181 regulations" is still widely used because the regulations had a major impact on safety programs in the United States.

Later in 1990, Congress enacted the Hazardous Materials Transportation Uniform Safety Act (HMTUSA), 49 U.S.C. App. § 5101 *et seq.*, which, among other things, made changes to the HMTA limiting the authority of states to pass legislation unless it is substantially the same as federal rules governing the marking, labeling, packaging, placarding and classification of hazardous materials for transport. Under the HMTUSA, highway routing is an area of joint federal and state jurisdiction. The HMTUSA authorized grants to states to be used to develop emergency response programs for spills and releases and to train public sector employees to respond properly to an emergency. In 1990, Congress also enacted the Sanitary Food Transportation Act (SFTA), 49 U.S.C. App. § 2801 *et seq*. Section 15 of the SFTA contained the Motor Carrier Safety Act of 1990 (MCSA).

By legislation signed by the President on August 26, 1994, the HMTA was reauthorized by the Hazardous Materials Transportation Authorization Act (HMTAA). The HMTAA made modest amendments to the HMTA including an exemption of foreign carriers from U.S. registration fees and requirements that the DOT implement new regulations on fiber drum packaging and tank car crashworthiness and defects.

The Motor Carrier Safety Improvement Act was enacted in 1999, effective January 1, 2000. Among other things, this Act and other legislation transferred the functions of the Federal Highway Administration to a new Federal Motor Carrier Safety Administration (FMCSA).

The effects of the DOT's programs extend well beyond transportation. The DOT's methods for identifying, measuring, controlling and warning against hazards are used in industrial and commercial workplaces and are recognized and used by the general public. For example, we all are all cautious when we see a "FLAMMABLE" label or a "POISON" label on a container, even though it is in a building long after delivery.

The DOT's programs, like those of OSHA, are characterized by skillfully devised requirements which allow safe transportation of hazardous materials through achievable manufacturing, handling and use restrictions. Thus, they contrast with laws which focus on prohibitions and restrictions that have the effect of prohibitions.

The HMTA's scope covers interstate commerce. The HMTA also expressly instructs the DOT to promulgate regulations covering hazardous materials in intrastate commerce. 49 U.S.C. § 5103(b)(1). The DOT has stated that its regulations apply to intrastate shipments, subject to a few exceptions. 49 C.F.R. §§ 171.1, 173.5 and 173.8.

The HMTA preempts state and local laws that, as applied or enforced, are an obstacle to compliance with its requirements. 49 U.S.C. § 5125(a). Indeed, the HMTA preempts state laws on many subjects unless they are substantially the same as the HMTA requirement. 49 U.S.C. § 5125(b). However, hazardous waste is also regulated by RCRA.

B. Related Federal Laws

In addition to the HMTA, several other federal laws affect transportation of hazardous materials including the following:

1. Sanitary Food Transportation Act. 49 U.S.C. § 5701 *et seq.*
2. Pipeline safety laws. 49 U.S.C. § 60101 *et seq.*
3. Ports and Waterways Safety Act. 42 U.S.C. § 1221 *et seq.*

4. Occupational Safety and Health Act. 29 U.S.C. § 651 *et seq.*

5. Alcohol and Controlled Substance Testing Laws. 49 U.S.C. §§ 20140 and 45101 *et seq.*

6. Nuclear Waste Policy Act of 1982. § 10101 *et seq.*

7. Resource Conservation and Recovery Act. 42 U.S.C. 6901 *et seq.*

8. Comprehensive Environmental Response, Compensation and Liability Act, 42 U.S.C. § 9601 *et seq.*

C. Related International Codes

The DOT has coordinated its programs with international organizations to a far greater extent than other government agencies. Among the international standards included in RSPA's regulations are the following: the Recommendations of the United National Committee of Experts on the Transportation of Dangerous Goods; the IMDG Code of the International Maritime Organization; the ICAO Technical Instructions of the International Civil Aviation Organization; the IAEA Regulations for the Safe Transport of Radioactive Material of the International Atomic Energy Agency; the ECE Agreements and Regulations on Carriage of Dangerous Goods by Road and Rail of the Economic Commission for Europe Committee of Experts on the Transport of Dangerous Goods; and the Transportation of Dangerous Goods Regulations of the Government of Canada.

D. Related Industry Standards

RSPA has long recognized that industry organizations have extensive expertise and strong motivation to protect the people and reputation of their industries. Thus, RSPA has included the standards of many industry organizations in its regulations and encourages and cooperates with their safety programs. Among the standards incorporated by reference in RSPA's regulations are those of the following organizations: Aluminum Association, American National Standards Institutes, American Pyrotechnics Associations, American Society of Mechanical Engineers, American Society for Testing and Materials, Inc., American Water Work Association, American Welding Society, Association of American Railroads, Compressed Gas Association, Inc., Institution of Makers of Explosives, National Board of Boiler and Pressure Vessel Inspectors, National Fire Protection Association, National Motor Freight Traffic Association, Truck Trailer Manufacturers Association, National Association of Corrosion Engineers, and Society of the Plastics Industry, Inc.

Some years ago, a predecessor of the American Chemistry Council established an important emergency response information service called CHEMTREC which maintains information about the characteristics of over 1,000,000 chemicals. Persons dealing with a spill, fire or other chemical accident call CHEMTREC at 800-424-9300 to receive emergency response information.

The American Trucking Association, the American Chemistry Council, the American Forest and Paper Association, the Synthetic Organic Chemical Manufacturers Association and many other industry organizations (including those named above) provide literature, seminars and/or training to members and sometimes also to the public on transportation safety.

E. RSPA's Regulations

1. Registration

RSPA's regulations require annual registration with the DOT of persons (shippers) who offer hazardous materials for transportation and persons (carriers) who transport hazardous materials. 49 C.F.R. § 107.601 *et seq*. They also require registration of manufacturers and repairers of certain cargo tank motor vehicle equipment. 49 C.F.R. § 107.501.

The regulations exempt from registration (1) federal, state and local government agencies and their employees, (2) persons domiciled outside the United States if their only shipments are imports; and (3) individual employees who lease their vehicles to others for use. 49 C.F.R. § 107.606. The registration regulations also exempt shipments by farmers in direct support of their farm operations and shippers of small quantities set at levels which vary with the degree of hazard. 49 C.F.R. § 107.601.

Registration is made by filing Form 5800.2. Total current fees are $2,000, but small businesses pay $300. RSPA assigns a registration number and issues a certificate of registration to each registrant. Registrants must retain their registration documents for three years. A copy of the registration certificate must be kept with each vehicle.

2. General Requirements for Shipments and Packagings

RSPA's regulations prescribe general requirements for shipments and packaging. 49 C.F.R. Part 173.

The general requirements contain several exceptions. One is for "materials of trade" carried on motor vehicles by persons who are not primarily engaged in a transportation business and who transport the materials as incidental to their primary business. This exemption allows persons to carry small quantities of hazardous materials in order to (1) protect the health and safety of the motor vehicle operator; (2) support the operation of the motor vehicle; or (3) support a business other than motor vehicle transportation. The exemption allows painters, plumbers, farmers, gardeners, repairmen and others to carry on their trades without undertaking the effort and cost of compliance. However, the exemption is subject to several conditions. For example, the regulations limit the exemption to specified quantities for particular materials. The materials must remain in their original packaging or packaging of equal or greater strength and integrity. The vehicle operator must be informed that the materials are on board and of applicable reportable quantity and RSPA requirements. The exemption is not available for hazardous waste. 49 C.F.R. §173.6.

The regulations also contain exceptions for small quantities of some materials (§ 173.4), some agricultural operations (§ 173.5), some oilfield service vehicles (§ 173.5a), some U.S. Government materials (§ 173.7), and some nonspecification packagings used in intrastate transportation.

The regulations forbid the offering for transportation or transportation of a few materials including some explosives, electrical devices and materials subject to self-accelerated decomposition. 49 C.F.R. § 173.21.

RSPA's regulations group most hazardous materials into nine classes: (1) explosives; (2) hazardous gases and cryogenic liquids; (3) flammable and combustible liquids; (4) flammable solids and materials which are spontaneously combustible or dangerous when wet; (5) oxidizers and organic peroxides; (6) poisonous materials and infectious substances; (7) radioactive materials; (8) corrosive materials; and (9) miscellaneous hazardous materials. 49 C.F.R. §§ 171.8 and 173.50 *et seq.*

Some of the classes are divided into divisions based on common characteristics. For example, Class 2 is divided into flammable gas (Division 2.1); nonflammable nonpoisonous compressed gas (Division 2.2); and gas poisonous by inhalation (Division 2.3). 49 C.F.R. § 173.115.

The materials included in each class are defined specifically, as illustrated by the flammable and combustible liquids included in Class 3. With some exceptions, a flammable liquid means a liquid having a flash point not more than 60.5 degrees Celsius (141 degrees Fahrenheit) or any material intentionally heated and offered for transportation or transported at or above its flash point in a bulk packaging. A combustible liquid means any liquid that is not in any other hazard class and has a flash point above 60.5 degrees Celsius (141 degrees Fahrenheit) and below 93 degrees Celsius (200 degrees Fahrenheit). A "flash point" means the minimum temperature at which a liquid gives off a vapor within a test vessel in sufficient concentration to form an ignitable mixture with air near the surface of the liquid. Several ASTM methods are prescribed for determining flash points. 49 C.F.R. § 173.120.

Some other examples may be helpful. In Class 5, an oxidizer means a material that may, generally by yielding oxygen, cause or enhance the combustion of other materials. 49 C.F.R. § 173.127. In Class 6, an infectious substance (also called an etiological agent) means a viable microorganism, or its toxin, which causes or may cause, diseases in humans or animals, or any other agent that causes or may cause severe, disabling or fatal disease. 49 C.F.R. § 173.134. In Class 7, radioactive material means any material having a specific activity greater than 0.002 microCuries per gram (uCi/g). 49 C.F.R. § 173.403. Examples of radioactive materials are the isotopes of plutonium, thorium and uranium. In Class 8, corrosive material means a liquid or solid that causes full thickness destruction of intact skin tissue at the point of contact or that has a severe corrosion rate on steel or aluminum based on test methods such as ASTM G-31-72. 49 C.F.R. § 173.136.

If a hazardous material is within two or more classes, the regulations establish a precedence system which requires compliance to protect against the most serious hazard. 49 C.F.R. § 173.2a.

3. Hazardous Materials Table

RSPA's regulations contain a lengthy hazardous materials table that lists many hundreds of materials which have been identified by RSPA as hazardous materials. For each material, the table shows the applicable hazard class and division, if any, or states that transportation is forbidden. The table also shows the applicable packaging group: Packing Group I (great danger), Packing Group II (medium danger), and Packing Group III (minor danger). 40 C.F.R. § 172.101.

The table shows the proper shipping name for each hazardous material or directs the user to the preferred proper shipping name. The table also specifies or references for each material the applicable requirements for labelling, packaging, storage aboard vessels, and quantity limits aboard aircraft. 40 C.F.R. § 172.101. The table is supplemented and explained by a lengthy list of special provisions. 40 C.F.R. § 172.102.

The table is quite useful. However, a shipper or transporter who does not find a substance or mixture in the table should not automatically assume that it is not subject to the regulations. For example, formulators of new substances or mixtures must test them using the methods prescribed by the regulations to determine whether they are hazardous materials. If so, they must comply with all applicable requirements.

4. Shipping Papers

RSPA's regulations do not provide or require standard forms for shipping papers. However, they require that shipping papers be prepared for each shipment of hazardous materials. They also prescribe basic requirements for description of the shipment and for a certification or declaration by the shipper as to the accuracy of the shipping papers. 49 C.F.R. § 172.201 *et seq*.

The description must provide the proper shipping name, hazard class or division, the 4-digit UN identification number, packing group (in roman numerals), and total quantity. No other information may be inserted within this information. The shipping paper must also contain the name of the shipper and an emergency response telephone number. The shipping papers must also state whether any one or more containers holds a "hazardous substance" in a quantity that exceeds a reportable quantity (RQ) under CERCLA and, if so, must state the "RQ" on the paper. 49 C.F.R. §172.200-.204.

The required certification is as follows:

> This is to certify that the above-named materials are properly classified, described, packaged, marked and labeled, and are in proper condition for transportation according to the applicable regulations of the Department of Transportation.

Additional language is required for air shipments and radioactive material shipments. The certification must be signed by a principal, officer, partner or employee of the shipper or its agent, but may be signed by mechanical means. 49 C.F.R. § 172.204. If a shipment is of hazardous waste, RSPA's regulations require use of the USEPA's Uniform Hazardous Waste Manifest Form. 49 C.F.R. § 172.205. 40 C.F.R. §§ 262.20-.23. The shipping paper requirements contain exceptions for small shipments such as ORM-D materials.

5. Marking

RSPA's regulations require that the shipper mark each package, freight container, and transport vehicle containing a hazardous material, but assigns marking responsibility to the carrier under some circumstances. 49 C.F.R. § 172.300 *et seq.*

The marking regulations differ somewhat for nonbulk and bulk packaging, but require use of the proper shipping name and four digit identification number. Exemption packaging may be marked "DOT-E" followed by the assigned exemption number. The marking must not be removed from bulk packaging unless (1) sufficiently cleaned of residue and purged of vapors to remove any potential hazard or (2) refilled with material requiring different marking or no marking to an extent that anything remaining is no longer hazardous. 49 C.F.R. § 172.301-.302.

Marking must be durable and in English words. It must be printed on or affixed to the surface of the packaging or be on a label, tag or sign. Marking must be in a color that sharply contrasts with the background color (such as white on black). It must also be unobscured by labels or attachments and be located at a distance from other marking that could reduce its effectiveness. 49 C.F.R. § 172.304.

Numerous detailed requirements apply to particular materials such as poisonous, radioactive, explosive and ORM-D materials, and marine pollutants. Materials such as molten sulfur, which are shipped at elevated temperatures, must be marked "HOT" 49 C.F.R. §§ 171.310 to 325. Specific marking requirements apply to portable and cargo tanks, tankcars and other bulk packagings. 49 C.F.R. §§ 171.326-.338.

6. Labelling

RSPA's regulations require shippers to label each nonbulk package, certain small bulk packaging, portable tanks, multiunit tankcar tanks, overpacks, freight containers, and unit load devices. The regulations prescribe specific labels for each kind of hazardous material in the nine hazard cases, subject to numerous exceptions. 49 C.F.R. §§ 172.400-.400a.

The regulations provide label specifications including placement, durability, design, size and color. Labels conforming to the specifications in the UN Recommendations may also be used. The regulations contain drawings of the labels such as the diamond shaped "Flammable" label with a stylized flame burst. They also include an "Empty" label. 49 C.F.R. §§ 172.406-.450. See the labels in DOT's Chart 11 at the end of this chapter.

The regulations prohibit use of any other label which could by its design, color or shape be confused with a required label. The prohibitions do not apply if a packaging is (1) unused or cleaned of all residue, (2) not visible during transportation, or (3) loaded and unloaded by a shipper which is also the consignee. The prohibitions also do not apply to packages labelled in compliance with UN, IMO, ICAO or TDG requirements. 49 C.F.R. § 172.401.

RSPA has developed over the years remarkable expertise in effective communications which it uses in its labelling, marking and placarding regulations. One method is simplicity. Two words should not be used when one will deliver an effective message. A second method is the use of illustrations and colors to draw attention to the message. A third method is consistency and avoidance of confusion. A fourth method is avoidance of overmeasurement and overwarning of hazards so that the public knows that labels, markings and placards are credible and must be taken seriously. The USEPA and some other environmental agencies have not yet learned to use these methods, but would benefit from doing so.

7. Placarding

RSPA's regulations require shippers to provide required placards for highway and rail shipments of hazardous materials. They also provide that a carrier may not accept hazardous materials for transport unless the placards are provided. 49 C.F.R. § 172.501 *et seq*. Highway and rail carriers may provide placards as a service to shipper customers, but the shippers remain responsible for fulfillment of the placarding requirements.

The placarding requirements apply to bulk packaging, freight container, unit load device, transport vehicle and railcar shipments of any quantity of hazardous material and must be applied on each side and each end. Tables in the regulations list the applicable placards for each of the nine hazard classifications. However, general "DANGEROUS" placards may be used for some mixed shipments. Exceptions apply to shipments containing less than 454 kg (1,001 pounds) and empty nonbulk packages containing only the residue of hazardous material. 49 C.F.R. § 172.504.

The regulations prescribe requirements for visibility, display, and maintenance of placards and specifications including durability, design, size and color. The regulations contain drawings showing the placards for each of the nine hazard classes and the "DANGEROUS" placard. However, placards meeting ICAO, IMDG or TDG requirements may be used. 49 C.F.R. §§ 172.516-.519. See the placards in DOT's Chart 11 at the end of this chapter.

The placarding requirements do not apply to shipments of infectious substances; ORM-D materials; limited quantities in compliance with 49 C.F.R. § 172.203(b); materials in packaging meeting special requirements prescribed in § 173.13; small quantities in compliance with 49 C.F.R. § 173.4; and combustible liquids in nonbulk packagings. 49 C.F.R. § 172.500.

The regulations prohibit use of any sign, advertisement, slogan or device that, by its color, design, shape or content could be confused with a required placard. However, the regulations contain exceptions including placarding which conforms to TDG, MDG or UN requirements. 49 C.F.R. § 172.502.

8. Emergency Response Information

Shippers, carriers and any other person who transfers, stores or handles any hazardous material during transportation must assure that required emergency response information is immediately available for use at all times when it is present. The information must include: (1) the description and technical name of the hazardous material; (2) a description of any immediate health hazards and/or risks of fire or explosion; (3) immediate precautions to take in response to an accident or incident; (4) intermediate methods for handling fires; (5) initial methods for handling spills or leaks not involving a fire or explosion; and (6) preliminary first aid measures. 49 C.F.R. § 172.602.

The information must be printed in English and be immediately available on the transport vehicle away from the package containing the hazardous material so that it can be used by carrier personnel and other emergency response personnel. RSPA provides an Emergency Response Guidebook that is helpful in meeting these requirements. The Guidebook can be obtained at U.S. Government bookstores and from other sources including the American Trucking Association. The Guidebook and other information are typically kept in the vehicle cab. 49 C.F.R. §§ 172.600-.604.

Each shipper must also provide an emergency response telephone number where callers may obtain further information about the hazardous materials and emergency response methods. 49 C.F.R. § 172.604. The number need only be monitored during the actual transportation of hazardous materials but that means for many shippers that monitoring must be provided 24 hours per day and often also 7 days per week. As a result, many shippers contract with CHEMTREC to fulfill the requirement.

> *COMMENT:* The author was formerly a member of a team that received emergency calls for a large national chemical manufacturer. Although the team did its work knowledgeably and conscientiously, the author appreciates the improvements implemented over the years by CHEMTREC.

9. Training

An important part of RSPA's regulations are the hazardous materials (HAZMAT) training requirements. 49 C.F.R. § 172.700-.704.

The regulations apply to each HAZMAT employer. This means an employer that employs any employee who during the course of employment affects hazardous material transportation including those who (1) load, unload or handle hazardous material; (2) manufacture, recondition or test containers, drums or packages represented or qualified for use in transporting hazardous material; (3) prepare hazardous material for transportation; (4) are responsible for the safe transportation of hazardous material; or (5) operate a vehicle used to transport hazards material. 49 C.F.R. § 171.8.

Each HAZMAT employer must arrange for each HAZMAT employee to be trained and tested to ensure that he or she is familiar with the general provisions of the regulations including the hazard classification system and is able to recognize hazardous materials. The training must also include knowledge of the specific requirements of the regulations applicable to the employee's functions, emergency response information, self-protection measures, and accident prevention methods and procedures.

Training must be provided within 90 days to new employees and to employees who change job functions. They must work under supervision of a trained employee until they receive their training. The training must be repeated and updated every three years.

Training in the requirements of the ICAO Technical Instructions or the IMDG Code is an acceptable alternative to function specific training. Training may not conflict with the requirements of the hazard communication regulations of OSHA or the USEPA and training in their requirements may be used to fulfill part of the requirements for HAZMAT training. Records evidencing the HAZMAT training must be prepared and maintained as long as an employee is employed as a HAZMAT employee plus 90 days.

All commercial motor vehicle drivers must demonstrate basic hazardous materials knowledge to obtain and maintain their driver's licenses. 49 C.F.R. § 383.111. To obtain a Hazardous Materials Endorsement, they must demonstrate a broad range of hazardous materials knowledge. 49 C.F.R. § 383.121.

10. Regulation of Shipments and Packaging

a. Shippers's Responsibilities

Shippers are responsible to prepare hazardous materials for shipment. 49 C.F.R. § 173.1. A shipper must first determine whether a material is hazardous and, if so, the classification and division. 49 C.F.R. § 173.2 and .22. If the material presents more than one hazard, the shipper must refer to the Precedence of Hazards Table for the applicable requirements. 49 C.F.R. § 173.2a.

In general, RSPA's shipment and packaging regulations are based on the UN Recommendations and are consistent with the ICAO Technical Instructions and the IMDG Code. 49 C.F.R. § 173.1(d).

Shippers are responsible for the selection of packaging that is authorized or exempt and has been manufactured, assembled and marked properly. With some exceptions, shippers may rely on the manufacturer's certification, specification, approval or exemption marking. When a carrier provides cargo tanks, a shipper may rely on the manufacturer's identification plate or the carrier's written certification, specification or exemption. However, shippers are responsible for all functions necessary to bring DOT specification and UN standard packaging into compliance as indicated by the manufacturer or distributor. 49 C.F.R. § 173.22.

Shippers must assure that each package is designed, constructed, maintained, filled with contents limited for outage or ullage, and closed so that, under normal conditions, there will be no release of hazardous materials. Shippers must also assure that the effectiveness of the package will not be substantially reduced and no mixture of gases or vapors in the package could significantly reduce the effectiveness of the packaging. 49 C.F.R. § 173.24. Shippers also have numerous other responsibilities for packaging including assurance that "empty" packagings do not contain residues that could be the source of flammable or explosive vapors or other hazards. 49 C.F.R. § 173.30.

Shippers often load or unload transport vehicles rather than the carriers. Some shippers also load or unload vessels, although it is less common except when the shipper owns or has a long term charter for a vessel. If a shipper loads or unloads, it must comply with the loading and unloading requirements for carriers as provided in the regulations. 49 C.F.R. § 173.29.

b. Rail Carriers' Responsibilities

RSPA's regulations place considerable responsibility upon rail carriers. They may not accept any shipment of hazardous material unless it is prepared in compliance with the regulations. 49 C.F.R. § 174.3.

Rail carriers must inspect each loaded and placarded railcar (and the adjacent cars) at the originating point and upon receipt at each interchange point. They may continue in transit only if in safe condition. 49 C.F.R. § 174.9.

Rail carriers must forward shipments of hazardous materials promptly and within 48 hours after acceptance, subject to some exceptions including weekends and holidays. They must require companies to remove shipments delivered at agency stations within 48 hours, except for weekends and holidays. They may not allow a shipment to be unloaded at a nonagency station unless the consignee is there to receive it and properly locked and secure storage facilities are provided. 49 C.F.R. §§ 174.14-.16.

Rail carriers may not accept hazardous material for transportation without properly prepared shipping papers. 49 C.F.R. §§ 174.24-.25. They must comply with general handling and loading requirements so that hazardous materials are loaded, blocked and braced. The railcars must be properly cleaned, marked and placarded. 49 C.F.R. §§ 174.55-.59. As applicable, hazardous materials must be stored and segregated in compliance with the regulations, including the Segregation Table. Explosive materials (Class I) must be stored according to special regulations including a Compatibility Table. 49 C.F.R. § 174.81.

Rail carriers must notify train crews of placarded cars; replace lost or destroyed labels and placards; report hazardous materials incidents; and take required actions when violations, leaks, damaged packages or flammable vapors occur. 49 C.F.R. §§ 174.26-.59.

Rail carriers must assure that unloading is performed by reliable, properly instructed persons. They must see that brakes are set, wheels are blocked, and caution signs are placed on the track or cars during unloading. Manhole covers and outlet valve caps may not be removed until interior pressure is relieved. Placards and car certifications must be removed after unloading unless the placards should be left in place to warn about remaining residue. 49 C.F.R. §§ 174.67.

Rail carriers must provide HAZMAT training to their HAZMAT employees. 49 C.F.R. § 172.700 *et seq.*

c. Aircraft Operators' Responsibilities

The quantities of hazardous materials shipped by air carriers is small in comparison to the enormous volumes shipped by rail, vessel or motor vehicles. However, when time is a high priority and the cost can be justified, many products are shipped by air that are hazardous materials. Even in small quantities, these materials must be handled with special care because air transportation itself presents risks different and sometimes greater than other methods of transportation.

RSPA's regulations provide that aircraft operators may not transport on an aircraft any hazardous materials that are not in compliance with the regulations. 49 C.F.R. § 175.3. They must comply with all applicable requirements unless the regulations specifically provide for another person to perform them. 49 C.F.R. § 175.20.

The regulations apply to U.S. registered aircraft wherever engaged in air commerce and to foreign and any other aircraft in the United States. However, there are exceptions for government-owned and operated aircraft not engaged in commercial purposes and some aircraft engaged in domestic or foreign government activities. 49 C.F.R. § 175.5. There are also exceptions for several kinds of hazardous materials. 40 C.F.R. § 175.10.

Aircraft operators may not accept hazardous material aboard an aircraft unless it is (1) authorized and within quantity limitations; (2) described and certified on properly prepared shipping papers; (3) properly labeled, marked and, if applicable, placarded; and (4) labeled "Cargo Aircraft Only" if not permitted aboard passenger aircraft. 40 C.F.R. § 175.30. The pilot-in-command must be informed about the hazardous materials and their shipping papers must be aboard the aircraft. Any discrepancies must be reported to the FAA. 49 C.F.R. §§ 175.33-.45.

The regulations prescribe loading, handling, stowage and unloading requirements. These rules impose quantity limitations and prescribe storage in compliance with compatibility requirements. Packages must be properly oriented, secured and located in the aircraft. Any package that appears to be damaged or leaking must be removed from the aircraft and the rest of the packages must be inspected to insure they are in proper condition and have not been contaminated. 49 C.F.R. §§ 175.75-.90.

Aircraft operators must provide HAZMAT training to their HAZMAT employees. 49 C.F.R. § 175.20.

d. Vessel Carriers' Responsibilities

RSPA's regulations provide that vessel carriers may not transport by vessel any shipment of hazardous material that is not in compliance with the regulations. 49 C.F.R. § 176.3. They must also comply with port security and safety regulations. 49 C.F.R. § 176.4. However, several exceptions may apply based on the kind of vessel or the tonnage and/or nature of activities of the vessel. For example, the regulations do not apply to public vessels not engaged in commercial service; vessels used exclusively for pleasure; some tug and towing vessels; some cable, dredge and other working vessels; and foreign vessels in compliance with the IMDG Code that transit U.S. territorial but not U.S. internal waters. The regulations also do not apply to vessels of 15 gross tons or less when not carrying passengers for hire and vessels of 500 gross tons or less when engaged in fishing. 49 C.F.R. § 176.5.

In general, foreign vessel carriers which comply with the IMDG Code may transport without compliance with most of the regulations. That is also true for Canadian vessel carriers which comply with Canada's TDG Regulations. However, there are some exceptions with which these carriers should check before shipping to the U.S. 49 C.F.R. § 176.11.

Vessel carriers must obtain proper shipping papers for each shipment, including the shipper's certificate. They must prepare and maintain on or near the bridge a dangerous cargo manifest, list or storage plan. They must inspect the hold, compartments and cargo after storage, every 24 hours thereafter, and upon entering port. They must meet a number of requirements in emergencies including notice and reporting to the nearest port captain. 49 C.F.R. § 176.24-.48.

Vessels often carry hazardous materials in larger quantities and for longer times and distances than rail, air and highway motor vehicle carriers. Thus, the regulations prescribe extensive handling and stowage requirements and segregation for incompatible materials. The regulations contain segregation tables to assist in compliance. 49 C.F.R. §§ 176.57-.84.

The National Cargo Bureau, Inc. is authorized to assist the USCG in(1) inspection of vessels for suitability for loading hazardous materials; (2) examination of stowage of hazardous materials; (3) recommending stowage requirements for hazardous materials cargo; and (4) issuing loading certificates. 49 C.F.R. § 176.18.

Vessel carriers must provide HAZMAT training to their HAZMAT employees. 49 C.F.R. § 176.13.

e. Highway Motor Vehicle Carriers' Responsibilities

Highway motor vehicle carriers transport the largest number of shipments of hazardous materials in the United States. Although many of the shipments are small, the shippers include many small companies which lack the experience and resources of the typical companies which ship by rail or vessel. The routes are also more likely to pass through populated nonindustrial areas. Thus, regulation of highway motor vehicle carriers is perhaps the most complex DOT responsibility. However, RSPA's regulations make a skillful effort to simplify compliance so that the numerous small shippers and small motor vehicle carriers can fulfill their duties daily with reasonable cost and effort.

RSPA's regulations apply to common, contract and private motor vehicle carriers. They may not accept for transportation any shipment of hazardous material that is not in compliance with the regulations. Each carrier, including each connecting carrier, must perform all duties and comply with all requirements unless the regulations specifically provide that another person is responsible. Motor vehicles must transport hazardous materials without unnecessary delay. 49 C.F.R. §§ 177.800-.801.

A motor vehicle carrier must assure that each shipment is accompanied by proper shipping papers, including the required certification. The shipping papers must be readily available to authorities if an accident or inspection takes place. 49 C.F.R. §§ 177.817.

A motor vehicle carrier may not move a vehicle containing hazardous material unless it is properly marked and placarded. However, in an emergency, the carrier can move a noncompliant vehicle to protect life or property or may obtain permission from the DOT or arrange an escort from a state or local authority. 49 C.F.R. §177.823.

Motor vehicle carriers must comply with detailed loading and unloading requirements if they perform those functions. The requirements, of course, differ for various vehicles and hazardous materials. Although the regulations are not so complex as those for vessels, motor vehicle carriers must also comply with segregation and compatibility requirements. The regulations provide a segregation table and also a compatibility table for explosives. 49 C.F.R. § 177.834-.848.

The regulations contain detailed provisions on such subjects as disabled vehicles, repairs and accidents, as well as leaks from packages. 49 C.F.R. §§ 177.854-.870.

Motor vehicle carriers must provide HAZMAT training to their HAZMAT employees, including their drivers. 49 C.F.R. § 177.801-.816.

An already complex regulatory program was further complicated in 1996 by enactment of the Federal Motor Carrier Safety Act which created the FMCSA. 49 U.S.C. § 501 *et seq.* Stated briefly, the Act and the FMCSA's regulations authorize states to administer equivalent programs if they adopt compatible laws and regulations and provide adequate funding and other resources to implement and maintain them. The FMCSA provides for federal grants to assist the states with their programs. Incompatible programs are preempted. If a state does not adopt an approved program, the FMCSA will administer its regulations directly.

The FMCSA has adopted extensive regulations which set national standards for use in state-administered programs and in directly administered programs. 49 C.F.R. Parts 350 to 399. Key topics are as follows:

1. *Drivers*: Qualifications (Part 391); licensing, testing and penalties (Part 383); driving of commercial motor vehicles (Part 392); driving and parking (Part 397); hours of service (Part 395); and controlled substance and a alcohol use and testing (Part 382).

2. *Carriers*: Federal Motor Carrier Identification Report, Form MCS-150 (Part 319); safety fitness rating procedures (Part 385); and financial responsibility (Part 387).

3. *Vehicles*: Construction, marking, operation, inspection, repair and maintenance standards (Parts 390 and 396).

4. *Migrant Workers*: Transportation of migrant workers (Part 398)

5. *Employees*: Employee safety and health standards (Part 399).

6. *State Program Conformity*: State compliance with the commercial driver's license programs. (Part 384); FMCSA-State cooperative agreements (Part 388).

7. *Routing and Preemption*: Routing of the transportation of hazardous materials. (Parts 355 and 356).

For most of the environmental laws, state administration has been a welcome opportunity to concentrate on real environmental improvements. However, the DOT and RSPA have been dedicated to public safety and health for decades. They have adopted conservative standards and enforced strictly, but have not seen industry as an opponent. They have worked effectively with industry organizations to improve safety methods. It remains to be seen whether state administration will be an improvement, except through coordination of driver licensing and training programs.

f. Packaging Standards

RSPA's regulations require that hazardous materials be transported in packaging and containers that meet its manufacturing and testing standards. 49 C.F.R. § 178.1. For decades, RSPA provided detailed packaging specifications in its regulations. However, since the adoption of the HM-181 Docket and the HMTUSA in 1990, the regulations prescribe many performance oriented packaging standards (POPS) by reference to the UN Recommendations. The authorization of POPS allows some freedom for innovation, provided that results achieving safety standards are attained.

Packaging must be marked to show the applicable DOT specification or UN standard. The marking must also identify the name and address or symbol of the manufacturer or, if it is UN standard packaging, of the agency certifying compliance. The markings must be stamped or otherwise applied to the packaging so as to assure that they are legible, permanent and accessible. Marking to indicate compliance with an UN standard, the ICAO Technical Instructions or the IMDG Code can be used to fulfill these requirements. 49 C.F.R. § 178.1-.3.

RSPA's technical specifications for packaging are famous for their detail. Readers who think a bag is just a bag, unless it is sold by Cartier or Escada, would be amazed to learn what RSPA requires for a 3-ply or 5-ply industrial bag. The specifications sometimes even prescribe how to make the materials used as packaging materials. They also contain performance standards, but only as a verification method because meeting the performance standards do not allow departure from the specifications. 49 C.F.R. §§ 177.33-.364.

The POPS adopted by RSPA are also very detailed, but there is some freedom for manufacturers to choose materials and methods, if the packaging meets the performance tests. 49 C.F.R. §§ 177.500-.523. To measure performance of packaging, the regulations prescribe drop testing, leak testing, hydrostatic pressure testing, stack testing, cooperage testing, vibration testing, and other special tests. For example, a drop test requires that a package or container be dropped from a prescribed height to determine whether it will burst or remain intact. 49 C.F.R. §§ 178.600-.609.

The regulations contain separate specifications for railroad tankcars which are coordinated with quasi-regulatory programs of the American Association of Railroads. They include general design requirements and specifications for various classes of tankcars. 49 C.F.R. Part 179.

F. Hazardous Waste Transportation

1. Compliance with the HMTA and RCRA

Shippers, carriers and other persons involved in the transportation of hazardous waste must comply with both the regulations of RSPA under the HMTA and the USEPA under RCRA. 49 C.F.R. §§ 171.3-.8. To make this clear, RSPA's regulations define "hazardous waste" as any material subject to the hazardous waste manifest requirements of the USEPA under RCRA. 49 C.F.R. § 171.8.

It is more difficult to compare other definitions. A "shipper" of hazardous waste under the HMTA may also be a generator under RCRA. However, RCRA's definition of a generator also includes a person who generates waste regardless whether it is transported or not. Further, RCRA imposes responsibilities on persons whom it calls "generators" and "transporters" that are different and more enduring than those imposed by the HMTA on shippers and carriers. Thus, shippers and carriers of hazardous waste typically allocate contractually between them the responsibilities and potential liabilities imposed by RCRA.

2. The USEPA's Hazardous Waste Regulations

The USEPA's regulations require a generator to determine whether its waste is hazardous even if it will remain at the facility where generated. 49 C.F.R. Part 261and 262. A generator must obtain an identification number from the USEPA for each facility where it generates hazardous waste.

A generator must determine whether the waste is hazardous according to detailed standards and methods prescribed in 49 C.F.R. Part 261. A generator who ships hazardous waste must prepare a uniform hazardous waste manifest on Form 8700-22 for each shipment and must comply with packaging, marking, labelling, placarding, recordkeeping and reporting requirements. 49 C.F.R. Part 262. The USEPA's regulations place corresponding requirements on persons who transport hazardous waste away from the site where generated. 49 C.F.R. § 260.10 and Part 263.

Wastes which the USEPA classes as hazardous under RCRA often present hazards that are far less imminent than most of the materials which RSPA classes as hazardous under the HMTA. The reason is that RSPA is primarily concerned with safe transportation and handling of materials during time periods which are typically brief. RSPA does not ignore chronic hazards, but focuses on exposure prevention which is almost always achievable during transportation which usually takes a few days and rarely more than a few weeks.

By contrast, the USEPA is concerned under RCRA about hazards of wastes for long after transportation, if any, has been completed. For example, the USEPA is concerned about the leaching characteristics that wastes may have in a landfill many years after disposal and even after the landfill is closed. Further, the USEPA bases its "cradle to the grave" regulatory system under RCRA on "worst case" assumptions that exposure will occur and have adverse effects on human health and the environment.

3. RSPA's Hazardous Waste Transportation Regulations

Persons who plan to ship hazardous waste must determine its proper classification under RSPA's regulations. As described previously, the shipper must first review the Hazardous Materials Table (49 C.F.R. § 172.101) and, if the waste is or contains a hazardous material listed and classified, must comply with the requirements indicated for the material in the Table. The shipping name must add the word "waste" to the name of the material. 49 C.F.R. § 172.101(c)(9).

If the waste contains a material that may be hazardous that is not listed in the Hazardous Materials Table, the shipper must nevertheless determine whether the material is hazardous by the methods prescribed in RSPA's hazard identification and classification regulations. If the material is hazardous, the shipper must comply with applicable requirements and add the word "waste" to the name of the material. 49 C.F.R. Part 173.

If a waste that is hazardous waste under RCRA is not, and does not contain, a material listed and classified in the Hazardous Materials Table or a material determined to be hazardous by the methods indicated by Part 173, then the shipper may describe it as "hazardous waste, liquid, n.o.s.," "hazardous waste, solid, n.o.s.," or "environmentally hazardous substance, n.o.s." Each of these wastes are in Class 9. See 49 C.F.R. § 173.8 and 173.140 to .144 and 173.155 and .156.

Once classified, the shipper must comply with all applicable RSPA regulations such as shipping papers, marking, labelling, placarding, recordkeeping and reporting as described previously. In general, the regulations of RSPA and the USEPA are sufficiently consistent that compliance with one system does not violate the other system. For example, the USEPA's Uniform Hazardous Waste Manifest Form 8700-22 is used as a shipping paper to fulfill RSPA's requirements. 40 C.F.R. § 172.205.

G. Recordkeeping, Reporting and Inspections

The HMTA provides that any person subject to its requirements must prepare and maintain records, prepare and submit reports, and provide to the DOT any information required by its provisions or by RSPA's regulations. 49 U.S.C. § 5121(b).

The HMTA authorizes DOT representatives to inspect properties and records relating to transportation of hazardous materials or to manufacturing or handling of containers used in transportation of hazardous materials. 49 U.S.C. § 5121(c).

H. Enforcement

Enforcement of the HMTA is allocated to the FRA for rail carriers and shipments; the FAA for air carriers and shipments; the USCG for water carriers and shipments; the FMCSA or state authorities for highway motor vehicle carriers and shipments; and RSPA for intermodal shipments.

The DOT may commence civil enforcement proceedings for knowing violations of the HMTA or any regulation or order thereunder, including investigations, subpoenas and violation notices. The DOT must allow the person to respond and to request a hearing before an administrative law judge whose decision is subject to appeal rights. The DOT may assess civil penalties from $250 to $27,500 per violation. 49 U.S.C. § 5123(a); 49 C.F.R. § 107.13-.329. RSPA has provided civil penalty guidelines at 49 C.F.R. § 107.133 and in Part 107, Appendix A. See also 60 Fed. Reg. 12,139 (1995).

The DOT may also issue warning letters or tickets for violations that do not have a direct or substantial impact on safety. Penalties for tickets are at reduced rates, but not less than $250. Recipients have 45 days to respond or pay. 49 C.F.R. § 107.309 and 310.

The DOT may request the U.S. Department of Justice to commence civil actions in the U.S. District Courts to enforce the HMTA, including DOT orders. However, the DOT can commence its own civil actions in the U.S. District Courts when it finds that an imminent hazard exists. 49 C.F.R. § 5123(d).

The amount of potential civil penalties can often be very large because the HMTA authorizes up to $27,500 per knowing violation per day for knowing violations. Like other federal statutes regulating industry, the HMTA does not require evidence of actual intent to break the law. The accused is held responsible for knowledge that a reasonable person acting in the circumstances and exercising reasonable care would have. 49 C.F.R. § 5123. A manufacturer was not excused from responsibility for proper packaging because it delivered drums to a domestic freight broker hired by a foreign customer to arrange air transportation. *NL Industries, Inc. v. U.S. Department of Transportation*. 901 F.2d 141 (D.C. Cir. 1990).

The HMTA also authorizes criminal proceedings for willful violations. Upon conviction, the defendant can be fined up to $25,000 and sentenced up to five years in prison. 49 C.F.R. § 5124. For a criminal conviction, actual wrongful intent must be proven. *U.S. v. Allied Chemical Corp.*, 431 F. Supp. 361 (W.D.N.Y. 1977).

I. Preemption

The HMTA preempts any requirement of a state or local government if compliance with the requirement and the HMTA or a regulation thereunder is impossible or if the requirement is an obstacle to compliance. 49 U.S.C. § 5125(a).

The HMTA also preempts any state or local requirement unless it is substantively the same as the HMTA provisions or DOT regulations governing the following:

1. The designation, description, and classification of hazardous material

2. The packing, repacking, handling, labeling, marking, and placarding of hazardous materials.

3. The preparation, execution, and use of shipping documents related to hazardous material, and requirements related to the number, contents, and placement of those documents.

4. The written notification, recording, and reporting of the unintentional release in transportation of hazardous material.

5. The design, manufacturing, fabricating, marking, maintenance, reconditioning, repairing, or testing of a package of container represented, marked, certified, or sold as qualified for use in transporting hazardous material. 49 U.S.C. § 5125(b).

State and local governments are not preempted from establishing, maintaining, and enforcing highway routing designations within the limits of § 5112 of the HMTA. 49 U.S.C. § 5125(c). Several federal courts have found preemption of routing and other requirements imposed by state and local governments because they did not comply with § 5112.

Several courts have held that the HMTA does not preempt state product liability law or laws regulating products. *Lyall v. Leslie's Poolmart, Inc.*, 984 F. Supp. 587 (E.D. Mich. 1997) and cases cited therein.

The HMTA authorizes state and local governments to apply to the DOT for a decision as to whether a requirement is preempted. 49 U.S.C. § 5125(d). A state or local government may also apply to the DOT for a waiver of preemption. 49 U.S.C. § 5125(e).

RSPA has adopted regulations on preemption standards, determinations and waivers. 49 C.F.R. § 107.201 *et seq.* See also the FMCSA's regulations on compatibility of state laws and regulations with the Federal Motor Carrier Safety Act. 49 C.F.R. Part 355.

EXHIBIT

1. DOT Chart 11 - Hazardous Materials Marking, Labeling & Placarding Guide

U.S. Department of Transportation
Research and Special Programs Administration

DOT CHART 11
Hazardous Materials Marking, Labeling & Placarding Guide

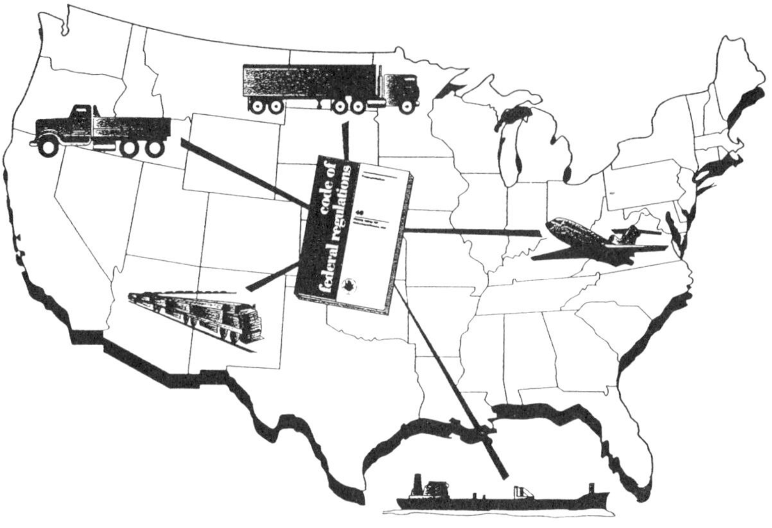

Refer to 49 CFR, Part 172:

Marking - Subpart D

Labeling - Subpart E

Placarding - Subpart F

Emergency Response - Subpart G

NOTE: This document is for general guidance only and must not be used to determine compliance with 49 CFR, Parts 100-185.

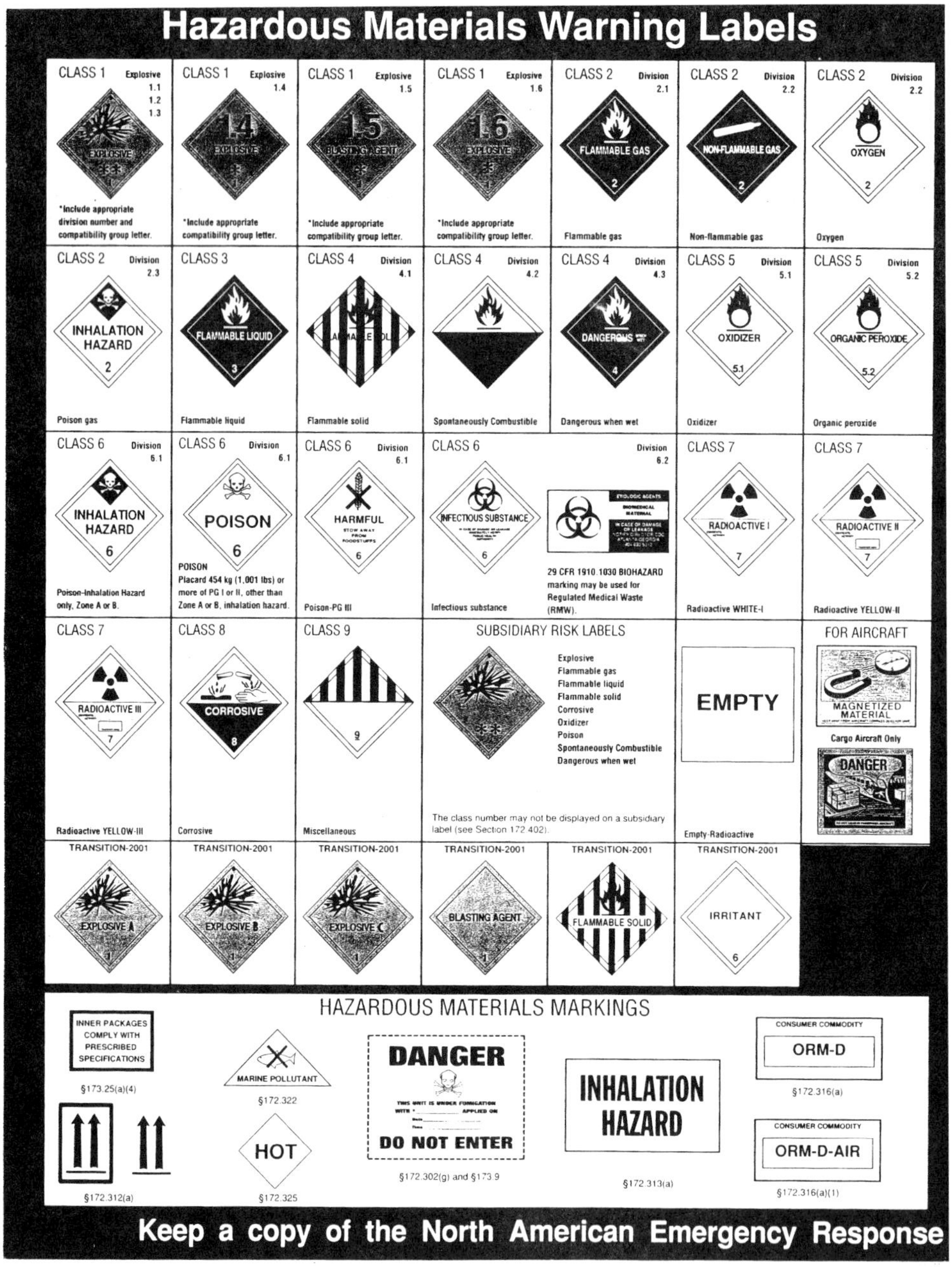
Hazardous Materials Warning Labels
CLASS 1 Explosive 1.1 1.2 1.3
EXPLOSIVE
*Include appropriate division number and compatibility group letter.
CLASS 1 Explosive 1.4
EXPLOSIVE
*Include appropriate compatibility group letter.
CLASS 1 Explosive 1.5
BLASTING AGENT
*Include appropriate compatibility group letter.
CLASS 1 Explosive 1.6
EXPLOSIVE
*Include appropriate compatibility group letter.
CLASS 2 Division 2.1
FLAMMABLE GAS
Flammable gas
CLASS 2 Division 2.2
NON-FLAMMABLE GAS
Non-flammable gas
CLASS 2 Division 2.2
OXYGEN
Oxygen
CLASS 2 Division 2.3
INHALATION HAZARD
Poison gas
CLASS 3
FLAMMABLE LIQUID
Flammable liquid
CLASS 4 Division 4.1
Flammable solid
CLASS 4 Division 4.2
Spontaneously Combustible
CLASS 4 Division 4.3
DANGEROUS WHEN WET
Dangerous when wet
CLASS 5 Division 5.1
OXIDIZER
Oxidizer
CLASS 5 Division 5.2
ORGANIC PEROXIDE
Organic peroxide
CLASS 6 Division 6.1
INHALATION HAZARD
Poison-Inhalation Hazard only, Zone A or B.
CLASS 6 Division 6.1
POISON
POISON Placard 454 kg (1,001 lbs) or more of PG I or II, other than Zone A or B, inhalation hazard.
CLASS 6 Division 6.1
HARMFUL
Poison-PG III
CLASS 6 Division 6.2
INFECTIOUS SUBSTANCE
Infectious substance
29 CFR 1910.1030 BIOHAZARD marking may be used for Regulated Medical Waste (RMW).
CLASS 7
RADIOACTIVE I
Radioactive WHITE-I
CLASS 7
RADIOACTIVE II
Radioactive YELLOW-II
CLASS 7
RADIOACTIVE III
Radioactive YELLOW-III
CLASS 8
CORROSIVE
Corrosive
CLASS 9
Miscellaneous
SUBSIDIARY RISK LABELS
Explosive
Flammable gas
Flammable liquid
Flammable solid
Corrosive
Oxidizer
Poison
Spontaneously Combustible
Dangerous when wet
The class number may not be displayed on a subsidiary label (see Section 172.402).
EMPTY
Empty-Radioactive
FOR AIRCRAFT
MAGNETIZED MATERIAL
Cargo Aircraft Only
DANGER
TRANSITION-2001
EXPLOSIVE A
TRANSITION-2001
EXPLOSIVE B
TRANSITION-2001
EXPLOSIVE C
TRANSITION-2001
BLASTING AGENT
TRANSITION-2001
FLAMMABLE SOLID
TRANSITION-2001
IRRITANT
HAZARDOUS MATERIALS MARKINGS
INNER PACKAGES COMPLY WITH PRESCRIBED SPECIFICATIONS
§173.25(a)(4)
§172.312(a)
MARINE POLLUTANT
§172.322
HOT
§172.325
DANGER
DO NOT ENTER
§172.302(g) and §173.9
INHALATION HAZARD
§172.313(a)
CONSUMER COMMODITY
ORM-D
§172.316(a)
CONSUMER COMMODITY
ORM-D-AIR
§172.316(a)(1)
Keep a copy of the North American Emergency Response

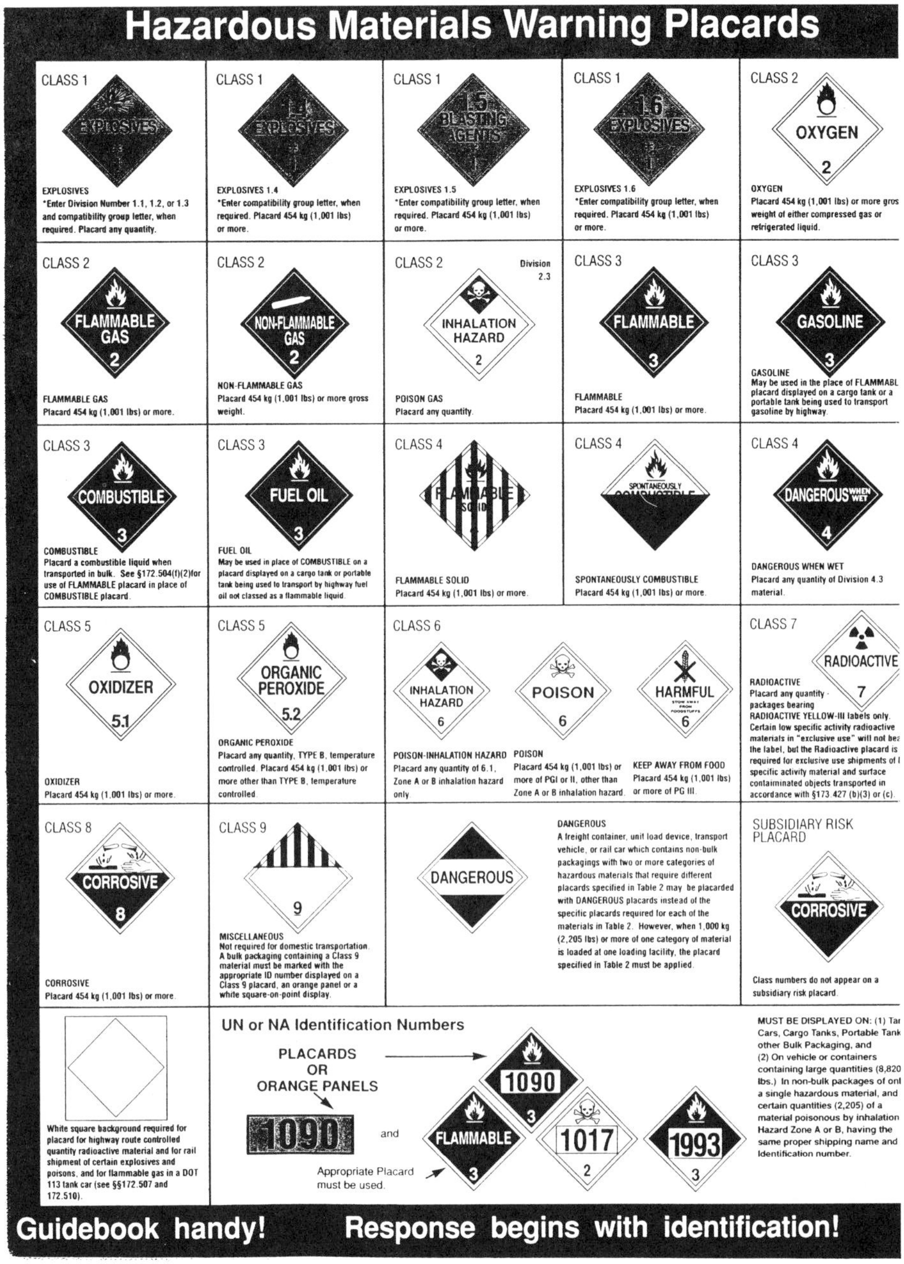
Hazardous Materials Warning Placards
CLASS 1
EXPLOSIVES
EXPLOSIVES
*Enter Division Number 1.1, 1.2, or 1.3 and compatibility group letter, when required. Placard any quantity.
CLASS 1
1.4
EXPLOSIVES
EXPLOSIVES 1.4
*Enter compatibility group letter, when required. Placard 454 kg (1,001 lbs) or more.
CLASS 1
1.5
BLASTING AGENTS
EXPLOSIVES 1.5
*Enter compatibility group letter, when required. Placard 454 kg (1,001 lbs) or more.
CLASS 1
1.6
EXPLOSIVES
EXPLOSIVES 1.6
*Enter compatibility group letter, when required. Placard 454 kg (1,001 lbs) or more.
CLASS 2
OXYGEN
2
OXYGEN
Placard 454 kg (1,001 lbs) or more gros weight of either compressed gas or refrigerated liquid.
CLASS 2
FLAMMABLE GAS
2
FLAMMABLE GAS
Placard 454 kg (1,001 lbs) or more.
CLASS 2
NON-FLAMMABLE GAS
2
NON-FLAMMABLE GAS
Placard 454 kg (1,001 lbs) or more gross weight.
CLASS 2
Division 2.3
INHALATION HAZARD
2
POISON GAS
Placard any quantity.
CLASS 3
FLAMMABLE
3
FLAMMABLE
Placard 454 kg (1,001 lbs) or more.
CLASS 3
GASOLINE
3
GASOLINE
May be used in the place of FLAMMABL placard displayed on a cargo tank or a portable tank being used to transport gasoline by highway.
CLASS 3
COMBUSTIBLE
3
COMBUSTIBLE
Placard a combustible liquid when transported in bulk. See §172.504(f)(2)for use of FLAMMABLE placard in place of COMBUSTIBLE placard.
CLASS 3
FUEL OIL
3
FUEL OIL
May be used in place of COMBUSTIBLE on a placard displayed on a cargo tank or portable tank being used to transport by highway fuel oil not classed as a flammable liquid.
CLASS 4
FLAMMABLE SOLID
FLAMMABLE SOLID
Placard 454 kg (1,001 lbs) or more.
CLASS 4
SPONTANEOUSLY
SPONTANEOUSLY COMBUSTIBLE
Placard 454 kg (1,001 lbs) or more.
CLASS 4
DANGEROUS WHEN WET
4
DANGEROUS WHEN WET
Placard any quantity of Division 4.3 material.
CLASS 5
OXIDIZER
5.1
OXIDIZER
Placard 454 kg (1,001 lbs) or more.
CLASS 5
ORGANIC PEROXIDE
5.2
ORGANIC PEROXIDE
Placard any quantity, TYPE B, temperature controlled. Placard 454 kg (1,001 lbs) or more other than TYPE B, temperature controlled.
CLASS 6
INHALATION HAZARD
6
POISON
6
HARMFUL
STOW AWAY FROM FOODSTUFFS
6
POISON-INHALATION HAZARD
Placard any quantity of 6.1, Zone A or B inhalation hazard only.
POISON
Placard 454 kg (1,001 lbs) or more of PGI or II, other than Zone A or B inhalation hazard.
KEEP AWAY FROM FOOD
Placard 454 kg (1,001 lbs) or more of PG III.
CLASS 7
RADIOACTIVE
7
RADIOACTIVE
Placard any quantity - packages bearing RADIOACTIVE YELLOW-III labels only. Certain low specific activity radioactive materials in "exclusive use" will not bea the label, but the Radioactive placard is required for exclusive use shipments of l specific activity material and surface contaiminated objects transported in accordance with §173.427 (b)(3) or (c).
CLASS 8
CORROSIVE
8
CORROSIVE
Placard 454 kg (1,001 lbs) or more.
CLASS 9
9
MISCELLANEOUS
Not required for domestic transportation. A bulk packaging containing a Class 9 material must be marked with the appropriate ID number displayed on a Class 9 placard, an orange panel or a white square-on-point display.
DANGEROUS
DANGEROUS
A freight container, unit load device, transport vehicle, or rail car which contains non-bulk packagings with two or more categories of hazardous materials that require different placards specified in Table 2 may be placarded with DANGEROUS placards instead of the specific placards required for each of the materials in Table 2. However, when 1,000 kg (2,205 lbs) or more of one category of material is loaded at one loading facility, the placard specified in Table 2 must be applied.
SUBSIDIARY RISK PLACARD
CORROSIVE
Class numbers do not appear on a subsidiary risk placard.
White square background required for placard for highway route controlled quantity radioactive material and for rail shipment of certain explosives and poisons, and for flammable gas in a DOT 113 tank car (see §§172.507 and 172.510).
UN or NA Identification Numbers
PLACARDS OR ORANGE PANELS
1090
and
Appropriate Placard must be used.
1090
3
FLAMMABLE
3
1017
2
1993
3
MUST BE DISPLAYED ON: (1) Tar Cars, Cargo Tanks, Portable Tank other Bulk Packaging, and (2) On vehicle or containers containing large quantities (8,820 lbs.) In non-bulk packages of onl a single hazardous material, and certain quantities (2,205) of a material poisonous by inhalation Hazard Zone A or B, having the same proper shipping name and Identification number.
Guidebook handy! Response begins with identification!

General Guidelines on Use of Warning Labels and Placards

LABELS

See 49 CFR, Part 172, Subpart E for complete labeling regulations.

- Until October 1, 1999, labels for materials poisonous by inhalation that conform to the requirements of the HMR in effect on September 30, 1997, may be used to satisfy the requirements of Subpart E.
- Those labels in boxes marked "TRANSITION-2001" on the chart are not authorized for use under Subpart E. (NOTE: these labels may be used IF they were affixed to a package offered for transportation and transported prior to October 1, 2001, and the package was filled with hazardous materials prior to October 1, 1991.)
- For classes 1,2,3,4,5,6 and 8, text indicating a hazard (e.g., "CORROSIVE") IS NOT required on a label. The label must otherwise conform to Subpart E [Section 172.405].
- Any person who offers a hazardous material for transportation MUST label the package, if required [Section 172.400(a)].
- The Hazardous Materials Table [Section 172.101] identifies the proper label(s) for the hazardous material listed.
- When required, labels must be printed on or affixed to the surface of the package near the proper shipping name [Section 172.406(a)].
- When two or more labels are required, they must be displayed next to each other [Section 172.406(c)].
- Labels may be affixed to packages when not required by regulations, provided each label represents a hazard of the material contained in the package [Section 172.401].

PLACARDS

See 49 CFR, Part 172, Subpart F for complete placarding regulations.

- Until October 1, 2001, placards for materials poisonous by inhalation, by all modes of transportation, may be used that conform to specifications for placards (1) in effect on September 30, 1991, (2) specified in the December 21, 1990 final rule, (HM-181) or (3) specified in the July 22, 1997 final rule (HM-206).
- All of the placards appearing on the Hazardous Materials Warning Placards chart may be used to satisfy the placarding requirements contained in Subpart F.
- Each person who offers for transportation or transports any hazardous material subject to the Hazardous Materials Regulations shall comply with all applicable requirements of Subpart F.
- Placards may be displayed for a hazardous material even when not required, if the placarding otherwise conforms to the requirements of Subpart F.
- For other than Class 7 or the OXYGEN placard, text indicating a hazard (e.g., "CORROSIVE") is not required on a placard [Section 172.519(b)].
- Any transport vehicle, freight container, or rail car containing any quantity of material listed in Table 1 must be placarded [Section 172.504].
- When the gross weight of all hazardous materials in non-bulk pkgs. covered in Table 2 is less than 454 kg (1,001 lbs), no placard is required on a transport vehicle or freight container [Section 172.504].

Effective October 1, 1994, and extending through October 1, 2001, these placards may be used for HIGHWAY TRANSPORTATION ONLY.

Illustration numbers in each square refer to Tables 1 and 2 below.

Inhalation Hazard Materials

Materials which meet the inhalation toxicity criteria have additional "communication standards" prescribed by the HMR. First, the words "Poison-Inhalation Hazard" must be entered on the shipping paper, as required by Section 172.203(m)(3). Second, packagings must be marked "Inhalation Hazard" or, alternatively, when the words "Inhalation Hazard" appear on the label or placard, the "Inhalation Hazard" marking is not required on the package. Transport vehicles, freight containers, portable tanks and unit load devices that contain a poisonous material subject to the "Poison-Inhalation Hazard" shipping description, must be placarded with a POISON INHALATION HAZARD or POISON GAS placard, as appropriate. This shall be in addition to any other placard required for that material in Section 172.504.

Table 1 (Placard any quantity)

Hazard class or division	Placard name
1.1	EXPLOSIVES 1.1
1.2	EXPLOSIVES 1.2
1.3	EXPLOSIVES 1.3
2.3	POISON GAS
4.3	DANGEROUS WHEN WET
5.2 (Organic peroxide, Type B, liquid or solid, temperature controlled)	ORGANIC PEROXIDE
6.1 (Inhalation Hazard, Zone A or B)	POISON INHALATION HAZARD
7 (Radioactive Yellow III label only)	RADIOACTIVE

Table 2 (Placard 1,001 pounds or more)

1.4	EXPLOSIVES 1.4
1.5	EXPLOSIVES 1.5
1.6	EXPLOSIVES 1.6
2.1	FLAMMABLE GAS
2.2	NON-FLAMMABLE GAS
3	FLAMMABLE
Combustible Liquid	COMBUSTIBLE
4.1	FLAMMABLE SOLID
4.2	SPONTANEOUSLY COMBUSTIBLE
5.1	OXIDIZER
5.2 (Other than organic peroxide, Type B, liquid or solid, temperature controlled)	ORGANIC PEROXIDE
6.1 (PG I or II, other than Zone A or B inhalation hazard)	POISON
6.1 (PG III)	KEEP AWAY FROM FOOD
6.2	NONE
8	CORROSIVE
9	CLASS 9
ORM-D	NONE

For complete details, refer to one or more of the following:

- Code of Federal Regulations, Title 49, Transportation, Parts 100-185. [All modes]
- International Civil Aviation Organization (ICAO) Technical Instructions for Safe Transport of Dangerous Goods by Air [Air]
- International Maritime Organization (IMO) Dangerous Goods Code [Water]
- Transportation of Dangerous Goods Regulations of Transport Canada. [All Modes]

U.S. Department of Transportation
Research and Special Programs Administration

Copies of this Chart can be obtained by writing
OHMIT/DHM-51,
Washington, D.C. 20590
or
Phone: **202-366-4900**
E-mail: **training@rspa.dot.gov**
Web site: **http//hazmat.dot.gov**

CHART 11
REV. JULY 1998

CHAPTER XIV
OCEAN DISPOSAL OF WASTE

A. The Marine Protection, Research and Sanctuaries Act

The Marine Protection, Research and Sanctuaries Act (MPRSA), 33 U.S.C. § 1401 *et seq.*, prohibits ocean disposal of radiological, chemical and biological warfare agents, high level radioactive wastes and medical wastes. The MPRSA requires a permit from the USEPA for ocean disposal of other substances. However, the U.S. Army Corps of Engineers is authorized to issue permits for ocean disposal of dredged material. The U.S. Coast Guard also participates in the administration and enforcement of the MPRSA.

The USEPA's regulations under the MPRSA are at 40 C.F.R. Part 220 *et seq.* No discussion of these regulations is provided because the USEPA has rarely granted permits for ocean disposal. In effect, the USEPA phased out ocean disposal of industrial waste during the 1980s and of municipal sewage sludge in the early 1990s.

The Corps of Engineers' permit regulations are at 33 C.F.R. Part 320 *et seq.* Ocean disposal is governed by 33 C.F.R. Part 325. The USEPA has authority to disapprove a dredging and filling permit granted by the Corps of Engineers. The USEPA's regulations for reviewing permits granted by the Corps of Engineers at 40 C.F.R. Part 225.

The Corps of Engineers continues to issue dredging and filling permits because, among other reasons, it is essential to maintain harbors open for shipping. As ships have grown larger, ports such as Boston, Baltimore, Elizabeth, New York, and Norfolk must dredge and fill to maintain existing channels and must also deepen channels.

Permits for dredging of mud and silt in the East and Hudson Rivers adjacent to Manhattan Island and their disposal in a 31 acre pit in Newark Bay near Elizabeth, New Jersey were issued with unusual promptness. *The New York Times*, October 2, 2001, page B7 and October 9, 2001, page B13. The need for the barge ports was to transport enormous quantities of debris from the ruins of the World Trade Center where the author taught courses for several years before September 11, 2001. The author recommends reading the articles which describe the kind of giant tasks which the Corps of Engineers is so often asked to undertake.

In the early days of the MPRSA, Waste Management, Inc. and other entrepreneurs who had encountered difficulty obtaining permits for disposal by landfill and by incineration within the United States sought permits to incinerate industrial hazardous waste on vessels at sea. Although it temporarily granted permits for limited evaluation programs, the USEPA was strongly opposed to incineration at sea. Thus, the USEPA cooperated with environmental organization allies who campaigned against ocean incineration. The USEPA then found that ocean incineration was equivalent to ocean dumping, denied the permits and declined to adopt final permit regulations for ocean incineration. The courts upheld the USEPA's decisions. *Seaburn, Inc. v. USEPA*, 712 F. Supp. 218 (D.D.C. 1989); *Waste Management, Inc. v. USEPA*, 669 F. Supp. 536 (D.D.C. 1987).

The U.S. Coast Guard has adopted regulations that would apply if ocean incineration should ever be permitted. 46 C.F.R. Part 150. However, it seems unlikely that serious efforts will be made in the near future. The USEPA has imposed regulatory restrictions and costs on land-based incineration facilities that prevent them from having any major advantage over competitive disposal methods. It is foreseeable that the USEPA would do the same if the MPRSA should be amended to require consideration of ocean incineration.

Any further consideration of ocean disposal by incineration or other means would also require consideration of the Convention for the Prevention of Marine Pollution by Dumping from Ships and Aircraft, a treaty signed in 1972 by many nations at Oslo, Norway, and the Convention on the Prevention of Marine Pollution by Dumping of Waste or Other Matter, a treaty signed by many nations (including the United States) in 1972 at London, England.

The MPRSA provides civil and criminal penalties for violations and authorizes seizure and forfeiture of vessels used to commit violations. 33 U.S.C. § 1415(a), (b) and (i).

The MPRSA authorizes civil suits by private persons in the U.S. District Courts including awards of attorneys fees. 33 U.S.C. § 1415(g). *Save our Sound Fisheries Ass'n v Callaway*, 429 F. Supp. 1136 (D.R.I. 1977). Private civil suits have often been successful. However, when environmental groups attacked permits on solely technical grounds and failed to recognize the importance of port activities, some courts decided against them. *Clean Ocean Action v. York*, 57 F.3d 328 (3d Cir. 1995); *National Wildlife Fed'n v. Benn*, 491 F. Supp. 1234 (S.D.N.Y. 1980). In the *Clean Ocean Action* decision, the U.S. Circuit Court of Appeals for the Third Circuit, which is usually pro-environmental, held that the environmental plaintiffs were correct in their arguments on analytical test methods, but denied an injunction against the Corps of Engineers on grounds that port activities have extraordinary economic importance to carriers, longshoremen and the public.

B. The Act to Prevent Pollution from Ships

The Act to Prevent Pollution from Ships (APPS) was adopted primarily to implement the Regulations for the Prevention of Pollution by Garbage from Ships which are annexed to the International Convention for the Prevention of Pollution from Ships, 1973, as amended by the Protocol of 1978. The APPS also includes provisions implementing the Protocol on Environmental Protection to the Antarctic Treaty signed in 1991 at Madrid, Spain. 33 U.S.C. § 1901 *et seq.* The APPS refers to these treaties as the MARPOL Protocol and the Antarctic Protocol.

The APPS applies to ships of United States registry or nationality, or operated by the authority of the United States, wherever located. The APPS also applies to other ships which are required to comply with one of more provisions while in the navigable waters, exclusive economic zone or any port or terminal of the United States. Exclusions apply to submarines owned or operated by the U.S. Navy and ships specifically excluded by the Protocols. However, the APPS requires the U.S. Navy to develop technologies and practices to reduce waste streams generated aboard ships and improved waste disposal processes. The restrictions do not apply during time of war or a declared national emergency.

The APPS declares it to be unlawful to violate the MARPOL Protocol or the Antarctic Protocol and authorizes ships inspections as part of its enforcement methods. 33 U.S.C. § 1907. The APPS imposes criminal fines and civil penalties for violations. Clearances may be refused or revoked if there is reasonable cause to believe that a ship, its owner, operator, or person in charge may be subject to a fine or penalty. 33 U.S.C. § 1908.

U.S. Coast Guard regulations under the APPS are at 33 C.F.R. Part 151.

CHAPTER XV
THE OCCUPATIONAL SAFETY AND HEALTH ACT

A. General

The Occupational Safety and Health Act (the "OSH Act") was enacted in 1970. 29 U.S.C. § 651 *et seq*. A related law, the Federal Mine Safety and Health Act (the "MSH Act") was enacted in 1977. 30 U.S.C. §§ 801 *et seq*. This chapter will discuss primarily the OSH Act which has broader coverage.

Primary responsibility to administer the OSH Act and the MSH Act is assigned to the U.S. Department of Labor (DOL) which does so through its Occupational Safety and Health Administration (OSHA) and its Mine Safety and Health Administration (MSHA).

Other scientific and administrative responsibilities are assigned to the National Institute for Occupational Safety and Health (NIOSH) which reports to the Centers for Disease Control and Prevention (CDC), an organization within the U.S. Department of Health and Human Services (DHHS).

Both OSHA and MSHA are part of the DOL which has extensive responsibilities to protect and enhance the welfare of workers throughout the United States. Thus, neither OSHA nor MSHA is an "independent" agency conceptually free of the policies of the executive branch of the U.S. Government. Thus, the OSH Act created the Occupational Safety and Health Review Commission (OSHRC) and the MSH Act created the Mine Safety and Health Review Commission (MSHRC) as "independent" commissions to review civil proceedings and penalties imposed by OSHA and MSHA, respectively.

States which wish to administer the OSH Act may apply to OSHA and demonstrate satisfactory legal authority and administrative and financial resources to do so effectively. About half the states now administer their own programs. In the other states, OSHA administers the OSH Act directly through its regional and local offices.

The OSH Act places upon each employer a general duty to furnish employment and a workplace free from recognized hazards causing or likely to cause death or serious physical harm. Both employers and employees must comply with the standards and the rules, regulations and orders of OSHA, although the obligations of employers are far more extensive.

OSHA has adopted many regulations under the Act. 29 C.F.R. Part 1900 *et seq.* They include safety and health standards; review and approval of state plans; inspections, citations and penalties; recording and reporting of occupational injuries and illnesses; accreditation of testing laboratories. An index to the numerous safety and health standards is provided following 29 C.F.R. § 1910.1500. MSHA's regulations are found at 30 C.F.R. Part 104 *et seq.*

B. Applicability of OSHA

OSHA applies very broadly to any employer having one or more employees. Thus, OSHA applies to thousands of very small employers often excluded from other laws such as professional and service firms, nonprofit organizations, and agricultural employers.

The definition of an employer excludes the United States or any state or subdivision of a state, but does include the U.S. Post Office. However, Executive Orders require federal government agencies to establish similar programs. Further, the OSH Act requires any state seeking OSHA's approval to administer the program to establish a program for its state and local employees. In some states, such as New York, the state has obtained approval from OSHA only to administer a program for state and local employees. OSHA directly regulates private employers in those states.

OSHA does not apply to self-employed individuals; domestic household workers in private residences; immediate family members of farmers; and persons who perform or participate in religious services. 49 C.F.R. Part 1975. However, when religious organizations employ workers for other activities, the OSH Act applies to them.

C. The "General Duty" Provision

OSHA actively enforces the "general duty" of employers to furnish employment and a place of employment free from recognized hazards causing or likely to cause death or serious harm. 29 U.S.C. § 654(a)(1).

OSHA must show the following to support an alleged violation of the general duty provision: (1) a hazard existed in the workplace; (2) the employer recognized the hazard; (3) the hazard was likely to cause death or serious harm; and (4) the employer had available a feasible method that was likely to protect its workers from the hazard.

Compliance with OSHA's standards will ordinarily be accepted as compliance with the general duty provision. However, if an employer recognizes that an OSHA standard has become inadequate to protect workers, compliance with the standard is not necessarily a defense to a charge of violation. *International Union, UAW v. General Dynamics*, 815 F.2d 1570 (D.C.Cir. 1988).

OSHA can use both direct and constructive knowledge to show that an employer recognized a hazard. An employer cannot deny recognition if its own employees and former employees admit knowledge of the hazard or if it is generally known in the industry. *McKie Ford, Inc. v. Secretary of Labor*, 191 F. 3d 853 (8th Cir. 1999); *Bethlehem Steel v. OSHRC*, 607 F.2d 871 (3rd Cir. 1979).

Whether a feasible abatement method was available has been a frequently contested issue, particularly as to the extent cost should be weighed as an element of feasibility. In early decisions, some federal appeals courts ruled that the cost of a protective method does not prevent feasibility if it is only burdensome but not prohibitive. *American Textile Manufacturers v. Donovan*, 452 U.S. 490, 101 S. Ct. 2478 (1981); *Industrial Union v. Hodgson*, 499 F.2d 467 (2d Cir. 1975); cert. den. 421 U.S. 922 (1975). However, other cases in which OSHA argued for engineering controls rather than personal protective equipment to abate excessive noise levels, some courts held that cost-benefit analysis must be used in determining feasibility. *Turner Co. v. Secretary of Labor*, 561 F.2d 82 (7th Cir. 1977); *Donovan v. Castle & Cook*, 692 F.2d 641 (9th Cir. 1982).

The federal courts have disagreed as to whether OSHA or the employee has the burden of proof on the issue of feasibility. *Modern Continental v. OSHRC*, 196 F.2d 274 (1st Cir. 1999).

When considering a feasibility defense, employers should recognize that the courts defer to the decision of OSHA if it is supported by substantial evidence. Thus, an employer will have to build a very strong case in order to prevail. *Union Tank Car v. OSHRC*, 192 F.3d 701 (7th Cir. 1999); *Puffer's Hardware, Inc. v. Donovan*, 742 F.2d 12 (1st Cir. 1984).

D. Safety and Health

1. Standards Groups

OSHA has issued its standards in four broad groups; General Industry (40 C.F.R. Part 1910); Construction (40 C.F.R. Part 1926); Agricultural Operations (49 C.F.R. Part 1928); and Maritime Employment (40 C.F.R. Part 1915). These groups allow the standards to focus on conditions in each industry. This is specially important for the construction industry which tends to have high accident rates.

2. National Consensus Standards

National consensus standards on safety and health were adopted by OSHA shortly after the Act became effective based on existing standards of other government agencies and industry organizations. A list of standards incorporated by reference to standards of ANSI, ASTM, NFPA and other industry organizations is provided at the end of 29 C.F.R. § 1910.1500.

3. Safety Standards

Safety standards adopted by OSHA are numerous and detailed. They include design and performance specifications for equipment used in the workplace such as machinery, tools, electrical systems, compressed gases, vehicles, and personal protective equipment worn by workers.

OSHA's safety standards are so fundamental that the public sometimes fails to recognize their importance. They provide for such steps as exits marked with signs and lights that can be seen in emergencies; guards on machines and handtools to prevent cutting of fingers and hands; coded insulation for electrical wiring; safety valves for compressed gas equipment; designs and methods for welding and cutting torches; first aid and medical resources; confined space entry; and personal protective equipment such as air purifying respirators, impermeable gloves and "moon suits" when full dress protection is needed.

OSHA's standards differ from those of the USEPA in that they do not require employers to apply for permits to carry on their activities. However, they require recordkeeping and reporting and are enforced by inspections, as described later in this Chapter.

4. Health Standards

OSHA's health standards are strict and are the most effective regulatory protection of health furnished by the federal government. Indeed, OSHA's health standards have sometimes been challenged in court by industry because of their strictness. A contributing factor to these challenges is the OSHA tradition of active enforcement against small and medium-sized businesses as well as large businesses. OSHA's broad inspection and enforcement policy benefits workers who most need protection. However, the policy results in active opposition by some small and medium-sized businesses who know that OSHA will require them to comply and fear the cost and difficulty of doing so.

Many of OSHA's health standards are found in 29 C.F.R. Part 1910, Subpart Z. Among them are the air contaminants, asbestos and lead standards which will be further described later in this chapter. The famous technology forcing vinyl chloride monomer standard and standards for inorganic arsenic, coke oven emissions, cotton dust, acrylonitrile, benzene, beta-propiolactone (BPA), N-nitrosodimethylamine (NTA) and others. These standards have affected not only the specific chemicals, but have been models for industry in formulating chemical products and designing processes for chemicals with similar characteristics. For example, manufacturers learned to formulate with materials having lower vapor emissions such as the use of methyl diisocyanate (MDI) over toluene diisocyanate (TDI) where worker exposure is likely. In recent years, chemical processes are more and more frequently designed as fully enclosed systems and to recapture and recycle materials that are not fully reacted.

5. The Hazard Communication Standard

Building on the experience of the Research and Special Projects Administration (RSPA) of the U.S. Department of Transportation and methods developed by industry, OSHA adopted in 1983 its Hazard Communication Standard (HCS). 29 C.F.R. § 1910.1200 The HCS has had great influence throughout the United States and elsewhere in the world. Before describing the HCS, some explanation of its significance is worthwhile.

The HCS achieved a cultural change through its recognition of worker and customer rights to know about chemical hazards. This recognition led to recognition of broader public rights to know. At the time, there was real and serious concern that the required disclosures would sacrifice trade secrets and allow irresponsible persons to create "scares." Those fears have come true to some extent, but the benefits of the HCS to industry, workers and the public have outweighed the disadvantages.

The HCS was formally adopted by OSHA in 1983 with deferred deadlines for compliance. However, some companies had been using its methods, such as enhanced labelling and material safety data sheets, since as early as the mid-1970s.

A key concept in the HCS was the requirement to disclose chronic hazards as well as imminent hazards. It soon became clear to many employers that they lacked adequate information about chronic hazards needed to comply with the HCS. Even though testing was not specifically required, employers and their industry organizations greatly increased their testing for both imminent and chronic hazards. Toxicology grew from a minor to a major profession over a relatively few years because sponsors were ready to pay for improved skills and equipment.

A second key concept was to clarify disclosure of hazards and the steps needed to protect against them. For example, warnings about flammable vapors from paints or other solvent-based products were improved from a simple "Keep away from fire" to specifically warn that the vapors might migrate to a pilot light located at some distance.

A third key concept was to require written compliance programs including formal employee training. Both employers and employees tended to dislike formal programs because they were often unimaginative, repetitive and time-consuming. However, when the programs became mandatory, employers and employees found ways to make them meaningful and effective.

The HCS applies broadly to employers including not only chemical manufacturers, importers and distributors, but also users of chemicals. Exemptions from other requirements of the OSH Act may not include HCS compliance.

The key mechanisms used to implement the HCS are hazard determination; written compliance programs; labelling and warning; material safety data sheets

(MSDS); employee information and training; recordkeeping, and inspections. OSHA's inspectors have been instructed to emphasize HCS compliance during inspections.

a. Hazard Determination

Compliance with the HCS begins with evaluation of chemicals to determine their physical and health hazards, both imminent and chronic. The HCS prescribes detailed methods for determining physical hazards. For example, the flashpoints for determining combustible or flammable liquids must be determined by using Tagliabue, Pensky-Martens or Setaflash closed cup testing equipment and specific ASTM methods.

Although testing is not required to determine health hazards, the available scientific evidence must be evaluated such as the following:

1. The definitions in Appendix A of the HCS of chemicals which must be considered a carcinogen, corrosive, highly toxic, an irritant, a sensitizer, or toxic.

2. The evaluation criteria in Appendix B of the HCS that require disclosure of the results of scientifically valid studies which report statistically significant conclusions, regardless of whether the employer agrees with them. However, *in vitro* studies alone do not establish that a substance is hazardous.

Chemical manufacturers, importers and employers must treat the following sources as establishing the chemicals listed in them as hazardous: (1) the list of toxic and hazardous substances in 29 C.F.R. Part 1910, Subpart Z and (2) the lists in the Threshold Limit Values (TLVs) for Chemical Substances and Physical Agents in the Work Environment published by ACGIH.

Chemical manufacturers, importers and employers must treat the following sources as establishing that a chemical is a carcinogen or potential carcinogen: (1) the National Toxicology Program (NTP) Annual Report on Carcinogens, (2) the International Agency for Research on Cancer (IARC) Monographs, and (3) the chemicals listed as carcinogens in 29 C.F.R. Part 1910, Subpart Z. The Registry of Toxic Effects of Chemical Substances published by NIOSH indicates whether a chemical has been found by NTP or IARC to be a potential carcinogen.

The NTP's reports are often published after long delays when scientific work has progressed beyond the descriptions in the report. The author recommends a call to the NTP scientists to determine which there have been significant subsequent developments. The author also recommends obtaining the IARC Monographs from IARC through the Internet.

b. Written Hazard Communication Program

Employer must develop, implement and maintain at each workplace a written hazard communication program that describes how the labelling and warning, MSDS, and employee information and training requirements will be met and which also includes (1) a list of the chemicals known to be present and (2) the methods the employer will use to inform employees of the hazards of non-routine tasks and the hazards of chemicals contained in unlabelled pipes. Employers in multi-employer workplaces must cooperate to ensure that all their employees are informed about the hazards of chemicals and the related protective measures.

c. Labels and Other Warnings

Each chemical manufacturer, importer or distributor must ensure that each container of hazardous chemicals is labeled, tagged or marked with (1) the identify of the hazardous chemical, (2) appropriate hazard warnings, and (3) the name and address of the manufacturer, importer or other responsible party. It must revise labels within three months after becoming aware of any significant new information. Each employer receiving hazardous chemicals has corresponding obligations to ensure that each container is properly labeled, tagged or marked to identify the hazardous chemicals and to provide appropriate warnings of their physical and health hazards. It may not remove or deface existing labels. Warning language must be in English, but employers may add information in other languages if they have employees who speak other languages.

d. Material Safety Data Sheets

Chemical manufacturers and importers must develop or obtain an MSDS for each hazardous chemical they produce or import. Employers must have an MSDS in the workplace for each hazardous chemical they use.

The MSDS must state the identity of the hazardous chemical as used on its label and its chemical and common name if it is a single substance. If it is a mixture which has been tested as a whole to determine its hazards, the MSDS must contain the chemical and common names of the ingredients which contribute to the known hazards and the common name of the mixture. If it is a mixture that has not been tested as a whole, the MSDS must contain the chemical and common names of (1) all ingredients determined to present a physical hazard and (2) all ingredients determined to be health hazards and which comprise:

1. 1% or more of the composition, except that carcinogens must be listed if the concentrations are 0.1% or more.

2. Less than 1% (0.1% for carcinogens) of the mixture if they could be released in concentrations which would exceed a PEL (OSHA) or a TLV (ACGIH) or could present a health risk to employees.

The MSDS must also describe the physical and chemical characteristics of the hazardous chemical; the physical hazards; the health hazards including symptoms and medical conditions aggravated by exposure to the chemical; the primary routes of entry; the PEL, TLV and any other recommended exposure limits; any listing as a potential carcinogen by the NTP, IARC or OSHA; any generally applicable safe handling and use precautions known to the manufacturer, importer or employer preparing the MSDS; any generally applicable control measures known to the preparer of the MSDS such as engineering controls, work practices or personal protective equipment; emergency and first aid procedures; the date of preparation of the MSDS or the last change to it; and the name, address and telephone number of preparer or other responsible party who can provide additional information and emergency procedures, if necessary.

The HCS contains detailed requirements for distribution of MSDS by and to chemical manufacturers, importers and distributors and their maintenance in workplaces immediately available to employees and readily accessible to OSHA representatives.

e. Employee Information and Training

Employers must provide employees with effective information and training on hazardous chemicals in their work area at the time of their initial assignment and whenever a health hazard is introduced into their work area. Employees must be informed of the HCS requirements, the operations in their work areas where hazardous chemicals are present, and the location and availability of the HCS program including the lists of hazardous chemicals and MSDS. (Most employers fulfill this requirement by maintaining in each work area a loose-leaf folder or book containing the MSDS with a table of contents listing them.)

Employee training must include (1) methods and observations to detect the presence or release of a hazardous chemical in the work area; (2) physical and health hazards; (3) measures to protect themselves from exposure; and (4) the details of the HCS programs developed by the employer including an explanation of the labeling and MSDS system and how they can obtain and use hazard information.

f. Trade Secrets

The HCS authorizes the manufacturer, importer or employer to withhold the specific chemical identity from the MSDS if it is a *bona fide* trade secret. However, if a treating physician or nurse determines that a medical emergency exists and the specific identity is necessary for emergency or first aid treatment, the manufacturer, importer or employer must immediately disclose the specific identity to the treating physician or nurse, but may require a written statement of need and a confidentiality agreement. In non-emergency situations, disclosure of the specific identity to health professionals may also be required under more formal procedures including an adjudication of any disputed issues by OSHA.

The HCS has four appendices. Appendix A is specially important because it contains health hazard definitions such as "acute," "chronic," "carcinogen," "highly toxic," "irritant," "sensitizer" and "toxic." It also includes a list of chemicals grouped by their target organ effects. For each group, examples of signs and symptoms of the effects and the names of some chemicals associated with the effects. For example, the first group is hepatotoxins which are chemicals that produce liver damage. Signs and symptoms are jaundice and liver enlargement. Named associated chemicals are carbon tetrachloride and nitrosamines.

A copy of a nonmandatory form of MSDS appears at the end of this chapter. Employers who provide the required information are free to add supplemental information and many do so. Some persons wonder why industry has not challenged the authority of OSHA to extend the duties of chemical manufacturers and importers beyond their own employees to include their customers. The answer is that manufacturers and importers are concerned about safety and health and their customers want and need MSDS information.

6. Air Contaminants Standard

OSHA has adopted numerous standards for air contaminants which typically prescribe permissible exposure limits (PELs) expressed as the concentration of the contaminant in a specified volume of work place air. The standards require use of administrative and engineering controls. However, if they are not feasible, the employer may comply by using protective equipment and other protective measures to keep employee exposures within the PELs. Examples of engineering controls are air collection, filtration and ventilation equipment. Examples of protective equipment are the numerous kinds of respirators for which specifications are approved by NIOSH. 29 C.F.R. § 1910.1000.

The air contaminant standard contains three lists of air contaminants and their PELs. For some substances, the exposure limit is a concentration based on an 8-hour, time weighted average (TWA). For some substances, the standard imposes a short term exposure limit (STEL) based on a 15 minute TWA. For some substances, there is a ceiling or "peak" exposure which may not be exceeded at any time.

Any equipment and technical measures used to achieve compliance must be approved for each particular use by a competent industrial hygienist or other technically qualified person. If respirators are used, their use must comply with OSHA's respirator standard at 29 C.F.R. § 1910.134. The respirator standard, among other things, incorporates by reference the certification procedures of NIOSH in 42 C.F.R. Part 84.

On January 19, 1989, OSHA adopted and published at 54 Fed. Reg. 2,332 a final rule revising and greatly expanding its Air Contaminants Standard to establish PELs for several hundred hazardous substances, many of which were the subject of preexisting more lenient standards. However, the revised Air Contaminants Standard was vacated by court order in *AFL v. OSHA*. 965 F.2d 962 (11th Cir. 1992). Many businesses have chosen to comply voluntarily with the vacated Standard or to follow other standards such as those of the American Conference of Government Industrial Hygienists. (ACGIH). OSHA is considering adoption of stricter PELs for some of the hazardous substances that were part of the vacated standard.

7. Chemical Process Standard

In 1992, OSHA adopted a major standard for the management of the hazards of processes which manufacture or use any chemicals on a list of 137 toxic or reactive chemicals or flammable liquids and gases in quantities of 10,000 pounds or more. Retail facilities are excluded.

OSHA's chemical process standard is designed to reduce the threat of accidental releases of chemicals in the workplace. The standard recognizes that chemical processes are continually changing in response to technology and, therefore, places responsibility on the employer to make detailed written analyses of hazards involved in their processes and to adopt operating procedures, employee training, emergency response plans, pre-startup review procedures, mechanical integrity inspection procedures, hot work permits, incident investigation procedures and compliance audits. The written procedures must include management of change so that changes of chemicals, equipment and other elements are evaluated for their effects on the whole process. The standard also provides for access to information and participation by employees and their representatives, typically a labor union. The analysis must be reviewed and updated when a process changes and at least every five years. 29 C.F.R. § 1910.119.

The USEPA subsequently adopted a similar process safety management. The USEPA's standard is discussed in an earlier chapter.

8. Hazardous Waste Operations Standard

In 1989, OSHA adopted regulations governing hazardous waste and emergency response operations, commonly called the "HAZWOPER standard." The HAZWOPER standard applies to cleanup operations at uncontrolled hazardous waste sites under CERCLA and state law programs; corrective actions at treatment, storage and disposal (TSD) facilities under RCRA; and emergency response operations involving hazardous substances regardless of location. The standard requires that employers establish a written safety and health program and take other steps including site characterization and analysis; site control; training of management, supervisors and workers; medical surveillance; establishment of engineering control, work practice and personal protective equipment programs; air monitoring; information programs; container handling procedures; decontamination procedures; emergency response plans; sanitation facilities; new technology programs; and other special programs. 29 C.F.R. § 1910.120.

Like all requirements of the OSH Act, the HAZWOPER standard does not apply to state and local government employers and their employees. However, states which administer their own occupational safety and health programs approved by OSHA have adopted standards corresponding to the HAZWOPER standard. The USEPA has adopted a standard which is the same as the HAZWOPER standard and which applies to state and local government employers and their employees in states which do not administer their own programs with OSHA approval. 40 C.F.R. Part 311.

9. The Asbestos Standards

OSHA has a general industry standard for exposure to airborne asbestos. 29 C.F.R. § 1910.1001. OSHA also has an asbestos standard for the shipyard industry. 40 C.F.R. § 1915.1001. The shipyard standard is specially appropriate because most of the employees who incurred real and serious asbestos illnesses over the years were employed in shipyards building and repairing ships for the U.S. Navy which refused to waive its government immunity and pay for the workers' illnesses. OSHA also has a standard for the construction industry. 29 C.F.R. § 1926.1101. The construction standard is the most important standard today because sale of asbestos products was discontinued in the 1970s and the most serious potential exposure is now of the employees of asbestos abatement contractors.

The standards set a PEL of 0.1 fibers per cubic centimeter of workplace air, measured as an 8-hour, time-weighted average. They also contain other detailed requirements including exposure monitoring, worker training, engineering controls, respiratory protection, protective work clothing and equipment, housekeeping, medical surveillance, medical removal protection, record preparation and maintenance, and reporting.

The asbestos standard for general industry also imposes responsibilities on real property owners to prepare and maintain records of asbestos-containing materials and to notify tenants of their presence in rented space.

10. The Lead Standards

OSHA has lead standards for general industry (40 C.F.R. § 1910.1025), the construction industry (40 C.F.R. § 1926.62) and shipyard employment (40 C.F.R. § 1915.1025).

Lead has been banned as a gasoline additive (tetraethyl lead) and in consumer paints (pigments and driers). However, lead is very useful, and perhaps even irreplaceable, in other uses such as corrosion protection, radiation protection, and automotive and industrial batteries. Thus, unlike products such as asbestos insulation and PCB dielectric and heat transfer fluids, lead continues to be actively mined, manufactured into products, and sold in the United States.

OSHA's lead standards set a PEL of 50 micrograms of lead per cubic meter (50 ppm) of workplace air, measured as an 8-hour time-weighted average. They also contain other detailed requirements including exposure monitoring, worker training, engineering controls, protective work clothing and equipment, housekeeping, medical surveillance, medical removal protection, record preparation and maintenance, and reporting.

The Lead Industries Association assists its members and others in developing programs which comply with and supplement the standard. Thus, the major mining, primary and secondary smelting, battery manufacturing and recycling, and other companies have active safety and health programs.

The most important application of the standards today is the protection of workers for lead-based abatement contractors which include some small firms which hire workers who will work for low wages because they lack education and/or experience. OSHA's strict enforcement is a vital protection for these workers.

11. Bloodborne Pathogens Standard

In 1992, OSHA also adopted a bloodborne pathogens standard limiting occupational exposure to blood and other potentially infectious materials. The standard was developed in response to highly publicized incidents involving alleged transmission of the HIV virus and Hepatitis B in hospitals and in medical and dental offices. However, OSHA did not restrict the standard to the health care industry. It applies to any employer whose employees are occupationally exposed to blood or other potentially infectious materials. 29 C.F.R. § 1910.1030.

12. The Ergonomics Standard

After consideration for several years, OSHA issued an ergonomics standard in late 2000 despite opposition by industry, many members of congress, and promises made during the campaign which led to the election of President George W. Bush. 29 C.F.R. § 1910.900. For further information, see OSHA's announcement and explanation of the standard which used over 600 pages of the Federal Register. 65 Fed. Reg. § 66,261 to 66,870 (Nov. 14, 2000). In early 2001, Congress rescinded the standard under the Congressional Review Act. OSHA is expected to reconsider and repropose a revised standard at some time in the future.

OSHA has for some years used the general duty provision to require employers to furnish a workplace free of serious ergonomic hazards. *Secretary of Labor v. Pepperidge Farms, Inc.*, 17 OSHC 1993 (1997); *Secretary of Labor v. Beverly Enterprises*, 19 OSHC 1161 (2000). However, use of the general duty provision arises typically in enforcement proceedings, often after injuries have occurred. Although many employers adopt new worker protections voluntarily, some do not do so even after they learn of enforcement proceedings against other employers. Thus, OSHA proposed a standard to achieve wider compliance.

Concern about the standard began with its title because ergonomics is an innovative field that seeks to adapt working conditions to the physical needs and capabilities of employees. Even without a standard, employers are generally interested in ergonomics because suitable working conditions attract and retain capable employees, improve efficiency, and reduce lost time and claims due to injuries and illnesses. However, the field is new and far from an exact science.

The standard proposed by OSHA was not focussed on all ergonomic conditions, although its name suggested that goal. The standard applied to musculoskeletal disorders such as carpal tunnel syndrome, trigger finger, tendonitis, sciatica and low back pain. There is general agreement among medical experts, OSHA and other government regulators and industry that these problems exist and can be painful and even disabling. On the other hand, it is difficult to diagnose them and determine their causes. Medical practitioners must rely heavily on patients' statements as to the extent of pain and impairment of capabilities. Further musculoskeletal disorders are not unique to workplaces and most result from normal living conditions, especially sports activities.

The rescinded standard would have required all general industry employers to furnish information about musculoskeletal injuries to their employees, including the provisions of the standard. If an employee reported a musculoskeletal disorder, the employer would have been obligated to investigate and determine whether the employee's work exposed him or her to musculoskeletal hazards such as repetitive motion, lifting, stretching or vibration. The employee would also have been required to adopt a detailed program similar to those required by the asbestos and lead standards including work hazard analysis, reduction and control. The program would have included employee participation and training. Employees determined to be injured would have been entitled to continue to receive full pay and benefits for 90 days, although they were otherwise eligible for workers compensation benefits.

E. Recordkeeping and Reporting

1. Recordkeeping

OSHA's regulations require that employers prepare and maintain records of work-related injuries and illnesses. The general recordkeeping requirements apply to employers with more than ten employees, but exempt some employers in service fields where work-related injuries are relatively uncommon. 29 C.F.R. § 1904.16. Separate recordkeeping requirements are imposed by OSHA's standards such as the asbestos and lead standards.

Effective January 1, 2002, OSHA revised Part 1904. The descriptions in the next paragraphs include these revisions. 66 Fed. Reg. 5,915 (Jan. 19, 2001).

The heart of OSHA's general recordkeeping requirements are its Forms 300, 301 and 300-A. The regulations require that employers maintain a Form 300 Log of Work-Related Injuries and Illness and record on it within seven days each recordable injury or illness. They must also prepare within seven days a Form 301 Injury and Illness Incident Report for each recordable injury or illness providing further information that summarizes the contents of the Form 300 Log. The Form 300-A Summary must be posted conspicuously where notices to employees are customarily posted and be maintained from February 1 to at least April 30.

An injury or illness is recordable if it is work-related and new and if it resulted in death; loss of consciousness; lost days from work; assignment to restricted work or a transfer of work; or medical treatment beyond first aid. If a work-related injury or illness is diagnosed by a physician or licensed health care professional, it must also be recorded although it does not meet the foregoing criteria.

In the author's experience, employers have tended over the years to record many relatively small injuries, but few illnesses. Their tendency is to recognize that cuts, bruises, falls and other physical injuries are work-related, but to believe that illnesses are not recordable. However, OSHA's regulations specifically require recording of any work-related (1) cut from a needle or other sharp object that was contaminated with another persons's blood or other potentially infectious material; (2) medical removal of an employee pursuant to an OSHA health standard; (3) hearing loss of ten decibels in an employee's ear; or (4) tuberculosis infection after exposure to a known or active case in another worker. 29 C.F.R. §§ 1904.8-.12.

Whether an injury or illness is work-related is often obvious, but is sometimes very difficult to determine. OSHA's regulations provide general criteria which must be used for recordkeeping purposes, including several exceptions. 29 C.F.R. § 1904.5.

OSHA's regulations provide for confidential treatment of information about some kinds of injuries and illnesses such as mental illness and HIV infections.

2. Reporting

Employers must report to OSHA within 8 hours any work-related death or any hospitalization of three or more employees. They can report by telephone to the nearest OSHA office or to the toll free number 1-800-321-6742.

Employers subject to specific OSHA safety and health standards must also fulfill the reporting requirements in those standards.

Employers selected at random to answer annual injury and illness survey forms sent by OSHA and the Bureau of Labor Statistics must do so in an accurate and timely manner. Companies that have a policy not to respond to surveys from private sources should instruct their employees not to discard government surveys which may be mandatory.

F. Cooperative Programs, Training, Inspections and Enforcement

1. Consulting and Voluntary Protection

Among OSHA's most important methods to achieve compliance are its consulting and voluntary protection programs. In an active economy such as prevails in the United States, thousands of people go into businesses every year and become employers. Many of the new employers are small or are founded by people whose prior experience did not include safety and health responsibilities. They need guidance to achieve compliance. On the other hand, some experienced employers voluntarily establish safety and health programs that go well beyond the standards established by OSHA. They have sought recognition of their programs by OSHA as a source of good employee relations and public relations and freedom from routine inspections.

OSHA funds state agencies and educational institutions to provide free consulting services, primarily to small or new employers. The consulting services are kept separate from OSHA's enforcement staff so that employers do not fear to use them. 29 C.F.R. Part 1908.

OSHA also has voluntary protection programs for employers. The Star Program is for employers who are leaders having successful, comprehensive and effective safety and health programs and who are willing to share their experience and expertise to encourage others toward success. The Merit Program is for employers who have a safety and health program that does not yet meet the qualifications for the Star Program and who want to work toward Star Program participation. The Demonstration Program provides an opportunity for companies and worksites to demonstrate the effectiveness of alternate methods of achieving safety and health program excellence that could be substituted for current Star methods. These Programs, including revisions made in the year 2000, are described at 65 Fed. Reg. 45,650 (July 24, 2000).

The Demonstration Program provides another contrast between OSHA's regulatory policies and those of the USEPA. In the author's experience, the OSHA staff welcomes new and improved technologies if they are demonstrated to be sound and protective of worker safety and health. The USEPA staff has refused even to consider improved technology that would require a change in its regulations, even though the technology was in successful use outside the United States and was safer and more effective then the existing methods mandated by the regulations.

OSHA also has a strategic Partnership Program. See OSHA Directive TED 8-00.2 (Nov. 1998).

OSHA encourages employers to perform voluntary self-audits. In 2000, OSHA issued a policy indicating that it will not issue citations for violations that an employer discovered and corrected during a voluntary self-audit if the employer also took steps to prevent recurrence of the violation. OSHA will also not ordinarily require that voluntary self-audit reports be delivered to its inspectors or be used as evidence against an employer if the employer has taken appropriate corrective actions.

2. Training

Many of OSHA's standards include requirements for training of employees and require the use of qualified employees to perform certain kinds of work, especially work of a supervisory or scientific nature. Employers must keep records to show that training obligations were performed.

OSHA regards training as important and its inspectors may issue citations if required training has not been performed. OSHA has published guidelines for voluntary training programs. See OSHA Publication 2254.

3. Inspections

OSHA and the state agencies administering OSHA-approved programs perform tens of thousands of inspections every year. The inspectors issue citations for violations found during the inspections and propose civil monetary penalties for them. They also require correction of the violations within specified time periods, subject to additional penalties if the corrections are not made in a timely manner. Citations must be issued with reasonable promptness.

The typical inspection is not previously announced so that the inspector can see the employer's operations and facilities as they usually exist. Inspections sometimes result from accidents or complaints by workers or labor unions. However, they may be made because the employer is in an industry known to be hazardous or because the employer has not been inspected for some time.

Much has been made by writers of the decision by the U.S. Supreme Court that employers have a constitutional right to require OSHA's inspectors to obtain a warrant to conduct an inspection. *Marshall v. Barlow's Inc.*, 436 U.S. 307 (1978). The Supreme Court is very protective of civil rights and apparently thought that employers should not have rights less than those granted routinely to professional criminals. However, exercise of the right is a rarity. Although an inspection may be a significant interruption of operations, the great majority of employers recognize it as having priority and cooperate with the inspector or inspection team including arrangements for compliance with "walk around" rights of employees and their labor union representatives. In fact, many employers use an inspection as an opportunity to make a good impression by showing the inspector that their programs equal or exceed OSHA's standards.

OSHA has issued a Field Inspection Reference Manual providing guidelines to its inspectors. Copies of the Manual are available for purchase at modest cost by employers who wish to use it to prepare for inspections.

Both at the federal and state levels, OSHA inspectors are generally courteous and professional. They expect and welcome similar conduct from employer representatives. In the early years, many OSHA inspectors were learning their work and suffered from inexperience. They tended to focus on obvious minor violations while overlooking nonobvious serious hazards. As time has passed, OSHA inspectors have gained experience and their work is quite effective.

In general, employers should obtain the inspector's objectives at the initial interview and go through the inspection as rapidly as the inspector is willing to proceed. When the inspector asks questions, the employer should answer them, but be sure the answers are correct and complete. If an answer requires help from an employee not present or information from a supplier or engineering firm, it is best to tell the inspector that any answer is preliminary and will be supplemented. It is prudent, of course, not to volunteer information that could expand or complicate the inspection. However, employer representatives should not hesitate to provide enough information to assure the inspector understands the processes, equipment and working conditions inspected and the employer's applicable safety and health programs. Some extra information can avoid a mistaken citation that would require considerable effort and cost to defend.

For multi-employer workplaces such as construction sites, OSHA may issue citations not only to the employer which caused a hazard but also to other employers whose workers were exposed to the hazard and employers (such as a general contractor) which have the authority to control the workplace and take corrective actions. OSHA Directive CPL 2-0.124 (Dec. 10, 1999). The "multi-employer worksite" doctrine has been upheld by several U.S. Courts of Appeals. Recent decisions include *Universal Construction v. OSHRC*, 182 F.3d 726 (10th Cir. 1999); *U.S. v. Pitt-Des Moines, Inc.*, 168 F.3d 976 (7th Cir. 1999); and *IBP, Inc. v. Herman*, 144 F.3d 861 (D.C. Cir. 1998). The Fifth Circuit rejected the doctrine in *Melerine v. Avondale Shipyards*, 659 F.2d 706 (5th Cir. 1981). The Seventh Circuit held the doctrine did not impose liability on a plant operator merely because it had the right to terminate the contract of an independent contractor whose employees refused to comply with "lockout/tagout" regulations. *IBP, Inc. v. Herman*, supra.

4. Enforcement

The OSH Act imposes penalties for violations that are based on the gravity of the violation:

1. Serious violations—$1,500 to $7,000 per violation
2. Nonserious violations—$0 to $7,000 per violation
3. Repeated violations—maximum penalties of $70,000 per violation
4. Willful violations—If serious, $25,000 to $70,000 per violation If nonserious, $5,000 to $7,000 per violation
5. Failure to correct a violation—$7,000 per day per violation.

Failure to provide sufficiently detailed written instructions in an employer's chemical process safety plan explaining how to activate a block and bleed system as part of the shutdown procedures for a chemical reactor and a related failure to provide refresher training have been held to be serious violations. *Albemarle Corp. v. Herman*, 221 F.3d 782 (5th Cir. 2000).

Provision of wrist harnesses, rather than chest or full body harnesses, to employees for confined space entry has been held to be a serous violation. *Union Tank Car Co. v. OSHRC*, 192 F.3d 701 (7th Cir. 1999).

NOTE: The *Union Tank* case is an example of the difficult questions that sometimes arise in selecting safety methods and equipment. OSHA concluded that a chest or full body harness is the preferred method because wrist harnesses may expose employees to additional injury during a rescue, but its rule allowed an employer to demonstrate that (1) use of a body harness is infeasible or creates a greater hazard and (2) use of a wrist harness is the safest and most effective alternative. An expert for OSHA supported OSHA's conclusion. An expert for Union Tank, which had a commendable safety record and programs, testified that wrist harnesses allowed an endangered worker to be extracted three to five seconds faster than body harnesses and that body harnesses, if not property worn, present a risk of snagging. Union Tank also offered evidence that it had safely used wrist harnesses in some real and simulated rescues. The court upheld the decision of OSHA's Administrative Law Judge to accept the testimony of OSHA's expert over Union Tank's expert. In the author's experience, however, the problems of snagging and the loss of seconds described by Union Tank's expert are serious matters that could cause death in some circumstances.

Violations which require separate actions to abate need not be grouped to assess a single penalty. *Dakota Underground, Inc. v. Secretary of Labor*, 200 F.3d 564 (8th Cir. 2000). A second violation of a regulation requiring machine guarding may be treated as a repeated violation even though the first failure was mechanical and the second was electrical. *Caterpillar, Inc. v. Herman*, 154 F.3d 400 (7th Cir. 1998).

Failure to correct is subject to penalties that can accumulate to a very large amount. Thus, employers should take corrective action rapidly. If the corrective action requires design and installation of equipment or other costly and time-consuming work, the employer should reach agreement with OSHA that the work will satisfactorily correct the hazard and on the time schedule for its implementation. Penalties for failure to correct will not then be imposed unless the employer fails to perform the work in a timely manner. If a delay occurs, the employer should promptly notify OSHA and may be able to obtain an extension if the delay was unavoidable.

The OSH Act authorizes OSHA to refer charges to the U.S. Department of Justice of criminal prosecution. A willful violation resulting in death of an employee can result in up to six months imprisonment and a $10,000 fine or, if it is a subsequent conviction, up to a year imprisonment and a $20,000 fine. Falsification of records required by OSHA can result in up to six months imprisonment and a $10,000 fine. Interfering with an inspector's duties or assaulting an inspector can result in up to three years imprisonment and a $5,000 fine. *U.S. v. Pitt-Des Moines, Inc.*, 168 F.3d 976 (7th Cir. 1999).

In egregious cases involving death or serious injuries, prosecutors may bring charges against employers and their management under state criminal laws. *People of the State of New York v. Pymm Thermometer Co.*, 76 N.Y. 2d 511, 561 N.Y.S. 2d 687, 563 N.E. 2d 1 (1990); *People v. Hegedus*, 432 Mich. 598, 443 N.W. 2d 127.

Unpreventable employee misconduct is a defense to a charge that an employer violated the OSH Act. Examples of defiant employee disregard of fire safety rules appear in court decisions such as *Union Tank Car v. OSHRC*, 192 F.3d 701 (7th Cir. 1999). Hindsight can often find some way, however, that an employer could have prevented an injury or illness. *L. R. Willson v. OSHRC*, 134 F.3d 1235 (4th Cir. 1998).

Employers can request review of citations informally within OSHA and can also appeal them to the OSHRC. An employer must notify the OSHRC within 15 days of its intention to contest the citation. 29 U.S.C. § 659(a). Most contested violations are resolved by settlement within OSHA. An appeal from a decision of the OSHRC may be made within 60 days to a U.S. Circuit Court of Appeals which will consider issues of mistake of law or whether the evidence supporting OSHA's case is so insubstantial as to mean its decision was arbitrary and capricious. Employers considering a court appeal must have either a mistake of law issue or a strong case on factual issues because the courts defer to the presumed expertise of OSHA as they do in cases involving other government agencies.

G. Private Litigation; Employee Complaint Protection; Refusal to Work

1. No Private Right of Action under the OSH Act

The OSH Act does not authorize or imply any right of employees or their representatives to commence lawsuits against employers. *Russell v. Bartley*, 494 F.2d 334 (6th Cir. 1974). However, they can submit complaints to OSHA and exercise their rights under collective bargaining agreements and other laws.

Employees and their labor union representatives may not challenge a settlement of a violation between an employer and OHSA under which the employer withdraws its defense and agrees to penalties and/or abatement, except that they may challenge the abatement schedule. *U.S. v. Williams*, 216 F.2d 1099 (D.C.Cir. 2000).

2. Protection for Employees Who Complain to OSHA

The OSH Act provides extensive protection against retaliation to employees who submit complaints to OSHA. 29 U.S.C. § 660. The remedies include reinstatement, if an employee was terminated, and lost pay and benefits. These rights are important in order to assure that employees do not fear to furnish information to OSHA. However, actual cases are sometimes clouded by the practice of some unions to submit questionable complaints to OSHA as a lever during labor negotiations and disputes. Some employees also submit complaints to OSHA in an effort to prevent a justified termination or layoff.

Violation of OSHA standards is often used as evidence to establish negligence, fault or a defect in tort cases. However, the courts generally refuse to treat a violation determination by OSHA as conclusive evidence. One reason is that employers usually settle OSHA citations as soon as possible if minor penalties are proposed, even though they might have grounds to contest them. Some employers fear that actively contesting citations could result in retaliation by OSHA.

3. Refusal to Work

Employees have a right to refuse in good faith to work under conditions which subject them to danger of death or serious injury and to be free from subsequent employer discrimination as a result of such a refusal. 29 C.F.R. § 1977.12. *Whirlpool Corp. v. Marshall*, 445 U.S. 1, 63 L.Ed. 2d 154 (1980).

H. Preemption

In 1992, the U.S. Supreme Court ruled that OSHA's HAZWOPER regulations preempted a state law imposing regulatory requirements on hazardous waste operations. *Gade v. National Solid Waste Management Ass'n*, 112 S.Ct. 2374, 120 L. Ed. 2d 73 (1992).

In earlier cases involving the HCS standard, there were disagreements among the U.S. Circuit Courts of Appeals as to the extent to which the OSH Act and OSHA's regulations preempt inconsistent or more burdensome state and local laws. The Third Circuit found preemption only to the extent that the HCS standard provided actual coverage. *New Jersey State Chamber of Commerce v. Hughey*, 774 F. 2d 587 (3d Cir. 1985). The Sixth Circuit preempted a local law and did not allow partial preemption. Thus, the extent to which the OSH Act preempts state and local regulatory laws which arguably supplement, rather than contradict, its provisions is not clear.

The anti-retaliation provisions of the OSH Act did not preempt a wrongful discharge claim under the common law of the State of Kansas. *Flenker v. Willamette Industries, Inc.*, 162 F.3d 1083 (10th Cir. 1998).

The authority of OSHA to issue citations to a company that operated oil and gas exploration barges in Louisiana's territorial waters was not preempted by limited regulatory authority of the U.S. Coast Guard. *Chao v. Mallard Bay Drilling, Inc.*, 534 U.S. 235, 151 L.Ed 2d 659 (2002).

I. State Administration

The OSH Act authorizes states to assume responsibility for occupational health and safety and health standards by submitting a plan, including necessary laws and regulations, for approval by OSHA. 29 C.F.R. Part 1901 *et seq*. The state plan must be at least as effective as the standards adopted by OSHA. Less than half of the states fully administer the OSH Act, although some additional states have been approved by OSHA to administer limited programs for their own state and local employees. Those states which have not chosen to administer their own programs are preempted from adopting occupational safety and health standards. However, the preemption does not prevent the enforcement of state criminal laws for conduct which also violates OSHA's health and safety standards.

EXHIBITS

1. Material Safety Data Sheet (Non-Mandatory Form)

Material Safety Data Sheet

May be used to comply with

OSHA's Hazard Communication Standard, 29 CFR 1910.1200. Standard must be consulted for specific requirements.

U.S. Department of Labor

Occupational Safety and Health Administration

(Non-Mandatory Form)

Form Approved

OMB No. 1218-0072

IDENTITY *(As Used on Label and List)*	Note: Blank spaces are not permitted. If any item is not applicable, or no information is available, the space must be marked to indicate that.

Section I

Manufacturer's Name	Emergency Telephone Number
Address *(Number, Street, City, State, and ZIP Code)*	Telephone Number for Information
	Date Prepared
	Signature of Preparer *(optional)*

Section II - Hazard Ingredients/Identity Information

Hazardous Components (Specific Chemical Identity; Common Name(s))	OSHA PEL	ACGIH TLV	Other Limits Recommended	%*(optional)*

Section III - Physical/Chemical Characteristics

Boiling Point		Specific Gravity (H_2O = 1)	
Vapor Pressure (mm Hg.)		Melting Point	
Vapor Density (AIR = 1)		Evaporation Rate (Butyl Acetate = 1)	
Solubility in Water			
Appearance and Odor			

Section IV - Fire and Explosion Hazard Data

Flash Point (Method Used)	Flammable Limits	LEL	UEL
Extinguishing Media			
Special Fire Fighting Procedures			
Unusual Fire and Explosion Hazards			

(Reproduce locally) OSHA 174, Sept. 1985

Section V - Reactivity Data

Stability	Unstable		Conditions to Avoid
	Stable		
Incompatibility *(Materials to Avoid)*			
Hazardous Decomposition or Byproducts			
Hazardous Polymerization	May Occur		Conditions to Avoid

	Will Not Occur		

Section VI - Health Hazard Data

Route(s) of Entry:	Inhalation?	Skin?	Ingestion?
Health Hazards *(Acute and Chronic)*			
Carcinogenicity:	NTP?	IARC Monographs?	OSHA Regulated?
Signs and Symptoms of Exposure			
Medical Conditions Generally Aggravated by Exposure			
Emergency and First Aid Procedures			

Section VII - Precautions for Safe Handling and Use

Steps to Be Taken in Case Material is Released or Spilled
Waste Disposal Method
Precautions to Be taken in Handling and Storing
Other Precautions

Section VIII - Control Measures

Respiratory Proctection *(Specify Type)*		
Ventilation	Local Exhaust	Special
	Mechanical *(General)*	Other
Protective Gloves	Eye Protection	
Other Protective Clothing or Equipment		
Work/Hygienic Practices		

Page 2 * U.S.G.P.O.: 1986 - 491 - 529/45775

2. OSHA Forms 300, 300A and 301 and Instructions

OSHA
Forms for Recording
Work-Related Injuries and Illnesses

U.S. Department of Labor
Occupational Safety and Health Administration

What's Inside...

In this package, you'll find everything you need to complete OSHA's *Log* and the *Summary of Work-Related Injuries and Illnesses* for the next several years. On the following pages, you'll find:

- **An Overview: Recording Work-Related Injuries and Illnesses** — General instructions for filling out the forms in this package and definitions of terms you should use when you classify your cases as injuries or illnesses.
- **How to Fill Out the Log** — An example to guide you in filling out the *Log* properly.
- **Log of Work-Related Injuries and Illnesses** — Several pages of the *Log* (but you may make as many copies of the *Log* as you need.) Notice that the *Log* is separate from the *Summary*.

- **Summary of Work-Related Injuries and Illnesses** — Removable *Summary* pages for easy posting at the end of the year. Note that you post the *Summary* only, not the *Log*.

- **Worksheet to Help You Fill Out the Summary** — A worksheet for figuring the average number of employees who worked for your establishment and the total number of hours worked.
- **OSHA's 301: Injury and Illness Incident Report** — Several copies of the OSHA 301 to provide details about the incident. You may make as many copies as you need or use an equivalent form.

Take a few minutes to review this package. If you have any questions, **visit us online at www.osha.gov** or **call your local OSHA office**. We'll be happy to help you.

U.S. Department of Labor
Occupational Safety and Health Administration

An Overview: Recording Work-Related Injuries and Illnesses

The Occupational Safety and Health (OSH) Act of 1970 requires certain employers to prepare and maintain records of work-related injuries and illnesses. Use these definitions when you classify cases on the Log. OSHA's recordkeeping regulation (see 29 CFR Part 1904) provides more information about the definitions below.

The *Log of Work-Related Injuries and Illnesses* (Form 300) is used to classify work-related injuries and illnesses and to note the extent and severity of each case. When an incident occurs, use the *Log* to record specific details about what happened and how it happened. The *Summary* — a separate form (Form 300A) — shows the totals for the year in each category. At the end of the year, post the *Summary* in a visible location so that your employees are aware of the injuries and illnesses occurring in their workplace.

Employers must keep a *Log* for each establishment or site. If you have more than one establishment, you must keep a separate *Log* and *Summary* for each physical location that is expected to be in operation for one year or longer.

Note that your employees have the right to review your injury and illness records. For more information, see 29 Code of Federal Regulations Part 1904.35, *Employee Involvement.*

Cases listed on the *Log of Work-Related Injuries and Illnesses* are not necessarily eligible for workers' compensation or other insurance benefits. Listing a case on the *Log* does not mean that the employer or worker was at fault or that an OSHA standard was violated.

When is an injury or illness considered work-related?

An injury or illness is considered work-related if an event or exposure in the work environment caused or contributed to the condition or significantly aggravated a preexisting condition. Work-relatedness is presumed for injuries and illnesses resulting from events or exposures occurring in the workplace, unless an exception specifically applies. See 29 CFR Part 1904.5(b)(2) for the exceptions. The work environment includes the establishment and other locations where one or more employees are working or are present as a condition of their employment. See 29 CFR Part 1904.5(b)(1).

Which work-related injuries and illnesses should you record?

Record those work-related injuries and illnesses that result in:

- death,
- loss of consciousness,
- days away from work,
- restricted work activity or job transfer, or
- medical treatment beyond first aid.

You must also record work-related injuries and illnesses that are significant (as defined below) or meet any of the additional criteria listed below.

You must record any significant work-related injury or illness that is diagnosed by a physician or other licensed health care professional. You must record any work-related case involving cancer, chronic irreversible disease, a fractured or cracked bone, or a punctured eardrum. See 29 CFR 1904.7.

What are the additional criteria?

You must record the following conditions when they are work-related:

- any needlestick injury or cut from a sharp object that is contaminated with another person's blood or other potentially infectious material;
- any case requiring an employee to be medically removed under the requirements of an OSHA health standard;
- tuberculosis infection as evidenced by a positive skin test or diagnosis by a physician or other licensed health care professional after exposure to a known case of active tuberculosis.

What is medical treatment?

Medical treatment includes managing and caring for a patient for the purpose of combating disease or disorder. The following are not considered medical treatments and are NOT recordable:

- visits to a doctor or health care professional solely for observation or counseling;
- diagnostic procedures, including administering prescription medications that are used solely for diagnostic purposes; and
- any procedure that can be labeled first aid. (*See below for more information about first aid.*)

What do you need to do?

1. Within 7 calendar days after you receive information about a case, decide if the case is recordable under the OSHA recordkeeping requirements.
2. Determine whether the incident is a new case or a recurrence of an existing one.
3. Establish whether the case was work-related.
4. If the case is recordable, decide which form you will fill out as the injury and illness incident report.

   You may use *OSHA's 301: Injury and Illness Incident Report* or an equivalent form. Some state workers compensation, insurance, or other reports may be acceptable substitutes, as long as they provide the same information as the OSHA 301.

How to work with the Log

1. Identify the employee involved unless it is a privacy concern case as described below.
2. Identify when and where the case occurred.
3. Describe the case, as specifically as you can.
4. Classify the seriousness of the case by recording the **most serious outcome** associated with the case, with column J (Other recordable cases) being the least serious and column G (Death) being the most serious.
5. Identify whether the case is an injury or illness. If the case is an injury, check the injury category. If the case is an illness, check the appropriate illness category.

U.S. Department of Labor
Occupational Safety and Health Administration

What is first aid?

If the incident required only the following types of treatment, consider it first aid. Do NOT record the case if it involves only:

- ▼ using non-prescription medications at non-prescription strength;
- ▼ administering tetanus immunizations;
- ▼ cleaning, flushing, or soaking wounds on the skin surface;
- ▼ using wound coverings, such as bandages, BandAids™, gauze pads, etc., or using SteriStrips™ or butterfly bandages.
- ▼ using hot or cold therapy;
- ▼ using any totally non-rigid means of support, such as elastic bandages, wraps, non-rigid back belts, etc.;
- ▼ using temporary immobilization devices while transporting an accident victim (splints, slings, neck collars, or back boards).
- ▼ drilling a fingernail or toenail to relieve pressure, or draining fluids from blisters;
- ▼ using eye patches;
- ▼ using simple irrigation or a cotton swab to remove foreign bodies not embedded in or adhered to the eye;
- ▼ using irrigation, tweezers, cotton swab or other simple means to remove splinters or foreign material from areas other than the eye;
- ▼ using finger guards;
- ▼ using massages;
- ▼ drinking fluids to relieve heat stress

How do you decide if the case involved restricted work?

Restricted work activity occurs when, as the result of a work-related injury or illness, an employer or health care professional keeps, or recommends keeping, an employee from doing the routine functions of his or her job or from working the full workday that the employee would have been scheduled to work before the injury or illness occurred.

How do you count the number of days of restricted work activity or the number of days away from work?

Count the number of calendar days the employee was on restricted work activity or was away from work as a result of the recordable injury or illness. Do not count the day on which the injury or illness occurred in this number. Begin counting days from the day after the incident occurs. If a single injury or illness involved both days away from work and days of restricted work activity, enter the total number of days for each. You may stop counting days of restricted work activity or days away from work once the total of either or the combination of both reaches 180 days.

Under what circumstances should you NOT enter the employee's name on the OSHA Form 300?

You must consider the following types of injuries or illnesses to be privacy concern cases:

- ▼ an injury or illness to an intimate body part or to the reproductive system,
- ▼ an injury or illness resulting from a sexual assault,
- ▼ a mental illness,
- ▼ a case of HIV infection, hepatitis, or tuberculosis,
- ▼ a needlestick injury or cut from a sharp object that is contaminated with blood or other potentially infectious material (see 29 CFR Part 1904.8 for definition), and
- ▼ other illnesses, if the employee independently and voluntarily requests that his or her name not be entered on the log.

You must not enter the employee's name on the OSHA 300 *Log* for these cases. Instead, enter "privacy case" in the space normally used for the employee's name. You must keep a separate, confidential list of the case numbers and employee names for the establishment's privacy concern cases so that you can update the cases and provide information to the government if asked to do so.

If you have a reasonable basis to believe that information describing the privacy concern case may be personally identifiable even though the employee's name has been omitted, you may use discretion in describing the injury or illness on both the OSHA 300 and 301 forms. You must enter enough information to identify the cause of the incident and the general severity of the injury or illness, but you do not need to include details of an intimate or private nature.

What if the outcome changes after you record the case?

If the outcome or extent of an injury or illness changes after you have recorded the case, simply draw a line through the original entry or, if you wish, delete or white-out the original entry. Then write the new entry where it belongs. Remember, you need to record the most serious outcome for each case.

Classifying injuries

An injury is any wound or damage to the body resulting from an event in the work environment.

Examples: Cut, puncture, laceration, abrasion, fracture, bruise, contusion, chipped tooth, amputation, insect bite, electrocution, or a thermal, chemical, electrical, or radiation burn. Sprain and strain injuries to muscles, joints, and connective tissues are classified as injuries when they result from a slip, trip, fall or other similar accidents.

U.S. Department of Labor
Occupational Safety and Health Administration

Classifying illnesses

Skin diseases or disorders

Skin diseases or disorders are illnesses involving the worker's skin that are caused by work exposure to chemicals, plants, or other substances.

Examples: Contact dermatitis, eczema, or rash caused by primary irritants and sensitizers or poisonous plants; oil acne; friction blisters, chrome ulcers; inflammation of the skin.

Respiratory conditions

Respiratory conditions are illnesses associated with breathing hazardous biological agents, chemicals, dust, gases, vapors, or fumes at work.

Examples: Silicosis, asbestosis, pneumonitis, pharyngitis, rhinitis or acute congestion; farmer's lung, beryllium disease, tuberculosis, occupational asthma, reactive airways dysfunction syndrome (RADS), chronic obstructive pulmonary disease (COPD), hypersensitivity pneumonitis, toxic inhalation injury, such as metal fume fever, chronic obstructive bronchitis, and other pneumoconioses.

Poisoning

Poisoning includes disorders evidenced by abnormal concentrations of toxic substances in blood, other tissues, other bodily fluids, or the breath that are caused by the ingestion or absorption of toxic substances into the body.

Examples: Poisoning by lead, mercury, cadmium, arsenic, or other metals; poisoning by carbon monoxide, hydrogen sulfide, or other gases; poisoning by benzene, benzol, carbon tetrachloride, or other organic solvents; poisoning by insecticide sprays, such as parathion or lead arsenate; poisoning by other chemicals, such as formaldehyde.

All other illnesses

All other occupational illnesses.

Examples: Heatstroke, sunstroke, heat exhaustion, heat stress and other effects of environmental heat; freezing, frostbite, and other effects of exposure to low temperatures; decompression sickness; effects of ionizing radiation (isotopes, x-rays, radium); effects of nonionizing radiation (welding flash, ultra-violet rays, lasers); anthrax; bloodborne pathogenic diseases, such as AIDS, HIV, hepatitis B or hepatitis C; brucellosis; malignant or benign tumors; histoplasmosis; coccidioidomycosis.

When must you post the Summary?

You must post the *Summary* only — not the *Log* — by February 1 of the year following the year covered by the form and keep it posted until April 30 of that year.

How long must you keep the Log and Summary on file?

You must keep the *Log* and *Summary* for 5 years following the year to which they pertain.

Do you have to send these forms to OSHA at the end of the year?

No. You do not have to send the completed forms to OSHA unless specifically asked to do so.

How can we help you?

If you have a question about how to fill out the *Log*,

- ❑ **visit us online at www.osha.gov** or
- ❑ **call your local OSHA office.**

U.S. Department of Labor
Occupational Safety and Health Administration

Optional

Calculating Injury and Illness Incidence Rates

What is an incidence rate?

An incidence rate is the number of recordable injuries and illnesses occurring among a given number of full-time workers (usually 100 full-time workers) over a given period of time (usually one year). To evaluate your firm's injury and illness experience over time or to compare your firm's experience with that of your industry as a whole, you need to compute your incidence rate. Because a specific number of workers and a specific period of time are involved, these rates can help you identify problems in your workplace and/or progress you may have made in preventing work-related injuries and illnesses.

How do you calculate an incidence rate?

You can compute an occupational injury and illness incidence rate for all recordable cases or for cases that involved days away from work for your firm quickly and easily. The formula requires that you follow instructions in paragraph (a) below for the total recordable cases or those in paragraph (b) for cases that involved days away from work, *and* for both rates the instructions in paragraph (c).

(a) *To find out the total number of recordable injuries and illnesses that occurred during the year,* count the number of line entries on your OSHA Form 300, or refer to the OSHA Form 300A and sum the entries for columns (G), (H), (I), and (J).

(b) *To find out the number of injuries and illnesses that involved days away from work,* count the number of line entries on your OSHA Form 300 that received a check mark in column (H), or refer to the entry for column (H) on the OSHA Form 300A.

(c) *The number of hours all employees actually worked during the year.* Refer to OSHA Form 300A and optional worksheet to calculate this number.

You can compute the incidence rate for all recordable cases of injuries and illnesses using the following formula:

Total number of injuries and illnesses ÷ Number of hours worked by all employees X *200,000 hours = Total recordable case rate*

(The 200,000 figure in the formula represents the number of hours 100 employees working 40 hours per week, 50 weeks per year would work, and provides the standard base for calculating incidence rates.)

You can compute the incidence rate for recordable cases involving days away from work, days of restricted work activity or job transfer (DART) using the following formula:

(Number of entries in column H + Number of entries in column I) ÷ Number of hours worked by all employees X *200,000 hours = DART incidence rate*

You can use the same formula to calculate incidence rates for other variables such as cases involving restricted work activity (column (I) on Form 300A), cases involving skin disorders (column (M-2) on Form 300A), etc. Just substitute the appropriate total for these cases, from Form 300A, into the formula in place of the total number of injuries and illnesses.

What can I compare my incidence rate to?

The Bureau of Labor Statistics (BLS) conducts a survey of occupational injuries and illnesses each year and publishes incidence rate data by various classifications (e.g., by industry, by employer size, etc.). You can obtain these published data at www.bls.gov or by calling a BLS Regional Office.

Worksheet

Total number of recordable injuries and illnesses in your establishment

[ ]

÷ X 200,000 =

[ ]

Hours worked by all your employees

Total recordable cases incidence rate

[ ]

Total number of recordable injuries and illnesses with a checkmark in column H or column I

[ ]

÷ X 200,000 =

[ ]

Hours worked by all your employees

DART incidence rate

[ ]

U.S. Department of Labor
Occupational Safety and Health Administration

How to Fill Out the Log

The *Log of Work-Related Injuries and Illnesses* is used to classify work-related injuries and illnesses and to note the extent and severity of each case. When an incident occurs, use the *Log* to record specific details about what happened and how it happened.

If your company has more than one establishment or site, you must keep separate records for each physical location that is expected to remain in operation for one year or longer.

We have given you several copies of the *Log* in this package. If you need more than we provided, you may photocopy and use as many as you need.

The *Summary* — a separate form — shows the work-related injury and illness totals for the year in each category. At the end of the year, count the number of incidents in each category and transfer the totals from the *Log* to the *Summary*. Then post the *Summary* in a visible location so that your employees are aware of injuries and illnesses occurring in their workplace.

You don't post the Log. You post only the Summary at the end of the year.

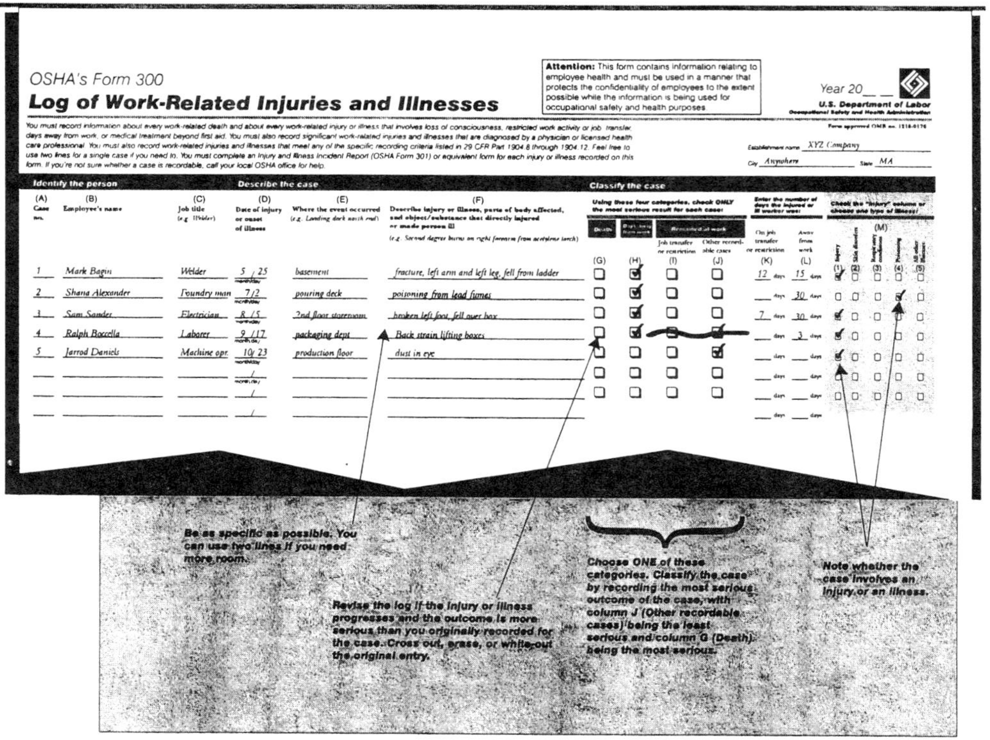

OSHA's Form 300

Log of Work-Related Injuries and Illnesses

Attention: This form contains information relating to employee health and must be used in a manner that protects the confidentiality of employees to the extent possible while the information is being used for occupational safety and health purposes.

Year 20__ __

U.S. Department of Labor
Occupational Safety and Health Administration

Form approved OMB no. 1218-0176

You must record information about every work-related death and about every work-related injury or illness that involves loss of consciousness, restricted work activity or job transfer, days away from work, or medical treatment beyond first aid. You must also record significant work-related injuries and illnesses that are diagnosed by a physician or licensed health care professional. You must also record work-related injuries and illnesses that meet any of the specific recording criteria listed in 29 CFR Part 1904.8 through 1904.12. Feel free to use two lines for a single case if you need to. You must complete an Injury and Illness Incident Report (OSHA Form 301) or equivalent form for each injury or illness recorded on this form. If you're not sure whether a case is recordable, call your local OSHA office for help.

Establishment name ____________

City ____________ State ____________

Identify the person		Describe the case				Classify the case										
						Using these four categories, check ONLY the most serious result for each case:				Enter the number of days the injured or ill worker was:		Check the "Injury" column or choose one type of illness: (M)				
						Death	Days away from work	Remained at work								
(A) Case no.	(B) Employee's name	(C) Job title (e.g., *Welder*)	(D) Date of injury or onset of illness	(E) Where the event occurred (*e.g., Loading dock north end*)	(F) Describe injury or illness, parts of body affected, and object/substance that directly injured or made person ill (*e.g., Second degree burns on right forearm from acetylene torch*)	(G)	(H)	Job transfer or restriction (I)	Other record-able cases (J)	On job transfer or restriction (K)	Away from work (L)	Injury (1)	Skin disorder (2)	Respiratory condition (3)	Poisoning (4)	All other illnesses (5)
			/ month/day			☐	☐	☐	☐	days	days	☐	☐	☐	☐	☐
			/ month/day			☐	☐	☐	☐	days	days	☐	☐	☐	☐	☐
			/ month/day			☐	☐	☐	☐	days	days	☐	☐	☐	☐	☐
			/ month/day			☐	☐	☐	☐	days	days	☐	☐	☐	☐	☐
			/ month/day			☐	☐	☐	☐	days	days	☐	☐	☐	☐	☐
			/ month/day			☐	☐	☐	☐	days	days	☐	☐	☐	☐	☐
			/ month/day			☐	☐	☐	☐	days	days	☐	☐	☐	☐	☐
			/ month/day			☐	☐	☐	☐	days	days	☐	☐	☐	☐	☐
			/ month/day			☐	☐	☐	☐	days	days	☐	☐	☐	☐	☐
			/ month/day			☐	☐	☐	☐	days	days	☐	☐	☐	☐	☐
			/ month/day			☐	☐	☐	☐	days	days	☐	☐	☐	☐	☐
			/ month/day			☐	☐	☐	☐	days	days	☐	☐	☐	☐	☐
			/ month/day			☐	☐	☐	☐	days	days	☐	☐	☐	☐	☐
					Page totals ➤	___	___	___	___	___	___	Injury (1)	Skin disorder (2)	Respiratory condition (3)	Poisoning (4)	All other illnesses (5)

Be sure to transfer these totals to the Summary page (Form 300A) before you post it.

Page ___ of ___

Public reporting burden for this collection of information is estimated to average 14 minutes per response, including time to review the instructions, search and gather the data needed, and complete and review the collection of information. Persons are not required to respond to the collection of information unless it displays a currently valid OMB control number. If you have any comments about these estimates or any other aspects of this data collection, contact: US Department of Labor, OSHA Office of Statistics, Room N-3644, 200 Constitution Avenue, NW, Washington, DC 20210. Do not send the completed forms to this office.

OSHA's Form 300A

Summary of Work-Related Injuries and Illnesses

Year 20__ __

U.S. Department of Labor
Occupational Safety and Health Administration

Form approved OMB no. 1218-0176

All establishments covered by Part 1904 must complete this Summary page, even if no work-related injuries or illnesses occurred during the year. Remember to review the Log to verify that the entries are complete and accurate before completing this summary.

Using the Log, count the individual entries you made for each category. Then write the totals below, making sure you've added the entries from every page of the Log. If you had no cases, write "0."

Employees, former employees, and their representatives have the right to review the OSHA Form 300 in its entirety. They also have limited access to the OSHA Form 301 or its equivalent. See 29 CFR Part 1904.35, in OSHA's recordkeeping rule, for further details on the access provisions for these forms.

Number of Cases

Total number of deaths	Total number of cases with days away from work	Total number of cases with job transfer or restriction	Total number of other recordable cases
______ (G)	______ (H)	______ (I)	______ (J)

Number of Days

Total number of days of job transfer or restriction	Total number of days away from work
______ (K)	______ (L)

Injury and Illness Types

Total number of . . .
(M)

(1) Injuries ______

(2) Skin disorders ______

(3) Respiratory conditions ______

(4) Poisonings ______

(5) All other illnesses ______

Establishment information

Your establishment name ______

Street ______

City ______ State ______ ZIP ______

Industry description (*e.g., Manufacture of motor truck trailers*) ______

Standard Industrial Classification (SIC), if known (*e.g., SIC 3715*) __ __ __ __

Employment information *(If you don't have these figures, see the Worksheet on the back of this page to estimate.)*

Annual average number of employees ______

Total hours worked by all employees last year ______

Sign here

Knowingly falsifying this document may result in a fine.

I certify that I have examined this document and that to the best of my knowledge the entries are true, accurate, and complete.

______ Company executive ______ Title

( ) ______ Phone / / Date

Post this Summary page from February 1 to April 30 of the year following the year covered by the form.

Public reporting burden for this collection of information is estimated to average 50 minutes per response, including time to review the instructions, search and gather the data needed, and complete and review the collection of information. Persons are not required to respond to the collection of information unless it displays a currently valid OMB control number. If you have any comments about these estimates or any other aspects of this data collection, contact: US Department of Labor, OSHA Office of Statistics, Room N-3644, 200 Constitution Avenue, NW, Washington, DC 20210. Do not send the completed forms to this office.

U.S. Department of Labor
Occupational Safety and Health Administration

Optional

Worksheet to Help You Fill Out the Summary

At the end of the year, OSHA requires you to enter the average number of employees and the total hours worked by your employees on the summary. If you don't have these figures, you can use the information on this page to estimate the numbers you will need to enter on the Summary page at the end of the year.

How to figure the average number of employees who worked for your establishment during the year:

❶ **Add** the total number of employees your establishment paid in all pay periods during the year. Include all employees: full-time, part-time, temporary, seasonal, salaried, and hourly.

The number of employees paid in all pay periods = ❶ ________

❷ **Count** the number of pay periods your establishment had during the year. Be sure to include any pay periods when you had no employees.

The number of pay periods during the year = ❷ ________

❸ **Divide** the number of employees by the number of pay periods.

❶ / ❷ ________ = ❸ ________

❹ **Round the answer** to the next highest whole number. Write the rounded number in the blank marked *Annual average number of employees.*

The number rounded = ❹ ________

For example, Acme Construction figured its average employment this way:

For pay period...	Acme paid this number of employees...
1	10
2	0
3	15
4	30
5	40
▼	▼
24	20
25	15
26	+10
	830

Number of employees paid = 830 ❶

Number of pay periods = 26 ❷

$\frac{830}{26}$ = 31.92 ❸

31.92 rounds to 32 ❹

32 is the annual average number of employees

How to figure the total hours worked by all employees:

Include hours worked by salaried, hourly, part-time and seasonal workers, as well as hours worked by other workers subject to day to day supervision by your establishment (e.g., temporary help services workers).

Do not include vacation, sick leave, holidays, or any other non-work time, even if employees were paid for it. If your establishment keeps records of only the hours paid or if you have employees who are not paid by the hour, please estimate the hours that the employees actually worked.

If this number isn't available, you can use this optional worksheet to estimate it.

Optional Worksheet

________ **Find** the number of full-time employees in your establishment for the year.

X ________ **Multiply** by the number of work hours for a full-time employee in a year.

________ This is the number of full-time hours worked.

\+ ________ **Add** the number of any overtime hours as well as the hours worked by other employees (part-time, temporary, seasonal)

________ **Round** the answer to the next highest whole number. Write the rounded number in the blank marked *Total hours worked by all employees last year.*

OSHA's Form 301
Injury and Illness Incident Report

Attention: This form contains information relating to employee health and must be used in a manner that protects the confidentiality of employees to the extent possible while the information is being used for occupational safety and health purposes.

U.S. Department of Labor
Occupational Safety and Health Administration

Form approved OMB no. 1218-0176

This *Injury and Illness Incident Report* is one of the first forms you must fill out when a recordable work-related injury or illness has occurred. Together with the *Log of Work-Related Injuries and Illnesses* and the accompanying *Summary*, these forms help the employer and OSHA develop a picture of the extent and severity of work-related incidents.

Within 7 calendar days after you receive information that a recordable work-related injury or illness has occurred, you must fill out this form or an equivalent. Some state workers' compensation, insurance, or other reports may be acceptable substitutes. To be considered an equivalent form, any substitute must contain all the information asked for on this form.

According to Public Law 91-596 and 29 CFR 1904, OSHA's recordkeeping rule, you must keep this form on file for 5 years following the year to which it pertains.

If you need additional copies of this form, you may photocopy and use as many as you need.

Completed by ______________________

Title ______________________

Phone (____)______-________ Date ___/___/___

Information about the employee

1) Full name ______________________

2) Street ______________________

City ______________ State ______ ZIP ______

3) Date of birth ___/___/___

4) Date hired ___/___/___

5) ☐ Male
☐ Female

Information about the physician or other health care professional

6) Name of physician or other health care professional ______________________

7) If treatment was given away from the worksite, where was it given?

Facility ______________________

Street ______________________

City ______________ State ______ ZIP ______

8) Was employee treated in an emergency room?
☐ Yes
☐ No

9) Was employee hospitalized overnight as an in-patient?
☐ Yes
☐ No

Information about the case

10) Case number from the *Log* ____________ *(Transfer the case number from the Log after you record the case.)*

11) Date of injury or illness ___/___/___

12) Time employee began work ____________ AM / PM

13) Time of event ____________ AM / PM ☐ Check if time cannot be determined

14) **What was the employee doing just before the incident occurred?** Describe the activity, as well as the tools, equipment, or material the employee was using. Be specific. *Examples:* "climbing a ladder while carrying roofing materials"; "spraying chlorine from hand sprayer"; "daily computer key-entry."

15) **What happened?** Tell us how the injury occurred. *Examples:* "When ladder slipped on wet floor, worker fell 20 feet"; "Worker was sprayed with chlorine when gasket broke during replacement"; "Worker developed soreness in wrist over time."

16) **What was the injury or illness?** Tell us the part of the body that was affected and how it was affected; be more specific than "hurt," "pain," or sore." *Examples:* "strained back"; "chemical burn, hand"; "carpal tunnel syndrome."

17) **What object or substance directly harmed the employee?** *Examples:* "concrete floor"; "chlorine"; "radial arm saw." *If this question does not apply to the incident, leave it blank.*

18) **If the employee died, when did death occur?** Date of death ___/___/___

Public reporting burden for this collection of information is estimated to average 22 minutes per response, including time for reviewing instructions, searching existing data sources, gathering and maintaining the data needed, and completing and reviewing the collection of information. Persons are not required to respond to the collection of information unless it displays a current valid OMB control number. If you have any comments about this estimate or any other aspects of this data collection, including suggestions for reducing this burden, contact: US Department of Labor, OSHA Office of Statistics, Room N-3644, 200 Constitution Avenue, NW, Washington, DC 20210. Do not send the completed forms to this office.

U.S. Department of Labor
Occupational Safety and Health Administration

If You Need Help...

If you need help deciding whether a case is recordable, or if you have questions about the information in this package, feel free to contact us. We'll gladly answer any questions you have.

- **Visit us online at www.osha.gov**
- **Call your OSHA Regional office and ask for the recordkeeping coordinator**

or

- **Call your State Plan office**

Federal Jurisdiction

Region 1 - 617 / 565-9860
Connecticut; Massachusetts; Maine; New Hampshire; Rhode Island

Region 2 - 212 / 337-2378
New York; New Jersey

Region 3 - 215 / 861-4900
DC; Delaware; Pennsylvania; West Virginia

Region 4 - 404 / 562-2300
Alabama; Florida; Georgia; Mississippi

Region 5 - 312 / 353-2220
Illinois; Ohio; Wisconsin

Region 6 - 214 / 767-4731
Arkansas; Louisiana; Oklahoma; Texas

Region 7 - 816 / 426-5861
Kansas; Missouri; Nebraska

Region 8 - 303 / 844-1600
Colorado; Montana; North Dakota; South Dakota

Region 9 - 415 / 975-4310

Region 10 - 206 / 553-5930
Idaho

State Plan States

Alaska - 907 / 269-4957

Arizona - 602 / 542-5795

California - 415 / 703-5100

*Connecticut - 860 / 566-4380

Hawaii - 808 / 586-9100

Indiana - 317 / 232-2688

Iowa - 515 / 281-3661

Kentucky - 502 / 564-3070

Maryland - 410 / 767-2371

Michigan - 517 / 322-1848

Minnesota - 651 / 284-5050

Nevada - 702 / 486-9020

*New Jersey - 609 / 984-1389

New Mexico - 505 / 827-4230

*New York - 518 / 457-2574

North Carolina - 919 / 807-2875

Oregon - 503 / 378-3272

Puerto Rico - 787 / 754-2172

South Carolina - 803 / 734-9669

Tennessee - 615 / 741-2793

Utah - 801 / 530-6901

Vermont - 802 / 828-2765

Virginia - 804 / 786-6613

Virgin Islands - 340 / 772-1315

Washington - 360 / 902-5554

Wyoming - 307 / 777-7786

*Public Sector only

Have questions?

If you need help in filling out the *Log* or *Summary*, or if you have questions about whether a case is recordable, contact us. We'll be happy to help you. You can:

- Visit us online at: **www.osha.gov**
- Call your regional or state plan office. You'll find the phone number listed inside this cover.

U.S. Department of Labor
Occupational Safety and Health Administration

CHAPTER XVI
LAWS RELATING TO LEAD

A. History

Since the days of the Athenian and Roman Empires, lead has been known as a useful and versatile metal, but also as a hazardous substance when misused. During the past century, lead and lead compounds have been widely used in batteries, electronic circuit boards, paint driers and pigments, cable sheathing, piping, solder, radiation shielding, printer's type, ammunition, television and crystal glass, stained glass, ceramics, electronic components, ammunition, sporting equipment and tetraethyl lead gasoline additives.

The benefits of lead should not be underestimated. The roofs of great cathedrals, such as St. Paul in London and Sancta Sophia in Constantinople (Istanbul), have endured for centuries because they were made of lead. Lead-acid batteries are a mainstay of the automotive industry and may yet have a role in future clean powered vehicles. Lead is used in traffic safety paint to produce the bright yellow lines on highways. Lead is used to shield humans from radiation such as the X-rays taken in hospitals and other medical and dental facilities. Lead is the most effective material used for the storage of radioactive materials and wastes.

B. Lead Exposure Sources and Health Effects

Exposure to lead may come from several sources. Workers in primary and secondary smelters, battery factories and other workplaces may inhale to dust and fumes if their employer does not provide effective engineering controls and personal protective equipment. Workers may orally ingest dust and fumes from hand to mouth activity. The general public near a facility such as a lead smelter may inhale airborne lead emissions if they are not controlled. The public may also be exposed to dust from deteriorated lead-based paint; soils affected by leaded gasoline; water contaminated by lead piping and solder; and food and food containers containing lead. Some studies have also concluded that lead can be transferred during pregnancy through the placenta.

Inhalation accounts for about 90% of lead intake and food and drinking water about 10%. The body absorbs about 5% to 15% of the amount ingested, but absorption by children may be higher. Much of the body burden is excreted rapidly, but some remains and excretes more slowly. Lead absorbed passes primarily into the bloodstream and links to red blood cells. Lead inhibits the production of heme which carries oxygen in red blood cells and may substitute itself for iron creating an iron deficiency. If exposure continues, lead will migrate into tissue and bone. When exposure ceases, the migration reverses and declines rapidly from blood and tissue, but more slowly from bone.

High levels of lead absorption may have acute toxic effects. Death can occur at blood lead levels approaching or exceeding 100 micrograms per deciliter (100 ug/dL), depending on individual susceptibility. At levels from 70 ug/dL to 100 ug/dL, symptoms may appear such as colic, wrist drop, gum lead lines, headaches, stomachaches, muscular weakness, and hypertension.

Symptomatic lead poisoning has become rare in the United States as public intake of lead and blood lead levels have declined dramatically for several decades. In the 1940s, the daily intake of lead from food alone was 200 to 500 ug/dL, but is less than 20 ug/dL today.

C. Health Effects of Low Level Exposure

Millions of children grow up throughout the United States in houses and apartments where lead-based paint is present. The great majority experience no adverse effects because their homes are well kept and their activities well supervised. However, some children of lower-income parents do not share their well-being. These children may have many problems. Some have parents who neglect to feed them properly and supervise their activities. As a result, some of them learn slowly and misbehave in school.

Adding to their problems, some of these children live in old apartments where lead-based paint has deteriorated and paint dust and chips exist on floors, window sills and other surfaces. Very young children may inhale the lead dust and may also ingest dust and chips by hand to mouth activity. Some very young children may chew on window sills. They may play on soil impacted by leaded gasoline or lead-based paint. Children who come from other countries may also eat food in traditional dishware and take traditional medicines containing lead or lead coatings. When their blood is sampled and tested during visits to doctors or in school health programs, it may be found to contain lead, although at levels below the levels that adversely affect the health of adults.

Beginning in the 1970s, numerous studies and surveys were published indicating that low levels of lead exposure may have effects on very young children that are more serious than their effects on adults and older children. The first of these studies was. "The relation of subclinical lead level to cognitive and sensorimotor impairment to black preschoolers," Perino and Ernhardt, *Journal of Learning Disorders*, Vol. 7,m pp. 708-712 (1974). Some studies concluded that low level lead exposure could have dramatic adverse effects on children's intelligence and behavior. However, the effects, if any, on very young children are difficult to measure because of confounding variables in the studies. *Lead and Human Health*, American Council on Science and Health pp. 12-15 (Dec. 1997). Professor Ernhardt, coauthor of the original publication, pointed out that confounding factors led some studies to overestimate the actual hazards to young children. In 1994, an English research team published the results of a systematic review of 26 epidemiological studies published since 1979 and reported that a doubling of body lead burden was associated with a mean deficit in full scale IQ of around 1-2 IQ points. The report said that uncertainty remained as to the real impact that lead makes on a child's neurological development. The report concluded that the priority that should be devoted to detection and intervention on children with moderately increased blood lead, compared with other social influences on childhood development, was open to debate. "Environmental Lead and Children's Intelligence: A Systematic Review of the Epidemicological Evidence," Pocock et al., *British Medical Journal*, Vol. 309, p. 1189 (Nov. 5, 1994).

In the 1960s and earlier, blood lead levels of 40 ug/dL were common among children. By the later 1980s and early 1990s, national health and nutrition examination surveys by the Centers for Disease Control and Prevention (CDC) published in 1994 showed that levels among children on a nationwide basis had declined to 2.8 ug/dL. However, levels were higher among urban children of lower income families, although they were far below the levels for children of earlier generations. See also the *Journal of the American Medical Association*, Vol. 272, No. 4, July 1994 and No. 6, August 1994.

In 1991, the Centers for Disease Control and Prevention (CDC) of the U.S. Department of Health and Human Services reduced its threshold action level for blood lead content in children under age 6 from 25 ug/dL to 10 ug/dL. The CDC stated that this action level called for rescreening of children and environmental investigation to provide lead hazard control. At 20 ug/dL, the CDC recommended more frequent testing of the child, family lead education, reference for social services (if necessary), and environmental investigation to provide lead hazard control. The CDC recommended that medical treatment of the children be initiated at a level of 45 ug/dL.

Some environmentalists and attorneys refer to a child with a blood lead concentration of 10 ug/dL as "lead poisoned," although that level is a precautionary action level. They quote the USEPA's statement that there is no known safe level in a manner that implies that any level is poisonous. Since their viewpoints have been widely publicized, many people having little familiarity with lead believe inaccurately that any lead exposure is poisonous.

The CDC action level has been used in several subsequent programs including the regulations of the U.S. Department of Housing and Urban Development described later in this chapter. See also the discussion of lead-based paint litigation later in this chapter.

D. Clean Air Act

USEPA regulations under the Clean Air Act (CAA) establish national ambient air quality standards (NAAQS) for lead as particulate matter, i.e., 150 ug/m^3, 24 hour average concentration (PM10) and 50 ug/m^3, annual arithmetic mean (PM10). 40 CFR § 50.6. They also establish an air quality standard for lead itself of 1.5 ug/cm^3, maximum arithmetic mean, quarterly average. 40 C.F.R. § 50.12.

USEPA regulations establish national emission standards for industrial processes which emit hazardous substances, including lead, to the atmosphere. 40 C.F.R. Part 60. For example, the standard for primary lead smelters is found at 40 CFR § 60.180.

The CAA phased out manufacture and sale of vehicle fuels containing the anti-knock compound, tetraethyl lead. Leaded gasoline was banned from sale for motor vehicle use after December 31, 1995. To replace tetraethyl lead, fuel producers used aromatic compounds such as benzene, toluene ethylbenzene and xylene and the oxygenate compound, methyl tertiary butyl ether (MTBE).

E. Clean Water Act

USEPA regulations under the Clean Water Act (CWA) include lead in the list of hazardous substances. 40 C.F.R. § 116.4. They also establish reportable quantities for spills of lead and lead compounds. 40 C.F.R. § 117.3.

Discharges of lead and lead compounds are among those governed by the national pollutant discharge elimination system. (40 C.F.R. Part 122); the water quality management and planning regulations (40 C.F.R. Part 130); the state water quality standards regulations (40 C.F.R. Part 131); the effluent guidelines and standards (40 C.F.R. Parts 401-471); and the sewage sludge management regulations (40 CFR § 503.13).

F. Safe Drinking Water Act

USEPA regulations under SDWA set a maximum contaminant level goal (MCLG) of zero for lead in drinking water. 40 CFR § 141.51. However, they provide technology-based controls rather than a maximum contaminant level (MCL).

Community water systems exceeding an action level of 0.015 mg/L must install and operate corrosion control equipment to minimize lead concentration in drinking water and send printed information to their customers about the lead in their drinking water. If corrosion control does not reduce the lead concentration below the action level, they must treat their source water. If the source water treatment does not succeed, they must undertake a program to replace their water lines that contain lead until the lead concentration is below the action level. Further discussion of the lead and copper rule is contained in the chapter on the Safe Drinking Water Act. 40 CFR § 141.80 *et seq.*

Drinking water pipes and pipe fittings containing more than 8% lead and school drinking water coolers and solder and flux containing more than 0.2% lead are prohibited. 42 U.S.C. §§ 300g-6 and 300j-21 *et seq*. Requirements imposed on the states to distribute information about water coolers and to adopt remedial action programs were declared unconstitutional. *ACORN v. Edwards*, 81 F.3d 1387 (5th Cir. 1996); *cert. denied*, sub. nom. *ACORN v. Foster*, 521 U.S. 1129 (1997).

G. Resource Conservation and Recovery Act

USEPA's regulations under Resource Conservation and Recovery Act (RCRA) for municipal solid waste landfills include lead and lead compounds in their surface water and groundwater standards, their design criteria for landfills, and their lists of hazardous constituents for which monitoring is required. 40 CFR Parts 257 and 258.

The USEPA's hazardous waste management system regulations include specific wastes containing lead or lead compounds in the hazardous waste lists in 40 CFR § 261.30 to 33. Other wastes containing lead or lead compounds may be hazardous wastes if they do not meet criteria determined by toxic characteristic leaching procedure (TCLP) tests prescribed in 40 CFR § 261.24.

Lead and lead compounds that are hazardous wastes are subject to the land disposal regulations. 40 C.F.R. Part 268. They are also subject to the universal waste management standards at 40 C.F.R. § 273.2. Standards for management of spent lead-acid batteries are prescribed at 40 C.F.R. § 266.80.

H. CERCLA

USEPA regulations establish reportable quantities for lead and lead compounds under the Comprehensive Environmental Response, Compensation and Liability Act (CERCLA). 40 CFR, Table 302.4. USEPA soil lead guidance documents for CERCLA sites refers to the TSCA guidelines for soil cleanup of 400 ppm in a play area and an average of 1,200 ppm of bare soil in the rest of a yard possible use as a relevant and appropriate standard, but the eventual remedial criteria must be developed according to CERCLA procedures and may be set at higher or lower levels. OSWER Directive 9355.4-12 (1994) and OSWER Directive 9200.4-27P (1998).

I. Occupational Safety and Health Act

OSHA's regulations include a general industry standard, a construction industry standard and a shipyard employment standard for lead exposure in workplace air. 29 C.F.R. §§ 1910.1025, 1926.62 and 1915.1025. In all three standards, the personnel exposure limit (PEL) is 50 ug/m^3, 8 hour TWA and the action level is 30 ug/m^3 8 hour TWA. Lead and lead compounds are among the materials covered by the hazard communication rules. 29 CFR § 1910.1200, Appendix A.

OSHA, when headed by Robert Reich, imposed some of its largest fines ever for alleged violations of the construction industry standard by small firms engaged in bridge renovation, i.e., \$3.7 million in *Reich v. Manganas Paint Co.* and \$6.0 million in *Reich v. E. Smalis Painting Co.*

J. Emergency Planning and Community Right-to-know Act

Lead and lead compounds are subject to some of the reporting requirements of the Emergency Planning and Community Right-to-Know Act. 40 C.F.R. Parts 370 and 372. In 2001, the USEPA decided to treat lead as a persistent and bioaccumulative chemical and lowered the reporting thresholds for lead and lead compounds. In doing so, the USEPA rejected comments that the change exceeded it legal authority and was not scientifically justified. 66 Fed. Reg. 4499 (Jan. 17, 2001); 40 C.F.R. § 372.28; also 64 Fed. Reg. 58,666 (Oct. 29, 1999).

K. Consumer Product Safety Act

The Consumer Product Safety Act, 15 U.S.C., § 2051 *et seq.* authorizes the Consumer Product Safety Commission (CPSC) to ban certain consumer products which it finds to be hazardous. Effective February 27, 1978, the CPSC banned lead-containing paint, i.e., paint and other coatings with a lead content in excess of 0.06% by weight of nonvolatile content or dried film, unless exempted. The ban also includes articles (such as toys or furniture) bearing lead-containing paint. 16 CFR Part 1303.

If labelled with prescribed warnings, the CPSC's regulations exempt (1) agricultural and equipment refinish coatings; (2) industrial and commercial building and equipment maintenance coatings; (3) graphic art coatings for such applications as billboards, road signs, and identification marking in industrial buildings; (4) touch up coatings for agricultural equipment, lawn and garden equipment, and appliances; and (5) catalyzed coatings for use on radio-controlled model powered aircraft.

The CPSC's regulations exempt without a labelling requirement (1) mirrors which are part of furniture articles and which bear lead-containing backing paint; (2) artists' paints and related materials; and (3) metal furniture articles (except children's furniture) bearing factory applied coatings.

L. Federal Food, Drug, and Cosmetics Act

The Federal Food, Drug and Cosmetics act authorizes the Food and Drug Administration (FDA) of the U.S. Department of Health and Human Services to adopt standards to protect the public from adulteration and misbranding of food, drugs, and cosmetics. 21 U.S.C. § 301 *et seq.* The FDA has adopted extensive regulations which prohibit some substances as additives to food, drugs or cosmetics, but which more often establish tolerances which allow use of the substances subject to concentration limits and other restrictions. For example, see 21 C.F.R. Parts 73 and 74 (color additives for food, drugs and cosmetics); Parts 170-190 (direct and indirect food additives including food contact packaging and substances generally recognized as safe); and Parts 500-589 (animal drugs, feeds and related products).

The FDA has prohibited the use of lead solder to manufacture cans for packaging foods. 40 C.F.R. § 73.2396. The FDA has also prescribed warning labels for ornamental and decorative ceramic ware. 21 C.F.R. § 109.16.

M. The Hazardous Materials Transportation Act

The Regulations of the Research and Special Programs Administration (RSPA) of the U.S. Department of Transportation under the Hazardous Materials Transportation Act list a number of lead compounds in the Hazardous Materials Table in 49 C.F.R. § 172.101. Reportable quantities for spills or releases of these compounds are listed in Appendix A, Table 1 to the Hazardous Materials Table. Some lead compounds are also listed as marine pollutants in Appendix B.

N. Toxic Substances Control Act

Numerous tasks relating to lead-based paint were assigned to the USEPA by amendments to the Toxic Substances Control Act (TSCA) enacted in 1992. TSCA defines lead-based paint as paint containing greater than 1.0 mg/cm3 or 0.5% by weight.

Among other steps, USEPA has issued booklets on home remodelling and protection of children. The USEPA has announced grants to nonprofit organizations to train abatement workers and grants to states for accreditation and certification for professionals. The USEPA has issued cleanup guidance for residential lead-based paint, lead-contaminated dust, and lead-contaminated soil.

The USEPA has issued regulations (1) defining lead-based paint hazards; (2) requiring distribution of information about lead-based paint before renovation of residential housing constructed before January 1, 1978 ("target housing); (3) disclosure of known lead-based paint and/or lead paint hazards upon sale or lease of target housing; and (4) lead-based paint activities, i.e., accreditation of training programs, certification of individuals and firms, work practice standards and requirements that lead-based paint activities be conducted only according to the prescribed procedures and standards and by certified individuals or firms. The USEPA's regulations also establish requirements for authorization of states and Indian Tribes to administer these programs. 40 C.F.R. Part 745.

The regulations identifying lead-based paint hazards were adopted to provide information and criteria. 40 C.F.R. § 745.61 *et seq.* They begin by stating that they do not require any property owner to evaluate property for the presence of lead-based paint hazards or to take action to control any conditions identified. The regulations identify the hazards in three categories:

1. *Paint-Lead Hazard.* A paint-lead hazard is, in summary, (a) any lead-based paint on a friction surface subject to abrasion if dust levels on the nearest horizontal surface underneath it equal or exceed the dust-lead hazard levels; (b) any damaged or deteriorated lead-based paint on an impact surface caused by a related building component; (c) any chewable lead-based painted surface with evidence of teeth marks; and (d) any other deteriorated lead-based paint in or on the exterior of any residential building or child-occupied facility.

2. *Dust-Lead Hazard.* A dust-lead hazard is surface dust in a residential building or child-occupied facility that contains a mass area concentration of lead equal to or exceeding 40 ug/ft^2 on floors or 250 ug/ft^2 on interior window sills, and 400 ug/ft^2 on window troughs, based on wipe samples.

3. *Soil-Lead Hazard.* A soil-lead hazard is bare soil on residential real property or the property of a child-occupied facility containing lead equal to or exceeding 400 ppm in a play area and an average of 1,200 ppm of bare soil in the rest of the yard, based on soil samples.

A child-occupied facility is defined in later regulations as a building, or portion of a building, constructed prior to 1978, visited regularly by the same child, six years of age or under, on at least two different days in any week if (1) each day's visit is at least 3 hours, (2) the combined weekly visit is at least 6 hours, and (3) the combined annual visits are at least 60 hours. Examples include day-care centers, preschools and kindergarten classrooms. 40 C.F.R. § 745.223.

The residential property renovation regulations apply to all renovations of target housing performed for compensation. They require that the renovator furnish the USEPA's pamphlet on lead-based paint hazards to the owner of each dwelling unit or, if the owner does not occupy the unit, to the adult occupant not more than 60 days before beginning the renovation. The renovator must obtain either a written acknowledgment of receipt of the pamphlet or a certificate of its mailing. The renovator must maintain records evidencing compliance for three years. Renovation means any modification of an existing structure that results in disturbance of painted surfaces, unless the renovator has a written determination from a certified lead-based paint inspector that the components affected by the renovation are free of lead-based paint. Exceptions apply to minor repair and maintenance that disrupt two square feet or less of painted surface per component and to emergency renovation operations. 40 C.F.R. § 745.80 *et seq.*

The renovation regulations require renovators to provide information, but do not require inspection, removal or abatement of lead-based paint. Owners of single-family homes, condominiums and others who must bear the cost generally choose not to remove or abate lead-based paint but rather to maintain it in good condition. However, tenants in multi-family housing sometimes press building owners to remove or abate, especially in rent-controlled buildings.

The real estate disclosure regulations require that every seller and lessor of "target housing" meet several requirements for the benefit of the buyer or tenant. "Target housing" means any housing constructed prior to 1978 except certain housing for the elderly and disabled and any 0-bedroom dwelling. The requirements are to furnish a lead hazard information pamphlet prepared by the USEPA, disclose the presence of any known lead-based paint or lead-based paint hazards in the housing, and permit a 10-day period to conduct a risk assessment or inspection. Contracts for purchase or sale of any interest in target housing must contain a prescribed warning statement and a statement signed by the purchaser that evidences compliance with the requirements of TSCA. A seller or lessor who disagrees with the information in the warning statement is not allowed to change it. Neither the law nor the regulations require that a seller or lessor remove or abate any lead-based paint identified during a risk assessment or inspection. In general, sellers and buyers and landlords and tenants agree that removal or abatement is not necessary because lead-based paint is not a significant hazard in any home where paint is maintained in good condition and children receive good care. 40 C.F.R. § 745.100 *et seq.*

The lead-based paint activity regulations provide for accreditation of training programs for persons engaged in lead-based paint inspection, risk assessment, abatement and related activities. They prescribe procedures for certification of individuals and firms and require that all lead-based paint activities be performed by certified individuals or firms. The regulations also provide work practice standards. Activities performed by owners within residential dwellings which they own and occupy are excluded unless a child residing in the building has been identified as having an elevated blood level. 40 C.F.R. § 745.220 *et seq.* An elevated blood level is defined as 20 ug/dL for a single *venous* test or 15-19 ug/dL in two consecutive tests taken 3 to 4 months apart. A finger stick test is not a venous test.

O. Lead-Based Paint Poisoning Prevention Act, U.S.C. § 4801 and the Residential Lead-Based Paint Reduction Act, U.S.C.§ 4851

These Acts provide for a wide variety of programs including the amendments to TSCA previously described. In addition, they provide for major programs of the Department of Housing and Urban Development (HUD) which govern the identification and abatement of lead-based paint in federally assisted housing and are found in many parts of 24 C.F.R.

HUD presented a Report to Congress dated December 7, 1990 of a Comprehensive and Workable Plan for the Abatement of Lead-Based Paint in Privately Owned Housing in response to 1987 amendments to the LBPPPA. In 1991, HUD issued The HUD Lead Based Paint Abatement Demonstration (FHA), August, 1991, reporting on multi-city abatement projects which it had sponsored. These reports contain extensive information for those interested in the abatement of lead-based paint.

HUD is also authorized to provide grants for studies and for rehabilitation of federally financed and subsidized housing under several laws including the National Housing Act (42 U.S.C. § 1441 *et seq.*) and the Housing and Community Development Act (42 U.S.C. § 5301 *et seq.*). These laws have perennially been amended and expanded by legislation such as the McKinney Homeless Assistance Amendments Act of 1988, the Cranston-Gonzalez National Affordable Housing Act of 1990, and the Housing and Community Development Act Amendments of 1992. Among the grant programs are Section 8 Grants, Community Development Block Grants and HOME Grants.

HUD has adopted extensive regulations on lead-based paint. At present, the regulations are centered in 40 C.F.R. Part 35. The first regulation corresponds to the regulation adopted under TSCA by the USEPA requiring sellers and lessors to disclose known lead-based paint and lead-based paint hazards and to afford an opportunity for a risk assessment or inspection upon a sale or lease of target housing. 40 C.F.R. § 35.80 *et seq.* The second regulation establishes general lead-based paint requirements for all of HUD's programs. 40 C.F.R. § 35.100 *et seq.* Several other regulations prescribe requirements applicable to federally assisted housing programs including properties which HUD owns or possesses as a result of mortgage foreclosures. The most important is the last regulation which prescribes methods and standards for lead-based paint hazard evaluation and hazard reduction activities. 40 C.F.R. § 35.1300 *eq seq.*

HUD's general requirement regulations at 40 C.F.R. § 35.100 *et seq.* contain several definitions that are important because HUD adopted them:

1. Lead-based paint means paint containing lead equal to or 1.0 mg/cm^3 or 0.5% (5,000 ppm) by weight.

2. A lead-based paint hazard means any condition that causes exposure to lead from dust-lead hazards, soil-lead hazards, or lead-based paint that is deteriorated or present in chewable surfaces, friction surfaces, or impact surfaces, that would result in adverse human health effects.

3. A dust-lead hazard is the same as the previously described criteria adopted by the USEPA under TSCA.

4. A soil-lead hazard is the same as the previously described criteria adopted by the USEPA under TSCA. However, if those levels are not applicable, HUD uses the following levels: 400 ug/g in play areas and 2000 ug/g in other areas with bare soil that total more than 9 square feet per residential property.

HUD's general requirements regulations begin by summarizing the levels of protection and hazard reduction requirements provided in the later regulations for specific federally assisted housing programs. 40 C.F.R. § 35.100. They establish several exemptions: (1) residential property for which construction was completed after January 1, 1978; (2) a zero-bedroom dwelling unit; (3) certain housing for the elderly or disabled persons unless a child less than age 6 resides or is expected to reside therein; (4) residential property found not to have lead-based paint by an inspection pursuant to the HUD Guidelines; (5) residential property where all lead-based paint has been identified, removed and clearance achieved according to HUD's regulations; (6) an unoccupied dwelling unit; (7) property or part of a property not used and not to be used for human residential habitation except that common areas in mixed use property are not exempt; (8) rehabilitation that does not disturb a painted surface; and (9) emergency actions immediately necessary to safeguard against imminent danger to human life, health or safety or to protect property from further structural damage. 40 C.F.R. § 35.115.

The general requirements regulations prescribe notification to occupants of evaluation and hazard reduction activities including provision of the USEPA's pamphlet. They prohibit any new use of lead-based paint. They prohibit the following methods of paint removal: (1) open-flame burning or torching; (2) machine sanding or grinding without a high efficiency particulate air (HEPA) local exhaust control; (3) abrasive blasting or sandblasting without HEPA local exhaust control; (4) heat guns operating above 1100 °F or charring the paint; (5) dry sanding or dry scraping with exceptions for very small areas; and (6) paint stripping in a poorly ventilated space using a volatile stripper and/or hazardous chemical as defined in the CPSC or OSHA regulations. They require that all evaluation and hazard reduction activities be performed in compliance with all applicable federal, state, tribal and local laws. They also provide, among other things, for waivers by HUD, monitoring and enforcement, and recordkeeping. 40 C.F.R. § 35.120 to .175.

HUD's program regulations prescribe requirements for evaluation and hazard reduction activities that vary considerably from program to program. Some programs require a risk assessment and implementation of interim controls to treat lead-based hazards identified in the risk assessment. These steps must be followed by ongoing maintenance. If the owner is notified by a public health department or other medical health care provider that a child less than 6 years of age living in a dwelling unit has an environmental intervention blood level, the owner must complete a risk assessment of that dwelling unit within 15 days. Within 30 days after receipt of the report, the owner must complete reduction of the identified lead-based paint hazards including a clearance report confirming treatment of the hazards with interim controls or abatement.

HUD's methods and standards for lead-based paint evaluation and hazard reduction activities are important not only for work in federally assisted target housing, but because many state, local and private entities use the methods and standards and the HUD Guidelines). The methods and standards apply to (1) inspections and risk assessments; (2) abatement; (3) interim controls; (4) standard treatments; (5) clearance; (6) occupant protection and worksite preparation;

(7) safe work practices; and (8) ongoing maintenance and reevaluation activities. 40 C.F.R. § 35.1300 *et seq.*

P. State Environmental and Health Laws

The states have adopted environmental laws implementing the federal environmental laws including the CAA, CWA, SWDA, RCRA and CERCLA. Many states also adopted health laws to regulate lead-based paint hazards. Some of these laws have established only limited programs. Others provide for comprehensive programs which may be found in the laws and in the implementing regulations adopted by applicable health, environmental, and housing agencies. In general, the more comprehensive laws and regulations are found in the northeastern states where anti-lead organizations receive both federal and state funding.

The comprehensive state programs typically require screening of children; mandatory reports of "lead poisoning" as defined in terms of micrograms per deciliter (ug/dL) of blood; inspection and evaluation of residences for lead-based paint as defined in terms of lead content by weight or per square centimeter; abatement of lead-based paint hazards as specified; notice to a designated agency prior to abatement work; licensing and training of abatement contractors and personnel; prohibition of retaliation by owners against tenants; and imposition of strict liability on owners under some circumstances.

The regulations in states such as Massachusetts and Maryland are quite detailed, particularly as to the methods, equipment and performance standards for abatement. For example, abatement rules often prescribe inspection methods and equipment (x-ray fluorescence analyzer, atomic absorption analyzer, or sodium sulfide); occupant and property removal or protection; methods for containment of the work area with polyethylene sheeting and sealants; warnings and restriction of access to the work area; the surface which must be abated; prohibited abatement methods; permitted abatement methods; cover materials useable for encapsulation; worker protection during abatement; cleanup requirements such as HEPA filters; reoccupancy inspection requirements; lead dust levels during and at the end of abatement work; disposal of wastes; record keeping; and issuance of certificates of compliance.

Q. Lead-Based Paint Litigation

1. Background

During the last two decades, although blood-lead levels in children have dropped far below levels in previous years, lead-based paint litigation has grown rapidly. In a common complaint, the plaintiff attorney alleges that the plaintiff was exposed as a very young child to dust or chips of lead-based paint and has (or had) some level of lead in his or her blood. The complaint alleges that the lead caused illness, impairment of mental capacity as measured by I.Q.

level or poor performance in school, and perhaps also behavioral problems demonstrated in school or other relationships. Some plaintiff attorneys contend that a child with any detectible level of lead in his or her blood is "lead poisoned." Other plaintiff attorneys limit their cases to children with a blood lead level over the CDC's "action level" of 10 ug/dL or children with higher blood lead levels that they allege to be evidence of lead poisoning.

2. Litigation Based on Conspiracy Theories

Lawsuits have been commenced against large paint manufacturers which were members of the Lead Industries Association seeking to impose alternative, enterprise or market share liability for lead-based paint sold many decades ago. These lawsuits have generally been unsuccessful. *Brenner v. American Cyanamid*, 699 N.Y.S. 2d 848 (4th Dept. 1999); *City of Philadelphia v. Lead Industries Association, Inc.*, 994 F.2d 112 (3d Cir. 1993); *Santiago v. Sherwin-Williams Company*, 782 F. Supp. 186 (D. Mass 1993), affirmed 3 F.3d 546 (1st Cir. 1993); However, see *City of New York v. Lead Industries Association, Inc.*, 190 A.D. 2d 173, 597 N.Y.S. 2d 698 (1st Dept. 1993) and 241 A.D.2d 387, 660 N.Y.S. 2d 422 (1st Dept. 1997). However, the Rhode Island Superior Court and Supreme Court refused to dismiss a lawsuit by the State of Rhode Island and trial is expected to commence during 2002.

3. Implied Claims under Federal Statutes

Some courts have found implied private rights of action under the federal lead-based paint laws. *Davis v. Philadelphia Housing Authority*, 121 F.3d 92 (3d Cir. 1997); *Aristil v. Housing Authority*, 54 F. Supp. 2d 1289 (M.D. Fla. 1999); *Sipes v. Russell*, 89 F. Supp. 2d 1199 (D. Kans. 2000). However, see *Santiago v. Hernandez*, 53 F. Supp. 2d 264 (S.D.N.Y. 1999).

4. Lawsuits Against Building Owners

Many lawsuits are being commenced against landlords with various results. Strict liability in tort has been imposed in some cases. *Bencosme v. Kokoras*, 400 Mass. 40, 507 N.E. 2d 748 (1987); *Hardy v. Griffin*, 41 Conn. Sup. 283, 569 A.2d 49 (1989) Strict liability was not allowed in other cases and the plaintiff was required to prove negligence. *Juarez v. Wavecrest*, 88 N.Y.2d, 649 N.Y.S. 2d 115 (1996); *Underwood v. Risman*, 605 N.E. 2d 832 (Mass. 1993); *Brown v. Marathon Realty, Inc.*, 170 A.D. 2d 426, 565 N.Y.S. 2d 219 (2d Dept. 1991); *Miller v. Beaugrand*, 169 A.D. 2d 537, 564 N.Y.S. 2d 390 (1st Dept. 1991).

Contributory negligence of a child's parents, including negligent parental supervision, is not imputed to a plaintiff child. However, parental conduct may provide evidence that a landlord did not breach a duty to a child or that a child's injuries were not caused by a landlord's breach. *Hill v. City of New York*, 201 A.D. 2d 329 (1st Dept. 1994); *Brown v. Marathon Realty*, 170 A.D. 2d 426 (2d Dept. 1991); *Alharb v. Sayegh*, 604 N.Y.S. 243 (2d Dept. 1984); *Davis v. Royal-Globe*, 223

So. 2d 859 (La. 1969). Contribution claims against negligent parents have been allowed in Massachusetts, but not in New York. *Ankiewicz v. Kinder*, 408 Mass. 792 (1990); *Franklin v. Krumanocker*, 114 A.D. 2d 611 (3d Dept. 1985).

Claims have been made successfully under a statutory warranty of habitability. *Curry v. Westchester Country Club*, 186 A.D. 2d 712, 589 N.Y.S. 2d 491 (2d Dept. 1993); *Carpenter v. Smith*, 191 A.D.2d 1036, 595 N.Y.S.2d 710 (4th Dept. 1993); *Stone v. Gordon*, 211 A.D.2d 881, 621 N.Y.S.2d 220 (3d Dept. 1995).

Liability under several other legal theories is also alleged in lead-based paint cases. They include a statutory or implied warranty of habitability; negligence *per se* based on violation of a statute or code; nuisance; strict liability for ultra hazardous substances; intentional infliction of mental distress; negligent infliction of emotional distress; and deprivation of rights, privileges or immunities secured by the Constitution or laws under the Civil Rights Act. 42 U.S.C. § 1983. Allegations under these theories may survive a motion to dismiss, but may be difficult to prove. *German v. Federal Home Loan Mortgage Corp.*, 885 F. Supp. 537 (S.D.N.Y. 1995).

The evidence required to prove that a landlord knew or had notice of the presence of lead-based and the presence of a very young child in an apartment is a key issue in lead-based paint litigation. The courts have generally held that a landlord may not be held liable without actual or constructive knowledge that a child was residing in an apartment. *Juarez v. Wavecrest Management*, 88 N.Y. 2d 628, 672 N.E. 2d 135 (1996); *Selvy v. Beigsel*, 283 Ill. App. 3d 532, 670 N.E. 2d 784 (1996). Mere notice of chipping, peeling or chalking paint is not usually sufficient to establish that a landlord had knowledge or notice of lead-based paint because many other kinds of paints have been used during the last 50 years. *Chapman v. Silber*, 97 N.Y. 2d 9, 734 N.Y.S. 2d 541 (2001); *Hines v. Rap Realty*, 684 N.Y.S. 2d 594 (2d Dept. 1999); appeal den. 695 N.Y.S. 2d 540 (1999); *Andrade v. Wong*, 675 N.Y.S. 2d 112 (2d Dept. 1998). However, if a statute or ordinance requires inspection for lead-based paint, a landlord has constructive notice of its presence. *Juarez v. Wavecrest*, supra. A few courts have found a duty to inspect for lead-based paint in the absence of a statute as part of a general duty of due care.

Expert testimony is important in lead-based paint litigation. The experts testify as to whether the injuries claimed were caused by lead-based paint and also as to the present and future effects of the injuries. Their qualifications and testimony is subject to under the "Daubert" standards set by the U.S. Supreme Court. *Daubert v. Merrell Dow*, 509 U.S. 579, 125 L. Ed. 2d 469 (1993). The courts continue to be quite liberal in allowing expert testimony. *Dombrowski v. Gould Electronics, Inc.*, 85 F. Supp. 2d 456 (M.D. Pa. 2000); *Walton v. Albany Community Dev. Agency*, 718 N.Y.S. 2d 456 (3d Dept. 2001). However, a court held that expert testimony was inadequate when the expert never examined the infant and was uncertain whether an initial high blood lead reading was an admittedly unreliable "micro finger stick" test. A later test showed only a 3 ug/dL blood lead concentration. *Arce v. New York City Housing Authority*, 696 N.Y.S.2d 67 (2d Dept. 1999).

Plaintiff attorneys often use neuropsychologists to testify in lead-based paint lawsuits and the courts often allow their testimony on medical issues although they are not admitted to practice medicine. For example, a federal district court in Pennsylvania accepted general testimony of two neuropsychologists as sufficient to establish injury and injury causation, although highly qualified medical experts and engineers testified specifically to the contrary for a defendant battery recycler. *Dombrowski v. Gould Electronics, Inc.*, 85 F. Supp. 2d 456 (M.D. Pa. 2000).

When a claim of illness, mental impairment or behavioral problems is made on behalf of a child, defense attorneys inquire whether the child is actually suffering these conditions and whether they resulted from exposure to lead-based paint or other causes. Thus, they seek to examine the child's health and school records. They also seek to examine health, occupational and school records of parents and health and school records of the child's brothers and sisters. Plaintiff attorneys strongly oppose access to these records. Even a sympathetic jury may find that a child was not injured by lead-based paint if his or her parents, brothers and sisters had the same IQ and learning problems without being exposed to lead-based paint. The courts generally authorize discovery of the child's medical and school records except to the extent restricted by a statute. *Monica W. v. Milovoi*, 685 N.Y.S. 2d 231 (1st Dept. 1999). A court may also authorize discovery of the academic records of a child's mother and siblings and require the mother to take an IQ test. However, a court may refuse to allow access to academic records of siblings. *Alexander v. Westminster Presbyterian Church*, 702 N.Y.S. 2d 727 (4th Dept. 1999); *Monica W. v. Milovoi*, supra. A court may also refuse to require a mother to take an IQ test based on an argument that it is a hardship and an invasion of privacy. *Andon v. 302-304 Mott Street Associates*, 94 N.Y. 2d 740, 709 N.Y.S. 2d 873 (2000).

5. Lawsuits to Obtain Insurance Coverage

Many lawsuits are being commenced against insurers seeking defense and indemnification against liability or to recover abatement costs under general liability policies.

To claim coverage, the insured must show that the child was exposed to lead-based paint during the policy term or that illness caused by lead-based paint manifested itself during the policy term. If both exposure and manifestation took place before the policy period, the courts may uphold an insurer's disclaimer of coverage even though the illness continued during the policy period. *St. Leger v. American Fire*, 870 F. Supp. 641 (E.D. Pa.); aff'd without opinion 61 F.3d 896 (3d Cir. 1995); *Hartford Mutual Ins. Co. v. Jacobson*, 73 Md App. 670, 536 Atl. 2d 120 (1988). However, if new exposure and injuries continue during the policy period, the later insurer must share coverage on a pro rata basis. *Scottsdale Insurance v. American Empire Surplus*, 811 Supp. 210 (D. Md. 1993).

Many general liability policies contain an "absolute" pollution exclusion. The courts have disagreed as to whether this exclusion allows an insurer to deny coverage of an insured for claims of injury by lead-based paint. Several courts have held that lead is a pollutant and that the exclusion clearly applies. *Auto-Owners Ins. v. Housing Authority, Tampa*, 231 F.3d 1298 (11th Cir. 2000); *Auto-Owners Ins. Co. v. Hanson*, 588 N.W. 2d 777 (Minn. 1999); *U.S. Liability v. Bourbeau* 49 F.3d 786 (1st Cir. 1995); *St. Leger v. American Fire*, 870 F. Supp. 641 (E.D. Pa. 1994), aff'd without opinion 61 F.3d 896 (3d Cir. 1995); *Oates v. State of New York*, 610 N.Y.S. 987 (1993); *Kaytes v. Imperial Casualty*, WL 780901 (E.D. Pa. 1994).

Other courts have ordered insurers to provide coverage by finding that lead-based paint is not a pollutant. *Atlantic Mutual v. McFadden*, 413 Mass 90, 596 N.E.2d 762 (1992); *Generali - U.S. Branch v. Caribe Realty*, 160 Misc. 2d 1056, 612 N.Y.S. 2d 296 (1994).

Some courts have ordered insurers to provide coverage by declaring the "absolute" pollution exclusion to be ambiguous, although its language is plain and very broad. *Lititz Mutual Ins. Co. v. Steely*, 567 Pa. 98, 785 A.2d 975 (Pa. 2001); *Byrd v. Blumenreich*, 317 N.J. Super. 496, 722 Atl.2d 548 (1999); *Sphere Drake Ins. Co. v. Y.L. Realty Co.*, 990 F. Supp. 240 (S.D.N.Y. 1997); *Schumann v. State of New York*, 610 N.Y.S. 2d 987 (N.Y. Claims Ct. 1994). In recent decades, several insurers which had written significant policy coverage in New Jersey went into liquidation or sustained serious losses. Several insurers have discontinued, or have announced plans to discontinue, offering insurance in New Jersey.

The New York Court of Appeals held that an insurer was obligated to defend the owners of an apartment building because a lead-based paint exclusion was not properly incorporated into its umbrella policy. *Westview Associates v. Guaranty Nat. Ins. Co.*, 95 N.Y. 2d 34, 717 N.Y.S. 2d 75 (2000).

6. Legislation and Litigation in New York

In the City of New York, there is a large volume of lead-based litigation because of a local ordinance (Local Law No.1) adopted in 1960 that prohibited lead-based paint in multiple dwellings occupied by children of age 6 or under, ignoring the obvious fact that thousands upon thousands of buildings may have lead-based paint in some or all of their apartment units and common areas. Indeed, the City owns large numbers of such buildings that it acquired by foreclosure because rent control and expenses forced the owners to abandon them. For many of these buildings, the cost of removal of lead-based alone is more than the value of the entire building. Few building owners actually know whether lead-based paint is present because lead-based paint gradually ceased to be used in residential buildings during the years from the 1950s to the 1970s and records are no longer available. Thus, building owners have generally taken no action to abate lead-based paint, although the great majority maintain paint in good condition. In 1999, the City adopted Local Law No. 38, a new ordinance establishing a program that would require landlords to abate lead-based paint in deteriorated condition and in dwellings where a child with an elevated blood-level resides. By invitation, the author submitted information to the City Council supporting the new ordinance as a practical step forward. However, anti-lead groups, who hope to force a massive inspection and removal program, obtained a court order setting aside the new ordinance. *New York City Coalition v. Vallone*, N.Y.L.J. 26:1 Oct. 16, 2000. However, on appeal, the order was aside and Local Law No. 38 was held valid. *New York City Coalition v. Vallone,* 741 N.Y.S. 2d 186, 2002 WL 453719 (1st Dept. 2002).

Recently, a bill was introduced before the City Council which has many new members, seeking to repeal Local Law No. 38 and impose much more extensive and costly abatement requirements on building owners.

The City of New York has often been held liable for injuries allegedly caused by lead-based paint in housing of its Housing Authority. The City's liability has not been extended to other housing. A complaint against the City for alleged failure to enforce provisions of its Health Code and Building Code relating to lead-based paint was dismissed on grounds that these statutes were enacted for the benefit of the general public and did not create a special duty to the plaintiffs. *Gibbs v. Paine*, 720 N.Y.S. 2d 184 (2d Dept. 2001).

In cases involving housing in the City of New York that is not a multiple dwelling, evidence of peeling or chipping paint and media reports about lead-based paint have been found insufficient to place a landlord on notice of hazardous conditions. *Hines v. Rap Realty*, 684 N.Y.S.2d 594 (2d Dept. 1999), appeal denied 695 N.Y.S.2d 540 (1999); *Andrade v. Wong*, 675 N.Y.S.2d 112 (2d Dept. 1998).

In New York State outside of the City of New York, a plaintiff attorney suing a landlord must prove several key facts. The landlord must have agreed to perform repairs and retained a right of access to make them. The landlord must have known that the apartment was built during a time when lead-based paint was used. The landlord must also have known that paint in the apartment was deteriorating; a young child was living in the apartment; and lead-based paint was hazardous to young children. *Chapman v. Silber*, 97 N.Y.2d 9 (2001). In reaching its decision, the Court of Appeals rejected arguments that landlords should be required to test for lead-based paint based on alleged "general knowledge" of the hazards of lead-based paint.

CHAPTER XVII
THE OIL POLLUTION ACT AND RELATED LAWS

The Oil Pollution Act (OPA) was adopted in 1990 as a reaction to the oil spill which resulted when the Exxon Valdez ran aground in Prince William Sound off the shore of Alaska.[1] Many of the provisions are found at 33 U.S.C. § 2701 *et seq.*, including the Great Lakes Oil Pollution Research and Development Act which begins at 33 U.S.C. § 2761 *et seq*. However, the OPA also included amendments to the Clean Water Act, 33 U.S.C. § 2701 *et seq*. and the Trans-Alaska Pipeline System Act, 43 U.S.C. § 1651 *et seq*.

The OPA consists of nine titles. Title I imposing liability for petroleum discharges and Title IV on oil tanker safety, manning and double hull requirements are most significant and controversial provisions.

Federal environmental laws closely related to the OPA include the CWA, CERCLA, the MPRSA; the APPS; the Deep Water Port Act (33 U.S.C. § 1501 *et seq.*); the Outer Continental Shelf Lands Act (43 U.S.C. § 1331 *et seq.* and § 1811 *et seq.*); the Intervention on the High Seas Act (33 U.S.C. § 1471 *et seq.*); the Port and Waterways Safety Act and Port and Tanker Safety Act, U.S.C. § 1221 *et seq.* and the Oceans Act of 2000 (33 U.S.C. § 857 *et seq.*).

These laws go beyond international treaties such as the International Convention on Civil Liability for Oil Pollution Damage, and the International Convention for Prevention of Pollution from Ships, 1973 and its Protocol of 1978 (known as "MARPOL 73/78"). However, a lawsuit under the OPA and the Outercontinental Shelf Lands Act to set aside an approval by the U.S. Department of the Interior for drilling in the Beaufort Sea was rejected in *Edwardsen v. U.S. Dept. of Interior,* 268 F.3d 781 (9th Cir. 2001).

---

1 The spill of oil by the Exxon Valdez cost Exxon over $3.4 billion for voluntary cleanup costs, governmental and private claims, and penalties and fines. The loss of its vessel and cargo was alone $46 million. These amounts were described by the Circuit Court of Appeals for the Ninth Circuit in holding that a jury award of $5 billion of punitive damages was excessive. *In re Exxon Valdez*, 270 F.3d 1215 (9th Cir. No. 97-35191, Nov. 7, 2001).

A. Liability Provisions (Title I)

Title I of the OPA provides that each party responsible for a vessel or facility from which oil is discharged, or which poses a substantial threat of an oil discharge, into navigable waters of the United States, the adjoining shorelines, or the exclusive economic zone claimed by the United States by Presidential Proclamation and treaties is liable for removal costs and damages. The liability is imposed upon each responsible party, thus making it likely that the liability is joint and several. The liability is imposed notwithstanding any other provision or rule of law. 33 U.S.C. § 2702(a). A spill only into groundwater is not a spill into navigable waters of the United States. *Rice v. Harkin Exploration,* 270 F.3d 264 (5th Cir. 2001).

Oil includes petroleum, fuel oil, sludge, refuse, and oil mixed with waste, but does not include dredge spoils or any component that is a hazardous substance under CERCLA. The Edible Oil Regulatory Reform Act of 1995 required the USEPA to differentiate between edible oils and other oils and greases, including petroleum, in applying standards. 33 U.S.C. § 2720.

Responsible parties include owners, operators and bareboat charterers of vessels; owners and operators of offshore oil facilities and oil pipelines; and persons licensed to operate deep water ports. The OPA defines a party responsible for an onshore facility and an offshore facility so as to include any person who is an owner or operator except governmental entities. 33 U.S.C. § 2701(32).

Removal costs incurred by the United States, a state, or an Indian Tribe under certain sections of the CWA, the Intervention on the High Seas Act or state law can be recovered by those governmental organizations. Removal costs can be recovered by other persons for acts taken in compliance with the National Contingency Plan. Specified claimants can recover damages for injury to, destruction of, loss of, or loss of use of, natural resources and real or personal property. Recovery is also authorized for loss of subsistence use of natural resources, lost revenues, lost profits and earning capacity, and net costs of providing additional public services. 33 U.S.C. § 2702(b). Punitive damages may not be recovered. *South Port Marine v. Gulf Oil Ltd.*, 234 F.3d 58 (1st Cir. 2000).

The liability does not apply to any discharge permitted by a permit issued under federal, state or local law. It also does not apply to a discharge from a vessel owned or bareboat chartered and operated by the U.S., a state or political subdivision thereof, or a foreign nation, except when the vessel is engaged in commerce. 33 U.S.C. § 2702(e).

The OPA defines a "vessel" to include every description of watercraft other than a public vessel. Thus, its application goes beyond large tanker vessels to include the working vessels of private businesses and recreational vessels owned by private citizens. For example, a tug boat owner was held liable for oil spill cleanup costs resulting from a collision with a cargo vessel. *National Shipping Co. v. Moran*

Trade Corp., 122 F.3d 1062 (4th Cir. 1997). The OPA also defines a "facility" extremely broadly so as to include even motor vehicles.

Even if a third party is *solely* responsible, the OPA requires that a responsible party pay removal costs and damages incurred by the United States and other claimants and then sue the third party based on subrogation to the rights of the United States and other claimants paid. 33 U.S.C. § 2702(d). The OPA contains act of God, act of war, and act of a third party defenses similar to those contained in CERCLA. However, the defenses are narrowed almost to the vanishing point by requirements that the responsible party prove that it not only exercised due care for the oil but also took precautions against foreseeable third party acts or omissions and their foreseeable consequences. Hindsight makes it very difficult to carry this burden of proof. 33 U.S.C. §2703. The OPA contains limits on liability, but the amounts are high and may be avoided by also suing under other laws. 33 U.S.C. § 2704. A vessel owner cannot limit its liability under the OPA by adopting limitations allowed by the Limitation of Liability Act. *Bouchard Transportation Co. v. Updegraff*, 147 F.3d 1344 (11th Cir. 1998). *In re Metlife Capital Corp.*, 132 F.3d 818 (1st Cir. 1998).

The Federal Court of Claims has strictly limited the third party defense to prevent private industry from defending against liability for removal costs and from recovering them from the U.S. Government. The Court found that an oil company had not made an adequate inspection when it failed to foresee that a flood would erode soil and rupture its pipeline, thus causing an oil spill. *Total Petroleum, Inc. v. U.S.*, 12 Ct. Cl. 178 (1987). Uncontroverted evidence that a railroad had fulfilled its duty of visual inspection of a tank car was not conclusive as to whether its measures were sufficient to meet its duty of reasonable care. *Southern Pacific v. U.S.*, 13 Ct. Cl. 402 (1987). A sudden rainstorm with very high winds that occurred while a vessel was transferring oil at a terminal facility was held not to qualify for the act of God defense. *Liberian Poplar Transports, Inc. v. U.S.*, 26 Ct. Cl. 223 (1992). However, the Court of Claims allowed an oil distributor to recover its costs for cleaning up a spill from oil delivery truck after an unavoidable collision with a vehicle which made an unlawful turn in front of the truck. *Grundy Oil Co., Inc. v. U.S.*, 14 Ct. Cl. 759 (1988).

The OPA contains two provisions of which provide some modest relief to private businesses and private citizens who are held liable without fault. Contribution actions against other persons who are or may be liable are authorized by 33 U.S.C. § 2709. Indemnification agreements are authorized by 33 U.S.C. § 2710. Thus, persons held liable without fault can share or shift the liability among themselves, but cannot escape the liability.

B. Natural Resource Damages

Title I of the OPA provides for the recovery of natural resource damages from responsible parties. 33 U.S.C. § 2706(d). Environmental organizations and plaintiff attorneys are vitally interested in these provisions which have potential for very large financial recoveries. In addition, natural resource trustees can use funds from the Oil Spill Liability Trust Fund to investigate and gather evidence to develop a claim.

The USEPA adopted brief provisions for the appointment of natural resource trustees and the assessment of natural resource damages in the National Oil and Hazardous Substances Contingency Plan (NCP). 40 C.F.R. § 300.600 to .665 and Appendix E, § 5.5.

In the late 1980s, the Department of the Interior (DOI) adopted regulations establishing procedures for assessing natural resource damages under CERCLA. The DOI's regulations supplement the NCP procedures for identification, study and response to a discharge of oil or a release of a hazardous substance. The regulations also provide procedures by which a natural resource trustee can determine compensation for injuries to natural resources that are not addressed by response actions pursuant to the NCP. The procedures are not mandatory, but must be used by federal and state natural resource trustees to obtain the rebuttable presumption in their favor provided in the response recovery provisions of CERCLA. 43 C.F.R. Part 11; 42 U.S.C. § 9607(f)(2)(C).

In 1996, the National Oceanic and Atmospheric Administration (NOAA) of the U.S. Department of Commerce adopted regulations on natural resource damage assessments. 15 C.F.R. Part 990. These regulations supersede the DOI's regulations at 43 C.F.R. Part 11 with regard to oil discharges covered by the OPA. However, for natural resource damages resulting from a discharge or release of a mixture of oil and hazardous substance, natural resources trustees must use 43 C.F.R. Part 11 to obtain the rebuttable presumption in their favor provided by the OPA. With some exceptions, NOAA's regulations withstood a court challenge in *General Electric v. Department of Commerce*, 128 F.3d 767 (D.C. Cir. 1997). See proposed amendments at 66 Fed. Reg. 39,464 (July 31, 2001).

C. Financial Responsibility (Title I)

The OPA imposes extensive financial responsibility requirements on owners and operators of vessels, offshore facilities and deepwater ports. 33 U.S.C. §§ 2716 and 2716a. The requirements apply to the responsible party for (1) any vessel over 300 gross tons except a non-self-propelled vessel (barge) that does not carry oil as cargo or fuel and (2) any vessel using the waters of the exclusive economic zone to tranship or lighter oil destined for a place subject to U.S. jurisdiction, 33 U.S.C. § 2716(a).

Each responsible party must provide to the Coast Guard evidence of financial responsibility sufficient to meet its maximum amount of OPA liability. However, a party responsible for more than one vessel need only meet the maximum liability of its vessel having the greatest maximum liability.

The OPA provides that financial responsibility may be established by any one or combination of the following methods which the Coast Guard for vessels and the USEPA for facilities determine to be acceptable: insurance, surety bond, guarantee, letter of credit, qualification as a self-insurer, or other evidence. The OPA limits the defenses available to a guarantor of the financial responsibility of a responsible party. 33 U.S.C. § 2716(e). However, it allows a guarantor to establish an aggregate limit with respect to an incident on the amount of financial responsibility provided to a responsible party. 33 U.S.C. § 2716(g).

Financial responsibility regulations of the U.S. Coast Guard are found at 33 C.F.R. Part 138 (vessels) and 33 C.F.R. § 135.201 (offshore facilities).

D. The Oil Spill Liability Fund (Title I)

Title I of the OPA contains provisions implementing the Oil Spill Liability Trust Fund created by Section 9509 of the Internal Revenue Code of 1986 (IRC, 1986) by providing provisions for uses of the Fund, claims procedures and related provisions. The Fund derived revenues from an excise tax imposed by § 4611 of the Internal Revenue Code of $0.5 per barrel on crude oil and certain other petroleum products. The IRC, 1986 imposes a limit of $1.0 billion per incident on government and private uses of, and claims against, the Fund. The IRC also provides that the tax does not apply during any calendar quarter if the unobligated balance in the Fund exceeds $1.0 billion.

The moneys in the Fund can be used to pay removal costs incurred in accordance with the NCP including monitoring costs of federal and state government agencies. They can also be used to pay the costs of natural resource trustees to develop natural resource damage claims. Other persons may also submit claims for removal costs if they can show they were incurred in a manner consistent with the NCP. A responsible party can also submit a claim if it incurred costs although it was entitled to a defense or limitation of liability. 33 U.S.C. §§ 2712 and 2708.

The regulations of the U.S. Coast Guard on the Fund are found at 33 C.F.R. Parts 133 to 136.

E. Prevention of Oil Pollution (Title IV)

Title IV of the OPA contains numerous provisions intended to prevent oil pollution. Many of them consist of amendments to Title 46 of the U.S. Code. They require the Coast Guard to apply stricter standards and procedures for the issuance and renewal of licenses, certificates of registry and merchant mariners' documents including limits to five year terms and suspension or revocation for alcohol or drug abuse. 46 U.S.C. §§ 7503 and 7701 to 7704. They require the Coast Guard to implement stricter manning standards for tank vessels and to evaluate the adequacy of standards of foreign countries for foreign tank vessels. 46 U.S.C. § 9101(a). They require the Coast Guard to establish minimum plating thickness standards for bulk oil cargo vessels and to require periodic gauging of the plating thickness of such vessels when over 30 years old. They require the

Coast Guard to issue minimum standards for overfill devices and tank level or pressure monitoring devices. With certain exceptions, they require new tank vessels and tank vessels undergoing a major conversion on or after June 30, 1990 to be double hulled. With certain exceptions, they require tank vessels of at least 5,000 gross tons without a double hull to be phased out over a 20 year period from 1995 to 2015 46 U.S.C. § 3701 *et seq.*

The Coast Guard has adopted regulations implementing the OPA. The regulations on licenses and certificates of registry for marine officers (including training schools, professional requirements, examinations and demonstrations of professional competence) are found at 46 C.F.R. Part 10. The regulations on certification of seamen are at 46 C.F.R. Part 12. The regulations on certification of tankermen are at 46 C.F.R. Part 13. The regulations on chemical testing for drugs and alcohol are at 46 C.F.R. Part 16.

The Coast Guard regulations prescribing minimum requirements for the manning of inspected and uninspected vessels are at 46 C.F.R. Part 15. These regulations prescribe not only the minimum complement of officers and crew deemed necessary for safe operation of a vessel but also the licensing and other qualifications they must have.

The Coast Guard regulations on vessel design, equipment, inspection and certification are found in several places. Regulations on tank vessels are found at 46 C.F. R Parts 30 to 39. Regulations on passenger vessels are at 46 C.F.R. Parts 70 to 80. Regulations on cargo and miscellaneous vessels are at 46 C.F.R. Parts 90 to 105. Regulations on mobile offshore drilling units are at 46 C.F.R. Parts 107 to 109. Special rules on barges, ships and vessels carrying bulk cargoes are at 46 C.F.R. Part 172.

The Coast Guard regulations on the design, equipment, installation and operation of tank vessels carrying oil in bulk are at 40 C.F.R. Part 157. These regulations contain the double hull requirements including interim measures for some tank vessels without double hulls carrying petroleum and other oils. 40 C.F.R. §§ 157.400 to 157.610. The OPA does not define a double hull. However, the regulations define a double hull to mean watertight protective spaces that do not carry any oil and which separate the sides, bottom, forward end, and aft end of tanks that hold any oil within the cargo tank length from the outer skin of the vessel as prescribed in § 157.10d. Detailed general specifications for double hulls are provided in § 157.10d.

A claim against the United States alleging a taking of single hull oil tankers as a result of the provisions of Title IV was held to be premature because the requirements have not yet taken affect. *Maritrans, Inc. v. United States*, 43 Fed. Claims Ct. 86 (1999).

The International Maritime Organization (IMO) has also scheduled a conversion of all tank vessels to double hulls by 2015, but will allow alternate designs that achieve the required spill protection at lower cost. The Coast Guard has not allowed alternatives to double hulls.

The states are free to impose operational requirements or tanker vessels, but the OPA preempts the states from imposing additional design requirements such as extra navigational and emergency equipment. *International Association of Independent Tanker Owners v. Loche*, 148 F.3d 1053 (9th Cir. 1998).

Some of the provisions in Title IV appear to be motivated at least partially to favor domestic ships and maritime professionals. For example, certain single hulled foreign vessels over 5,000 tons must be escorted in Northwestern waters by two tugs. Certain vessels must use a U.S. or Canadian pilot on the Great Lakes. Certain vessels are required to have a licensed master or mate on the bridge in addition to the pilot.

F. Removal of Oil Discharges (Title IV)

Title IV of the OPA establishes primary authority of the federal government over the mitigation or prevention of oil discharges and the removal of oil discharges. 33 U.S.C. § 1321. However, state laws are not preempted. 33 U.S.C. § 1321(o). Removal is required to be in accordance with the NCP and is also subject to the National Planning and Response System contained in the Coast Guard regulations at 33 C.F.R. Part 155. 40 C.F.R. § 302. In order to encourage cooperation, the OPA provides that a person is not liable for removal costs or damages which result from actions taken or omitted in the course of rendering care, assistance or advice consistent with the NCP or as otherwise directed by the USEPA. 33 U.S.C. § 1321(c)(4).

Coastal marine transportation facilities and vessels handling, storing or transporting oil in bulk as cargo are required to develop and implement discharge response plans addressing, among other things, "worst case" discharges. For example, secondary containment must be adequate to hold the entire contents of the largest single tank within the containment system. 33 U.S.C. § 1321(j)(5); 40 C.F.R. Parts 154 and 155.

G. Other Regulations

The Coast Guard's regulations on deepwater ports, including pollution prevention equipment and oil transfer operations, are at 33 C.F.R. Parts 148 to 150.

H. Criminal and Civil Penalties

1. Criminal Penalties

The OPA imposes numerous and draconian civil and criminal penalties for a variety of violations. For example, negligent discharge of oil is treated as a criminal offense. 33 U.S.C. § 1319(c)(1). A knowing violation is treated as a felony. 33

U.S.C. § 1319(c)(2). Like other environmental laws, a "knowing" violation does not require proof that the person accused knew that he, she or it was breaking the law, but only that the person knew is was taking the action that resulted in the violation.

If a person who commits a "knowing" violation has actual knowledge that the actions pose a serious threat to human health and life, the person is subject to significantly increased fines and imprisonment periods. 33 U.S.C. § 1319(c). If a person who commits a "knowing" violation knows that another person is placed in imminent danger of death or serous bodily harm, the fine for an individual is up to $250,000 and imprisonment is up to 15 years. For an organization, the fine is up to $1,000,000. 33 U.S.C. § 1319(c).

Failure to notify the appropriate federal agency of an oil discharge is subject to a fine up to $250,000 and imprisonment up to five years for individuals and a fine up to $500,000 for organizations. 42 U.S.C. § 1321(b)(5).

Similar criminal penalties are imposed for violation of the vessel manning regulations. 42 U.S.C. § 1321. Thus, vessel owners and operators who may wish to economize face not only opposition from labor unions and employees but also criminal penalties imposed without regard to fault.

2. Civil and Administrative Penalties

Permit violations are subject to civil penalties and administrative penalties up to $25,000 per day of violation. 33 U.S.C. § 1319(d) and (g). Oil discharges and failures to comply with regulations are subject to administrative penalties up to $10,000 per day up to $25,000 for a Class I penalty and $125,000 for a Class II penalty. 33 U.S.C. § 1321(b)(6). Failure to comply with the financial responsibility requirements is subject to civil penalties up to $25,000 per day. 33 U.S.C. § 2716a. Smaller civil penalties apply to violations of the manning requirements. 33 U.S.C. § 8101 *et seq.*

Oil discharges, failures to remove discharges, and failures to comply with orders or regulations are also subject to court imposed civil penalties up to $25,000 per day of violation or $1,000 per barrel of oil spilled or three times the cleanup costs incurred by the Oil Spill Liability Trust fund. If a violation results from gross negligence or willful misconduct, the civil penalties are a minimum of $100,000 and $3,000 per barrel of oil discharged.

Under the Debt Collection Improvement Act, the amounts of civil penalties are adjusted for inflation every four years. The 1998 adjustment was 10%. Thus, for example, $25,000 maximum penalties were increased to $27,500.

A court upheld a civil penalty on the operator of an oil terminal for a discharge that caused a light sheen of oil in a small area of Curtis Bay, Baltimore, Maryland. The discharge resulted from a 10 gallon spill by a customer that overflowed the facility's oil water separator as a result of a heavy rain. *BP Exploration v. Dept. of Transportation*, 44 F. Supp. 2d 34 (D.D.C. 1999).

3. Small Vessels and Facilities; Small Discharges

Some owners and operators of small vessels and facilities believe that the OPA applies to corporations such as Exxon Mobil that own and operate large vessels and facilities. However, the law also applies to owners and operators of small vessels and facilities and criminalizes small oil spills.

The captain of the M/V Venture Pride was convicted of failing to report an oil discharge at Cruz Bay, St. Johns in the U.S. Virgin Islands. *U.S. v. Frederick*, 38 F. Supp. 2d 396 (D.V.I. 1999). A leak or spill of only a few gallons that creates a "sheen" on water will support a conviction. *Orgulf Transport v. U.S.*, 711 F. Supp. 344 (W.D. Ky 1989); *U.S. v. Chotin Transport*, 649 F. Supp. 356 (S.D. Ohio 1986).

CHAPTER XVIII
LAWS PROTECTING WILDLIFE, FISH, PLANTS AND MARINE MAMMALS

A. The Endangered Species Act

1. Background

The Endangered Species Act, 16 U.S.C. § 1531 *et seq.*, (ESA) creates a number of federal regulatory programs. The most fundamental is its prohibition of actions including the import, export, possession, sale or "taking" of endangered species of fish, wildlife and plants. The Act is administered by the Fish & Wildlife Service of the U.S. Department of the Interior (FWS). FWS's regulations are found at 50 C.F.R. Part 10 *et seq.* and Part 402 *et seq.* The ESA was adopted with widespread public support after extensive campaigns by environmental groups describing a need to protect animals such as eagles, seals, whooping cranes, swans and buffaloes.

The National Marine Fisheries Service (NMFS) of the National Oceanographic and Atmospheric Administration (NOAA) of the U.S. Department of Commerce also administers the ESA as to certain marine and anadromous species. The NMFS has adopted regulations on the taking and importing of marine mammals (50 C.F.R. Part 216); general endangered and threatened marine species (50 C.F.R. Part 222); threatened marine and anadromous species (50 C.F.R. Part 223); endangered marine and anadromous species (50 C.F.R. Part 224); and designated critical habitat (50 C.F.R. Part 226). The FWS and the NMFS have adopted joint regulations on anadromous fisheries (50 C.F.R. Part 401); interagency cooperation (50 C.F.R. Part 402); state programs (50 C.F.R. Part 403); listing endangered and threatened species (50 C.F.R. Part 424); and the endangered species exemption process. (50 C.F.R. Parts 450 to 453).

To avoid duplication and repetition, this chapter discusses the ESA in terms of its administration by the FWS which has a role that is broader and more familiar to the public than the role of the NMFS. However, readers should keep in mind that it is the NMFS which has responsibilities such as listing and designating critical habitat for (1) marine and anadromous fish such as sturgeon and salmon;

(2) marine mammals such as whales, seals and sea lions; and (3) sea turtles. See 50 C.F.R. §§ 223.102 and 224.101.

2. Listing of Endangered and Threatened Species

The ESA provides for the FWS to publish lists of all species that it has determined to be endangered or threatened. Listing of a species is a key first step to imposing restrictions on commercial or industrial use of land determined to be the critical habitat of the species.

The ESA states that an "endangered species" is any species in danger of extinction throughout all or a significant portion of its range other than insects determined by the FWS to be pests whose protection would present an overriding risk to man. 16 U.S.C. § 1532(6). 50 C.F.R. § 424.02(e). A "threatened species" is any species likely to become an endangered species in the foreseeable future throughout all or a significant part of its range. 16 U.S.C. § 1532(20).

A "species" includes any subspecies of fish, wildlife or plants and any distinct population segment of any species of vertebrate fish or wildlife which interbreeds when mature. 16 U.S.C. § 1532(16).

Based on these definitions, the FWS has very extensive authority to list fish, animals, and plants as endangered or threatened species. The FWS is not limited to a true biological species. For example, the FWS may list a subspecies or any group that it finds to be a distinct population segment (DPS) or an evolutionary significant unit (ESU). 56 Fed. Reg. 58,612 (1991); 61 Fed. Reg. 4721 (1996). This freedom to subdivide allows the FWS to impose land use control restrictions in areas where a fish, animal or plant is scarce, even though it exists in larger numbers and under favorable conditions in other areas.

The FWS also need not show that a "species" is actually endangered or threatened. The FWS may list on the basis of any of five criteria: (1) actual or threatened destruction, modification or curtailment of habitat or range; (2) overutilization for commercial, recreational, scientific or educational purposes; (3) disease or predation; (4) inadequacy of existing regulatory protection; or (5) other natural or manmade factors affecting continued existence. 40 C.F.R. § 424.11(c). When the FWS considered planned future actions to protect a species, environmental groups obtained court orders limiting it to consideration of existing regulatory mechanisms. *Southwest Center v. Babbitt*, 939 F. Supp. 49 (D.D.C. 1996); *Biodiversity Legal Foundation v. Babbitt*, 943 F. Supp. 23 (D.D.C. 1996); *Friends of Wild Swan, Inc. v. U.S. Fish and Wildlife Service*, 945 F. Supp. 1388 (D. Ore. 1996).

The ESA authorizes the FWS to make emergency listings of species without following the required rulemaking procedures. 16 U.S.C. § 1533(b)(7). *City of Las Vegas v. Lujan*, 891 F.2d 927 (D.C. Cir. 1989).

The FWS has listed nearly two thousand endangered and threatened species, but has not limited the lists to the popular animals envisioned by the public.

The FWS has listed numerous predatory animals and pests such as hawks, wolves, bears, reptiles and rats. The lists are at 50 C.F.R. § 17.11 (wildlife) and § 17.12 (plants). For an example of a listing proposal, see the proposal to list the San Bernardino kangaroo rat. 66 Fed. Reg. 46,251 (Sept. 4, 2001).

As mentioned earlier, the NMFS has listed certain marine and anadromous fish, marine mammals and sea turtles as threatened or endangered species. The lists appear at 50 C.F.R. §§ 223.102 and 224.101.

3. Critical Habitat

For each "endangered species" or "threatened species" the FWS must designate a "critical habitat" which means the areas containing features essential to the conservation of the species and may require special management considerations or protection. 16 U.S.C. § 1532(5)(A). *Sierra Club v. U.S. Fish & Wildlife Service*, 245 F.3d 434 (5th Cir. 2001); *Forest Guardians v. Babbitt*, 174 F.3d 1178 (10th Cir. 1999). The ESA states that the FWS must base its designation of critical habitat on the best scientific data available after considering its economic impact. 16 U.S.C. § 1533(b)(2); 50 C.F.R. § 424.12(a). *New Mexico Cattle Growers v. U.S. Fish & Wildlife*, 248 F.3d 1277 (10th Cir. 2001).

As criteria for determining "critical habitat," the FWS has adopted regulations saying that it may consider (1) space for normal behavior and individual and population growth; (2) food, water, light, minerals or other nutritional or physiological requirements; (3) cover or shelter; (4) sites for breeding, reproduction or rearing of offspring, germination and seed dispersal; and (5) habitats protected from disturbance or representative of the historical and ecological distribution of the "endangered species." The FWS also considers roosting sites, nesting grounds, spawning sites, feeding sites, seasonal wetland and dryland, vegetation, soil type, and water quantity and quality. 50 C.F.R. § 424.12(b).

Using these broad considerations, the FWS may designate thousands of square miles as critical habitat for an "endangered species" or a "threatened species" indigenous to the United States. The area must be delineated in a map published in the Federal Register. 50 C.F.R. § 424.12(c). The FWS does not designate a critical habitat for "endangered species" outside the United States.

FWS designations of critical habitats and maps appear at 50 C.F.R. §§ 17.94 to .96. NMFS critical habitat designations are at 50 C.F.R. Part 226.

4. Limited Need to Consider Scientific Data

Court decisions have interpreted the statutory requirement of the best scientific data to favor listing of numerous species and designation of expansive "critical habitats" for them. For example, the FWS may use estimates rather than actual counts of "endangered species" and must designate critical habitat based on limited scientific data presently available without waiting for better data to be developed over a period of time. *Southwest Center v. Babbitt*, 215 F. 3d 58 (D.C. Cir. 2000); *Conner v. Burford*, 848 F. 2d 1441 (9th Cir. 1988).

5. Social and Economic Impacts

The FWS is not authorized to consider economic impact when deciding whether to list an "endangered species." Consideration of economic impact applies only to the designation of critical habitat. 50 U.S.C. § 1533(b)(12). *New Mexico Cattle Growers v. U.S. Fish & Wildlife*, supra.

Although the FWS is required to consider the economic impact of its designation of critical habitat, it is not authorized to consider the social impact. Once the FWS prepares and considers an analysis of the economic impact, it can designate "critical habitat" notwithstanding adverse social and economic impacts such as loss of employment and revenues at businesses in the restricted area. *Douglas County v. Lujan*, 810 F. Supp. 1470, reversed in part, 48 F.3d 1495 (9th Cir. 1995); cert. denied 516 U.S. 1042, 733 L. Ed. 2d 655 (1996). The fact that Congress itself had appropriated large sums of money for the Tellico Dam, which was nearly completed in an area needing economic development, was not enough economic impact to persuade the U.S. Supreme Court that it took precedence over the critical habitat of a small fish called a snail darter. *TVA v. Hill*, 437 U.S. 153, 57 L. Ed. 2d 117(1977).

Nevertheless, the FWS must analyze all of the economic impacts of critical habitat designation. It may not use a "baseline approach" designed to exclude economic impacts of listing an endangered species that the FWS presumed to be coextensive with a critical habitat listing. *New Mexico Cattle Growers v. U.S. Fish & Wildlife*, supra. The court explained that the FWS had for some years deferred adoption of critical habitat for many listed species on grounds that it was unnecessary because the prohibitions of its "jeopardy standard" in 50 C.F.R. § 402.02 were coextensive with the prohibitions of its "adverse modification" standard for designated critical habitat. Thus, when designating critical habitat for the southwestern flycatcher, the FWS determined that the designation would have no economic impact. The court held that the "baseline approach" violated the plain language of the ESA and the intent of Congress to require that critical habitat be designated and that cost be considered at that stage of the process.

6. Prohibited Conduct

The ESA contains numerous prohibitions against conduct that might affect a listed species or its critical habitat. The prohibitions include (1) importing, exporting or "taking" any endangered species; (2) possessing, selling, delivering, carrying, transporting or shipping any endangered species unlawfully taken in the course of any commercial activity or activity involving interstate or foreign commerce in endangered species; (3) any violation of the regulations of the

FWS. 16 U.S.C. § 1538(a). The prohibitions are subject to exceptions for species before specified dates. 16 U.S.C. § 1538(b).

The prohibitions include any violation of the Convention on International Trade in Endangered Species of Wild Flora and Fauna. 16 U.S.C. § 1538(c). They also include engaging in business as an importer of fish, wildlife, plants or African elephant ivory without permission from the FWS other than imports of shellfish and fishery products not listed as endangered or threatened species and imported for human or animal consumption or taken in waters under U.S. jurisdiction or on the high seas for recreational purposes. 16 U.S.C. § 1538(d). The prohibitions also include any attempt, solicitation or conduct that causes a violation. 16 U.S.C. § 1538(g).

The FWS has adopted regulations interpreting the prohibitions and creating some exceptions. 50 C.F.R. §§ 17.21, 17.31,17.61, 17.71, 17.82 and 17.104. The FWA and the regulations authorize any person to "take" endangered species in defense of his or her own life or the lives of others. *Shuler v. Babbitt*, 49 F. Supp. 2d 1165 (D. Mont. 1998). However, the authorization does not extend to defense of property and a rancher was convicted of violation of the ESA for shooting a wolf after wolves killed over 80 of his sheep. *U.S. v. McKittrick*, 142 F.3d 1170 (9th Cir. 1998); cert. den. 525 U.S. 1072, 142 L. Ed. 2d 667. See also *Christy v. Hodel*, 857 F.2d 1324 (9th Cir. 1989) upholding a fine imposed on another sheep farmer for killing a grizzly bear.

The ESA states that the term "take" means to harass, harm, pursue, hunt, shoot, wound, kill, trap, capture, or collect, or to attempt to engage in such conduct. 16 U.S.C. § 1532 (19). The FWS' regulations define the term "harass" expansively to mean any intentional or negligent act or omission which creates the likelihood of injury to wildlife by annoying it to such an extent as to interrupt its normal behavioral patterns, subject to some exceptions for animal husbandry practices, breeding procedure and veterinary care. 50 C.F.R. § 17.3. The regulations define the term "harm" as any act which actually kills or injures wildlife including significant habitat modification or degradation where it actually kills or injures wildlife by significantly impairing essential patterns including breeding, feeding or sheltering. 50 C.F.R. § 17.3.

The prohibition against "taking" includes "incidental takings" such as relocation of a listed endangered species or modification of its habitat. *City of Las Vegas v. Lujan*. 891 F.2d 927 (D.C.Cir. 1989). Lighting a beachfront was held to be a "taking" because it changed the night habitat of sea turtles. *Loggerhead Turtle v. County Council*, 148 F.3d 1231 (11th Cir. 1998). A lawsuit could be brought against logging because it presented an imminent threat of injury to Northern Spotted Owls by impairing their essential behavioral patterns. *Forest Conservation Council v. Roseboro Lumber*, 50 F.3d 781 (9th Cir. 1995). A lawsuit could also be brought based on claims that logging constitutes a taking of coho salmon. *Coho Salmon v. Pacific Lumber Co.*, 61 F. Supp. 2d 1001 (N.D. Cal. 1999). A railroad which spilled corn on railroad tracks was found to have "taken" bears killed while feeding on the spilled corn, although an injunction was denied in view of costly corrective actions by the railroad to prevent any future threat to the bears. *National Wildlife Federation v. Burlington Northern*, 23 F.3d 1508 (9th Cir. 1998).

Indirectly caused harm may also be a "taking." For example, the State of Hawaii was found to have taken palila birds because it maintained goats and sheep which ate seedlings of mumane trees which were part of the habitat of the palila birds. *Palila v. Hawaii Dept. of Land and Natural Resources*, 852 F.2d 1106 (9th Cir. 1988). Unintended and indirect harm to red-cockaded woodpeckers and northern spotted owls by modification of their habitat was upheld as a taking by the U.S. Supreme Court. *Babbitt v. Sweet Home Chapter*, 515 U.S. 687 (1995).

The *Sweet Home Chapter* decision by the U.S. Supreme Court left open for case-by-case resolution such related issues as whether wildlife actually have been, or will be, killed or injured and whether particular activities have a causal relation to such harm. For example, when plaintiffs failed to present credible evidence that deer hunting on the Quabbin Reservation in Massachusetts had or would cause injury to bald eagles by ingestion of lead slugs, a judgment against them was upheld. *American Bald Eagle v. Bhatti*, 9 F.3d 163 (1st Cir. 1993).

6. Experimental Populations

The ESA provides that the FWS may authorize the release of any population of an endangered or a threatened species outside the current range if the release will further the conservation of such species. 16 U.S.C. § 1539(j)(2)(A). For example, the FWS has used this authority to release experimental populations of wolves in spite of considerable opposition from ranchers, farmers and other persons affected by the releases.

Before authorizing such a release, the FWS must identify the population and determine whether it is essential to the continued existence of an endangered or threatened species. Each member of an experimental population is treated as a threatened species, but the FWS is not authorized to designate a critical habitat for an experimental population unless it has determined that the experimental population is essential to the continued existence of a species. 16 U.S.C. § 1539(j)(2)(B) and (C).

The FWS was entitled to transport gray wolves from Canada into the United States to create an experimental population. *U.S. v. McKittrick*, 142 F.3d 1170 (9th Cir. 1998); cert den. 525 U.S. 1072, 142 L. Ed. 2d 667.

The constitutionality of a regulation adopted by the FWS to establish a population of red wolves that limited their taking on private land was upheld in *Gibbs v. Babbitt*, 214 F.3d 483 (4th Cir. 2000). In its opinion, the court pointed out that, among other things, the regulation authorized not only the taking of the red wolves in defense of a person's own life and the lives of others but also authorized private landowners to take red wolves on their property when in the act of killing livestock or pets.

7. Permits, Exemptions and Other Exceptions

a. Permits

The FWS is authorized to issue permits allowing an otherwise prohibited act (1) if it is for scientific purposes or to enhance the propagation or survival of the affected species, or (2) if it is a taking incidental to, and not the purpose of, the carrying out of an otherwise lawful activity. A permit applicant must submit to the FWS a conservation plan that, among other things, specifies the likely impacts from the taking and steps the applicant will take to minimize and mitigate such impacts, including the funding available to implement the steps. The FWS may issue the permit only if it makes several findings with respect to the application and the conservation plan including a finding that the taking will not appreciably reduce the likelihood of survival and recovery of the species in the wild. 16 U.S.C. § 1539(a).

FWS has published its general permit procedures at 50 C.F.R. Part 13. Special provisions authorizing permits for scientific purposes, enhancement of propagation or incidental taking of endangered wildlife are at 50 C.F.R. § 17.22. Special provisions authorizing permits for scientific purposes, enhancement of propagation or survival, economic hardship, zoological exhibition, educational purposes, or incidental taking of threatened species are at 50 C.F.R. § 17.32. Applicants for permits must include a habitat conservation plan which, among other things, describes the impacts likely to result from the taking, the steps the applicant will take to minimize and mitigate the impacts, and the funding available to implement the steps. To provide guidelines to applicants, the FWS has published a Habitat Conservation Handbook.

b. Hardship Exemptions; Exemptions for Alaska Natives

The ESA authorizes the FWS to issue limited hardship exemptions to persons who have entered into a contract with respect to a species of fish, wildlife or plant before the publication in the Federal Register of notice of consideration of the species as an endangered species. 66 U.S.C. § 1539(b). The ESA also contains exceptions from the taking and import prohibitions for any Indian, Aleut or Eskimo who is an Alaskan Native who resides in Alaska and any non-native permanent resident of an Alaskan village if the taking is for subsistence purposes. There is also an exception for sales of native articles of handicrafts and clothing. 16 U.S.C. § 1539(c).

c. Exemptions Granted by the Endangered Species Committee

In 1978, Congress amended the ESA to authorize a federal agency, a state governor, or a permit or license applicant whose application for a federal permit or license has been denied based on the ESA to submit an application to the FWS for an exemption that may be granted by the Endangered Species Committee. The Committee members are the chief administrators of federal government departments and agencies, including the USEPA. The application and review procedures are extremely difficult and the Committee has only rarely granted an exemption. 16 U.S.C. §1536(e); 50 C.F.R. Parts 450-453.

8. Conservation Programs, Recovery Plans and Consultation

The ESA requires the U.S. Department of the Interior to develop and implement recovery plans for the conservation and survival of each listed species unless it finds that a recovery plan will not promote conservation of the species. 16 U.S.C. § 1533(f)(1). The FWS generally prepares a recovery plan within three years after a listing. The courts have held that the timing, content and implementation of the plans are discretionary and that the plans are guidelines and not mandatory. *Fund for Animals, Inc. v. Rice*, 85 F.3d 535 (11th Cir. 1996); *Oregon NRC v. Turner*, 863 F. Supp. 1277 (D. Ore. 1994). In general, the courts have rejected lawsuits claiming that the federal government agencies were obligated to go beyond their plans to include measures demanded by environmental groups. *Hawksbill Sea Turtle v. FEMA*, 11 F. Supp. 2d 529 (D.V.I. 1998).

The ESA requires the U.S. Department of the Interior, the U.S. Department of Commerce and other federal government agencies to use their authorities in furtherance of its purposes by carrying out programs for conservation of listed species. 16 U.S.C. 1536(a)(1). The authorization of these programs is not intended, however, to expand the powers granted to these agencies. *Platte River Whooping Crane Trust v. FERC*, 962 F.2d 27 (D.C. Cir. 1992).

The ESA requires federal government agencies to consult with the FWS and to avoid activities that jeopardize listed species or destroy or adversely modify their critical habitat. The consultation is required for any discretionary action authorized, funded or carried out by the agency. 16 U.S.C. § 1536(a)(2). The FWS regulations are at 40 C.F.R. Part 402. The FWS has also published a Consultation Handbook. Among other things, a biological assessment must be prepared for each major construction activity if a listed endangered or threatened species or critical habitat may be in the activity area. The FWS has sought to expand its consultation role into a veto power by adopting a regulation indicating that a federal agency which determines that it cannot comply with a jeopardy biological opinion of the FWS must notify the FWS of its decision and may apply for an exemption. 50 C.F.R. § 402.15.

The courts have often supported the FWS and environmental groups in claims that federal agencies must consult on a wide range of agency actions. *Klamath Water Users v. Patterson*, 191 F.3d 1115 (9th Cir. 1999); *NRDC v. Houston*, 146 F. 3d 1118 (9th Cir. 1998); *O'Neil v. U.S.*, 50 F.3d 677 (9th Cir. 1995); *Lane County Audubon v. Jamison*, 958 F.2d 290 (9th Cir. 1992); *Pacific Rivers Council v. Thomas*, 30 F.3d 1050 (9th Cir. 1994).

On the other hand, several environmental groups have sought court orders requiring federal agencies to consult with the FWS on matters for which the agencies had no discretionary authority. Their objective was to "bootstrap" the consultation obligation into a vehicle by which the environmental groups and the FWS could block projects which the other federal agencies did not have authority to block. The courts have so far declined these efforts to expand the consultation obligations. *Sierra Club v. Babbitt*, 65 F.3d 1502 (9th Cir. 1995); *Platte River Whooping Crane Trust v. FERC*, supra.

9. Penalties and Enforcement

a. Civil and Criminal Penalties

Any person who knowingly violates the ESA or any permit or implementing regulation as to an endangered species may be assessed a civil penalty by the FWS of up to $25,000 for each violation and a criminal fine up to $100,000 and up to one year of imprisonment. A person who knowingly commits these violations as to a threatened animal or plant may be assessed a civil penalty up to $12,000 and a criminal fine up to $25,000 and up to six months imprisonment. Certain recordkeeping regulations are excepted from these civil and criminal penalties. 16 U.S.C. § 1540(a) and (b). If a person is engaged in business as an importer or exporter of fish, wildlife or plants, there is no requirement that the violation be knowing. 16 U.S.C. § 1549(a) and (b). The criminal law increases the maximum fine for a knowing violation as to an endangered species from $50,000 to $100,000. 18 U.S.C. § 3571(b)(5). Any person who otherwise violates the ESA or any regulation, permit or certificate issued thereunder may be assessed a civil penalty up to $500 per violation by the ESA. The penalties are adjusted every four years pursuant to the Debt Collection Improvement Act of 1996.

The FWS is authorized to pay rewards to any person who furnishes information leading to an arrest, criminal conviction, civil penalty assessment, or forfeiture of property for any violation of the ESA or any regulation thereunder. 16 U.S.C. § 1540(d).

The ESA also authorizes extensive enforcement powers including detention for inspection of any package, crate or container and searches, seizures and arrests with or without a warrant. ESA also authorizes forfeiture of property seized such as guns, traps, nets and other equipment, vessels, vehicles, aircraft and other means of transportation used in violation of its provisions. 16 U.S.C. § 1540(e).

Two U.S. Circuit Courts of Appeals have held that a defendant can be convicted of a criminal violation of the ESA without proof of wrongful intent. The Fifth Circuit held that a defendant could be convicted of possession of a loggerhead sea turtle if he knew he was in possession of the turtle regardless of whether he knew it was an endangered species or that was unlawful to possess it. *U.S. v. Nguyen*, 916 F.2d 1016 (5th Cir. 1990). The Fifth Circuit reached a similar conclusion in a later case involving *U.S. v. Ivey*, 949 F.2d 759 (5th Cir. 1991). The Ninth Circuit held that a defendant should be convicted of shooting a gray wolf if he knew he was shooting an animal, even though he may have believed it was a wild dog. *U.S. v. McKittrick*, 142 F.3d 1170 (9th Cir. 1998).

The ESA allows a limited defense to both civil and criminal penalties. If it can be shown by a preponderance of the evidence that the defendant committed an act based on a good faith belief that he was acting to protect himself or herself or a family member or other individual from bodily harm, then no civil penalty shall be imposed and there should be no criminal conviction. 16 U.S.C. § 1540(a)(3) and (b)(3).

10. Land Use Control and The ESA

The ESA is an important factor in efforts to achieve land use control.

The construction of "Westway" in New York City was blocked by a coalition of environmentalists, local commercial groups and political leaders who wanted to trade the construction funds for mass transit subsidies. These groups professed concern that Westway would adversely affect sea bass in the Hudson River. Concern for sea bass did not block other projects on the Hudson River waterfront such as Battery Park City, the North River Sewage Treatment Plant, redevelopment of old piers such as the Chelsea Pier, and the redevelopment of the Westside Highway.

Another example was the "snail darter" which was the subject of a lawsuit to block the Tellico Dam. *Hill v. TVA*, 549 F.2d 1064 (6th Cir. 1977), aff'd 437 U.S. 153, 57 L. Ed. 2d 117. Still another example was use of the "spotted owl" to block logging projects in the forests of the Pacific Northwest in spite of opposition by companies which lost business and their workers who lost employment. See, e.g., *National Audubon Society v. Espy*, 998 F.2d 699 (9th Cir. 1993).

A bird called the Southwestern Willow Flycatcher was the subject of an unsuccessful lawsuit involving the area near Lake Mead and the Hoover Dam. *Southwest Center v. Bureau of Reclamation*, 143 F.3d 515 (9th Cir. 1998).

A campaign on behalf of a small fish called the Alabama Sturgeon did not prevent the Alabama Tombigbee Rivers canal project which is of immense importance to the economies of Alabama, Mississippi and other states. One phase of the long battle is described in *Alabama Tombigbee Rivers Coalition Dept. of Interior*, 26 F.3d 1103 (5th Cir. 1999).

11. Trade in Endangered Species

The U.S. is a party to the Convention on International Trade in Endangered Species which is implemented by 16 U.S.C. § 1537 and the FWS regulations at 50 C.F.R. Part 23.

12. Citizen Suits

The ESA authorizes any person to file a lawsuit in a U.S. District Court seeking to enjoin a violation of the ESA by any person, including the United States, or to require the U.S. Department of Interior to take enforcement actions or perform other duties required by the ESA. 16 U.S.C. § 1540(g). The U.S. Supreme Court described the provision as remarkably broad. *Bennett v. Spear*, 520 U.S. 154, 137 L. Ed. 2d 281 (1997).

The ESA requires a 60 day notice to the proposed defendants before filing the lawsuit so that they may take corrective actions, if appropriate. Some environmental groups have declined or failed to give the notice and their lawsuits were dismissed. *Southwest Center v. Bureau of Reclamation*, 143 F.3d 515 (9th Cir. 1998); *Save the Yaak Committee v. Block*, 840 F.2d 714 (9th Cir. 1988); Sanctions on counsel for failure to give notice were upheld in *Maine Audubon Society v. Purslow*, 907 F.2d 265 (1st Cir. 1990).

The plaintiff in a citizen's suit must demonstrate that it has standing to sue. This is a constitutional requirement. The plaintiff must show that (1) it suffered injury in fact to a legally protected interest that is actual or imminent and not conjectural or hypothetical; (2) the injury was caused or "fairly traceable" to the defendant's action; and (3) the injury will likely be redressed by a favorable judicial ruling.

For example, the U.S. Supreme Court held that two Oregon irrigation districts and two ranch operators had standing to challenge a biological opinion and conclusions of the FWS relating to the Klamath Irrigation Project that would deprive them of water supplies which they had used for years. The Court rejected an argument that private water users should be treated less favorably than environmental groups. *Lujan v. Defenders of Wildlife*, 504 U.S. 555, 119 L. Ed. 2d 351 (1992).

Electric power purchasing cooperatives had standing to challenge a biological opinion prepared by the National Marine Fisheries Service and related actions by other federal government agencies in response to the listing of three populations of Snake River salmon as endangered species. However, summary judgment against them was upheld because the issues had become moot. *Pacific Northwest Generating Co-Op v. Brown*, 38 F.3d 1058 (9th Cir. 1994).

The U.S. Supreme Court held that plaintiff environmentalists who had visited Egypt to see the Nile Crocodile and Sri Lanka to see the Asian Elephant and Leopard and alleged that they planned to visit again at unspecified times did not have standing to challenge a regulation of the FWS excluding federal agency actions outside the United States from consultation obligations under the ESA. The Court also denied standing because a favorable decision vacating the rule and requiring consultation would be unlikely to affect the foreign projects of concern to the plaintiffs because the federal agencies were funding only a small part of the cost of the projects. *Bennett v. Spear*, 520 U.S. 154, 137 L. Ed. 2d 281

(1997). A similar result was reached in *Humane Society v. Babbitt*, 46 F.3d 93 (D.C. Cir. 1995).

B. The Marine Mammal Protection Act

1. Background

The Marine Mammal Protection Act (MMPA) imposes a moratorium on the taking and importation of marine mammals and marine mammal products, subject to several exceptions and exemptions. 16 U.S.C. § 1361 *et seq.* The MMPA is administered by the National Marine Fisheries Service (NMFS) of the National Oceanographic and Atmospheric Administration (NOAA) of the U.S. Department of Commerce and the Marine Mammal Commission. State laws regulating marine mammals are preempted.

2. Definitions

The term "marine mammal" means any mammal which (1) is morphologically adopted to the marine environment (such as sea otters) or (2) primarily inhabits the marine environment (such as polar bears), including any part such as its fur or skin. Examples of marine mammals are whales, dolphins, seals, sea lions, sea turtles, sea otters and polar bears. The term "take" means to harass, hunt, capture or kill or an attempt to do any of those actions. The term "harassment" means any act of pursuit, torment or annoyance which (1) has the potential to injure a marine mammal or marine mammal stock in the wild or (2) has the potential disturb a marine mammal or marine mammal stock in the wild by causing disruption of behavioral patterns such as migration, breathing, nursing, breeding, feeding or sheltering. 16 U.S.C. § 1362.

The prohibition against taking has been interpreted very broadly. For example, feeding wild dolphins was held to be a taking because it disturbed their normal behavior and could make them less able to search for food or their own. *Strong v. U.S.*, 5 F.3d 905 (5th Cir. 1995).

3. Exceptions and Exemptions

There are several exceptions to the taking moratorium. For example, the NMFS may issue permits for importation for scientific research, public display, photography for educational or commercial purposes, or enhancing the survival or recovery of a species or stock. The NMFS may also issue permits for "incidental taking" in the course of commercial fishing operations, but such permits are subject to numerous requirements and to programs designed to reduce incidental kill and incidental serious injury to insignificant levels approaching zero. 16 U.S.C. § 1371.

Limited exemptions apply to (1) Indians, Aleuts and Eskimos in coastal areas of Alaska; (2) taking imminently necessary in self-defense or to save the life of another person in immediate danger if the taking is reported to the NMFS within 48 hours; or (3) taking imminently necessary to avoid serious injury, additional injury or death to a marine mammal entangled in fishing gear or debris. 16 U.S.C. § 1371.

4. Prohibitions

The MMPA prohibits any person, vessel or other conveyance subject to the jurisdiction of the United States to take any marine mammals on the high seas. With some exceptions such as treaty, the MMPA also prohibits any person to take or import marine mammals or marine mammal products taken in waters or on lands under U.S. jurisdiction or by use of any port, harbor or place subject to U.S. jurisdiction. The MMPA also prohibits importation of pregnant or nursing mammals; depleted species or stock; inhumane taking; and importation of illegally taken mammals. 16 U.S.C. § 1372.

5. NMFS Regulations

The MMPA requires the Department of Commerce to adopt regulations on the taking of marine mammals. 16 U.S.C. § 1373. The MMPA prescribes the factors to be considered in prescribing regulations and allowable restrictions. These factors were intended to guide the NMFS, but not to authorize it to restrict commercial fishing so extensively that it could not supply food to the growing population of the United States.

The NMFS has adopted regulations on the taking and importing of marine polar bears; sea and marine otters; walrus; and West Indian Amazonian and West African Manatees. 50 C.F.R. Part 18. Regulations establishing sanctuaries and refuges for manatees in Florida are at 50 C.F.R. §17.100 *et seq.* Regulations on the taking and importing of whales, porpoises, seals and sea lions are at 50 C.F.R. Part 216. The NMFS has also adopted regulations under the MMPA and ESA as follows: general endangered and threatened marine species (50 C.F.R. Part 222); threatened marine and anadromous species (50 C.F.R. Part 223); endangered marine and anadromous species (50 C.F.R. Part 224); and designated critical habitat (50 C.F.R. Part 226). The FWS and the NMFS have adopted joint regulations on anadromous fisheries (50 C.F.R. Part 401); interagency cooperation (50 C.F.R. Part 402); state programs (50 C.F.R. Part 403); listing endangered and threatened species (50 C.F.R. Part 424); and the endangered species exemption process. (50 C.F.R. Parts 450 to 453).

The "taking" regulations of the NMFS cover a wide array of subjects:

1. Taking for subsistence purposes at the Pribilof Islands
2. Dolphin safe tuna labelling
3. Small takes of marine mammals
4. Taking of ringed seals incidental to on-ice seismic activities

5. Taking incidental to space vehicle and test flight activities

6. Taking incidental to power plant operations

7. Taking of bottlenose and spotted dolphins incidental to oil and gas activities

8. Taking of marine mammals incidental to underwater detonation of conventional explosives by the Department of Defense

9. Taking of marine mammals incidental to shock testing the USS Seawolf

10. Taking of marine mammals incidental to construction and operation of offshore oil and gas facilities in the U.S. Beaufort Sea.

6. Permits

The MMA authorizes the NMFS to issue permits which authorize the taking or importation of marine mammals for purposes such as commercial fishing, scientific research, public display, or enhancing survival of species on stock, subject to numerous conditions 16 U.S.C. § 1374. The NMFS has provided for a number of permits on its regulations at 50 C.F.R. Part 216.

In 1994, Congress amended the MMPA to remove the requirement that an incidental take permit be obtained for commercial fishing because the NMFS's decisions on permits were making commercial fishing into a "threatened industry." Congress substituted a registration requirement and take reduction plans designed to reduce mortality and serious injury to marine mammals incidental to commercial fishing to insignificant levels within seven years. 16 U.S.C. § 1387.

The International Dolphin Conservation Act. 16 U.S.C. § 1411 *et seq.* and related amendments to the MMPA close the U.S. market to tuna fish caught by using purse seine equipment which tends to entrap dolphins along with the tuna. In 1995, a federal appellate court upheld the authority of the NMFS to issue an order closing the U.S. tuna market to foreign competitors using purse seine equipment. *American Tunaboat Association v. Brown*, 67 F.3d 1404 (9th Cir. 1995).

7. The Marine Mammal Commission

The MMPA created the Marine Mammal Commission. The Commission is responsible to review the activities of the United States pursuant to laws and treaties relating to marine mammals. The Commission must also conduct a continuing review of the condition of the stocks of marine mammals; methods for their protection and conservation; humane means for taking marine mammals; research and development programs under the MMPCA; and applications for permits for scientific research, public display, or enhancing the survival of a species or stock. The Commission is also authorized to conduct other reviews and studies and to consult with and make recommendations to the NMFS and other federal officials on subjects such as the lists of endangered and threatened species maintained under the ESA. 16 C.F.R. § 1402.

Several provisions of the MMPA require the NMFS to consult with the Commission during proceedings to consider permits and other matters. The NMFS and other federal officials must respond to recommendations of the Commission and must explain in detail the reason why any of its recommendations are not followed or adopted.

In appointing members of the Commission, the President is required, among other things, to appoint individuals who are not in a position to profit from the taking of marine mammals. The NMMPA is silent on profitable relations with environmental organizations, consulting firms, law firms and universities.

8. Citizen's Suits

The MMPA does not provide for enforcement by citizen's suits. *Strahan v. Coxe*, 127 F.3d 155 (1st Cir. 1997); cert. den. 525 U.S. 830 and 978.

9. Enforcement

The NMFS may impose a civil penalty up to $10,000 upon anyone who violates the MMPA. Each violation is a separate offense. Upon any failure to pay a penalty, the NMFS may request the Department of Justice to institute a civil action to collect the penalty. 16 U.S.C. § 1375(a).

Any person who knowingly violates the MMPA is subject to a criminal fine up to $20,000 for each violation or imprisonment up to one year, or both. 16 U.S.C. § 1375(b).

Any vessel subject to U.S. jurisdiction employed in the unlawful taking of any marine mammal shall have its entire cargo or the monetary value thereof subject to seizure and forfeiture and to a civil penalty up to $25,000. Port clearance may be withheld until the penalty is paid or a satisfactory surety bond posted. 16 C.F.R. § 1376.

C. Other Laws

Laws for the protection of fish and wildlife are very numerous. Title 16, Conservation, of the U.S. Code alone contains approximately 80 such laws. It is beyond the capacity of this chapter to describe all of them. However, brief descriptions of some of the more significant laws are provided in this section.

1. The Lacey Act

The Lacey Act states that it is unlawful for any person to import, export, transport, sell, receive, acquire or purchase any fish or wildlife taken, possessed, transported or sold in violation of any federal law or treaty, state or tribal law, or foreign law and to attempt to do any of such acts. 18 U.S.C. § 42 and 16 U.S.C. § 3371 *et seq.* The Act is enforced by civil and criminal penalties. To prove a criminal violation, the government must show that the defendant knew that he, she or it was engaging in the conduct that constituted the violation, but need not prove that the defendant knew the law or intended to break the law. Some examples of convictions under the Lacey Act are as follows:

1. A seller of catfish caught in excess of a daily quantity limit on seine fishing fixed by Wisconsin law. *U.S. v. Monsoor*, 77F.3d 1031 (7th Cir. 1996).

2. A big-game hunting promoter who imported animal hides and horns of animals illegally killed in Pakistan and which he omitted from his customs declaration form on return to the United States. *U.S. v. Mitchell*, 39 F.3d 465 (4th Cir. 1994).

3. A guide who arranged and conducted deer hunts without providing licenses required by the State of Montana. *U.S. v. Atkinson*, 966 F.2d 1270 (9th Cir. 1992).

4. Squid fishers who sold salmon captured in violation of a regulation of the Republic of China (Taiwan). *U.S. v. Lee*, 937 F.2d 1388 (9th Cir. 1991).

A federal appellate court held that wrongful intent (*mens rea*) must be proven to support a conviction for a criminal violation of the Lacey Act. Although ignorance of the law is not a defense, ignorance of facts involved in the defendant's conduct is a defense. Thus, the court held that an importer that arranged an air shipment of frogs which died could not be convicted of knowing transportation under inhumane or unhealthful conditions only by proof that defendant knew of the transportation. It must also be proven that the defendant knew the conditions were inhumane or unhealthful. *U.S. v. Bronx Reptiles, Inc.*, 217 F.3d 82 (2d Cir. 2000). Another federal appellate court held that a hunter could not be convicted for having purchased guiding and outfitting services, which were lawful acts, because he subsequently used them for unlawful hunting and shipment of animals. *U.S. v. Romano*, 137 F.3d 677 (1998).

2. The Bald and Golden Eagle Protection Act

The Bald and Golden Eagle Protection Act prohibits taking, possessing, selling, purchasing, exporting or importing bald or golden eagles or their parts, nests or eggs. 16 U.S. C. § 668. The FWS may issue permits allowing taking of these eagles under limited circumstances. Violation of the Act is subject to civil and criminal penalties. 16 U.S.C. § 668. The Act and other environmental laws have been credited with significant recovery of populations of bald eagles once listed as endangered under the Endangered Species Act.

3. The Migratory Bird Treaty Act

The Migratory Bird Treaty Act (MBTA) prohibits taking, killing, hunting, capturing, pursuing, selling, purchasing, shipping, importing or exporting of migratory birds protected by treaties between the United States and Canada, Japan, Mexico and Russia. The MTBA also protects the nests, eggs and parts of the birds protected by the treaties. 16 U.S.C. § 703 *et seq.* The MTBA applies to conduct such as that of hunters and poachers and cannot be used to enjoin timber sales and logging authorized by the U.S. Forest Service on grounds that the logging would disrupt nesting migratory birds. *Newton County Wildlife Ass'n v. U.S. Forest Service*, 113 F.3d 110 (8th Cir. 1997).

The courts have disagreed as to whether *scienter* must be proven to convict a defendant of violating the MTBA:

> *Misdemeanors*: One federal appellate court held that scienter must be proven. *U.S. v. Gannett*, 984 F.2d 1402 (5th Cir. 1993). Another federal appellate court held that a defendant can be convicted without proof of intent to violate the MTBA. *U.S. v. Corrow*, 119 F.3d 796 (10th Cir. 1997); cert. den. 522 U.S. 1133 (1998).
>
> *Felonies*: Although the MTBA requires that a felony violation be "knowing," an appellate court ruled that a conviction is valid without proof that a defendant knew that his conduct was unlawful if the facts involved in the violation (such as an illegally baited field) were discoverable by reasonable effort. *U.S. v. Lee*, 217 F.3d 284 (5th Cir. 2000); *U.S. v. Pitrone*, 115 F.3d 1 (1st Cir. 1997).

A federal appellate court enjoined a plan adopted by the U.S. Department of Agriculture for controlling Canada Geese which have become so numerous that their eating reduces crop supplies and their droppings damage water quality including drinking water supplies. In a lawsuit by environmental organizations, the court held that the plan could not be adopted without a permit granted by the FWS under the MBTA and an FWS policy not to require federal agencies to obtain permits was contrary to the MBTA. *Humane Society v. Glickman*, 217 F.3d 882 (D.C. Cir. 2000). However, see contrary opinions in *Sierra Club v. Martin*, 110 F.3d 1551 (11th Cir. 1997) and *Newton County Wildlife Ass'n v. U.S. Forest Service*, 113 F.3d 110 (8th Cir. 1997).

A related law is the Migratory Bird Conservation Act. 16 U.S.C. § 715 *et seq.*

4. National Wildlife Refuge System and Restoration Acts

The National Wildlife RefugSe System Act (NWRSA) provides for the administration by the FWS of various areas that are refuges for fish and wildlife. The NWRSA imposes restrictions on transfers of acquired refuge system lands; restricts certain activities in refuge areas such as mining, mineral leasing, hunting and fishing except as authorized by permits; and requires the FWS to adopt and implement comprehensive conservation plans for related complexes of refuge lands. 16 U.S.C. § 668 dd.

The Wildlife Restoration Act (WRA) is a law establishing a wildlife restoration fund to pay for FWS and state management of wildlife restoration projects and denying funds to states which do not adopt and implement such programs. The state funds are matching grants. 16 U.S.C. § 669 *et seq.* One federal district court held that no private right of action exists under the FWA. *Illinois State Rifle Ass'n v. State of Illinois*, 717 F. Supp. 634 (N.D. Ill. 1989).

D. Side Effects

The wildlife protection and other environmental laws obtain their primary political support from residents of the large city and suburban areas of the United States. These residents idealize wildlife and other natural conditions which they see during vacations and otherwise experience through films, books and other information.

The restrictions imposed by the environmental laws on farming, hunting, fishing, logging, mining and development in small town and rural areas has led to hardship and strong resentment among the populations in those areas. This can be seen on a map of the election results for the year 2000. The big city states on the two coasts voted for the environmentalist candidate, Albert Gore, and the small town and rural states voted for George Bush who promised more recognition of state and local conditions in environmental regulation.

CHAPTER XIX
NOISE CONTROL LAWS

There are several federal laws which regulate excessive noise. The program with the broadest application is the OSHA's occupational noise exposure regulation under the Occupational Safety and Health Act. 29 C.F.R. § 1910.95. Among other things, the regulation imposes permissible noise exposure limits (PNELs) ranging from 115 dbA for exposure of 15 minutes or less to 90 dbA for exposure of eight hours. The regulation establishes an action level at 85 decibels per 8 hour time weighted average (TWA), or an equivalent dose of 50%, without regard to attenuation provided by personal protective equipment. When the action level is equalled or exceeded for any employee, an employer must develop and implement a hearing conservation program including monitoring, employee notification, audiometric testing, training, furnishing hearing protectors at no cost to employees, and recordkeeping and retention.

The Department of Labor is required by the Mine Safety and Health Act, 30 U.S.C. § 846, to develop and implement noise standards for mines. The standard adopted by the Mine Safety and Health Administration (MSHA) is found at 30 C.F.R. Part 62. Like OSHA, MSHA's regulations establish an action level which is an 8-hour time weighted average sound level of 85 dBA, or an equivalent dose of 50%. If the action level is equalled or exceeded for any miner, a mine operator must enroll the miner in a hearing conservation program including miner notification, monitoring, provision and use of hearing protectors, audiometric testing, training, and recordkeeping.

Another program was established by the Noise Control Act which requires the USEPA to adopt regulations setting noise emission standards for certain equipment sold in interstate commerce. 42 U.S.C. § 4901 *et seq*. The USEPA has adopted regulations applicable to rail and motor carrier transportation equipment, motor carrier equipment and construction equipment and regulations for certification of low noise emission equipment. The USEPA has also established noise emission control regulations applicable to medium and heavy trucks and motorcycles. The regulations prescribe warranty and labelling requirements. 40 C.F.R. § 201 *et seq*.

The Department of Transportation is required to develop and promulgate highway noise level standards. 23 U.S.C. § 109(i). The Federal Highway Administration, recently replaced by the Federal Motor Carrier Safety Administration, has adopted the procedures for abatement of highway traffic noise and construction noise. 23 C.F.R. Part 772.

The Federal Aviation Administration (FAA) is required, with certain exceptions, to issue regulations proposed by the USEPA to provide control and abatement of aircraft noise and sonic boom. 49 U.S.C. § 44715. The FAA's responsibilities were extensively supplemented by the Aviation Safety and Noise Abatement Act of 1979 and the Airport Noise and Capacity Act of 1990. 49 U.S.C. § 47501 *et seq* and § 47521 *et seq*. The FAA's regulations for aircraft certification are at 14 C.F.R. Part 36. The FAA's regulations on airport noise compatibility planning are at 14 C.F.R. Part 150. The FAA's regulations on notice and approval of airport noise and access restrictions are at 14 C.F.R. Part 161.

The Department of Labor is required by the Mine Safety and Health Act, 30 U.S.C. § 846, to develop and implement noise standards for mines. The standard adopted by the Mine Safety and Health Administration (MSHA) is found at 30 C.F.R. Part 62. Like OSHA, MSHA's regulation establish an action level which is an 8-hour time weighted average sound level of 85 dBA, or an equivalent dose of 50%. If the action level is equalled or exceeded for any miner, a mine operator must enroll the miner in a hearing conservation program including miner notification, monitoring provision and use of hearing protectors, audiometric testing, training, and recordkeeping.

CHAPTER XX

LAWS GOVERNING RADIOACTIVE MATERIALS AND WASTES

A. Introduction

Radioactive materials occur naturally throughout the world in the form of heavy elements such as radium, uranium and thorium. To use them, they must be mined, milled, concentrated, enriched and processed to increase their radioactivity level. Prior to 1954, the mining and production of radioactive materials in the United States was primarily for weapons systems used by predecessors of the U.S. Department of Defense (DOD).

In 1954, the U.S. Congress adopted the Atomic Energy Act (AEA) to foster peaceful uses of radioactive material. The Atomic Energy Commission (AEC) was appointed to administer the Act. The AEC sponsored and regulated a wide range of peaceful uses including nuclear fuels to generate electric power and a multitude of medical, pharmaceutical and industrial applications. The safety record for industrial use of radioactive materials has been far better than the record of other major industrial and governmental operations of similar size and complexity. However, public perception of the hazards of radioactive materials has been affected by their early use in weapons and by political controversy. Thus, laws and regulations governing radioactive materials and wastes have grown greatly in number and detail.

The basis for environmental regulation of radioactive materials and wastes is derived primarily from federal laws including the following:

Atomic Energy Act of 1954 (AEA), 42 U.S.C. § 2011 *et seq.*

Energy Reorganization Act of 1974 (ERA), 42 U.S.C. § 5801 *et seq.*

Energy Policy and Conservation Act of 1975 (EPCA), 42 U.S.C. § 6201 *et seq.*

Uranium Mill Tailings Radiation Control Act (UMTRCA), 42 U.S.C. § 2022 and § 7901 *et seq.*

Low Level Radioactive Waste Policy Act of 1980 (LLRWPA), 42 U.S.C. § 2021b-j

Nuclear Waste Policy Act of 1982 (NWPA), 42 U.S.C. § 10101 *et seq.*

Omnibus Low Level Radioactive Waste Interstate Compact Act of 1986, 42 U.S.C. § 2021

Energy Policy Act of 1992, 42 U.S.C. § 13201 *et seq.*

Several federal agencies regulate radioactive materials and wastes. The Nuclear Regulatory Commission (NRC), which succeeded to the regulatory responsibilities of the AEC under the Energy Reorganization Act of 1974, regulates its several thousand licensees including nuclear power generating facilities. The Department of Energy (DOE) regulates the many facilities which it owns or operates through contractors or for which has been required to assume responsibility. These facilities include laboratories, nuclear fuel production facilities and weapons production and testing facilities. Examples are the Los Alamos, Idaho, Sandia and Lawrence Livermore national laboratories and the DOE plants at Savannah River, South Carolina; Oak Ridge, Tennessee; Fernald, Ohio; Rocky Flats, Colorado; Los Alamos, New Mexico; and Hanford, Washington. (The DOE is responsible for many sites listed on the NPL maintained by the USEPA under CERCLA). The Department of Defense (DOD) regulates numerous sites related to its use, testing and storage of weapons systems and nuclear fuel for high performance submarines. The USEPA has authority under the AEA and the UMTRCA to adopt standards of general application to radioactive materials and waste as well as authority under the other environmental laws which it administers.

B. Radiation and Radioactivity

Radioactivity is the emission of ionizing radiation from atoms which have an unstable nucleus with a neutron imbalance. These atoms decay over a period of years by emitting radiation consisting of alpha particles, beta particles and gamma rays.

Exposure to radiation is commonly measured in rems and millirems. Concentrations of radioactive materials in soil or groundwater are commonly measured in pico Curies per gram (pCi/g) and picoCuries per liter (pCi/L).

Radiation is everywhere. Humans are exposed to radiation all day and every day, almost always without harm. Indeed, humans need and benefit greatly from nonionizing radiation in the form of light from the sun and artificial sources. They also benefit greatly from electricity, although wires carrying electricity generate harmless electromagnetic fields (EMF) around them that is another example of nonionizing radiation.

Humans are also daily exposed to ionizing radiation, a more energetic form of adiation, from the sun and outer space. Less frequently, they are exposed to ionizing radiation when X-rays are taken in doctor's or dentist's office or a hospital. Many common building materials, such as bricks, emit radiation.

C. NRC Licensing of Radioactive Materials

1. Licensed Material

The AEA prohibits any person from transferring, delivering, receiving, possessing, importing or exporting any source material, special nuclear material or byproduct material except as authorized by a license issued by the NRC. Source material is uranium or thorium (and ores containing them at 0.5% by weight) that can be used to produce nuclear fuels, but which has not been enriched to be fissionable. Special nuclear material is plutonium, uranium-233, and enriched uranium that can be used as nuclear fuel. Byproduct is any material yielded in, or made radioactive by exposure to radiation incident to, the process of producing or using special nuclear material. Byproduct material also includes tailings or wastes processed by extraction or concentration of uranium or thorium from ore processed primarily for its source material content. The NRC regulations call all three categories "licensed material. "

2. Exemptions

The NRC has adopted several exemptions from the licensing requirements for low quantities of source material and byproduct material and low concentrations of radioactivity in byproduct materials. 20 U.S.C. §§ 2077(d), 2092 and 2111.20 C.F.R. §§ 30.14 to 30.19 and 40.13.

The low quantity and low concentration exemptions for byproduct material and source material are essentially use exemptions and do not authorize import into the United States or manufacture of products containing exempt quantities. 10 C.F.R. §§ 30.14(b) and (d), 30.18(c) and (d), 40.13(c)(9). The NRC also contends that they do not authorize disposal of radioactive material in the absence of a specific exemption or permit authorizing disposal.

With some exceptions, the AEA does not apply to the DOE and its prime contractors. See the definition of a "person" and "persons" in 10 C.F.R. §§ 30.11, 40.11 and § 70.11. 42 U.S.C. § 2140(a). However, the NRC is authorized to license some DOE facilities which store high-level radioactive waste.

Common and contract carriers, freight forwarders, warehousemen, and the U.S. Post Office are exempt from the licensing and other requirements of the NRC's regulations to the extent they transport or store in the regular course of carriage for others. 10 C.F.R. §§ 30.13, 40.12 and 70.12.

3. Licensees and Kinds of Licenses

There are about 22,000 licensed users of radioactive materials subject to the AEA. About one-third are licensed directly by the NRC and the rest are licensed by state government agencies under the cooperation agreements described later in this chapter.

The NRC's regulations provide for general licenses, specific licenses, and exemptions. A general license is created by a regulation authorizing classes of persons to receive, possess and/or transfer radioactive material in compliance with the requirements of the regulation. An application to the NRC is not usually required for general license. For example, the NRC regulations provide general licenses allowing exports and imports of a number of radioactive materials if the license requirements are met. Other exports or imports require specific licenses. 10 C.F.R. Part 10. For another example, the NRC regulations provide general licenses for a number of byproduct materials. 10 C.F.R. Part 31.

A specific license is a license issued to a particular person authorizing receipt, possession and/or transfer of radioactive material in compliance with its terms. The NRC regulations contain several parts providing for the grant of specific byproduct licenses for purposes such as oil well sand consolidation resins; radioactive drugs; self-luminous products; gas and aerosol detectors; broad scope byproduct uses; industrial radiography; medical and dental uses; irradiation; and well logging. See 10 C.F.R. Parts 30 to 37. The NRC regulations aiso provide for domestic licensing of source material and special nuclear material. 10 C.F.R. Parts 40 and 70.

4. Production and Utilization Facilities

Persons planning to construct and/or operate a production or utilization facility must first obtain a construction and/or operating permit from the NRC. 40 C.F.R. Part 50. However, limited preconstruction activities are allowed. 40 C.F.R. § 50.10.

5. Nuclear Power Plants and Reactors

The NRC has regulations for the licensing of nuclear power plants and reactors. 10 C.F.R. Parts 52 to 55. The NRC also has environmental protection regulations for domestic licensing and related regulatory functions including the preparation of environmental impact statements in compliance with the National Environmental Policy Act. 10 C.F.R. Part 51.

6. NRC's Radiation Protection Regulations

The NRC's radiation protection regulations are found at 10 C.F.R. Part 20. Each licensee must establish a radiation protection program. Using engineering controls to the extent practicable, each licensee must maintain occupational and public doses at levels that are as low as reasonably achievable (ALARA). The occupational annual dose limit for adults is the lesser of (1) the total effective dose equivalent of 5 rems or (2) the sum of the deep dose equivalent and the committed dose equivalent to any individual organ or tissue other than the eye lens equal to 50 rems. The annual limit for the eye lens is an eye dose equivalent of 15 rems. The annual limit for the skin of the whole body or to the skin of any extremity is a shallow dose equivalent of 50 rems. The dose limits for an individual member of the public are (1) an annual total effective dose limit from a licensed operation not exceeding 0.1 rem and (2) a one hour dose in any unrestricted area not exceeding 0.002 rem. 10 C.F.R. §§ 20.1101 to .1301. In 2001, the NRC proposed to amend the methods used to calculate the shallow dose equivalent for skin exposure, but did not change the limit. 66 Fed. Reg. 36502 (July 12, 2001).

Each licensee must comply with exposure control requirements. The licensee must use, to the extent practical, process or other engineering controls to do so. When such controls are not practical, the licensee must maintain the dose equivalent ALARA by control of access, limitation of exposure times, use of respiratory protection equipment, and other means. The licensee must also comply with storage and control requirements including caution signs, posting requirements, container labels, and package receiving and opening procedures. Each licensee must comply with waste disposal requirements including restrictions on discharge to sanitary sewage and procedures on transfers for disposal including use of manifests. Each licensee must maintain prescribed records and must notify the NRC of incidents and exposures and of any radiation levels or radioactive materials concentrations that exceed permissible limits. 10 C.F.R. § 1601 *et seq.*

The Appendices to 40 C.F.R. Part 20 provide useful information:

Appendix A. Assigned Respirator Protection Factors

Appendix B. Annual Limits on Intake and Derived Air Concentrations of Radionuclides for Occupational Exposure; Effluent Concentrations; Sewerage Release Concentrations

Appendix C. Quantities of Licensed Material Requiring Labelling

Appendix D. NRC Regional Offices

Appendix G. Requirements for Transfers of Low-Level Radioactive Waste for Disposal at Licensed Land Disposal Facilities and Manifests.

7. NRC's Decommissioning Regulations

The NRC regulations require each licensee to prepare a decommissioning plan providing for disposal of radioactive material when its license terminates including elimination of any residual radioactive contamination. The licensee must provide financial assurance to secure performance of its decommissioning plan by surety bond, financial guaranty or other satisfactory method. The licensee must keep records of the decommissioning and must perform a radiation survey upon completion to demonstrate to the NRC that building and outdoor areas are suitable for release for unrestricted use. 40 C.F.R. Parts 61, 70 and 72.

8. NRC's Independent Spent Fuel Storage Installation Regulations

The NRC has regulations under which it grants licenses for independent spent fuel storage installations (ISFSIs). The ISFSIs may be located at the site of a licensed nuclear power reactor or at other sites which meet the licensing requirements. The regulations include specifications for the casks in which radioactive materials must be stored. The regulations also provide for licenses to the DOE for monitored retrievable storage installations (MRSs) to receive, transfer, package and possess power reactor spent fuel, high-level radioactive waste, and other radioactive materials associated with their storage. 40 C.F.R. Part 72. The regulations on ISFSIs are of interest because political opposition to the establishment of a central depository and MRSs has meant continuing storage of spent nuclear fuel at nuclear power plants throughout the United States that may become permanent.

9. NRC's General Nuclear Waste Repository Guidelines

In 1981, the NRC adopted general guidelines for the recommendation of sites for nuclear waste repositories. 10 C.F.R. Part 60. These regulations were amended significantly in 2001 and are discussed again later in this chapter.

10. NRC's Regulations for Yucca Mountain

In 2001, the NRC adopted regulations to be used in licensing the DOE for the Yucca Mountain geological repository for disposal of spent nuclear fuel and high level radioactive waste. 10 C.F.R. Part 63; 66 Fed. Reg. 55753 (Nov. 2, 2001). They are discussed later in this chapter.

D. The DOE's Regulations

The DOE has adopted regulations applicable to its own nuclear activities. They include nuclear activities procedures; nuclear safety management; occupational radiation protection; extraordinary nuclear occurrences; general guidelines for the recommendation of sites for nuclear waste repositories; standard contracts for disposal of spent nuclear fuel and/or high level radioactive waste; and byproduct material. 10 C.F.R. Parts 820 to 962. The DOE's regulations providing general guidelines for recommendation of the suitability of the Yucca Mountain Site for a nuclear waste depository are at 10 C.F.R. Part 963 and are described later in this chapter. See also 66 Fed. Reg. 57297 (Nov. 14, 2001).

E. State Licensing of Radioactive Materials

The AEA provides for regulation of radioactive materials, including nuclear power plants, by the NRC, DOE and other instrumentalities of the federal government. However, the states may regulate naturally occurring radioactive material (NORM) and accelerator produced radioactive material. 42 U.S.C. § 2021(b).

The AEA provides for cooperative agreements between the NRC and the states under which the NRC may cede to them the right to regulate source material, special nuclear material in quantities below those needed for a critical mass, and byproduct material. 42 U.S.C. § 2021. In the absence of a cooperative agreement, state regulation is preempted. *Northern States Power v. Minnesota*, 447 F.2d 1143 (8th Cir. 1971), aff'd 405 U.S. 1035 (1972).

F. The USEPA's Radiation Protection Regulations

In 1977, the USEPA adopted environmental radiation protection standards for nuclear power operations requiring them to operate in a manner that maintains public exposure to radiation within annual dosage limits. 40 C.F.R. Part 190. These regulations apply to "uranium fuel cycle operations. " The cycle includes milling uranium ore, chemical conversion of uranium, isotopic enrichment of uranium, fabrication of uranium fuel, generation of electricity by a light-water-cooled nuclear power plant using uranium fuel, and reprocessing of spent uranium fuel, to the extent that they directly support the production of electric power for public use utilizing nuclear energy. § 190.02. The standards do not apply to mining operations, operations at waste disposal sites, transportation in support of these operations, or the reuse of recovered non-uranium special nuclear and byproduct materials from the cycle. The key standard requires that environmental operations be conducted to provide responsible assurance that the annual dose equivalent to any member of the public will not exceed 25 millirems to the whole body, 75 millirems to the thyroid, and 25 millirems to any other organ. § 190.10.

In 1985, the USEPA adopted environmental protection standards for management and disposal of spent nuclear fuel, high-level and transuranic radiative wastes (Part 191). Two years earlier in 1983, the USEPA had adopted health and environmental protection standards for uranium and thorium mill tailings (Part 192). These regulations became the basis for subsequent regulations adopted by the USEPA as well as cleanup criteria under CERCLA.

In 1996, the USEPA adopted criteria for certification and recertification of compliance with the Part 191 waste disposal regulations by the Waste Insulation Pilot Plant in New Mexico. (Part 194). In 2001, the USEPA adopted public health and radiation protection standards for the proposed geological radioactive waste repository at Yucca Mountain, Nevada (Part 197). These regulations are discussed again later in this chapter.

The USEPA also adopted regulations on radon proficiency programs. (Part 195) These brief regulations do not provide effective protection against sale to the public of unnecessary products and services based on perceptions that radon is more hazardous and difficult to remediate than it really is. The USEPA has published literature that provides partial help by recommending some relatively practical remediation methods.

G. The Clean Air Act

The Clean Air Act (CAA) includes radionuclides in its list of hazardous air pollutants for which the USEPA is required to adopt national emissions standards, often called "NESHAPs. " 42 U.S.C. § 7412. The USEPA has adopted NESHAPs for emissions of radon and other radionuclides from several kinds of facilities such as underground uranium mines; DOE facilities; federal facilities other than DOE facilities; phosphogypsum stacks; uranium mill tailings; and operating mill tailings. 40 C.F.R. Part 61 and Appendices.

H. The Clean Water Act

The Clean Water Act (CWA) requires that a national pollutant discharge system (NPDES) permit be obtained from the USEPA before discharging any pollutant. The CWA's definition of a "pollutant" includes radioactive materials. 40 C.F.R. § 1382(6). However, the definition of a "pollutant" in the USEPA's regulations excludes source, special nuclear and byproduct materials regulated by the Nuclear Regulatory Commission under the AEA. 40 C.F.R. § 122.2. The exclusion was upheld as consistent with the legislative history of the CWA by the U.S. Supreme Court. *Train v. Colorado PIRG*, 426 U.S. I, 48 L.Ed.2d 434 (1976).

The exclusion also applies to uranium mill tailings. *Waste Action Project v. Dawn Mining Corp.*, 137 F.3d 1426 (9th Cir. 1998). However, the exclusion does not apply to discharges of radium or accelerator-produced isotopes. 40 C.F.R. § 122.2.

I. The Safe Drinking Water Act

The Safe Drinking Water Act (SDWA) requires the USEPA to establish drinking water regulations. The USEPA has adopted regulations establishing a maximum contaminant level (MCL) of 5 pCi/L for combined radium-226 and radium—228 and 15 pCi/L for gross alpha particle activity excluding radon and uranium. The MCL for beta particle and photon radioactivity from man-made radionuclides is an average annual concentration that will not produce an annual dose equivalent to the total body or any internal organ greater than 4 millirems per year. 40 C.F.R. § 141.66.

The USEPA proposed in 1991 a MCL for radon—222 in drinking water of 300 pCi/L. However, subsequent amendments to the SDWA required the USEPA to perform and publish a risk reduction and cost analysis of radon in drinking water. The USEPA published the analysis at 64 Fed. Reg. 9559 (Feb. 26, 1999). In its request for comments, the USEPA said that states which have an approved multimedia mitigation (MMM) program may develop alternate maximum concentration levels (AMCLs) for radon in drinking water.

J. The Resource Conservation and Recovery Act

The Resource Conservation and Recovery Act (RCRA) excludes from its definition of "solid waste" source, special nuclear and byproduct material as defined in the AEA. 42 U.S.C. § 6903(7). The USEPA's regulations provide the same exclusion. 40 C.F.R. § 261.4. Since the excluded materials are not solid waste, they are not subject to the USEPA's solid waste or hazardous waste regulations under RCRA.

However, if radioactive materials are mixed with other solid waste (including hazardous waste), the mixed waste is subject to regulation under RCRA. 42 U.S.C. § 6903(41).

For example, the USEPA's regulations requiring treatment of hazardous waste before land disposal included treatment standards for radioactive high level wastes generated during the reprocessing of fuel rods (D002-D011) that contain regulated hazardous constituents including arsenic or other hazardous heavy metals. 40 C.F.R. § 268.40 (Table).

K. Comprehensive Environmental Response, Compensation and Liability Act

The Comprehensive Environmental Response, Compensation and Liability Act (CERCLA) contains a definition of a "hazardous substance" that is sufficiently broad to include radioactive materials. 42 U.S.C. § 9601(14). The definition of a "release," however, excludes a release of source, special nuclear and byproduct materials as defined in the AEA. 42 U.S.C. § 9601(14). The USEPA's regulations contain the same exclusions and also a partial exclusion of any release of such material from a processing site designated under §§ 102(a)(1) or 302(a) of the UMTRCA. Like RCRA, if a release is a mixture of excluded radioactive materials and other hazardous substances, it is subject to CERCLA.

Several dozen sites are listed in the Federal Facilities Section of the National Priorities List (NPL) because of contamination with mixtures of radioactive materials and other hazardous substances. Among these sites are 16 which are owned or operated by the DOE including some national laboratories and facilities which once made important contributions to national defense and development of nuclear materials for peaceful purposes such as the Oak Ridge Reservation, the Savannah River Site, and the Paducah Gaseous Diffusion Plant.

When remediating an NPL site, the National Contingency Plan (NCP) provides that remediation of contamination be based upon applicable or relevant and appropriate requirements (ARARs). 40 C.F.R. § 300.430. In addition to the general standards applicable to carcinogens, the USEPA's health and environmental protection standards for uranium and thorium mill tailings may be proposed as ARARs and used unless other standards are shown to be more appropriate. For background, see "Establishment of Cleanup Levels for CERCLA Sites with Radioactive Contamination," OSWER Directive 9200. 4-18 (Aug. 22, 1997).

In 1988, the USEPA furnished additional guidance on the use of soil cleanup criteria for NPL sites. The USEPA said that all remedial actions must be protective of human health and the environment and comply with ARARs unless a waiver is justified. Cleanup levels and ARARs are determined on a site-specific basis. The USEPA pointed out that the surface soil concentration criterion of 5 pCi/g of radium-226 in 40 C.F.R. Part 192 is a health-based standard. However, the subsurface concentration criterion of 15 pCi/g is not a health-based standard but was developed to allow use of field testing at uranium mill tailing sites. Accordingly, the USEPA will regard the use of 15 pCi/g as an ARAR only under circumstances where its use can be expected to achieve an actual subsurface cleanup level below 5 pCi/g.

L. The Occupational Safety and Health Act

The Occupational Safety and Health Act (the "OSH Act") provides authority for the Occupational Safety and Health Administration (OSHA) of the U.S. Department of Labor to adopt standards requiring employers to protect the safety and health of workers in their workplaces. 29 U.S.C. § 651 *et seq.*

OSHA has a regulation requiring employers to protect their employees from exposure to nonionizing radiation. 29 C.F.R. § 1910.97.

OSHA's hazard communication standard does not apply to ionizing and nonionizing radiation. 29 C.F.R. § 1910.1200. However, some employers elect to disclose radiation hazards in material safety data sheets.

OSHA has adopted hazardous waste operations regulations, called the "HAZWOPER" regulations, which require employers to implement detailed programs to protect workers against the hazards involved in working to remediate or otherwise handle hazardous waste, including radioactive waste. 29 C.F.R. § 1910.120.

M. Transportation of Radioactive Materials and Waste

Transportation of radioactive materials is regulated by U.S. Department of Transportation (DOT) under the Hazardous Materials Transportation Act (HMTA). 49 U.S.C. § 5101 *et seq.* Their transportation is also regulated by the NRC under the AEA.

1. DOT Transportation Regulations

The Research and Special Program Administration (RSPA) of the DOT has extensive and detailed regulation applicable to shippers, carriers, packaging manufacturers and others involved in transportation of radioactive materials and wastes. 49 C.F.R. Part 171 *et seq.* Under RSPA's regulations, radioactive materials are Class 7 materials. See the lists in the Hazardous Materials Table in 49 C.F.R. § 172.101. See also the list of radionuclides and reportable quantities in Appendix A, Table 2 to §172.101. RSPA's regulations are enforced by the Federal Railroad Administration, the Federal Aviation Administration, the U.S. Coast Guard, and the Federal Motor Carrier Safety Administration.

RSPA's regulations provide that shippers of Class 7 materials must comply with all the usual requirements for shipments of hazardous materials. The shipping papers must also contain extra entries such as the words "RADIOACTIVE MATERIAL;" the name of each radionuclide in the radioactive material; a description of the physical and chemical form of the material unless it is in special form; the activity contained in each package in Curies; the applicable label; the transport index for each package bearing certain labels; additional warnings and instructions for fissile materials or the words "fissile exempt;" a notation of the package identification marking for each package approved by the NRC or DOE; and a notation of the package identification by the International Atomic Energy Agency (IAEA) for each export shipment or shipment in a foreign package.

Carriers must also meet extra requirements for Class 7 materials including placarding, training and routing requirements. The routing requirements are prescribed by the states in the manner described later in this chapter.

2. NRC Packaging and Transportation Regulations

The NRC has regulations applicable to packaging and transportation of licensed material, including fissile material. They contain exemptions for physicians and for low level material having a specific activity not greater than 0.002 uCi/g. The regulations also contain application procedures for package approval; package approval standards; package, special form and low specific activity material tests; operating controls and procedures; and quality assurance requirements. The NRC's regulations are in addition to, and not in substitution for, the requirements of other agencies such as the DOT or the U.S. Post Office. 40 C.F.R. Part 71.

Among other provisions, the regulations require each licensee to provide advance notice to the governor of each state of the shipment of irradiated reactor fuel and certain other nuclear wastes through or across the boundary of the state before the shipment leaves the licensee's plant or other place of use or storage. The advance notice provides time for state officials to prevent protests by anti-nuclear activists from becoming violent. 10 C.F.R. § 71.97.

N. Disposal of Spent Nuclear Fuel and Radioactive Wastes

1. Background

A matter of national concern is lack of permanent disposal facilities for spent nuclear fuel and high level and low level radioactive wastes. High level waste includes irradiated reactor fuel, certain liquid wastes from solvent extraction cycles, and solid wastes into which the liquid wastes have been converted. Low level wastes are wastes not classified as high level waste, transuranic waste, spent fuel, or byproduct materials such as uranium and thorium mill tailings.

2. NRC Regulations

As described earlier, the NRC's licensing regulations include provisions on decommissioning. The NRC also has licensing requirements for land disposal of radioactive waste (10 C.F.R. Part 61) and for emergency access to non-federal and regional low-level waste disposal facilities (40 C.F.R. Part 62). Although described as storage, the NRC's licensing requirements for IFSFIs and MSRs are the equivalent of disposal regulations in the absence of significant progress to develop permanent disposal sites for high-level and low-level radioactive waste. 10 C.F.R. Part 72.

The NRC's most politically controversial regulations are those on disposal of high-level radioactive waste in geological repositories. These regulations are focussed on the site at Yucca Mountain, Nevada and are discussed later in this chapter. 10 C.F.R. Parts 60 and 63.

3. DOE Regulations and Orders

DOE regulations include its guidelines for the recommendation of sites for nuclear waste repositories. 10 C.F.R. Part 960. In the mid-1990s, the DOE proposed a new regulation on radiation protection of the public and the environment to become 10 C.F.R. Part 834. The DOE has issued several regulatory orders. DOE Order 5400.4 applies to CERCLA policies and procedures prescribed by the NCP. DOE Order No. 5400.5 prescribes standards and requirements for radiation protection of the public and the environment. DOE Order No. 5820.2A prescribes radioactive waste management requirements including the performance objectives of the NRC's land disposal regulations at 40 C.F.R. Part 61.

4. USEPA Regulations

Under the AEA, the USEPA adopted regulations applicable to disposal of spent nuclear fuel, high level and transuranic wastes, often called the high level radioactive waste rule. 40 C.F.R. Part 191. Under the AEA and UMTRCA, the USEPA also adopted health and environmental protection standards for the control and cleanup of uranium and thorium mill tailings at certain inactive sites being remediated by the DOE and for uranium and thorium byproduct materials at certain active sites of NRC licensees. 40 C.F.R. Part 192.

During the 1990s, under the AEA, the EPA staff drafted a Radiation Site Cleanup Regulation to become 40 C.F.R. Part 196. The NRC and the USEPA said that this Regulation would not apply to NRC licensees if the USEPA become satisfied with the adequacy of the NRC's decommissioning rules. The USEPA has not adopted Part 196.

In 1996, the USEPA adopted regulations establishing criteria for the certification and recertification of the waste isolation plant's compliance with the Part 191 disposal regulations. 40 C.F.R. Part 194. These regulations were used in the certification of the DOE's Waste Isolation Pilot Plant (WIPP) at Carlsbad, New Mexico used for transuranic wastes. Transuranic wastes are generally harmless wastes such as clothing worn by workers in nuclear weapons activities.

5. The Yucca Mountain Geological Repository Site

In 1983, the U.S. Congress adopted the NWPA to sponsor the selection and development of disposal sites for high level radioactive waste. The NWPA originally directed the DOE to recommend five sites to be characterized as permanent disposal sites, but subsequent amendments focussed on the characterization of a site at Yucca Mountain, Nevada. The NWPA also directed the DOE to develop plans for monitored retrievable storage (MRS) sites that would not be permanent disposal sites.

Programs of the DOE to implement the NWPA have been extremely costly. Billions of dollars have been spent since 1987 on characterization of the Yucca Mountain site. The delays have been caused by political opposition which has attacked every step taken by the DOE by publicity, lobbying and lawsuits. For just one example, the State of Nevada enacted a law prohibiting the storage of high level radioactive waste and commenced litigation against the DOE, but was unsuccessful. *Nevada v. Watkins*, 914 F.2d 1545 (9th Cir. 1990); *Nevada v. Watkins*, 943 F.2d 1080 (9th Cir. 1991). Requests by the State of Nevada to the DOE for funding of its "oversight" activities have been partially granted and partially denied. A denial of $6.0 million of funds was upheld in *State of Nevada v. U.S. Dept. of Energy*, 133 F.3d 1201 (9th Cir. 1998).

The NWPA obligated the federal government to develop and license five geologic repositories for spent nuclear fuel and high level radioactive waste (HLRW). The sites were to be characterized by the DOE which would then be licensed by the NRC to operate them. In 1987 amendments, Congress directed the DOE to limit its work to the site at Yucca Mountain. In the meantime, the DOE entered into contracts with public utilities and other generators of spent nuclear fuel and high level radioactive waste across the nation and they paid fees into the Nuclear Waste Fund maintained by the U.S. Treasury to cover the costs of developing, constructing and operating the site and which recently totalled about $17 billion. 40 C.F.R. Part 961. The deadline for DOE to commence fulfilling its contractual obligations was January 31, 1998.

Political opponents continued to raise questions about the performance of the Yucca Mountain site over 10,000 years. An environmental group obtained a court order partially vacating USEPA release standards that were a basis for NRC licensing regulations. The USEPA then contracted with the National Academy of Sciences (NAS) for a report advising on the technical basis for the health and safety standards at the site. The NAS recommended in its report of August 1,

1995 that the basis of regulation be changed from release limits to assessment of adverse health risks. Both the NRC and USEPA then reconsidered their regulatory programs.

DOE did not complete its site characterization by the deadline of January 31, 1998. Thus, the DOE did not meet its statutory and contractual obligations to commence accepting spent nuclear fuel and HLRW by the deadline. Electric utility companies filed lawsuits against the DOE seeking mandamus orders to the DOE to fulfill its obligations. The court found that the DOE had breached its statutory and contractual obligations. However, the court refused to issue the requested order and limited the plaintiffs to monetary damages perhaps recoverable by lawsuits in the Federal Court of Claims. *Northern States Power Co. v. DOE*, 128 F.3d 754 (D.C. Cir. 1997); *Indiana Michigan Power Co. v. DOE*, 88 F. 3d 1272 (D.C. Cir. 1995).

Under a new presidential administration, remarkable regulatory progress was made during 2001. The USEPA adopted its public health and environmental radiation protection regulations for Yucca Mountain as 40 C.F.R. Part 197. 66 Fed. Reg. 32132 (June 13, 2001). With those regulations in place, the NRC could and did adopt its criteria to license the DOT for Yucca Mountain. 10 C.F.R. Part 63. 66 Fed. Reg. 55733 (Nov. 2, 2001). This enabled the DOE to adopt amendments to its general guidelines for the recommendation of sites for nuclear waste repositories at 10 C.F.R. 960 and to adopt new suitability guidelines for the Yucca Mountain Site as 10 C.F.R. Part 963. 66 Fed. Reg. 57297 (Nov. 14, 2001).

In December 2001, the State of Nevada sued the DOE in the Circuit Court for the District of Columbia to stop the progress. Among other things, Nevada claims that the guidelines are unlawful because they provide for engineered barriers as well as natural barriers to isolate the stored radioactive wastes. The DOE recognizes that engineered barriers should not be used to compensate for certain site deficiencies. However, the DOE said there is no requirement that site performance be cased solely on natural barriers and it is proper to use both natural and engineered barriers to enhance site performance. Opponents also raised technical questions such as the determination of groundwater travel time. The DOE replied that its viability assessment had found no conditions that would disqualify the site, although it would continue to study matters such as groundwater flow and transport.

The Governor of Nevada announced a national advertising program that will describe claimed hazards of transporting high-level radioactive waste. As part of the publicity, the Governor described a report by the General Accounting Office (GAO) as saying that the Yucca Mountain project should be postponed because many scientific and engineering issues are yet to be resolved. The GAO report was prepared at the request of Nevada's Congressional representatives who seek to block the project. The DOE announced in January 2002 that it would go forward.

Pending licensing of the Yucca Mountain site, the DOE and over 100 nuclear power plants must rely on "temporary storage" facilities that are gradually becoming permanent, although they are not designed to be permanent. The problems of the DOE were increased when it was required to accept spent fuel rods containing enriched uranium from foreign research reactors as part of the nuclear nonproliferation programs. A lawsuit by the State of South Carolina and environmental organizations to block acceptance of 409 foreign rods that the DOE planned to store at its Savannah River Site near Aiken, South Carolina was rejected. *State of South Carolina v. O'Leary*, 64 F.3d 892 (4th Cir. 1995).

When the DOE completes the site characterization of the Yucca Mountain site, it must apply to the NRC for a license under its regulations governing licensing of the DOE for disposal of high level radioactive wastes in geologic depositories pursuant to the NWPA. 40 C.F.R. Part 60 and proposed Part 63. Among other things, the regulations provide for participation by states and affected Indian Tribes. This licensing proceeding will presumably provide a forum for further political opposition.

6. Disposal of Low-Level Radioactive Wastes

In 1980, the U.S. Congress adopted the LLRWPA to provide for the selection and development of sites for the disposal of low level radioactive waste. As amended in 1985, the LLRWPA makes each state responsible to provide capacity for disposal of low level radioactive waste generated within its borders. However, the LLRWPA authorizes the states to enter into regional compacts under which a state may agree to develop a host site for waste from within its own borders and from the other compact member states. It also authorizes compact states to refuse waste from outside the compact regions. Many states entered into compacts, but the only existing disposal sites are the site operated by the South Carolina Energy Office (with assistance from Chem Nuclear) at Barnwell, South Carolina and the site operated by Envirocare of Utah, Inc. at Clive, Utah. Thus, hospitals, laboratories, universities and industries which generate low level radioactive waste in several states (such as New York) do not have access to any site and must store the waste under "temporary" arrangements.

The LLRWPA divided LLRW into Classes A, B and C with Class A having the lowest radioactivity level and Class C having the highest. The LLRWPA made the federal government (essentially the DOE) responsible for Class C waste. More than 90% of the LLRW for which the states were left with responsibility was in the lowest level, Class A.

The LLRWPA provided funding for the states to use in developing LLRW disposal sites. The LLRWPA also originally required that any state which failed to provide a disposal site would be required to "take title" to LLRW if requested by the generator or owner. However, the U.S. Supreme Court held that the "take title" provision was a violation of the states rights under the U.S. Constitution. *New York v. U.S.*, 505 U.S. 144, 120 L.Ed.2d 120 (1992). The Supreme Court upheld the rest of the LLRWPA including provisions that states which fail to meet its deadlines are subject to loss of funding.

Due to political opposition and highly publicized overestimates of hazards, the establishment of disposal sites for medical and other low level radioactive wastes has been needlessly stalemated throughout the nation. Safe, sound and conservatively designated facilities have been blocked in States such as New York. Despite their lack of progress and even opposition to establishing LLRW sites, some compact commissions and states have sued the DOE to obtain funds provided by the LLRWPA. DOE decisions to deny funds were upheld by the federal courts in *Appalachian States LLRW Comm. v. O'Leary*, 93 F.3d 103 (3d Cir. 1996) and *Central Midwest Interstate LLRW Comm. v. Pena*, 113 F.3d 1468 (7th Cir. 1997).

O. Federal Public Liability Action, Insurance and Indemnification

The Price Anderson Act (PAA) provides a federal cause of action for any lawsuit asserting liability arising out of or resulting from a nuclear incident or precautionary evacuation, subject to some exceptions. Original and removal jurisdiction are in the federal district court for the district where the nuclear incident takes place. 42 U.S.C. § 2210(n)(2). The substantive rules for decisions in the action are derived from the law of the state in which the incident occurs, unless such law is inconsistent with the provisions of the PAA.

The PAA recognizes that most liability insurance policies exclude coverage of bodily injury and property damage related to radioactive materials and that coverage con be obtained only by special arrangements. The PAA requires that licensees and holders of construction permits maintain financial protection of such type and in such amounts as the NRC requires to cover public liability claims. The amount of primary financial protection required is the amount available from private insurers, although the NRC is authorized to establish a lesser amount. For large nuclear power generating facilities with a rated capacity of 100,000 electrical kilowatts ro more, the required amount is the maximum amount available at reasonable cost and on reasonable terms from private sources. The primary financial protection may include private contractual indemnities, self-insurance or other proof of financial responsibility as the NRC prescribes. The NRC is also authorized to require licensees to maintain additional private liability insurance under an industry retrospective rating program providing for wholly or partially deferred premium charges. 42 U.S.C. § 2210 (a) and (b).

The PAA requires the NRC to indemnify licenses insured licenses between August 30, 1954 and August 1, 2002 from public liability for nuclear incidents in excess of the level of financial protection required of the licensee. The aggregate indemnity limit per nuclear incident is $50 million, excluding costs of investigating and settling claims and defending suits for damage. However, the indemnity amount is reduced by the amount of the licensee's required financial protection in excess of the $60 million. The foregoing provisions also apply to any production or utilization facility issued a construction permit between August 30, 1954 and August 1, 2002 that is licensed after August 1, 2002. 42 U.S.C. § 2710(c).

The DOE is authorized until August 1, 2002 to enter into agreements of indemnification with any person who may conduct activities under a DOE contract that involve risk of public liability and that are not subject to the NRC financial protection requirements or agreements of indemnification described earlier. Funding for these indemnification agreements are funded by the Nuclear Waste fund.

The PAA limits the aggregate public liability of a large nuclear power generating facility (100,000 kW or more) to the maximum financial protection which it is required to provide under 42 U.S.C. § 2210(b). The limit for contractors indemnified by the NRC is the amount of required financial protection plus the indemnity. The limit for other licensees required to maintain financial protection is $500 million plus the amount up to $60 million of the financial protection required of the licensee. 42 U.S.C. § 2210(e). The NRC is authorized to collect a fee from all persons with whom an indemnification is executed. The basic fee is $30 per year per thousand kilowatts of thermal energy capacity for nuclear power plants. The NRC is authorized to reduce the fee for other licensees. 42 U.S.C. § 2210(f). The NRC is required to exempt nonprofit educational institutions from the financial protection requirements and to indemnify each such institution from public liability in excess of $250,000 arising form nuclear incidents, subject to and aggregate limit per nuclear incident of $500 million. 42 U.S.C. § 2210(k). Limits are placed on awards of legal costs, precautionary evacuation costs, liability of lessors, and punitive damages. 42 U.S.C. § 2210(s), (q), (r) and (s).

The NRC has adopted regulations establishing the amounts of financial protection required for nuclear reactors, construction permit holders, plutonium processing and fuel fabrication plants, and uranium enrichment plants. The regulations provide that financial protection may be furnished and maintained by an effective liability insurance policy from private sources, adequate resources, or other means approved by; the NRC. The regulations also prescribe the methods to provide proof of financial protection such as delivery to the NRC of certificate by the insurer and a copy of the policy. The regulations provide forms of indemnity agreements which are attached as appendices. They also provide for license guarantees of deferred premium payments and for NRC guarantee and reimbursement agreements. 10 C.F.R. § 140.10-.22.

The NRC's regulations also provide for NRC indemnity agreements with federal agencies and nonprofit educational institutions and for determining whether there has been an "extraordinary nuclear occurrence. " 10 C.F.R. §§ 140. 51-.87.

The NRC's regulations list its civil remedies and penalties for violations and the criminal penalties for violations 10 C.F.R. § 140.87-.89.

A. Nuclear energy Liability Policy for Facilities

B. Indemnity Agreement with Licensees Furnishing Insurance Policies as Proof of Financial Protection

C. Indemnity Agreement with Licensees Furnishing Proof of Financial Protection as Licensee's Resources

D. Indemnity Agreement with Federal Agencies

E. Indemnity Agreement with Nonprofit Educational Institutions

F. Indemnity Locations

G. Indemnity Agreement with Plutonium Licensees Furnishing Insurance Policies as Proof of Financial Protection

H. Indemnity Agreement with Plutonium Licensees Furnishing Resources as Proof of Financial Protection.

I. Master Nuclear Energy Liability Insurance Policy (Secondary Financial Protection) of these Nuclear Energy Liability Insurance Association.

The PAA has withstood constitutional challenges by plaintiff attorneys who wished to sue in state court and to be free of its limits. *Duke Power v. Carolina Environmental Study Group*, 438 U.S. 59, 57 L.Ed.2d 595 (1978); *O'Conner v. Commonwealth Edison*, 13 F.3d 1090 (7th Cir. 1994), cert. denied 129 L.Ed.2d 838; *In re TMI Litigation*, 940 F.2d 832 (3d Cir. 1991), cert. denied 121 L.Ed.2d 491.

Creation of the federal cause of action by the PPA does not supervene the exclusivity provisions of a state worker's compensation laws. Thus, a lawsuit for medical monitoring by current and former employees of a nuclear weapons plant was decided by summary judgement in favor of the defendant manufacturer which was granted immunity from common law suits by the workers compensation law. *Building and Construction Dept., AFL-CIO v. Rockwell International*, 7 F. 3d 1487 (10th Cir., 1993).

Some leading court decisions in personal injury lawsuits have dealt with efforts to avoid the provisions of the PAA stating that public liability actions arising out of nuclear incidents may be commenced or removed to the federal district courts. 42 U.S.C. §§ 2210(n)(2), 2214(hh) and 2214(q). Rejecting an effort to sue uranium mine operators for damages in a tribal court of the Navajo Nation, the U.S. Supreme Court ruled that the federal district court should not have deferred removal until the tribal court decided whether it had jurisdiction because Congress had clearly placed jurisdiction in the federal district court. *El Paso Natural Gas Co. v. Neztsosie*, 526 U.S. 473, 143 L.Ed.2d 635 (1999).

An attempt was made to justify a lawsuit in a Texas state court by arguing that personal injuries alleged by employees of two uranium mining and processing companies were not a "nuclear incident" because they occurred over 40 years and because Texas regulates its own uranium industry under a cooperative agreement with the NRC. Both arguments were rejected in *Acuna v. Brown & Root Inc.*, 200 F.3d 335 (5th Cir. 2000).

The standard of care in a lawsuit against a public utility company operating a nuclear power plant is conclusively established by the federal safety regulations. Thus, a personal injury lawsuit was dismissed for failure to allege that an electrician plaintiff was exposed to radiation in excess of federal limits. *Roberts v. Florida Power*, 146 F.3d 1305 (11th Cir. 1998). See also *Kennedy v. Southern California Edison Co.*, 219 F.3d 988 (9th Cir. 2000) *In re TMI*, 67 F.3d 1103 (3d Cir. 1995); *O'Conner v. Commonwealth Edison*, 13 F. 3d 1090 (7th Cir. 1994). This standard contrasts sharply with the standard of care which the courts apply to private industry which can be held liable even though in compliance with governmental standards.

The standard of care applicable to alleged improper disposal of radioactive thorium tailings is determined by the NRC regulations rather than the USEPA regulations. *Carey v. Kerr McGee Chemical*, 60 F. Supp. 2d 800 (N.D. Ill. 1999).

P. Nuclear Weapons Stockpiles and Facilities

Under treaties and domestic policies, the United States has for at least two decades been curtailing its nuclear weapons programs. In recent years, the primary activities have been a stockpile stewardship and management program and the clean up of eight major facilities formerly active in the nuclear weapons programs. These facilities are the Los Alamos, Sandia and Lawrence Livermore National Laboratories and the Savannah River Plant at Aiken, South Carolina; the Y-12 Plant at Oak Ridge, Tennessee; the Kansas City Plant at Kansas City, Missouri; the Pantex Plant at Amarillo, Texas; and the Nevada Test Site at the Las Vegas, Nevada.

Q. Medical Use of Byproduct Material

In 2002, the NRC adopted revised regulations on medical use of byproduct material based on "risk informed" and "performance based" risk assessment methods, 67 Fed. Reg. 20250 (April 24, 2002). The USEPA said that medical applications of radioisotopes has grown rapidly and approximately 11,000,000 patients undergo medical procedures involving byproduct material annually for diagnosis and treatment of diseases such as cancer. Some persons who commented on the proposed regulations took the position that the NRC should conduct a formal risk assessment before adopting the regulations, but the NRC did not do so.

CHAPTER XXI

ENVIRONMENTAL REVIEWS FOR BUSINESS TRANSACTIONS

A. Reasons for Environmental Reviews

In recent years, it has become customary to conduct environmental reviews before buying commercial or industrial property; acquiring a business; making loans or equity investments to finance property or business acquisitions; and other transactions. Buyers, lenders and equity investors have several reasons for these reviews:

1. Risk of unexpected owner or operator liability for cleanup costs and risk of succession to other environmental liabilities and obligations.

2. Risk of acquiring or taking a collateral interest in property which is contaminated or subject to other environmental liabilities that unexpectedly reduce its value.

3. Risk of acquiring or providing loan or equity financing for a property or business that cannot be operated as expected for lack of environmental permits or inability to comply with the requirements of environmental laws, regulations or permits.

Companies considering joint venture agreements, toll conversion agreements, and leases that provide for the tenant to operate all or part of a property, may also arrange for environmental reviews for similar reasons.

B. Limited Reviews Using ASTM Methods

1. ASTM Standard Practices and Guidelines

During the 1980s, methods and checklists for environmental reviews were gradually developed by buyers, lenders, investment firms, environmental consulting firms, and law firms based on their own experience and objectives. Not surprisingly, they differed in scope as well as methods and checklist details. These differences raised questions about what should be done in order to perform effective reviews at reasonable cost and what might qualify for the "innocent purchaser" defense under CERCLA and similar state law provisions.

During the 1990s, the American Society for Testing Materials, Inc. (ASTM) published several standard practices and guides:

1. ASTM E1527-93, a standard practice for phase I environmental site assessments that was updated in 1994, 1997 and 2000 and is now ASTM E1527-00.
2. ASTM E1528-93, a standard transaction screen process for environmental site assessments that was updated and became ASTM E1528-00.
3. ASTM E 1903-97, a standard guide for phase II environmental site assessments.

The practices and the guide were developed by Subcommittee E 50.02 on Commercial Real Estate Transactions under the jurisdiction of ASTM Committee E-50 on Environmental Assessment.

2. Phase I Environmental Site Assessments

ASTM E1527-00 and its prior versions have been widely used throughout the United States by environmental consulting firms performing environmental assessments for buyers of office buildings, shopping centers, and multi-occupant residential buildings and centers. In the author's experience, ASTM E1528-96 and ASTM E 1903-97 have been used much less frequently. For further information on the history, the author recommends an article titled "ASTM Issues Revised Standards for Environmental Assessments," Schnapf, Environmental Due Diligence Reporter (BNA), 231:1175.

ASTM E1527-00 defines a standard of good and customary practice for conducting an environmental site assessment of a property with a goal to identify recognized environmental conditions. ASTM E1527-00 defines a recognized environmental condition as the presence or likely presence of any hazardous substances or petroleum products on a parcel of property under conditions that indicate an existing or past release, or a material threat of a release, of any hazardous substances or petroleum products on the property or into the ground, groundwater or surfacewater of the property. Leaking underground storage tanks are common examples of recognized environmental conditions.

ASTM E1527-00 does not include (1) asbestos-containing materials, (2) radon, (3) lead-based paint, (4) lead in drinking water, and (5) wetlands. However, many buyers, lenders and investors instruct environmental consulting firms to add one or more of these items to the work. If added, the assessment of these items will, like other phase I items, be a general review to identify recognized environmental conditions and will not include physical sampling and testing or a formal risk assessment of hazards.

ASTM E1527-00 prescribes that a phase I environmental site assessment have four components: (1) a standard database records review; (2) a site reconnaissance; (3) interviews with current owners and occupants of the property and local government officials; and (4) an evaluation and report.

Many firms obtain standard computer-generated reports from Environmental Data Resources, Inc. (EDR) to meet most of the requirement for a records review because EDR provides reviews of such federal databases as NPL, CERCLIS, CORRACTS, RCRIS and ERNS and such state databases as SHWS, SWF/LF, CBS UST,MOSF UST and VCP. EDR also provides historical Sanborn maps.

The site reconnaissance includes a "walkthrough" at the site and a "window shield" review of neighboring properties. The site reconnaissance depends importantly on the experience of the personnel performing the assessment. Interviews of current owners and occupants are often accompanied by questionnaires, but do not usually include a review of operating records. Interviews of local government officials are sometimes a weak spot in the assessment because the firm cannot reach the knowledgeable officials within the time allowed for the assessment. Further, some states do not release information except in response to a freedom of information request that may take several weeks to process.

The report is usually a lengthy written document describing the assessment in detail and ending with findings and conclusions as to the presence or absence of recognized environmental conditions, recommendations regarding any recognized environmental conditions, and recommendations as to any need for further investigation. Vicinity and site maps, photographs, the EDR report, and sometimes other documents are included as exhibits.

Numerous environmental consulting firms perform phase I environmental site assessments throughout the United States. The fees are quite modest, typically $1,500 to $3,500. A few leading environmental firms have declined to perform phase I assessments except for specially valued customers because the compensation does not fairly pay them for the extent of work they believe should be performed. Some other firms do the work reluctantly, but routinely recommend a phase II assessment whenever any question arises. Some observers have commented ruefully that the "The purpose of a phase I assessment is to recommend a phase II assessment."

3. Phase II Environmental Site Assessments

A phase II environmental site assessment usually involves sampling and testing of the structures, containers, soil, surfacewater or groundwater where potential recognized environmental conditions were found in order to determine whether hazardous substances, petroleum products and other substances such as asbestos or lead are present and, if so, where and at what concentrations. Depending on the results of this assessment, remedial action may be necessary or prudent. In addition, if a release is detected, there may be reporting obligations to the USEPA and/or state and local environmental agencies who may then require further investigation and remediation.

The author often recommends that buyers, lenders and investors decline to authorize phase II sampling and testing until full reviews of applicable records of owners, occupants and environmental government agencies have been performed. The reason is that sampling and testing is costly and time-consuming and may not provide the information needed to evaluate the items of concern. For example, if an underground storage tank at an adjacent property has leaked, the logical first step is to read the remediation files for the adjacent property to learn the kind and volume of the substance released, whether its migration is a significant threat, and the remedial steps being taken to control and remediate the release. If a responsible cleanup is being performed at the adjacent property, it may be unnecessary to determine whether trace contamination has migrated to the property being assessed because natural attenuation will eliminate it after the source of the leakage at the adjacent property is removed or controlled.[1]

Similarly, sampling and testing of suspect PCB-containing equipment, asbestos containing materials, and lead-based paint is usually unnecessary for properties where the buildings were constructed during the last two decades or the operations are commercial or industrial. Monsanto Company, the only manufacturer of PCB fluids in the United States, withdrew them from the market in the 1970s. Manufacturers of friable asbestos-containing materials withdrew them from the market in the 1970s. Manufacturers of lead-based paints phased them out of residential use in the 1960s and 1970s and they were banned from sale as consumer products in early 1978. At commercial or industrial properties and even some residential properties, electrical equipment containing PCB dielectric fluids, asbestos-containing materials and lead-based paint can be managed in place in compliance with USEPA and OSHA regulations. Thus, sampling and testing is usually necessary only if they will be disturbed by such activities as renovation or demolition.

In recent years, environmental consulting firms often propose a phase II assessment for any detailed review of occupant or government records. For example, if there is a leaking underground storage tank at an adjacent upgradient property, the firm will propose a phase II assessment consisting of a review of the file of the remediation case manager at the office of the state or local government agency supervising the cleanup and closure. Customers sometimes wonder why this work was not included in the phase I assessment. However, government files for cleanup work may be difficult to obtain and may also be quite extensive and cover periods of several years. The author usually recommends that buyers, lenders and investors approve reasonable extra fees for these detailed record reviews because they are likely to produce information that is more significant and ultimately less costly than the information resulting from sampling and testing of soil and groundwater.

---

1 If sampling and testing is performed first, samples may be taken in the wrong locations. Further, clean test results cannot assure against subsequent migration of contamination from the adjacent property. Test results showing contamination must usually be followed in any event by an investigation and evaluation of the remedial actions at the adjacent property.

C. "Due Diligence" Reviews of Industrial Businesses

Phase I and phase II assessments are not intended to evaluate, and their scope does not include, ongoing compliance with the environmental laws by industrial businesses. For example, their scope does not include:

1. Whether a business has all required permits for air emissions, water effluent discharges, and hazardous and nonhazardous wastes and is in compliance with them.

2. Whether the business complies with the recordkeeping and reporting requirements of the environmental laws and regulations.

3. Inspections of operating compliance by environmental government agencies, any resulting civil or criminal penalties, and the effort and the scope and cost of any required corrective actions.

4. Liabilities of the business for offsite disposal of hazardous substances.

5. The effort and cost of overall environmental compliance activities and increased effort and cost likely to result from new regulations scheduled to come into effect.

6. Effects of environmental laws on the business such as possible need to discontinue products, close plants, or operate facilities at reduced capacity in order to stay within permit limits.

7. Capabilities and effectiveness of personnel responsible for compliance with environmental laws.

8. Voluntary programs to protect human health and the environment where government programs do not exist or are limited.

9. The steps required to transfer permits and otherwise allow a buyer or lender enforcing workout or foreclosure rights to operate an industrial or commercial business which is subject to environmental regulations.

To illustrate, if an industrial business does not have a necessary permit for emissions of pollutants to the ambient air or a discharge of contaminated effluent to a river or sewer, an environmental agency could order a shutdown of the unpermitted emission or discharge. More likely, the agency will impose a fine and order submission of a permit application and installation of required control equipment and procedures in accordance with a time schedule. As a result, the business may have to undertake major effort and expense while the control equipment is being designed, approved and installed.

For another illustration, the buyer of a business may plan to increase the production of a seller manufacturing facility which has been operated at only partial capacity. However, if an air emission or effluent discharge permit contains restrictions that limit any production increase, the buyer may find it impossible or difficult and costly to achieve the plan.

As one more illustration, many industrial businesses arranged for disposal of hazardous substances for many years at municipal landfills and other offsite locations. These disposal sites are gradually being remediated across the nation under CERCLA and state laws. The USEPA, state agencies and private firms that undertake the remediation usually demand that persons which arranged for disposal of the hazardous substances reimburse all or part of their cleanup costs. Buyers and other persons who succeed to the liabilities of an acquired business are at risk of these cleanup cost claims.

Many environmental consulting firms which perform phase I and II assessments do not have personnel with qualifications and experience to perform environmental "due diligence" reviews for industrial properties. Unfortunately, some firms attempt to supplement their phase I assessments by a review of operating compliance that does not include all necessary items and relies on unverified information obtained through interviews with seller or borrower personnel. Reliance on these reviews can create serious risks for buyers, lenders and investors.

EXHIBITS

1. Checklist for an Environmental "Due Diligence" Review

Emissions of Pollutants to Ambient Air

- ☐ Identify point source emissions and fugitive emissions and the identities, concentrations and volumes of the hazardous substances and pollutants emitted.
- ☐ Identify the control processes and equipment for the emissions and their cost and efficiency.
- ☐ Review construction permits for the point sources and control equipment.
- ☐ Review operating permits including the emission limits and monitoring and reporting requirements.
- ☐ Determine whether compliance is based on standards for sources existing in 1972 or other standards such as new source performance standards.
- ☐ Review monitoring records and reports.
- ☐ Review any history of excursions over permit limits and any violation proceedings and corrective actions.
- ☐ Review adverse effects, if any, of the permit limits on capacity and operating rates and the capital operating costs to upgrade facilities to achieve compliance at higher capacity and operating rates.
- ☐ Review the possible necessity and capital and operating costs of upgrading facilities to meet new source performance standards, maximum achievable control technology, prevention of significant deterioration, and other requirements, if they are not being met and there is a need to increase capacity or operating rates.
- ☐ Review permits and controls on fugitive emissions.
- ☐ Review effects of "no significant deterioration" rules if the plant is in a nonattainment area for one or more pollutants.
- ☐ Review compliance with any applicable national emission standards for hazardous air pollutants (NESHAPs), if applicable, such as the carbon monoxide or the nitrogen oxides standard.
- ☐ Review compliance with th e accidental release regulations.
- ☐ Review compliance with the acid deposition control (acid rain) and stratospheric ozone (Montreal Protocol) regulations.

Discharges of Pollutants to Water

- ☐ Identify direct point source discharges of pollutants to an ocean, lake, river or stream and stormwater and other nonpointsource discharges.
- ☐ Identify discharges of pollutants to sewer systems leading to publicly owned treatment works (POTWs).
- ☐ Review permits, ordinances or regulations of POTWs restricting discharges to sewers and imposing sewer charges and pretreatment requirements.
- ☐ Identify equipment and facilities used to control and pretreat direct and indirect discharges. Does the business have collection and treatment systems? What are the capabilities of the systems? Do they neutralize acid or caustic effluent? Do they skim or filter solids? Do they treat and biodegrade organics?
- ☐ Review national pollution discharge elimination system (NPDES) permits including the pollutant limits and monitoring and reporting requirements. Review monitoring records and reports.

- ❑ Review exceedances over permit limits and any violation proceedings.
- ❑ Determine whether there are other dischargers to the receiving waters and the effects of their discharges.
- ❑ Determine whether the POTW is complying with its NPDES permit and, if not, whether it plans to tighten restrictions on any indirect dischargers.
- ❑ Review stormwater permits.
- ❑ Review the Spill Control Plan and Program.
- ❑ Identify any tidal or freshwater wetlands and transition areas on the seller's properties and any historical or proposed dredging, filling or other disturbances.
- ❑ Review processes and equipment and the capital and operating costs required to achieve compliance.

Management of Hazardous and Nonhazardous Solid Wastes

- ❑ Identify solid wastes generated, both hazardous and nonhazardous, and test procedures used to characterize wastes.
- ❑ Obtain EPA generator identification number.
- ❑ Review any treatment, storage and disposal (TSD) facilities located on seller's properties, if any exist, except for storage less than 90 days; review the TSD permit and compliance history. Has the seller complied with "corrective action" requirements for the entire facility?
- ❑ Review the TSD facilities for compliance such as secondary containment, leachate control systems, labeling, etc. Review the closure and postclosure plan and funding arrangements.
- ❑ Review registrations and records relating to underground storage tanks (USTs). What are and were the contents? Are the USTs registered? Are the USTs active or inactive? Have the inactive USTs been properly closed? Have active USTs been upgraded to meet the corrosion control, secondary containment and other RCRA requirement that became effective December 22, 1998?
- ❑ Review aboveground storage tanks. What are their contents? Are they properly constructed, including adequate secondary containment?
- ❑ Review arrangements for offsite disposal of hazardous waste and compliance with manifest and labeling requirements. Identify present and former waste transporters and disposal sites. Are any of the disposal sites listed in the National Priority List (NPL) or the CERCLIS database or any state "minisuperfund" or other cleanup list? How costly are the disposal arrangements? What methods are used at the present disposal sites? What is their capacity and how long will they remain available?
- ❑ Review arrangements for offsite disposal of nonhazardous waste. Identify present and former transporters and disposal sites. Are any of the disposal facilities listed on any federal, state or local list for cleanup? What disposal methods are used at the disposal facilities? Are any of the disposal sites nearing capacity and planning to close or to adopt stricter specifications for acceptable wastes? How costly are the disposal arrangements?
- ❑ Review waste minimization and recycling activities. Can raw materials and intermediates not fully converted to products be returned to early stages of the process and blended with similar materials? Does the process produce coproducts or byproducts? Are any wastes reclaimed or recycled? If wastes are transported for reclamation or recycling at offsite locations, identify the transporters and the locations. How do they accomplish the reclamation or recycling? Does it involve land application or use as fuel? Obtain copies of permits and beneficial use determinations.
- ❑ Verify compliance with small generator regulations, if applicable.

Community Right-to-Know

- ☐ Review any history of releases including continuous releases, of hazardous chemicals and compliance with requirements for notification of state and local emergency response officials.
- ☐ Review compliance with supplier notification requirements.
- ☐ Review material safety data sheets (MSDS) of hazardous chemicals from suppliers and evidence of their delivery to state and local officials.
- ☐ Review Tier One/Tier Two reports to state and local officials.
- ☐ Review Form R/Form A Toxic Chemical Release Inventory Forms and their filing with state and local officials including the inventory of hazardous chemicals and any reported releases.
- ☐ Review compliance with record keeping requirements.

Owner, Operator, Arranger for Disposal and Transporter Liability for Hazardous Substance Releases

- ☐ Review the National Priority List (NPL) and the CERCLIS database for the properties of the business to be acquired and properties near them. Review state "minisuperfund" and other property cleanup lists for the same purpose.
- ☐ Walk through the seller's or borrower's properties to understand the present and historical manufacturing processes including raw materials, finished products and intermediates and onsite and offsite disposal practices. Be alert to evidence of historical onsite landfills, buried containers, dumping and spills.
- ☐ Perform a "windshield" review of neighboring properties to learn about their manufacturing processes and products. Investigate further, if necessary.
- ☐ Review available business directories, aerial photographs, Sanborn maps and other data showing the history of properties.
- ☐ Obtain lists of present and former waste haulers and disposal sites used for hazardous and nonhazardous wastes generated by the seller or borrower.
- ☐ Determine whether the seller or borrower has received any CERCLA § 104 letters from the EPA or has been named as a potentially responsible party (PRP) at any site listed or under review by the EPA or a state or local environmental agency.
- ☐ If the seller or borrower is responsible for any remedial activity, what are the levels of the soil, surfacewater, groundwater or other contamination? How do the levels compare to the residential and nonresidential cleanup guidelines used by state agencies or ARARs used by the USEPA at NPL sites? What progress has been made to accomplish investigation and the cleanup? Have a RI/FS, RAW or ROD been prepared? What are the estimated cleanup costs? What share of the cleanup costs is likely to be allocated to the seller and any successors to the seller's obligations?
- ☐ Will the transaction trigger cleanup obligations under responsible property transfer laws such as those in Connecticut, Illinois, Indiana and New Jersey? Are the seller's properties subject to any lien or superlien under the environmental laws?

Toxic Substances Control Act (TSCA)

- ☐ Determine whether all chemical substances produced or used appear on the TSCA inventory or are eligible for exemptions such as the research and development exemption or the polymer exemption.
- ☐ Review compliance with premanufacturing notice (PMN) requirements for any new chemical substances and any consent orders or significant new use regulations (SNURs) under which they are being manufactured, used or sold.

- ❑ Determine whether any products are or may be subject to testing orders by the EPA.
- ❑ Determine whether seller is in compliance with the import certification and export notification regulations, if applicable.
- ❑ Determine whether seller is in compliance with Section 8(e) reporting requirements.
- ❑ Determine whether seller has filed all required inventory update reports (IURs) and preliminary assessment information reports (PAIRs).
- ❑ Determine whether seller's properties have any transformers, capacitors or other electrical equipment containing polychlorinated biphenyl (PCB) dielectric fluid and, if so, whether seller is in compliance with applicable regulations. If the equipment is owned by a public utility, verify the status with the utility.

Asbestos; Lead; Radioactive Materials

- ❑ Determine whether the seller's properties may have asbestos containing materials (ACMs). Are they hazardous (i.e., friable) or nonhazardous (i.e., nonfriable)? Does the seller have an operations and maintenance program? Are there any plans for demolition, renovation or repairs that may disturb the ACMs?
- ❑ Determine whether seller historically manufactured, sold, applied, removed or used ACMs or acquired any business engaged in these activities? Is there any history of asbestos-related claims or lawsuits?
- ❑ Determine whether seller's properties may have lead-based paint (LBP). Is the LBP intact or in deteriorated condition? Does the seller have an operations and maintenance program? Are there any plans for demolition, renovation or remodeling that may disturb LBP? Does the drinking water contain lead at a concentration in excess of the EPA's "action level" of 15 parts per billion.
- ❑ Determine whether seller historically manufactured products containing lead or used lead in its processes. Is there any history of claims or lawsuits?
- ❑ Determine whether seller's business has used any radioactive materials or equipment or generated any radioactive wastes. Does seller have a license from the Nuclear Regulatory Commission (NRC) or a state having a regulatory agreement with the NRC?
- ❑ Determine whether seller historically manufactured radioactive materials or equipment or used radioactive materials in its processes. Is there any history of worker exposure or claims?

Worker Safety

- ❑ OSHA Form 300 Log, Form 301 Reports and Form 300-A Summary Reports.
- ❑ OSHA (or state agency) inspection reports.
- ❑ Insurer inspection reports.
- ❑ Safety committee minutes and reports.
- ❑ Workers Compensation "Loss Runs"
- ❑ Compliance with OSHA's hazard communication system including MSDS and labeling requirements.
- ❑ Compliance with OSHA's process safety management (PSM) regulations including "lock-out/tagout" and "confined space entry" rules, if applicable.
- ❑ Air test results if manufacturing processes result in workplace air emissions.
- ❑ Repetitive stress (ergonomic) injuries, i.e., carpal tunnel syndrome.
- ❑ Equipment for the engineering control of health hazards.
- ❑ Personal protective equipment including respirators.

Potential Effects of Recent and Planned Environmental Regulatory Programs

How will the business be affected by recent and planned environmental regulatory programs such as:

- ❑ Regulation of air emissions of particulate matter at 2.5 microns rather then 10 microns?
- ❑ Power shortages and price increases resulting from USEPA enforcement programs against electric utilities which increased capacity to meet growing customer needs?
- ❑ Restrictions on effluent discharges to water resulting from TMDLs that will require that industrial firms which are in compliance with their permits to share the new and stricter limits with uncontrolled agricultural and stormwater effluent discharges?
- ❑ Workers compensation claims that may result when ergonomic regulations are adopted by OSHA?
- ❑ Reduced availability and increased costs of landfill, incineration and other disposal facilities?
- ❑ Increased reliance on imports as regulation continues to reduce the capacity of manufacturers in the United States to produce power, fuels, petrochemicals and chemicals?

2. Freedom of Information Act (FOIA) Web Submittal Form

U.S. Environmental Protection Agency
Freedom of Information Act

Recent Additions | Contact Us | Print Version   Search: [ ] GO
EPA Home > Compliance and Enforcement

Planning & Results
Compliance Assistance
Compliance Incentives & Auditing
Compliance Monitoring
Civil Enforcement
Cleanup Enforcement
Criminal Enforcement
Environmental Justice
NEPA

Information Resources
About Us

Newsroom
Where You Live
Tips and Complaints
Training

Freedom of Information Act (FOIA) Web Submittal Form

Use this form to submit your request for FOIA information to the EPA FOIA Office. Replys will be via U.S. mail.

Please complete the following fields (red colored field names are required). When you are finished, click on the "Submit" button at the bottom of the form.

Name: [   ]
Company or Organization: [   ]
Address: [   ]
City: [   ]
State: [   ]
Country: [USA]
Zip/Postal Code: [   ]
Telephone Number: [   ]
Please include Country Code if number is outside U.S.

Media(s) of Interest
(Check all that apply)
☐ Air   ☐ Water   ☐ Toxics and Pesticides
☐ Hazardous Waste   ☐ Superfund

Data System(s) of Interest
(Check all that apply)
☐ AFS   ☐ BRS   ☐ CERCLIS   ☐ Civil Docket   ☐ ERNS
☐ FFIS   ☐ LST   ☐ NARS   ☐ NCDB   ☐ OSHA
☐ PCS   ☐ RCRIS   ☐ SETS   ☐ SSTS   ☐ TRIS
☐ IDEA - For Integrated Data and Enforcement Analysis

Message Body: [   ]

Do not submit FOIA request in hardcopy or by fax, if this electronic form is used. Submitting your FOIA in hardcopy or fax, in addition to this form will result

U.S. Environmental Protection Agency

Finding Answers

Serving Illinois, Indiana, Michigan, Minnesota, Ohio, Wisconsin and 35 Tribes

Contact Us | Print Version Search: GO

EPA Home > Region 5 >> About Region 5 > Finding Answers > FOIA

Experts List

Library

Top Questions

Publications

Contact Us

Submit a Comment

Freedom of Information (FOIA)

Freedom of Information Act (FOIA)

- What is FOIA?
- How do I submit a FOIA request?
- How soon will I get a response?
- What do I need to include in my request?
- What are the costs involved?
- How else can I get this information?

SUBMIT A FOIA REQUEST

What is FOIA?

Under the Federal Freedom Of Information Act (FOIA), 5 U.S.C. 552, the public is allowed to receive copies of records in the possession of the agencies of the U.S. Government, including EPA. In general, documents must be released to a person requesting the document, unless the document falls into one of the release exemptions set forth in FOIA. With some exceptions, EPA is allowed to charge fees to requestors in order to recover the direct costs of search, duplication, and review of the documents requested.

In accordance with Federal regulations set forth at 40 C.F.R. Part 2, FOIA requests to EPA must be **in writing** and sent to the Freedom of Information Officer.

How do I submit a FOIA request?

You have several ways to submit your FOIA request for records in the possession of EPA's Region 5 office (for the states of IL, IN, MN, WI, MI, and OH):

***Option 1:* Online Form:**
You will receive a confirmation copy of the completed form via e-mail.

Option 2: E-Mail: r5foia@epa.gov

Option 3: Fax: (312) 886-1515

Option 4: Mail via Postal Service to:

Freedom of Information Officer
U.S. EPA Region 5 (MI-9J)
77 West Jackson Blvd.
Chicago, IL 60604-3590

If you elect to use the e-mail form, fax, or e-mail, please **do not** mail a follow-up letter. Please direct any questions to the **Freedom of Information hotline at (312) 886-6686.**

Please note: EPA Region 5's holdings contain only environment-related information regarding the states of Illinois, Indiana, Michigan, Minnesota, Ohio, and Wisconsin. If your request does not meet these criteria, but you do not know where to obtain the information you desire, please send us an e-mail (option #2 above) and we will do our best to assist you.

How soon will I get a response?

On October 2, 1997, the FOIA Amendments of 1996 went into effect. A key change for Region 5 and all Executive Branch agencies is that the base response time will be adjusted from 10 to 20 business days. Automatic extensions will no longer be available. For more information, please see:

Electronic FOIA Amendments of 1996
Summary of Electronic FOIA Amendments EXIT disclaimer

What do I need to include in my request?

In your FOIA request, please provide the full and complete name(s) of the facility(ies) you are inquiring about, the complete address(es), and a specific statement regarding which documents you wish to receive. Since many facilities are regulated under more than one Federal environmental law, please indicate the program or programs from which you desire to request records. If you need database lists for a ZIP code area, please include the state and the needed databases. Please also indicate whether you would like these lists as a printout or on a diskette.

What are the costs involved?

Your request should also include a statement regarding your willingness to pay statutory fees for the information requested. If you are in a commercial category, EPA charges either $4 per half hour or $10 per half hour, depending on the technical expertise used. We also charge fifteen cents per copy.

3. FOIA by E-mail

U.S. Environmental Protection Agency

Finding Answers

Serving Illinois, Indiana, Michigan, Minnesota, Ohio, Wisconsin and 35 Tribes

Contact Us | Print Version Search: GO

EPA Home > Region 5 >> About Region 5 > Finding Answers > FOIA > FOIA by e-mail

Experts List
Library
Top Questions
Publications
Contact Us
Submit a Comment
Freedom of Information (FOIA)

FOIA by e-mail

CAUTION: Any information you submit is not secure, and could be observed by a third party.

This form will send e-mail to **r5foia@epa.gov**

More information on FOIA

Your Name

Your Company Name

Your Mailing Address

Your City

Your State

Your ZIP Code

Your E-Mail Address

Your Phone Number

Please provide the full and complete name(s) of the property(ies) you are inquiring about with the complete address(es).

Since many facilities are regulated under more than one Federal environmental law, please indicate the program office or program offices from which you desire to request records.

- Air and Radiation Division
- Superfund Division
- Water Division
- Waste, Pesticides and Toxics Division (RCRA, TSCA, FIFRA)
- Other (i.e., legal, public affairs, etc.)
- Unsure (describe request fully in next box)

Any additional information:

Fee Commitment in dollars; see sample charges below. Requests will not be completed without a fee commitment. You will be contacted if this box is incomplete or if the estimated fees exceed your commitment.

If the information you request is for a commercial use, EPA charges either $4 per half hour or $10 per half hour, depending on the technical expertise used. We also charge fifteen cents per copy.

Send FOIA Request | Reset

CHAPTER XXII
RISK ASSESSMENT—HUMAN HEALTH AND THE ENVIRONMENT

A. Introduction

Risk assessment applies systematic methods to identify, measure and evaluate the risk which chemical substances present to human health and the environment. Risk assessment as well as risk management are important factors in the environmental decision making process. Other factors are also considered including public perception, employment, available financial resources, and legal and political considerations.

The USEPA separates the processes of risk assessment and risk management. The USEPA groups with risk management any factors that reduce risk below theoretical "worst case" scenarios. The USEPA uses default assumptions based on "worst case" scenarios during risk assessments to assure that the results are conservative.

An underlying concept in risk assessment is the "precautionary principle" that conservative methods should be used to adequately protect human health and the environment against unforeseen factors and other uncertainties that are inherent to the process. Everyone from environmental advocates to industrial business executives agrees that the "precautionary principle" should be used, even though it results in overstatement of risk. However, they do not agree on the extent to which conservative methods should be used. Recently, the USEPA has sought to relieve the disagreement by providing explanations of the extent to which precautionary methods are used and their effects on the results. The explanations may help the public to distinguish between risks that are imminent and probable and risks that are long term and based on "worst case" analyses.

An important use of risk assessments is to set protective standards for human health risks and environmental risks. Standard setting usually begins with a risk assessment and then goes on to consider risk management and public policy factors. Risk management is discussed later in this chapter. Public policy factors have led to the adoption of many technology-based standards rather than standards based solely on risk to human health or the environment. In setting technology-based standards, a judgment is made that the risk shown in the risk assessment can be adequately managed by properly designed and operated facilities and equipment, hazard communication methods, and personal protective equipment.

B. Human Health

1. The Risk Assessment Process

Assessment of risk to human health can be divided into four phases: (1) hazard identification; (2) dose-response assessment; (3) exposure assessment; and (4) risk characterization. The four risk assessment steps are sometimes combined. For example, the USEPA recommended combining hazard identification with dose-response assessment when assessing developmental toxicity risk. See *Final Guidelines for Assessing Developmental Toxicity Risk Assessment*, 56 Fed. Reg. 63,798 (Dec. 5, 1991); Chemical Reg. Rep. (BNA), 39:3401.

Hazard Identification. Hazard identification consists of preparation, collection and qualitative evaluation of information and studies which bear on the capacity of a chemical to produce adverse health effects. The information should include physical-chemical properties; structure-activity relationships; metabolic and pharmacokinetic properties; and toxicological effects. The studies should include available animal studies and epidemiological studies. The evaluation should include the methodology and validity of the studies. For example, were the tests *in vitro* or *in vivo*? Were the studies short or long term? Were the studies designed to identify acute, subchronic or chronic hazards? Were degradation products and metabolites considered? In cancer studies, how were lesions counted and how was other evidence of carcinogenicity evaluated after small animals were sacrificed? Were epidemiological studies case-control , cohort or intervention studies? Did epidemiological studies adequately control for confounding factors? The assessor should identify any significant data gaps and the assumptions used in reaching conclusions. The assessor should also determine whether the data may support alternative conclusions. At the end, the assessor should reach conclusions identifying the hazards including the extent to which confidence in the identification is justified.

Dose-Response Assessment. Dose response assessment evaluates quantitatively the relationship between dose and the adverse health effects of a chemical. Dose-response assessment is performed differently for noncarcinogenic and carcinogenic chemical substances.

For noncarcinogens, reference doses (RfDs) and reference concentrations (RfCs) are determined for comparison to exposures in order to establish a level of exposure that should not result in adverse health effects over a lifetime. RfDs and RfCs are calculated by dividing an uncertainty factor into the dose or concentration which produces a no observed effect level (NOEL), a no observed adverse effect level (NOAEL), or a lowest observed adverse effect level (LOAEL). These levels are doses or concentrations above which there are no statistically or biologically significant increases in the frequency or severity of adverse effects on an exposed population as compared to a corresponding control population. RfDs and RfCs are expressed as mg/kg/day. Uncertainty factors are conservative dividers or multipliers used in risk assessment to provide an extra margin of public safety. The USEPA uses uncertainty factors that increase the assessment of risk many times.

Dose-response assessment for chemical substances considered to be carcinogens is performed by different methods because the USEPA and environmental organizations decline to agree that RfDs and RfCs should be determined for them. Instead, the USEPA describes carcinogenic risk as a "probability," expressed as a ratio such as 1 in 1,000,000, that a human will develop cancer from exposure to dose level of a specific chemical substance over a lifetime. In assessing whether a substance may be a carcinogen and the risk that it may cause cancer in humans, the USEPA uses multiple conservative default assumptions. If a substance has a structure similar to a carcinogen, the USEPA will assume that it may also be a carcinogen. Epidemiological case control and cohort studies are accorded considerable weight, even though there are confounding factors, if their results are "consistent with" a statistically significant incidence of cancer in any human group or subgroups. Carcinogenic effects attributed to any group or subgroup are assumed to predict cancer in any other exposed group. It is assumed that any carcinogenic effects in small laboratory animals are predictive of cancer in humans, even though the animals have characteristics significantly different from humans. Studies of laboratory animals (usually rats and mice) involve force feeding or other exposure to the maximum doses which they can tolerate without death, even though the dosage is far higher and more frequent than human experience and may cause the animals to suffer severe adverse health effects. When the animals are sacrificed and examined for tumors, both benign and malignant tumors are counted as malignant. Human equivalent doses are extrapolated from the animal test results. In extrapolating to low doses from force fed and other gavage doses of a chemical administered to laboratory animals, the USEPA generally uses a simple linear method, or may use a model such as the multistage model developed by Armitage and Doll, that incorporates a 95% upper bound confidence level.

The USEPA sometimes allows departures from its default assumptions and has stated that proof of a negative is neither reasonable nor required. However, the USEPA requires clear and convincing evidence that an alternative should replace a default assumption and has stated the evidence should be generally accepted in a peer review. Thus, the assessment process inevitably causes some substances to be considered human carcinogens, although they may not be. The assessment process also greatly overstates risk. For further information, see *Guidelines on Assessing Chemical Carcinogens, Chapter 6*, Office of Science and Technology Policy, USEPA, 50 Fed. Reg. 10372 (March 14, 1985). See also the draft revised Guidelines for Assessing Cancer Risk, July 1999 and the USEPA's notice of its decision to use them as interim guidance published at 66 Fed. Reg. 59593 (Nov. 29, 2001).

Readers interested in the USEPA's risk assessment of specific chemicals should consult its Integrated Risk Information System (IRIS) database.

Exposure Assessment. Exposure assessment is a quantitative estimate and interpretation of the intake and uptake of a chemical by individuals or population groups through identified exposure pathways including their frequency and duration. Intake includes oral ingestion and inhalation. Uptake also includes absorption of a chemical through the skin, eye and other tissues. Because exposure assessment is closely related to dose-response assessment, it is important to distinguish between potential dose, applied dose and internal (absorbed) dose and to consider the extent to which a chemical is bioavailable. The result of an exposure assessment may be expressed as a concentration or a dose. For example, an exposure limit in a standard may be stated as a concentration in milligrams or micrograms per cubic meter or liter or may be stated as parts per million or parts per billion. It may also be expressed as a dose in milligrams per day or in milligrams per kilogram of body weight per day.

Exposure assessment is commonly performed by using or developing a model suitable for the exposure pathway or pathways and designed to include data for the concentration or dose and for frequency and duration. Exposure assessments by the USEPA and environmental organizations use extremely conservative assumptions including "worst case" intake and uptake exposures occurring frequently over lengthy time periods. For example, they assume daily exposure for decades or a lifetime, although exposure in real life is far less frequent and enduring. The USEPA has published guidelines on exposure assessment which allow more realistic choices. See *Guidelines for Exposure Assessment, Section 4.3*, Office of Health and Environmental Assessment, USEPA, 57 Fed. Reg. 22888 (May 29, 1992); Chemical Reg. Rep. (BNA) 39:3501. Other information used in exposure assessment includes data on background levels, body burdens or biomarkers, and pharmacokinetic relationships.

Risk Characterization. Risk characterization is the final step and the workproduct of the risk assessment process. It is the process of describing the conclusions of a risk assessment and its strength and limitations. The USEPA emphasizes that risk characterization should be kept separate from risk management and other information used in environmental decision-making. A risk characterization presents summaries of the major components of the risk assessment (i.e., hazard identification, dose-response and exposure assessment) together with a quantitative estimate of risk. It should describe key assumptions and their rationales; the extent of scientific consensus; the uncertainties identified; and alternative assumptions and their effects on conclusions and estimates. It should outline specific ongoing or potential research that would probably clarify significantly the extent of uncertainty in the risk estimation. The USEPA emphasizes that risk descriptions should address risk to individuals; populations; population subgroups that may be highly exposed or highly susceptible; and specific situations which may have a low probability of occurrence but high consequences if they occur. *Guidance on Risk Characterization*, USEPA, Feb. 26, 1992, Chemical Reg. Rep. (BNA), Feb. 26, 1992.

The USEPA's Administrator, Carol M. Browner, issued a memorandum on risk characterization policy dated March 21, 1995 that included the following statement:

> "While I believe that the American public expects us to err on the side of protection in face of scientific uncertainty, I do not want our assessments to be unrealistically conservative. We cannot lead the fight for environmental protection into the next century unless we use common sense in all we do."

The issuance of such a statement during the Clinton/Gore Administration was a significant policy adjustment. The Memorandum also acknowledged that key stakeholders in environmental issues were entitled to information about the processes by which the USEPA makes its decisions and called upon the USEPA's administrators to adopt as values transparency in the decision-making process and clarity in communication. *Memorandum on Risk Characterization Policy*, Office of the Administrator, USEPA, Chem. Reg. Rep. (BNA), March 21, 1995.

On the same day, the USEPA also issued a policy for risk characterization and updated guidance on risk characterization. The policy emphasized clarity, comparability and consistency. It also provided lists of questions that should be answered and information that should be discussed or described in risk characterizations.

The guidance substantially reaffirmed the USEPA's previous methods including linear extrapolation models for chemicals considered to be carcinogens; the use of high end (above the 90th or 95th percentile) estimates for exposure; and the use of uncertainty multipliers. However, the guidance described the use of central tendency estimates as an alternative. The policy also described the use of probabilistic methods accomplished by appropriate modeling (e.g., Monte Carlo simulation or parametric statistical methods) for exposure assessments.

In the author's experience, the USEPA staff has become somewhat more receptive to replacing default assumptions in recent years when valid studies are presented. Risk assessment information published in the Federal Register also shows that the USEPA is disclosing its overstatements of risk. However, the USEPA does not yet include the disclosures in introductory or final summaries, but makes the disclosures in the midst of lengthy textual discussions. Thus, the media (who usually read only titles, captions and summaries) and the public continue to be unaware of the extent and effects of the USEPA's use of conservative methods throughout the risk assessment process including risk characterization.

C. Guidelines on Children, Reproductive Toxicity and Neurotoxicity

Assessing Risks to Children. The National Academy of Sciences (NAS) and the USEPA have pointed out that children may be more or less sensitive than adults when exposed to a chemical and their responses may be different from those of adults. These differences result from many factors including differences in pharmacokinetics, pharmacodynamics, body composition, and maturity of biochemical and physiological functions such as metabolic rates and pathways. For example, the USEPA said that children eat more food and drink more water per unit of body weight and the variety of the food they consume is more limited than adults. They may inhale or absorb substances more than adults. Because they are not fully developed, their growth and development may be affected by chemicals that do not create symptomatic illness. Accordingly, the USEPA issued a policy on October 20, 1995, effective November 1, 1995, to consider risks to infants and children as part of its risk assessments and to do so separately unless it states clearly why it is unnecessary to do so. *Policy on Assessing Risks to Children*, Office of the Administrator, USEPA, Oct. 20, 1995; Chemical Reg. Rep. (BNA), 39:3771.

To implement the 1995 policy and Executive Order 13045 dated April 21, 1997, the USEPA issued guidance for rule writers titled "Protection of Children from Environmental Health Risks and Safety Risks." This Executive Order supplemented Executive Order 12898 titled "Federal Actions to Address Environmental Justice in Minority Populations and Low Income Populations." The guidance focussed on actions that are economically significant and that address an environmental health or safety risk that may have disproportionate risk to children. For this purpose, disproportionate means that children's exposure, uptake and/or susceptibility is greater than that of adults.

Reproductive Toxicity. On October 31, 1996, the USEPA published guidelines on risk assessment of reproductive toxicity. The USEPA announced that, among other things, the guidelines combined female and male reproductive systems; integrated the hazard identification and dose-response sections; and assumed as a default that an agent (chemical) for which sufficient data were available for only one sex may also affect reproductive function in the other sex.

As background information, the USEPA said that a variety of problems are associated with reproductive system disorders including nutrition, environment, socioeconomic status, lifestyle and stress. Human reproduction disorders include reduced fertility; impotence; menstrual disorders; spontaneous abortion; low birth weight and other developmental defects; premature reproductive senescence; and various genetic diseases.

The guidelines begin with "hazard characterization" and call for qualitative examination of all available experimental animal and human data (including observed effects, associated doses, routes, timing and duration of exposure) to determine if an agent causes reproductive toxicity in a species and, if so, under what conditions. Using criteria in the guidelines, the health-related databases can be characterized as sufficient or insufficient for use in risk assessment. Quantitative dose-response analysis is then used to determine a NOAEL and/or LOAEL, but the USEPA may determine and use a benchmark dose rather than a NOAEL. If the data are sufficient and, if reproductive toxicity occurs at the lowest toxic dose level, an RfD or RfC can be derived by dividing the NOAEL or benchmark dose by uncertainty factors to account for interspecies differences in response, intraspecies variability, and database deficiencies. A nonlinear dose-response is assumed. Exposure assessment then identifies and describes the populations exposed or potentially exposed and the type, magnitude, frequency and duration.

In assessing reproductive toxicity exposure, some unique considerations should be evaluated such as age dependent variation; differences between prenatal or neonatal exposure and later exposure; delayed effects of acute exposure on sperm; reversibility; and effects of agents that bioaccumulate when exposure duration is increased. For female exposure, unique considerations include relating exposure to a stage of life (such as prenatal, prepubescent, reproductive or menopausal) and physiologic states (such as nonpregnant, pregnant or lactating).

The risk characterization should, among other things, describe highly exposed and highly susceptible subgroups. *Guidelines on Reproductive Toxicity Risk Assessment*, USEPA, October 31, 1996; Chemical Reg. Rep. (BNA), 39:3801.

Neurotoxicity. On May 14, 1998, the USEPA issued guidelines on neurotoxicity risk assessment. In its introduction, the USEPA said that the National Research Council (NRC) had published a 1994 report titled "Science and Judgment in Risk Assessment" that had, among other things, recommended an approach that would be more holistic, less linear, and more interactive. The USEPA said that the guidelines describe a more interactive approach in which hazard characterization includes deciding whether a chemical has an effect by qualitative consideration of dose-response relationships, route and duration of exposure. This approach acknowledges that determining a hazard often depends on whether a dose-response relationship is present and combines the important information with potential human exposure scenarios. It also avoids labelling chemicals as "neurotoxicants" on a purely qualitative basis.

In its description of quantitative dose-response analysis, the USEPA commented on its use of a benchmark dose approach because of limitations associated with use of the NOAEL. The USEPA said the benchmark dose approach takes into account the availability in the data and the slope of the dose-response curve and provides a more consistent basis for calculation of the RfD or RfC.

In its description of assumptions, the USEPA said, among other things, that it assumed that behavioral, neurophysiological, neurochemical, and neuroanatomical manifestations are of concern. In the past, the tendency was to consider only neuropathological changes as endpoints of concern. Later, the USEPA described functional neurotoxic effects as including somatic/autonomic, sensory, motor, and/or cognitive functions. This expansion is consistent with theories argued for some years by plaintiff attorneys and neuropsychologists that behavioral problems and cognitive shortfalls (i.e., low IQ) are grounds for lawsuits, even in the absence of neuropathological evidence identifiable by an expert neurologist.

The USEPA said that it assumed that, in the absence of data to the contrary, humans are as sensitive as the most sensitive animal species tested. It also assumed a nonlinear dose-response relationship, as it does with other noncancer endpoints.

Under its description of hazard characterization methods, the USEPA gave as examples of human studies a number of highly controversial studies. Despite its earlier comment avoiding labels, the USEPA said that organochlorines, organophosphates, carbamates, pyrethroids, certain fungicides, and some fumigants are all known neurotoxicants. See *Guidelines on Neurotoxicity Risk Assessment*, May 14, 1998, Chemical Reg. Rep. (BNA), 39:3901.

Readers seeking background on neurotoxicology will find helpful an article titled "An Integrative Approach to Neurotoxicology," Dorman, *Toxicologic Pathology*, Society of Toxic Pathologists, Vol. 28, pp. 37-40 (2000); reprinted with some modifications, *CIIT Activities*, Vol. 20, No. 3, pp. 1-7 (2000). In this article, Dr. David Dorman discusses the model neurotoxicants acrylamide, trimethyltin, MPTP, and ivermectin to illustrate the need for a multidisciplinary approach to determine whether a chemical is neurotoxic. The article also discusses an investigation of manganese being performed at the Chemical Industry Institute of Technology.

D. Pharmacokinetic Modelling

An interesting recent article described the advantages of physiologically based pharmacokinetic (PBPK) modelling to improve the reliability of extrapolations across dose, species, and exposure routes that are generally required in chemical risk assessment. The authors described use of a PBPK model by the USEPA in a risk assessment of methylene chloride resulting in risk assessments lower than those obtained by the default approach by nearly a factor of 10. The authors said the USEPA has also used PBPK models for vinyl chloride and 2-butoxyethanol. They said that OSHA adapted the PBPK model used by the USEPA in making rules for methylene chloride. "A Consistent Approach for the Application of Pharmacokinetic Modelling in Cancer and Noncancer Risk Assessment," Clewell *et al.*, *Environmental Health Perspectives*, Vol. 110, No. 1, Jan. 2002.

E. Risk Assessment of New Chemical Substances

Risk assessment is a key part of the review of new chemical substances for which premanufacturing notices (PMNs) are submitted to the USEPA under Section 5 of the Toxic Substances Control Act (TSCA). The submitter usually provides with the PMN a number of tests intended to enable the New Chemicals Branch of the USEPA to assess the risks of the new chemical. After determining a structural analogue, the Branch reviews the data submitted and other available data to determine whether they are sufficient to permit a reasoned evaluation of the human health and environmental effects of the substance. If the data are sufficient and the substance does not present unreasonable hazards, the USEPA will notify the submitter and will add the substance to the TSCA Inventory upon notice from the submitter that it has commenced commercial manufacture or import.

The USEPA's regulations do not prescribe specific tests that must be submitted with a PMN. Rather, they require submission of all test data and other data in the submitter's possession or control and a description of other data concerning the health and environmental effects of the new chemical substance that are known to or reasonably ascertainable by the submitter. A submitter usually goes beyond the minimum legal requirements and obtains and provides all test data and other information that it anticipates the USEPA will need for use in its risk assessment model. The tests should be performed by methods meeting the USEPA's guidelines. A list of the tests included in the USEPA's Health Effects Testing Guidelines is contained in Appendix A to this chapter.

If the test data and other information are insufficient, the USEPA may require submission of additional test data. For example, the USEPA may require submission of information described in the environmental effects testing guidelines. 40 C.F.R. Part 797. When it has sufficient information to determine the hazards which can be evaluated based on short and intermediate termed tests, the USEPA often enters into consent orders with submitters of PMNs allowing them to commence manufacture or import while performing costly long term studies to complete the database.

F. Risk Assessment to Set Pesticide Tolerances

Readers interested in examples of risk assessment information will find interesting the USEPA's summaries of pesticide petitions that are published from time to time in the Federal Register. Brief and relatively simple examples are the summaries of the tolerance petition for acetamiprid by Aventis Crop Science and for azoxystrobin and its isomer by the Interregional Research Project Number 4 that were published at 66 Fed. Reg. 29213 and 29317, May 30, 2001.

Each summary begins with a description of the residue chemistry including plant metabolism, analytical method and magnitude of residues. Extraction of acetamiprid from crops was accomplished with methanol, filtration, partitioning and cleanup and analysis was by gas chromatography/electron capture detection (GC/ECD) methods. For azoxystrobin, analysis was performed by gas chromatography/nitrogen phosphorus detection (GC/NPD) and high performance liquid chromatography/ultra violet detection (HPLC/UVD) methods.

The summaries then describe the toxicological profile including acute toxicity; genotoxicity; reproductive and developmental toxicity; subchronic toxicity; chronic toxicity; animal metabolism; metabolite toxicology; and endocrine disruption. Readers will see acute toxicity data expressed as lethal dose (LD_{50}) and lethal concentration (LC_{50}) test results. Readers will see the use of NOAEL and LOAEL data for neurotoxicity, reproductive and developmental toxicity, subchronic toxicity, and chronic toxicity. Readers will also see the use of long-term (18 month and 2 year) mouse and rat studies for chronic toxicity.

The next descriptions are of aggregate exposure including dietary exposure (food and drinking water) and nondietary exposure (outdoor ornamentals). Readers will see reference dose (RfD) data and its derivation from NOAELs and the use of several models.

The discussions under cumulative effects for both acetamiprid and azoxystrobin said that no determination had been made whether either of them has a common method of toxicity with other substances because methods for doing so have not been developed.

The safety determination concluded for both acetamiprid and azoxystrobin that there was a reasonable certainty that no harm will occur to the U.S. population or to infants and children. Exposure to each substance is likely to be far less than its RfD. The discussion of acetamiprid said that feeding studies of rats and mice showed no evidence of carcinogenicity or mutagenicity. The discussion of azoxystrobin said the USEPA's Safety Factor Committee had removed the lOx safety factor multiplier prescribed by the Food Quality Protection Act because the USEPA had a complete database and its effects on infants and children and its toxic properties did not raise concerns about the adequacy of the standard 100 x multiplier.

The USEPA published the final rule adopting tolerances for acetamipride residues at 67 Fed. Reg. 14649, March 27, 2002. The notice describes in detail the aggregate risk assessment and determination of safety made by the USEPA. An extensive and interesting risk assessment of the herbicide 2,4-dichlorophenoxyacetic acid (2,4-D) to support an extension of a time-limited tolerance of 0.02 parts per million (20 ppb) for use in or on soybeans was published 67 Fed. Reg. 10623, March 8, 2002. The USEPA extended the tolerance to December 31, 2004. In its discussion of cancer risk, the USEPA described the use of margin of exposure (MOE) calculations, a non-linear approach, rather than linear default risk methodology, under certain specific circumstances. The USEPA's summary showed 2,4-D as a Group D chemical not classified as to human cancer. In its determination of safety, the USEPA concluded that there is a reasonable certainty that no harm will result to the general population, and to infants and children, from aggregate exposure to 2,4-D residues. The USEPA also concluded that GC/ECD method ENC-2/93 is an adequate analytical enforcement methodology to enforce the time-limited tolerance on soybean seed. The time-limited extension will allow time for an industry task force to submit additional field residue trials and two species oncogenicity studies for evaluation by the USEPA.

G. Cumulative Risk Assessment

The Food Quality Protection Act of 1996 (FQPA) requires that the USEPA evaluate cumulative risks among groups of pesticides having a common toxicity mechanism. Under this directive, the USEPA recently announced that organophosphates present risks to young children both through dietary and residential exposure from sources such as pet products. The evaluation did not show risks through drinking water, but the USEPA plans further study of exposure through drinking water.

Manufacturers of organophosphate pesticides have withdrawn the registrations for many of their products because the USEPA staff has targeted them for several years and it seems unlikely that costly development of further scientific supporting continued registration would change their view.

H. Ecological Risk Assessment

Ecological risk assessment requires a greater range of information and assessment methods than are required for assessment of risk to human health. The reason is that there are many ecological receptors, including wildlife and plant life, which have widely different characteristics. They are affected not only by chemicals, but also by biological and physical factors. They interact with each other and consume each other in the food chain.

Ecological risk assessments are used to determine cleanup levels for hazardous waste sites. They are used in setting air emission and water discharge permit standards. They are also used in the preparation of environmental impact statements under the National Environmental Policy Act and similar state laws.

An ecological risk assessment for a hazardous waste site begins with investigation and characterization of the site including identification of chemical contaminants in the soil, surfacewater and groundwater. This is followed by identification of the hazards of the chemicals to the ecological receptors which may be exposed to them. Examples of ecological receptors include wildlife and especially birds and animals which are endangered or threatened species. They include small invertebrates such as earthworms that aerate soil and provide food for birds. They include fish including very small fish such as fathead minnows, small crustaceans such as mysid shrimp, and small aquatic invertebrates such as ceriodaphnia dubia. They also include sensitive aquatic areas such as wetlands and stream sediments.

The identification of the chemical hazards must be related to the characteristics and susceptibilities of the receptors. For example, doses of chemicals that have no effect on humans or large animals and fish may be toxic to small animals and fish and especially to very small and sensitive terrestrial and marine organisms. The toxicity may result in mortality or it may affect other characteristics such as reproductivity.

The identification of potential receptors should consider the pathways through which animals and fish may be exposed. Like humans, most animals can be exposed by ingestion, inhalation and dermal absorption. Fish may be exposed by ingestion and respiration. Like humans, both animals and fish can suffer asphyxiation if chemicals deprive them of oxygen.

The identification may also consider the food chain. As plants grow, they may take up chemical substances from the soil, surfacewater and groundwater. Some animals or fish may then eat the contaminated plants. In turn, some animals or fish may eat the animals or fish which feed on the contaminated plants.

To evaluate the potential exposure of identified receptors at a hazardous waste site, fate and transport analysis is used. This analysis determines how chemical substances may move to air, soil, surfacewater, groundwater and perhaps other media and estimates the concentrations of chemical substances that may actually reach the receptors. Fate and transport analysis involves consideration of many factors such as volatility; convection; absorption; adsorption; solubility; permeability; hydraulic conductivity; persistence or biodegradability of the chemical substances, and bioaccumulation.

The exposure concentrations can then be used to calculate chemical intake by combining them with data on the extent, frequency, duration and pathway of exposure. This information can be used to calculate toxicity quotients for the ecological receptors.

I. Risk Assessment and Hazardous Waste Sites

When CERCLA and other federal and state hazardous waste cleanup laws were first adopted, some environmental organizations urged that contaminated sites be remediated to their previous natural state. However, experience showed that such an objective was impossible for many sites and was technologically infeasible or prohibitively expensive for almost all sites.

The environmental organizations did not easily relinquish their objective and urged stricter enforcement. As a result, billions of dollars were spent by potentially responsible parties on remedial investigation and feasibility studies, litigation, and civil and criminal penalties. As the years passed, sites remained on the National Priority List (NPL) and similar state lists because there was no agreement on "how clean is clean." Then, the public began to question why once valuable industrial and commercial properties could not be restored to use as creators of employment, tax revenues and productive activities.

In response, the USEPA and state environmental agencies began to adopt standards for site remediation. Under CERCLA, the USEPA directed that remediation meet applicable or relevant and appropriate regulatory (ARAR) standards such as its drinking water standards at NPL sites. These standards were developed by health-based risk assessments and were extremely conservative and strict.

The state environmental agencies also began to adopt soil and groundwater cleanup standards and borrowed extensively from standards adopted by the USEPA. For example, the New York State Department of Environmental Conservation adopted groundwater standards equal to the federal drinking water standards regardless of whether the groundwater is in a residential or industrial area and regardless of whether it is used for drinking water. The New Jersey Department of Environmental Protection adopted some groundwater standards that are even stricter than the USEPA's drinking water standards because its staff believe that the USEPA is too lenient in setting standards. Thus, the groundwater standard for chlorinated solvents, trichloroethylene and tetrachloroethylene, in New Jersey is one part per billion as compared to the federal drinking water standard of five parts per billion. The standard applies even in urban areas where municipal drinking water is supplied from deep aquifers and shallow groundwater is not used for drinking water.

Because both the federal and state cleanup standards were derived from very conservative risk assessments, there has been little progress in remediating NPL sites and state administered hazardous waste sites in spite of expenditures of billions of dollars. For example, technologies effective to reduce contaminant concentrations in soil and groundwater to levels well below one part per million are often ineffective or prohibitively expensive when required to reach standards of only a few parts per billion.

During the economic recession that began in the late 1980s and continued into the early 1990s, state legislatures began to question why cleanups at thousands of properties were so long delayed. The legislatures began to adopt "brownfields" legislation intended to expedite the return of contaminated properties to productive use. Lacking information to challenge the risk assessment methods, the legislatures mandated that environmental regulators adopt separate standards for residential and nonresidential properties. The legislatures also mandated that environmental regulators recognize that risk can be managed at commercial and industrial properties by risk management methods such as engineering and institutional controls.

In some states, environmental regulators cooperated with the "brownfields" legislation. As a result, industrial properties in Michigan and other "rust belt" states were returned to productive use. Other state agencies were reluctant, but most adopted residential and nonresidential soil cleanup criteria, recognized engineering and institutional controls, and allowed groundwater classification exception areas, provided that the landowner recorded deed notice restrictions warning about the contamination remaining at the properties. However, progress continues to be limited in states such as New Jersey because their agencies insist that properties be investigated and characterized for years before allowing remediation to proceed.

Some states have adopted risk-based corrective action (RBCA) standards. The regulatory agencies in states such as Connecticut, New York and New Jersey have been unwilling to adopt RBCA standards, preferring to handle each site on a prolonged case by case basis. Thus, many sites in these states continue to remain unremediated and inactive.

The USEPA has announced several federal "brownfields" programs. Congress has appropriated many millions of dollars that the USEPA disburses as grants for pilot projects and to sponsor participation by environmental groups. However, after two decades, only about 250 of over 1,500 NPL sites have been remediated and delisted. Real progress is unlikely until risk assessment methods and the cleanup standards derived from them are brought closer to reality.

CHAPTER XXIII

INSURANCE, TAX, ACCOUNTING AND PUBLIC DISCLOSURE ISSUES AND VALUATION OF ENVIRONMENTALLY IMPACTED PROPERTIES

A. Insurance

1. Background

In the early 1970s, insurers recognized that environmental liabilities were presenting kinds and amounts of risks that their underwriters could not evaluate. Thus, they began to include pollution exclusions in their policies. Some courts held that the early pollution exclusions were ambiguous and unenforceable, so the insurers then included "absolute" pollution exclusions written in broader language. Most courts have upheld the "absolute" pollution exclusions, except when insurers have used them to attempt to avoid traditionally covered liabilities.

As the environmental laws multiplied throughout the United States, it became very difficult and, during some periods, impossible to obtain environmental insurance coverage. No one could predict what products or conditions might become liabilities or what methods might be required to remedy them. As the administration of the environmental laws gradually matured, it became possible to identify and evaluate some risks and to offer policies covering them. However, the environmental insurance market continues to be limited.

Environmental insurance coverage is offered in separate policies that insurers usually issue only after careful due diligence reviews of applications and supporting information to identify and evaluate the risks to be underwritten. Unlike other fields of insurance where policies contain standard provisions that are seldom changed, it is common to negotiate and draft special provisions and policy language to cover environmental risks. This extra effort is intended to provide the expected coverage to insured persons while protecting the insurers against claims beyond the coverage which they are willing to underwrite.

As this chapter is written, the insurers offering environmental insurance are relatively few in number. Commerce & Industry Insurance Company, a subsidiary of American International Group, Inc. (AIG), is the most active insurer. Greenwich Insurance Company and Indian River Insurance Company, subsidiaries of XL Capital Company, are also active. Other insurers such as Kemper Environmental Insurance Company, Zurich America, Hartford, Liberty, Gulf, Seneca and Chubb, Inc. appear in the market, but are less active or are active in "niche" markets. Insurance brokers familiar with the environmental insurance markets include Willis, Aon, Marsh, MLW Services, and Environmental Insurance Agency, Inc.

2. New Insurance Coverage

Currently offered environmental insurance coverage can be grouped in three broad categories: (1) cleanup cost "cap" coverage, (2) pollution legal liability coverage, and (3) liability coverage for environmental contractors and service providers.

Cleanup Cost "Cap" Coverage. Cleanup cost "cap" insurance is a form of "stop loss" coverage. It has an important role in facilitating transactions such as property sales, mortgage loans and other financing transactions, mergers and acquisitions, and securitization of mortgage pools. For example, the owner of a shopping center may wish to sell the property, but a gasoline station and a dry cleaning shop in the center leaked contamination into the soil and groundwater under the property. Investigation and remedial work are in progress in cooperation with the state environmental agency. The prospective buyer has arranged financing and is ready to close the purchase. However, the environmental cleanup work may take two years to accomplish and the buyer and its lender are unwilling to assume the risk of a cost overrun.

An insurer considering the risk will usually require that the full site investigation be completed and that a remedial action workplan and cost estimate be completed and approved by the state environmental agency and any other agencies or persons having a right to approve them. The insurer will satisfy itself that the seller, buyer or other person or persons responsible for the cleanup have sufficient knowledge and financial resources and the cleanup contractor is competent. The insurer will also review the investigation and the soundness of the remedial action workplan and cost estimate. If the estimated cleanup cost is, for example, $1,800,000, the insurer may then offer a policy agreeing to pay all cleanup costs in excess of $2,000,000. The insured persons would then bear the risk of a cost overrun up to $200,000 and the insurer would bear the risk in excess of that amount. From the insurer's viewpoint, the $200,000 protects it in a manner similar to a "deductible" or "self-insured retention" amount. The policy is issued at the closing of the sale of the shopping center property and names the buyer, the mortgage lender and perhaps others as insured persons. Thus, they are protected from an unexpected large cost overrun.

A cleanup cost "cap" insurance policy can help to meet financial responsibility requirements required by state laws of persons obligated to remediate contaminated properties because the insurers usually have strong credit ratings. Of course, the insured must meet the financial responsibility requirements for payments up to the "cap" amount.

The policy does not usually provide defense or reimbursement of defense costs for lawsuits or administrative proceedings related to disputes about responsibility for cleanup actions and expenditures. Some insurers may decline to issue "cost cap" policies for an aggregate limit less than a threshold such as $1,000,000 or $2,000,000.

Pollution Legal Liability Coverage. Pollution legal liability coverage is derived from traditional commercial general liability concepts and insures against bodily injury and property damage liability and also carefully defined and limited cleanup cost liability. The policy is written in a "claims made" form requiring that the pollution conditions must occur and the claim must be made within the policy term or any late notice ("tail coverage") period or periods. The policy will usually also provide for defense of third party claims. It is important to assure that the insurer commits to defend and to pay liabilities on behalf of the insured and not merely to indemnify the insured.

Before a commitment to issue a policy is issued, the insurer customarily requires at least a phase I environmental site investigation and perhaps also a phase II investigation. The insurer will carefully evaluate the environmental conditions reported and may exclude or limit coverage of some or all of them. However, some insurers have recently been offering master policies to major secured lenders under programs which provide for rapid and limited review of the borrowers and their properties.

A policy which became available some years ago offered at relatively modest premium cost a coverage of liability for pollution conditions arising within an insured property, but only to the extent they caused bodily injury, property damage and perhaps cleanup costs outside of the property. The policy was sometimes called "Bhopal" coverage. The assumption was that bodily injury to onsite workers was covered by workers compensation benefits and onsite property damage should be covered by casualty insurance or self-insured.

A broad form of pollution legal liability policy includes a selection of coverages. The coverages may include:

(1) Third party claims for onsite bodily injury and property damage

(2) Third party claims for offsite bodily injury and property damage.

(3) Third party claims for offsite cleanup resulting from new conditions.

(4) Third party claims for offsite cleanup resulting from preexisting conditions.

(5) Claims for onsite cleanup of new conditions based on discovery or a third party claim.

(6) Claims for onsite cleanup of unknown preexisting conditions based on discovery or a third party claim.

(7) Third party claims for onsite cleanup costs at non-owned locations.

(8) Pollution conditions resulting from transported cargo

The policy typically provides for defense of third party claims within the selected coverages. The defense costs will be charged against the occurrence and aggregate limits.

After reviewing the coverage list, the applicant indicates in its application the coverages it wants. After review of the application and the investigation materials, the insurer informs the applicant of the coverages that it is willing to include in the policy and any special exclusions. The insurer will also state the occurrence and aggregate limits, the deductibles or self-insured retentions, and the premium.

If an applicant seeks coverage of preexisting pollution conditions, the insurer may agree to cover bodily injury and property damage although the environmental assessment reports reveals some pollution conditions. However, the insurer will agree only if it decides that risk of bodily injury or property damage is acceptable. The insurer may also agree to cover cleanup costs for preexisting conditions, but will satisfy itself that there are no known preexisting conditions or that any identified preexisting pollution conditions have been fully remediated. Evidence of full remediation includes a no further action letter from the environmental agency supervising the remedial work.

Pollution legal liability coverage obligates the insurer to pay only for cleanup costs that are legally required by the environmental laws. The author recommends that a specially drafted endorsement be added to each policy clarifying how the legal requirements will be determined. For example, the endorsement should state whether the insurer will pay for remediation of soil to meet residential cleanup criteria or only to meet nonresidential or risk-based corrective action criteria. The endorsement should state whether the insurer will pay for remediation of groundwater to meet the strictest criteria, usually based on the federal drinking water standards, or more lenient classification exceptions allowed for properties in industrial areas. The author recommends that the endorsement obligate the insurer to pay for all investigation and remediation required by federal, state and local government agencies, so that the insurer cannot decline payment on grounds that the agencies required work beyond the requirements of the environmental laws. This is an important provision because the USEPA and some state agencies frequently require extra investigation and remediation work, but persons performing the work have no practical means to challenge their decisions.

When drafting language for coverage provisions, it helps to recognize the difficulty of identifying when leaks into subterranean soil and groundwater occured and when and if they will or may have migrated throughout a property or to adjacent properties.

Exclusions must also be negotiated and drafted carefully. Proposed policy forms may exclude such items as radioactive materials, asbestos-containing materials, lead-based paint and mold, which liability is unpredictable.

Environmental liability insurance can sometimes be used to meet financial responsibility requirements required by federal and state environmental laws for the operation of solid and hazardous waste facilities and underground storage tank systems and for the cleanup of contaminated properties.

Contractor and Service Provider Coverage. There are thousands of contractors and service providers in the environmental field. They need insurance coverage for their own benefit and the benefit of their customers in order to operate successfully. Examples of these firms are as follows:

1. Large consulting and engineering firms such as URS Corporation (formerly Dames & Moore and Woodward-Clyde Consultants); Gannett Fleming Engineers (formerly Eder Associates); Clayton Consulting Group; CH_2M Hill; Camp Dresser & McKee; and Roy F. Weston, Inc.

2. Small environmental consulting firms performing limited services such as phase I environmental site assessments.

3. Construction and installation contractors.

4. Testing laboratories such as Triangle Laboratories at Research Triangle Park, North Carolina.

5. Transporters of solid and hazardous wastes.

6. Asbestos and lead-based paint abatement contractors.

7. Storage tank removal contractors.

Customers of these contractors and product and service providers regularly require them to furnish certificates evidencing their coverage and may also require an endorsement naming them as additional insured persons.

These contractors and product and service providers need the traditional errors and omissions coverage long expected by their customers. They also need coverage for personal injury and property damage, contractual liability, and pollution liability including cleanup costs. The transporters also need coverage for air emissions, spills, leaks, fires and explosions involving their cargoes while in transit and during loading and unloading operations including cleanup costs.

In the 1970s and 1980s, the insurance industry became very cautious about insuring environmental contractors and service providers and coverage was scarce and very expensive. The insurers continue today to be cautious, but coverage availability has improved. The premiums are expensive, but have come to be accepted.

The insurance industry provides several kinds of policies to meet the needs of environmental contractors and product and service providers. For example, capable service providers can obtain errors and omissions coverage including pollution liability. They can also obtain policies that combine errors and omissions coverage and liability coverage including contractual liability and pollution liability. Many of the policy forms are "claims made." The policies, of course, contain occurrence and aggregate limits with defense costs charged to the limits.

Once a difficult risk, the author understands that asbestos abatement consultants, inspectors and contractors can obtain insurance coverage without undue difficulty. They follow methods that have been prescribed in the asbestos regulations of OSHA and the asbestos NESHAP and AHERA regulations of the USEPA. The "Green Book" published by the USEPA helped to remove some of the anxiety that once made asbestos abatement a prohibitively risky service.

The author also understands that lead-based paint consultants, inspectors, risk assessors and abatement contractors are able to obtain insurance coverage. However, this risk is difficult because plaintiff attorneys are initiating large numbers of lawsuits claiming that lead-based paint is responsible for reducing intelligence levels and causing behavioral problems among children in lower income urban neighborhoods. The lawsuits have been directed primarily at landlords, but abatement contractors have sometimes become defendants. See Chapter XVI.

B. Tax

Business and property owners and operators must frequently make expenditures for pollution control facilities and equipment and to remediate property which is contaminated. The Internal Revenue Service (IRS) that many of these expenditures may not be treated as expenses deductible in determining income, but must be capitalized and depreciated as capital assets.

For example, a groundwater treatment facility with a life substantially beyond the current year is a capital expenditure. Rev. Ruling 94-38, 1994-2 Cum. Bull. 38. The same is true of air emission control equipment; effluent discharge control or pretreatment equipment; and waste treatment facilities and equipment. In letter rulings, the IRS has also required taxpayers to treat amounts paid to remove asbestos and remediate PCB dielectric fluid and dry cleaning fluid contamination as capital expenditures.

A federal district court held that a dairy corporation was required to treat as capital expenditures the costs it incurred to remediate contamination which preexisted its purchase of dairy property. The court reasoned that the expenditures did not merely restore the property to its condition at the time of purchase, but increased its value. *United Dairy Farmers, Inc. v. U.S.*, 2000-1 U.S.T.C. (CCH) § 50,538 (S.D. Ohio 2000).

A federal appellate court held that environmental remediation costs that were part of the renovation of a former electric power plant to prepare it for sale were capital expenditures. *Dominion Resources, Inc., v. U.S.*, 2000-2 U.S.T.C. (CCH) § 50,638 (4th Cir. 2000).

On the other hand, a manufacturer was allowed current deductions for costs to remediate soil and groundwater contamination that it had caused at its own property. The expenses did not make long term improvements, but only restored the land to its preexisting condition. Rev. Ruling 94-38, supra.

The IRS furnishes guidance on the deductibility of remediation costs in response to requests made in accordance with Rev. Proc. 98-17, 1998-1 Cum. Bull. 405.

In 1997, the Congress and the President added a new Section 198 to the Internal Revenue Code allowing taxpayers to elect to deduct any "qualified remediation expenditure" as a currently deductible expense rather than as chargeable to capital account. The election may be made for a "qualified contaminated site" which means a site located in a "targeted area" meaning an area with high unemployment or a minority group population. There is no requirement that state environmental agencies review or approve the expenditures, but Section 198 requires that each taxpayer obtain a statement from the state environmental agency that the area where its expenditures were made is an eligible "targeted area." See Rev. Proc. 98-47, I.R.B. 1998-37, Sept. 14, 1998 issued by the IRS providing procedures for the election.

In 1998, the IRS issued a broader based ruling allowing all taxpayers to expense costs incurred to replace underground storage tanks ("USTs") containing waste byproducts including the cost of removal, cleanup and disposal of the old USTs and acquiring, installing and filling new USTs. This ruling allows the expense deduction without regard to the area of the nation where the expenses are made. See Rev. Ruling 98-25, I.R.B. 1998-19, May 11, 1998.

C. Accounting

The basic accounting authority applicable to the environmental laws and regulations is Statement of Financial Accounting Standards (SFAS) No. 5, "Accounting for Contingencies." SFAS No. 5 states that an estimated loss from a loss contingency shall be accrued by a charge to income if it is probable that an asset has been impaired or a liability has been incurred and the amount of the loss can be reasonably estimated. SFAS No. 5 also provides for disclosures of information relating to loss contingencies.

It is very difficult to apply SFAS No. 5 to environmental contingencies because both probability and amount are usually unpredictable. The environmental laws and regulations focus intensely on some injuries and threats to human health and the environment, but do not apply to many others that are far more serious. The costs of corrective actions and civil penalties and fines vary depending on the policies adopted by federal, state and local environmental agencies and even by individual administrators and case managers acting on behalf of these agencies.

In Staff Accounting Bulletin No. 92, June 8, 1993, the SEC provided some "common sense" answers on accounting and disclosure of environmental loss contingencies. *First*, the SEC staff said that a probable contingent liability and a probable offsetting recovery should not ordinarily be offset and treated as a net single amount, but should be presented separately with appropriate disclosures. *Second*, a company which is jointly and severally liable for a contaminated site need not recognize a liability for costs which it has a reasonable basis to believe will be apportioned to other responsibility parties, but the company must disclose any defenses the other parties may have to payment and any insolvency or other factor limiting their ability to pay. SEC Release No. SAB 92, 17 C.F.R. Part 211.

In 1996, the Financial Accounting Standards Board issued Statement of Position (SOP) 96-1 providing accounting guidance on the accrual of environmental remediation liabilities including their recognitiom, measurement and disclosure. A liability accrued in accordance with SFAS No. 5 should include all costs including estimated legal fees and without a setoff for potential recoveries.

D. Public Disclosure by SEC Registered Companies

Companies with securities registered with the Securities and Exchange Commission (SEC) under the Securities Act of 1933 and Securities Exchange Act of 1934 are required to make several kinds of disclosures of the effects of environmental laws and regulations on their businesses. The requirements include such matters as material obligations for environmental expenses and capital expenditures and any pending legal proceedings including any proceedings known to be contemplated by government authorities.

In a description of business, an SEC registered company is required to disclose the material effects that compliance with federal, state and local environmental laws may have on its capital expenditures, earnings and competitive position. The company must disclose any material expenditures for environmental control facilities for the remainder of its current fiscal year, its succeeding fiscal year and such further years as may be material. It may also be required to describe material environmental permits and their restrictions and the related compliance costs. It may be required to describe shortages and increased costs of power or raw materials caused by environmental laws. It may be required to describe declining or lost sales of key products due to adverse publicity by environmental groups. In recent years, some companies have disclosed plant closings, layoffs and decisions to file in bankruptcy because of the environmental laws and actions of environmental organizations, especially those relating to asbestos and nuclear power. SEC Regulation S-K, Item 101, 17 C.F.R. § 229.101.

An SEC registered company must disclose a pending or government-contemplated legal proceeding (including an administrative proceeding if (1) the proceeding is material to its business or financial condition; (2) the proceeding involves potential damages, monetary sanctions, capital expenditures, deferred charges or charges to income (excluding interest and costs) that exceed 10% of its consolidated current assets; or (3) the proceeding includes a governmental party and potential monetary sanctions unless the company reasonably believes such sanctions will be less than $100,000. In the disclosure, the company may group similar proceedings. See SEC Regulation S-K, Item 103, 17 C.F.R. § 229.103.

In a management discussion and analysis, an SEC registered company is required to explain demands, commitments events or uncertainties that are likely to affect its liquidity and any material commitments for capital expenditures and the anticipated source of funds needed to fulfill such commitments. It is also required to discuss material changes, trends and uncertainties that have affected or are likely to affect its financial condition and results of operations. Thus, a company may explain, for example, that earnings for the current year are lower than for the previous year because of environmental expenses. For another example, it may disclose that its liquidity has been adversely affected by a need to make commitments for environmental expenditures and that there is uncertainty whether it will be able to obtain financing from lenders concerned about its potential environmental liabilities. SEC Regulation S-K, Item 303, 17 C.F.R. § 229.303.

For further information, see SEC Release No. 34-10116, 38 Fed. Reg. 12100 (April 20, 1973) and SEC Release 34-16224, 44 Fed. Reg. 56924 (Sept. 27, 1979).

A company which fails to meet its disclosure obligations may be sued for violation of the SEC Rule 10-b-5. A successful defense of such a lawsuit was made in *Levine v. NL Industries Inc.*, 926 F.2d 199 (2d Cir. 1991). The American Society for Testing Materials, Inc. recently adopted a Standard Guide for Disclosure of Environmental Liabilities, ASTM E 2173.

E. Valuation of Environmentally Impacted Property

Capitalization of income (cash flow) is widely used as a method for valuing industrial and commercial properties which generate a reliably predictable revenue stream. The method is specially appropriate for any property whose owner has entered into a long-term "triple net" lease to a tenant with strong credit standing. Indeed, if a lease is very favorable to the owner, contamination may have no adverse effect on the owner and its impact may fall on the tenant. Use of this method is inappropriate if revenues from the property cannot be projected with reasonable confidence.

The comparable value method is the other widely used method for valuing industrial and commercial properties. The valuation professional collects information about recent sales of properties that are as closely comparable as possible to the property being valued. Many factors can and should be considered in determining comparability. They include location; acreage; buildings and other improvements; utilities; access to markets and transportation; access to raw materials; availability of capable workers; and the characteristics of the surrounding area. A problem in using the comparable value approach for contaminated properties is that many are located in older urban areas where few property sales are made. In addition, other comparable properties may also have some contamination or other environmental problems that are difficult to evaluate.

It has been suggested that replacement or reproduction cost could be used as a valuation method. Replacement or reproduction cost is information that can be useful in valuation, but it is not a valuation method. Experience often shows that the cost of replacing or reproducing older properties may far exceed their income producing or resale value. When that happens, management will usually not replace or reproduce the property.

The courts have held that the proper measure of damages for permanent injury to real property is the lesser of the decline in value and the cost of restoration. *Scribner v. Summers*, 138 F.3d 471 (2d Cir. 1998) and cases cited therein.

Valuation of some environmentally impacted properties is a simple task. For example, if a small quantity of asbestos-containing materials or a small spill of gasoline or oil has occurred, the property value can be determined by traditional methods, i.e., capitalization of income (cash flow) and/or comparable values. The estimated cleanup cost can then be subtracted. Thus assumes that the federal, state and local regulatory authorities will allow the cleanup to be performed at reasonable and predictable cost and within a reasonable time period.

Cleanup cost is difficult, and sometimes impossible, to determine reliably when a property is heavily contaminated or the contamination consists of complex contaminant mixtures, high-profile contaminants, or contaminants that are difficult to investigate and remediate. For example, a property soaked with contamination from former gasoline station operations can be remediated. However, extensive delineation may be required to trace the contamination plume through soil and groundwater and perhaps to nearby properties. Selection and implementation of a remedial workplan may also be difficult and uncertain, especially if the contaminants are difficult to remove by conventional methods. The cost may also increase if staff personnel at the USEPA or a state agency supervising the investigation and remediation do not respond promptly to reports and proposals or require that work be expanded or repeated.

Cleanup cost is ultimately also affected by any rights of the owner to shift the costs of investigation and remediation to other responsible parties or to recover contributions to its costs from them or from insurers or indemnitors.

When a property is extensively contaminated, its fair market value is significantly reduced because potential buyers, tenants and mortgage lenders will be reluctant to undertake the risk of the uncertainties and delays involved in investigation and remediation. The loss of value may be greater than the eventual cost of investigation and remediation.

Real property tax assessment proceedings have recently been a forum for debate on the issues involved in the valuation of contaminated property. The New York Court of Appeals upheld a valuation using capitalization of income to determine the value of a property in an uncontaminated state followed by subtraction in each year of the full estimated cleanup cost. In reaching that conclusion, the Court of Appeals rejected the tax assessor's arguments that only the amount spent each year should be deducted or at least the total cost should be discounted to present value. *Commerce Holding v. Assessors of Babylon*, 88 N.Y.2d 932 (1996). The Minnesota Supreme Court held that a property leased for an annual rental income of $114,000 should be assessed as having no market value because estimated cleanup costs for contamination were approximately twice its value if uncontaminated. *Westling v. County of Mille Lacs*, 543 N.W. 2d 91 (Minn. 1996). An U.S. Bankruptcy Court determined the assessable value of a site on the National Priority List by capitalizing gross income for each year and subtracting an "environmental adjustment" of $139,000 per year as a straight line amortization of the total estimated cleanup of $1,390,000. The Bankruptcy Court then reduced the result by 20% for each year because of a "stigma" that would continue after remediation had taken place. *Custom Distribution Services, Inc. v. City of Perth Amboy*, 216 B.R. 136 (D.N.J. 1997).

The author has worked with valuation experts for many years and taught advanced finance courses which included valuation methods. Based on experience, the author agrees with the *Commerce Holding* decision, except that the Court of Appeals should have directed that cleanup costs payable in future years should be discounted to present value. The author agrees with the *Westling* decision that a property which is burdened by cleanup costs greater than its fair market value should be assessed at no value, but recommends inquiry as to whether the cost burden actually falls on the landowner or may fall on tenants, subtenants or other persons. The author considers the 10-year straight-line proration of the estimated cleanup cost allowed in the *Custom Distribution* decision to have been an insufficient reduction of value because it did not reflect the full discount a buyer would have demanded if the property were sold during any of the applicable years. In "real world" negotiations, a buyer would have insisted on price reduction equal to the full $1,390,000, discounted to present value to the extent that part of the amount could be deferred for payment in years after the purchase.

In the *Custom Distribution* decision, the Bankruptcy Court decided that an additional 20% reduction of value was appropriate because the property was listed on the National Priority List and would be likely to carry a "stigma" as a former "Superfund" site even after full remediation. There are numerous court decisions in lawsuits seeking to recover damages for an alleged "stigma" attached to contaminated property or to property located near contaminated property. The courts have disagreed as to whether such claims are allowable and, if so, the circumstances that justify a recovery of damages.

Some courts have said that stigma damages may be awarded if a contaminated property cannot be fully remediated to restore its preexisting market value. *Scribner v. Summers*, 138 F. 3d 471 (2d Cir. 1998); *Bradley v. Armstrong Rubber Co.*, 130 F. 3d 168 (5th Cir. 1997). The reason is that there will be a permanent reluctance of potential buyers to buy, or pay full value for, a property which is not fully remediated.

A landowner in Pennsylvania recovered damages by proof that a stigma would actually remain temporarily or permanently after its property was fully remediated. The court said that the proof must, however, go beyond a mere showing that there had been some negative publicity about the property. *In re Paoli Yard PCB Litigation*, 113 F.3d 444 (3d Cir. 1997).

Claims for stigma damages based on fear of contamination without evidence of actual contamination causing physical damage to the plaintiffs' property were rejected in *Berry v. Armstrong Rubber Co.*, 989 F.2d 822 (5th Cir. 1993), cert. den. 510 U.S. 117 (1994) and *Adams v. Star Enterprise,* 51 F.3d 417 (4th Cir. 1995). See also *Halliday v. Norton Co.*, 265 A.D.2d 614, 696 N.Y.S.2d 549 (3d Dept. 1999) and *Adkins v. Thomas Solvent Co.*, 440 Mich. 293, 487 N.W.2d 715 (1992).

The New York Court of Appeals has held that a landowner was entitled to recover direct and consequential damages from the Power Authority of the State of New York for reduction of market value of their property due to public perception of a health risk from exposure to electromagnetic emissions from power lines over the property. The Power Authority had used its eminent domain authority to obtain easements over the plaintiffs' property to construct the power lines. The Court said that the issue in eminent domain proceedings is full compensation to the landowner for the value of the property taken, not the reasonableness of fear that affects the value. The Court said that proof of a personal or quirky fear is insufficient, but proof of a prevalent public or market perception is sufficient, scientific certitude or reasonableness notwithstanding. *Criscuola v. Power Authority,* 81 N.Y.2d 649, 602 N.Y.S.2d 588 (1993). However, plaintiffs and plaintiff attorneys who assert such questionable claims may find them rejected by their fellow citizens sitting as jury members. *In re Paoli R.R. Yard PCB Litigation*, 113 F.3d 444 (3d Cir. 1997).

CHAPTER XXIV
POLLUTION CONTROL PROCESSES AND EQUIPMENT

A. Air Emission Control Processes and Equipment

1. Background

Dry air at sea level contains by volume about 78.08% nitrogen, 20.95% oxygen, 0.33% carbon dioxide, and small amounts of other gases such as argon, neon, helium, methane, krypton, hydrogen, nitrous oxide, xenon and ozone. Ambient air typically contains moisture, especially at warmer temperatures, as we know from the high humidity levels in weather reports for summer months. Air can itself be liquified by processes involving compression and cooling.

According to Boyle's Law, the volume of a gas varies inversely with pressure if temperature is constant. According to Charles' Law, the pressure of a gas is proportional to its absolute temperature if volume is constant. According to Avogadro's Law, equal volumes of gases contain the same number of molecules regardless of their chemical and physical properties if they are at the same temperature and pressure. These laws apply to ideal or theoretical gases, but allow some useful generalizations. For example, as temperature increases, volume will increase and density will decrease. A temperature decrease will have the opposite effects. For another example, as pressure increases, volume will decrease and density will increase. A pressure decrease will have the opposite effects.

In real life, gases do not perform precisely like ideal gases. However, the gases which are natural air components and the gases most often found in air as contaminants perform with enough similarities to ideal gases to make the generalities useful in practical decisions. For example, the author recalls responding to a problem at a chemical plant that was found to have insufficient dry air to convert maleic acid to maleic anhydride due to high summer humidity in Illinois. Efforts to dry the air by passing it over trays of silica gel did not solve the problem. It became necessary to purchase and install an air compressor at additional capital and operating cost, but the compressor produced the necessary volume of cold dry air.

Air and other gases move from place to place by transport processes. Advection is the transport of a gas from a place of high pressure to a place of low pressure. Diffusion is the transport of gas from a place of high density to a place of low density. These are physical transport mechanisms and do not depend on outside forces. Dispersion is the transport of a gas due to changes in air velocity, turbulence and other outside forces. The chimney or tall vertical stack has been used for centuries as a simple and effective method to disperse particulate matter and other air contaminants.

2. Processes that Minimize Generation of Air Pollutants

Process technology is valued for performance characteristics including product quality, capacity, yield from raw materials, yield from utilities, coproducts, capital cost and operating cost. Process technology licensors provide process guarantees to their customers to assure them that the technology will perform as promised.

Historically, many manufacturing processes provided far less than 100% yield from raw materials. For example, early distillation processes which produced straight run gasoline left behind a lot of valuable hydrocarbons contained in petroleum. Development of catalytic cracking and reforming processes made it possible to produce more gasoline from these hydrocarbons. Development of the petrochemical and synthetic polymer industries made it possible to use still more of the hydrocarbons.

Many processes for internal recovery and productive use of raw material constituents have been in existence for so long that we take them for granted. Few remember that hydrocarbons containing such valuable petrochemicals as benzene, ethylene and propylene were discarded for many years. Still today, refineries in some areas of the world flare large quantities of natural gas to the atmosphere.

A variety of factors contribute to decisions to make productive use of raw material constituents that would otherwise become air or water pollutants or solid waste. For example, some processes which manufactured ammonia and urea from natural gas historically converted well less than half of the raw material per pass through the reactor, so it was essential to install equipment to recapture and recirculate the raw material in order to make the process economical. On the other hand, processes for the manufacture of formaldehyde from methanol for many years converted well over 90% of the raw material, so that installation of equipment to recapture and recirculate unreacted methanol was of marginal economic value when the capital and operating cost of the recirculation equipment was compared to the value of the product manufactured from the recirculated raw material.

The adoption of clean air laws affected the financial evaluation of chemical processes such as those described in the previous paragraph. Strict limits imposed on emissions of chemical substances created incentives to recapture and recirculate unreacted or partially reacted raw materials even though the value of the products produced from them was less than the capital and operating cost of the necessary equipment.

3. Air Ventilation Equipment

The first step in cleaning the air within a workplace and controlling its emission to the outside atmosphere is to collect it by use of fans and blowers or other equipment which force contaminated air by positive or negative pressure into a hood and through ductwork and perhaps also a plenum area. Ventilation equipment may transport the contaminated air directly to the outside atmosphere if the contamination is below applicable emission standards. If not, it will transport the contaminated air to air pollution control equipment of the kinds described later in this chapter.

There are many different designs for collection and ventilation equipment, including fans and blowers. The equipment must operate continuously, reliably and economically. Thus, relatively sophisticated control equipment is used on many systems to assure efficient operation and minimize risks such as fire that are ever-present when handling airborne dust or vapors. In recent years, considerable progress has also been made to control noise created by these systems.

4. Air Emission Control Equipment

(a) Particulate Matter

Many air emissions contain contaminants in the form of small particles. Some particles, such as asbestos fibers and flyash, are the subject of separate regulatory standards. Some are subject to particulate matter standards such as the USEPA's standards for PM_{10} and $PM_{2.5}$.

Equipment used to control air emissions of particulate matter include (1) cyclone equipment; (2) baghouse and other fabric filtration equipment; (3) electrostatic precipitator equipment; and (4) venturi and other wet scrubber equipment.

Cyclone equipment uses centrifugal force to separate particulate matter by spinning air (or another gas) that is passing through the equipment so that the particulate matter moves outward from the vortex to the interior walls and the air remains in the center. The clean air then exits by straight flow or reverse flow. The particulate matter is collected by gravity or other means and handled as solid waste or recycled. Cyclone equipment is very widely used because it is relatively simple and reliable and both capital and operating cost are low.

Fabric filtration equipment ranges from large fiberglass bag filter systems with medium efficiency to small high efficiency particulate air (HEPA) equipment and ultra low penetration air (ULPA) equipment capable of removing over 99.9% of particulate matter from air. In this equipment, a stream of contaminated air flows through filter media which may be fiberglass, woven or nonwoven fibers such as cotton or cellulose, ceramic or plastic materials. Contaminants are separated because they are too large to pass through the porous filter media and form a cake on its surface that can be removed by shaking, pulse-cleaning or other means. The author worked years ago with reverse air cleaning baghouse equipment that was difficult to maintain at full efficiency, but newer versions of this equipment operate more effectively. A familiar example of small filtration equipment is the HEPA filtration equipment used to meet the strict air purification requirements for asbestos and lead-based paint abatement work.

Electrostatic precipitator equipment is best known for its use in removing fly ash and other particulate matter contaminants from electric generation plants burning coal as fuel. It is also used in the cement, chemical, paper, steel and other industries. The equipment operates by applying an electric charge to the particulate matter in a passing air stream. The particulate matter is then attracted to, and collects on, a surface with an opposite electric charge. High voltage current is used. The equipment has a relatively high capital cost, but can be designed to separate particulate matter with efficiency over 99.9%. Rapping equipment is used to remove the particulate matter from the collecting plate. Electrostatic precipitators can also be used to separate other contaminants such as acid mists, dusts and fumes. The separated materials can then be handled as waste or recycled into useful products. For example, the author worked for several years with a company which recovered sulfuric acid from the stack gases of a large electric utility. The recovered acid was reacted with magnesium oxide to form magnesium sulfate pellets which were transported to a sulfuric acid plant. The pellets were then fed into a fluid bed reactor which produced sulfur dioxide to be used in making sulfuric acid and magnesium oxide which was transported back to the electric utility for reuse.

Venturi and other wet scrubber equipment operates by passing an air stream contaminated with particulate matter through a water spray. In most equipment, drops of water contact and absorb the particles. The clean air then exits and the water drops containing the particles are collected and removed. Venturi scrubbers are widely used in rod, slot or orifice designs. Spray towers are also commonly used. Scrubber equipment is generally economical as to both capital and operating costs. A significant additional advantage is that wet scrubber equipment can collect both particulate matter and industrial gases, including high temperature gases, and do so without the extent of concern about fire risk inherent in dry systems. On the other hand, scrubber equipment may suffer from corrosion and have operating problems during cold weather. The equipment also creates a wet slurry that must be handled as waste or recycled, but which may have to be dried if transportation is necessary because water is heavy.

(b) Gases, Vapors and Mists

Equipment commonly used to control air emissions of gases, vapors and mists includes (1) absorption equipment; (2) adsorption equipment, thermal (high temperature) oxidation equipment, and (4) catalytic (medium temperature) oxidation equipment.

Absorption equipment generally separates gases, vapors and mists from an air stream by absorbing them into water or another liquid such as caustic solution. Dry or partially dry absorption equipment is also used. Wet absorption equipment can provide odor control and has less risk of fire than dry equipment. Wet absorption equipment may suffer from corrosion and have operating problems in cold weather.

Adsorption equipment separates gases, vapors and mists from an air stream by adsorbing them onto the surface of a material such as activated carbon or silica gel. The gas, vapor or mist can then be desorbed by steam or hot air and handled as waste or recycled. This allows the adsorbent to be reused. Some adsorbent systems are designed for automatic regeneration so that tandem equipment can be operated continuously. A common use of adsorption equipment is in groundwater remediation systems which pump groundwater contaminated with volatile hydrocarbons through canisters containing activated carbon. Although the activated carbon has a very large surface area, the canisters must be changed periodically because their adsorption capacity declines as surface area in used.

Thermal oxidation equipment destroys gases, vapors and mists by burning them to carbon dioxide and water. Their use is important for the disposal of toxic substances. They operate at high temperatures, commonly at 1200°F to 1800°F but sometimes even exceeding 2000°F. They are costly to operate, although operating cost may be reduced if the substance being burned has fuel value. Most thermal oxidizers are designed with regenerative capability. The cost factor may be partially offset by high efficiency because thermal oxidation can destroy very high percentages of the substances fed to them. However, even highly efficient equipment has itself very small emissions of air contaminants which may be combustion products. For example, environmental groups have often opposed permits for thermal oxidation facilities burning polyvinyl chloride and other plastic materials and have given as a reason their emissions of chlorodioxins at concentrations in low parts per trillion.

Catalytic oxidation equipment also destroys gases, vapors and mists by burning them to carbon dioxide and water. They are also used to burn toxic substances. However, they operate at significantly reduced temperatures, commonly between 500°F and 1000°F, because the oxidation is enhanced by a catalyst, often a noble metal, on a bed of ceramic or other material. Catalytic oxidation is used to save the fuel and other costs involved in high temperature thermal oxidation, although the savings are partially offset by catalyst and catalyst bed costs. Historically, the destructive efficiency of catalytic oxidation equipment was somewhat less than thermal oxidation equipment and it was more difficult to operate. However, the equipment has improved with the passage of time.

5. Test Equipment

A wide variety of test equipment is used for measurements related to air pollution control equipment. Some equipment is used as part of the operating systems and some is used for safety purposes. The equipment is used for such measurements as air flow volumes and rates; particulate sizes (aerodynamic and physical); particulate and gas concentrations; temperatures; and pressures. Users are generally free to select or design most test equipment to meet their needs.

Test equipment which will be used to perform air monitoring tests required by the USEPA must be able to perform in compliance with the USEPA's test methods prescribed in 40 C.F.R. Part 60. The USEPA's methods do not contain equipment specifications, but prescribe sampling and testing methods in detail. Customers purchasing equipment to be used in fulfilling the monitoring and reporting requirements of the USEPA should verify that the equipment can do so correctly and reliably.

B. Water Treatment Facilities and Equipment

1. Water Effluent Discharge Sources

Environmental regulation has focussed primarily on requiring control and treatment of industrial water effluent. However, there are other important kinds of water treatment facilities and equipment. Examples include municipal drinking treatment facilities; municipal sewage treatment works; agricultural and other stormwater runoff control systems; and groundwater remediation systems to remove contamination from leaks and spills.

2. Drinking Water Treatment Facilities and Equipment

Treatment of water to be used for drinking water begins with coagulation and flocculation in a system such as a flash mixing system. The coagulation step neutralizes the electrical charge of small particles in colloidal suspension. The flocculation step uses flocculant chemicals to agglomerate the small particles into large relatively dense particles that can readily be separated from the water during clarification. The mixing can be done by several kinds of mechanical, hydraulic, water jet diffusion or static equipment. A widely used inorganic flocculant chemical, called aluminum sulfate or "alum," is made by several manufacturers throughout the nation including a business for which the author served as an officer for almost a decade. Newer flocculant products include polyaluminum chloride (PAC) and organic compounds called "polyelectrolytes."

The water is then transported to a clarification system where the water is separated from the flocculated suspended solids. Clarification may be done in sedimentation tanks or air flotation equipment. A sedimentation tank separates suspended solids from water primarily by gravity. The suspended solids settle to the bottom of the tank from where they are removed as sludge and the water is transported to the filtration system. Air flotation equipment separates suspended solids by causing them to float on the surface of the water from where they are removed by skimming and handled as sludge. The flotation is accomplished by introducing air saturated water into the bottom of the tank so that air bubbles lift light flocculated solids upward to the tank surface from where they are skimmed and pumped to the filtration system.

The filtration process is important because it must remove all significant remaining particulate impurities including such contaminants as cryptosporidia. The filtration is accomplished by pumping the water through one or more tanks containing a bed of sand or another granular filter media material such as pulverized coal, activated carbon or diatomaceaus earth. Chlorine disinfectants and polymeric filtration aids can be added during the filtration process. Caustic compounds may also be added to adjust the pH.

The water must also be disinfected to protect the public from natural hazards such as escherichia coli, cryptosporidia and legionella. Despite opposition from environmental organizations such as Greenpeace, chlorine is the primary disinfectant. Other disinfectant chemicals include chlorine dioxide, sodium hypochlorite, and ozone. Ultraviolet light equipment is also used to disinfect water. Environmental organizations also object to the alternatives, but water treatment operators cannot yield to them because failure to disinfect water will rapidly result in public illness and death such as happened during the cryptosporidia outbreak a few years ago in Milwaukee.

Another important step is fluoridation by adding solid or liquid fluoride compounds. Once widely opposed by environmentalists, fluoridation has achieved an enormous improvement of dental health throughout the United States. Before the author's generation, average citizens seldom reached middle age without false teeth. The author's generation lived with fillings, pulled teeth and root canal work. Younger generations seldom even have dental caries if they use good dental hygiene practices.

Drinking water is usually stored in a large concrete tank called a clearwell from where it can be supplied for public use. Sludge from the processes may be discharged to a sewer; dried and transported to a landfill as nonhazardous solid waste; or recycled into useful byproducts.

3. Municipal Sewage Treatment Works and Equipment

Municipal sewage treatment uses some of the same processes and equipment used in other water treatment processes. However, sewage treatment must be more extensive and flexible than other processes and the equipment must more often be able to withstand upset conditions.

Raw sewage may need pretreatment in a mixing and equalization tank or basin where steps such as pH adjustment are taken. This is specially likely if the sewage includes effluent from industrial discharges which are not subject to the pretreatment requirements of the federal and state clean water laws. The raw sewage then passes through screens and grit removal equipment which separate large debris that is discharged into sewers including packaging and cloth materials, clay, sand and even metal objects such as pins.

The sewage wastewater goes to clarification equipment where solids are separated by gravity in a sedimentation tank or by skimming from air flotation equipment. These processes are enhanced by the use of coagulant and flocculant chemicals such as alum or polyelectrolytes which become part of the sludge which is removed by settling or skimming.

The sewage wastewater receives secondary biotreatment in trickling filter or other equipment containing aerobic bacteria. These systems, including activated sludge processes, are selected for their efficiency in biological oxidation demand (BOD) removal. The wastewater then goes to another screening step, called polishing. Nutrients may be removed by phosphorous or nitrates. Finally, the wastewater is disinfected using chlorine, chlorine compounds, ozone, or hydrogen peroxide and ultraviolet radiation.

The solids removed during the sewage treatment processes include the large solids removed by the screens; smaller solids from the grit removal equipment; skimmed material; settled material; and treated sludge from the secondary treatment process. The large and small solids may be disposed of at a landfill or by incineration. However, sewage sludge contains large quantities of fecal material and has a foul smell. The sludge usually goes through further processing by aerobic stabilization or anaerobic digestion to improve its characteristics before disposal. Some sludge is disposed of by transportation to a landfill. Some sludge is incinerated or disposed of by wet oxidation or pyrolysis (burning in the absence of oxygen), but these processes involve transportation cost and problems such as odor control and regulated air emissions. Treated sludge is also spread on land as fertilizer and is also used in compost blends and soil amendment products. The USEPA's regulations at 40 C.F.R. Part 503 include requirements applicable to land application of biosolids derived from sewage sludge.

Readers interested in land treatment of municipal (and industrial) wastewater and biosolids will find helpful a book titled "Land Treatment Systems for Municipal and Industrial Wastes," Crites, Reed and Bastian, McGraw-Hill, 2000; Two of the authors are managers with environmental engineering firms and the third is a senior USEPA official who assists communities with innovative methods of treatment of wastewater and beneficial reuse of biosolids.

4. Industrial Wastewater Treatment Facilities and Equipment

Industrial wastewater treatment facilities and equipment have many different designs, some of which are quite innovative. They have traditionally been grouped into primary, secondary and tertiary (or advanced) treatment methods.

Primary treatment includes pH neutralization and removal of suspended solids, oil and grease, and heavy metals. It may also include equalization in basins or tanks so that raw water effluent has relatively consistent characteristics. Neutralization is accomplished by adding acids such as sulfuric acid or hydrochloric acid or caustic materials such as caustic soda. Large suspended solids are removed by screens, washers and hydrocyclones, often in series. Suspended solids are also removed by coagulation and flocculation, followed by removal in a sedimentation pond or tank or air flotation system. Flocculation and air flotation may be combined in a single tank.

The wastewater is then filtered in equipment using sand or some other granular filter media. For operations where oil and grease is the only problem, an oil-water separator can be used instead of the multiple steps described. Heavy metals can be removed by processes such as precipitation, ion exchange or chelation.

During primary treatment, a treatment facility may also chemically reduce or oxidize hazardous wastes. However, oxidation is most commonly accomplished by aeration. During the 1970s and 1980s, industrial manufacturers installed many lined treatment basins with floating aerators, often in combination with biooxidation secondary treatment.

Secondary and tertiary treatment processes are designed to detoxify or otherwise improve the characteristics of wastewater so that it can meet permit requirements for discharge to a sewer or to a stream, river or lake. Activated sludge basins ("bug ponds") or tanks with aerators are widely used in secondary treatment of organic compounds, such as phenol. The microorganisms in the activated sludge oxidize the organic compounds to nonhazardous material which can be discharged, dried and handled as solid waste, or recycled for beneficial reuse. Trickling filter, carbon adsorption, solvent extraction, membrane reverse osmosis and ultrafiltration methods are also used. These treatment processes may sufficiently reclaim materials to permit reuse for their original purposes such the regeneration of spent solvents.

Many industrial sludge materials such as alum sludge or paper sludge have valuable characteristics for beneficial use such as relative consistency of composition. Municipal sludges (biosolids) have less uniform characteristics and must be treated with care to avoid hazards including pathogens and vectors (rats).

5. Groundwater and Surfacewater Control and Treatment

There are several methods for groundwater control and treatment. The control methods include capping with materials such as concrete, asphalt and compacted clay (including the footprint of structures and roadways) in order to prevent intrusion by surfacewater including stormwater. They also include subsurface drains (such as french drains) and barriers (such as slurry walls). The treatment methods include pumping and treating of volatiles by air stripping, activated carbon adsorption or bioremediation and of metals by methods such as precipitation. The treatment methods also include bioremediation in place.

Control methods for stormwater runoff and other surfacewater include channels, berms, detention ponds, grading and vegetation. Treatment methods include skimming, filtration and aeration. Enhancement methods for wetlands include removal of dumped trash, installation of a better variety of vegetation including replacement of phragmites with aspartina aeterniflora, and restoration of habitat suitable for endangered or threatened species.

Treatment of groundwater by air stripping is accomplished by installing extraction wells and pumping the contaminated water to the surface where it can be passed through a packed or trayed stripping tower, an aeration tank or basin, or an activated carbon adsorption tank or canister. The removed groundwater can also be treated by other methods such as steam stripping, chemical oxidation or biooxidation.

Filtration by activated carbon adsorption is commonly used for treatment of extracted groundwater because the equipment is readily available in tanks or canisters and is relatively economical. The tiny carbon granules have very large surface area. As the contaminated water passes through the porous carbon bed, the contaminant adsorbs to the carbon. When the carbon bed reaches its adsorptive capacity, the contaminated carbon is removed and replaced with clean activated carbon. The contaminated carbon can be sent for disposal or regenerated.

Pump and treat methods are fairly effective for removal from groundwater of volatile and semi-volatile organic compounds and even dissolved metal. However, their effectiveness is limited to removing free product from spills of substances such as gasoline and reducing high concentrations to lower levels. Pump and treat methods have difficulty attaining the extremely low groundwater remediation criteria used by the USEPA at NPL and RCRA corrective action sites and by state agencies at sites where they use criteria based on the USEPA's drinking water standards. Further, pump and treat methods have limited effectiveness for remediation of chlorinated solvents and other dense nonaqueous phase liquids (DNAPLs) because they are heavier than water and sink through groundwater until they reach and form pools on impervious surfaces such as bedrock or clay.

Biological treatment presents several alternative methods for remediation of groundwater. The methods include bioventing, biosparging, phytoremediation and monitored natural attenuation. These methods rely upon, and some of them enhance, natural biodegradation of organic materials which occurs fairly rapidly for some compounds but slowly for highly stable compounds such as some chlorinated hydrocarbon compounds Except for natural attenuation, these methods are primarily soil treatment methods, but benefit groundwater by remediating soil contamination which is a passive source for groundwater contamination. Further, biosparging systems inject air into the saturated zone, thus enhancing biodegradation in this zone which is permeated by shallow groundwater. These methods are discussed further under Soil Remediation Methods and Equipment.

C. Soil Remediation Methods and Equipment

Before commencing remediation of soil contamination, the USEPA and state agencies require investigation and characterization of the soil to identify the contaminants, their concentrations and the extent of their migration horizontally and vertically. Initial work may be done with photoionization detector (PID) and geoprobe equipment. When prompt test results are needed, portable gas chromatograph equipment may be used to test samples. When more precise work is required, borings are drilled and soil samples collected at selected depths including soil just above groundwater. The samples are split and sent under chain of custody procedures to a licensed testing laboratory for testing by methods prescribed in the USEPA's SW-846. The test equipment ranges from simple equipment to GC/ECD and GC/MS equipment which can identify and quantify substances in parts per trillion.

Soil remediation can be accomplished by soil washing which involves its removal and processing in equipment using water which may also contain solvents, surfactants and chemical extractants. The clean soil is then restored to the site. Soil washing is likely to be feasible where a large quantity of contaminated soil is present and transportation to, and operation of, the washing equipment at the site is technically and financially feasible including the means and cost of disposal of the washwater.

A variety of chemical treatment methods can be used to remediate soil contaminated with heavy metals. The metals can be precipitated, dissolved, chelated, oxidized or reduced by treating them with suitable processes and reagents.

Soil remediation can also be also be accomplished by thermal methods including incineration, catalytic oxidation, and low temperature desorption. Here also, the technical and financial feasibility must be carefully considered including the availability of thermal equipment suitable for efficient destruction of the contaminant, possible effects of the contaminant on the equipment, emissions from the equipment, and disposal of residues of the burnt soil.

Biological treatment of soil on site has a fundamental advantage over soil removal. The treatment upgrades the soil quality rather than moving the contaminated soil to another location where it must be managed. Biological treatment on site can be performed while leaving the soil in place or by removing the soil for treatment on site and then restoring the soil. Biological treatment can also be performed using aerobic systems and anaerobic systems. Aerobic systems use microorganisms and oxygen to oxidize synthetic organic (xenobiotic) substances. Anaerobic systems use microorganisms in the absence of oxygen to convert synthetic organic substances to carbon dioxide and methane. For example, contaminated soil can be removed and treated on site in an aerobic bioreactor or anaerobic digestor, if there is extensive contamination and other factors also justify transporting the equipment to the site and operating it there. Soil can be treated in place by aerobic methods such as bioventing by air injection into the soil in the shallow vadose zone or air sparging by air injection into soil in the deeper saturated zone. The air injection supplies the oxygen needed to enhance aerobic microbial action.

Biological treatment requires care to maintain the microorganism populations and encourage their activities. Microorganisms tend to be sensitive and become ineffective and even die when maintained under less than optimal conditions. Accordingly, they must be maintained under favorable temperature, moisture and pH conditions. It may be necessary to feed nutrients to them and to protect them from doses of organic or metallic contaminants other than those to which they have adapted. For example, a steam line can be run through an activated sludge pond to maintain warm temperature during winter. Microorganisms adapted to a compound such as phenol or vinyl acetate must be protected from inadvertent introduction of a substance such as formaldehyde solution which would cause the population to die.

In recent years, there has been growing interest in phytoremediation, i.e., the use of plants to extract metallic or other contaminants from soil or to assist microorganisms in biodegrading them. Environmentalists have long been concerned about plants, such as soy bean or mustard plants, that can take up metals or other contaminants from soil as they grow, thus potentially affecting the food chain. Phytoremediation uses this uptake capacity for beneficial purposes. Plants are intentionally grown on soil with shallow contamination which is absorbed into the plants through their roots. The plants are then harvested and handled for disposal by incineration or at a permitted landfill. During their growth period, the plants can also serve their long recognized function of soil stabilization.

Once blocked as a "no action" alternative by environmentalists, monitored natural attenuation has become a widely used remedial alternative at thousands of sites. To be allowed to use natural attenuation, a proponent may be required to demonstrate that biodegradation is occurring and can be expected to attain cleanup criteria within a reasonable time when compared to other methods. For example, the New Jersey Department of Environmental Protection requires that samples be tested for four consecutive calendar quarters and show declining contaminant concentrations.

Engineering controls (such as capping and slurry walls) and institutional controls (such as recorded deed notice restrictions) have been used at many sites in recent years when the USEPA or state environmental agencies allow monitored contamination to remain in place at concentrations above the cleanup criteria for residential property. These controls create long term obligations requiring regulatory supervision. They have relieved some of the pressure on the USEPA and state agencies to modify the risk assessment methods which are the basis for the cleanup criteria which cannot be met.

D. Waste Management and Disposal Facilities and Equipment

Both the USEPA and industry deserve credit for improving the management of solid and hazardous waste since the 1970s. USEPA deserves special credit for adopting regulations that industry could meet, although they required extensive effort and cost. Thus, the waste management regulations have spent less time in court and shown more progress than other regulatory programs.

Industry has greatly reduced generation of solid and hazardous waste by designing processes that produce greater yields of useful products from raw materials. Some processes improve yield by converting higher percentages of raw materials or by recovering and recirculating raw materials. Other processes treat hazardous waste to convert it to nonhazardous solid waste. These processes are sometimes held as trade secret information.

Since the adoption of RCRA and its regulations, solid and hazardous waste is routinely characterized by sampling and analytical testing before transportation and disposal. Standard test methods are used such as closed cup flammability test methods and toxic characteristic leaching procedure methods.

Drums, bags and other product containers are better made and are commonly stored inside warehouse facilities or on impervious pads surrounded by berms or dikes. Ships, barges, railcars and truck trailers are better made and less likely to leak or spill during transportation and loading and unloading operations. Many of these improvements resulted from the cooperation between industry organizations and the Research and Special Programs Administration of the U.S. Department of Transportation in developing performance-based packaging (container) standards.

Use of underground storage tanks has been reduced. When used, underground storage tanks are installed, or upgraded, to have corrosion protection and, leak monitoring equipment as well as secondary protection against leaks and spills. With growing frequency, aboveground storage tanks are fabricated or upgraded to have leak monitoring equipment and secondary containment within concrete dikes. The author served for several years as an officer of a company which installed and operated large acid storage tanks that required as much capital and operating cost as some entire manufacturing facilities during previous decades.

Nonhazardous waste continues to be transported in large quantities for disposal at landfills. These landfills are designed to meet the requirements of state regulations and the USEPA's regulations under RCRA at 40 C.F.R. Parts 257 and 258. Hazardous waste continues to be transported for disposal at fully secure landfills, but in quantities that have been greatly reduced in recent years. Indeed, there are only a few landfills which are permitted to accept hazardous waste such as the landfills at Emelle, Alabama and Arlington, Oregon. Hazardous waste facilities must comply with the USEPA's regulations at 40 C.F.R. Parts 264 to 273.

Modern landfills are designed at both process and detailed engineering levels to perform effectively and to comply with federal, state and local regulations. At hazardous waste landfills, waste is evaluated for compatibility and placed in cells that are separated from each other by barriers. The bottom of the landfill is isolated from the surrounding soil, bedrock and groundwater by primary and secondary liners with leachate collection and monitoring systems. The liner materials usually include layers of compacted clay and plastic materials such as du Pont's Hypalon® chlorosulfonated polyethylene product. The liners are selected for resistance to chemicals, tearing and cracking in response to freeze-thaw cycles. Daily cover and capping materials must meet composition and performance specifications and be installed as provided in the landfill design. Sanitary landfills must have facilities to control dust and to collect and safely vent methane gas which could otherwise present flammability and asphyxiation hazards. The cap material must be overlaid with topsoil and planted with grass and other vegetation.

Landfills have progressed greatly during the last three decades. The author wondered at one time if there would ever be a synthetic liner material that did not rip or crack. Early landfills sometimes experienced collapses due to underflowing water or underplanned slope construction. So much methane was generated by some sanitary landfills that the author participated on early project to extract and purchase methane (500 BTU) from a landfill at Irwindale, California for use as fuel at nearby manufacturing facilities. In recent years, some landfills have been so well designed, operated and closed that commercial and recreational facilities such as parks and golf courses have been built on them. The public has reacted favorably to these uses of former landfills and calls them "Mount Trashmores".

Solid and hazardous waste can be disposed of by thermal methods by burning in the presence of oxygen or by pyrolysis in the absence of oxygen. It is also possible to reclaim contaminated noncombustible materials by burning the contaminants and recovering the materials. Thermal methods include high temperature incineration and low temperature catalytic combustion. They are used primarily to destroy organic waste in solid, liquid or vapor form. There may be a significant cost saving if the organic waste can serve as the fuel, either entirely or with a small quantity of purchased supplemental fuel. Although some incineration and other thermal equipment has a combustion efficiency of 99.99%, combustion is never totally complete. Thus, thermal methods have encountered criticism by environmental organizations because they generate carbon dioxide, small quantities of carbon monoxide, water vapor opacity, and a variety of other emissions depending on the wastes being burnt. For example, they may generate emissions of sulfur dioxide, nitrogen oxides, and acids such as hydrochloric acid. When polyvinyl chloride plastics are burnt, there may also be emissions of infinitesimal quantities of chlorinated dioxins. There are many different designs of thermal equipment including equipment which injects liquid or vapor and the rotary ceramic refractory kiln or fluid bed equipment which is commonly used to burn solid waste. Many incinerators have heat recovery equipment and secondary combustion chambers to improve their cost and combustion efficiency. They may also have air emission control and monitoring equipment as well as safety equipment.

E. Recycling

Recycling has been a cornerstone of industry for over a century. For example, the oil industry once used simple processes to distill gasoline and to produce fuel oil and discarded the residues. However, early in the 1900s, the refineries developed cracking, reforming and other processes to use the residual hydrocarbons to produce more and better aviation fuel and gasoline. Later, they used the residues to produce petrochemicals and synthetic polymers that are now used in every material in the United States. For example, synthetic polymers derived from formerly discarded petroleum hydrocarbons are used to make cloth, leather, plastic, paint, ink, adhesives, furniture, vehicles, boats, and construction materials.

The most efficient recycling processes recover useful materials before they reach the "end of the pipe" and are discarded as waste. The recovery processes are numerous and may involve sequential further processing of unused materials. Many processes internally recover materials by methods such as screening, filtration, distillation or flotation. They are then recirculated to the production stages of the process.

Recycling of materials which have become waste has also been a major activity for many decades. For example, the iron and steel industry processed mine tailings to ship taconite for decades. The copper industry also processed mine tailings. For several decades, a large segment of the steel industry has used scrap as its raw material rather than mined iron. For several decades, the paper industry has recovered waste paper and used it to make tissue paper and other paper products. The lead industry has long had battery collection, breaking and secondary smelting processes which recycle used batteries. Useful waste materials are recovered by a variety of processes such as screening, magnetic separation or planned separation at the source.

Optimal recycling involves use of waste materials to make products that meet commercial specifications and can be sold in competitive markets for a price that provides a net payment to the recycler. However, some waste is recycled by processes that upgrade it only enough to allow the product to be sold for applications which have relatively low economic value such as landfill daily cover or as cement kiln or incinerator fuel. For those applications, the recycler may have to pay the customer to take the product and the amount will be based on the seller's avoided cost and the buyer's saving compared to other available materials.

As described, many recycling businesses developed before the adoption of the environmental laws. Like other businesses, they adapted to environmental regulation and some have been able to continue to operate.

Many environmental laws contain provisions intended to encourage recycling. Environmental groups have made recycling a popular theme. However, entrepreneurs who have founded new recycling businesses of the kinds encouraged by the environmental laws have found success difficult to achieve. Some could not obtain an adequate and reliable supply of reasonably priced waste materials. Some could not obtain customers willing to buy their recycled products consistently and for adequate prices, even when subsidized by preferential treatment in government purchasing programs and the right to use "Green Advertising" such as the familiar "Chasing Arrows" emblem.

> *NOTE:* The Federal Trade Commission and the Better Business Bureau regulate the use of "Green Advertising" to limit its use to qualifying recyclers.

Serious burdens borne by recyclers are regulation and adverse publicity. Other new businesses can usually operate on a "shoestring" in their early years and can market their products free of adverse publicity resulting from causes beyond their control. New recycling businesses must meet strict permit or exemption requirements and conduct their activities under the watchful eyes of the regulatory agencies from their earliest days. Some are driven out of business because they cannot meet complex regulatory requirements. Further, they never know when one or more environmental groups may commence a publicity campaign against the waste materials they are recycling or against their products or similar products because they contain trace amounts of contaminants. Such adverse publicity can be devastating because recyclers are already selling products perceived by customers as "second hand."

Congress took a limited step to aid recycling by adopting the Superfund Recycling Equity Act which provides a limited exemption from arranger liability under CERCLA to persons who arrange recycling of recyclable material. 42 U.S.C. § 9627. In effect, the exemption protects persons who deliver materials to recyclers in the careful manner required will not be liable for response costs if the recycler's property should become subject to a cleanup under CERCLA.

CHAPTER XXV

INDUSTRY MEMBERSHIP ORGANIZATIONS AND STANDARDS ORGANIZATIONS

A. Industry Membership Organizations

There are many industry membership organizations in the United States. They include the Air Transport Association of America, the Aluminum Association, the American Association of Railroads, the North American Diecasting Association, the American Forest and Paper Association, (AF&PA), the American Institute of Chemical Engineers (AICHE), the American Pyrotechnics Association (APA), the American Society of Mechanical Engineers (ASME), the American Trucking Association (ATA), the American Waterworks Association (AWWA), the Association of the Pulp and Paper Industry (TAPPI), the Chlorine Institute, the Federation of Paint and Coatings Societies, the Fiberclay Council, the Lead Industries Association (LIA), the National Association of Corrosion Engineers (NACE), the National Fire Protection Association (NFPA), the National Motor Freight Traffic Association, Inc., the Society for the Plastics Industry (SPI), the Synthetic Organic Chemical Manufacturers Association, and the Truck Trailer Manufacturers Association.

B. Programs of Industry Membership Organizations

The length of this book does not allow the author to describe the programs of all the industry membership organizations. The author decided to use as examples some of the programs of the American Chemistry Council because of the national importance of its CHEMTREC® Emergency Communications Center and its high production volume chemical testing program.

The American Chemistry Council (ACC) founded and has conducted for over two decades the Chemical Emergency Communications Center, called CHEMTREC®. CHEMTREC provides emergency response information, technical assistance and emergency medical assistance to persons first responding to incidents involving hazardous materials. The service is provided without charge 24 hours per day, every day of the year, anywhere in the United States, Canada, Puerto Rico and the Virgin Islands through the toll free number (800) 424-9300 (Emergency). Callers outside the United States and ships at sea can call (703) 527-3887. Emergency collect calls are accepted. A copy of the CHEMTREC Emergency Assistance

Guidelines are provided at the end of this chapter. The author was part of the emergency response team for a major chemical company and is familiar with the kinds of calls that are made to the CHEMTREC Center. They result from vehicle collisions, train derailments, factory or warehouse fires and other incidents for which prompt, accurate and experienced information is urgently needed. The calls come from many different sources including truck drivers and dispatchers; train engineers and switching yard supervisors; police and fire department personnel; and medical professionals. Thus, the personnel who handle calls for the Center must be very knowledgeable and also communicate effectively with people having widely different backgrounds.

The ACC and its members are leaders in the high-production volume (HPV) chemicals voluntary testing program that will provide test data to the USEPA on approximately a thousand chemical substances for which testing had not been performed. The HPV program has been delayed by lawsuits by "animal rights" activists who seek to stop the use of rats and mice in health testing. When the program is allowed to go forward, it will add greatly to the health and safety data available to the public.

The ACC sponsors a program called "Responsible Care." The program emphasizes product stewardship and management systems to achieve continued improvement of environmental, health and safety (EH&S) performance. The program fosters outreaching communication between its participating members and government and the public.

The ACC collects, summarizes and reports facts and figures on subjects such releases of hazardous substances, accidents and injuries so that the public will have access to accurate information on these subjects. The ACC plans to expand these information programs to include additional data on air, water and waste emissions and other environmental data.

In response to the attack on the World Trade Center on September 11, 2001, the ACC joined with other organizations to publish Site Security Guidelines for the U.S. Chemical Industry and Transportation Security Guidelines. The ACC also works the U.S. Drug Enforcement Agency to combat illegal drugs and with the U.S. Department of State on treaties to ban chemical weapons.

C. Intermediary Roles of Industry Membership Organizations

Industry membership organizations have played essential roles in the development and implementation of environmental standards. As environmental organizations persuaded the U.S. Congress and state legislatures to adopt environmental laws, the next step was for the USEPA and state environmental agencies to adopt regulations requiring industry to comply and to impose civil and criminal penalties for failure to do so.

However, the environmental laws seldom clearly stated what the USEPA or state environmental agencies should require, or the steps that industry should take, to achieve compliance. Their broad restrictions on air pollutant omissions, water effluent discharges and disposal of solid and hazardous wastes could not be performed immediately without closing facilities and creating unemployment and shortages of essential goods and services. As the USEPA and state environmental agencies undertook their responsibilities, they recognized that it was important to prioritize and define the tasks that industry should accomplish and set schedules for their implementation. However, regulatory personnel needed to learn about industry's facilities, operations and products in order to adopt regulations that would be strict but not harm the overall economy.

Responding to this need, industry membership organizations undertook two roles. They coordinated the work to assemble and provide meaningful information about their industries. In doing so, they advocated viewpoints held in their industries, but they also presented valuable information that was much needed by the regulators. They also established programs to educate their members about regulatory requirements and practical methods to achieve compliance. The author worked with several industry organizations to help them develop educational programs including conferences and literature.

The roles undertaken by the industry membership organizations are difficult. They often face criticism from members who believe they should persuade legislators and regulators to withdraw or modify environmental programs. They face skepticism from some legislators and regulators who see them only as advocates for their industries and who sometimes decline to use their information, even though complete and accurate. Environmental groups oppose them, often in harsh accusatory terms. Industry organizations typically respond by courteously providing more factual information and seeking middle ground. By doing so, they find legislators and regulators who want to be better informed and are willing to focus on achievable objectives.

By performing the two roles, industry membership organizations have helped to advance environmental programs from general mandates to realistic programs that bring measurable benefits to human health and the environment.

D. Standards Organizations

There are a number of organizations which set national or international standards for use by industrial or government organizations that wish to use them. Some are self-maintaining nonprofit organizations. Others are industry membership organizations. Many of them have been developing standards for decades including years before the environmental laws were adopted. Their standards are usually well-respected and are voluntarily adopted and widely followed. Except for the right of membership organizations to exclude companies from membership, the standards organizations have no power to enforce their standards, so their work is useful but is not a substitute for government regulation. Government regulators often develop their own standards, but sometimes adopt previously existing standards or use them in developing regulatory requirements.

The best known international standards organization is the International Organization on Standardization (called "ISO"). In the United States, the best known standards organizations are the American National Standards Institute (ANSI) of Bethesda, Maryland; the American Society for Quality Control (ASQC) of Milwaukee, Wisconsin; the American Society for Testing Materials, Inc. (ASTM) of West Conshohocken, Pennsylvania; and NSF International of Ann Arbor, Michigan.

Numerous other organizations set standards in the United States. For example, the National Association of Corrosion Engineers (NACE) sets corrosion standards. The National Fire Protection Association (NFPA) sets fire standards.

E. The ISO 14000 Standards

The ISO 14000 standards are a series of environmental management standards published by the International Organization for Standardization (ISO) headquartered at Geneva, Switzerland. ISO is an organization which develops standards that can be adopted and used by private industry and by government organizations, if they wish to do so. ISO previously adopted quality system standards, the ISO 9000 series, which use similar methods and have been widely adopted throughout the world.

The ISO 14000 standards do not prescribe specific environmental policies. That is the responsibility of the organizations which use the standards. They also do not specify detailed steps to be performed by employees performing daily environmental responsibilities because that is the function of a compliance manual.

ISO 14001 provides specifications and guidance on environmental management systems and requires establishment of:

1. Environmental policies meeting several criteria and their documentation and communication to employees and the public.

2. Procedures or processes to identify environmental requirements and their impacts applicable to activities, products and services and documented programs to set and achieve environmental objectives and targets.

3. A structure and resources to manage environmental issues including personnel training; internal and external communication procedures; document control procedures; implementation procedures; and accident prevention and response procedures.

4. Documented procedures for monitoring and measuring processes impacting the environment; investigating and correcting nonconformance; maintaining records; and conducting system audits.

5. A process for management to review and evaluate the system.

An instructor teaching ISO standards once commented that ISO considers that actions not recorded in writing do not exist. ISO emphasizes written policies and communications because unwritten information can easily be misunderstood or forgotten.

Other standards in the ISO 14000 series cover such subjects as environmental auditing (14010 to 14012); environmental site assessments (14015); product life cycle analysis (14040 to 14043); and environmental labels, declarations and claims (14020 to 14025).

Certification that an organization in the United States has successfully adopted and implemented ISO 14000 compliance is provided, after careful review, by the American International Standards Institute (ANSI) headquartered at Bethesda, Maryland.

F. ASTM'S Environmental Site Assessment Standards

ASTM has adopted standards for performing phase I and phase II environmental site assessments that are widely used throughout the United States. These standards are described in Chapter XXI.

G. Chemical Industry Institute of Technology (CIIT)

About three decades ago, members of the chemical industry established and continue to support an outstanding environmental research organization called the Chemical Industry Institute of Technology (CIIT) which has built an outstanding research staff and performs advanced original research projects. CIIT is located at Research Triangle Park, North Carolina and puslishes the CIIT Activities describing its research projects and other activities.

CHAPTER XXVI
OTHER ENVIRONMENTAL LAWS AND TREATIES

In addition to those described in this book, there are numerous other laws and treaties which affect the environment. Some of them are as follows:

Consumer Product Safety Act

Federal Food, Drug, and Cosmetic Act

North American Free Trade Agreement

World Bank Group Environmental Guidelines

Kyoto Protocol

For example, the Consumer Product Safety Commission was the agency that in 1978 banned the sale of lead-based paint for consumer use. The Food and Drug Administration has adopted extensive regulations protecting the public against misbranded and adulterated food and establishing tolerances for food additives including standards for food contact packaging and other materials.

The North American Free Trade Agreement (NAFTA) between Canada, Mexico and the United States contains extensive environmental provisions and for co-operation between the nations in environmental matters.

The World Bank Group (The International Bank for Reconstruction and Development, the International Development Association, the International Finance Corporation, and the Multilateral Investment Guarantee Agency) have detailed environmental guidelines that must be met by applicants seeking financing for development projects.

The Kyoto Protocol is a treaty sponsored by the United Nations Framework Convention on Climate Change and includes agreements made at Bonn, Germany and Marrakesh, Morocco. The Protocol requires member nations to reduce emissions of carbon dixoide and other so-called "greenhouse gas" emissions that environmentalists believe are causing "Global Warming." There is opposition to the Protocol by persons who are not persuaded that there is a real warming trend caused by emissions of industrial gases and persons who object to inequalities in the Protocol's reduction system. In the United States, the Bush Administration has criticized the Protocol and the U.S. Congress has not approved it.

CHAPTER XXVII
LIMITATIONS IMPOSED BY THE U.S. CONSTITUTION

The U.S. Supreme Court and the lower federal courts have consistently upheld the constitutionality of the environmental laws when challenged in lawsuits making broad-based arguments based on potential interpretation and application in a manner that would violate the U.S. Constitution.

During the last century, Mr. Dooley, the creation of the famous humorist, Finley Peter Dunne, observed that the Supreme Court reads the election returns. When Congress adopts laws prepared in response to public concerns, the U.S. Supreme Court customarily exercises judicial restraint in early efforts to raise constitutional issues. This technique allows government agencies and the lower courts to implement the laws while using care to interpret and apply them within constitutional principles. Generally, they do so.

As time passes, serious issues inevitably arise. However, most of them can be resolved on narrow grounds. For example, vague wording in a law can be interpreted broadly or narrowly so as to keep the law within constitutional bounds. Improper actions by government agencies can be nullified because of failure to follow their own regulations or by denying enforcement of regulations unauthorized by the law.

Because of these practical judicial techniques, few questions ultimately require constitutional review. Further, such questions tend to arise only after ample opportunity for government agencies and others to implement programs achieving the broad remedial objective of the laws. The passage of time also allows an opportunity to develop experience and evidence useful in deciding how constitutional principles should be applied.

In recent years, the Supreme Court has rendered decisions holding that some actions taken because of the environmental laws have exceeded constitutional bounds. In 1992, the Supreme Court held that an additional fee of $72 per ton imposed by the State of Alabama on out-of-state hazardous waste disposed of at a licensed privately-owned site at Emelle, Alabama was invalid because it constituted an impermissible discrimination against interstate commerce in violation of the U.S. Constitution. *Chemical Waste Management, Inc. v. Hunt*, 504 U.S.

334, 112 S. Ct. 2009, 119 L.Ed.2d 121 (1992); See also *Oregon Waste Systems v. Oregon Dept. of Environmental Liability*, No. 9370, 1994 U.S. LEXIS 2659 (4/4/94). Provisions of the Illinois Clean Coal Act encouraging the installation of stack emission scrubbing equipment in order to allow public utilities to purchase high-sulfur coal mined in Illinois over low-sulfur coal mined in western states were also held to discriminate impermissibly against interstate commerce. *Alliance for Clean Coal v. Miller*, 44 F.3d 591 (7th Cir. 1994).

In 1992 and 1994, the Supreme Court held that "waste flow" laws and regulations adopted in Michigan and New York were invalid because they discriminated against out-of-state waste in violation of the U.S. Constitution. *Fort Gratiot Sanitary Landfill v. Michigan Dept. of Natural Resources*. 504 U.S. 353, 112 S. Ct. 2019, 119 L. Ed 2d 139 (1992); *C&A Carbone, Inc. v. Town of Clarkstown*, 511 U.S. 383, 114 S. Ct. 1677 128 L. Ed. 2d 399 (1994). The "waste flow" laws presented a difficult question. They were adopted by many states to encourage municipalities to construct waste treatment and disposal facilities. To encourage confidence among investors purchasing bonds to finance the facilities, state legislatures adopted "waste flow" laws granting franchise monopolies to each municipal facilities for all waste generated in its district and prohibiting each from accepting waste from generations outside the district. However, the benefit of having local waste treatment and disposal facilities was affected by inefficient high cost operations and a tendency to impose much higher fees on private industry than on local residents. Industrial waste generators and long distance trucking companies challenged the "waste flow" laws and did so successfully in the *Fort Gratiot* and *C&A, Carbone* cases.

In 1992, the U.S. Supreme Court reviewed a lawsuit by an owner of two residential lots on a barrier island alleging that the South Carolina Beachfront Management Act barred erection of any permanent habitable structures on the lots. The Court held that regulations which deprive an owner of all economically viable use of his properties entitle him to fair compensation. *Lucas v. South Carolina Coastal Council*, 505 U.S. 1003, 112 S. Ct. 2886, 120 L. Ed. 2d 798 (1992).

In 1994, the U.S. Supreme Court ruled that an environmental requirement that a landowner dedicate to the public a bicycle path as a condition for development of property could be a "taking" which constitutionally entitled the landowner to fair compensation. *Dolan v. City of Tigard*, 512 U.S. 374, 114 S. Ct. 2309, 129 L. Ed. 2d 304 (1994). In 1994, the federal government was ordered by the U.S. Court of Claims to pay a property owner for loss of value after the U.S. Army Corps of Engineers denied a fill permit for installation of a septic system at a residential lot, thus destroying the only economically viable use of the property. *Bowles v. United States*, 31 Fed. Cl. 37 (1994). See also *Creppel v. U.S.*, 41 F.3d 627 (Fed. Cir. 1994).

The U.S. Supreme Court later held that a "taking" action is not barred by a claimant's acquisition of title after the effective date of regulations restricting economic use. However, a claimant who showed only that wetlands regulations of the Rhode Island Coastal Resources Management Council prevented development of property with 74 single-family dwellings did not establish that the regulations deprived him of all economic use because they permitted him to build a substantial residence on part of the property. *Palazzolo v. Rhode Island*, 533 U.S. 606, 121 S. Ct. 2448, 150 L. Ed. 2d 592 (2001). See also *Suitum v. Tahoe Regional Planning Agency*, 520 U.S. 725, 117 S.Ct. 1639, 137 L. Ed. 2d 980 (1997).

Recently, the U.S. Supreme Court held that temporary moratoria on land development by a state government planning agency while formulating a comprehensive land use plan were not *per se* takings of property requiring compensation, even though the moratoria were for relatively lengthy time periods. *Tahoe Sierra Preservation Council v. Tahoe Regional Planning Agency*, 122 S. Ct. 1465, 70 USLW 4260 (2002).

CHAPTER XXVIII
STATE LAWS

A. State General Environmental Laws

As explained earlier, the states have adopted laws implementing the major federal environmental laws and have appointed agencies to administer and enforce them. The agencies have adopted regulations implementing the state laws and have generally been successful in obtaining approval from the USEPA to administer the federal programs. Thus, in most states, regulation of the programs established by the CAA, CWA, SDWA, RCRA and other laws is administered by the state agencies.

Although the state programs generally follow the federal patterns, there are numerous differences which reflect historical developments and adaptations to local conditions. Thus, it is beyond the scope of this book to attempt to cover the multitude of state laws and regulations.

The reader should be aware that the state environmental agencies are major, fully staffed organizations with considerable expertise and experience. They typically have headquarters in the state capital where senior administration, and perhaps also central engineering and laboratory facilities, are located. They also have regional, district and/or local offices which perform inspection, enforcement and other functions.

The state environmental agencies often assume a leadership role in regional, state or local matters where their "hands on" experience may provide more insight than is available to the USEPA. For example, the Pennsylvania Department of Environmental Resources has developed streamlined permitting methods applicable to companies which produce a wide and changing variety of chemical products. The Illinois Pollution Control Board has established regulation of categories of special wastes which require more management than ordinary solid wastes, but less management than hazardous wastes, thus providing an economical waste disposal alternative. The Minnesota Department of Natural Resources sponsored special disposal methods for wastes resulting from abatement of lead-based paint.

The New Jersey Department of Environmental Protection, known for its strict enforcement policies, has developed some programs designed to facilitate compliance. For example, under memoranda of agreement which require cost reimbursement at reasonable rates, the Department provides review of voluntary compliance work including site investigation and remediation plans. The New York State Department of Environmental Conservation has programs to encourage recycling.

A number of states established statutory programs to provide funding for cleanup of leaks from underground storage tanks. However, these programs were only partially successful because applications for funds far exceeded the needs anticipated when the programs were established. Thus, the state environmental agencies administering these programs found it necessary to apply the limited available resources to situations having relatively high priority and defer remediation of the others unless the owner or operator was willing to perform the cleanup at its own expense.

B. Real Estate Transfer Laws

A few states have adopted laws which require that industrial and commercial real property must be inspected for contamination with hazardous substances at the time of a sale and certain other transfers. Transfers which may create a cleanup obligation include a change in ownership of a corporation or other entity which owns or operates the property, a lease expiration, a bankruptcy, or a shutdown or curtailment of operations.

For example, even a sale of corporate ownership by out-of-state shareholders or a merger may require compliance with a law such as the New Jersey Industrial Site Recovery Act (ISRA). In New Jersey, ISRA provides that an owner or operator planning to close operations or to sell or transfer ownership or operations of an industrial establishment classified under certain standard industrial codes (if minimal hazardous substance activities have taken place) must file a notice and a negative declaration with the Department of Environmental Protection (DEP). If the property is not contaminated, the owner or operator can submit appropriate information and request approval of the negative declaration by the DEP. If the property is contaminated, a preliminary site assessment must be conducted and a cleanup plan and cost estimate must be prepared in accordance with the DEP's technical requirements for site remediation and approved by the DEP. The owner or operator must agree to reimburse the DEP's surveillance costs. A letter of credit, bond, trust fund or other evidence of financial responsibility in an amount equal to the estimated cleanup cost must be provided as a remediation funding source to assure performance of the cleanup. The DEP will allow a transfer of the property once it has satisfactory assurances for the cleanup. When the cleanup is performed in compliance with the technical requirements, the DEP will provide a no further action letter and covenant not to sue. ISRA contains several exemptions under which the cleanup obligation may be excused, deferred or limited, but almost all of them require DEP approval which is difficult to obtain. An attempt to close operations, sell or transfer without compliance is voidable by the buyer or the DEP and punishable by fines. 13 NJSA § 13:1K-6 *et seq.*

The Connecticut Transfer Act does not void a sale, but requires the seller of an establishment where hazardous substances have been used to provide to the buyer prior to the sale a disclosure form concerning hazardous wastes at the property. A copy must be filed with the Department of Environmental Protection within 15 days after the sale. If the property is contaminated, the buyer (or another responsible person such as the seller) must certify to the Department that it will take cleanup action as required by the Department. Noncompliance renders the seller liable to the buyer and to fines. 22a Conn. Gen. Stat. Annot., § 22a - 134 *et seq*. The cleanup work is usually performed by a firm that has qualified as a licensed environmental professional ("LEP") which can certify compliance subject to review by the Department.

The State of Indiana has an Environmental Hazardous Disclosure and Responsible Party Transfer Law which requires disclosure of environmental defects to buyers. 13 Indiana Code § 13-7-22.5-1 *et seq*. The State of Illinois has a Responsible Property Transfer Act that requires delivery of a document disclosing environmental information to buyers and a copy is filed with the Illinois Environmental Protection Agency. 765 ILCS, § 90/1 *et seq*. See also California Health and Safety Code, § 25359.7 and Michigan Compiled Laws Annot., § 699.610c.

Many states have adopted laws requiring sellers of residential property to furnish written statements disclosing environmental conditions to prospective buyers. For example, New York has a Real Property Disclosure Act requiring every seller of residential property to provide to a prospective buyer a lengthy and detailed property condition disclosure statement. *Real Property Law*, Art. 14, § 460. The statement must be signed by the seller and buyer and attached to the sale contract. The Act provides that a seller who does not deliver the statement must give the buyer a $500 credit against the purchase price at the closing. The Act states that it does not prevent a seller and buyer from making agreements with respect to the physical condition of the property to be sold including a sale "as is." The statement says that it is not a warranty and does not substitute for inspections obtained by the buyer. A copy of the statement appears at the end of this Chapter.

C. Lien and Superlien Laws

Some state laws grant to the state environmental agency a lien or a "superlien" securing cleanup costs expended by the agency for abandoned or other hazardous waste sites. The lien or superlien may apply to the property where the costs were incurred and perhaps also to other properties of the owner or operator. A superlien is a lien that has retroactive priority over mortgages and security interests held by banks and other lenders recorded before the recording of the superlien.

The states having superlien laws are Connecticut (C.G.S.A. § 22a-452a); Louisiana (La. Rev. State. Annot. § 30-2281); Maine (Me. Rev. Stat. Annot. Title 38, § 1371); Massachusetts (Mass. Gen. Laws, Ch. 21E, § 13); Michigan (Mich. Comp. Laws § 324.20138); New Hampshire (N.H. Rev. Stat. Annot. § 147-B:10-b); New Jersey (N.J. Rev. Stat. § 58:10-23. 11f(f)); and Texas (Tex. Health & Safety Code Annot. § 361.753).

EXHIBIT

1. Property Condition Disclosure Statement (New York)

NYS Department of State
Division of Licensing Services
84 Holland Avenue
Albany, NY 12208-3490
(518) 474-4429
www.dos.state.ny.us

Property Condition Disclosure Statement

Name of Seller or Sellers: ____________________

Property Address: ____________________

____

General Instructions:

The Property Condition Disclosure Act requires the seller of residential real property to cause this disclosure statement or a copy thereof to be delivered to a buyer or buyer's agent prior to the signing by the buyer of a binding contract of sale.

Purpose of Statement:

This is a statement of certain conditions and information concerning the property known to the seller. This Disclosure Statement is not a warranty of any kind by the seller or by any agent representing the seller in this transaction. It is not a substitute for any inspections or tests and the buyer is encouraged to obtain his or her own independent professional inspections and environmental tests and also is encouraged to check public records pertaining to the property.

A knowingly false or incomplete statement by the seller on this form may subject the seller to claims by the buyer prior to or after the transfer of title. In the event a seller fails to perform the duty prescribed in this article to deliver a Disclosure Statement prior to the signing by the buyer of a binding contract of sale, the buyer shall receive upon the transfer of title a credit of $500 against the agreed upon purchase price of the residential real property.

"Residential real property" means real property improved by a one to four family dwelling used or occupied, or intended to be used or occupied, wholly or partly, as the home or residence of one or more persons, but shall not refer to (a) unimproved real property upon which such dwellings are to be constructed or (b) condominium units or cooperative apartments or (c) property on a homeowners' association that is not owned in fee simple by the seller.

Instructions to the Seller:

a. Answer all questions based upon your actual knowledge.
b. Attach additional pages with your signature if additional space is required.
c. Complete this form yourself.
d. If some items do not apply to your property, check "NA" (Non-applicable). If you do not know the answer check "Unkn" (Unknown).

Seller's Statement:

The seller makes the following representations to the buyer based upon the seller's actual knowledge at the time of signing this document. The seller authorizes his or her agent, if any, to provide a copy of this statement to a prospective buyer of the residential real property. The following are representations made by the seller and are not the representations of the seller's agent.

GENERAL INFORMATION

1. How long have you owned the property? .... ____________

2. How long have you occupied the property? .... ____________

3. What is the age of the structure or structures? .... ____________
   Note to buyer – If the structure was built before 1978 you are encouraged to investigate for the presence of lead based paint..

4. Does anybody other than yourself have a lease, easement or any other right to use or occupy any part of your property other than those stated in documents available in the public record, such as rights to use a road or path or cut trees or crops? .... ☐ Yes ☐ No ☐ Unkn ☐ NA

5. Does anybody else claim to own any part of your property? *If Yes, explain below* .... ☐ Yes ☐ No ☐ Unkn ☐ NA

____

____

DOS-1614 (1/02) PAGE 1 OF 6

Property Condition Disclosure Statement

6. Has anyone denied you access to the property or made a formal legal claim challenging your title to the property? *If Yes, explain below* .... ☐ Yes ☐ No ☐ Unkn ☐ NA

7. Are there any features of the property shared in common with adjoining landowners or a homeowner's association, such as walls, fences or driveways? *If Yes, describe below* ...... ☐ Yes ☐ No ☐ Unkn ☐ NA

8. Are there any electric or gas utility surcharges for line extensions, special assessments or homeowner or other association fees that apply to the property? *If Yes, explain below* ..... ☐ Yes ☐ No ☐ Unkn ☐ NA

9. Are there certificates of occupancy related to the property? *If No, explain below* .... ☐ Yes ☐ No ☐ Unkn ☐ NA

ENVIRONMENTAL

Note to Seller:

In this section, you will be asked questions regarding petroleum products and hazardous or toxic substances that you know to have been spilled, leaked or otherwise been released on the property or from the property onto any other property. Petroleum products may include, but are not limited to, gasoline, diesel fuel, home heating fuel, and lubricants. Hazardous or toxic substances are products that could pose short or long-term danger to personal health or the environment if they are not properly disposed of, applied or stored. These include, but are not limited to, fertilizers, pesticides and insecticides, paint including paint thinner, varnish remover and wood preservatives, treated wood, construction materials such as asphalt and roofing materials, antifreeze and other automotive products, batteries, cleaning solvents including septic tank cleaners, household cleaners and pool chemicals and products containing mercury and lead.

Note to Buyer:

If contamination of this property from petroleum products and/or hazardous or toxic substances is a concern to you, you are urged to consider soil and groundwater testing of this property.

10. Is any or all of the property located in a designated floodplain? *If Yes, explain below* ..... ☐ Yes ☐ No ☐ Unkn ☐ NA

11. Is any or all of the property located in a designated wetland? *If Yes, explain below* .... ☐ Yes ☐ No ☐ Unkn ☐ NA

12. Is the property located in an agricultural district? *If Yes, explain below* .... ☐ Yes ☐ No ☐ Unkn ☐ NA

13. Was the property ever the site of a landfill? *If Yes, explain below* .... ☐ Yes ☐ No ☐ Unkn ☐ NA

DOS-1614 (1/02) PAGE 2 OF 6

Property Condition Disclosure Statement

14. Are there or have there ever been fuel storage tanks above or below the ground on the property? .... ☐ Yes ☐ No ☐ Unkn ☐ NA
    - If Yes, are they currently in use? .... ☐ Yes ☐ No ☐ Unkn ☐ NA
    - Location(s) ______________________________
    - Are they leaking or have they ever leaked? *If Yes, explain below* .... ☐ Yes ☐ No ☐ Unkn ☐ NA

15. Is there asbestos in the structure? *If Yes, state location or locations below* .... ☐ Yes ☐ No ☐ Unkn ☐ NA

16. Is lead plumbing present? *If Yes, state location or locations below* .... ☐ Yes ☐ No ☐ Unkn ☐ NA

17. Has a radon test been done? *If Yes, attach a copy of the report* .... ☐ Yes ☐ No ☐ Unkn ☐ NA

18. Has motor fuel, motor oil, home heating fuel, lubricating oil or any other petroleum product, methane gas, or any hazardous or toxic substance spilled, leaked or otherwise been released on the property or from the property onto any other property? *If Yes, describe below* .... ☐ Yes ☐ No ☐ Unkn ☐ NA

19. Has the property been tested for the presence of motor fuel, motor oil, home heating fuel, lubricating oil, or any other petroleum product, methane gas, or any hazardous or toxic substance? *If Yes, attach report(s)* .... ☐ Yes ☐ No ☐ Unkn ☐ NA

STRUCTURAL

20. Is there any rot or water damage to the structure or structures? *If Yes, explain below* ...... ☐ Yes ☐ No ☐ Unkn ☐ NA

21. Is there any fire or smoke damage to the structure or structures? *If Yes, explain below* ..... ☐ Yes ☐ No ☐ Unkn ☐ NA

22. Is there any termite, insect, rodent or pest infestation or damage? *If Yes, explain below* .... ☐ Yes ☐ No ☐ Unkn ☐ NA

23. Has the property been tested for termite, insect, rodent or pest infestation or damage? .... ☐ Yes ☐ No ☐ Unkn ☐ NA
    If Yes, please attach report(s)

24. What is the type of roof/roof covering (slate, asphalt, other)? .... ______
    - Any known material defects? .... ______
    - How old is the roof? .... ______

DOS-1614 (1/02) PAGE 3 OF 6

Property Condition Disclosure Statement

- Is there a transferable warrantee on the roof in effect now? *If Yes, explain below* ...... ☐ Yes ☐ No ☐ Unkn ☐ NA

____

____

25. Are there any know material defects in any of the following structural systems: footings, beams, girders, lintels, columns or partitions? *If Yes, explain below* .... ☐ Yes ☐ No ☐ Unkn ☐ NA

____

____

MECHANICAL SYSTEMS AND SERVICES

26. What is the water source? *(Circle all that apply)* .... well, private, municipal, other: ____________
    - If municipal, is it metered? .... ☐ Yes ☐ No ☐ Unkn ☐ NA
27. Has the water quality and/or flow rate been tested? *If Yes, describe below* .... ☐ Yes ☐ No ☐ Unkn ☐ NA

____

____

28. What is the type of sewage system? *(Circle all that apply)* .... public sewer, private sewer, septic, cesspool
    - If septic or cesspool, age? .... ____________
    - Date last pumped? .... ____________
    - Frequency of pumping? .... ____________
    - Any known material defects? *If Yes, explain below* .... ☐ Yes ☐ No ☐ Unkn ☐ NA

____

____

29. Who is your electrical service provider? .... ____________
    - What is the amperage? .... ____________
    - Does it have circuit breakers or fuses? .... ____________
    - Private or public poles? .... ____________
    - Any known material defects? *If yes, explain below* .... ☐ Yes ☐ No ☐ Unkn ☐ NA

____

____

30. Are there any flooding, drainage or grading problems that resulted in standing water on any portion of the property? *If Yes, state locations and explain below* .... ☐ Yes ☐ No ☐ Unkn ☐ NA

____

____

31. Does the basement have seepage that results in standing water? *If Yes, explain below* ..... ☐ Yes ☐ No ☐ Unkn ☐ NA

____

____

Are there any known material defects in any of the following? *If Yes, explain below. Use additional sheets if necessary* ....

32. Plumbing system? .... ☐ Yes ☐ No ☐ Unkn ☐ NA
33. Security system? .... ☐ Yes ☐ No ☐ Unkn ☐ NA
34. Carbon monoxide detector? .... ☐ Yes ☐ No ☐ Unkn ☐ NA

DOS-1614 (1/02) PAGE 4 OF 6

Property Condition Disclosure Statement

35. Smoke detector? .... [] Yes [] No [] Unkn [] NA

36. Fire sprinkler system? .... [] Yes [] No [] Unkn [] NA

37. Sump pump? .... [] Yes [] No [] Unkn [] NA

38. Foundation/slab? .... [] Yes [] No [] Unkn [] NA

39. Interior walls/ceilings? .... [] Yes [] No [] Unkn [] NA

40. Exterior walls or siding? .... [] Yes [] No [] Unkn [] NA

41. Floors? .... [] Yes [] No [] Unkn [] NA

42. Chimney/fireplace or stove? .... [] Yes [] No [] Unkn [] NA

43. Patio/deck? .... [] Yes [] No [] Unkn [] NA

44. Driveway? .... [] Yes [] No [] Unkn [] NA

45. Air conditioner? .... [] Yes [] No [] Unkn [] NA

46. Heating system? .... [] Yes [] No [] Unkn [] NA

47. Hot water heater? .... [] Yes [] No [] Unkn [] NA

____

____

____

____

48. The property is located in the following school district ______________________ [] Unkn

Note: Buyer is encouraged to check public records concerning the property (e.g. tax records and wetland and floodplain maps).

The seller should use this area to further explain any item above. If necessary, attach additional pages and indicate here the number of additional pages attached.

____

____

____

____

____

____

____

____

DOS-1614 (1/02) PAGE 5 OF 6

Property Condition Disclosure Statement

Seller's Certification:

Seller certifies that the information in this Property Condition Disclosure Statement is true and complete to the seller's actual knowledge as of the date signed by the seller. If a seller of residential real property acquires knowledge which renders materially inaccurate a Property Condition Disclosure Statement provided previously, the seller shall deliver a revised Property Condition Disclosure Statement to the buyer as soon as practicable. In no event, however, shall a seller be required to provide a revised Property Condition Disclosure Statement after the transfer of title from the seller to the buyer or occupancy by the buyer, whichever is earlier.

Seller's Signature

X ______________________________ *Date* ______________

Seller's Signature

X ______________________________ *Date* ______________

Buyer's Acknowledgment:

Buyer acknowledges receipt of a copy of this statement and buyer understands that this information is a statement of certain conditions and information concerning the property known to the seller. It is not a warranty of any kind by the seller or seller's agent and is not a substitute for any home, pest, radon or other inspections or testing of the property or inspection of the public records.

Buyer's Signature

X ______________________________ *Date* ______________

Buyer's Signature

X ______________________________ *Date* ______________

DOS-1614 (1/02) PAGE 6 OF 6

CONNECTICUT DEPARTMENT OF CONSUMER PROTECTION

RESIDENTIAL PROPERTY CONDITION DISCLOSURE REPORT

Seller's Name: ______________________

Property Address: ______________________

____

The Uniform Property Condition Disclosure Act (Public Act No. 95-311) requires the seller of residential property to provide this disclosure to the prospective purchaser prior to the prospective purchaser's execution of any binder, contract to purchase, option, or lease containing a purchase option. These provisions apply to the transfer of residential real property of four dwelling units or less made with or without the assistance of a licensed broker or salesperson. The seller will be required to credit the purchaser with the sum of $300.00 at closing if the seller fails to furnish this report as required by this act.

Please note that Connecticut law requires the owner of any dwelling in which children under the age of 6 reside to abate or manage materials containing toxic levels of lead.

Pursuant to the Uniform Property Condition Disclosure Act, the seller is obligated to disclose here any knowledge of any problem regarding the following:

YES	NO	UNKN	I.	GENERAL INFORMATION
			1.	How long have you occupied the property?_____Age of structure______
☐	☐	☐	2.	Does anybody other than yourself have any right to use any part of your property, or does anybody else claim to own any part your property? If yes, explain______
☐	☐	☐	3.	Is the property in a flood plain area or an area containing wetlands?______

YES	NO	UNKN	II.	SYSTEM / UTILITIES
☐	☐	☐	4.	HEATING SYSTEM problems? Explain______ a.Heating System and Fuel Type______ b.Is there any underground fuel tank? If yes, location and age______
☐	☐	☐	5.	HOT WATER HEATER problems? Explain______ Type of Hot Water Heater______Age______
☐	☐	☐	6.	PLUMBING SYSTEM problems? Explain______
☐	☐	☐	7.	SEWAGE SYSTEM problems? Explain______ a.Type of sewage disposal system (central sewer, septic, cesspool, etc.)______ b. If private (a)Name of service company______ (b)Date last pumped______Frequency______
☐	☐	☐	8.	AIR CONDITIONING problems? Explain______ Air Conditioning Type: Central_____ Window_____ Other______

☐	☐	☐	9.	ELECTRICAL SYSTEM problems? Explain________________
☐	☐	☐	10.	DRINKING WATER problems? Quality or Quantity? Explain________________
☐	☐	☐	11.	ELECTRONIC SECURITY SYSTEM problems? Explain________________
☐	☐	☐	12.	CARBON MONOXIDE OR SMOKE DETECTOR problems? Explain________________
☐	☐	☐	13.	FIRE SPRINKLER SYSTEM problems? Explain________________
YES	**NO**	**UNKN**	**III.**	**BUILDING / STRUCTURE / IMPROVEMENTS**
☐	☐	☐	14.	FOUNDATION/SLAB problems/settling? Explain________________
☐	☐	☐	15.	BASEMENT Water/Seepage/Dampness? Explain amount, frequency and location.________________
☐	☐	☐	16.	SUMP PUMP problems? If yes, explain________________
☐	☐	☐	17.	ROOF leaks, problems? Explain________________ Roof type________________Age________________
☐	☐	☐	18.	INTERIOR WALLS/CEILING problems? Explain________________
☐	☐	☐	19.	EXTERIOR SIDING problems? Explain________________
☐	☐	☐	20.	FLOOR problems? Explain________________
☐	☐	☐	21.	CHIMNEY/FIREPLACE/WOOD OR COAL STOVE problems? Explain________________
☐	☐	☐	22.	Any knowledge of FIRE/SMOKE damage? Explain________________
☐	☐	☐	23.	PATIO/DECK problems? Explain________________ If made of wood, is wood treated or untreated?________________
☐	☐	☐	24.	DRIVEWAY problems? Explain________________
☐	☐	☐	25.	TERMITE/INSECT/RODENT/PEST INFESTATION problems? Explain________________
☐	☐	☐	26.	IS HOUSE INSULATED? Type________________Location________________
☐	☐	☐	27.	ROT AND WATER DAMAGE problems? Explain________________
☐	☐	☐	28.	WATER DRAINAGE problems? Explain________________
☐	☐	☐	29.	Are ASBESTOS CONTAINING INSULATION OR BUILDING MATERIALS present?________________ If yes, location________________
☐	☐	☐	30.	Is LEAD PAINT present? If yes, location________________
☐	☐	☐	31.	Is LEAD PLUMBING present? If yes, location________________
☐	☐	☐	32.	Has test for RADON been done? If yes, attach copy. State whether a radon control system is in place.________________

The Seller should use this area to further explain any item above. Attach additional pages if necessary and indicate here the number of additional pages attached.

I. Seller's Certification

To the extent of the Seller's knowledge as a property owner, the Seller acknowledges that the information contained above is true and accurate for those areas of the property listed. In the event a real estate broker or salesperson is utilized, the Seller authorizes the brokers or salespersons to provide the above information to prospective buyers, selling agents or buyer's agents.

DATE__________ SELLER__________________ (Signature) SELLER__________________ (Type or Print)

DATE__________ SELLER__________________ (Signature) SELLER__________________ (Type or Print)

II. Responsibilities of Real Estate Brokers

This report in no way relieves a real estate broker of his or her obligation under the provisions of Section 20-328-5a of the Regulations of Connecticut State Agencies to disclose any material facts. Failure to do so could result in punitive action taken against the broker, such as fines, suspension or revocation of license.

III. Statements Not to Constitute a Warranty

Any representations made by the seller on this report shall not constitute a warranty to the buyer.

IV. Nature of Disclosure Report

This residential disclosure report is not a substitute for inspections, tests, and other methods of determining the physical condition of the property.

V. Buyer's Certification

The buyer is urged to carefully inspect the property and, if desired, to have the property inspected by an expert. The buyer understands that there are areas of the property for which the seller has no knowledge and that this disclosure statement does not encompass those areas. The buyer also acknowledges that the buyer has read and received a signed copy of this statement from the seller or seller's agent.

DATE__________ BUYER__________________ (Signature) BUYER__________________ (Type or Print)

DATE__________ BUYER__________________ (Signature) BUYER__________________ (Type or Print)

Questions or Comments? Consumer Problems? Call the Department of Consumer Protection at 1-800-842-2649

CHAPTER XXIX
FUTURE TRENDS

In addition to their specific objectives, the environmental laws and regulations are part of the political, social and economic history and future of the U.S. Like other nations, the U.S. has benefitted greatly from industrial and scientific development. However, while solving the problems of its own and prior generations, each generation fails to foresee some needs of future generations. The most important result of the environmental laws may be the requirement that foresight be applied to the environment.

Past generations did not ignore the environment to the extent that environmentalists tend to believe. They saw that the natural environment presented imminent and chronic hazards in their daily lives. The author recommends that readers interested in earlier perceptions of the environment read "On the Banks of Plum Creek," Laura Ingalls Wilder, Harper & Row and particularly Chapter 25, "The Glittering Cloud" and the following Chapters. These Chapters show the harsh impacts of the natural environment which made people welcome pesticides, fertilizers and other developments which sheltered them from the natural environment.

After the great depression and "dust storms" of the 1930's followed by World War II, the people of the U.S. were glad to turn their efforts to industry and science. They achieved an abundance of food, effective medicines, affordable clothing and housing, education, high speed travel and communication, and many other improvements of living conditions previously unknown in the U.S. and other nations except to wealthy people. However, development came so fast that few saw its environmental side effects which harmed human health and the environment. Thus, the environmental laws and regulations were adopted.

During the first three decades, the environmental laws have been applied primarily to private industry. However, as environmental government agencies have sought to require compliance by federal, state and municipal governments and by the general public, they have encountered criticism and requests for reforms. Three reforms have the greatest priority. The first is to establish realistic risk assessment methods. The second is to match regulatory mandates with funding to pay for compliance. The third is to provide fair compensation to persons whose property is taken in order to achieve environmental objectives. So far, environmentalists have resisted these reforms, but their credibility will be strengthened and their environmental objectives will become more attainable if they support the reforms.

CHAPTER XXX
CONCLUSION

In conclusion, the author hopes that this book will provide to its readers a convenient tool to work with the U.S. environmental laws and reference sources where further information can be found. More than most other nations, the U.S. prefers to be governed by laws (and regulations) rather than the judgmental decisions of persons holding government responsibilities. Thus, effort devoted to understanding the laws and regulations is worthwhile because, once adopted, they are widely followed by those who regulate and those who are regulated, regardless of their personal beliefs. The author also hopes that the book well illustrates the process of change that is characteristic of U.S. laws and regulations because the general attitude of compliance depends significantly on freedom to seek change through legislative, regulatory and judicial processes.

Edward E. Shea, Esq.

May 2002

TABLE OF CASES

A

A&W Smelter v. Clinton, 146 F.3d 1107 (9th Cir. 1998) . . . . 171 - 172

ABB Industrial v. Prime Technology, 120 F.3d 351 (2d Cir. 1997) 196, 198

Acme Printing Ink Co. v. Menard, Inc., 870 F. Supp. 1465 (E.D. Wis. 1994) 196

ACORN v. Edwards, 81 F.3d 1387 (5th Cir. 1996), cert. denied, sub. nom. ACORN v. Foster, 521 U.S. 1129 (1997). 348, 481

Acuna v. Brown & Root, Inc., 200 F.3d 335 (5th Cir. 2000) 543

Acushnet Co. v. Mohasco Corp., 191 F.3d 69 (1st Cir. 1999) 192, 201

Acushnet River and New Bedford Harbor Proceedings, In re, 712 F. Supp. 1010 (D. Mass. 1989) 209

Adams v. Star Enterprise, 51 F.3d 417 (4th Cir. 1995) 588

Adkins v. Thomas Solvent Co., 440 Mich. 293, 487 N.W.2d 715 (1992) 588

AFL v. OSHA. 965 F.2d 962 (11th Cir. 1992). 447

Akzo Nobel Coatings, Inc. v. Aigner Corp., 30 F.3d 761 (7th Cir. 1994) 213

Akzo Nobel Coatings, Inc. v. Aigner Corp., 197 F.3d 302 (7th Cir. 1999). . . . 200 - 201

Alabama Tombigbee Rivers Coalition v. Dept. of Interior, 26 F.3d 1103 (5th Cir. 1999) 514

Albemarle Corp. v. Herman, 221 F.3d 782 (5th Cir. 2000) 455

Alexander v. Westminster Presbyterian Church, 702 N.Y.S. 2d 727 (4th Dept. 1999) 491

Alharb v. Sayegh, 604 N.Y.S. 243 (2d Dept. 1984) 489

All Indian Pueblo Council v. U.S., 975 F.2d 1437 (10th Cir. 1992) 13

Alliance for Clean Coal v. Miller, 44 F.3d 591 (7th Cir. 1994) 614

Allstead, Inc. v. EPA, No. 94-3179, 1994 U.S. App. LEXIS 12385 (6th Cir., 3/26/94) . . 36

Almond Hill School v. U.S. Dept. of Agriculture, 768 F.2d 1030 (9th Cir. 1985) 13

AM International, Inc. v. Datacard Corp., 106 F.3d 1342 (7th Cir. 1997) 193

American Auto Mfrs. Ass'n., 152 F.3d 196 (2d Cir. 1998). 53

American Bald Eagle v. Bhatti, 9 F.3d 163 (1st Cir. 1993). 510

American Canoe Ass'n. v. EPA, 54 F. Supp. 2d 621 (E.D. Va. 1999) 109

American Corn Growers v. EPA, _F.3d_, 2002 WL 1040579 (D.C. Cir. 2002). 34

American Iron & Steel Institute v. E.P.A., 115 F.3d 979 (D.C. Cir. 1997) 99, 106

American Iron & Steel Institute v. EPA, 526 F.2d 1022 (3d Cir. 1975) 98

American Mining Congress v. E.P.A., 824 F.2d 1177 (D.C. Cir. 1987). 121

American Mining Congress v. EPA, 965 F.2d 759 (9th Cir. 1992) 112

American Petroleum Institute v. EPA, 198 F.3d 275 (D.C. Cir. 2000). 51

American Textile Manufacturers v. Donovan, 452 U.S. 490, 101 S. Ct. 2478 (1981) 441

American Tunaboat Association v. Brown, 67 F.3d 1404 (9th Cir. 1995) 518

American Water Works Ass\rquote n v. EPA, 40 F.3d 1266 (D.C. Cir. 1994) 337

American Wildlands v. EPA, 260 F.3d 1192 (10th Cir. 2001) 111

Andon v. 302-304 Mott Street Associates, 94 N.Y. 2d 740, 709 N.Y.S. 2d 873 (2000) 491

Andrade v. Wong, 675 N.Y.S. 2d 112 (2d Dept. 1998). 490, 493

Ankiewicz v. Kinder, 408 Mass. 792 (1990) 490

Anne Arundel County v. USEPA, 963 F.2d 412 (1992). 179

Anspec Co. v. Johnson Controls, Inc., 922 F.2d 1240 (6th Cir. 1991) 208

Appalachian Power v. EPA, 2000 U.S. App. LEXIS 6826 (D.C. Cir., April 14, 2000) . . . 61

Appalachian Power v. Train, 545 F.2d 1351 (4th Cir. 1976). 100

Appalachian States LLRW Comm. v. O'Leary, 93 F.3d 103 (3d Cir. 1996) 540

Aragon v. U.S., 146 F.3d 819 (10th Cir. 1998). 219

Arce v. New York City Housing Authority, 696 N.Y.S.2d 67 (2d Dept. 1999) 491

Aristil v. Housing Authority, 54 F. Supp. 2d 1289 (M.D. Fla. 1999) 489

Arkansas Platte & Gulf v. Van Waters & Rogers, 981 F.2d 1177 (10th Cir. 1993) . . . 396

Arkansas Wildlife Federation v. ICI Americas, Inc., 29 F.3d 376 (1994), cert. denied 513 U.S. 1147 (1994). 118

Arst v. Pipefitters Welfare Educ. Fund, 25 F.3d 417 (7th Cir. 1994) 207

Artesian Water Co. v. New Castle County, 659 F. Supp. 1269 (D. Del. 1987). 194

Association of Battery Recyclers v. EPA, 208 F.3d 1047 (D.C. Cir. 2000) 121

Atlantic Mutual v. McFadden, 413 Mass 90, 596 N.E.2d 762 (1992) 492

Atlantic Richfield Co. v. American Airlines, Inc., 98 F.3d 564 (10th Cir. 1996) 193

Atlantic Richfield v. Blorenski, 847 F. Supp. 1261 (E.D. Pa. 1994) 195

Atlantic States Legal Foundation v. Eastman Kodak, 12 F.3d 353 (2d Cir. 1994), cert. denied 115 S.Ct. 62 (1994). 101

Auto-Owners Ins. Co. v. Hanson, 588 N.W. 2d 777 (Minn. 1999) 492

Auto-Owners Ins. v. Housing Authority, Tampa, 231 F.3d 1298 (11th Cir. 2000). . . 492

Axel Johnson, Inc. v. Carroll Carolina Oil Co., 191 F.3d 409 (4th Cir. 1999). . . 191, 196

B

B.F. Goodrich v. Betkoski, 99 F.3d 88 (2d Cir. 1996), cert. denied, 118 S. Ct. 2318, 141 L. Ed. 2d 694. . . . . 200, 209

B.F. Goodrich v. Murtha, 815 F. Supp. 539 (D.C. Conn. 1993) 172

Babbitt v. Sweet Home Chapter, 515 U.S. 687 (1995). 510

Bancamerica Commercial Corp. v. Mosher Steel, Inc., 100 F.3d 792 (10th Cir. 1996) 195

Bancamerica v. Mosher Steel, Inc., 99 F.3d 505 (2d Cir. 1996) 201

Beazer East, Inc. v. Mead Corp., 34 F.3d 206 (3d Cir. 1994) 209

Bedford Affiliates v. Sills, 156 F.3d 416 (2d Cir. 1998) 192, 195, 201

Bell Petroleum, Matter of, 3 F.3d 889 (5th Cir. 1993), later proceedings 64 F.3d 202 (5th Cir. 1995) 201

Bencosme v. Kokoras, 400 Mass. 40, 507 N.E. 2d 748 (1987). 489

Bennett v. Spear, 520 U.S. 154, 137 L. Ed. 2d 281 (1997). . . . . 515 - 516

Bergsoe Metal Corp., In re, 910 F.2d 668 (9th Cir. 1990). 205

Berkovitz v. U.S., 486 U.S. 531 (1988). 219

Berry v. Armstrong Rubber Co., 989 F.2d 822 (5th Cir. 1993), cert. denied 510 U.S. 117 (1994) 588

Bethlehem Steel v. OSHRC, 607 F.2d 871 (3d Cir. 1979) 441

Biodiversity Legal Foundation v. Babbitt, 943 F. Supp. 23 (D.D.C. 1996). 506

Board of Trustees v. National Gypsum, 733 F. Supp. 1413 (D. Kans. 1990). 332

Boeing Co. v. Cascade Corp., 207 F.3d 1177 (9th Cir. 2000) 200, 204

Borden Ranch v. U.S. Army Corps, 261 F.3d 810 (9th Cir. 2001) 114

Bouchard Transportation Co. v. Updegraff, 147 F.3d 1344 (11th Cir. 1998) 497

Bowles v. United States, 31 Fed. Cl. 37 (1994) 614

BP Exploration v. Dept. of Transportation, 44 F. Supp. 2d 34 (D.D.C. 1999) 502

Bradley v. Armstrong Rubber Co., 130 F.3d 168 (5th Cir. 1997) 588

Brenner v. American Cyanamid, 699 N.Y.S. 2d 848 (4th Dept. 1999) 489

Brown v. Marathon Realty, Inc., 170 A.D. 2d 426, 565 N.Y.S. 2d 219 (2d Dept. 1991) 489

Browning-Ferris Industries v. Ter Maat, 195 F.3d 953 (7th Cir. 1999) 208

Building and Construction Dept., AFL-CIO v. Rockwell International, 7 F.3d 1487 (10th Cir. 1993) 542

Burlington Northern RR Co. v. Woods Industries, 815 F. Supp. 1384 (E.D. Wash. 1993) 195

Burnette v. Carothers, 192 F.3d 52 (2d Cir. 1999) 219

Byrd v. Blumenreich, 317 N.J. Super. 496, 722 Atl.2d 548 (1999). 492

C

C&A Carbone, Inc. v. Town of Clarkstown, 511 U.S. 383, 114 S. Ct. 1677, 128 L. Ed. 2d 399 (1994) 614

California v. Sierra Club, 451 U.S. 287, 68 L. Ed. 2d 101 (1981). 3

Carey v. Kerr McGee Chemical, 60 F. Supp. 2d 800 (N.D. Ill. 1999). 543

Carlyle Piermont Corp. v. Federal Paper Board, 742 F. Supp. 814 (S.D.N.Y. 1990) . . 195

Carpenter v. Smith, 191 A.D.2d 1036, 595 N.Y.S.2d 710 (4th Dept. 1993) 490

Carr v. Alta Verde Industries, 931 F.2d 1055 (5th Cir. 1991) 98

Carson Harbor Village, Ltd. v. Unocal Corp., 270 F.3d 863 (9th Cir. 2001) 196

Carter-Jones Lumber v. Dixie Distributing, 166 F.3d 840 (6th Cir. 1999) . 172, 199, 208

Carter-Jones Lumber v. LTV Steel Co., 237 F.3d 745 (6th Cir. 2001) 207

Catellus Development v. U.S., 34 F.3d 748 (9th Cir. 1994) 199

Caterpillar, Inc. v. Herman, 154 F.3d 400 (7th Cir. 1998) 456

Celebrezze v. National Lime, 68 Ohio 3d 377, 627 N.E. 2d 538 (1994) 36

Centerior Serv. Co. v. Acme Scrap Iron, 153 F.3d 344 (6th Cir. 1998). 192, 203

Central and Southwest Services v. U.S.E.P.A., 220 F.3d 683 (5th Cir. 2000) 284

Central Midwest Interstate LLRW Comm. v. Pena, 113 F.3d 1468 (7th Cir. 1997) . . 540

Chao v. Mallard Bay Drilling, Inc., 534 U.S. 235, 151 L. Ed. 2d 659 (2002) 458

Chapman v. Silber, 97 N.Y. 2d 9, 734 N.Y.S. 2d 541 (2001) 490, 493

Chateaugay, In re, 944 F2d 997 (2d Cir. 1991) 217

Chemical Manufacturers Ass'n v. EPA, 859 F.2d 977 (D.C. Cir. 1988) 262

Chemical Manufacturers Ass'n v. EPA, 899 F.2d 1344 (5th Cir. 1990). 262

Chemical Manufacturers Association v. EPA, 28 F.3d 1259 (D.C. Cir. 1994) 40

Chemical Waste Management v. E.P.A., 976 F.2d 2 (D.C. Cir. 1992) 142

Chemical Waste Management v. Templet, 967 F.2d 1058, (5th Cir. 1992), cert. denied, 61 USLW 3498 (1993) 146

Chemical Waste Management, Inc. v. Hunt, 504 U.S. 334, 112 S. Ct. 2009, 119 L. Ed. 2d 121 (1992) 614

Christy v. Hodel, 857 F.2d 1324 (9th Cir. 1989). 509

Ciba-Geigy Corp. v. EPA, 874 F.2d 277 (5th Cir. 1989) 388

Ciba-Geigy Corp. v. USEPA, 46 F.2d 1209 (D.C. Cir. 1995) 339

City of Chicago v. Environmental Defense Fund, 511 U.S. 328, 114 S. Ct. 1588, 128 L. Ed. 2d 302 (1994). 122

City of Greenville v. W.R. Grace & Co., 827 F.2d 975 (4th Cir. 1987) 331

City of Las Vegas v. Lujan, 891 F.2d 927 (D.C. Cir. 1989) 506, 509

City of Los Angeles v. U.S. Dept of Agriculture, 950 F. Supp. 1005 (C.D. Cal. 1996) 15

City of New York v. Exxon Corp., 744 F. Supp. 474 (S.D.N.Y. 1990) 172

City of New York v. Keene Corporation, 32 Misc. 2d 745, 505 N.Y.S. Supp. 2d 782, aff'd 513 N.Y.S. 2d 1004 (1st Dept. 1987) 331

City of Philadelphia v. Lead Industries Association, Inc., 994 F.2d 112 (3d Cir. 1993) 489

City of Philadelphia v. New Jersey, 119 L. Ed. 2d 121 (1992) 147

City of Toledo v. Beazer Materials, 923 F. Supp. 1013 (N.D. Ohio 1996) 196

Clarkstown v. C&A Carbone, Inc., 511 U.S. 383, 128 L. Ed. 2d 399 (1994) 146

Clean Air Implementation Project v. EPA, 1996 WL 393118, 65 USLW 2059 (D.C. Cir. 1996) 60

Clean Ocean Action v. York, 57 F.3d 328 (3d Cir. 1995) 436

CMC Heartland Partners, In re, 966 F.2d 1143 (7th Cir. 1992) 217

Coho Salmon v. Pacific Lumber Co., 61 F. Supp. 2d 1001 (N.D. Cal. 1999) 509

Colorado Environmental Coalition v. Romer, 796 F. Supp. 457 (D. Colo. 1992) . . . 348

Commander Oil v. Barlo Equipment, 215 F.3d 321 (2d Cir. 2000) 196

Commerce Holding v. Assessors of Babylon, 88 N.Y.2d 932 (1996). 587

Commonwealth of Virginia v. E.P.A., 108 F.3d 1397 (D.C. Cir. 1997) 53

Commonwealth of Virginia v. EPA, 108 F.3d 1397 (D.C. Cir. 1997) 30

Community Ass'n v. Henry Bosna Dairy, 65 F. Supp. 2d 1129 (E.D. Wash. 1999) . . . 98

Concerned Area Residents v. Southview Farm, 34 F.3d 114 (2d Cir. 1994). . . . 98, 110

Concrete Sales v. Blue Bird Body Co., 211 F.3d 1333 (11th Cir. 2000) 198, 200

Connecticut Coastal Fishermen's Ass'n. v. Remington Arms, 777 F. Supp. 173 (1991) aff'd in part, reversed in part 989 F.2d 1305 (1st cir. 1991) 118

Conner v. Burford, 848 F.2d 1441 (9th Cir. 1988). 508

Con-Tech Sales v. Cockerham, 715 F. Supp. 701 (E.D. Pa. 1989) 196

Control Data Corp. v. S.C.S.C. Corp., 53 F.3d 930 (8th Cir. 1995) 207

Corporation of Mercer University v. National Gypsum, 877 F.2d 35 (11th Cir. 1989) 332

Corrosion Proof Fittings v. E.P.A., 947 F.2d 1201 (5th Cir. 1991). 330

Corrosion Proof Fittings v. E.P.A., 947 F.2d 1201 (5th Cir. 1991). 285

County Line Investment Co. v. Wagco Land, 933 F.2d 1508 (10th Cir. 1991). 194

Cox v. City of Dallas, 256 F.3d 281 (5th Cir. 2001) 148

Creppel v. U.S., 41 F.3d 627 (Fed. Cir. 1994) 614

Criscuola v. Power Authority, 81 N.Y.2d 649, 602 N.Y.S.2d 588 (1993). 588

Curry v. Westchester Country Club, 186 A.D. 2d 712, 589 N.Y.S. 2d 491 (2d Dept. 1993) 490

Custom Distribution Services, Inc. v. City of Perth Amboy, 216 B.R. 136 (D.N.J. 1997) 587

D

D'Agnillo v. U.S. Dept. of Housing and Urban Dev., 965 F. Supp. 535 (S.D.N.Y. 1997) 13

Daigle v. Shell Oil, 972 F.2d 1527 (10th Cir. 1992) 193

Dakota Underground, Inc. v. Secretary of Labor, 200 F.3d 564 (8th Cir. 2000). . . . 456

Darbouze v. Chevron, 1998 WL 512941 (E.D. Pa. Aug. 19, 1998). 196

Daubert v. Merrell Dow, 509 U.S. 579, 125 L. Ed. 2d 469 (1993) 490

Davis County v. EPA, 101 F.3d.1395 (D.C. Cir. 1996). 36

Davis v. Philadelphia Housing Authority, 121 F.3d 92 (3d Cir. 1997) 489

Davis v. Royal-Globe, 223 So. 2d 859 (La. 1969) 490

Defenders of Wildlife v. EPA, 882 F.2d 1294 (8th Cir. 1989) 388

Dent v. Beazer Materials, 156 F.3d 523 (4th Cir. 1998) 197, 201

Dolan v. City of Tigard, 512 U.S. 374, 114 S. Ct. 2309, 129 L. Ed. 2d 304 (1994). . . 614

Dombrowski v. Gould Electronics, Inc., 85 F. Supp. 2d 456 (M.D. Pa. 2000) . . 490 - 491

Dominion Resources, Inc. v. U.S., 2000-2 U.S.T.C. (CCH) § 50,638 (4th Cir. 2000) . . 583

Donahey v. Bogel, 987 F.2d 1250 (6th Cir. 1993), vacated 114 S. Ct. 2688 (1994) . . 195

Donovan v. Castle & Cook, 692 F.2d 641 (9th Cir. 1982) 441

Douglas County v. Babbitt, 48 F.3d 1495 (9th Cir. 1995). 12

Douglas County v. Lujan, 810 F. Supp. 1470, reversed in part, 48 F.3d 1495 (9th Cir. 1995), cert. denied 516 U.S. 1042, 733 L. Ed. 2d 655 (1996) 508

Driscoll v. Adams, 181 F.3d 1285 (11th Cir. 1999) 97

Du Bois v. U.S. Dept. of Agriculture, 102 F.3d 1273 (1st Cir. 1996) 14

Du Bois v. U.S. Dept. of Agriculture, 102 F.3d 1273 (1st Cir. 1996) 97

Duke Power v. Carolina Environmental Study Group, 438 U.S. 59, 57 L. Ed. 2d 595 (1978) 542

Dunn v. Hovic, 1 F.3d 1371 (3d Cir. 1993) 333

Durfey v. E.I. du Pont, 59 F.3d 121 (9th Cir. 1995) 193

E

E.I. du Pont v. Train, 430 U.S. 112 (1977) . . . . 100 - 101

E.P.A. v. Smithfield Food, Inc., 191 F.3d 516 (4th Cir. 1999) 115

EDF v. Costle, 636 F.2d 1229 (D.C. Cir. 1980). 106

Edison Electric Institute v. EPA, D.C. Cir No. 96-1062, July 25, 1998 107

Edwardsen v. U.S. Dept. of Interior, 268 F.3d 781 (9th Cir. 2001) 495

El Paso Natural Gas Co. v. Neztsosie, 526 U.S. 473, 143 L. Ed. 2d 635 (1999) 542

Environmental Defense Fund v. EPA, 548 F.2d 998 (D.C. Cir. 1976) 389

Ethyl Corp. v. Browner, 67 F.3d 941 (D.C. Cir. 1995). 49

Exxon Valdez, In re, 270 F.3d 1215 (9th Cir. 2001) 495

F

Fertilizer Institute v. Browner, 163 F.3d 774 (3d Cir. 1998) 236

Fertilizer Institute v. Browner, No. 98-1067 1999 U.S. Dist. LEXIS 9298 (D.D.C. April 15, 1999) 236

Fina, Inc. v. ARCO, 200 F.3d 266 (5th Cir. 2000) 210

First United Methodist Church Board v. U.S. Gypsum, 360 S.E. 2d 325 (1987) 332

First United Methodist Church v. U.S. Gypsum, 882 F.2d 862 (4th Cir. 1989) 172

Flenker v. Willamette Industries, Inc., 162 F.3d 1083 (10th Cir. 1998) 458

Flint Ridge v. Scenic Rivers, 426 U.S. 776, 49 L. Ed. 2d 205 (1976) 12

FMC Corp. v. Aero Industries, Inc., 998 F.2d 842 (10th Cir. 1993) 207

Forest Conservation Council v. Roseboro Lumber, 50 F.3d 781 (9th Cir. 1995) . . . 509

Forest Guardians v. Babbitt, 174 F.3d 1178 (10th Cir. 1999) 507

Fort Gratiot Sanitary Landfill, Inc. v. Michigan Department of Natural Resources, 504 U.S. 353, 112 S.Ct. 2019, 119 L. Ed. 2d (1992) 146, 614

Fox Bay Partners v. U.S. Corps of Engineers, 831 F. Supp. 605 (N.D. Ill. 1993) 3

Franklin County v. American Premier Underwriters, 240 F.3d 574 (6th Cir. 2001) . . 193

Franklin v. Krumanocker, 114 A.D. 2d 611 (3d Dept. 1985). 490

Freeman v. Glaxo Wellcome, Inc., 189 F.3d 160 (2d Cir. 1999). 172

Freeport-McMoran v. B-B Paint Corp., 56 F. Supp. 2d 823 (E.D. Mich. 2000). 183

Friends of Santa Fe County v. LAC Minerals, 892 F. Supp. 1333 (D.N.M. 1995) 97

Friends of the Earth v. Archer-Daniels-Midland, 780 F. Supp. 95 (N.D.N.Y. 1992) . . 118

Friends of the Earth v. Crown Central Petroleum, 95 F.3d 358 (5th Cir. 1996) 118

Friends of the Earth v. Laidlaw Environmental, 528 U.S. 167, 145 L. Ed. 2d 610 (2000) 218

Friends of the Earth v. Laidlaw Environmental, 890 F. Supp. 470 (D.S.C., 1995) . . . 118

Friends of Wild Swan, Inc. v. U.S. Fish and Wildlife Service, 945 F. Supp. 1388 (D. Ore. 1996) 506

Fund for Animals, Inc. v. Rice, 85 F.3d 535 (11th Cir. 1996) 512

G

Gade v. National Solid Waste Management Ass'n, 112 S.Ct. 2374, 120 L. Ed. 2d 73 (1992) 458

General Electric v. Department of Commerce, 128 F.3d 767 (D.C. Cir. 1997) 498

General Electric v. EPA, 290 F.3d 377 (D.C. Cir. 2002) 284

Generali - U.S. Branch v. Caribe Realty, 160 Misc. 2d 1056, 612 N.Y.S. 2d 296 (1994) 492

George's Pest Control Service v. USEPA, 572 F.2d 204 (9th Cir. 1977) 393

Geraghty & Miller v. Conoco, Inc., 234 F.3d 917 (5th Cir. 2000) 204

German v. Federal Home Loan Mortgage Corp., 885 F. Supp. 537 (S.D.N.Y. 1995). . 490

Gibbs v. Babbitt, 214 F.3d 483 (4th Cir. 2000) 510

Gibbs v. Paine, 720 N.Y.S. 2d 184 (2d Dept. 2001) 493

Gideon v. Johns-Manville, 761 F.2d 1129 (5th Cir. 1985) 333

Giudice v. BFG Electroplating, 732 F. Supp. 556 (W.D. Pa. 1989). 205

GNB Battery v. Gould, Inc., 65 F.3d 617 (7th Cir. 1995). 210

Gopher Oil Co. v. Union Oil Co., 955 F.3d 519 (8th Cir. 1992) 201

Grenier v. Vermont Log Buildings, Inc., 96 F.3d 559 (1st Cir. 1996) 396

Grundy Oil Co., Inc. v. U.S., 14 Ct. Cl. 759 (1988). 497

Gwaltney of Smithfield Ltd. v. Chesapeake Bay Foundation, Inc., 484 U.S. 49, 98 L. Ed. 2d 306 (1987) 6

H

Halliday v. Norton Co., 265 A.D.2d 614, 696 N.Y.S.2d 549 (3d Dept. 1999) 588

Harbour Gateway v. USEPA, 167 F.3d 602 (D.C. Cir. 1999) 179

Hardy v. Griffin, 41 Conn. Sup. 283, 569 A.2d 49 (1989) 489

Harley-Davidson, Inc. v. Minstar, Inc., 41 F.3d 341 (7th Cir. 1994) 209

Harmon Industries v. Browner, 191 F.3d 894 (8th Cir. 1999). 116

Hartford Mutual Ins. Co. v. Jacobson, 73 Md App. 670, 536 Atl. 2d 120 (1988) . . . 491

Hawkins v. Leslie's Pool Mart, Inc., 184 F.3d 244 (3rd Cir. 1999). 396

Hawksbill Sea Turtle v. FEMA, 11 F. Supp. 2d 529 (D.V.I. 1998) 512

Hayes v. EPA, 48 Env't Rep. Cases (BNA) 1078 (N.D. Okla. 1998) 109

Hayes v. Whitman, 204 F.3d 1017 (10th Cir. 2001). 109

Hazardous Waste Treatment Council v. E.P.A. 861 F.2d 270 (D.C. Cir. 1988) 144

Hazardous Waste Treatment Counsel v. E.P.A., 886 F.2d 355 (D.C. Cir. 1989) 142

Hemingway Transport, Inc., In re, 993 F.2d 915 (1st Cir. 1993) 218

Hendler v. U.S., 175 F.3d 1374 (Fed. Cir. 1999). 220

Hendler v. U.S., 951 F.2d 1364 (Fed. Cir. 1991). 220

Hill v. City of New York, 201 A.D. 2d 329 (1st Dept. 1994) 489

Hill v. TVA, 549 F.2d 1064 (6th Cir. 1977), aff'd 437 U.S. 153, 57 L. Ed. 2d 117 . . . 514

Hines v. Rap Realty, 684 N.Y.S.2d 594 (2d Dept. 1999), appeal denied 695 N.Y.S.2d 540 (1999) 490, 493

Hoffman Homes, Inc. v. Environmental Protection Agency, 999 F.2d 256 (7th Cir. 1993) 97

Hughes River v. Glickman, 81 F.3d 437 (4th Cir. 1996). 14

Hughey v. JMS Development, 78 F.3d 1522 (1st Cir. 1996) 111

Humane Society v. Babbitt, 46 F.3d 93 (D.C. Cir. 1995). 516

Humane Society v. Glickman, 217 F.3d 882 (D.C. Cir. 2000) 521

I

Idylwoods Associates v. Mader Capital, 915 F. Supp. 1290, reconsidered in part 956 F. Supp. 410 (W.D.N.Y. 1996) 198

IBP, Inc. v. Herman, 144 F.3d 861 (D.C. Cir. 1998) 455

Idaho Sporting Congress v. Thomas, 137 F.3d 1146 (9th Cir. 1998) 13

Illinois State Rifle Ass'n v. State of Illinois, 717 F. Supp. 634 (N.D. Ill. 1989) 521

Indiana Michigan Power Co. v. DOE, 88 F.3d 1272 (D.C. Cir. 1995) 538

Industrial Union v. Hodgson, 499 F.2d 467 (2d Cir. 1975), cert. denied 421 U.S. 922 (1975) 441

International Association of Independent Tanker Owners v. Loche, 148 F.3d 1053 (9th Cir. 1998) 501

International Fabricare Institute v. USEPA, 972 F.2d 384 (D.C. Cir. 1992) 339

International Union, UAW v. General Dynamics, 815 F.2d 1570 (D.C. Cir. 1988). . . 441

J

Johnson v. Monsanto Chemical, 129 F. Supp. 2d 189 (N.D.N.Y 2001) 396

Joslyn Manufacturing Corp. v. T.L. James & Co., 893 F.2d 80 (5th Cir. 1990). 206

Joslyn Mfg. Co. v. Koppers Co., Inc., 40 F.3d 750 (5th Cir. 1994) 196, 210

Juarez v. Wavecrest Management, 88 N.Y. 2d 628, 672 N.E. 2d 135 (1996) . . 489 - 490

Juliano v. Montgomery-Otsego-Scholarie, 983 F. Supp. 319 (N.D.N.Y. 1997). 220

K

Kaiser Aluminum v. Catellus Development, 976 F.2d 1338 (9th Cir. 1992) 197

Kalamazoo River Study Group v. Menasha Corp., 228 F.3d 648 (6th Cir. 2000) . . . 192

Kalamazoo River Study Group v. Rockwell International, 274 F.3d 1043 (6th Cir. 2001) 201

Kaytes v. Imperial Casualty, WL 780901 (E.D. Pa. 1994) 492

Kelley v. E.P.A., 15 F.3d 1100 (D.C. Cir. 1994), rehearing denied, 25 F.3d 1088 (D.C. Cir. 1994), cert. denied, (January 17, 1995) 205

Kelley v. Sellin, 42 F.3d 1501 (6th Cir. 1995), cert. denied, 515 U.S. 1159 (1995) . . . 13

Kelley v. U.S., 618 F. Supp. 1103 (W.D. Mich. 1985) 98

Kelley v. Wagner, 930 F. Supp. 293 (E.D. Mich. 1996) 213

Kennedy v. Southern California Edison Co., 219 F.3d 988 (9th Cir. 2000) 543

Kent County v. USEPA, 963 F.2d 391 (1992) 179

Kerr-McGee Chemical v. Lefton Iron, 14 F.3d 321 (7th Cir. 1994) 198, 209

Key Tronic Corp. v. U.S., 511 U.S. 809, 128 L. Ed. 2d 797 (1994) 193

King v. E.I. Du Pont, 996 F.2d 1346 (1st Cir. 1993) 396

Kingman Park v. EPA, 29 Envtl. L. Rep. 10716 (Nov. 1999) 109

Klamath Water Users v. Patterson, 191 F.3d 1115 (9th Cir. 1999) 512

L

Landsford-Coaledale Joint Water Authority v. Tonolli Corp., 4 F.3d 1209 (3rd Cir. 1993) 197

Lane County Audubon v. Jamison, 958 F.2d 290 (9th Cir. 1992) 512

Lawrence Corp., In re, 239 B.R. 720 (Bkrtcy. D.N.J. 1999) 218

Lead Industries Ass'n. v. EPA, 647 F.2d 1130 (D.C. Cir. 1980) 28

LEAF v. EPA, 118 F.3d 1467 (11th Cir. 1997) 346, 348

Lentz v. Mason, 961 F. Supp. 709 (D.N.J. 1997) 196

LES v. Reilly, 968 F.2d 985 (9th Cir. 1992), cert. denied 507 U.S. 950 (1993) 353

Leslie Salt Co. v. U.S., 896 F.2d 354 (9th Cir. 1990) 97

Levine v. NL Industries Inc., 926 F.2d 199 (2d Cir. 1991) 585

Lewis v. American Cyanamid Co., 715 A.2d 967 (N.J. 1998) 396

Liberian Poplar Transports, Inc. v. U.S., 26 Ct. Cl. 223 (1992) 497

Lititz Mutual Ins. Co. v. Steely, 567 Pa. 98, 785 A.2d 975 (Pa. 2001) 492

Loggerhead Turtle v. County Council, 148 F.3d 1231 (11th Cir. 1998) 509

Long Beach v. Dorothy B. Godwin California Living Trust, 32 F.3d 1364 (9th Cir. 1994) 196

Long Island Soundkeeper Fund v. New York Athletic Club, 42 Env. Rep. Cases (BNA) 1421, 1996 WL 131863 (S.D.N.Y. March 22, 1996) 98

Loretto v. Teleprompter Manhattan, 458 U.S. 419 (1982) 220

Louisiana-Pacific Corp. v. Asarco, Inc., 204 F.3d 1565 (9th Cir. 1994) 194

Louisiana-Pacific Corp. v. Asarco, Inc., 909 F.2d 1260 (9th Cir. 1990) 209

Love v. Thomas, 858 F.2d 1347 (9th Cir. 1988) 389

Lowe v. Sporicidin International, 47 F.3d 124 (4th Cir. 1995) 396

Lucas v. South Carolina Coastal Council, 505 U.S. 1003, 112 S. Ct. 2886, 120 L. Ed. 2d 798 (1992) 614

Lujan v. Defenders of Wildlife, 504 U.S. 555, 119 L. Ed. 2d 351 (1992) . . . 13, 218, 515

Lujan v. National Wildlife Federation, 497 U.S. 871, 111 L. Ed. 2d 695 (1990) 218

Lyall v. Leslie's Poolmart, Inc., 984 F. Supp. 587 (E.D. Mich. 1997) 429

M

Mahary, Inc. v. Van Wert Solid Waste, 249 F.3d 544 (6th Cir. 2001) 147

Maine Audubon Society v. Purslow, 907 F.2d 265 (1st Cir. 1990) 515

Maritrans, Inc. v. United States, 43 Fed. Claims Ct. 86 (1999) 500

Marriott Corp. v. Simkins Industries, Inc., 929 F. Supp. 396 (S.D. Fla. 1996) 207

Marsh v. Oregon Natural Resources Council, 490 U.S. 360, 104 L. Ed. 2d 377 (1989) . . . . 13 - 14

Marshall v. Barlow's, Inc., 436 U.S. 307 (1978) 454

Matter of Investigation Pursuant to Clean Air Act, 728 F. Supp. 626 (D. Idaho 1990) 62

Mattoon v. City of Pittsfield, 980 F.2d 1 (1st Cir. 1992) 348

McDonald v. Monsanto Co., 27 F.3d 1021 (5th Cir. 1994) 396

McGill v. EPA, 593 F.2d 631 (5th Cir. 1979) 388

McKay v. U.S., 199 F.3d 1376 (Fed. Cir. 1999) 220

McKie Ford, Inc. v. Secretary of Labor, 191 F.3d 853 (8th Cir. 1999) 441

Mead Corp. v. Browner, 100 F.3d 152 (D.C. Cir. 1996) 179

Meghrig v. KFC Western, 516 U.S. 479, 134 L. Ed.2d 121 (1996) 148

Melerine v. Avondale Shipyards, 659 F.2d 706 (5th Cir. 1981) 455

Metlife Capital Corp., In re, 132 F.3d 818 (1st Cir. 1998) 497

Metropolitan Edison v. People Against Nuclear Energy, 460 U.S. 766 (1983) 12

Miccosukee Tribe v. South Florida Water Mgt. Dist., 2002 U.S. App. LEXIS 1588 (11th Cir. 2002) 97

Michigan v. EPA, 213 F.3d 663 (D.C. Cir. 2000) 32

Midlantic National Bank v. NJDEP, 474 U.S. 494, 88 L. Ed. 2d 859 (1984) 218

Miller v. Beaugrand, 169 A.D. 2d 537, 564 N.Y.S. 2d 390 (1st Dept. 1991) 489

Minyard Enterprises v. Southeastern Chemical, 184 F.3d 373 (4th Cir. 1999) 192, 196, 203

Mobil Oil Corp. v. EPA, 35 F.3d 579 (D.C. Cir. 1994) 123

Modern Continental v. OSHRC, 196 F.2d 274 (1st Cir. 1999) 441

Monica W. v. Milovoi, 685 N.Y.S. 2d 231 (1st Dept. 1999) 491

Motor Vehicle Manufacturers v. NYS Dept. of Env. Cons., 17 F.3d 521 (2d Cir. 1994) 53

N

National Audubon Society v. Espy, 998 F.2d 699 (9th Cir. 1993) 514

National Gypsum Co. v. USEPA, 968 F.2d 40 (1992). 179

National Lime Ass'n v. EPA, 233 F.3d 625 (D.C. Cir. 2001) 39

National Lime Ass'n. v. EPA, 627 F.2d 416 (D.C. Cir. 1980). 35

National Mining Ass'n v. EPA, 59 F.3d 1351 (D.C. Cir. 1995) 35

National Mining Ass'n. v. EPA, 59 F.3d 1351 (D.C. Cir. 1995) 37

National Mining Ass'n v. Corps of Engineers, 145 F.3d 1399 (D.C. Cir. 1998) 97

National Petrochemical & Refineries Assoc. v. Environmental Protection Agency, 287 F.3d 1130 (D.C. Cir. 2002) 50

National Sea Clammers Ass'n. v. New York, 616 F.2d 1222 (3d Cir. 1980) 4

National Shipping Co. v. Moran Trade Corp., 122 F.3d 1062 (4th Cir. 1997) 497

National Solid Waste Management v. Meyer, 165 F.3d 11151 (7th Cir. 1999) 147

National Wildlife Fed. v. USEPA, 925 F.2d 470 (D.C. Cir. 1991). 345

National Wildlife Fed. v. USEPA, 980 F.2d 765 (D.C. Cir. 1992). 345

National Wildlife Federation v. Burlington Northern, 23 F.3d 1508 (9th Cir. 1998) . 510

National Wildlife Federation v. Gorsuch, 693 F.2d 156 (D.C. Cir. 1982) 97

National Wildlife Fed'n v. Benn, 491 F. Supp. 1234 (S.D.N.Y. 1980) 436

Natural Resources Defense Council v. EPA, 966 F.2d 1292 (9th Cir. 1992) 111

Nevada v. Watkins, 914 F.2d 1545 (9th Cir. 1990) 537

Nevada v. Watkins, 943 F.2d 1080 (9th Cir. 1991) 537

New Jersey State Chamber of Commerce v. Hughey, 774 F.2d 587 (3d Cir. 1985) . . 458

New Jersey Turnpike Authority v. PPG Industries, 1999 U.S. App. LEXIS 30389 (3d Cir. 1999) 183

New Mexico Cattle Growers v. U.S. Fish & Wildlife, 248 F.3d 1277 (10th Cir. 2001) 507

New York City Coalition v. Vallone, 741 N.Y.S. 2d 186, 2002 WL 453719 (1st Dept. 2002) 493

New York v. Lashins Arcade, 91 F.3d 353 (2d Cir. 1996) 198

New York v. Shore Realty, 759 F.2d 1032 (2d Cir. 1985) 191, 207

New York v. U.S., 505 U.S. 144, 120 L. Ed. 2d 120 (1992) 539

New York v. Westwood Squibb, 62 F. Supp. 2d 1035 (W.D.N.Y. 1999), aff'd 964 F.2d 85 (2d Cir. 1992) 209

Newton County Wildlife Ass'n v. U.S. Forest Service, 113 F.3d 110 (8th Cir. 1997) 521

NJDEP v. Ventron Corp., 94 N.J. 473, 468 A.2d 150 (1983) 208

NL Industries, Inc. v. U.S. Department of Transportation, 901 F.2d 141 (D.C. Cir. 1990) 428

No Spray Coalition, Inc. v. The City of New York, 252 F.3d 148 (2d Cir. 2001). . . . 148

Norfolk Southern v. Shulimson Brothers Co., 1 F. Supp. 2d 553 (W.D.N.C. 1998) . . 198

North Shore Gas Co. v. Salomon, Inc., 152 F.3d 642 (7th Cir. 1998) 209

Northwestern Mutual v. Atlantic Research, 847 F. Supp. 389 (E.D. Va., 1994) 197

NRDC v. EPA, 194 F.3d 130 (D.C. Cir. 1999) 31

NRDC v. Houston, 146 F.3d 1118 (9th Cir. 1998) 512

Nurad, Inc. v. William E. Hooper & Sons. Co, 966 F.2d 837 (4th Cir. 1992) . . 196 - 197

Nutra Sweet Co. v. X-L Engineering Corp., 933 F. Supp. 1409 (N.D. Ill. 1996) 207

O

Oates v. State of New York, 610 N.Y.S. 987 (1993) 492

O'Conner v. Commonwealth Edison, 13 F.3d 1090 (7th Cir. 1994), cert. denied 129 L. Ed. 2d 838 542

Ohio v. Kovacs, 469 U.S. 274, 85 L. Ed. 2d 649 (1985) 217

Oregon NRC v. Turner, 863 F. Supp. 1277 (D. Ore. 1994) 512

Oregon Waste Systems v. Oregon Dept. of Environmental Liability, No. 9370, 1994 U.S. LEXIS 2659 (4/4/94). 614

Organic Chemical Site PRP Group v. Total Petroleum, Inc., 58 F. Supp. 2d 755 (W.D. Mich. 1999) 172

Orgulf Transport v. U.S., 711 F. Supp. 344 (W.D. Ky 1989) 503

Owen Electric Steel v. Browner, 37 F.3d 146 (4th Cir. 1994) 121

P

Pacific Legal Foundation v. Andrus, 657 F.2d 829 (6th Cir. 1981) 12

Pacific Northwest Generating Co-Op v. Brown, 38 F.3d 1058 (9th Cir. 1994) 515

Pacific Rivers Council v. Thomas, 30 F.3d 1050 (9th Cir. 1994). 512

Palazzolo v. Rhode Island, 533 U.S. 606, 121 S. Ct. 2448, 150 L. Ed. 2d 592 (2001) 615

Palila v. Hawaii Dept. of Land and Natural Resources, 852 F.2d 1106 (9th Cir. 1988) 510

Paoli R.R. Yard PCB Litigation, In re, 113 F.3d 444 (3d Cir. 1997) 588

Papas v. Upjohn Co., 985 F.2d 516 (11th Cir. 1993) 396

Pennsylvania v. Conroy, 24 F.3d 568 (3d Cir. 1994). 218

People of the State of New York v. Pymm Thermometer Co., 76 N.Y. 2d 511, 561 N.Y.S. 2d 687, 563 N.E. 2d 1 (1990) 456

People v. Hegedus, 432 Mich. 598, 443 N.W. 2d 127. 456

Philadelphia Electric Co. v. Hercules, 762 F.2d 303 (3d Cir. 1985), cert denied 474 U.S. 980 (1985) 209

Pierson Sand v. Pierson Township, 43 Env. Rep. Cases (BNA) 1559 (6th Cir. 1996). . 194

Pierson Sand v. Pierson Township, 851 F. Supp. 850 (W.D. Mich. 1994) 197

Piney Run v. County Commissioners, 268 F.3d 255 (4th Cir. 2001) 97, 101, 118

Platte River Whooping Crane Trust v. FERC, 962 F.2d 27 (D.C. Cir. 1992) 512

PMC, Inc. v. Sherwin-Williams Co., 151 F.3d 610 (7th Cir. 1998) . . . 193, 201, 204, 210

Pneumo Abex Corp. v. Bessemer & Lake Erie RR Co., 936 F. Supp. 1250 (E.D. Va. 1996). 193

Pneumo Abex Corp. v. High Point, Thomasville & Denton RR Co., 142 F.3d 769 (4th Cir. 1998) 172

Prairie Wood Products v. Glickman, 971 F. Supp. 457 (D. Ore. 1997) 12

Prairie Wood v. Glickman, 971 F. Supp. 457 (D. Ore. 1997) 13

Price Road Neighborhood Ass'n v. U.S. Dept. of Transportation, 113 F.3d 1505 (9th Cir. 1997) 14

Price v. Navy Department, 39 F.3d 1101 (9th Cir. 1994) 193

Prisco v. A&D Carting, 168 F.3d 593 (2d Cir. 1999). 200

Public Citizen v. Office of the U.S. Trade Representative, 970 F.2d 916 (D.C. Cir. 1992) 15

Public Citizen v. U.S. Trade Representative, 5 F.3d 549 (D.C. Cir. 1993). 15

Public Interest Research Group v. Magnesium Elektron, Inc., 123 F.3d 111 (3d Cir. 1997) 118

Public Service Co. v. Gates Rubber Co., 175 F.3d 1177 (10th Cir. 1999) . . . . 194 - 195

Puffer's Hardware, Inc. v. Donovan, 742 F.2d 12 (1st Cir. 1984) 441

Q

Quivira Mining v. EPA, 765 F.2d 126 (10th Cir. 1985) 97

R

Racich v. Celotex Corp., 887 F.2d 393 (2d Cir. 1989). 333

Reading Co., Matter of, 115 F.3d 1111 (3d Cir. 1997). 204, 217

Reardon v. U.S., 947 F.2d 1509 (1st Cir. 1991) 204

Redwing Carriers v. Saraland Apartments, 94 F.3d 1489 (11th Cir. 1996) . . . 197 - 198

Reorganized Church v. U.S. Gypsum, 882 F.2d 335 (8th Cir. 1989). 332

Reserve Mining Co. v. Environmental Protection Agency, 514 F.2d 492 (8th Cir. 1975) 4

Rice v. Harkin Exploration, 270 F.3d 264 (5th Cir. 2001) 496

Roanoke River Basin Ass'n v. Hudson, 940 F.2d 58 (4th Cir. 1991) 3

Roberts v. Florida Power, 146 F.3d 1305 (11th Cir. 1998) 543

RSR Corp. v. Avanti Development, Inc., 69 F. Supp. 2d 1119 (S.D. Ind. 1999) 172

Rumpke of Indiana v. Cummins Engine, 107 F.3d 1235 (7th Cir. 1997). 192

Russell v. Bartley, 494 F.2d 334 (6th Cir. 1974) 457

S

San Francisco Baykeeper v. EPA, 54 ERC 1225 (9th Cir. 2002) 109

Santiago v. Hernandez, 53 F. Supp. 2d 264 (S.D.N.Y. 1999) 489

Santiago v. Sherwin-Williams Company, 782 F. Supp. 186 (D. Mass 1993), aff'd 3 F.3d 546 (1st Cir. 1993) 489

Save Our Sound Fisheries Ass'n. v. Callaway, 429 F. Supp. 1136 (D.R.I. 1977) 436

Save the Yaak Committee v. Block, 840 F.2d 714 (9th Cir. 1988). 515

Schalk v. Reilly, 900 F.2d 1091 (7th Cir. 1990), cert. denied 498 U.S. 987 (1990) . . 218

Schiavone v. Pearce, 79 F.3d 248 (2d Cir. 1996) 210

Schumann v. State of New York, 610 N.Y.S. 2d 987 (N.Y. Claims Ct. 1994). 492

Scottsdale Insurance v. American Empire Surplus, 811 Supp. 210 (D. Md. 1993) . . 492

Scribner v. Summers, 138 F.3d 471 (2d Cir. 1998). 586, 588

Seaburn, Inc. v. USEPA, 712 F. Supp. 218 (D.D.C. 1989) 436

Secretary of Labor v. Beverly Enterprises, 19 OSHC 1161 (2000). 450

Secretary of Labor v. Pepperidge Farms, Inc., 17 OSHC 1993 (1997) 450

Selvy v. Beigsel, 283 Ill. App. 3d 532, 670 N.E. 2d 784 (1996) 490

Shaw v. Dow Brands, Inc., 994 F.2d 364 (7th Cir. 1993) 396

Shell Oil Company v. EPA, 950 F.2d 741 (D.C. Cir. 1991) 123, 130

Shuler v. Babbitt, 49 F. Supp. 2d 1165 (D. Mont. 1998). 509

Sierra Club v. Abston Construction, 620 F.2d 41 (5th Cir. 1980). 97

Sierra Club v. Babbitt, 65 F.3d 1502 (9th Cir. 1995) . . . . 12 - 13, 513

Sierra Club v. Cedar Point Oil, 73 F.3d 546 (5th Cir. 1996) 117

Sierra Club v. Colorado Refining, 838 F. Supp. 1428 (D. Colo. 1993) 98

Sierra Club v. EPA, 167 F.3d 658 (D.C. Cir. 1996) 36, 39

Sierra Club v. EPA, 992 F.2d 337 (D.C. Cir. 1993) 105, 122

Sierra Club v. Martin, 110 F.3d 1551 (11th Cir. 1997) 521

Sierra Club v. U.S. Dept. of Transportation, 753 F.2d 120 (D.C. Cir. 1985) 13

Sierra Club v. U.S. Fish & Wildlife Service, 245 F.3d 434 (5th Cir. 2001) 507

Sierra Club v. Whitman, 268 F.3d 898 (9th Cir. 2001) 118

Simmons v. U.S. Corps of Engineers, 120 F.3d 664 (7th Cir. 1997) 14

Sipes v. Russell, 89 F. Supp. 2d 1199 (D. Kans. 2000). 489

Smith Douglass, Inc., In re, 856 F.2d 12 (4th Cir. 1988) 218

Smith Kline Beecham Corp. v. Rohm & Haas Co., 89 F.3d 154 (3d Cir. 1996). 210

Smith Land and Improvement Corporation v. Celotex Corporation,
851 F.2d 86 (3d Cir. 1988). 208

Solid Waste Agency of Northern Cork County v. U.S. Army Corps of Engineers,
531 U.S. 159 (2001) 5

Solid Waste Agency of Northern Illinois v. U.S. Army Corps of Engineers,
531 U.S. 159 (2001). 97

South Florida Water Mgmt Dist. v. Montalvo, 84 F.3d 402 (11th Cir. 1996) 200

South Port Marine v. Gulf Oil Ltd., 234 F.3d 58 (1st Cir. 2000) 496

Southwest Center v. Bureau of Reclamation, 143 F.3d 515 (9th Cir. 1998). 514

Southern Pacific v. U.S., 13 Ct. Cl. 402 (1987). 497

Southwest Center v. Babbitt, 215 F.3d 58 (D.C. Cir. 2000) 508

Southwest Center v. Babbitt, 939 F. Supp. 49 (D.D.C. 1996) 506

Southwest Center v. Bureau of Reclamation, 143 F.3d 515 (9th Cir. 1998). 515

Sphere Drake Ins. Co. v. Y.L. Realty Co., 990 F. Supp. 240 (S.D.N.Y. 1997). 492

St. Joseph Hosp. v. Celotex Corp., 874 F.2d 764 (11th Cir. 1989) 332

St. Leger v. American Fire, 870 F. Supp. 641 (E.D. Pa. 1994),
aff'd without opinion 61 F.3d 896 (3d Cir. 1995) . . . . 491 - 492

State of Minnesota v. Kalman W. Abrams Metals, Inc., 155 F.3d 1019
(8th Cir. 1998) 193

State of Minnesota v. Kalman W. Abrams Metals, Inc., 155 F.3d 1024
(8th Cir. 1998) 194

State of Nevada v. U.S. Dept. of Energy, 133 F.3d 1201 (9th Cir. 1998) 537

State of South Carolina v. O'Leary, 64 F.3d 892 (4th Cir. 1995). 539

Steel Co. v. Citizens for a Better Environment, 523 U.S. 83, 118 S. Ct. 1003,
140 L. Ed. 2d 210 (1998) 218, 235

Stone v. Gordon, 211 A.D.2d 881, 621 N.Y.S.2d 220 (3d Dept. 1995) 490

Stone v. Naperville Park District, 38 F. Supp. 2d 651 (N.D. Ill. 1999) 98

Strahan v. Coxe, 127 F.3d 155 (1st Cir. 1997), cert. denied 525 U.S. 830 and 978 . . 519

Suitum v. Tahoe Regional Planning Agency, 520 U.S. 725, 117 S.Ct. 1639, 137 L. Ed. 2d 980 (1997) 615

Sun Co. v. Browning Industries, 124 F.3d 1187 (10th Cir. 1997) 203

Swanson v. U.S. Forest Service, 87 F.3d 339 (9th Cir. 1996). . . . . 13 - 14

T

Tahoe Sierra Preservation Council v. Tahoe Regional Planning Agency, 122 S. Ct. 1465, 70 USLW 4260 (2002) 615

Taracorp, Inc. v. NL Industries, Inc., 73 F.3d 738 (7th Cir. 1996) 210

Tex Tin Corp. v. USEPA, 935 F.2d 1321 (1991) and 992 F.2d 353 (1993) 179

The Old Timer, Inc. v. Blackhawk-Central City, 51 F. Supp. 2d 1109 (D. Colo. 1999) 116

Tippins v. USX Corp. No. 93-3609, 1994 U.S. App. LEXIS 24550 (3d Cir., Sept. 12, 1994) 200

TMI Litigation, In re, 940 F.2d 832 (3d Cir. 1991), cert. denied 121 L. Ed. 2d 491 . . 542

TMI, In re, 67 F.3d 1103 (3d Cir. 1995) 543

Total Petroleum, Inc. v. U.S., 12 Ct. Cl. 178 (1987) 497

Town of New Windsor v. Tesa Tuck, Inc., 935 F. Supp. 310 (S.D.N.Y. 1996) 198

Towrico Electronics, Inc., In re, 8 F.3d 146 (3d Cir. 1993) 217

Train v. Colorado PIRG, 426 U.S. 1, 48 L. Ed. 2d 434 (1976) 532

Transportation Leasing v. California, 32 Env. Rep. (C.D. Cal. 1990). 172

Trinity American Corp. v. USEPA, 150 F.3d 389 (4th Cir. 1998). 347

Troy Corp. v. Browner, 120 F.3d 277 (D.C. Cir. 1997), petition for rehearing on IPBC denied 129 F.3d 1290 (D.C. Cir. 1997) 236

Trust Co. Bank v. U.S. Gypsum Co., 950 F.2d 1144 (5th Cir. 1992) 332

Turner Co. v. Secretary of Labor, 561 F.2d 82 (7th Cir. 1977) 441

TVA v. EPA, 2002 U.S. App. LEXIS 249 (11th Cir. Jan. 8, 2002) 35

TVA v. Hill, 437 U.S. 153, 57 L. Ed. 2d 117 (1977) 508

U

United Technologies Corporation v. Browning-Ferris Industries, Inc., 33 F.3d 96 (1st Cir. 1994), cert. denied 513 U.S. 1183 (1995) 192

U.S. Department of Energy v. Ohio, 503 U.S. 607, 118 L. Ed. 2d 255 (1992) 6

U.S. Liability v. Bourbeau, 49 F.3d 786 (1st Cir. 1995) 492

U.S. v. Cello-Foil Products, 100 F.3d 1227 (6th Cir. 1996) 200

U.S. v. 150 Acres of Land, 204 F.3d 698 (6th Cir. 2000). 173, 196, 198, 204

U.S. v. A&N Cleaners, 788 F. Supp. 1317 (S.D.N.Y. 1992) 195

U.S. v. Aceto Agricultural, 699 F. Supp. 1384 (S.D. Iowa), aff'd in part 872 F.2d 1373 (8th Cir. 1988) 199

U.S. v. Alcan Aluminum Corp., 964 F.2d 252 (3d Cir. 1992). 171

U.S. v. Alcan Aluminum Corp., 990 F.2d 711 (2d Cir. 1993) 171, 192, 201

U.S. v. Allied Chemical Corp., 431 F. Supp. 361 (W.D.N.Y. 1977) 428

U.S. v. AM General, 34 F.3d 472 (7th Cir. 1994) 36

U.S. v. Atkinson, 966 F.2d 1270 (9th Cir. 1992). 520

U.S. v. Bestfoods, Inc., 524 U.S. 51, 118 S.Ct. 1876 (1998) 206, 208

U.S. v. Bliss, 667 F. Supp. 1298 (E.D. Mo. 1987) contra, U.S. v. Mottolo, 695 F. Supp. 615 (D.N.H. 1988) 199

U.S. v. Broderick Investment, 862 F. Supp. 272 (D. Colo. 1994) 198

U.S. v. Bronx Reptiles, Inc., 217 F.3d 82 (2d Cir. 2000) 520

U.S. v. Carolina Transformer Co., 978 F.2d 832 (4th Cir. 1992) 197, 207, 209

U.S. v. CDMG Realty, 96 F.3d 706 (3d Cir. 1996) 198

U.S. v. Chapman, 146 F.3d 1166 (9th Cir. 1998) 194

U.S. v. Chotin Transport, 649 F. Supp. 356 (S.D. Ohio 1986) 503

U.S. v. CMDG Realty Co., 96 F.3d 706 (3d Cir. 1996) 196

U.S. v. Corbin Farm Service, 444 F. Supp. 510 (E.D. Cal. 1978) 395

U.S. v. Corrow, 119 F.3d 796 (10th Cir. 1997), cert. denied 522 U.S. 1133 (1998) 521

U.S. v. Crown Roll Leaf, Inc., 29 ERC 2018 (D. N.J. 1987) 208

U.S. v. Dean, 969 F.2d 187 (6th Cir. 1992) 148

U.S. v. Edison, 108 F.3d 1336 (11th Cir. 1997) 97

U.S. v. Elias, 269 F.3d 1003 (9th Cir. 2001) 147

U.S. v. Fleet Factors, 901 F.2d 1550 (11th Cir. 1990) 205

U.S. v. Frederick, 38 F. Supp. 2d 396 (D.V.I. 1999) 503

U.S. v. GAF Corp., 389 F. Supp. 1379 (S.D. Tex. 1975) 98

U.S. v. Gannett, 984 F.2d 1402 (5th Cir. 1993) 521

U.S. v. Gaubert, 499 U.S. 135 (1991) 219

U.S. v. Glidden Co., 3 F. Supp.2d 823 (N.D. Ohio 1997). 204

U.S. v. Gurley, 43 F.3d 1188 (8th Cir. 1994), cert. denied, 516 U.S. 817 (1995) 197, 208

U.S. v. Hanousek, 176 F.3d 1116 (9th Cir. 1999) 117

U.S. v. Hanson, 262 F.3d 1217 (11th Cir. 2001) 147

U.S. v. Hardage, 750 F. Supp. 1444 (W.D. Okla. 1990), aff'd in part and reversed in part on other issues, 982 F.2d 1436 (10th Cir. 1992). 200

U.S. v. Heuer, 3 F.3d 723 (9th Cir. 1993) 148

U.S. v. Hong, 242 F.3d 528 (4th Cir. 2001) 147

U.S. v. Hopkins, 53 F.3d 533 (2d Cir. 1995) 117

U.S. v. ITT Rayonier, Inc., 627 F.2d 996 (9th Cir. 1980) 116

U.S. v. Iverson, 162 F.3d 1015 (9th Cir. 1998) 117

U.S. v. Ivey, 949 F.2d 759 (5th Cir. 1991) 514

U.S. v. Kayser-Roth Corp., 724 F. Supp. 15 (D. R.I. 1989), aff'd 910 F.2d 24 (1st Cir. 1990), cert. denied, 498 U.S. 1084 206

U.S. v. Lambert, 915 F. Supp. 797 (S.D.W. Va. 1996) 4

U.S. v. Laughlin, 10 F.3d 961 (2d Cir. 1993) 148

U.S. v. Lee, 217 F.3d 284 (5th Cir. 2000) 521

U.S. v. Lee, 937 F.2d 1388 (9th Cir. 1991) 520

U.S. v. Lowe, 118 F.3d 399 (5th Cir. 1997) 193

U.S. v. M/V Big Sam, 681 F.2d 432 (5th Cir. 1982) 4

U.S. v. Maryland Bank & Trust Co., 632 F. Supp. 573 (D. Md. 1986) 205

U.S. v. McKittrick, 142 F.3d 1170 (9th Cir. 1998), cert. denied 525 U.S. 1072, 142 L. Ed. 2d 667 . . . . 509 - 510, 514

U.S. v. Mexico Feed & Seed Co., Inc., 980 F.2d 478 (8th Cir. 1992) 197, 209

U.S. v. Mirabile, 15 E.L.R. 20,992 (E.D. Pa. 1985) 205

U.S. v. Mitchell, 39 F.3d 465 (4th Cir. 1994) 520

U.S. v. Monsanto Co., 858 F.2d 160 (4th Cir. 1988) 191, 196

U.S. v. Monsoor, 77 F.3d 1031 (7th Cir. 1996) 520

U.S. v. Nguyen, 916 F.2d 1016 (5th Cir. 1990) 513

U.S. v. Occidental Chemical Corp., 200 F.3d 143 (3d Cir. 1999) 174

U.S. v. Occidental Chemical, 965 F. Supp. 408 (W.D.N.Y. 1997) 170

U.S. v. Outboard Marine Corp., 789 F.2d 497 (7th Cir. 1986) 4

U.S. v. Peterson Sand, 806 F. Supp. 1346 (N.D. Ill. 1992) 196

U.S. v. Pitrone, 115 F.3d 1 (1st Cir. 1997) 521

U.S. v. Pitt-Des Moines, Inc., 168 F.3d 976 (7th Cir. 1999) . . . . 455 - 456

U.S. v. Plaza Health, 3 F.3d 643 (2d Cir. 1993) 97

U.S. v. R.W. Meyer, Inc., 889 F.2d 1497 (6th Cir. 1989) 173, 196

U.S. v. Rohm and Haas, 2 F.3d 1265 (3d Cir. 1993) 195

U.S. v. Romano, 137 F.3d 677 (1998) 520

U.S. v. Saul, 955 F. Supp. 1076 (E.D. Ark., 1996) 393

U.S. v. Sinskey, 119 F.3d 712 (8th Cir. 1997) 117
U.S. v. TIC Investment Corp., 866 F. Supp. 1173 (N.D. Iowa 1994) 197
U.S. v. Town of Lowell, 637 F. Supp. 254 (N.D. Ind. 1985) 116
U.S. v. USX Corp., 68 F.3d 811 (3d Cir. 1995) 207
U.S. v. Wagner, 29 F.3d 264 (7th Cir. 1994) 148
U.S. v. Weintraub, 273 F.3d 139 (2d Cir. 2001) 328
U.S. v. Weitzenhoff, 1 F.3d 1523 (9th Cir. 1993) 117
U.S. v. Western Processing Co., 761 F. Supp. 713 (W.D. Wash. 1991) 172
U.S. v. Williams, 216 F.2d 1099 (D.C. Cir. 2000) 457
U.S. v. Wilson, 133 F.3d 251 (4th Cir. 1997) 97, 117
U.S. v. Wright, 988 F.3d 1036 (10th Cir. 1993) 346
Underwood v. Risman, 605 N.E. 2d 832 (Mass. 1993) 489
Union Tank Car Co. v. OSHRC, 192 F.3d 701 (7th Cir. 1999) . . . . 441, 456 - 457
United Dairy Farmers, Inc. v. U.S., 2000-1 U.S.T.C. (CCH) § 50,538 (S.D. Ohio 2000) 583
United Haulers Association, Inc. v. Oneida-Herkimer Solid Waste Management Authority, 261 F.3d 245 (2d Cir. 2001) cert. denied, 122 S.Ct. 815, 151 L. Ed. 2d 699 (2002) 147
United States v. Brace, 41 F.3d 341 (3d Cir. 1994) 5
United States v. Members of the Estate of Boothby, 16 F.3d 19 (1st Cir. 1994) 3
United States v. Riverside Bayview Homes, Inc., 474 U.S. 121, 88 L. Ed. 2d 419 (1985) 4
United Technologies Corporation v. Browning-Ferris Industries, Inc., 33 F.3d 96 (1st Cir. 1994), cert. denied 513 U.S. 1183 (1995) 203
Universal Construction v. OSHRC, 182 F.3d 726 (10th Cir. 1999) 455
Uricam Corp. v. W.R. Grace & Co., 739 F. Supp. 1493 (W.D. Okla. 1990) 332

V

Van Abbema v. Fornell, 807 F.2d 633 (7th Cir. 1986) 3
Vermont Yankee Nuclear Corporation, 435 U.S. 519 (1978) 14
Virgin Islands Tree Boa v. Witt, 918 F. Supp. 879 (D.V.I. 1996), aff'd, 82 F.3d 408 (3d Cir. 1996) 13

W

Wall Tube, In re, 831 F.2d 118 (6th Cir. 1987) 218
Wall v. EPA, 265 F.3rd 426 (6th Cir. 2001) 31
Walton v. Albany Community Dev. Agency, 718 N.Y.S. 2d 456 (3d Dept. 2001) . . . 490

Washington State Dept. of Transportation v. Washington Natural Gas Co., 59 F.3d 793 (9th Cir. 1995) . . . . 193 - 194

Waste Action Project v. Dawn Mining Corp., 137 F.3d 1426 (9th Cir. 1998) 532

Waste Management v. City of York, 910 F. Supp. 1035 (M.D. Pa. 1995) 213

Waste Management, Inc. v. USEPA, 669 F. Supp. 536 (D.D.C. 1987) 436

Western Greenhouses v. U.S., 878 Supp. 917 (N.D. Tex. 1995). 219

Western Radio v. Espy, 79 F.3d 896 (9th Cir. 1996), cert. denied 136 L. Ed. 2d 38 (1996) 15

Westfarm Associates v. Washington Suburban Sanitary Com'n., 66 F.3d 669 (4th Cir. 1995), cert. denied, 517 U.S. 1103 (1995) 192, 198

Westling v. County of Mille Lacs, 543 N.W. 2d 91 (Minn. 1996) 587

Westview Associates v. Guaranty Nat. Ins. Co., 95 N.Y. 2d 34, 717 N.Y.S. 2d 75 (2000) 492

Whirlpool Corp. v. Marshall, 445 U.S. 1, 63 L. Ed. 2d 154 (1980). 458

Whitman v. American Trucking Association, 531 U.S. 457, 149 L. Ed. 2d 1(2001). . . 29

Wichita v. U.S. Gypsum, 72 F.3d 1491 (10th Cir. 1996). 332

Williams Pipe Line Co. v. Bayer Corp., 964 F. Supp. 1300 (S.D. Iowa 1997) 98

Willson, L. R., v. OSHRC, 134 F.3d 1235 (4th Cir. 1998) 457

Wilshire Westwood Associates v. Atlantic Richfield Co., 881 F.2d 801 (9th Cir. 1989) 172

Wisconsin Electric v. Reilly, 893 F.3d 901 (7th Cir. 1990) 35

Wisconsin Public Intervenor v. Mortier, 501 U.S. 597, 111 S.Ct. 2476 (1991) 396

Worm v. American Cyanamid, 5 F.3d 744 (4th Cir. 1993). 396

Wright v. Inman, 923 F. Supp. 1295 (D. Nev. 1996) 14

Y

Yates v. Island Creek Coal Co., 485 F. Supp. 995 (W.D. Va. 1980). 4

TREATIES, LAWS AND EXECUTIVE ORDERS

A

B

C

I

L

M

N

O

P

SUBJECT INDEX